2018
INDEX OF
U.S. MILITARY STRENGTH

DAVIS INSTITUTE FOR NATIONAL SECURITY AND FOREIGN POLICY

The Heritage Foundation

2018
INDEX OF
U.S. MILITARY STRENGTH

DAVIS INSTITUTE FOR NATIONAL SECURITY AND FOREIGN POLICY

edited by
Dakota L. Wood

We are honored to dedicate the
2018 Index of U.S. Military Strength
to The Honorable J. William Middendorf II.

Contents

Contributors

Heritage Experts

Dakota L. Wood is Senior Research Fellow for Defense Programs in the Center for National Defense, of the Kathryn and Shelby Cullom Davis Institute for National Security and Foreign Policy, at The Heritage Foundation. He served for two decades as an officer in the U.S. Marine Corps, including service as a strategic analyst for the Commandant of the Marine Corps and the Secretary of Defense's Director of Net Assessment.

James Jay Carafano, PhD, is Vice President for the Davis Institute and E. W. Richardson Fellow at The Heritage Foundation. He served for 25 years as a U.S. Army officer and has taught at a number of universities, including the National Defense University.

Thomas W. Spoehr, Lieutenant General, U.S. Army (Ret.), is Director of the Center for National Defense. Before joining The Heritage Foundation, he served America for more than 36 years in the Army.

Frederico Bartels is Policy Analyst for Defense Budgeting in the Center for National Defense. Before joining The Heritage Foundation, he served for three years as a Policy Analyst with Concerned Veterans for America.

Thomas Callender is Senior Research Fellow for Defense Programs in the Center for National Defense. Before joining Heritage, he served for five years as Director for Capabilities in the Capabilities and Concepts Directorate of the Office of the Deputy Under Secretary of the Navy for Policy.

Dean Cheng is a Senior Research Fellow in the Asian Studies Center of the Davis Institute. He specializes in China's military and foreign policy.

Luke Coffey is Director of the Douglas and Sarah Allison Center for Foreign Policy of the Davis Institute. He joined Heritage after service as Senior Special Advisor to the Secretary of State for Defence of the United Kingdom.

Michaela Dodge is Senior Policy Analyst for Defense and Strategic Policy in the Center for National Defense. She specializes in missile defense, nuclear weapons modernization, and arms control.

Nile Gardiner, PhD, is Director of the Margaret Thatcher Center for Freedom of the Davis Institute. He served as foreign policy researcher in the Private Office of former Prime Minister Margaret Thatcher of the United Kingdom.

Bruce Klingner is Senior Research Fellow for Northeast Asia in the Asian Studies Center. He served for two decades at the Central Intelligence Agency and the Defense Intelligence Agency.

Daniel Kochis is a Policy Analyst in European Affairs in the Margaret Thatcher Center for Freedom, where he specializes in trans-Atlantic security issues including NATO, U.S.–Russia relations, and the Arctic.

Walter Lohman is Director of the Asian Studies Center. He has served on the staff of the Senate Committee on Foreign Relations, in the Office of Senator John McCain, and as Executive Director of the U.S.–ASEAN Business Council.

James Phillips is Senior Research Fellow for Middle Eastern Affairs in the Allison Center. He has also served at the Congressional Research Service and at the East–West Center.

Brian Slattery is a former Policy Analyst for National Security in the Center for National Defense, where he supported production of the *Index of U.S. Military Strength* for four years.

John Venable is Senior Research Fellow for Defense Policy in the Center for National Defense. A 25-year veteran of the U.S. Air Force and F-16 pilot, he served in three combat operations, was commander of the Thunderbirds, and earned the rank of colonel before retiring.

Rachel Zissimos is a Research Associate in the Center for National Defense. She focuses on Department of Defense Energy and Industrial Base policy in addition to supporting production of the *Index of U.S. Military Strength*.

External Reviewers and Expert Contributors

Patrick M. Cronin, PhD, is a Senior Advisor and Senior Director of the Asia–Pacific Security Program at the Center for a New American Security (CNAS).

G. Alexander Crowther, PhD, is Senior Research Fellow for NATO/Europe and Cyber at the Institute for National Strategic Studies at the National Defense University.

Harry Foster is Director of Analysis at the Telemus Group.

Brad Glosserman is Executive Director of the Pacific Forum at the Center for Strategic and International Studies.

David Isby is a Washington-based defense analyst and consultant.

David E. Johnson, PhD, is a Senior Fellow at the Center for Strategic and Budgetary Assessments.

Roy D. Kamphausen is Senior Vice President for Research and Director of the Washington, D.C., Office of the National Bureau of Asian Research.

Jeff M. Smith is Director of Asian Security Programs and Kraemer Strategy Fellow at the American Foreign Policy Council.

Douglas E. Streusand, PhD, is a Professor of International Relations at the U.S. Marine Corps Command and Staff College.

Larry M. Wortzel, PhD, is Adjunct Research Professor at the U.S. Army War College.

Acknowledgments

While no publication of this type is possible without the contributions of a great many people, there usually are a few special contributors whose talents, work ethic, and willingness to go the extra mile make it something quite special.

Policy Analyst for National Security Brian Slattery was the linchpin of production success, working with the authors, editors, and graphics and production professionals who made this *Index* a reality, both in print and on the Web. Rachel Zissimos, Research Associate in the Center for National Defense, contributed with specialized research, writing, fact-checking, ably handling production management duties as needed, and overseeing additional research by interns brought on to support the project. On that note, Heritage Young Leaders Program interns Zachary Olden, Andrew Nagode, and Jordan Bernstein contributed significant research that helped to inform the findings of the *2018 Index*.

As with past editions, Senior Copy Editor William T. Poole was instrumental not only in maintaining a consistent tone throughout this multi-author document—a challenging feat all its own—but also in checking every reference to ensure accuracy of reporting and coherence throughout the *Index* while also updating text that, though still current, can become stale when carried from one year to the next. Data Graphics Services Manager John Fleming, ably assisted by Data Graphics Specialist and Editorial Associate Luke Karnick, once again gave visual life to text and statistics to convey a message with maximum impact. Creative Director Melissa Bluey, assisted by the detailed efforts of Art Director Jay Simon and Digital Strategy Director Maria Sousa, ensured that the presentation of *Index* materials was tuned to account for changes in content delivery as our world becomes increasingly digital, portable, and driven by social media.

We believe that this *Index* helps to provide a better informed understanding and wider appreciation of America's ability to "provide for the common defence" that undergirds The Heritage Foundation's vision of "an America where freedom, opportunity, prosperity, and civil society flourish." Judging by reception of the *Index* during this past year—some 480,000 unique visitors to the *2017 Index* website alone, a sixfold increase over our inaugural *Index* released in 2015—we are encouraged that so many Americans are similarly concerned about the state of affairs in and the multitude of factors affecting our country.

The Heritage Foundation seeks a better life for Americans, which requires a stronger economy, a stronger society, and a stronger defense.

To help measure the state of the economy, our Institute for Economic Freedom and Opportunity publishes the annual *Index of Economic Freedom*.

To help measure the state of society, our Institute for Family, Community, and Opportunity publishes the annual *Index of Culture and Opportunity*.

And to help Americans everywhere more fully understand the state of our defenses, our Kathryn and Shelby Cullom Davis Institute for National Security and Foreign Policy is publishing this fourth annual edition of the *Index of U.S. Military Strength*.

In addition to acknowledging all of those who helped to prepare this edition, very special recognition is due to Mr. Philip and Dr. Patricia Bilden and two Heritage members who wished to remain anonymous, whose generous financial support made the *2018 Index of U.S. Military Strength* possible.

Finally, as always, The Heritage Foundation also expresses its profound appreciation to the members of the U.S. armed forces who continue to protect the liberty of the American people in an increasingly dangerous world.

Preface

Edwin J. Feulner, PhD

Since the inaugural *2015 Index of U.S. Military Strength*, subsequent editions have demonstrated an unsettling trend, and the *2018 Index* leaves no room for interpretation: Our military has undoubtedly grown weaker. Service chiefs confirm these findings in testimony and reports to Congress. Yet, despite widespread agreement, critical maintenance and modernization efforts continue to be deferred and underfunded. Personnel and platforms decline in number as threats proliferate. The result is a force of growing age and declining capability, tasked with greater responsibilities but apportioned fewer resources.

Meanwhile, our competitors and enemies are spending more and acting more aggressively. Russian technological advances in ground combat vehicles rival and may even surpass our own; North Korea's nuclear weapons threaten regional forces as well as the U.S. homeland; and China is cementing its territorial claims in contested waters, militarizing islands, and building the beginnings of a blue-water navy.

Although the U.S. remains the world's dominant military power, recent developments should demonstrate that this status in not assured. In 2017, General Joseph Dunford, Chairman of the Joint Chiefs of Staff, warned that "without sustained, sufficient, and predictable funding...we will lose our ability to project power" within the next five years.

Global power projection enables the military to defeat threats before they can reach U.S. shores, protect shipping lanes that support global commerce, and provide reassurance and support to U.S. allies. It is a critical component of America's security and economic prosperity—and it is at risk.

As U.S. military strength continues to deteriorate, more and more people are taking notice. Since November 2016, when the *2017 Index* was launched online, there have been nearly 950,000 page views—a fivefold increase since the inaugural 2015 edition.

There is also movement on Capitol Hill. Both the House and Senate versions of the FY 2018 appropriations bills authorize defense spending that is above statutorily enacted budget caps and even above the levels requested in the President's budget. Congress understands the sad current state of military readiness and the consequences of sustained underinvestment in military capabilities and programs. Yet it continues to trip on its own shoelaces.

It continues to be our aim to inform Congress about the issues facing our military and nation, but after five years of arbitrary defense budget caps, it is time for Congress to stop discussing the problem and do something to solve it. The problem is clear, and the solution is simple: *Fund the military at a level that matches the importance of securing the country and our national interests.* In other words, stop squabbling and pass a budget that will truly provide for the common defense.

Edwin J. Feulner, PhD, President
The Heritage Foundation
October 2017

Introduction

The United States maintains a military force primarily to protect the homeland from attack and to protect its interests abroad. Although there are secondary uses for the military—such as assisting civil authorities in times of emergency or deterring enemies—that amplify other elements of national power such as diplomacy or economic initiatives, America's armed forces exist above all else so that the U.S. can physically impose its will on an enemy and change the conditions of a threatening situation by force or the threat of force.

Each year, The Heritage Foundation's *Index of U.S. Military Strength* gauges the ability of the U.S. military to perform its missions in today's world and how the condition of the military has changed from the preceding year.

The United States prefers to lead through "soft" elements of national power: diplomacy, economic incentives, and cultural exchanges. When soft approaches such as diplomacy work, that success often owes much to the knowledge of all involved that U.S. "hard power" stands ready, if silently, in the diplomatic background. Soft approaches cost less in manpower and treasure than military action costs and do not carry the same risk of damage and loss of life, but when confronted by physical threats to U.S. national security interests, soft power cannot substitute for raw military power. In fact, an absence of military power or the perception that one's hard power is insufficient to protect one's interests often invites challenges that soft power is ill-equipped to address. Thus, hard power and soft power are complementary and mutually reinforcing.

The continuing decline of America's military hard power is thoroughly documented and quantified in this report. More difficult to quantify, however, are the growing threats to the U.S. and its allies that are engendered by the perception of American weakness abroad and doubts about America's resolve to act when its interests are threatened. The anecdotal evidence is consistent with direct conversations between Heritage scholars and high-level diplomatic and military officials from countries around the world: The perception of American weakness is destabilizing many parts of the world, prompting old friends to question their reliance on America's assurances. For decades, the perception of American strength and resolve has served as a deterrent to adventurous bad actors and tyrannical dictators. Regrettably, both that perception and, as a consequence, its deterrent effect are eroding. The result is an increasingly dangerous world threatening a significantly weaker America.

It is therefore critical to understand the condition of the United States military with respect to America's vital national security interests, the threats to those interests, and the context within which the U.S. might have to use hard power. It is likewise important to know how these three areas—operating environments, threats, and the posture of the U.S. military—change over time, given that such changes can have substantial implications for defense policies and investments.

In the opening paragraph of the U.S. Constitution, "We the People" stated that among their handful of purposes in establishing the Constitution was to "provide for the common defence." The enumeration of limited powers for the federal government in the Constitution includes the powers of Congress "To declare

War," "To raise and support Armies," "To provide and maintain a Navy," "To provide for calling forth the Militia," and "To provide for organizing, arming, and disciplining, the Militia" and the power of the President as "Commander in Chief of the Army and Navy of the United States, and of the Militia of the several States, when called into the actual Service of the United States." With such constitutional priority given to defense of the nation and its vital interests, one might expect the federal government to produce a standardized, consistent reference work on the state of the nation's security. Yet no such single volume exists, especially in the public domain, to allow comparisons from year to year. Recently, the Department of Defense has moved to restrict reporting of force readiness even further. Thus, the American people and even the government itself are prevented from understanding whether investments made in defense are achieving their desired results.

What is needed is a publicly accessible reference document that uses a consistent, methodical, repeatable approach to assessing defense requirements and capabilities. The Heritage Foundation's *Index of U.S. Military Strength*, an annual assessment of the state of America's hard power, fills this void, addressing both the geographical and functional environments relevant to the United States' vital national interests and threats that rise to a level that puts or has the strong potential to put those interests at risk.

Any assessment of the adequacy of military power requires two primary reference points: a clear statement of U.S. vital security interests and an objective requirement for the military's capacity for operations that serve as a benchmark against which to measure current capacity. A review of relevant top-level national security documents issued by a long string of presidential Administrations makes clear that three interests are consistently stated:

- Defense of the homeland;

- Successful conclusion of a major war that has the potential to destabilize a region of critical interest to the U.S.; and

- Preservation of freedom of movement within the global commons: the sea, air, outer-space, and cyberspace domains through which the world conducts business.

Every President has recognized that one of the fundamental purposes of the U.S. military is to protect America from attack. While going to war has always been controversial, the decision to do so has been based consistently on the conclusion that one or more vital U.S. interests are at stake.

This *Index* embraces the "two-war requirement"—the ability to handle two major wars or two major regional contingencies (MRCs) successfully at the same time or in closely overlapping time frames—as the most compelling rationale for sizing U.S. military forces. In the *2015 Index*, Dr. Daniel Gouré provided a detailed defense of this approach in his essay, "Building the Right Military for a New Era: The Need for an Enduring Analytic Framework," which is further elaborated upon in the military capabilities assessment section. The basic argument, however, is this: The nation should have the ability to engage and defeat one opponent and still have the ability to guard against competitor opportunism (i.e., to preclude someone's exploiting the perceived opportunity to move against U.S. interests while America is engaged elsewhere).

The *Index* is descriptive, not prescriptive, reviewing the current condition of its subjects within the assessed year and describing how conditions have changed from the previous year, informed by the baseline condition established by the inaugural *2015 Index*. In short, the *Index* answers the question, "Have conditions improved or worsened during the assessed year?"

This study also assesses the U.S. military against the two-war benchmark and various metrics explained further in the military capabilities section. Importantly, this study measures the hard power needed to win conventional wars rather than the general utility of the military relative to the breadth of tasks it might be (and usually is) assigned to advance U.S. interests short of war.

Assessing the World and the Need for Hard Power

The assessment portion of the *Index* is composed of three major sections that address the aforementioned areas of primary interest: America's military power, the operating environments within or through which it must operate, and threats to U.S. vital national interests. For each of these areas, this publication provides context, explaining why a given topic is addressed and how it relates to understanding the nature of America's hard-power requirements.

The authors of this study used a five-category scoring system that ranged from "very poor" to "excellent" or "very weak" to "very strong" as appropriate to each topic. This particular approach was selected as the best way to capture meaningful gradations while avoiding the appearance that a high level of precision was possible given the nature of the issues and the information that was publicly available.

Some factors are quantitative and lend themselves to discrete measurement; others are very qualitative in nature and can be assessed only through an informed understanding of the material that leads to an informed judgment call.

Purely quantitative measures alone tell only a part of the story when it comes to the relevance, utility, and effectiveness of hard power. Assessing military power or the nature of an operating environment using only quantitative metrics can lead to misinformed conclusions. For example, the mere existence of a large fleet of very modern tanks has little to do with the effectiveness of the armored force in actual battle if the employment concept is irrelevant to modern armored warfare. (Imagine, for example, a battle in rugged mountains.) Also, experience and demonstrated proficiency are often decisive factors in war—so much so that numerically smaller or qualitatively inferior but well-trained and experienced forces can defeat a larger or qualitatively superior adversary.

However digital and quantitative the world has become thanks to the explosion of advanced technologies, it is still very much a qualitative place, and judgment calls have to be made in the absence of certainty. We strive to be as objective and evenhanded as possible in our approach and transparent in our methodology and sources of information so that readers can understand why we came to the conclusions we reached and perhaps reach their own. The end result will be a more informed debate about what the United States needs in military capabilities to deal with the world as it is. A detailed discussion of scoring is provided in each assessment section.

In our assessment, we begin with the operating environment because it provides the geostrategic stage upon which the U.S. attends to its interests: the various states that would play significant roles in any regional contingency; the terrain that enables or restricts military operations; the infrastructure—ports, airfields, roads, and rail networks (or lack thereof)—on which U.S. forces would depend; and the types of linkages and relationships the U.S. has with a region and major actors within it that cause the U.S. to have interests in the area or that facilitate effective operations. Major actors within each region are identified, described, and assessed in terms of alliances, political stability, the presence of U.S. military forces and relationships, and the maturity of critical infrastructure.

Our assessment focuses on three key regions—Europe, the Middle East, and Asia—because of their importance relative to U.S. vital security interests. This does not mean that we view Latin America and Africa as unimportant. Rather, it means that the security challenges within these regions do not currently rise to the level of direct threats to America's vital security interests as we have defined them. We addressed their current condition in the *2015 Index* and will provide an updated assessment when it is warranted.

Next is a discussion of threats to U.S. vital interests. Here we identify the countries that pose the greatest current or potential threats to U.S. vital interests based on two overarching factors: their behavior and their capability. We accept the classic definition of "threat" as a combination of intent and capability, but while capability has attributes that can be quantified, intent is difficult to measure. We concluded that "observed behavior" serves as a reasonable surrogate for intent because it is the clearest manifestation of intent.

We based our selection of threat countries and non-state actors on their historical behavior and explicit policies or formal statements vis-à-vis U.S. interests, scoring them in two areas: the degree of provocative behavior that they exhibited during the year and their ability to pose a credible threat to U.S. interests irrespective of intent. For example, a state full of bluster but with only a moderate ability to act accordingly poses a lesser threat, while a state that has great capabilities and a pattern of bellicose behavior opposed to U.S. interests still warrants attention even if it is relatively quiet in a given year.

Finally, we address the status of U.S. military power in three areas: capability (or modernity), capacity, and readiness. Do U.S. forces possess operational capabilities that are relevant to modern warfare? Can they defeat the military forces of an opposing country? Do they have a sufficient amount of such capabilities? Is the force sufficiently trained and its equipment materially ready to win in combat? All of these are fundamental to success even if they are not de facto determinants of success (something we explain further in the section). We also address the condition of the United States' nuclear weapons capability, assessing it in areas that are unique to this military component and critical to understanding its real-world viability and effectiveness as a strategic deterrent.

Topical Essays

The *2018 Index* departs from the previous *Index* themes of strategic, regional, and functional topics to focus on the domains in and through which military operations are conducted. Nearly all discussions of military power and the forces used to wield it focus on the forces themselves or the areas of competition between forces as evolving technologies are harnessed to gain advantage over an enemy. Seldom does one read about the domains themselves that shape the nature of employment and the characteristics of the forces used. The characteristics of the domains both facilitate and inhibit operations, impose constraints, and make demands on time, energy, firepower, cost, size, and durability associated with military actions.

Our authors take on the challenge of describing the various operating domains available to military forces—land, sea, air, space, and cyberspace—and how they inform the design of platforms, the size and endurance of forces, and expectations for how easily (or not) the U.S. military can accomplish objectives.

- Dr. James Jay Carafano leads off with "America's Joint Force and the Domains of Warfare," an overview of the concept of "jointness," an idea much larger than U.S. forces simply acting in concert with each other. Per Dr. Carafano, "The future focus of jointness will be on ensuring that U.S. armed forces retain the ability to operate effectively in all domains in a theater...and to exploit the ability to use advantages in one domain to operate in another."

- Dr. David E. Johnson, in "An Overview of Land Warfare," notes that "the land domain has the greatest ability to create operational friction." Land is not only where people live, but also where challenges to the conduct of war are most apparent. Land forces must contend directly with cities, forests, mountains, deserts, and the impact of weather. The physicality of the land domain makes operations hard, but once forces are established, dislodging them is quite difficult as well.

- The vastness of the oceans and the characteristics of water impose their own challenges on the projection of military power via the seas. In "The Naval Warfare Domain," Thomas Callender explores how the breadth, depth, salinity, and physical properties of the maritime domain affect naval forces and how they operate. Callender explains how the seas have their own "terrain" that provides cover and avenues through which to advance, much as land does for ground forces, while also imposing obstacles to rapid movement and sustained presence.

- Harry Foster provides a deeply informed primer on the complexities of air operations with "The Air Domain and the Challenges of Modern Air Warfare." "*The speed* possible in the air domain shrinks time" and provides advantages in vantage, maneuverability, flexibility, and range but also imposes limitations on payload, persistence, and the ability to mask one's actions in such a transparent medium. Foster provides the "why" for each of these and concludes with thoughts on the evolving nature of competition in this domain.

- In "Space 201: Thinking About the Space Domain," Dean Cheng provides the basis for understanding how space can be leveraged to support the protection of national security interests and why it is so costly to do so. Space, arguably the harshest and most technically challenging of operating environments, is crucial to modern military operations. Cheng helps the reader understand why maintaining mastery of it, especially relative to competitors, is essential.

- Finally, Dr. G. Alexander Crowther tackles the always mentioned but consistently misunderstood world of cyber in "National Defense and the Cyber Domain." Dr. Crowther outlines the players, roles, and infrastructure of the cyber domain but takes the discussion further in pointing out that "[h]umans are the weakest link in the cybersecurity system. Unlike the physical world, in which potential human activity is limited by geographic and space limitations...[e]veryone who has a desktop, laptop, or smartphone is an actor and a potential problem." He concludes by observing that "[a]lthough military leaders understand the importance of cyber and information, not all understand the scope of the opportunities and challenges that cyber provides." This essay should help in that regard.

Scoring U.S. Military Strength Relative to Vital National Interests

The purpose of this *Index* is to make the national debate about defense capabilities better informed by assessing the ability of the U.S. military to defend against current threats to U.S. vital national interests within the context of the world as it is. Each of the elements can change from year to year: the stability of regions and access to them by America's military forces; the various threats as they improve or lose capabilities and change their behavior; and the United States' armed forces themselves as they adjust to evolving fiscal realities and attempt to balance readiness, capacity (size and quantity), and capability (how modern they are) in ways that enable them to carry out their assigned missions successfully.

Each region of the world has its own set of characteristics that include terrain; man-made infrastructure (roads, rail lines, ports, airfields, power grids, etc.); and states with which the United States has relationships. In each case, these traits combine to create an environment that is either favorable or problematic when it comes to U.S. forces operating against threats in the region.

Various states and nonstate actors within these regions possess the ability to threaten—and have consistently behaved in ways that threaten—America's interests. Fortunately for the U.S., these major threat actors are currently few in number and continue to be confined to three regions—Europe, the Middle East, and Asia—thus enabling the U.S. (if it will do so) to focus its resources and efforts accordingly.

As for the condition of America's military services, they continue to be beset by aging equipment, shrinking numbers, rising costs, and problematic funding: four factors that have accelerated over the past year at a time when threats to U.S. interests continue to rise.

These four elements interact with each other in ways that are difficult to measure in concrete terms and impossible to forecast with any certainty. Nevertheless, the exercise of describing them and characterizing their general condition is worthwhile because it informs debates about defense policies and the allocation of resources that are necessary for the U.S. military to carry out its assigned duties. Further, as seen in this *2018 Index*, noting how conditions have changed from the preceding year helps to shed light on the effect that policies, decisions, and actions have on security affairs involving the interests of the United States, its allies and friends, and its enemies.

It should be borne in mind that each annual *Index* assesses conditions as they are for the assessed year. This *2018 Index of U.S. Military Strength* describes changes that occurred during the preceding year, with updates current as of mid-September 2017.

Assessments for U.S. Military Power, Global Operating Environment, and Threats to Vital U.S. Interests are shown in the Executive Summary. Factors that would push things toward "bad" (the left side of the scales) tend to move more quickly than those that improve one's situation, especially when it comes to the material condition of the U.S. military.

Of the three areas measured—U.S. Military Power, Global Operating Environment, and Threats to Vital U.S. Interests—the U.S. can directly control only one: its own military. The condition of the U.S. military can influence the other two because a weakened America arguably emboldens challenges to its interests and loses potential allies, while a militarily strong America deters opportunism and draws partners to its side from across the globe.

Conclusion

During the decades since the end of the Second World War, the United States has underwritten and taken the lead in maintaining a global order that has benefited more people in more ways than at any other period in history. Now, however, that American-led order is under stress, and some have wondered whether it will break apart entirely. Fiscal and economic burdens continue to plague nations; violent, extremist ideologies threaten the stability of entire regions; state and nonstate opportunists seek to exploit upheavals; and major states compete to establish dominant positions in their respective regions.

America's leadership role remains in question, and its security interests are under significant pressure. Challenges are growing, old allies are not what they once were, and the U.S. is increasingly bedeviled by debt that constrains its ability to sustain its forces commensurate with its interests.

Informed deliberations on the status of the United States' military power are therefore desperately needed. This *Index of U.S. Military Strength* can help to inform the debate.

Methodology

The assessment portion of the *Index of U.S. Military Strength* is composed of three major sections that address America's military power, the operating environments within or through which it must operate, and threats to U.S. vital national interests.

The authors of this study used a five-category scoring system that ranged from "very poor" to "excellent" or "very weak" to "very strong" as appropriate to each topic. This particular approach was selected to capture meaningful gradations while avoiding the appearance that a high level of precision was possible given the nature of the issues and the information that was publicly available.

Some factors are quantitative and lend themselves to discrete measurement; others are very qualitative in nature and can be assessed only through an informed understanding of the material that leads to a judgment call. Further, conditions in each of the areas assessed are changing throughout the year, so any measurement is based on the information at hand and must necessarily be viewed as a snapshot in time. While this is not entirely satisfactory when it comes to reaching conclusions on the status of a given matter, especially the adequacy of military power (and will be quite unsatisfactory for some readers), we understand that senior officials in decision-making positions will never have a comprehensive set of inarguable hard data on which to base a decision.

Purely quantitative measures alone tell only part of the story when it comes to the relevance, utility, and effectiveness of hard power. In fact, assessing military power or the nature of an operating environment using only quantitative metrics can lead to misinformed conclusions. Raw numbers are a very important component, but they tell only a part of the story of war. Similarly, experience and demonstrated proficiency are often decisive factors in war, but they are nearly impossible to measure.

This *Index*'s assessment of the **global operating environment** focused on three key regions—Europe, the Middle East, and Asia—because of their importance relative to U.S. vital security interests.

For **threats to U.S. vital interests**, the *Index* identifies the countries that pose the greatest current or potential threats to U.S. vital interests based on two overarching factors: their behavior and their capability. The classic definition of "threat" considers the combination of intent and capability, but intent cannot be clearly measured, so "observed behavior" is used as a reasonable surrogate since it is the clearest manifestation of intent. The selection of threat countries is based on their historical behavior and explicit policies or formal statements vis-à-vis U.S. interests, scoring them in two areas: the degree of provocative behavior that they exhibited during the year and their ability to pose a credible threat to U.S. interests irrespective of intent.

Finally, the **status of U.S. military power** is addressed in three areas: capability (or modernity), capacity, and readiness. All three are fundamental to success even if they are not de facto determinants of success, something we explain further in the section. Also addressed is the condition of the United States' nuclear weapons capability, assessing it in areas that are unique to this military component and critical to understanding its real-world viability and effectiveness as a strategic deterrent.

Assessing the Global Operating Environment

Not all of the factors that characterize an operating environment are equal, but each contributes to the degree to which a particular operating environment is favorable or unfavorable to future U.S. military operations. Our assessment of the operating environment utilized a five-point scale, ranging from "very poor" to "excellent" conditions and covering four regional characteristics of greatest relevance to the conduct of military operations:

1. **Very Poor.** Significant hurdles exist for military operations. Physical infrastructure is insufficient or nonexistent, and the region is politically unstable. The U.S. military is poorly placed or absent, and alliances are nonexistent or diffuse.

2. **Unfavorable.** A challenging operating environment for military operations is marked by inadequate infrastructure, weak alliances, and recurring political instability. The U.S. military is inadequately placed in the region.

3. **Moderate.** A neutral to moderately favorable operating environment is characterized by adequate infrastructure, a moderate alliance structure, and acceptable levels of regional political stability. The U.S. military is adequately placed.

4. **Favorable.** A favorable operating environment includes good infrastructure, strong alliances, and a stable political environment. The U.S. military is well placed in the region for future operations.

5. **Excellent.** An extremely favorable operating environment includes well-established and well-maintained infrastructure; strong, capable allies; and a stable political environment. The U.S. military is exceptionally well placed to defend U.S. interests.

The key regional characteristics consisted of:

a. **Alliances.** Alliances are important for interoperability and collective defense as allies would be more likely to lend support to U.S. military operations. Various indicators provide insight into the strength or health of an alliance. These include whether the U.S. trains regularly with countries in the region, has good interoperability with the forces of an ally, and shares intelligence with nations in the region.

b. **Political Stability.** Political stability brings predictability for military planners when considering such things as transit, basing, and overflight rights for U.S. military operations. The overall degree of political stability indicates whether U.S. military actions would be hindered or enabled and considers, for example, whether transfers of power in the region are generally peaceful and whether there been any recent instances of political instability in the region.

c. **U.S. Military Positioning.** Having military forces based or equipment and supplies staged in a region greatly facilitates the ability of the United States to respond to crises and, presumably, achieve successes in critical "first battles" more quickly. Being routinely present in a region also assists in maintaining familiarity with its characteristics and the various actors that might try to assist or thwart U.S. actions. With this in mind, we assessed whether or not the U.S. military was well-positioned in the region. Again, indicators included bases, troop presence, prepositioned equipment, and recent examples of military operations (including training and humanitarian) launched from the region.

d. **Infrastructure.** Modern, reliable, and suitable infrastructure is essential to military operations. Airfields, ports, rail lines, canals, and paved roads enable the U.S. to stage, launch operations from, and logistically sustain combat operations. We combined expert knowledge of regions with publicly available information on critical infrastructure to arrive at our overall assessment of this metric.

Assessing Threats to U.S. Vital Interests

To make the threats identified herein measurable and relatable to the challenges of operating environments and adequacy of American military power, *Index* staff and outside reviewers evaluated separately the threats according to their level of provocation (i.e., their observed behavior) and their actual capability to pose a credible threat to U.S. interests on a scale of 1 to 5, with 1 representing a very high threat capability or level of belligerency. This scale corresponds to the tone of the five-point scales used to score the operating environment and military capabilities in that 1 is bad for U.S. interests and 5 is very favorable.

Based on these evaluations, provocative behavior was characterized according to five descending categories: benign (5); assertive (4); testing (3); aggressive (2); and hostile (1). Staff also characterized the capabilities of a threat actor according to five categories: marginal (5); aspirational (4); capable (3); gathering (2); and formidable (1). Those characterizations—behavior and capability—form two halves of the overall threat level.

Assessing U.S. Military Power

Also assessed is the adequacy of the United States' defense posture as it pertains to a conventional understanding of "hard power," defined as the ability of American military forces to engage and defeat an enemy's forces in battle at a scale commensurate with the vital national interests of the U.S. The assessment draws on both quantitative and qualitative aspects of military forces, informed by an experience-based understanding of military operations and the expertise of the authors and internal and external reviewers.

It is important to note that military effectiveness is as much an art as it is a science. Specific military capabilities represented in weapons, platforms, and military units can be used individually to some effect. Practitioners of war, however, have learned that combining the tools of war in various ways and orchestrating their tactical employment in series or simultaneously can dramatically amplify the effectiveness of the force committed to battle.

The point is that a great number of factors make it possible for a military force to locate, close with, and destroy an enemy, but not many of them are easily measured. The scope of this specific project does not extend to analysis of everything that makes hard power possible; it focuses on the status of the hard power itself.

This *Index* assesses the state of military affairs for U.S. forces in three areas: capability, capacity, and readiness.

Capability. Capability is scored based on the current state of combat equipment. This involves four factors: the age of key platforms relative to their expected life span; whether the required capability is being met by legacy or modern equipment; the scope of improvement or replacement programs relative to the operational requirement; and the overall health and stability (financial and technological) of modernization programs.

This *Index* focused on primary combat units and combat platforms (e.g., tanks, ships, and airplanes) and elected not to include the array of system and component upgrades that keep an older platform viable over time, such as a new radar, missile, or communications suite. New technologies grafted onto aging platforms ensure that U.S. military forces keep pace with technological innovations relevant to the modern battlefield, but at some point, the platforms themselves are no longer viable and must be replaced. Modernized sub-systems and components do not entirely substitute for aging platforms, and it is the platform itself that is usually the more challenging item to field. In this sense, primary combat platforms serve as representative measures of force modernity just as combat forces are a useful surrogate measure for the overall military that includes a range of support units, systems, and infrastructure.

In addition, it is assumed that modernization programs should replace current capacity at a one-to-one ratio; less than a one-to-one replacement assumes risk, because even if the newer system is presumably better than the older, until it is proven in actual combat, having fewer systems lessens the capacity of the force, which is an important factor if combat against a peer competitor carries with it the likelihood of attrition. For modernization programs, only Major Defense Acquisition Programs (MDAPs) are scored.

The capability score uses a five-grade scale. Each service receives one capability score that is a non-weighted aggregate of scores for four categories: (1) Age of Equipment, (2) Modernity of Capability, (3) Size of Modernization Program, and (4) Health of Modernization Program. General criteria for the capability categories are:

Age of Equipment

- **Very Weak:** Equipment age is past 80 percent of expected life span.

- **Weak:** Equipment age is 61 percent–80 percent of expected life span.

- **Marginal:** Equipment age is 41 percent–60 percent of expected life span.

- **Strong:** Equipment age is 21 percent–40 percent of expected life span.

- **Very Strong:** Equipment age is 20 percent or less of expected life span.

Capability of Equipment

- **Very Weak:** Majority (over 80 percent) of capability relies on legacy platforms.

- **Weak:** 60 percent–79 percent of capability relies on legacy platforms.

- **Marginal:** 40 percent–59 percent of capability is legacy platforms.

- **Strong:** 20 percent–39 percent of capability is legacy platforms.

- **Very Strong:** Less than 20 percent of capability is legacy platforms.

Size of Modernization Program

- **Very Weak:** Modernization program is significantly too small or inappropriate to sustain current capability or program in place.

- **Weak:** Modernization programs are smaller than current capability size.

- **Marginal:** Modernization programs are appropriate to sustain current capability size.

- **Strong:** Modernization programs will increase current capability size.

- **Very Strong:** Modernization programs will vastly expand capability size.

Health of Modernization Program

- **Very Weak:** Modernization programs facing significant problems; too far behind schedule (five-plus years); cannot replace current capability before retirement; lacking sufficient investment to advance; cost overruns including Nunn–McCurdy breach. (A Nunn–McCurdy breach occurs when the cost of a new item exceeds the most recently approved amount by 25 percent or more or if it exceeds the originally approved amount by 50 percent or more. See Title 10, U.S.C. § 2433, Unit Cost Reports (UCRs).)

- **Weak:** Facing procurement problems; behind schedule (three–five years); difficult to replace current equipment on time or insufficient funding; cost overruns enough to trigger an Acquisition Program Baseline (APB) breach.

- **Marginal:** Facing few problems; behind schedule by one–two years but can replace equipment with some delay or experience some funding cuts; some cost growth but not within objectives.

- **Strong:** Facing no procurement problems; can replace equipment with no delays; within cost estimates.

- **Very Strong:** Performing better than DOD plans, including lower actual costs.

Capacity. To score capacity, the service's size (be it end strength or number of platforms) is compared to the force size required to meet a simultaneous or nearly simultaneous two-war or two–major regional contingency (MRC) benchmark. This benchmark consists of the force needed to fight and win two MRCs and a 20 percent margin that serves as a strategic reserve. A strategic reserve is necessary because deployment of 100 percent of the force at any one time is highly unlikely. Not only do ongoing requirements like training or sustainment and maintenance of equipment make it infeasible for the entirety of the force to be available for deployment, but committing 100 percent of the force would leave no resources available to handle unexpected situations.

Thus, a "marginal" capacity score would exactly meet a two-MRC force size, a "strong" capacity score would equate to a plus–10 percent margin for strategic reserve, and a "very strong" score would equate to a 20 percent margin.

Capacity Score Definitions
- **Very Weak:** 0 percent–37 percent of the two-MRC benchmark.

- **Weak:** 38 percent–74 percent of the two-MRC benchmark.

- **Marginal:** 75 percent–82 percent of the two-MRC benchmark.

- **Strong:** 83 percent–91 percent of the two-MRC benchmark.

- **Very Strong:** 92 percent–100 percent of the two-MRC benchmark.

Readiness. The readiness scores are from the military services' own assessments of readiness based on their requirements. These are not comprehensive reviews of all readiness input factors, but rather rely on the public statements of the military services regarding the state of their readiness.

It should be noted that even a "strong" or "very strong" score does not indicate that 100 percent of the force is ready; it simply indicates that the service is meeting 100 percent of its own readiness requirements. Often, these requirements assume that a percentage of the military at any one time will not be fit for deployment. Because of this, even if readiness is graded as "strong" or "marginal," there is still a gap in readiness that will have significant implications for immediate combat effectiveness and the ability to deploy quickly. Thus, anything short of meeting 100 percent of readiness requirements assumes risk and is therefore problematic.

Further, a service's assessment of its readiness occurs within its size or capacity at that time and as dictated by the Defense Strategic Guidance, National Military Strategy, and related top-level documents generated by the Administration and senior Defense officials. It does not account for the size-related "readiness" of the force to meet national security requirements assessed as needed by this *Index*. Thus, for a service to be assessed as "very strong" would mean that 80 percent–100 percent of the existing force in a service meets that service's requirements for being "ready" even if the size of the service is less than that required to meet the two-MRC benchmark. Therefore, it is important for the reader to keep this in mind when considering the actual readiness of the force to protect U.S. national security interests against the challenges presented by threats around the world.

Readiness Score Definitions
- **Very Weak:** 0 percent–19 percent of service's requirements.

- **Weak:** 20 percent–39 percent of service's requirements.

- **Marginal:** 40 percent–59 percent of service's requirements.

- **Strong:** 60 percent–79 percent of service's requirements.

- **Very Strong:** 80 percent–100 percent of service's requirements.

Executive Summary

"The U.S. military is only marginally able to meet the demands of defending America's vital national interests."

The United States maintains a military force primarily to protect the homeland from attack and to protect its interests abroad. There are secondary uses—for example, to assist civil authorities in times of disaster or to deter opponents from threatening America's interests—but this force's primary purpose is to make it possible for the U.S. to physically impose its will on an enemy when necessary.

It is therefore critical that the condition of the United States military with respect to America's vital national security interests, threats to those interests, and the context within which the U.S. might have to use "hard power" be understood. Knowing how these three areas—operating environments, threats, and the posture of the U.S. military—change over time, given that such changes can have substantial implications for defense policies and investment, is likewise important.

Each year, The Heritage Foundation's *Index of U.S. Military Strength* employs a standardized, consistent set of criteria, accessible both to government officials and to the American public, to gauge the ability of the U.S. military to perform its missions in today's world. The inaugural 2015 edition established a baseline assessment on which each annual edition builds, assessing the state of affairs for its respective year and measuring how key factors have changed from the previous year.

What the *Index* Assesses

The *Index of U.S. Military Strength* assesses the ease or difficulty of operating in key regions based on existing alliances, regional political stability, the presence of U. S. military forces, and the condition of key infrastructure. Threats are assessed based on the behavior and physical capabilities of actors that pose challenges to U.S. vital national interests. The condition of America's military power is measured in terms of its capability or modernity, capacity for operations, and readiness to handle assigned missions successfully. This framework provides a single-source reference for policymakers and other Americans who seek to know whether our military power is up to the task of defending our national interests.

Any discussion of the aggregate capacity and breadth of the military power needed to address threats to U.S. security interests requires a clear understanding of precisely what interests must be defended. Three vital interests have been specified consistently and in various ways by a string of Administrations over the past few decades:

- **Defense** of the homeland;

- **Successful conclusion** of a major war that has the potential to destabilize a region of critical interest to the U.S.; and

- **Preservation** of freedom of movement within the global commons (the sea, air, outer-space, and cyberspace domains) through which the world conducts its business.

To defend these interests effectively on a global scale, the United States needs a military force of sufficient size, or what is known in the Pentagon as capacity. The many factors involved make determining how big the military should be a complex exercise, but successive Administrations, Congresses, and Department of Defense staffs have managed to arrive at a surprisingly consistent force-sizing rationale: an ability to handle two major wars or major regional contingencies (MRCs) simultaneously or in closely overlapping time frames. This two-war or two-MRC requirement is embraced in this *Index*.

At the core of this requirement is the conviction that the United States should be able to engage and decisively defeat one major opponent and simultaneously have the wherewithal to do the same with another to preclude opportunistic exploitation by any competitor. Since World War II, the U.S. has found itself involved in a major "hot" war every 15–20 years while simultaneously maintaining substantial combat forces in Europe and several other regions. The size of the total force roughly approximated the two-MRC model. Accordingly, our assessment of the adequacy of today's U.S. military is based on the ability of America's armed forces to engage and defeat two major competitors at roughly the same time.

This *Index*'s benchmark for a two-MRC force is derived from a review of the forces used for each major war that the U.S. has undertaken since World War II and the major defense studies completed by the federal government over the past 30 years. We concluded that a standing (i.e., Active Duty component) two-MRC–capable Joint Force would consist of:

- **Army:** 50 brigade combat teams (BCTs);

- **Navy:** at least 346 surface combatants and 624 strike aircraft;

- **Air Force:** 1,200 fighter/ground-attack aircraft; and

- **Marine Corps:** 36 battalions.

This recommended force does not account for homeland defense missions that would accompany a period of major conflict and are generally handled by Reserve and National Guard forces. Nor does it constitute the totality of the Joint Force, which includes the array of supporting and combat-enabling functions essential to the conduct of any military operation: logistics; transportation (land, sea, and air); health services; communications and data handling; and force generation (recruiting, training, and education), to name a very few. Rather, these are combat forces that are the most recognizable elements of America's hard power but that also can be viewed as surrogate measures for the size and capability of the larger Joint Force.

The Global Operating Environment

Looking at the world as an environment in which U.S. forces would operate to protect America's interests, the *Index* focused on three regions—Europe, the Middle East, and Asia—because of the intersection of our vital interests and actors able to challenge them.

Europe. For the most part, Europe remains a stable, mature, and friendly environment, home to America's oldest and closest allies, although the migrant and refugee crises are straining the economies and societies of many European nations. The U.S. is tied to Europe by treaty, robust economic bonds, and deeply rooted cultural linkages. In general, America's partners in the region are politically stable; possess mature (though increasingly debt-laden) economies; and have fairly modern (but shrinking) militaries. America's longtime presence in the region, Europe's well-established basing and support infrastructure, and the framework for coordinated action provided by NATO make the region quite favorable for military operations. A more muscular, belligerent Russia has caused a review of U.S. force posture on the continent, spurring reinvestment of U.S. military capabilities through programs like the European Reassurance Initiative.

The Middle East. The Middle East, by contrast, continues to be a deeply troubled

Operating Environment: Europe

	VERY POOR	UNFAVORABLE	MODERATE	FAVORABLE	EXCELLENT
Alliances				✓	
Political Stability				✓	
U.S. Military Posture			✓		
Infrastructure				✓	
OVERALL				✓	

Operating Environment: Middle East

	VERY POOR	UNFAVORABLE	MODERATE	FAVORABLE	EXCELLENT
Alliances			✓		
Political Stability	✓				
U.S. Military Posture			✓		
Infrastructure			✓		
OVERALL			✓		

Operating Environment: Asia

	VERY POOR	UNFAVORABLE	MODERATE	FAVORABLE	EXCELLENT
Alliances				✓	
Political Stability			✓		
U.S. Military Posture				✓	
Infrastructure				✓	
OVERALL				✓	

Global Operating Environment

	VERY POOR	UNFAVORABLE	MODERATE	FAVORABLE	EXCELLENT
Europe				✓	
Middle East			✓		
Asia				✓	
OVERALL				✓	

Global Operating Environment

VERY POOR	UNFAVORABLE	MODERATE	FAVORABLE	EXCELLENT
			FAVORABLE	

area riven with conflict, ruled by authoritarian regimes, and home to a variety of terrorist and other destabilizing entities. Though the United States does enjoy a few strong partnerships in the region, its interests are beset by security and political challenges, transnational terrorism rooted in the region, and the maturing threat of a nuclear Iran. Offsetting these challenges to some extent are the U.S. military's experience in the region and the basing infrastructure that it has developed and leveraged for nearly 25 years, although these positive elements are decaying as a consequence of continued upheaval in Syria; Iran's pursuit of weapons that threaten both the U.S. and Europe, as well as its continued support of such terrorist groups as Hezbollah; and the increasingly problematic political environment in countries that historically have hosted U.S. forces (Qatar, for example).

Asia. Though the region includes longstanding U.S. allies that are stable and possess advanced economies, the tyranny of distance makes U.S. military operations in the region difficult in terms of the time and sealift and airlift required, a challenge that is only exacerbated as the size of the U.S. military continues to shrink. The region is critical to U.S. economic interests because Asian markets account for 40 percent of U.S. trade; consequently, the increasingly aggressive postures of China and North Korea have caused concern. In 2017, China was more overtly aggressive in pressing its claims to disputed islands and waters. Both South Korea and Japan have expressed alarm over North Korea's intentions, especially with respect to its missile program. Combined with a slight decrease in political stability across the region, Asia as an operating environment has trended toward more challenging for the U.S. in 2017.

Summarizing the condition of each region enables us to get a sense of how they compare in terms of the challenge the U.S. would have in projecting military power and sustaining combat operations in each one.

As a whole, the global operating environment currently rates a score of "favorable," meaning that the United States should be able to project military power anywhere in the world as necessary to defend its interests without substantial opposition or high levels of risk, but conditions could easily tip this aggregate score into the "moderate" category if conditions continue to degrade in both Asia and the Middle East in 2018.

Threats to U.S. Interests

Our selection of threat actors discounted troublesome states and non-state entities that lacked the physical ability to pose a meaningful threat to vital U.S. security interests. This reduced the population of all potential threats to a half-dozen that possessed the means to threaten U.S. vital interests and exhibited a pattern of provocative behavior that should draw the focus of U.S. defense planning. This *Index* characterizes their behavior and military capabilities on five-point, descending scales.

All of the six threat actors selected—Russia, China, Iran, North Korea, and terrorist groups in the Middle East and Afghanistan—remained actual or potential threats to U.S. interests over the past year. All amply demonstrated a commitment to expanding their capabilities to pursue their respective interests that directly challenged those of the U.S. All also continued or increased their aggressive behavior when compared to the 2016 *Index*.

Worryingly, all of the six noted threat actors now rank "high" on the scale of threats to U.S. interests, with Russia coming close to being elevated to "severe" from its past score of "high."

Russia and China continue to be the most worrisome, both because of the ongoing modernization and expansion of their offensive military capabilities and because of the more enduring effect they are having within their respective regions. Russia has maintained its active involvement in the conflict in Ukraine, has been more assertive in the Baltic Sea region, and has continued to insert itself into the Syrian conflict. China's provocative behavior continues to include militarization of islands that it has built in highly disputed international waters of the South China Sea. China

Threat Categories

Behavior	HOSTILE	AGGRESSIVE	TESTING	ASSERTIVE	BENIGN
Capability	FORMIDABLE	GATHERING	CAPABLE	ASPIRATIONAL	MARGINAL

Behavior of Threats

	HOSTILE	AGGRESSIVE	TESTING	ASSERTIVE	BENIGN
Russia		✓			
Iran		✓			
Middle East Terrorism		✓			
Af-Pak Terrorism		✓			
China			✓		
North Korea		✓			
OVERALL		✓			

Capability of Threats

	FORMIDABLE	GATHERING	CAPABLE	ASPIRATIONAL	MARGINAL
Russia	✓				
Iran		✓			
Middle East Terrorism			✓		
Af-Pak Terrorism			✓		
China	✓				
North Korea		✓			
OVERALL		✓			

Threats to U.S. Vital Interests

	SEVERE	HIGH	ELEVATED	GUARDED	LOW
Russia		✓			
Iran		✓			
Middle East Terrorism		✓			
Af-Pak Terrorism		✓			
China		✓			
North Korea		✓			
OVERALL		✓			

Threats to U.S. Vital Interests

SEVERE	HIGH	ELEVATED	GUARDED	LOW

also continues its aggressive naval tactics to intimidate such neighboring countries as Japan and the Philippines and continues to bully other countries that try to exercise their right to navigate international waters in the region.

North Korea has executed an alarming number of missile tests: 18 as of early August 2017 compared to 21 for all of 2016. These tests have demonstrated the commitment of Kim Jong-un's regime to fielding a force of short-range, medium-range, and long-range ballistic, cruise, and submarine-launched missiles, presumably with the ability to carry nuclear warheads. The latest tests have hinted at North Korea's ability to reach targets in the United States. These developments, combined with its increasingly hostile rhetoric toward the West over the past year, make North Korea the most volatile threat addressed in the *Index*.

Terrorism based in Afghanistan continues to challenge the stability of that country. To the extent that various groups based in the region straddling the border with Pakistan remain potent and active, they also remain a threat in being to the stability of Pakistan, which is a matter of concern given Pakistan's status as a nuclear power and its sustained frictions with India, also a nuclear power.

In addition, Iran's efforts to develop more advanced military capabilities and its active support of the various terrorist groups operating in the Middle East continue to undermine regional security conditions and therefore to threaten the regional interests of the U.S.

With these threats taken together, the globalized threat to U.S. vital national interests as a whole during 2017 remained "high."

The Status of U.S. Military Power

Finally, we assessed the military power of the United States in three areas: capability, capacity, and readiness. We approached this assessment by military service as the clearest way to link military force size, modernization programs, unit readiness, and (in general terms) the functional combat power (land, sea, and air) represented by each service. We treated the United States' nuclear capability as a separate entity given its truly unique characteristics and constituent elements, from the weapons themselves to the supporting infrastructure that is fundamentally different from the infrastructure that supports conventional capabilities.

These three areas of assessment (capability, capacity, and readiness) are central to the overarching questions of whether the U.S. has a sufficient quantity of appropriately modern military power and whether military units are able to conduct military operations on demand and effectively.

As reported in all previous editions of the *Index*, the common theme across the services and the U.S. nuclear enterprise is one of force degradation resulting from many years of underinvestment, poor execution of modernization programs, and the negative effects of budget sequestration (cuts in funding) on readiness and capacity. While the military has been heavily engaged in operations, primarily in the Middle East but elsewhere as well, since September 11, 2001, experience is both ephemeral and context-sensitive. Valuable combat experience is lost as the servicemembers who individually gained experience leave the force, and it maintains direct relevance only for future operations of a similar type: Counterinsurgency operations in Iraq, for example, are fundamentally different from major conventional operations against a state like Iran or China.

Thus, although the current Joint Force is experienced in some types of operations, it lacks experience with high-end, major combat operations, and it is still aged and shrinking in its capacity for operations.

In the aggregate, the United States' military posture is rated **"marginal"** and is trending toward **"weak,"** a condition unchanged from the *2017 Index*.

Overall, the *2018 Index* concludes that the current U.S. military force is likely capable of meeting the demands of a single major regional conflict while also attending to various presence and engagement activities but that it would be very hard-pressed to do more and certainly would be ill-equipped to handle two nearly simultaneous major regional contingencies. The limits imposed on defense spending and the programmatic volatility created by continuing resolutions, passed in lieu of formal budgets approved on schedule, have kept the military services small, aging, and under significant pressure. Essential maintenance continues to be deferred; the availability of fewer units for operational deployments increases the frequency and length of deployments; and old equipment continues to be extended while programmed replacements are either delayed or beset by developmental difficulties.

The military services have continued to prioritize readiness for current operations by shifting funding to deployed or soon-to-deploy units while sacrificing the ability to keep non-deployed units in "ready" condition; delaying, reducing, extending, or canceling modernization programs; and sustaining the reduction in size and number of military units. While Congress and the new Administration have taken some positive steps to fund readiness in 2017 more robustly, they have not overturned the Budget Control Act that caps defense spending. Without a real commitment to increases in modernization, capacity, and readiness accounts over the next few years, America's military branches will continue to be strained to meet the missions they are called upon to fulfill.

As currently postured, the U.S. military is only marginally able to meet the demands of defending America's vital national interests.

We characterized the services and the nuclear enterprise on a five-category scale ranging from "very weak" to "very strong," benchmarked against criteria elaborated in the full report. These characterizations should not be construed as reflecting the competence of individual servicemembers or the professionalism of the services or Joint Force as a whole; nor do they speak to the U.S. military's strength relative to other militaries around the world. Rather, they are assessments of the institutional, programmatic, and material health or viability of America's hard military power.

Our analysis concluded with these assessments:

- **Army as "Weak."** The Army's score remained "weak" for reasons similar to those cited in previous editions of the *Index*. The Army has continued to trade end strength and modernization for improved readiness in some units for current operations. However, accepting risks in these areas has enabled the Army to keep only one-third of its force at acceptable levels of readiness, and even for units deployed abroad, the Army has had to increase its reliance on contracted support to meet maintenance requirements. Budget cuts have affected combat units disproportionately: Over the past few years, a 16 percent reduction in total end strength has led to a 32 percent reduction in the number of brigade combat teams and similar reductions in the number of combat aviation brigades. In summary, the Army is too small for the tasks it is assigned, its equipment continues to age, and it struggles to improve the readiness of its operating forces. Concerned by the prospect of a "hollow force" (i.e., units that exist on paper but are woefully understaffed), Army officials, instead of using a 2017 congressional authorization to increase end strength by creating more units, chose merely to increase the level of staffing in existing units.

- **Navy as "Marginal."** The Navy's readiness score returned to the *2016 Index*'s score of "marginal." While the Navy is maintaining a solid global presence (slightly more than one-third of the fleet is deployed on any given day), it has little ability to surge to meet wartime demands. As in 2016, the Navy's decision to defer maintenance has kept ships at sea but also has affected the Navy's ability to deploy. With scores of "weak" in capability (largely because of old platforms and troubled modernization programs) and "marginal" in capacity, the Navy remained just able to meet operational requirements in 2017. Continuing budget shortfalls in its shipbuilding account will hinder the Navy's ability to improve its situation, both materially and quantitatively, for the next several years—an even larger problem considering that the Navy has revised its assessment of how many ships it needs to 355 instead of the 308 for which it has been budgeting in its 30-year shipbuilding plan.

- **Air Force as "Marginal."** Although the Air Force's overall score remains the same as last year's, a clearer picture of the USAF's aircraft inventory yielded a significant drop in deliverable fighter capacity: The Air Force possesses 923 combat-coded tactical fighter aircraft, 236 below last year's capacity assessment and 277 below the *Index* assessment of 1,200 needed to meet a two-MRC level of military strength. While the Air Force's readiness score remained "marginal," this assessed area continues to trend downward due to increasing evidence of training and maintenance shortfalls, as well as pilots' own assessments of their forces obtained by The Heritage Foundation through personal interviews. Combined with a continued capability score of "marginal," the Air Force's overall military strength score continues to trend downward at a time when America's dominance in the air domain is increasingly challenged by the technological advances of potential adversaries.

- **Marine Corps as "Weak."** The Corps continues to deal with readiness challenges driven by the combined effects of high operational tempo and low levels of funding. Aviation remained the largest challenge for the Corps in 2017 as maintenance and flight hour shortfalls combined with old platforms to cause the service to self-assess a dire state of readiness. The Corps' modernization programs are on track, but it will take several years for new equipment to be produced and fielded; ground combat systems, in particular, are long overdue for replacement. Unlike in past years, the Corps did not publicly provide detailed information about the status of its active-duty force with respect to its state of readiness for combat. The Corps has said the deploy-to-dwell ratio for its active force has dipped below 1:2, revealing increased stress on the force. This, combined with a clear assessment of poor aviation readiness, drove the Marine Corps' overall strength score from "marginal" to "weak" in 2017, making it the only service to drop to a lower category.

- **Nuclear Capabilities as "Marginal."** Warhead modernization, warhead/system testing, and adequate investment in the intellectual and talent underpinnings of the nuclear enterprise continue to be the chief problems facing America's nuclear capability. Delivery platform modernization continued to receive strong support from Congress and the Administration during 2017, with major investments in next-generation bomber and ballistic-missile submarine programs, but the force depends on a very limited set of weapons (in number of designs) and models that are quite old, in stark contrast to the aggressive programs of competitor states. Of continued concern is the "marginal" score for "Allied Assurance" at a time when Russia has rattled its nuclear saber in a number of recent provocative exercises; China has been more aggressive in militarily pressing its claims to the South and East China Seas; North Korea is investing heavily in a submarine-launched ballistic missile capability; and Iran retains its nuclear infrastructure program as a key feature of the Joint Comprehensive Plan of Action (JCPOA) meant to restrain Iran's nuclear program. The aggressive pace of North Korea's missile testing, which purportedly is tied to its nuclear aspirations, is of particular concern.

U.S. Military Power

	VERY WEAK	WEAK	MARGINAL	STRONG	VERY STRONG
Army		✓			
Navy			✓		
Air Force			✓		
Marine Corps		✓			
Nuclear			✓		
OVERALL			✓		

U.S. Military Power: Army

	VERY WEAK	WEAK	MARGINAL	STRONG	VERY STRONG
Capacity		✓			
Capability			✓		
Readiness		✓			
OVERALL		✓			

U.S. Military Power: Navy

	VERY WEAK	WEAK	MARGINAL	STRONG	VERY STRONG
Capacity			✓		
Capability		✓			
Readiness			✓		
OVERALL			✓		

U.S. Military Power: Air Force

	VERY WEAK	WEAK	MARGINAL	STRONG	VERY STRONG
Capacity			✔		
Capability			✔		
Readiness			✔		
OVERALL			✔		

U.S. Military Power: Marine Corps

	VERY WEAK	WEAK	MARGINAL	STRONG	VERY STRONG
Capacity		✔			
Capability			✔		
Readiness		✔			
OVERALL		✔			

U.S. Military Power: Nuclear

	VERY WEAK	WEAK	MARGINAL	STRONG	VERY STRONG
Warhead Surety				✔	
Delivery Platform Reliability				✔	
Warhead Modernization		✔			
Delivery Systems Modernization				✔	
Nuclear Weapons Complex		✔			
National Labs Talent			✔		
Force Readiness			✔		
Allied Assurance			✔		
Nuclear Test Readiness		✔			
OVERALL			✔		

America's Joint Force and the Domains of Warfare

James Jay Carafano, PhD

The term "joint" has been well established in the U.S. military lexicon for many decades. While the word's meaning may remain a constant, its significance for the American military is changing.

The essays on the dimensions of warfare in the *2018 Index of U.S. Military Strength* reflect a crucial dynamic that affects thinking about how militaries ought to be employed. Dominance in war will not be gained through domination of a single domain. The future focus of jointness will be on ensuring that U.S. armed forces retain the ability to operate effectively in all domains in a theater (land, sea, air, subsurface, cyberspace, and space) and to exploit the ability to use advantages in one domain to operate in another. For the U.S., having the capacity to check an adversary or take the initiative across all domains will be essential to establishing a competitive advantage in future conflicts.

The Dimensions of War

One of the great truisms of war was expressed by the British military historian B. H. Liddell Hart: "The real target in war is the mind of the enemy commander, not the bodies of his troops."[1] This maxim touches the core of understanding the nature of warfare. War is a competition. War is a competition between adversaries, a contest of action and counteraction that concludes or changes based on the agency of competitors, and this competition unfolds in the domains accessible to each competitor: land, sea, air, space, and cyberspace. Dominating in war is not about dominating a domain. It is about dominating an enemy.

In contemporary conflict, as competitors increasingly gain access to all domains of warfare, it becomes more likely that adversaries will seek to offset a competitor's dominance in one domain by acting more aggressively in another space. As transnational terrorists like ISIS have lost physical ground in the Middle East, for example, they have redoubled their cyber operations to stay in the fight against the West. Alternatively, competitors might redouble their efforts to defeat an adversary's capacity to dominate them in a particular domain. This has become a feature of Chinese military strategy, which seeks to prevent adversaries from achieving a dominant advantage in space, air, sea, and cyber operations in the Asia–Pacific theater.

Thus, dominance in one or more domains is important, but to dominate an enemy, the ability to conduct operations in more than one domain at a time, to shift between them, and to use one domain to affect another is more important.

The elements of the U.S. armed forces increasingly operate across domains, each service specializing in one but increasingly having an effective presence in the others and/or relying on the other services to create opportunities for exploitation and to prevent an enemy from using a domain for their own purposes. No one service bears sole responsibility for military operations in any domain. Each of the uniformed military services, for example, uses cyberspace. All conduct or depend on space operations. Forces from land bases can affect operations at sea. Naval forces can influence land battles. Air force operations routinely have an impact on multiple domains.

The nature of contemporary warfare has implications for how the armed forces address jointness now and in the future. Further, the evolution of the joint force and how the U.S. military thinks about conducting joint operations has significant consequences for how national leaders understand military strength and its utility in securing national interests.

Evolution of the Joint Concept

For the Pentagon, "joint" "[c]onnotes activities, operations, organizations, etc., in which elements of two or more Military Departments participate."[2] In the case of the United States, that means the Army, Air Force, and Navy Departments, the last of which includes the Navy and Marine Corps. The U.S. Coast Guard, when operating in concert with them, also could be considered part of the joint force. U.S. Special Operations Forces (e.g., SEALs and Rangers) are provided by the services; when they operate across service components or with conventional forces (e.g., Army brigades), they are also conducting joint operations.

The U.S. military's appreciation of jointness is built on a historical understanding of Western warfare and its own contemporary experiences. While joint operations, the cooperative use of forces operating in their respective domains, may not be as old as war itself, there are certainly many antecedents from the times of ancient warfare. Most notably, histories of the Peloponnesian Wars, the decades-long struggle between alliances led by the Greek city-states Athens (primarily a naval power) and Sparta (the dominant land power), turned on joint operations.[3]

Athens and Sparta. One instructive example of joint operations in the ancient world was the land–sea campaign in Sicily from 415 BC to 413 BC. An Athenian expeditionary force was dispatched to secure the strategic island off the coast of Italy that, some of their leaders argued, would provide a decisive advantage in the war with Sparta. The Athenian force was joint, composed of a naval force of some 100 triremes (Greek war galleys, or rowed fighting ships); numerous transport and cargo ships; and more than 5,000 hoplite infantrymen and additional archers and slingers that could conduct ground operations.[4]

Once establishing themselves in Sicily, the Athenians were slow to advance on their main objective, the city of Syracuse. This allowed time for the Spartans to dispatch reinforcements to their Syracusan allies. The Athenians lost the land battle against the superior combined land force of Sparta and Syracuse. When they tried to withdraw by sea, the Spartans, having developed their own navy, intercepted the retreating fleet, soundly defeating the Athenians in a massive sea battle.

Using the Athenian naval assets to maneuver ground units into a superior position was a classic exercise in joint operations, leveraging forces that operate in one domain to provide a competitive advantage to forces operating in another. But coordinating different forces and operating in different domains is complex. Effective command and control of the Athenian expeditionary force broke down, leaving it vulnerable to the Spartan counterstrike.[5] In this respect, the operation illustrated both the potential advantages and possible pitfalls of employing joint forces in a campaign.

Joint operations, principally cooperation between land and sea forces, have been a feature of Western warfare through the ages. U.S. military history also includes exemplars of joint operations, notably including the defeat of the British at Yorktown in 1781[6] and the siege of Vicksburg in 1863.[7]

Yorktown. The siege of Yorktown included both joint operations and combined operations (operations involving forces of more than one nation). After a vigorous campaign in Virginia, British forces withdrew to the

Yorktown Peninsula to rearm and refit, resupplied and protected by British naval forces. As the Continental Army conducted a forced march from New York to the Tidewater region in the Chesapeake Bay to block the British by land, a French fleet intercepted and destroyed reinforcements dispatched to the British at Yorktown by sea. While the Continental Army laid siege to the garrison by land, the French Navy blockaded Yorktown by sea. Pressed by the advance of combined American–French forces and cut off from reinforcement and resupply, the British surrendered, a catastrophic military defeat that led to the end of the war and the securing of American independence.

Napoleon in Egypt. The battles of the American Revolution presaged the transition from the early modern era of warfare to the Napoleonic Age, which saw significant innovation in both land and sea warfare in terms of technology, tactics, and logistics. The practice of joint operations—such as Napoleon's aborted invasion of Egypt in 1798, in which the future emperor transported an army of over 30,000 by sea only to see the force eventually cut off and defeated in detail—looked not much different from the conduct of joint operations in previous decades.[8]

In many ways, the American Civil War continued the practices and tactics of the Napoleonic era. One area in which there were glimpses of change was in the conduct of joint operations, which indicated the potential promise of coordinating land and sea operations to achieve strategic objectives—practices that would emerge more fully during the two great world wars of the 20th century.

Vicksburg. The most illustrative battle was the siege of Vicksburg.[9] A joint land–naval force isolated and reduced the Confederate strong point at Vicksburg, Mississippi. The victory gave the Union control of the Mississippi River, effectively cutting the Confederacy in two. Not only did the battle preview new technology, such as armored ships and rifled cannon, but Union operations demonstrated the effective coordination, command, and control of joint forces, with General Ulysses

Grant succeeding where Athens and Napoleon had failed.

Throughout the evolution of war in the early modern and Napoleonic eras and into the modern era, joint operations were a matter of practice, but there was scant emphasis on the development of doctrine, tactics, training, or force development. Even massive joint operations, such as the Gallipoli campaign of 1915–1916 during World War I, were largely improvised.[10]

Gallipoli. While war on the European Western Front stagnated in trench combat, operations in the Dardanelles were intended to knock the Ottoman Empire out of the war by employing the swift maneuver of forces that could be achieved by joint operations. A British-led Allied expeditionary force moved to secure Gallipoli, a strategically important peninsula that controlled Mediterranean access to the Black Sea, but the operation was protracted and suffered from numerous delays, giving the Turks time to move adequate defenses into place, after which the battle devolved into trench warfare that soon resembled the stalemate on the Western Front. Though the Allies had the means to transport a land force by sea and support its employment from the sea, and enjoyed effectively uncontested use of the sea, their failure to move swiftly, decisively, and in well-practiced form ceded all of the important advantages to the Turks, who used their control of the land to greater effect.[11]

World War II. The modern age of warfare arrived during World War II when operations in several theaters required the integrated use of land, sea, and air forces. Most notably in the Pacific Theater, amphibious operations to sustain land campaigns from the sea, designed to seize a beachhead in order to conduct more expanded operations ashore, required joint operations as a matter of course.

Dramatic advances in airpower during the 1930s added a new dimension to warfare. Forces and supplies could be moved by air, either air-landed or inserted by glider or parachute forces. Airpower could also provide airborne reconnaissance and fire support for both land

and sea services (e.g., sub hunting and attack by air of an opposing fleet).

Another but little discussed aspect of emerging joint warfare was the electromagnetic dimension, from radio communications to intercept, radar, and electronic jamming. Forces had to learn how to operate across a new dimension of war that did not transit a geographical space and was not the purview of any one service. This was a sign of times to come, as all of the services would find themselves operating increasingly in multiple domains, which requires a great degree of coordination and deconfliction.

In response to the demands of the war, the military services developed operations, command and control organizations, equipment, doctrine, and training to facilitate joint operations. However, while military operations and campaigning were joint, many other aspects of military operations including education, intelligence, and logistics were often done as single-service activities or only loosely integrated.

The Post–World War II Era. Even after the experience of the Second World War, military thought continued to focus on the competition between domains for dominance in warfare. The classics still mattered. The Army favored Prussian military theorist Carl von Clausewitz, who focused his writing on victory in land battles;[12] the Navy had Alfred Thayer Mahan, who concentrated on control of the sea;[13] and new-to-the-scene airpower enthusiasts referenced Giulio Douhet, who championed victory through airpower.[14] With the invention of nuclear weapons, strategists like Bernard Brodie argued for the strategic dominance of nuclear weapons.[15]

Despite the prevalence of joint operations during World War II, little was done to institutionalize joint operations. The Defense Reorganization Act of 1958, under the tutelage of President Dwight David Eisenhower, drawing in part on his extensive experience with joint operations during the war as Supreme Allied Commander Europe, advanced efforts to establish unified command for joint forces, but little more.[16]

Goldwater–Nichols. Lack of effective joint operations at the operational level was one of the significant criticisms of U.S. military activities during the Vietnam War. The issue was famously addressed in Arthur T. Hadley's book *The Straw Giant*.[17] Among the many reforms instituted by the Goldwater–Nichols Department of Defense Reorganization Act of 1986 was a legislative effort to institutionalize jointness in the armed forces.[18] The legislation addressed the Unified Command Plan (the global command and control of U.S. forces); education, professional development, and training; and acquisition of weapon systems, platforms, and related equipment.[19] Thus, after Goldwater–Nichols, jointness emphasized integration of the military services across the full range of defense activities, not just warfighting.

The case for jointness, introduced by the Senate Armed Services Committee staff that spearheaded the Goldwater–Nichols legislative effort, was illustrated by the aborted Iranian hostage rescue operation (1980), popularly called the disaster at Desert One.[20] All of the services participated in the ad hoc effort to put together a special operation to rescue U.S. embassy employees who had been taken hostage in Tehran during the Iranian Revolution. Although the operation was joint, it failed.

In truth, however, the mission's most critical shortfalls had little to do with a failure of joint operations. The Marine helicopters were operating at the extreme edge of their operational range; that, combined with bad luck and some miscues on the ground, doomed the mission. Nevertheless, the story was one of dramatic and embarrassing failure and helped to galvanize support for the legislation, which was actively opposed by the Pentagon and the services, which viewed jointness as an imposition on their responsibilities for managing and employing military forces.

Despite opposition from the Pentagon, the legislation was passed and signed into law. This effort coincided with the Reagan defense buildup, which increased the size of the military force, as well as funding for operations and training, and greatly advanced the modernization of key military platforms (ships, planes, and armored vehicles).[21] Flush with resources and responding to the challenge and demands of jointness imposed by Goldwater–Nichols, the military responded adroitly.

Goldwater–Nichols largely succeeded in institutionalizing joint warfare. From professional military education to operations in the field, U.S. military activities today are inherently joint. Further, the U.S. military has decades of extensive combat experience in joint operations at the operational and tactical levels across the spectrum of conflict. Joint integration has been so successful that when major defense reforms (e.g., Goldwater–Nichols II) are suggested, they rarely substantively address joint matters.[22]

Of course, innovations in jointness did not erase the intellectual debate about which dimensions of war ought to be considered the most important and which service forces would dominate future conflict. The debate was renewed in the wake of the First Gulf War (1991). Air Force advocates, with the introduction of the proliferated use of precision-guided weapons, argued that post–Cold War military operations would be dominated by airpower. This vision was reflected in the Air Force-sponsored Gulf War Air Power Survey.[23] In contrast, the official Army history, *Certain Victory*, argued for the returned dominance of land power.[24] The Navy, which played a subordinate role in the conflict, looked beyond the "lessons" of the war to make the case that U.S. security in the post–Cold War world would be protected by sea-centric military dominance.[25]

The renewed debate about domain dominance that emerged after the Gulf War was as likely a reflection of competition between the services for scarce defense dollars as it was influenced by new technologies and warfighting concepts. In the wake of the war, the Pentagon suffered from an end-of-the-Cold War "peace dividend" that saw a reduction in forces and military spending throughout the 1990s.[26] Increasingly, the services squabbled over pieces of an increasingly smaller budget pie, with each service arguing in part that it delivered

more bang for the buck because of its capacity to dominate battle space in its domain.

Despite the renewal of interservice intellectual rivalry, in practice, the trend toward increasing jointness in the development and employment of forces continued. There were many controversial aspects to military operations in Afghanistan and Iraq following the terrorist attacks of September 11, 2001, but shortfalls in the capacity to undertake joint operations were far down the list of items noted by critics.

Joint Future

While some military reformers and theorists continue to propose ways of war predicated on dominance of particular domains, most modern military thinking envisions future operations that are inherently joint. In recent years, for example, the U.S. Army and Marine Corps have advanced the concept of Multi-Domain Battle, the notion that the U.S. should be prepared to fight in an environment in which all domains are contested.[27] Whether the Army–Marine concept is useful remains a subject of some debate (and would eventually have to be proven in battle anyway), but it does reflect mainstream military thinking: The U.S. armed forces must have the expertise, capabilities, and capacity to operate in all domains in a contested theater and to leverage those domains more effectively than the enemy can. Developing and sustaining that capacity will be the key goal of joint future.

As previewed by Multi-Domain Battle, joint future will likely focus on the challenge of employing the armed forces in environments where operations are contested in multiple domains. Planning for military operations may likely be based on assumptions that the U.S. will not enjoy superiority,[28] much less supremacy,[29] in one or more domains. The services will likely focus more on what they can contribute to operations across the dimensions of war rather than arguing the unique contributions of their capabilities in a single domain. The U.S. military will likely continue to look at a mix of operational practices, technologies, force structure, and capacity to achieve and sustain a competitive edge across the dimensions of warfare.

Most likely, other aspects of jointness will fade in priority: Logistics, infrastructure, education, planning, and training will become more inherently joint as a matter of practice. Joint future will focus on inter-domain dependencies and cross-dimension operations and effects.

A careful reading of the domain essays in this edition of the *Index of U.S. Military Strength* suggests both the challenges and opportunities involved in building U.S. military strength for the next fight. These range from human resources to warfighting systems, from alliances to enemies, from technological improvement to intellectual innovation. The essays raise important questions for the future of the joint force concept and its role in protecting the vital interests of the United States.

Endnotes

1. B. H. Liddell Hart, *Thoughts on War* (London: Faber and Faber, 1944), quoted in Air University, Cyberspace and Information Operations Study Center, "Influence Operations," http://www.au.af.mil/info-ops/influence.htm#top (accessed July 8, 2017).

2. See "joint," in U.S. Department of Defense, *DOD Dictionary of Military and Associated Terms*, June 2017, p. 125, http://www.dtic.mil/doctrine/new_pubs/dictionary.pdf (accessed July 6, 2017).

3. See, for example, *The Landmark Thucydides: A Comprehensive Guide to the Peloponnesian War*," ed. Robert B. Strassler (New York: Touchstone, 1998).

4. Ibid., p. 375.

5. Edward S. Creasy, *The Fifteen Decisive Battles of the World: From Marathon to Waterloo* (Hertfordshire, UK: Oracle Publishing Ltd, 1996), pp. 54–82.

6. "The Winning of Independence, 1777–1783," Chapter 4 in *American Military History Volume 1: The United States Army and the Forging of a Nation, 1775–1917*, ed. Richard W. Stewart (Washington: United States Army, Center of Military History, 2005), pp. 98–102, http://www.history.army.mil/books/AMH-V1/PDF/Chapter04.pdf (accessed July 10, 2017).

7. Christopher R. Gabel, *The Vicksburg Campaign: November 1862–July 1863* (Washington: United States Army, Center of Military History, 2013), http://www.history.army.mil/html/books/075/75-8/CMH_Pub_75-8.pdf (accessed July 10, 2017).

8. David G. Chandler, *The Campaigns of Napoleon: The Mind and Method of History's Greatest Soldier* (New York: Scribner, 1966), Part 4, "Oriental Interlude: The Six Acres of Land."

9. Gabel, *The Vicksburg Campaign*, pp. 59–61.

10. Martin Gilbert, *Churchill: A Life* (London: Minerva, 1992), pp. 291, 299–302.

11. Martin Gilbert, *The First World War: A Complete History* (New York: Henry Holt, 1994), pp. 146–153.

12. Carl von Clausewitz, *On War*, ed. and trans. Michael Howard and Peter Paret (Princeton, NJ: Princeton University Press, Reprint Edition, 1989).

13. Alfred Thayer Mahan, *The Influence of Sea Power Upon History, 1660–1783* (Mineola, NY: Dover, 1987).

14. Giulio Douhet, *The Command of the Air*, trans. Dino Ferrari (New York: Coward-McCann, 1942), https://permanent.access.gpo.gov/airforcehistory/www.airforcehistory.hq.af.mil/Publications/fulltext/command_of_the_air.pdf (accessed July 8, 2017).

15. Bernard Brodie, *Strategy in the Missile Age* (Santa Monica, CA: RAND Corporation, 1959), http://www.rand.org/content/dam/rand/pubs/commercial_books/2007/RAND_CB137-1.pdf (accessed July 8, 2017).

16. Defense Reorganization Act of 1958, Public Law 85–599, 72 Stat. 514, 85th Cong., August 6, 1958, https://www.govinfo.gov/content/pkg/STATUTE-72/pdf/STATUTE-72-Pg514.pdf (accessed July 8, 2017).

17. Arthur T. Hadley, *The Straw Giant* (New York: Random House, 1986).

18. Goldwater–Nichols Department of Defense Reorganization Act of 1986, Public Law 99–433, 100 Stat. 92, 99th Cong., October 1, 1986, http://history.defense.gov/Portals/70/Documents/dod_reforms/Goldwater-NicholsDoDReordAct1986.pdf (accessed July 8, 2017).

19. Edward J. Drea, Ronald H. Cole, Walter S. Poole, James F. Schnabel, Robert J. Watson, and Willard J. Webb, *History of the Unified Command Plan 1946–2012*, U.S. Department of Defense, Office of the Chairman of the Joint Chiefs of Staff, Joint History Office, 2013, http://www.jcs.mil/Portals/36/Documents/History/Institutional/Command_Plan.pdf (accessed July 8, 2017).

20. Stuart L. Koehle and Stephen P. Glick, "Why the Rescue Failed," *The American Spectator*, September 14, 2012, https://spectator.org/34807_why-rescue-failed/ (accessed July 8, 2017).

21. Jonathan Reed Winkler, "Reagan and the Military," Chapter 10 in *A Companion to Ronald Reagan*, ed. Andrew L. Johns (Hoboken, NJ: Wiley Blackwell, 2015), pp. 167–183.

22. Colin Clark, "Carter to Reshape US Military: Goldwater–Nichols II," *Breaking Defense*, April 5, 2016, http://breakingdefense.com/2016/04/carter-to-reshape-us-military-goldwater-nichols-ii/ (accessed July 8, 2017).

23. Thomas A. Keaney and Eliot A. Cohen, *Gulf War Air Power Survey Summary Report*, Washington, DC, 1993, http://www.dtic.mil/dtic/tr/fulltext/u2/a273996.pdf (accessed July 8, 2017).

24. General Robert H. Scales, *Certain Victory: The US Army in the Gulf War* (Fort Leavenworth, KS: U.S. Army Command and General Staff College Press, Select Reprint, 1994), http://usacac.army.mil/cac2/cgsc/carl/download/csipubs/CertainVictory.pdf (accessed July 8, 2017).

25. Peter D. Haynes, "American Naval Thinking in the Post–Cold War Era: The U.S. Navy and the Emergence of a Maritime Strategy, 1989–2007," PhD dissertation, Naval Postgraduate School, Monterey, CA, June 2013, http://calhoun.nps.edu/bitstream/handle/10945/34675/13Jun_Haynes_Peter_PhD.pdf?sequence=1 (accessed July 11, 2017).

26. The term "peace dividend" refers to the post–Cold War period of the 1990s when, under the presumption that the world was entering a prolonged era of peace, the U.S. government drew down the funding for and size of the military to reduce the national deficit. For two differing perspectives, see Ann Markusen, "How We Lost the Peace Dividend," *The American Prospect*, July–August 1997, http://prospect.org/article/how-we-lost-peace-dividend (accessed July 8, 2017), and Lynn Woolsey, "Bill Clinton and the Decline of the Military," *Human Events*, December 21, 2006, http://humanevents.com/2006/12/21/bill-clinton-and-the-decline-of-the-military/ (accessed July 6, 2017).

27. United States Army, Training and Doctrine Command, "Multi-Domain Battle," updated June 23, 2017, http://www.tradoc.army.mil/multidomainbattle/ (accessed July 6, 2017).

28. For definitions of "superiority" across various domains, see U.S. Department of Defense, *DoD Dictionary of Military and Associated Terms*, *passim*.

29. See, for example, "air supremacy," in ibid., p. 14.

An Overview of Land Warfare

David E. Johnson, PhD

"The past is never dead. It's not even past."
—William Faulkner[1]

Since the dawn of time, as historian T. R. Fehrenbach wrote in *This Kind of War*, "the object of warfare [has been] to dominate a portion of the earth, with its peoples, for causes either just or unjust. It is not to destroy the land and people, unless you have gone wholly mad."[2] Fehrenbach was analyzing U.S. involvement in the Korean War, and in his preface, he draws a lesson from that war—fought in a time of great-power competition between nuclear-armed adversaries—that bears revisiting today:

> The great test placed upon the United States was not whether it had the power to devastate the Soviet Union—this it had—but whether the American leadership had the will to continue to fight for an orderly world rather than to succumb to hysteric violence.... Yet when America committed its ground troops into Korea, the American people committed their entire prestige, and put the failure or success of their foreign policy on the line.[3]

Over the past 15 years, the United States has become an expeditionary power, largely based in the Continental United States, accustomed to projecting power by dominating the air, maritime, space, and cyber domains. U.S. superiority was routinely contested only in the land domain, albeit largely by irregular adversaries, insurgents, and terrorists. U.S. domain supremacy is eroding, if not ending, with the renewal of great-power competition with state actors—principally China and Russia—that can contest U.S. operations to some degree in all domains. This reality will shape how land forces contribute to U.S. security now and into the future.

Where We All Live

Of all the domains, the land domain has the greatest ability to create operational friction. It is the environment that informed Clausewitz's admonition that "Everything in war is very simple, but the simplest thing is difficult."[4] Soldiers and Marines cannot "slip the surly bonds of earth."[5] It is the domain where humans live, and operating there almost certainly results in human interaction—for good or ill.

The Inherently Complex Physical Aspects of Terrain. The land domain, unlike other physical domains (air and maritime) is highly variable, and its very nature forces adaptation by ground forces. According to the Army's 2005 working definition:

> ["Complex terrain" is comprised of] those areas that severely restrict the Army's ability to engage adversaries at a time and place of its choosing due to natural or man-made topography, dense vegetation or civil populations, including urban, mountains, jungle, subterranean, littorals and swamps. In some locales, such as the Philippines, all of these features can be present within a ten-kilometer radius.[6]

Retired Army Lieutenant General Patrick M. Hughes succinctly summed up the implications of operating in complex terrain: "It is dam (*sic*) hard to find a vacant lot to hold a war in...and in this new era of warfare, that's the last thing the enemy wants anyway."[7] Additionally, superiority in the other domains does not simplify the demands that land places on ground forces.

Operations in Afghanistan, both now and during occupation by the Soviet Union, show the effects of complex terrain. The absence of roads and the mountainous terrain make helicopters important in movement of forces, medical evacuation, and resupply. However, the weather and terrain (cool and thin air at high altitudes affecting lift) also make flying helicopters much more difficult than in Iraq (hot air at low altitudes with good lift).[8]

The continued global trend toward urbanization means that dense urban terrain is a likely future operational environment. "In the future," Army Chief of Staff General Mark Milley noted in October 2016, "I can say with very high degrees of confidence, the American Army is probably going to be fighting in urban areas."[9] While dense urban terrain can affect all of the domains, it creates particularly difficult challenges for land forces, as recent U.S. experiences in Mogadishu, Fallujah, Baghdad, and Mosul demonstrate.

Dense urban areas enable an adversary to hide, both physically and among the population, move unobserved, and achieve positions of advantage over friendly forces. Dense urban terrain occludes target acquisition by reducing targetable signatures and target exposure times. Beyond slowing the advance of ground forces, urban areas have a canalizing effect on mobility that not only affects approach speed, but significantly increases the risk to maneuver elements. It slows ground operations and often involves clearing buildings one by one, putting friendly ground forces at risk. Subterranean features like subways and sewer tunnels, multistory buildings, and "urban canyons" only further complicate operations in cities, as experienced by Germany in Stalingrad during World War II and by Russia in Grozny during its Chechen Wars.[10]

Weather. Weather, notoriously unpredictable and ever changing, can conspire with terrain to complicate the inherent challenges of land domain operations. Weather can impede the ability to employ maritime and air domain capabilities in support of ground operations and can make ground maneuver difficult. A sandstorm caused a pause in ground maneuver during the coalition drive to Baghdad in 2003.[11] Furthermore, as the Germans realized during Operation Barbarossa, winter in Russia can be a formidable adversary. Weather and tides were critical decision points for the invasion of Normandy in June 1944 and Incheon in September 1950. Bad weather enabled the German offensive in the Ardennes in late 1944 by grounding Allied air support.

Fog, rain, dust storms, sandstorms, and darkness can affect the ability to see the enemy and employ air support and can limit the effective range of weapons that require line of sight to the target. In addition, cold and heat can affect the performance of soldiers and increase logistical demands: Hot weather, for example, increases the demand for water.

Opportunities and Challenges. The principal opportunity that land forces offer is the ability to impose a decision on adversaries that the other domains cannot: taking and holding ground, destroying enemy forces in detail, and controlling and protecting populations. Many of the types of military operations required by U.S. policy and joint doctrine shown in Table 1 can be accomplished, in whole or in part, only with elements operating in the land domain.

Politically and strategically, operations in the land domain signal U.S. commitment because land forces, once deployed, can be difficult to extract. They are there for the duration. Ground forces are also essential for deterrence, even in relatively small numbers. As Charles Krauthammer has noted:

> Today we have 28,000 troops in South Korea.... Why? Not to repel an invasion. They couldn't. They're not strong enough. To put it very coldly, they're there to die. They're a deliberate message to the enemy that if you invade our ally you will have to kill a lot of Americans first. Which will galvanize us into a full-scale war against you.[12]

At the tactical and operational levels, the physical qualities of the land domain can

TABLE 1

Examples of Military Operations and Activities

- Stability activities
- Defense support of civil authorities
- Foreign humanitarian assistance
- Recovery
- Noncombatant evacuation
- Peace operations

- Countering weapons of mass destruction
- Chemical, biological, radiological, and nuclear response
- Foreign internal defense
- Counter-drug operations
- Combating terrorism

- Counterinsurgency
- Homeland defense
- Mass atrocity response
- Security cooperation
- Military engagement

SOURCE: U.S. Department of Defense, Joint Chiefs of Staff, "Joint Operations, Joint Publication 3–0," January 17, 2017, p. V–2, http://www.dtic.mil/doctrine/new_pubs/jp3_0.pdf (accessed August 14, 2017).

🏛 heritage.org

provide opportunities that other domains do not, such as physical protection. Adversaries and friendly forces can hide from observation and avoid accurate attack from the other domains, particularly the air domain. Fortifications, foxholes, barriers, gullies, subways, buildings, etc., all provide the ability to avoid the effects of enemy weapons. There are no foxholes in the sky.[13]

This was the case in the 2006 Lebanon War, when Hezbollah hid rockets and other systems in forested areas and in bunkers to avoid detection by and attack from Israel's air force. Similarly, the Islamic State (ISIS) went to ground in Mosul, using congested, dense urban areas and hiding among the people to avoid destruction from the air and to force Iraqi ground forces to clear the city block by block. The Germans used the "impassable" Ardennes Forest to marshal forces for their attack and achieved surprise over Allied forces. Similarly, the North Vietnamese used the cover of thick jungles to move troops and supplies into South Vietnam throughout the Vietnam War, despite U.S. air supremacy.

The land can also be used to conceal hazards like mines, booby traps, and obstacles that impede movement. There are also other inherent advantages for land forces in comparison with forces from other domains because they can:

- Maneuver on the land and take advantage of terrain;

- Counter adversary maneuver and protect against adversary special operations forces (SOF) activities;

- Build partner capacity by training and advising;

- Operate more easily without the highly "nodal" structures of air and maritime forces;

- Harden, conceal, and disperse their capabilities;

- Network with terrestrial links (e.g., buried fiber optics) that are hard to access and disrupt;

- Stockpile relatively large amounts of ammunition that can be protected;

- Reload, resupply, and refuel in theater and away from large, vulnerable bases;

- Maneuver in the absence of overhead intelligence, surveillance, and reconnaissance (ISR) and global positioning system data with analog systems and target enemy forces; and

- Enable operation in the other domains from ground positions (e.g., counter integrated air defense fires).

These advantages, however, are not without their challenges. The forces and capabilities have to be in place on the ground with sufficient capacity to turn the land force element into more than a speed-bump deterrent. Furthermore, as noted, the land domain's principal challenges are posed by its inherent nature. Movement, the sustainment of forces, protection from the elements—and the adversary—all make land operations different from those in the other domains.

The nature of operations on land, shaped by the ability of land forces to traverse expanses of varied terrain quickly, makes the positioning of forces a critical matter. Being close to an expected area of action confers important advantages over a competitor who is farther away. Consider the physical posture of U.S. forces in Europe just three decades ago. During the Cold War, U.S. ground forces were essentially toe-to-toe with the Warsaw Pact along the German border, with substantial forces prepared to reinforce from the United States. Since the end of the Cold War, U.S. ground forces have been based mostly in the Continental United States. The difference between U.S. levels in Europe toward the end of the Cold War and those maintained there today are startling.

Until the resurgence of Russia, a reduced posture seemed adequate to protect U.S. interests while minimizing the costs of overseas bases. The current U.S. posture in NATO, however, is now problematic, particularly in Eastern Europe in the face of recent Russian adventurism.

The Baltic States, made members of NATO in its post–Cold War expansion, are vulnerable with little U.S. or NATO presence to provide a deterrent. The lone rotational U.S. Army armored brigade combat team in Poland and the Baltics is the only capability on the ground to deter Russia, aside from the modest Polish and Baltic State defense forces. War games held by a variety of organizations have repeatedly demonstrated that Russian forces could likely reach the outskirts of Baltic capital cities in 60 hours or less, leaving U.S. and allied forces little time to deploy.[14] Although the armed forces of the Russian Federation are much smaller than those maintained by the Soviet Union during the Cold War, they are physically located on NATO's eastern flank. Today, the two permanently stationed U.S. brigades, neither of which is armored, are distant from the Baltics in Germany and Italy. Geography alone thus suggests a high probability that the Russians could rapidly present NATO with a fait accompli if they chose to invade the Baltics.

Restoring a credible deterrent in Europe is an expensive proposition. It would require stationing more forces in Europe (particularly in NATO's frontline states), negotiating basing rights, establishing prepositioned equipment sets in sufficient quantities, and a host of other tasks to convince the Russians that military aggression is not a good option while restoring Allied confidence in American resolve. Deterring in Eastern Europe is different from defending along the German border during the Cold War. The distance from the United States is greater, and reinforcements would have to come across land from Western Europe or risk attempting to arrive by air or sea under a formidable Russian anti-access/area-denial (A2/AD) complex that covers much of Eastern Europe and the Baltic Sea.

Today, U.S. forces deploy from bases at home to conduct operations globally, which include rotational forces in Afghanistan and Iraq and modest forward-stationed ground forces in South Korea and those already mentioned in Europe. This view that forces were better maintained at home but kept available for global deployment was a logical consequence of the collapse of the Soviet Union. It was further buttressed by the conclusion that China's military rise was principally a challenge for the air, maritime, space, and cyber domains, even though ground forces could contribute with maneuver forces, SOF, long-range fires, and complementary capabilities in electronic warfare, cyber, and intelligence, reconnaissance, and surveillance.[15]

As important as the physical positioning of forces is the ability of those forces to win in battle, which depends in no small measure on their technological edge when compared with the enemy's forces. Investments in ground force modernization are urgently required to reverse the situation described by Lieutenant General H. R. McMaster in testimony before Congress in 2016: "We are outranged and outgunned by many potential adversaries."[16] After a decade of relative peace followed by 15 years of counterinsurgency operations, modernization of U.S. Army capabilities for high-end conventional combat has repeatedly been shelved in favor of other priorities.

The Nature of Adversaries and Implications for Operations

The characteristics of the adversary, like terrain, create an inherent complexity that determines what can be done, what cannot be done, and the difficulty of the operation. As the old saying goes, the enemy always gets a vote.

Understanding enemy strengths, capabilities, locations, activities, and possible courses of action are key questions for commanders to understand as they frame their own plans.[17] What has become increasingly apparent since the 2006 Lebanon War is that there are three broad categories of adversaries that the United States could confront in the future: non-state irregular, state-sponsored hybrid, and state forces.

Importantly, the nature of the enemy and his will to continue fighting often can be countered and defeated only by ground forces. Protracted air operations can be costly and eventually result in diminishing returns. Naval power has little, if any, ability to overturn enemy seizure or control of land. This is also true for cyber and space.

Non-State Irregular Adversaries. These are the main types of adversaries the United States has fought since 9/11, including the Taliban, al-Qaeda, and now the Islamic State. The Russians faced this type of adversary in the mujahedeen during the early stages of its Cold War–era war in Afghanistan, as did the Israelis during the intifadas in the West Bank and Gaza. These adversaries are generally limited to small arms; rocket-propelled grenades (RPGs); improvised explosive devices (IEDs); and the occasional mortar, rocket, or

man-portable air defense system (MANPADS). Their activity is limited primarily to operations in the land domain.

Operations to counter non-state/irregular forces often require large numbers of ground forces for protracted periods, as seen in Afghanistan and Iraq. The luster of rapid victories in Afghanistan (2001) and Iraq (2003) quickly faded as insurgencies grew in both countries. U.S. counterinsurgency doctrine demands forces on the ground to augment, train, and advise the supported government and its security forces until they can take the lead with less direct U.S. assistance, and operational demands can be significant:

> Counterinsurgents can apply pressure on an insurgency by conducting raids on cell members; recovering enemy caches; interdicting supply routes; searching or seizing resources from cars, homes, and personnel entering the area of operations; isolating the insurgents from access to markets, smugglers, and black-market goods; and by conducting offensive operations that diminish guerrilla numbers.[18]

These activities, focused on protecting the population, require significant numbers of ground forces, as seen in the 2006 U.S. Army and Marine Corps counterinsurgency doctrine: "Twenty counterinsurgents per 1,000 residents is often considered the minimum troop density required for effective COIN operations; however as with any fixed ratio, such calculations remain very dependent upon the situation."[19] The Surge in Iraq succeeded in large part because it "achieved a 50 per thousand ratio in Iraq, with 30 million people being protected by 600,000 counterinsurgents (160,000 coalition troops, 340,000 Iraqi security forces, and 100,000 Sons of Iraq)."[20]

Conventional ground forces are augmented by special operations forces that "provide conventional forces with important cultural and advising capabilities. They also provide important offensive capabilities. SOF capable of conducting direct action might be able to conduct raids and gain intelligence that conventional forces cannot execute."[21]

Insurgents are often fixed in the close fight and defeated using direct and indirect fires (artillery and air strikes). Rarely is a U.S. platoon or larger formation at risk.[22]

If the objective of U.S. policy is to change conditions on the ground in an enduring way, large numbers of ground forces are likely to be needed.[23] Nevertheless, over time, the goal is that most (eventually all) land forces will be indigenous, with U.S. land forces providing trainers and advisers and supporting the operations of local forces by employing enablers from the other domains. This transition is occurring now in Iraq in the fight against ISIS, and it is a major goal of the International Security Assistance Force in Afghanistan.

One of the most difficult aspects of countering an insurgency is maintaining the political will to endure the costs in blood and treasure of a protracted conflict. As that will fades, political restrictions on force levels and engagements may result, easing the pressure on insurgent groups. The burden on the counterinsurgent is that he must win, while the insurgent need only avoid losing to maintain influence.

State-Sponsored Hybrid Adversaries. State-sponsored or other hybrid forces may reflect many of the attributes and behaviors of an insurgent force yet possess a significantly higher level of lethality and sophistication. Russian-backed separatists in Ukraine and Hezbollah represent two modern hybrid forces, and U.S.-backed anti-Soviet mujahedeen in Afghanistan were an early example.

The challenge posed by these adversaries is qualitatively different from the challenge posed by irregular opponents—similar to major combat operations but at a lower scale and with a mix of niche but sustainable high-end capabilities such as anti-tank guided missiles (ATGMs), MANPADS, and intermediate-range or long-range surface-to-surface rockets provided by a state actor that may allow hybrid forces to employ lethal force from greater range and with greater survivability.[24] Hybrid adversaries not only attempt to hide from overhead ISR systems by using terrain or mixing with the civilian population, but also may seek to jam or otherwise counter key ISR capabilities directly.

Land forces, using combined arms maneuver, are required to make these adversaries visible and then defeat them in close combat augmented by indirect fires (artillery and air strikes). The United States has not fought adversaries approximating the hybrid capabilities of Hezbollah or the Ukrainian separatists since it confronted North Vietnamese main force units during the Vietnam War. These types of adversaries can also inflict substantial casualties, as seen in the destruction of Ukrainian battalions by separatist rocket fire.[25]

The U.S. military has not suffered mass casualties of the kind these systems could impose since the Korean War, and the U.S. Army, in particular, is increasingly aware that it needs new capabilities (e.g., active protection for combat vehicles against RPGs and ATGMs) to operate against state-sponsored hybrid adversaries. As Acting Secretary of the Army Patrick J. Murphy and Army Chief of Staff General Mark A. Milley acknowledged in their 2017 posture statement, "While we are deliberately choosing to delay several modernization efforts, we request Congressional support of our prioritized modernization programs to ensure the Army retains the necessary capabilities to deter and if necessary, defeat an act of aggression by a near-peer."[26]

Beyond military capabilities, hybrid adversaries may also enjoy political advantages that make wholly defeating them difficult. Hybrid forces may have cross-border sources of supply that are difficult to interdict. Further, they may enjoy the support of the local populace, as Hezbollah does in Lebanon. If they are seen as the legitimate government or at least as a strong political actor, their defeat could be regionally destabilizing.

State Adversaries. Events in Ukraine, Syria, and the Pacific have drawn U.S. attention once more to high-end state adversaries (Russia, China, North Korea, and Iran) that have capabilities ranging from small arms to nuclear weapons. They have long studied U.S. capabilities and are modernizing their militaries to contest the United States across all

FIGURE 1

Phasing an Operation Based on Predominant Military Activities

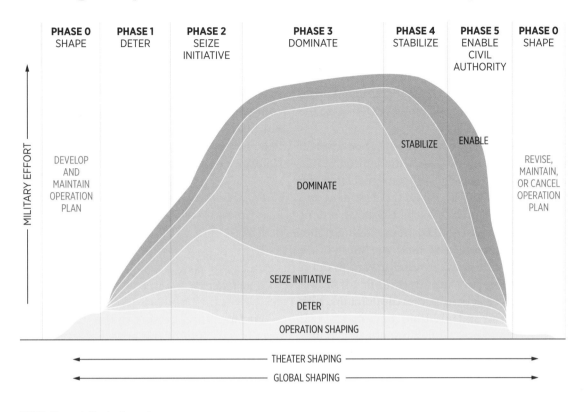

NOTE: Figure is illustrative only.
SOURCE: U.S. Department of Defense, Joint Chiefs of Staff, "Joint Operations, Joint Publication 3–0," January 17, 2017, p. V-13, http://www.dtic.mil/doctrine/new_pubs/jp3_0.pdf (accessed August 14, 2017).

🏛 heritage.org

domains, seeking in particular to undermine the advantages that the U.S. military has enjoyed since Operation Desert Storm, including but not limited to uncontested use of close-in air bases and logistics facilities, overhead and/or persistent ISR, and relatively unprotected, high-bandwidth communications.

Again, the Russians present a particularly difficult challenge because of their proximity to Eastern European NATO members, the lack of NATO forces on the ground in Eastern Europe, and the comparatively small militaries of the NATO frontline states. As noted, this situation is different from the U.S. speed bump in South Korea, where substantial Republic of Korea forces deter North Korean action.

Although land forces in the Pacific can make contributions in many areas, they are central to deterring Russian activity in NATO. This will require forward-positioned land forces that are large enough and capable enough to convince Russia that the game is not worth the candle—a case not made clearly in Georgia, Ukraine, and Syria.

Old Concepts and Better Adversaries

Complicating deterrence demands in Eastern Europe and the Pacific is the advent of a tough, layered A2/AD environment designed to thwart U.S. operations.[27] This challenges the long-standing U.S. operational phasing model shown in Figure 1.

What is important in this figure is the requirement for a steady increase of military effort during Phase I (deter) and Phase II (seize the initiative) before reaching Phase III (dominate). In large-scale operations since the end of the Cold War, Phase II and Phase III have required moving the majority of forces, particularly land forces and their sustainment, from the Continental United States (CONUS) to the theater of operations.

Operations Desert Shield and Desert Storm are good examples of how the United States has employed this phasing construct since the end of the Cold War. While the President and the executive branch of the U.S. government worked to establish coalitions, basing rights, and other agreements, the Department of Defense began to move forces forward to deter Saddam Hussein from attacking Saudi Arabia. This involved activity across the domains, with significant air and maritime components rushing to theater and a quickly deployable buffer force on the ground, initially provided by the rapidly deployable 82nd Airborne Division, backed by overwhelming U.S. superiority in all other domains.

Over the next five months, the U.S. coalition built up sufficient forces and sustainment capacity to seize the military initiative and then dominate in air and ground offensive operations against the Iraqi force occupying Kuwait. What is extremely important from this example—and from the initial operations in virtually all large-scale U.S. operations since World War II—is the fact that the United States initially had unchallenged supremacy in all but the land domain, and this dominance enabled a sanctuary for the buildup of forces sufficient to win in Phase III.

This will not be the case against near-peer regional adversaries. U.S. abilities to project power into their regions or steadily build up combat power and sustainment capacity will be confronted by formidable A2/AD capabilities that could interdict reinforcements as they close on the conflict zone. Thus, there is likely to be greater emphasis in the future on having greater combat power forward not just for deterrence, but to also conduct the initial stages of a conflict while the joint force seeks to regain freedom of maneuver, an arduous process of methodically degrading or defeating the enemy's efforts to impede U.S. operations.

This rising challenge of reinforcement stems from the emergence and adoption of new technologies across all domains that are contesting U.S. capabilities to deploy and operate. Secretary of Defense James Mattis testified in June before the House Armed Services Committee that:

> For decades, the United States enjoyed uncontested or dominant superiority in every operating domain or realm. We could generally deploy our forces when we wanted, assemble them where we wanted, and operate how we wanted. Today, every operating domain is contested.[28]

Furthermore, getting to the operational area is only half of the problem; operating there will also be heavily contested. In his written testimony, Secretary Mattis elaborated, noting that "the introduction of long-range air-to-surface and surface-to-surface guided weapons, advanced armored vehicles and anti-tank weapons, and tactical electronic warfare systems" threatens U.S. dominance on land.[29]

General Joseph Dunford, Chairman of the Joint Chiefs of Staff, shares Mattis's concern, testifying in the same session that "[i]n just a few years, if we don't change our trajectory, we will lose our qualitative and quantitative competitive advantage." He also said that the Budget Control Act denies the U.S. military the "sustained, sufficient and predictable funding" that it needs. If this situation is not rectified, Dunford warned, the United States will lose "our ability to project power," and the U.S. military will be "much smaller" or "a hollow force."[30] The Army's *Future Force Development Strategy* sums up what this means for a service whose role is sustained land combat:

> The Army faces the triple effect of a reduced force combined with an aging combat fleet and a severe reduction of research and

development spending. This reduction comes just as revisionist powers are aggressively challenging the world order and modernizing their own militaries. Modernization resources are close to historic lows since 1945. The Army requires resources in order to maintain tactical overmatch.[31]

Thus, there is an urgent need for new concepts and capabilities across the U.S. armed forces that can be used to solve the access challenge. For land forces, these concepts and modernization initiatives will need to assist the U.S. Army and Marine Corps to operate and win in increasingly contested land environments while under threat from combined arms fires that include missile, air, and other potential challenges.

Air and naval forces can mitigate the access challenges posed by increasingly capable competitors, but only to the extent that they can get enemy targets within range of the weapons they carry (increasingly a problem for naval forces in particular) and sustain an effective posture overhead (a growing problem for air forces). Thus, the Army must have better organic capabilities that are relevant to conducting land warfare in the modern age. To improve warfighting capabilities for these future battlefields, the Army has established modernization priorities to close the capability gaps that U.S. land forces face against capable adversaries:

1. Air and Missile Defense (SHORAD, short-range air defense);

2. Long-Range Fires such as improvements to multiple launch rocket systems (MLRS) and advanced weapons like the Army Tactical Missile System (ATACMS);

3. Munitions;

4. Mobility, Lethality, and Protection of brigade combat teams (BCTs);

5. Active Protection Systems, Air and Ground;

6. Assured position, navigation, and timing (PNT);

7. Electronic Warfare/Signals Intelligence;

8. Cyber (offensive and defensive);

9. Assured Communications (i.e., protected from enemy compromise or denial); and

10. Vertical lift (e.g., next-generation helicopters or tiltrotor aircraft).[32]

Together, these capability areas will help to improve Army resiliency in the event joint control of other enabling domains is disrupted. Further, they would provide the Army (and the Marine Corps) with the ability to impose cross-domain effects on an adversary in support of joint operations, such as through ground-based counter-air and electromagnetic warfare systems. As air and naval forces can enable land operations, so too can land forces facilitate operations in other domains by leveraging their ability to bring "fires" to bear against targets that threaten platforms and forces operating in the air and naval domains. It is not enough just to develop next-generation systems, however. The Army and Marine Corps must integrate these capabilities together in functional warfighting concepts, exercise those concepts, and then prepare to fight that way in the field.

How Are the Domain and Related Warfare Concepts Changing?

The resurgence of Russia has brought the role of land operations to the fore again, back to the war Fehrenbach described in *This Kind of War*, which highlighted the centrality of the land domain and the need to put boots (and fires, electronic warfare, and other land-based capabilities) on the ground to achieve policy objectives and enable success in the other domains:

> Americans in 1950 rediscovered something that since Hiroshima they had forgotten: you may fly over a land forever; you may bomb

it, atomize it, pulverize it and wipe it clean of life—but if you desire to defend it, protect it, and keep it for civilization, you must do this on the ground, the way the Roman legions did, by putting your young men into the mud.[33]

Technology and special operations forces will not provide universal solutions. These are the central points that make land forces a key component of a force that deters adversaries, as U.S. ground forces have done on the Korean Peninsula since the Korean War and did in NATO during the Cold War. Ground forces are also important to compel adversaries if deterrence fails; Operation Desert Storm accomplished this by physically forcing Iraqi forces out of Kuwait.

Arguments abound that dominance in new domains—airpower following World War II or cyber today—can render land power all but obsolete by deterring or defeating adversaries or at least sufficiently degrading their capabilities to the point that they are no longer a significant threat to the interests of the United States or its partners. The protracted aftermaths of the initial "victories" in Afghanistan and Iraq, both states with only limited capabilities to contest U.S. operations in other domains, have not yet put these arguments to rest, despite the difficulty with which the United States pursued its policy objectives. Possible future conflicts with peer competitors, who will possess far more sophisticated domain-denial capabilities, will likely bear little resemblance to recent U.S. warfighting experiences and reflect the difficulties of achieving victories through a single dominant domain.

Additional arguments similar to those extolling the primacy of technology have risen in the post–9/11 world as the United States has begun to rely on relatively small numbers of highly trained special operations forces in its fight against disparate insurgent and terrorist organizations. Special forces have enormous utility because they can direct precision attacks by air and maritime forces and can also conduct precision raids to kill or capture high-value targets. Both special forces and small detachments of conventional ground forces can deploy to train and advise partner forces and enable their use of our capabilities without becoming directly engaged in combat themselves. Yet special forces cannot hold terrain against determined adversaries and cannot retake land seized through acts of aggression.

Thus, an assessment of the continued relationship between ground forces and the attainment of U.S. policy objectives is fundamental to understanding the full portfolio of capabilities and capacities that the United States will likely require in the future. Land forces will continue to be a vital part of future conflicts, whether they are the supported element of a principally land-based war or serve as an enabling force assisting other elements to retake control of the skies and seas of a littoral conflict. Many elements of military competition in the 21st century will be defined by air, naval, and cyber forces, but the fate of lands and peoples will continue to be determined principally by the staying power of land forces.

The Nature of the Competition

The global military challenges that confront the United States are evolving, and they are doing so in different ways. Managing these disparate challenges will be an added complication for the joint force. Today, just as Japan and Nazi Germany represented unique challenges in the 1930s and 1940s, a rising China and resurgent Russia pose problems that are dramatically different from anything else that the United States has faced since the end of the Cold War. Coupled with these near-peer competitors are the continued challenges posed by North Korea, Iran, turmoil in the Middle East, and global terrorism.

Concepts and capabilities that work in one setting and the mix of land with other forms of military power may have little relevance in other settings. What is clear is that capabilities that put the joint force at risk against even midtier competitors are proliferating. The need for force modernization to restore overmatch in the land domain is urgent. Also needed are new concepts for how to employ these modernized forces—with the understanding that what might work against one adversary might not work against another.

Understanding the problem is the first step in developing solutions. In the land domain, as already discussed, distance, terrain, weather, and the nature of our adversaries combine to create complex problems that often only land forces can solve.

In the *2017 Index of U.S. Military Strength*, Antulio Echevarria discussed the central importance of and challenges involved in crafting new operational concepts to "provide a way to convert military strength into military power: the ability to employ military force where and when we want to employ it."[34] While noting the success of some U.S. concepts like Air-Land Battle, he highlights the failure of Effects-Based Operations and the incomplete nature of Air-Sea Battle.[35] What all of these concepts share is that they began as a way that U.S. forces wanted to fight and then later evolved into general-purpose solutions for confronting any adversary.

The recently published Army–Marine Corps white paper, "Multi-Domain Battle: Combined Arms for the 21st Century," recognizes the military problem that the current and future operating environments pose for the United States across the domains: "U.S. ground combat forces, operating as part of a joint, interorganizational, and multinational teams [*sic*], are currently not sufficiently trained, organized, equipped, nor postured to deter or defeat highly capable peer enemies to win in future war."[36] The paper also includes a "Solution synopsis":

Multi-Domain Battle: Combined Arms for the 21st Century requires ready and resilient Army and Marine Corps combat forces capable of outmaneuvering adversaries physically and cognitively through the extension of combined arms across all domains.... Through credible forward presence and resilient battle formations, future Army and Marine Corps forces integrate and synchronize capabilities as part of a joint team to create temporary windows of superiority across multiple domains and throughout the depth of the battlefield in order to seize, retain, and exploit the initiative; defeat enemies; and achieve military objectives.[37]

While a good starting point, however, the Multi-Domain Battle concept is just the beginning. Much work remains to be done as the United States is now in a competition for the first time since the Cold War with adversaries who can challenge, and perhaps defeat, America's armed forces in their local regions.

Conclusion

For the first time since the 1940s, the United States faces the prospect of peer competitors in the Pacific and Europe that can challenge U.S. capabilities in their regions. Coupled with these high-end adversaries are other actors, ranging from rogue states (North Korea and Iran) to hybrid adversaries (Hezbollah) to irregular terrorist threats (al-Qaeda, the Taliban, and ISIS). In this evolving security environment, the land domain will be particularly important both in crafting concepts and capabilities to support U.S. deterrence regimes and in defeating America's enemies if deterrence fails.

Time and current resourcing levels, however, are not on our side. If the United States does not approach these challenges with the urgency required, it will forfeit its credibility as a great power.

Endnotes

1. William Faulkner, *Requiem for a Nun* (New York: Vintage Books, 2011), p. 73. I want to thank my colleagues Ryan Boone, Tom Mahnken, Whitney McNamara, and Rick Russo for their helpful comments on earlier versions of this essay.

2. T. R. Fehrenbach, *This Kind of War: The Classic Military History of the Korean War* (Dulles, VA: Potomac Books, 2008), p. 290.

3. Ibid., p. x.

4. Carl von Clausewitz, *On War*, trans. Michael Howard and Peter Paret (Princeton, NJ: Princeton University Press, 1976), p. 119.

5. Peter Armenti, "John Gillespie Magee's 'High Flight,'" Library of Congress, September 3, 2013, https://blogs.loc.gov/catbird/2013/09/john-gillespie-magees-high-flight/ (accessed June 19, 2017).

6. Brad Andrew, "It's More Than Urban...," *Military Intelligence Professional Journal*, Vol. 31, No. 2 (April–June 2005), pp. 61–62, https://fas.org/irp/agency/army/mipb/2005_02.pdf (accessed June 19, 2017).

7. Ibid.

8. Mark Thompson, "Why Flying Choppers in Afghanistan Is So Deadly," *Time*, October 27, 2009, http://content.time.com/time/nation/article/0,8599,1932386,00.html (accessed June 19, 2017).

9. Michelle Tan, "Army Chief: Soldiers Must Be Ready to Fight in 'Megacities'," *Army Times*, October 5, 2016, http://www.defensenews.com/articles/army-chief-soldiers-must-be-ready-to-fight-in-megacities (accessed June 19, 2017).

10. For recent studies on urban operations, see David E. Johnson, Matthew Wade Markel, and Brian Shannon, *The 2008 Battle of Sadr City: Reimagining Urban Combat* (Santa Monica, CA: RAND Corporation, 2013), http://www.rand.org/content/dam/rand/pubs/research_reports/RR100/RR160/RAND_RR160.pdf (accessed June 19, 2017); Gian Gentile, David E. Johnson, Lisa Saum-Manning, Raphael S. Cohen, Shara Williams, Carrie Lee, Michael Shurkin, Brenna Allen, Sarah Soliman, and James L. Doty III, *Reimagining the Character of Urban Operations for the U.S. Army: How the Past Can Inform the Present and Future* (Santa Monica, CA: RAND Corporation, 2017), http://www.rand.org/content/dam/rand/pubs/research_reports/RR1600/RR1602/RAND_RR1602.pdf (accessed June 19, 2017); and Colonel Marc Harris, Lieutenant Colonel Robert Dixon, Major Nicholas Melin, Command Sergeant Major Daniel Hendrex, Sergeant Major Richard Russo, and Michael Bailey, *Megacities and the United States Army: Preparing for a Complex and Uncertain Future* (Washington: Chief of Staff of the Army, Strategic Studies Group, June 2014), https://www.army.mil/e2/c/downloads/351235.pdf (accessed June 20, 2017).

11. CNN Student News, "U.S. Troops Weather Sandstorm, Cross Euphrates River," March 25, 2003, http://www.cnn.com/2003/fyi/news/03/25/iraq.war/ (accessed June 20, 2017).

12. Charles Krauthammer, "To Die for Estonia?" *The Washington Post*, June 2, 2017, p. A19, https://www.washingtonpost.com/opinions/global-opinions/to-die-for-estonia/2017/06/01/465619a6-46f1-11e7-a196-a1bb629f64cb_story.html?utm_term=.7cb38c158156 (accessed June 19, 2017).

13. From the book title: George C. Henry, *No Foxholes in the Sky and Guns of Ploesti* (Dallas: G. C. Henry, 2007).

14. For output from one such war game, see David A. Shlapak and Michael W. Johnson, *Reinforcing Deterrence on NATO's Eastern Flank: Wargaming the Defense of the Baltics* (Santa Monica, CA: RAND Corporation, 2016), https://www.rand.org/content/dam/rand/pubs/research_reports/RR1200/RR1253/RAND_RR1253.pdf (accessed June 20, 2017).

15. See Evan Braden Montgomery, *Reinforcing the Front Line: U.S. Defense Strategy and the Rise of China*, Center for Strategic and Budgetary Assessments, 2017, p. 38, http://csbaonline.org/research/publications/reinforcing-the-front-line-u.s.-defense-strategy-and-the-rise-of-china (accessed June 20, 2017), and Timothy M. Bonds, Joel B. Predd, Timothy R. Heath, Michael S. Chase, Michael Johnson, Michael J. Lostumbo, James Bonomo, Muharrem Mane, and Paul S. Steinberg, *What Role Can Land-Based, Multi-Domain Anti-Access/Area Denial Forces Play in Deterring or Defeating Aggression?* (Santa Monica, CA: RAND Corporation, 2017), https://www.rand.org/pubs/research_reports/RR1820.html (accessed June 20, 2017).

16. Sydney J. Freedberg Jr., "McMaster: Army May Be Outnumbered AND Outgunned in Next War," *Breaking Defense*, April 6, 2016, http://breakingdefense.com/2016/04/mcmaster-army-may-be-outnumbered-and-outgunned-in-next-war/ (accessed June 20, 2017).

17. U.S. Department of the Army, Field Manual No. 3-0, *Operations*, June 2001, p. 5-4, http://cnqzu.com/library/Anarchy%20Folder/Combat/Operations%20-%20FM%203-0.pdf (accessed June 19, 2017).

18. U.S. Department of the Army, Field Manual No. 3-24/U.S. Marine Corps, Warfighting Publication No. 3-33.5, *Insurgencies and Countering Insurgencies*, May 2014, p. 5-4, https://fas.org/irp/doddir/army/fm3-24.pdf (accessed June 20, 2017).

19. Ibid., p. 1-13.

20. Conrad C. Crane, *Cassandra in Oz: Counterinsurgency and Future War* (Annapolis, MD: United States Naval Institute Press, 2016), p. 288, https://www.usni.org/store/books/transforming-war-series/cassandra-oz (accessed June 19, 2017).

21. U.S. Department of the Army/U.S. Marine Corps, *Insurgencies and Countering Insurgencies*, p. 6-6.

22. David E. Johnson, *Hard Fighting: Israel in Lebanon and Gaza* (Santa Monica, CA: RAND Corporation, 2011), pp. 148–149, http://www.rand.org/content/dam/rand/pubs/monographs/2011/RAND_MG1085.sum.pdf (accessed June 19, 2017).

23. See James T. Quinlivan, "Force Requirements in Stability Operations," *Parameters*, Vol. 25, No. 4 (Winter 1995–1996), pp. 59–69, http://ssi.armywarcollege.edu/pubs/parameters/Articles/1995/quinliv.htm (accessed June 20, 2017). Quinlivan's analysis informed Army and Marine Corps doctrine on this topic: "Twenty counterinsurgents per 1000 residents is often considered the minimum troop density required for effective [counterinsurgency] operations; however as with any fixed ratio, such calculations remain very dependent upon the situation.... As in any conflict, the size of the force needed to defeat an insurgency depends on the situation." U.S. Department of the Army/U.S. Marine Corps, *Insurgencies and Countering Insurgencies*, pp. 1–13. See also David E. Johnson, "Fighting the 'Islamic State': The Case for U.S. Ground Forces," *Parameters*, Vol. 45, No. 1 (Spring 2015), p. 14, https://ssi.armywarcollege.edu/pubs/parameters/Issues/Spring_2015/4_Special-Commentary_Johnson.pdf (accessed June 19, 2017): "One could argue that they were not met across Iraq during the surge, but within Baghdad, considered by many to be the center of gravity of the war, there were approximately 131,000 U.S.–Iraqi security forces in a city with a population of some 7,000,000, which came close to the doctrinal ratio."

24. Johnson, *Hard Fighting*, pp. 153–154. "The term hybrid threat captures the seemingly increased complexity of operations, the multiplicity of actors involved, and the blurring between traditional elements of conflict. **A *hybrid* threat is the diverse and dynamic combination of regular forces, irregular forces, terrorist forces, or criminal elements unified to achieve mutually benefitting threat effects.**" Emphasis in original. U.S. Department of the Army, Army Doctrine Reference Publication No. 3-0, *Operations*, November 2016, p. 1-3, http://www.apd.army.mil/epubs/DR_pubs/DR_a/pdf/web/ADRP%203-0%20FINAL%20WEB.pdf (accessed June 25, 2017). Italics and bold in original.

25. U.S. Army Training and Doctrine Command, Army Capabilities Integration Center, Maneuver, Aviation, and Soldier Division, *The U.S. Army Combat Vehicle Modernization Strategy*, September 15, 2015, p. 15, http://www.arcic.army.mil/app_Documents/CVMS_SEP_Master.pdf (accessed June 23, 2017), and Amos C. Fox, "The Russian–Ukrainian War: Understanding the Dust Clouds on the Battlefield," Modern War Institute, January 17, 2017, https://mwi.usma.edu/russian-ukrainian-war-understanding-dust-clouds-battlefield/ (accessed June 19, 2017).

26. The Honorable Patrick J. Murphy, Acting Secretary of the Army, and General Mark A. Milley, Chief of Staff, United States Army, statement "On the Posture of the United States Army" before the Committee on Armed Services, U.S. Senate, 114th Cong., 2nd Sess., April 7, 2016, p. 6, https://www.armed-services.senate.gov/imo/media/doc/Murphy-Milley_04-07-16.pdf (accessed June 25, 2017).

27. Eric S. Edelman and Whitney Morgan McNamara, *U.S. Strategy for Maintaining a Europe Whole and Free*, Center for Strategic and Budgetary Assessments, 2017, pp. 13–26, http://csbaonline.org/research/publications/u.s.-strategy-for-maintaining-a-europe-whole-and-free/publication (accessed June 25, 2017). See also David E. Johnson, "The Challenges of the 'Now' and Their Implications for the U.S. Army," RAND Corporation *Perspective* No. 184, 2016, https://www.rand.org/pubs/perspectives/PE184.readonline.html (accessed June 25, 2017). Other state adversaries like North Korea and Iran, while perhaps not as formidable as China and Russia, can present significant challenges. Both possess large land forces, air defenses, and large amounts of long-range artillery, rockets, and missiles. North Korea also has nuclear weapons.

28. James Mattis, Secretary of Defense, statement in support of President's FY 2018 budget request before the Committee on Armed Services, U.S. Senate, June 13, 2017, p. 5, https://www.armed-services.senate.gov/imo/media/doc/Mattis_06-13-17.pdf (accessed August 15, 2017).

29. Ibid., p. 6.

30. Patrick Tucker, "Dunford: Without Better Funding, U.S. Will Lose 'Competitive Advantage' in Just a Few Years," *Defense One*, June 12, 2017, http://www.defenseone.com/politics/2017/06/without-better-funding-us-will-lose-competitive-advantage-just-few-years-top-general/138618/ (accessed June 25, 2017).

31. U.S. Army, *Future Force Development Strategy*, May 2017, p. 4.

32. U.S. Department of the Army, Assistant Secretary of the Army (Financial Management and Comptroller), *FY 2018 President's Budget Highlights*, May 2017, p. 18, https://www.asafm.army.mil/documents/BudgetMaterial/fy2018/pbhl.pdf (accessed August 15, 2017).

33. Fehrenbach, *This Kind of War*, p. 290.

34. Antulio J. Echevarria II, "Operational Concepts and Military Strength," in *2017 Index of U.S. Military Strength*, ed. Dakota L. Wood (Washington: The Heritage Foundation, 2016), p. 41.

35. Ibid., p. 43.

36. U.S. Army, Training and Doctrine Command, "Multi-Domain Battle: Combined Arms for the 21st Century," white paper, February 24, 2017, p. 3, http://www.tradoc.army.mil/MultiDomainBattle/docs/MDB_WhitePaper.pdf (accessed June 19, 2017).

37. Ibid., p. 4. Italics in original.

The Naval Warfare Domain

Thomas Callender

The maritime domain, in and through which operations on and under the oceans and seas are conducted, presents unique challenges as well as advantages to maritime nations and military forces. The domain is generally subdivided into two primary categories: littoral (coastal) and open ocean ("blue-water"). The littorals are defined by relatively shallow waters and close proximity to the coasts and include the territorial waters of coastal nations. Open-ocean operations, as the name suggests, are marked by waters beyond the maritime boundaries of nations, with their extreme depths and vast spaces.

While the maritime domain demands some common capabilities and operational concepts for all naval forces, littoral and blue-water environments require very different forces and warfighting strategies. The maritime domain drives some common characteristics for naval vessels: relatively large size and payloads compared to land and air platforms, slow speed, limited organic sensor range, long-range communications requirements, and naval logistics. In addition, the maritime domain shapes naval concepts of operations with tactics such as layered defense, forward presence, and sea control.

Importance of the Maritime Domain

Since prehistoric times, the world's oceans and seas have played a critical part in the development of mankind and many of man's dominant civilizations. Evidence suggests that the earliest man-made boats date back as far as 45,000 years.[1] Initially, these vessels were used for coastal fishing, but as they became larger and more sophisticated, people used them to trade with other coastal civilizations. Once man learned to navigate beyond sight of land and to harness the wind, exploration and trade routes developed across the Mediterranean Sea, the Arabian Sea, the Indian Ocean, and the Pacific Ocean. Maritime exploration also led to human migration between continents and island archipelagos.

The development of larger vessels made it possible to transport greater quantities of commodities both faster and more cheaply than was possible over land routes. These maritime trade routes eliminated the need to transit through the sovereign territory of other nations and pay often exorbitant tolls. However, the movement of large amounts of precious commodities by sea soon led to the rise of piracy. Just as land armies arose to defend national borders and trade routes, armed naval vessels soon arose to help protect these maritime trade routes. From the Ancient Egyptians to the Greeks and on to the rise of the British Empire, dominant maritime trade and naval power were critical to the rise and expansion of these empires.

The oceans and seas still play a vital role in the prosperity and protection of most of the world's population. Of the world's 195 nations, 147 border an ocean or sea, and 40 percent of the world's population lives within 100 kilometers (62 miles) of an oceanic coast.[2] In addition, maritime trade through international shipping lanes comprises over 90 percent of global commerce.[3] In a modern world that appears to be dominated by wireless communications and satellite broadcasts, 99 percent of all international data (phone, texts, and Internet) is transported over approximately 200 undersea fiber optic cables at speeds eight times faster than satellites.[4] While typically very robust, these submarine cables are susceptible to landslides and other seismic events.

Challenges and Advantages of the Maritime Environment

For those whose experience with the oceans is limited to the coasts, the vastness of the world's oceans is difficult to convey. The five recognized oceans (Atlantic, Pacific, Arctic, Indian, and Southern) cover 71 percent of the Earth's surface with an average depth of 13,000 feet.[5] The Atlantic Ocean covers "approximately 41,105,000 square miles," and the Pacific Ocean covers "more than 60 million square miles," or approximately 20 percent and 46 percent, respectively, of the Earth's surface.[6] For comparison, the Pacific Ocean is larger than all of the Earth's land masses combined;[7] the continental United States covers only 3,120,426 square miles (1.58 percent) of the Earth's surface.[8]

The vastness of the world's oceans presents both advantages and challenges. The immense oceanic distances and limited speed of ships (10–15 knots on average for transoceanic travel) create natural barriers of time and space. For example, these barriers prevented transoceanic exploration and colonization for centuries until shipbuilding technology and seafaring techniques became advanced enough to withstand storms, navigate safely, and carry sufficient supplies to survive weeks or months of travel. While land forces can resupply along their route with local fresh water and food, transoceanic vessels must be self-sufficient for extended periods, carrying or making adequate fresh water, food, and fuel.

The limited speed of naval vessels limits their rapid responsiveness or repositioning. For example, the great circle route (the

shortest distance between two points on the curved surface of the Earth) between Norfolk, Virginia, and the Strait of Gibraltar at the entrance to the Mediterranean Sea is 3,326 nautical miles. For a ship traveling at an average speed of 12 knots—a common economical speed for commercial shipping—it would take 11.5 days to make this transit, while a modern jet passenger aircraft traveling at 500 knots would take approximately six hours and 40 minutes.

This time and distance effect requires preplanning or prepositioning of naval forces if a nation desires a timely transoceanic response to maritime crises. For the United States, this has meant development of a forward-deployed blue-water Navy. Maintaining a credible deterrent force constantly deployed near potential naval adversaries enables the U.S. to respond rapidly to maritime security crises before they approach America's shores. This could not be accomplished with naval forces that remain predominantly in their home ports or near territorial waters.

The expanse of the oceans and the lack of landmarks once a sailor gets beyond sight of land present unique navigational challenges when traversing thousands of miles of ever-changing ocean surface. The fact that the ocean's surface varies from one second to the next and does not offer any geographical reference points has led to the development of rather sophisticated navigation techniques and technologies. Satellite navigation systems such as the Global Positioning System (GPS) provide a highly accurate real-time ship's position for both military and commercial vessels. GPS and related technologies have afforded military naval vessels the required positioning, navigation, and timing (PNT) accuracy that enables use of precision-guided munitions and coordinated military operations.

With the advent and subsequent proliferation of GPS-denial or degradation technologies, it has become essential for modern military vessels to have backup navigation systems that are resilient and reliable even in the face of enemy actions. Celestial navigation—the determination of one's position on the Earth's surface based on the position of celestial bodies, typically the sun, moon, or specific stars—is one such technique that relies on a clear sky and a highly accurate chronometer. An essential skill for sailors across the centuries, celestial navigation is again being taught to young sailors as navies recognize that they cannot rely solely on GPS. Another critical GPS-denied navigation method is inertial navigation, which provides the speed and position of a ship or other platform by measuring its acceleration in all three dimensions. Once extremely large and expensive, current solid-state inertial navigation units are getting smaller and cheaper, enabling their use on small surface vessels and even on unmanned undersea vehicles (UUVs).

The vast ocean expanses have also provided a measure of stealth for naval vessels, although this is becoming less and less true. For years, most modern naval vessels relied primarily on organic radar and electronic support measures (ESM) systems to locate and target adversary naval vessels at over-the-horizon (OTH) ranges beyond the line of sight. Maritime patrol craft and carrier aviation early-warning aircraft were able to extend the ability of these warships to locate and engage adversaries, but the ocean is a very big place, and even with radar, finding a comparatively small ship was still a challenge.

With the rise of intelligence, surveillance, and reconnaissance (ISR) satellites, this "stealth via vastness" was further reduced. The limited number of ISR satellites, however, precluded continuous coverage of any specific area, affording naval vessels opportunities in specific time and location windows to avoid detection.

The current proliferation of commercial and military electro-optic/infrared, radar, and electronic intelligence (ELINT) satellites is providing greater coverage of and more frequent revisit rates to the world's oceans. In addition, maritime domain awareness technologies such as the Automatic Identification System (AIS) provide the location and identity of commercial shipping, thereby helping to clarify the maritime picture. The proliferation of ISR unmanned aerial vehicles (UAVs) is also changing maritime surveillance by greatly increasing the capacity for real-time OTH ISR and targeting information for naval platforms. Not only can long-range land-based UAVs provide ISR coverage hundreds of miles from shore for 12 hours or more at a time, but smaller UAVs are being fielded that can be launched and recovered from naval platforms, providing naval fleets with organic ISR and cueing.

While these systems still have gaps in coverage and some require complex algorithms to scour the vast amounts of imagery required for open-ocean searches, it is getting harder for a large surface naval vessel such as an aircraft carrier to hide in the open ocean. To this end, many modern navies are regularly practicing electromagnetic emission control (EMCON) operations as well as developing technologies and tactics to deny or degrade ISR satellites and related platforms.

The ocean's depths provide their own condition of stealth for submarines and other undersea platforms such as UUVs, enabling undersea forces to move unseen and relatively undetected by adversary forces. This is because the environment below the ocean's surface is drastically different from the world above it. While light and radio waves can travel thousands of miles through the Earth's atmosphere, they penetrate the ocean's depths only from several inches to a maximum of several hundred feet depending on the frequency of the electromagnetic wave (light or radio waves). For example, only a minuscule fraction of sunlight penetrates the ocean's depths beyond approximately 650 feet, and for much of the ocean's depths, visibility is less than 100 feet in any direction. Radar and other radio transmissions cannot be used to search for objects or to communicate with submerged submarines or other undersea platforms. Although this limits the ability of submarines or other undersea platforms to communicate with ships, aircraft, or land-based headquarters, it also hides them from all but the most advanced search techniques.

While the air is the domain of radio waves and light, the ocean's depths are the domain of sound. Sound is the most effective means to communicate or to detect objects across the vast expanse of the oceans. Compared to light and radio waves, sound can travel from thousands of yards up to thousands of miles in water. For example, the vocalization of blue whales (at frequencies as low as 14 Hz) has been detected thousands of miles away.[9] Sound also travels eight times faster in water than in air, and sound waves travel faster as temperature, water pressure, and salinity increase. The deeper, warmer, and saltier the water, the faster sound travels.

The variance in ocean temperature and pressure with depth and geographic location can be exploited to benefit naval operations. Differences in temperature and pressure cause sound waves to bend (or refract) toward the area of slower speed of sound. This bending of sound waves can create "acoustic blind spots" as well as deep-sea sound channels where sound energy is easily transmitted for long distances. Lower-frequency sound travels further in water than higher-frequency sound does. Submarines, surface ships, and aircraft hunting for submarines, as well as land-based command centers communicating with submarines, will use these characteristics to hide from acoustic search or to pulse acoustic energy into the water to affect communications or locate an object.

Background ocean noise can mask quieter noise sources such as submarines. The primary factors contributing to ocean background noise are the sea state (how big the waves are); the amount of local shipping traffic; seismic events such as undersea earthquakes, volcanic eruptions, rock slides, and thermal vents; other noisy maritime evolutions such as fishing and offshore drilling; and even the animal life of the ocean including clicking shrimp, whales, and other marine mammals like porpoises.

Finally, undersea topography can affect the transmission of sound. The ocean's bottom varies from extraordinarily deep trenches to broad plains and undersea mountains, with the floor rising dramatically at times to form walls that stretch upward to the continental shelves. Acoustically, the shallow littoral waters behave differently from the deep oceans as sound waves repeatedly bounce off rocky bottoms and the ocean's surface or are attenuated by muddy sea floors. As on land, these undersea terrain features can affect the transmission of sound and the flow of currents, which in turn can affect temperature gradients as water flows, rises, and falls. The complexity and variability of ocean waters drives undersea naval forces to monitor these changes continuously and alter their tactics and operating profile to exploit any acoustic advantage as effectively as possible.

There are two main types of sound navigation and frequency ranging (SONAR) that provide an acoustic "picture" of the undersea world. The first is passive sonar, which essentially is listening for any noise sources on or below the ocean's surface. Passive sonar provides only the direction from which the sound came.

Active sonar provides a much more complete picture of the undersea environment. Like bats and whales, ships and submarines can transmit sound and then listen for the return echo as the sound wave bounces off an object. Most surface vessels, from small pleasure boats to large commercial transports and naval vessels, use high-frequency active sonar (tens to hundreds of kHz) "depth sounders" to determine the ocean depth beneath them. Active sonars used by submarines and other naval vessels are typically in the 1 kHz to 10 kHz range, with some high-definition sonars in the 100 kHz to 1 GHz or higher range. While the higher frequencies give better resolution of the ocean bottom and other undersea objects, their effective range is less than 100 meters. Conversely, low-frequency active sonars (less than 1,000 Hz) can potentially detect submarines at tens of thousands of yards in proper acoustic conditions.

The disadvantage of active sonar is that the transmitting platform gives away its own presence and position. Since they do not want to surrender their acoustic stealth, U.S. submarines therefore operate their active sonar only in very select tactical situations.

The global maritime commons differ greatly from land, where nations have very visible geographic boundaries, and long-standing protocols—codified in laws, treaties, and recognized practices—govern how countries interact with each other. Whereas almost all of the Earth's land masses are claimed by one nation or another, the vast majority of the 139.7 million square miles of its oceans are international waters and not subject to any one nation's laws or control.[10] This means that ships can sail almost anywhere without needing the permission of or being subject to restrictions or obligations imposed by any one nation.

The 1982 United Nations Convention on the Law of the Sea (UNCLOS) defines a nation's territorial sea as a belt of coastal waters extending at most 12 nautical miles from its coast. The United States has not ratified UNCLOS because of concerns about some of its provisions, but it does recognize the agreement's conventions on territorial limits and freedom of navigation as customary international law and has established similar sovereign rights in U.S. law. While territorial waters are regarded as the nation's sovereign territory, foreign ships (both military and civilian) are allowed innocent passage through them, or transit passage for straits, under specific guidelines. This sovereignty extends to the airspace and seabed.

UNCLOS also establishes an Exclusive Economic Zone (EEZ) in which a coastal state assumes jurisdiction over the exploration and exploitation of marine resources in its adjacent section of the continental shelf, taken to be a band extending 200 miles from the shore. Another important aspect of UNCLOS and international maritime law is freedom of navigation, according to which ships flying the flag of any sovereign state shall not be subject to interference by other states.

Since no one nation's laws apply to these international waters, they are governed by several multilateral treaties. The most important is the 1972 Convention on the International Regulations for Preventing Collisions at Sea, which establishes among other things the "rules of the road" or navigation rules to be followed by ships and other vessels at sea to prevent collisions between vessels. Since there are no marked traffic lanes or stoplights on the open seas, all ships must remain vigilant with respect to the course and speed of other vessels. As the USS *Fitzgerald*'s June 2017 fatal collision with a Philippine container ship demonstrates, even routine at-sea training operations are dangerous and require a minimum safe level of proficiency.[11]

In short, international maritime laws afford the U.S. Navy the ability to project power in response to crises or attempt to deter potential adversaries by sailing U.S. warships anywhere around the globe without having to obtain the permission of any other nation. In similar manner, they also afford maritime competitors the opportunity to sail their naval platforms off the U.S. coast. Visible examples of this are the recent periodic deployments of Russian submarines off the east coast of the U.S. near U.S. naval bases (e.g., Kings Bay, Georgia).

While some nations focus their navies on coastal defense against adversaries operating near their coasts and territorial waters, the U.S. Navy has taken a different approach. The Navy's maritime strategy since World War II has focused on maintaining a continuous forward naval presence that strives to deter adversaries and, if necessary, engage them in the open ocean or near their own coasts, keeping the fight and threat far from U.S. shores. At present, no other nation can conduct routine, sustained naval operations far from its home waters as does the U.S. However, some near-peer competitors like Russia could attempt to deploy small numbers of nuclear-powered submarines off the U.S. coast to launch missiles armed with conventional explosives against targets of vital importance to the U.S. In light of this threat, the U.S. Navy and U.S. Northern Command (USNORTHCOM) maintain the ability to find and target adversary undersea forces closer to the U.S. homeland.

Implications of the Maritime Domain for Naval Forces

The ocean and its unique characteristics place demands on and drive the design of a nation's navy. This is most readily apparent in the difference between a littoral or coastal defense navy and a blue-water or global open-ocean navy.

A coastal navy is focused on protecting a country's territorial waters and adjacent international waters. How far a nation's maritime area of concern extends from its coast will depend on the nation's strategic focus and the size of its navy. A coastal navy that operates within several hundred miles from the coast can consist of smaller vessels such as fast attack craft, frigates, and diesel submarines. Since they generally will operate at sea for days to weeks rather than months, they do not require the size and ability to carry large amounts of supplies, fuel, and ammunition.

Coastal waters typically are more protected from severe storms and seas; as a result, coastal naval vessels can be smaller and less robust than open-ocean warships. Also, since they operate closer to shore, these naval vessels will be less dependent on satellite communications and long-range ISR than are their blue-water counterparts, which operate thousands of miles from their military commanders. If necessary, these navies can use line-of-sight UHF or VHF communications with aircraft or other surface vessels to pass urgent communications. Smaller fast attack craft employ shorter-range (tens of miles) OTH anti-ship missiles that can receive targeting information from onboard or, in some cases, even shore-based radars. Larger frigates will operate farther from shore and can support longer-range OTH weapons that can engage adversary surface vessels at ranges in excess of 100 miles, requiring timely and accurate targeting information from other ships, aircraft, or space-based ISR.

Diesel submarines are perfectly suited to the coastal defense mission. Usually operating in a defensive posture off a strategic area of the coast or near a choke point, diesel submarines can operate at very slow speeds (five knots or

less) that allow them to conserve their battery energy, which provides propulsion and electrical power while submerged. In areas where the continental shelf extends into diesel submarine patrol areas, modern diesel submarines can even bottom themselves to conserve energy even further.

A modern diesel submarine operating on its battery or Air Independent Propulsion (AIP)[12] is extremely quiet and difficult to detect by passive sonar, especially when operating in or near congested coastal waters. A modern diesel submarine armed with wake-homing torpedoes requires only a moderately proficient crew to attack an adversary's surface ship as it transits through a choke point. A coastal defense approach can be supported by land-based aircraft (fighters, maritime patrol craft, and helicopters); OTH radars; and anti-ship cruise missiles. A coastal navy also does not require a large fleet of logistics ships, because its ships and submarines can return quickly to port for fuel, supplies, and weapons.

Naval mines are extremely well suited to a coastal defense strategy whose primary mission is to keep potential adversaries out of its area of concern or far enough away that they are unable or degraded in their ability to conduct maritime strikes ashore. Naval mines are relatively cheap compared to modern precision-guided munitions, and a littoral minefield can easily be laid by small naval vessels or even by militia vessels (civilian vessels that can be used for some low-end military missions). Just one ship hitting a mine effectively shuts down a choke point or area of concern until it can be confirmed that all mines are cleared. Since the high-frequency sonars required to detect undersea mines have limited range, it can take weeks or months to survey and clear a suspected minefield. This mission gets even harder if the local adversary has surface dominance over the minefield area, thus preventing the use of mine countermeasure ships.

Since the transit time to and from coastal navy's bases to desired operating areas is relatively short (hours to days), a smaller force can maintain a specific defensive posture.

Additionally, coastal navies can surge additional forces quickly if needed and have them on station within hours. Finally, coastal defense navies can use undersea acoustic arrays in or near their territorial waters to provide early warning of adversary submarines or unmanned undersea vehicles approaching their coastlines or critical undersea infrastructure.

A blue-water or global open-ocean navy like the U.S. Navy has very different demands that drive the design of its vessels as well as the overall structure of the force. Since these warships operate thousands of miles from their nearest naval base for months at a time, they must be larger than their coastal counterparts for a variety of reasons. First, blue-water naval vessels must be large enough to withstand the worst possible storms and seas; a ship with a maximum speed of 20–30 knots may not be able to outrun a hurricane or other large storm. They must also have larger crews to support sustained 24-hour operations for months on end and perform preventive maintenance to ensure maximum operational readiness.

Since forward-deployed warships cannot count on getting supplies from a port in their forward operating areas during a time of conflict, they must be able to carry sufficient supplies (food, spare parts, etc.) to operate for several months if necessary and must carry sufficient fuel for an operating range of several thousand miles to enable transoceanic crossings without refueling. Blue-water naval vessels also require weapons magazines that are large enough for them to perform their initial warfighting missions.

These warships are usually multimission, since operational commanders must have the flexibility to respond rapidly to numerous military contingencies without waiting weeks for the warship with the "right mission capability" to arrive. While not every ship can perform every mission, having a mix of numerous multimission ships forward deployed enables these naval forces to respond to the vast majority of contingencies. Blue-water navies also require a large logistics fleet to resupply warships with food, fuel, repair parts, and ammunition while underway, thereby enabling them to remain forward deployed and on station for months on end.

The level of training required for blue-water sailors to attain the required proficiency to operate safely and effectively in the harsh open-ocean environment is significantly greater than the level needed for short-duration littoral operations. This training must include at-sea local area operations to simulate the conditions they will face on deployment to ensure that the crew is proficient in all potential missions they could be called on to perform.

An open-ocean global navy requires a much larger force structure than its coastal counterpart. The typical rule of thumb for naval force structure is that it takes a minimum of four ships of a given class to have any one of those ships deployed. This accounts for one vessel in major extended maintenance, one on deployment, one just returned from deployment, and one preparing for deployment. Since it takes weeks for a ship to transit to a forward-deployed area, the geographic combat commanders must maintain a specific minimum number of deployed ships and submarines of various classes so that they can respond immediately to a major combat operation. Even in peacetime, the strategic deterrent provided by a sufficiently large forward naval presence can cause potential adversaries to refrain from taking hostile or other undesirable actions.

Blue-water submarines also have different demands on their designs compared with their coastal counterparts. Nuclear propulsion is more advantageous for a blue-water submarine than diesel electric or an air-independent battery recharge method.

- As noted, it can take weeks to transit an ocean even at an average speed of 12–15 knots. A diesel submarine can transit at that average speed for less than one day before it must slow and come near the surface to recharge its battery. A nuclear submarine, however, can operate at its maximum speed for days or weeks without surfacing if required to transit rapidly across the globe.

- With its greater propulsion power (~40,000 shaft horsepower compared to 4,000 for a diesel boat), a nuclear submarine can be much larger (~7,800 tons submerged) than a diesel submarine (less than 2,000 tons submerged) and therefore carry more weapons and a larger crew.

- A nuclear submarine's greater available power also enables it to have sufficient atmosphere control and fresh water–producing equipment to allow lengthy submerged operations.

The key drawback of a nuclear submarine compared to a diesel submarine is the noise generated by its power plant. The reactor support equipment and steam plant are inherently much louder than a diesel submarine operating an electric motor on the battery. These systems can be made extremely quiet and more closely approach the minimal noise levels of a diesel submarine, but the engineering is much more complicated and expensive. For example, it took the Russian/Soviet Navy and now the Chinese People's Liberation Army Navy (PLAN) decades to develop the expertise to quiet their nuclear submarines so that they could not be heard tens of thousands of yards away.

Similar demands drive the design of open-ocean aircraft carriers. Most immediately noticeable is the size of a modern carrier. For an aircraft carrier to provide sufficient power-projection capability anywhere on the globe, it must be able to store, launch, and maintain a variety and large quantity of aircraft in a carrier air wing. For example, a U.S. Navy carrier air wing typically consists of 68 aircraft of six different types.[13] Steam-driven catapults to launch aircraft and an arrested landing system to enable their recovery aboard ship provide significant decreases over traditional runways, but a minimum distance is still needed for aircraft to take off and land on the carrier's deck (modern U.S. carriers are more than 1,000 feet long). The carrier must also hold sufficient aviation fuel and ordnance to support carrier flight operations for several days without

resupply, and the manpower required to operate both the carrier and the carrier air wing is substantial: A typical U.S. carrier deploys with over 5,000 personnel.

All of these requirements result in a vessel that is 60,000 tons to over 100,000 tons for the *Nimitz* class.[14] The large size, need for extended periods of high speed for carrier operations, and power requirements of support equipment (especially the catapult system) make nuclear power attractive for modern carriers.

A credible blue-water or global open-ocean navy is expensive to build, train, and maintain, but it provides the capability for global power projection and enduring forward presence.

Increasing Maritime Competition and Threats

The world's oceans have never been more critical to its prosperity and security. Global maritime traffic has increased almost fourfold over the past 20 years,[15] with even more dramatic increases in the Indian Ocean and the East and South China Seas. The sea-lanes connecting Asia with North America, the Mediterranean, and Northern Europe flow through the Suez Canal and account for over 15 percent of today's global shipping traffic.[16] These global shipping lanes are extremely congested and subject to increased risk of collisions, terrorism, or piracy as they pass through critical choke points. Each year, for example, 50,000 ships transit the Strait of Malacca, averaging more than 135 per day, and the Suez Canal handles upwards of 75 ships per day.[17] World seaborne trade accounts for 80 percent of global merchandise trade, some 10 billion tons of cargo.[18]

Although global maritime piracy has decreased significantly over the past few years due to the efforts of multinational naval task forces such as Combined Task Force 151 off the east coast of Africa and actions by the commercial shipping industry, piracy remains a prevalent concern. Some areas such as the Gulf of Guinea are seeing increased activity. The threat of maritime piracy affects shipping costs by causing commercial shipping companies to route their ships farther out into the open ocean to avoid these small pirate vessels, thus creating longer and less efficient routes; to deploy armed guards and other self-defense measures; and to transit areas of increased threat at faster speeds that burn more fuel per distance traveled.

The search for oil, gas, and mineral resources has fueled an unprecedented increase in undersea exploration. The commercial use of remotely operated vehicles (ROVs) and UUVs to explore the ocean's bottom and to inspect and maintain deep-sea oil rigs has helped drive the technological maturation and increasing capabilities of small to medium-sized UUVs. Rapidly improving UUV and ROV technology also makes it possible for a growing number of state and non-state actors to find and cut undersea cables clandestinely.

The 2006 magnitude 7.0 Taiwan earthquake severed eight submarine cables in multiple places, resulting in a severe Internet disruption in China. It took 11 special cable-laying ships 49 days to repair the damage.[19] If an adversary or natural disaster cut the majority of cables to the continental United States or even to Hawaii, where U.S. Pacific Command Headquarters is located, it would likely take months to find and repair the damage. Trillions of dollars of international financial transactions would be affected, and secure military communications would be dangerously reduced. It should be noted that of the 56 commercial cable-laying/repair ships in operation worldwide, only one is registered in the U.S., and the U.S. government owns only one cable-repair ship, the USNS *Zeus*.[20] Just how many repair ships the commercial undersea industry would dedicate to such U.S.-focused repairs is therefore uncertain at best.

The search for undersea natural resources has political and legal implications. According to the United States Geological Survey, as much as one-fifth of the planet's undiscovered petroleum reserves may reside in the Arctic: roughly 90 billion barrels of oil and 1,670 trillion cubic feet of natural gas.[21] Under international maritime law, Canada, Denmark, Norway, Russia, and the United States all have a legal claim to this valuable seafloor territory. UNCLOS allows these nations to file claims for additional territory out to 350 nautical miles if they can prove their continental shelves extend into the Arctic seabed. To date, Russia, Denmark, and Norway have submitted claims to an extended continental shelf in the Arctic, providing yet another potential source of maritime conflict.

In the South China Sea, China has staked claims to maritime territory that includes the Spratly Islands, Paracel Islands, and Scarborough Shoal. These claims overlap with the EEZ claims of Brunei, Indonesia, Malaysia, the Philippines, and Vietnam. In addition to fishing rights, potentially lucrative oil and natural gas deposits are at stake. In the past few years, the Chinese have begun island-building projects on the Subi, Mischief, and Fiery Cross reefs to advance their disputed territorial claims. While the Chinese have claimed that these islands are being built for civilian purposes, to increase safety for ships transiting the waterway, analysis of recent construction shows airfields, radars, and hardened shelters that indicate a military focus.

Key Naval Warfare Competitors and Challenges for the U.S. Navy

The rapid maturation and proliferation of certain technologies have affected the maritime environment and security challenges for the U.S. The proliferation of commercial satellites has greatly improved the ability of many nations to conduct open-ocean command, control, communications, computers, intelligence, surveillance, and reconnaissance (C4ISR). Space-based electro-optical and synthetic aperture radar sensors permit wide-area search for surface vessels because, unlike the land with its forests, mountains, and other masking terrain, there is nowhere to hide on the ocean's surface. Commercial satellite communications provide global communications capabilities to nations and navies that do not possess their own, as well as redundant communications for near-peer adversaries.

Forty of the world's coastal nations currently possess submarines.[22] The capabilities and proficiencies of these submarine fleets vary significantly from nation to nation, but modern export submarines and weapon systems provide even a very small navy with a credible naval threat. The vast majority of these submarines are quiet diesel submarines that operate in coastal defense missions.

Since the passive radiated noise of modern diesel submarines is extremely low when operating on the battery, resulting in exceptionally short passive sonar detection ranges of less than 2,000 yards, active sonar is the most effective means by which to search for and locate diesel submarines. Their limited speed and endurance (most can sprint at speeds in excess of 20 knots only for less than one hour) prevent them from effectively evading a searching platform using active sonar. In addition, efforts by Russia and China to quiet their nuclear submarines have reduced their passive detection ranges, making open-ocean search and localization by U.S. naval forces more difficult and requiring the use of multiple anti-submarine warfare (ASW) assets, such as the Surveillance Towed Array Sensor System (SURTASS), maritime patrol aircraft, and destroyers.

Underwater acoustic arrays have become more prevalent in the littoral areas of most of the world's continents. Although the vast majority of these arrays are for oceanographic research, submarines operating in their vicinity could possibly be detected. Modern air-based and space-based surface search radars also have the ability to detect submarines operating at periscope depth, provided one knows exactly where to look or can apply sophisticated data analysis techniques designed to detect the unique radar signature of an exposed submarine periscope or antenna mast as it interacts with a constantly changing ocean surface.

Some argue that advancing non-acoustic anti-submarine warfare (NAASW) capabilities will soon make the oceans transparent,[23] but the laws of physics and projected technologies do not support this assessment. While the probability of detecting a submarine either acoustically or by means of NAASW increases significantly for a submarine operating in the littorals off near-peer adversaries, especially at periscope depth, a submarine or other undersea platform remains comparatively much harder to detect than even the stealthiest aircraft. The undersea environment continues to provide a significant military advantage to navies that are able to operate in it effectively.

The proliferation of precision-guided munitions, especially land-based and sea-based anti-ship cruise missiles (ASCMs), and other advanced weapons technologies provides an increasing threat to U.S. naval forces, especially when operating in choke points and the littorals. Just as the flat ocean expanses make it easy to see surface ships, they also provide an unobstructed field of fire for adversaries with the ability to field ASCMs. Since ships cannot hide at sea, they must have the capability to defend against these increasingly capable weapons. Although unsuccessful, the October 2016 Houthi missile attack from land-based launchers in Yemen against the USS *Mason* while it was operating in the Red Sea clearly illustrates the reality of this threat.[24] The development of long-range (greater than 1,000-mile) anti-ship ballistic missiles presents a potential threat to carrier strike groups and other surface naval forces.

Rapidly maturing UAV technologies and their proliferation to both state and non-state actors presents another growing maritime threat. Small military and commercial micro-UAVs can easily be "weaponized," allowing them either to drop small explosives on ships or other targets or to serve as "kamikaze" UAVs. These small and slow UAVs are hard to detect with traditional air-search radars, which are focused on larger and fast-moving military aircraft and missiles. While the very small commercial UAVs have a rather limited range of less than five miles, their range and endurance are rapidly increasing, and even today, they could be launched from shore or from a nearby civilian vessel against a naval vessel transiting a choke point.

Key Nations That Affect
U.S. Navy Design and Missions

Iran. The Iranian Navy is a regional navy that has been shaped by its maritime operating environment on the Arabian Gulf and the Gulf of Oman. Aided by land-based aircraft and a very capable Russian-built integrated air defense system, the Iranian fleet consists primarily of coastal patrol frigates, fast attack craft, fast inshore attack craft, and submarines. Iranian diesel submarines and mini-submarines armed with torpedoes and anti-ship missiles are ideal platforms with which to lie in wait undersea in Iranian territorial waters and hold the Strait of Hormuz at risk. The Iranian Navy has been observed employing its fast attack craft (FAC) and fast inshore attack craft (FIAC) in swarm tactics meant to overwhelm the capacity of adversary warships to target and engage incoming vessels and their anti-ship cruise missiles.

Although the Iranian Navy possesses only a few dedicated mine-laying vessels, it could employ its FAC/FIAC and other vessels to deploy the over 2,000 naval mines in its inventory.[25] Naval mines would be extremely effective in controlling the relatively narrow Strait of Hormuz, as evidenced by the damage inflicted on the USS *Samuel B. Roberts* when it struck an Iranian floating contact mine in April 1988. Although not a naval capability, Iran's ballistic missile capabilities and their potential threat to Europe have led to a ballistic missile defense (BMD) mission for specified U.S. Navy cruisers and destroyers.

Russia. The Russian Navy, like Iran's, has been shaped by its unique maritime operating environment. With much of the Barents Sea covered with ice for part of the year, providing a "bastion" for its nuclear strategic submarines, it is logical that Russia has prioritized its submarine force over a large surface blue-water navy. A resurgent Russian Navy has focused its modernization efforts on submarines and small surface combatants (frigates and corvettes). Its new *Yazen*-class nuclear guided missile submarine is assessed as being extremely quiet and capable of launching conventional or tactical nuclear long-range cruise missiles. The new *Borei*-class nuclear ballistic missile submarine demonstrates Russia's continued prioritization of a submarine strategic nuclear deterrent.

The new Russian Maritime Doctrine illustrates the Russian Navy's focus on the Arctic and Atlantic Oceans with the ultimate goal of restoring its blue-water capabilities.[26] In the Black and Baltic Seas, the Russian Navy would assist any future efforts for Russian influence and territorial expansion in Eastern Europe. The past few years have seen a dramatic increase in provocative and sometimes unsafe engagements between Russian warships and fighter aircraft and U.S. Navy warships and maritime patrol aircraft in the Mediterranean, Baltic, and Black Seas.

China. Over the past two decades, the Chinese military has focused its modernization efforts on developing capabilities to disrupt the U.S. military's power projection forces in the Western Pacific, with a focus on its carrier strike groups and C4ISR enterprise. China's emphasis on denying U.S. access to the South China Sea and East China Sea has concentrated primarily on land-based anti-ship and anti-land ballistic missiles with effective ranges out to over 1,000 miles as well as land-based fighter aircraft best suited for control of the close-in air domain. Long-range land-based OTH radars and airborne early-warning aircraft and satellites provide the necessary detection and targeting data for these long-range weapons.

The development of these long-range, land-based anti-ship capabilities has lessened China's dependence on naval platforms (destroyers, frigates, fast attack craft, and diesel submarines) to disrupt or deny U.S. naval power projection in the South China sea. The Chinese saw the advantages presented by the South China Sea's maritime environment in the context of their strategy and developed new technologies to take advantage of them: the vast capacity advantage that land-based aircraft and anti-ship weapons can provide over a forward-deployed blue-water navy with limited weapons' magazines and extended logistic tail.

Although not critical to support this area denial strategy against the U.S., the PLAN has been slowly developing blue-water naval capabilities: indigenous aircraft carriers, advanced guided missile destroyers, and quiet nuclear attack submarines to supplement its regional naval force structure. These blue-water capabilities help China to protect its growing economic interests in Africa and other maritime areas far beyond the second island chain. It remains to be seen whether China is able to develop the logistics foundation to support a truly forward-deployed naval power—logistics ships, a network of friendly forward bases, and the operational proficiency to project naval power effectively far from its homeland—or whether platforms such as its aircraft carriers are merely symbols of China's economic and military strength.

Implications for U.S. Fleet Design

Given the characteristics of the maritime domain and the evolving challenges affecting the U.S. Navy's ability to protect U.S. national security interests, the Navy must likewise evolve to remain relevant.

The Navy must be able to operate in all subsets of the maritime domain—constricted choke points and archipelagos, the littorals, the Arctic seas, the expansive open ocean, and the complex depths of the undersea world—as well as to defeat potential maritime adversaries with capabilities ranging from swarms of fast attack craft to near-peer competitors' long-range anti-ship missiles. This should drive a force structure comprised of a mix of multimission naval platforms possessing the defensive and offensive capabilities necessary to control the sea when and where necessary and to project power from the sea against any competitor that attempts to deny the U.S. access to regions, markets, and allies.

The fleet must be large enough for forward-deployed naval forces to provide an enduring, credible deterrent to potential adversaries in all critical geographic maritime regions of concern. A sufficiently large, forward-deployed force also enables the Navy to respond rapidly to emerging and unforeseen crises wherever and whenever such response is needed.

Since the U.S. Navy always prefers to play the "away game," keeping enemies as far from the U.S. as possible, there is a pressing requirement for increased magazine size on naval platforms and secure intra-theater weapons replenishment and reload capability. Conflicts in distant theaters typically do not allow time for ships to return to a regionally local port, much less the U.S., for resupply. A robust logistics and airborne tanker fleet and a resilient and secure C4ISR enterprise provide the essential foundation for global maritime operations far from land-based defenses and logistics support.

Fortunately, the Navy's senior leadership has recognized these challenges and is striving to develop new naval strategies and capabilities to maintain America's advantages in this domain. These efforts include Distributed Lethality;[27] Design for Maintaining Maritime Superiority;[28] Undersea Domain Operating Concept (UDOC);[29] and Electromagnetic Maneuver Warfare (EMW).[30]

The key to success in all of these efforts will be a commensurate commitment by the U.S. Congress to provide adequate and stable funding so that the Navy can maintain a healthy, well-trained fleet of sufficient size and capability to secure U.S. interests in the maritime domain.

Endnotes

1. John Noble Wilford, "On Crete, New Evidence of Very Ancient Mariners," *The New York Times*, February 15, 2010, http://www.nytimes.com/2010/02/16/science/16archeo.html (accessed July 30, 2017).

2. Center for International Earth Science Information Network at Columbia University (CIESIN), Socioeconomic Data and Applications Center (SEDAC), "Percentage of Total Population Living in Coastal Areas," http://sedac.ciesin.columbia.edu/es/papers/Coastal_Zone_Pop_Method.pdf (accessed July 30, 2017).

3. International Chamber of Shipping, "Key Facts," 2017, http://www.ics-shipping.org/shipping-facts/key-facts (accessed July 30, 2017).

4. Declan McCullagh, "NSA Eavesdropping: How It Might Work," *CNet Magazine*, February 7, 2006, https://www.cnet.com/news/nsa-eavesdropping-how-it-might-work/ (accessed July 30, 2017).

5. U.S. Department of Commerce, National Oceanic and Atmospheric Administration, National Ocean Service, "How Many Oceans Are There?" revised July 6, 2017, http://oceanservice.noaa.gov/facts/howmanyoceans.html (accessed July 30, 2017).

6. U.S. Department of Commerce, National Oceanic and Atmospheric Administration, National Ocean Service, "How Big Is the Atlantic Ocean?" revised June 17, 2015, https://oceanservice.noaa.gov/facts/atlantic.html (accessed July 31, 2017); U.S. Department of Commerce, National Oceanic and Atmospheric Administration, National Ocean Service, "How Big Is the Pacific Ocean?" revised July 6, 2017, https://oceanservice.noaa.gov/facts/biggestocean.html (accessed July 31, 2017).

7. The Earth's total landmass is estimated to be 149 million square kilometers, or 57.5 million square miles, less than the 60 million square miles of the Pacific Ocean. See U.S. Central Intelligence Agency, *The World Factbook 2018*, entry for "World" statistics, "Geographic Overview," https://www.cia.gov/library/publications/the-world-factbook/geos/xx.html (accessed August 6, 2017).

8. U.S. Department of Commerce, U.S. Census Bureau, "State Area Measurements and Internal Point Coordinates," https://www.census.gov/geo/reference/state-area.html (accessed August 5, 2017). The Census Bureau estimates the total landmass of the continental United States (to include the District of Columbia) to be 3.12 million square miles. The CIA estimates the Earth's surface area to be 510 million square kilometers, or 197 million square miles. See CIA, *World Factbook 2018*, "Geographic Overview."

9. *National Geographic*, "Blue Whales and Communication," Video Highlights from *Kingdom of the Blue Whale*, March 26, 2011, http://www.nationalgeographic.com.au/science/blue-whales-and-communication.aspx (accessed July 31, 2017).

10. Global Development Research Center, "The World's Oceans," https://www.gdrc.org/oceans/world-oceans.html (accessed July 28, 2017); Sea Around Us, "High Seas," 2016, http://www.seaaroundus.org/data/#/highseas (accessed August 2, 2017).

11. U.S. Navy, "Special Report: USS Fitzgerald Collision," Navy Live: The Official Blog of the U.S. Navy, June 17, 2017, http://navylive.dodlive.mil/2017/06/17/uss-fitzgerald/ (accessed July 31, 2017).

12. Edward C. Whitman, "Air Independent Propulsion: AIP Technology Creates a New Undersea Threat," *Undersea Warfare Magazine*, Vol. 4, No. 1 (Fall 2001), http://www.public.navy.mil/subfor/underseawarfaremagazine/Issues/Archives/issue_13/propulsion.htm (accessed July 31, 2017).

13. U.S. Navy, "Aircraft Carriers–CVN," *Fact File*, last updated January 31, 2017, http://www.navy.mil/navydata/fact_display.asp?cid=4200&tid=200&ct=4 (accessed August 6, 2017).

14. Ibid.

15. Becky Oskin, "Ship Traffic Increases Dramatically, to Oceans' Detriment," Live Science, November 18, 2014, https://www.livescience.com/48788-ocean-shipping-big-increase-satellites.html (accessed July 31, 2017).

16. Jean-Paul Rodrigue and Theo Notteboom, "Strategic Maritime Passages," Chapter 1, Application 2, in *The Geography of Transport Systems*, ed. Jean-Paul Rodrigue, Hofstra University, Department of Global Studies and Geography, https://people.hofstra.edu/geotrans/eng/ch1en/appl1en/ch1a2en.html (accessed July 28, 2017).

17. Ibid.

18. United Nations Conference on Trade and Development, *Review of Maritime Transport 2016*, p. 6, http://unctad.org/en/PublicationsLibrary/rmt2016_en.pdf (accessed August 6, 2017).

19. Michael Sechrist, "New Threats, Old Technology: Vulnerabilities in Undersea Communication Cable Network Management Systems," Discussion Paper, Harvard Kennedy School, Belfer Center for Science and International Affairs, February 2012, http://www.belfercenter.org/publication/new-threats-old-technology-vulnerabilities-undersea-communication-cable-network (accessed July 28, 2017); Douglas Main, "Undersea Cables Transport 99 Percent of International Data," *Newsweek*, April 2, 2015, http://www.newsweek.com/undersea-cables-transport-99-percent-international-communications-319072 (accessed July 28, 2017).

20. International Cable Protection Committee, "Cableships of the World," updated May 26, 2017, https://www.iscpc.org/cableships-of-the-world/ (accessed July 28, 2017).

21. Robert Lamb, "5 Most Coveted Offshore Petroleum Reserves," How Stuff Works, September 15, 2008, http://science. howstuffworks.com/environmental/energy/5-offshore-petroleum-reserves.htm (accessed July 28, 2017).

22. Global Fire Power, "Total Submarine Strength by Country," 2017, http://www.globalfirepower.com/navy-submarines.asp (accessed July 28, 2017).

23. Sydney J. Freedberg Jr., "Transparent Sea: The Unstealthy Future of Submarines," *Breaking Defense*, January 22, 2015, http:// breakingdefense.com/2015/01/transparent-sea-the-unstealthy-future-of-submarines/ (accessed July 31, 2017).

24. Hope Hodge Seck, "USS Mason Fired on a Third Time Near Yemen, CNO Says," Military.com, October 16, 2016, http://www.military. com/daily-news/2016/10/16/uss-mason-fired-on-a-third-time-near-yemen-cno-says.html (accessed July 28, 2017).

25. Sydney J. Freedberg Jr., "Sowing the Seas with Fire: The Threat of Sea Mines," *Breaking Defense*, March 30, 2015, http:// breakingdefense.com/2015/03/sowing-the-sea-with-fire-how-russia-china-iran-lay-mines-and-how-to-stop-them/ (accessed July 31, 2017).

26. Sean MacCormac, "The New Russian Naval Doctrine," Center for International Maritime Security, updated November 24, 2015, http://cimsec.org/new-russian-naval-doctrine/18444 (accessed July 31, 2017).

27. U.S. Navy, Commander, Naval Surface Forces, *Surface Force Strategy: Return to Sea Control*, January 9, 2016, p. 9, http://www. navy.mil/strategic/SurfaceForceStrategy-ReturntoSeaControl.pdf (accessed July 31, 2017).

28. Admiral John M. Richardson, Chief of Naval Operations, *A Design for Maintaining Maritime Superiority*, Version 1.0, January 2016, http://www.navy.mil/cno/docs/cno_stg.pdf (accessed July 31, 2017).

29. News release, "Undersea Domain Operating Concept Approved by Chief of Naval Operations," U.S. Navy, September 9, 2013, http://www.navy.mil/submit/display.asp%3Fstory_id%3D76420 (accessed July 31, 2017).

30. See *Naval Warfare Development Command's NEXT*, Vol. 3, No. 2 (Summer/Fall 2015), issue devoted to "Advancing Electronic Maneuver Warfare," https://www.nwdc.navy.mil/NeXT%20Assets/archive/NWDC_Mag_SUMMER_FALL%202015%20APP.pdf (accessed July 31, 2017).

The Air Domain and the Challenges of Modern Air Warfare

Harry Foster

It is difficult to imagine a modern world without flight and its associated technologies. The *speed* possible in the air domain shrinks time: A modern airliner travels 25 times faster than the fastest cruise ship on the Atlantic and seven times faster than the fastest locomotive in the 1950s. Militarily, operating in the air domain provides *vantage*: the ability to see not only over the next hill, but also over the horizon. It provides *maneuverability* unencumbered by mountain ranges, roads, river crossings, or rocky shoals at sea. Although navalists frequently remind us that 70 percent of the world is covered by oceans, 100 percent of the world is covered by air. The air domain is physically linked to every other domain, thus providing *flexibility* in operations, while its *range* provides an avenue for access anywhere in the world, anytime.

Over the past century, exploitation of the air domain's speed, vantage, maneuverability, flexibility, and range changed the nature of warfare. Specifically, it:

- Created new asymmetries that broke the stalemate of trench warfare after World War I, enabling combined-arms maneuver warfare that is with us today;

- Extended the reach of fleets and shore defenses beyond the sight of observation towers or the range of naval surface fires, making control of the air a requisite for operations on the sea;

- Allowed rapid insertion and resupply of forces at great distance from supporting bases; and

- Allowed air forces to go "over not through" the front lines of opposing armies, disrupting rearward logistics, denying maneuver, and taking war directly to capitals.

Today, from a military perspective, the degree to which the United States can exploit the air domain in its favor to find and hold at risk any target (fixed, mobile, hardened, and deep inland) anywhere on the globe is a key differentiator that makes it a military superpower.

Understanding the complexity of modern air power begins with a basic understanding of the air domain itself. This means understanding the air domain's unique attributes; how one can access and use the domain while exploring the limits of height and speed for platforms that operate in it; the domain's unique attributes of speed, range, persistence, and payload that have allowed the United States to dominate conflicts for the past 25 years; and current key shifts in the domain, driven by the evolution of technology and the return of state-based competition, and their implications for future military requirements.

Attributes of the Air Domain

The Atmosphere: Home to the Air Domain. The Department of Defense defines the air domain as "the atmosphere, beginning at the Earth's surface, extending to the altitude where its effects upon operations become negligible."[1] At its most fundamental level, the atmosphere is composed of air, a mixture of gases consisting of 21 percent oxygen, 78 percent nitrogen, and 1 percent argon, carbon dioxide, and other gases.[2]

The composition of air is perhaps its most extraordinary and important characteristic because it determines the very nature of the domain and dictates what can and cannot be done in it and drives the characteristics of the platforms that fly through it. Because these gases have mass, the distribution of the atmosphere is not uniform. For example, due to gravitational effects, nearly 50 percent of atmospheric mass is contained below 18,000 feet at the equator, 90 percent is contained below 52,000 feet, and 99.99 percent is contained below 330,000 feet or an altitude of 100 kilometers.[3] While some international organizations such as the Fédération Aéronautique Internationale define 100 kilometers as the beginning of space, the United States does not recognize a formal boundary either by treaty or by policy.[4]

The atmosphere is divided into several layers that are of varying degrees of significance to military operations.

- The lowest level, the troposphere, varies in height from the surface to 60,000 feet at the equator to 30,000 feet over the poles. All weather occurs in the troposphere. The top of the troposphere, called the tropopause, is the "cap" where summer thunderstorms flatten out to form an anvil shape. In the troposphere, the wind blows west to east in the Northern Hemisphere and east to west in the Southern Hemisphere. Temperature decreases by about 3.5 degrees Fahrenheit with every 1,000 feet of climb. Wind speed changes significantly with altitude, averaging 75 miles per hour from the west at 35,000 feet over the central United States in winter to as much as 200 miles per hour in the strongest jet streams.

- Above the troposphere is the stratosphere, which extends to about 180,000 feet. The stratosphere is where the ozone layer is located, and it is free from clouds and weather. Wind diminishes significantly with altitude in the stratosphere. Most of today's military operations occur in the troposphere and the stratosphere.

- Above the stratosphere at an altitude of about 34 miles is a region of the atmosphere that has proven easy to transit but difficult to operate in persistently. In this region, there is enough air to cause drag and surface heating but not enough to support aerodynamic control or air-breathing engine combustion.

- Sitting above the stratosphere, extending to 260,000 feet, is the mesosphere. Here, meteors burn up due to atmospheric heating. The ionosphere, which causes high-frequency radio waves to bounce off the atmosphere enabling long-range amateur radio operations, begins in this region.

- Above the mesosphere lies the final layer of the atmosphere, the thermosphere, which extends to as much as 600 miles above the Earth depending on solar activity. Atmospheric drag caused by gases in the lower portion of this layer limits the lowest unpowered, stable satellite orbit to roughly 120 miles.

Accessing the Air Domain for Military Advantage. From its earliest days, competition in the air domain has been enabled by constantly advancing technology. Warfighting in the air domain, however, is fundamentally a human endeavor, and as one learns about airspace technologies, it is important to keep technology in perspective. Technology enables access to and exploitation of the air domain, but humans marshal this technology to gain advantage over others as a tool of statecraft and war. Competition in the air domain therefore centers on maintaining or denying this advantage and depends not only on mastery of technology, but also on its artful and creative organization and application in strategy and tactics.

The characteristics of air and the atmosphere make five modes of access to the air domain possible: lighter-than-air flight, heavier-than-air flight, missiles, ground-fired or sea-fired projectiles, and the electromagnetic spectrum.

Lighter-than-air flight is achieved by trapping gases lighter than oxygen and nitrogen, like hydrogen or helium, or heated air in a sealed casing. Because the gas inside the casing is lighter than the surrounding air, lift is produced. The volume of air contained in that casing, coupled with the characteristics of the gas inside, determines its lifting ability. This allows exploitation of the air domain using hot-air balloons, gas-filled balloons, or powered airships (dirigibles and blimps). Lighter-than-air aircraft can provide persistence and relatively heavy lift, but this means of access is both slow and heavily affected by weather.

Lighter-than-air flight was exploited in World War I by Germany, which used dirigibles, or powered airships, to bomb central London, and in World War II by the United States, which used blimps for antisubmarine warfare patrols.[5] Although the speed of heavier-than-air platforms made them dominant over their lighter-than-air brothers, a role remains for balloons and powered airships today. Tethered balloons (aerostats) extending up to 14,000 feet line the U.S. border with Mexico and have been used in Iraq to provide persistent surveillance coverage.[6] Powered airships used by the logging industry to extract harvested timber from remote areas could provide a slow-speed, heavy-lift logistics option for military purposes.[7] High-altitude balloons also offer military utility as a backup to space-based capabilities like communications satellites.[8]

Heavier-than-air flight, on the other hand, uses aerodynamic forces to produce and sustain lift. Aerodynamic lift is produced by moving an airfoil (wing) through volume of air or fluid. Design differences between the upper and lower surfaces of the airfoil force the air to move faster across the upper surface as the wing is propelled through the air. This creates an area of lower pressure on the top of the wing that generates lift. There are other factors involved, but if one produces enough aerodynamic lift to overcome the force of gravity, then a heavier-than-air machine can fly.[9]

There are two other forces at play in the creation of aerodynamic lift: the thrust required to propel a wing though the air to generate lift and the drag that the wing creates through the process of creating lift. Thus, balancing the problems of lift, gravity, thrust, and drag makes flight possible using vehicles that are powered (airplanes, cruise missiles, helicopters, tilt rotors, and quad copters) and unpowered (towed gliders, lifting bodies, and air-delivered guided munitions). Aircraft provide a reusable form of access to the air domain and offer an incredible degree of flexibility with regard to speed, range, payload, and endurance for military operations.

Missiles use the brute force of expanding, burning gases provided by liquid-fueled or solid-fueled rocket engines to overcome the effects of gravity and gain access to the air domain. As the vehicle accelerates, it takes on aerodynamic characteristics and can be controlled using aircraft-like control surfaces until it reaches mid-stratosphere. Above this altitude, small thrusters or gimbaled engines controlled by guidance systems allow the highest levels of precision in movement and endgame placement.

Missiles deliver high-speed effects in both the air and space domains without the risk associated with manned flight, but there are trade-offs. Lift is created on the sheer power of their engines, making this form of access markedly less efficient than winged aircraft. Moreover, missiles used for attack or defense are not reusable; an aircraft can return to base and reload with ordnance, but a missile is a one-time shot.[10]

Projectiles like bullets, mortars, rockets, and bombs use a controlled explosive charge, propellant, or the momentum gained by a parent platform to overpower the aerodynamic effects of weight and drag temporarily in order to enter and transit the air domain. Aimed downward, air-launched munitions provide an additional and incredibly potent axis of fire against land-based and sea-based targets. Aimed upward, ground-fired projectiles provide a low-cost, effective way to deny an enemy use of the air domain in a limited area. For example, the vast majority of aircraft losses in Vietnam were due to anti-aircraft artillery rather than surface-to-air missile defenses.

Today, new technologies like electromagnetic rail guns can fire projectiles from land-based or sea-based platforms at hypersonic speeds to attack other surface targets or defend against low-flying, supersonic cruise missiles and high-speed ballistic missile warheads.[11] In addition, long-range, precision-guided rocket artillery teamed with unmanned intelligence, surveillance, and reconnaissance (ISR) capabilities like satellites or "drones" are changing the way armies view fires.[12]

Finally, *the electromagnetic spectrum* provides a less obvious but equally powerful method of accessing the air domain to enable, disrupt, or deny air operations. This includes use of voice and data communications to direct and employ forces; optical, infrared, laser, and radar-based sensors to detect objects in the air domain and guide weapons; high-power lasers to deny optical sensors or to attack incoming aircraft, missiles, or bombs;[13] high-powered microwaves to disrupt operation of airborne vehicles and weapons;[14] electromagnetic decoys to confuse an opponent's systems;[15] and modern jamming techniques to deny, disrupt, or spoof radars, communication, and space-based navigation systems like the Global Positioning System (GPS).

The electromagnetic spectrum can be manipulated through combinations of low-observable (stealth) technology and active electromagnetic countermeasures to increase the survivability of both aircraft and munitions against increasingly sophisticated air defenses. This electromagnetic method of accessing the air domain also enables cyberspace effects to shape every aspect of offensive and defensive air operations.

Leveraging these five methods of access, nations develop offensive and defensive capabilities to gain or deny advantage across the spectrum of warfighting domains, but the air domain is more complex than simply pitting system against system. Sanctuary or advantage can lie in operating at high or low altitude, operating at speed, operating from range versus operating forward, hiding in the noise of the electromagnetic spectrum, or increasing weapons accuracy to reduce repeated exposure to the threat.

The U.S. has taken several different investment strategies within the air domain since the 1950s. From the opening days of the jet age through the 1970s, it pursued a "higher, farther, faster" strategy. As the Soviet Union mastered its integrated air defense system (IADS), U.S. efforts moved to a low-altitude strategy that stayed in place through the opening days of Operation Desert Storm, when precision and stealth capabilities became dominant. A closer look at the limits of altitude and speed in the air domain therefore helps one to understand the constraints of the operating environment.

Defining the Air Domain's Upper Limit. Defining the upper limit of the air domain, "where its effects on operations becomes limited," is difficult. As noted, most military operations occur in the troposphere and lower stratosphere. Commercial aircraft operate up to about 40,000 feet, while military aircraft routinely operate as high as 60,000 feet. "Controlled airspace" over the United States ends at 65,000 feet. Operations above this altitude are sometimes called "near space."

The glider-like wings of the U-2 aircraft enable it to operate at the very edge of controlled flight while flying at subsonic speeds in the 70,000-foot regime.[16] Due to the thinning atmosphere, however, operations above this altitude require either increasing supersonic speeds with altitude to produce adequate lift or, paradoxically, no speed at all. For example, the Mach 3.0 SR-71 operated near 85,000 feet,[17] while the Mach 3.0 Mig-25 holds the absolute manned takeoff to altitude record of 123,523 feet.[18] On the other hand, the highest manned balloon reached 135,890 feet,[19] and unmanned balloons have reached the top of the stratosphere at over 176,000 feet.[20]

Going higher still requires different forms of propulsion and materials. Rocket planes carried aloft by a mother ship, like the 1960s-era X-15 (transported to high altitude by a B-52 bomber) or Virgin Galactic's Spaceship One flights, operate in the mesosphere and beyond in what are known as "suborbital" operations. Spaceship One holds the altitude record for an air-launched rocket plane at 367,487 feet or 70 miles, but it does not have the ability to persist in this regime for any meaningful length of time.[21]

Achieving persistence in the flight regime above the stratosphere is technically difficult, but it can be realized through atmospheric "skipping" where platforms use their speed to "skip" off denser layers of atmosphere at hypersonic speeds like a rock skipping across water. Such a capability offers a range of military benefits between the air and space domains (roughly 34 miles to 120 miles above the Earth), making it possible to maneuver and maintain altitude without the limitations of orbital mechanics that are imposed by operations in space.[22]

A hypersonic glide vehicle (HGV), a capability being pursued by the United States, Russia, and China, can be deployed from an intermediate-range ballistic missile to enable such atmospheric skipping.[23] An alternative approach might be found in new propulsion techniques such as air-breathing, plasma-fueled engines, which are in early research and development.[24]

Defining the Speed Limit in the Air Domain. Mach numbers play a crucial role in understanding the difficulty of going higher and faster in the atmosphere. A Mach number is a speed expressed as the percentage of the speed of sound. For example, Mach .82, a typical airliner speed, is 82 percent of the speed of sound.

Mach 1.0 occurs at 667 knots (nautical miles per hour) at sea level.[25] Above Mach 1.0 in the atmosphere, shock waves form on the nose and tail of an aircraft. If these shock waves reach the ground, sonic "booms" are heard and felt along the flight path as the shock waves pass by in close succession.

The basic formulation of aerodynamics that balances lift, draft, gravity, and thrust works well up to speeds of about .80 Mach or the beginning of the "trans-sonic" speed regime. Here, compressibility of air becomes a factor. Unlike water, air compresses as its velocity over a surface increases. As one goes faster, this changes the drag profile of traditional airfoils, requiring substantially more energy to sustain speed or go faster. In addition, shock waves begin to form in this flight regime that disrupt normal airflow over the airfoil.

For traditional, straight-wing airfoils, these pressures shift suddenly as one approaches the speed of sound, resulting in buffeting and loss of control. This phenomenon sets the speed limit of propeller-driven aircraft, even in a steep dive, due to drag increases and shock wave formation on the propeller blades.[26] Thus, "the sound barrier" was a significant obstacle in military aviation until it was broken in October 1947 thanks to propellerless propulsion, thin wing designs, and new control surfaces.[27]

Today, aircraft designed to go faster than .80 Mach have swept wings and other design features to reduce the effects of transonic drag. Since airliners cruise at speeds of .8 to .87 Mach, research into the transonic drag reduction, transonic airfoil optimization, and engine efficiency in the transonic regime remains important for airplane and engine companies.

Two speed regimes are relevant militarily in the air domain above Mach 1.0: supersonic (Mach 1.2–Mach 5.0) and hypersonic (Mach 5.0–Mach 10.0). Each regime poses different problems for designers.

Supersonic speed increases the range of air-to-air missiles, improves responsiveness for intercepts, expands the flight envelope for operations, and allows sustained high-altitude flight.

In the supersonic regime, designers must solve the problem of creating a subsonic airstream in the engine to support combustion despite air entering the engine at supersonic speed. To accomplish this, most military fighter aircraft utilize afterburning turbofans, which use a combination of inlet design and a spinning compressor to squeeze and slow the airflow coming into the engine to subsonic speed before injecting fuel and burning it.[28] Afterburning turbofans are far less efficient than the subsonic "high bypass" turbofans used by the airlines, although research is underway to improve their efficiency during subsonic flight.[29]

As one goes faster than about Mach 3.0, however, turbofan engines reach material limits to handle high heat and pressures. To go faster with an air-breathing engine, a ramjet is required. A ramjet uses a movable fixed inlet to achieve compression without rotating parts. Combustion still occurs in subsonic air, however. Ramjets can operate to Mach 6.0 but work best in the Mach 2.0–Mach 4.0 range. For example, a combined-cycle turbojet/ramjet engine enabled the SR-71 to reach speeds above Mach 3.0. While Mach 3.0 speed provided survivability against air defenses through the 1980s, this speed regime would become well within the capability of air defense systems like the Russian SA-20 and U.S. Patriot and Aegis by the 1990s.[30]

To improve survivability and reduce reaction time for today's most contested airspace, one must maneuver at hypersonic speeds. The cost to operate above Mach 5.0 within the atmosphere has risen at exponential rates with increasing speed due to shifts in structural material requirements to mitigate extreme heat and special requirements for air-breathing engines to handle extreme speeds.[31] Both China and the United States are actively pursuing research to reduce cost in these areas.[32]

To reduce the cost of hypersonic speed, air-breathing engines are more desirable than rocket engines because they produce more thrust for a given amount of weight. Moreover, the combination of speed and better fuel efficiency enables a hypersonic vehicle to travel longer distances on a small amount of fuel, in turn allowing for vehicles that are more compact.[33] For example, a powered hypersonic vehicle travels 560 miles on only eight minutes of fuel at Mach 7.0.

To achieve this, a scramjet engine that can sustain combustion in supersonic airflows is needed. Because these engines do not operate below Mach 4.5, a scramjet-powered hypersonic vehicle requires a rocket-motor "kick start" to accelerate to its engine start speed. Research into these engines is ongoing. In 2004, NASA's X-43 achieved 10 seconds of powered flight at Mach 9.6, the fastest jet-powered flight on record.[34] In 2013, the Air Force X-51A testbed achieved 240 seconds of hypersonic flight with a scramjet at Mach 5.1, the longest powered flight of a scramjet on record. Given the capability of improving modern air defenses and the growing importance of striking mobile targets, air-breathing hypersonic vehicles and weapons are likely to become an area of intense competition.[35]

Denominators for Exploitation of the Air Domain

Having discussed the speed and altitude attributes of the air domain, one must consider the denominators that are needed to exploit it. These break down into two major areas: being able to project power through range, persistence, and payload and being able to see and act using the electromagnetic spectrum.

Range, Persistence, and Payload. The ability of aircraft in the air domain to operate and survive at range and persist over time with intelligence, surveillance, and reconnaissance sensors and flexible weapons is key to exploiting the domain. This capability connects the air domain with other domains through missions like counterair, strike, close air support, ISR overwatch, airborne anti-submarine warfare, assault aviation, or airborne cyberspace operations. Twenty-five years after Desert Storm, the success of U.S. operations in largely permissive air environments has solidified the perception that American air power is an omnipresent force with an unblinking eye that wields a rapid, precision hammer.

TABLE 2

Effect of Distance on Sortie Production

Distance from Base (nautical miles)	Total Sortie Duration (hours)*	Sorties per Aircraft/Day**	Pilot Manning (per aircraft)***
650	4.7	~2.90	1.5
1,300	7.4	~2.00	2.0
1,950	10.1	~1.55	2.5
2,600	12.8	~1.25	3.5

* Assumes 2.0 hour on-station time.
** Assumes 1.5 hour regeneration time and 6.0 hours maintenance non-availability per day per aircraft. Times vary by aircraft, maintenance manning, and carrier deck cycles.
*** 12.0 hour sustained pilot duty day, 125 hours maximum per 30 days.
SOURCE: Author's calculations.

 heritage.org

Unlike the land and sea domains, where persistence consists of holding ground or patrolling in a geographically limited area, persistence in the air is about radius of action that leverages the speed and vantage that the air domain provides. For example, an aircraft loitering at 20,000 feet that is 80 miles away from a U.S. ground patrol in Syria is within easy radio contact of the ground patrol, can immediately bring sensors to bear, and can arrive overhead at Mach 1.0 in eight minutes. Should tensions escalate, other airborne forces can mass quickly. Should fuel run low, air refueling tankers arrive to provide inflight refueling. Thus, the operation can quickly scale and protract, especially in permissive environments (areas where there is little or no threat to U.S. air operations). Range and persistence make this possible.

Range and persistence are related concepts that revolve around fuel. For example, a pilot can travel point to point at speed, translating fuel into range, or orbit around a point at speed, translating fuel into persistence. Thus, fuel on board, expressed as combat radius or the unrefueled mission radius of action, is critical to exploitation of the air domain as well as to force posture and basing. For example, the United States developed air refueling in the 1950s to allow basing of jet bombers in depth from all sides of the Soviet Union. Without air refueling, aircraft could be based only within the range of the aircraft, which was strategically disadvantageous. As air refueling capability was incorporated into fighters, the idea of assured air refueling allowed designers to trade fuel capacity (which translates to weight) for airframe maneuverability (which also translates to weight) that was needed for air-to-air combat. Thus, the combat radius of most of today's U.S. fighters is 550–650 nautical miles. As a result, operations beyond this range require refueling about every two hours.

These basic time, combat radius, and distance economics incentivized a 60-year U.S. reliance on forward basing and forward carrier stations to project power in the air domain.[36] (See Figure 2.) There were good reasons for this approach. Operating from range taxes human endurance. In 2001, for example, fighters operating from the Arab Peninsula to Afghanistan had to transit 1,200 miles each way to fly around Iran. Thus, a six-hour mission time over Afghanistan required an 11-hour sortie that consisted of four to five air refuelings from four to five different air refueling aircraft. These air refueling aircraft transited similar distances with similar sortie durations. Thus, sustained operations from range require more pilots, more aircraft, and more fuel.

Forward basing, on the other hand, allows commanders to use aircraft and pilots multiple times per day.[37] This enables a high tempo of operations and allows persistence through multiple revisits or cycling of aircraft across the battlespace. Forward-based air refueling tankers enhance this capability for fighter/attack-sized aircraft, allowing aircraft to operate well beyond their organic combat radii and ensuring that enough fuel is always airborne and available. (See Figure 2.)

The ability to base forward also allowed the United States to divest aircraft with large payloads like the Navy's A-6 and the Air Force's fleet of bombers, since a higher number of sorties from fighter-sized aircraft at forward bases could make up the difference in payload. Recognizing this fact, China has invested in a new generation of ballistic and cruise missiles designed to hold forward bases and aircraft carriers at risk through massed, raid-style attacks designed to overwhelm active defenses.[38] In addition, China is taking other measures to increase U.S. force requirements by expanding the range of contested airspace. (See Figure 2.)

As forward bases come under increasing threat, which in turn drives increased basing distances, pressure on the air refueling force becomes extreme unless the organic combat radius of combat aircraft is increased. Protecting large air refueling tankers is difficult. Sheltering of forward-based air refueling tankers has proven unaffordable at scale thus far and was not attempted during the Cold War.[39] Left unsheltered, these aircraft are particularly susceptible to attacks using a variety of weapons, ranging from ballistic and cruise missiles to rockets and mortars to sniper rifles. In addition, the short combat radii of today's force increase the vulnerabilities of tankers in flight, since they must operate closer to the expanded threat envelopes of modern threat systems to provide adequate fuel for operations as illustrated in Figure 2.

Improved combat radius may therefore become increasingly important to exploitation of the air domain for power projection. Fortunately, the capabilities of modern missiles are rendering fighter maneuverability less important, allowing airframe weight to be traded for fuel. However, a greater emphasis is needed on larger payloads to make up for the potential loss of high-sortie production from forward bases and on unmanned operations to improve human abilities to sustain protracted operations from range.

The Electromagnetic Spectrum. In addition to projecting range, persistence, and payload, exploiting the air domain requires the capability to see, decide, and act. It is therefore difficult to separate operations in the air domain from the electromagnetic spectrum or the electromagnetic spectrum from weather. The relevant portions of the electromagnetic spectrum within the context of the air domain include visible light; infrared light, which is used for sensing temperature; and all radio frequencies, which enables communications and various forms of radar. From eyeballs to radar, if it is detected in the air domain, it is by and through the electromagnetic spectrum.

Weather, on the other hand, presents hazards like thunderstorms and severe icing, as well as wind and temperature, that affect operations. Most important, however, it shapes the degree to which the electromagnetic spectrum can be exploited. The line of sight distance to the horizon from an aircraft operating at 35,000 feet is 229 miles, but how much of this distance is usable? Looking up into the stratosphere, a great deal may be: The weather is generally clear, and the background is cold and free from clutter, perfect conditions for visible, infrared, and radar sensors.

Looking down toward the thicker atmosphere and the ground is another matter. In the visible spectrum, dust and clouds may obscure the view. For example, clouds cover most of North Korea more than 50 percent

FIGURE 2

How the U.S. Projects Air Power

Historically, the U.S. has been able to project air power by using airfields, carriers, and air refueling systems to minimize the size of contested space — the area in which aircraft would engage in conflict.

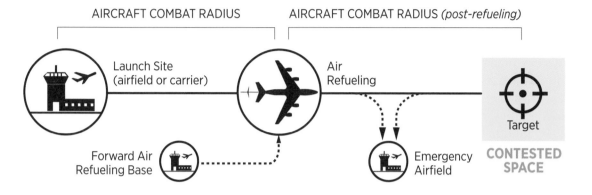

China is investing in missile systems that would significantly hinder the U.S.'s forward operating launch points, which would as a result make the contested space much larger.

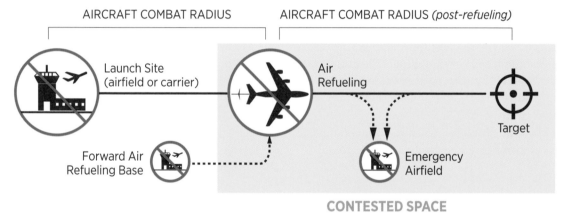

🐦 heritage.org

of the time from May to September. In the infrared spectrum, water vapor may attenuate temperature signatures, and clouds may block them completely. In the radar spectrum, synthetic aperture radar provides a means to see through clouds, but power dissipates rapidly with range (i.e., $1/\text{range}^4$), and rain attenuates signals at higher frequencies. In addition, airborne radars must contend with the "ground clutter" moving below them, complicating their operation.

Moreover, aircraft are limited in the amount of power they can produce and the sizes of radar antenna they can carry. Thus, antenna size tends to herd aircraft radars into a narrow range of operating frequencies and power. This means that a true all weather, day/night ISR capability requires a combination of sensors to be effective and that aircraft may be required to fly close to an area of interest for its sensors to "see" it, especially if the target is mobile.

Meanwhile, actors accessing the electromagnetic spectrum on the ground or at sea are not limited by power or radar size as aircraft are. They can develop powerful radars to detect and target air vehicles and employ severe jamming to disrupt airborne radar and precision navigation like the Global Positioning System. In addition, ground-based radars have the advantage of looking up away from clutter. This dynamic of air-based and ground-based competition in the air domain through the electromagnetic spectrum is what eventually forced the development of stealth.

As competition between nation-states intensifies, the competition to place sensors close enough to "find" targets, especially mobile ones, versus defensive efforts to prevent these actions will continue. Stealth, enhanced by active electronic countermeasures, remains relevant and essential for survivability in this environment in order to hold mobile and deep targets at risk. Other approaches, such as hypersonic speed or employing large numbers of vehicles to saturate defenses, also enhance survivability and may become key contributors to this competition. The question then becomes: How may the character of the domain change as technology advances?

Key Shifts Likely to Affect the Air Domain

Because exploitation of the air domain depends on technology that is constantly advancing, competition in the domain has never stood still. As technology accelerates and renewed nation-state competition drives new moves to counter U.S. capabilities, at least four key shifts are underway that are likely to alter the character of the air domain.

First, exploitation of the air domain is no longer just about aircraft. The proliferation of mobile advanced air defenses, mobile ballistic missiles, land-launched and sea-launched hypersonic boost glide systems, and air-launched powered hypersonic vehicles provides new means to deny air refueling, attack forward bases, and deny forward carrier stations through the air domain. This undercuts the force posture assumptions on which the present force is built. Given this development, increased combat radius of aircraft, larger payloads, and expanded use of long-range unmanned systems improve the ability of the U.S. to operate from range.

Second, the most important targets are mobile. The increasing importance of countering the above-described mobile targets increases the importance of ISR and the ability to direct forces in contested environments. Fully leveraging the leading edge of technology in the electromagnetic spectrum improves the ability of the U.S. to hold these targets at risk. This includes technologies for advanced sensors, penetrating stealth, survivability to "stand in," and alternatives to GPS navigation.

Third, weapons in flight are under increased risk. The maturation of directed energy and improved capability of ground-based point defenses may cause traditional weapons to come under increased threat. Increasing weapon speed or employing saturation tactics with large "flocks" of weapons improves the probability of weapon arrival. Either approach requires survivability to "stand in" or penetrate, increased payloads, and greater depths of weapons magazines.

Fourth, the threat from "low end" uses of the air domain is growing. The rise of machine learning, object recognition, and improved battery technology may enable small drones or quad copters to contest the air domain at the tree level. This capability may be used to disrupt airfields and to project power locally even in permissive environments. Research into countering machine learning and new capabilities to counter emerging small, swift, and robotic capabilities improves the ability of the U.S. to adjust to this threat.

Conclusion

The ability of military forces to exploit the air domain has revolutionized warfare over the past century. Exploiting the domain to find and hold targets as risk at global ranges remains a differentiator of U.S. power. Shifting technology, however, threatens to erode this advantage and presents challenges to the U.S. model of power projection. Sustaining that advantage will require more stealth platforms with C4ISR (command, control, communications, computers, intelligence, surveillance, and reconnaissance) capabilities and the ability to adapt to unforeseen changes in the air domain, as well as those it supports.

Endnotes

1. U.S. Department of Defense, *DOD Dictionary of Military and Associated Terms*, July 2017, p. 10, http://www.dtic.mil/doctrine/new_pubs/dictionary.pdf (accessed July 26, 2017).

2. North Carolina State University, "Climate Education for K–12: Composition of the Atmosphere," last modified August 9, 2013, http://climate.ncsu.edu/edu/k12/.AtmComposition (accessed July 26, 2017).

3. U.S. Department of the Air Force, *Weather for Aircrews*, Air Force Handbook 11-203, Volume 1, March 1, 1997, p. 9, http://www.dtic.mil/dtic/tr/fulltext/u2/a423996.pdf (accessed July 26, 2017).

4. S. Sanz Fernández de Córdoba, "100km Altitude Boundary for Astronautics," Fédération Aéronautique Internationale, http://www.fai.org/icare-records/100km-altitude-boundary-for-astronautics (accessed July 21, 2017). For a summary of conventions and treaties on air and space boundaries, see Paul Stephen Dempsey, "The Definition and Delimitation of Outer Space," presentation before the U.N. Committee on the Peaceful Uses of Outer Space, Vienna, Austria, March 30, 2017, http://www.unoosa.org/documents/pdf/copuos/lsc/2017/tech-05.pdf (accessed July 26, 2017).

5. The use of an observation balloon in the Battle of Fleurus to report on Austrian movements in 1794 marked the first asymmetric use of the air domain. Countermeasures began as snipers were used in the American Civil War to contest tethered balloon surveillance.

6. See Dave Long, "CBP's Eye in the Sky," U.S. Department of Homeland Security, U.S. Customs and Border Protection, https://www.cbp.gov/frontline/frontline-november-aerostats (accessed July 26, 2017).

7. See Mike Kendrick, "A New Age of Airships Is Ready for Lift-off," *The Telegraph*, March 31, 2016, http://www.telegraph.co.uk/technology/2016/03/31/a-new-age-of-airships-is-ready-for-lift-off/ (accessed July 26, 2017).

8. See Google's Project Loon, designed to deliver Internet using high-altitude balloons, at Project Loon, "What Is Project Loon: Balloon-Powered Internet for Everyone," https://x.company/loon/ (accessed July 26, 2017).

9. For those who are interested in why this is so, see Veritasium, "Why Does a Wing Actually Work?" August 3, 2012, https://www.youtube.com/watch?v=aFO4PBolwFg (accessed July 26, 2017).

10. Rocket-powered missiles fly trajectories that are based on their purpose. Air-to-air, air-to-surface, and surface-to-air missiles and missiles designed for ballistic missile defense fly customized profiles that balance maintaining sensor coverage on the target, preserving energy, and achieving an intercept of their intended target. Surface-to-surface missiles, on the other hand, fly either ballistic or maneuvering profiles. Ballistic profiles, such as those flown by a German V2 or Iraqi SCUD missile of Operation Desert Storm fame, describe a predictable arc based on the equations of motion and may transit space at apogee or the highest point in their arc. Maneuvering profiles, on the other hand, may be employed to fly an unpredictable flight path (such as the boost glide trajectory mentioned earlier), conserve energy, enable sensor coverage for warhead guidance, or defeat defenses. Finally, space-bound missiles transiting the air domain on their way to an orbital speed of 17,000 miles per hour must not go too fast or too low in the atmosphere as side loads due to wind can exceed the vibration or structural limits of a supersonic missile. This region of "maximum dynamic pressure" usually requires rocket designers to throttle down their engines until the missile is past 40,000 feet.

11. U.S. Department of the Navy, Office of Naval Research, "Electromagnetic Railgun," https://www.onr.navy.mil/en/Media-Center/Fact-Sheets/Electromagnetic-Railgun (accessed July 29, 2017); Sam LaGrone, "Pentagon: New Rounds for Old Guns Could Change Missile Defense for Navy, Army," USNI News, updated July 19, 2016, https://news.usni.org/2016/07/18/pentagon-new-rounds-old-guns-change-paradigm-missile-defense-navy-army (accessed July 29, 2017).

12. Kyle Mizokami, "The Army Is Getting a New Long-Range Tactical Missile," *Popular Mechanics*, June 16, 2017, http://www.popularmechanics.com/military/weapons/a26960/army-new-long-range-tactical-missile-deepstrike/ (accessed June 16, 2017).

13. For an example, see Kevin McCaney, "Navy Cranks Up the Power on Laser Weapon," *Defense Systems*, June 28, 2016, https://defensesystems.com/articles/2016/06/28/navy-150-kilowatt-laser-weapon-test.aspx (accessed August 1, 2017).

14. George Seffers, "CHAMP Prepares for Future Flights," *Signal*, February 1, 2016, http://www.afcea.org/content/?q=Article-champ-prepares-future-fights (accessed August 1, 2017).

15. Joe Pappalardo, "Drones Can Now Jam Enemy Radar," *Popular Mechanics*, November 14, 2013, http://www.popularmechanics.com/flight/drones/a9772/drones-can-now-jam-enemy-radar-16157656/ (accessed June 8, 2017).

16. Fact Sheet, "U-2S/TU-2S," U.S. Air Force, September 23, 2015, http://www.af.mil/About-Us/Fact-Sheets/Display/Article/104560/u-2stu-2s/ (accessed August 1, 2017).

17. Paul R. Kucher, "Blackbird Records," SR-71 Online: An Online Aircraft Museum, last modified October 2, 2011, https://www.sr-71.org/blackbird/records.php (accessed August 1, 2017).

18. GlobalSecurity.org, "MiG-25 FOXBAT," last modified February 4, 2016, http://www.globalsecurity.org/military/world/russia/mig-25.htm (accessed August 1, 2017).

19. John Markoff, "Parachutist's Record Fall: Over 25 Miles in 15 Minutes," *The New York Times*, October 24, 2014, https://www.nytimes.com/2014/10/25/science/alan-eustace-jumps-from-stratosphere-breaking-felix-baumgartners-world-record.html (accessed July 24, 2017).

20. Lighter-Than-Air Society, "Japan Sets New Balloon Altitude Record: 53.7 kms," September 22, 2013, http://www.blimpinfo.com/uncategorized/japan-sets-new-balloon-altitude-record/ (accessed July 24, 2017).

21. Fédération Aéronautique Internationale, "FAI Record ID #9881: Altitude Above the Earth's Surface With or Without Maneuvres of the Aerospacecraft," http://www.fai.org/fai-record-file/?recordId=9881 (accessed August 1, 2017).

22. Paige Carter, "Bringing Hypersonic Flight Down to Earth," *Science and Technology Review*, January/February 2000, pp. 20–22, https://str.llnl.gov/str/pdfs/01_00.pdf (accessed June 8, 2017).

23. Bradley Perrett, Bill Sweetman, and Michael Fabey, "U.S. Navy Sees Chinese HGV as Part of Wider Threat," *Aviation Week and Space Technology*, January 27, 2014, http://aviationweek.com/awin/us-navy-sees-chinese-hgv-part-wider-threat (accessed June 8, 2017).

24. Sandrine Ceurstemont, "Plasma Jet Engines That Could Take You from the Ground to Space," *New Scientist*, May 17, 2017, https://www.newscientist.com/article/mg23431264-500-plasma-jet-engines-that-could-take-you-from-the-ground-to-space/ (accessed August 1, 2017).

25. As with the maritime domain, operations within the air domain use nautical miles per hour or "knots" to quantify speed. One nautical mile is equal to one minute of latitude, 6,076 feet, or 1.15 statute miles on a car's odometer. The true speed of sound in knots varies by altitude and pressure. Notwithstanding this, a rule of thumb in aviation is to view the Mach number with the decimal point moved one place to the right as "nautical miles per minute" along the ground, discounting the effect of headwinds or tailwinds. Thus, .82 Mach is roughly 8.2 miles per minute, which equates to 492 knots along the ground with zero wind when multiplied by 60 minutes.

26. The speed record for a turboprop aircraft in level flight is held by the TU-114 at 478 knots or .73 Mach. See Aerospaceweb.org, "Tupolev Tu-114 Rossiya," last modified March 17, 2011, http://www.aerospaceweb.org/aircraft/jetliner/tu114/ (accessed August 1, 2017). Helicopters experience a different problem related to airfoil speed, called dissymmetry of lift. Helicopter blades can experience a condition in which the blade going forward in the direction of flight produces more lift than the blade going opposite the direction of flight. This can place the helicopter out of control when operating at speed unless countermeasures are taken in design.

27. There are claims that the jet-powered ME-262 exceeded the speed of sound in dives during World War II, but experts doubt that this happened. Shock waves prevented the testing of high-speed performance in wind tunnels of the time, and high speed in dives claimed many lives during World War II and in follow-on testing. For more, see PBS, "Faster Than Sound," *NOVA*, October 14, 1997, https://www.youtube.com/watch?v=_WFBe6cDrBg (accessed August 1, 2017).

28. Air entering the intakes of a turbofan engine is slowed by inlet shape, doors, or small flaps on the engine surface. A spinning compressor then sucks in the air and squeezes it, but this compression creates significant heat and pressure. For example, in the latest production F-16s, the air is squeezed 30 times before it is burned. The combustion process increases the temperature of this high-pressure air to nearly 2,750 degrees Fahrenheit before it exits into the afterburner section. This produces about 14,000 pounds of "non-afterburning" thrust, or about 3.5 times the engine's weight. Bumping large amounts of fuel into this hot exhaust and burning it in an afterburner increases thrust to nearly 32,000 pounds—more than seven times the engine's weight. Engines like this deliver tremendous performance across a wide operating envelope, enabling aircraft like the F-16 to fly at supersonic speeds from the surface to 50,000 feet. See General Electric, "F110-GE-129 Turbofan Engines," https://www.geaviation.com/sites/default/files/datasheet-F110-GE-129.pdf (accessed July 24, 2017).

29. As demand for greater range increases, the Air Force Research Laboratory is exploring a "three stream" afterburning turbofan engine that shares some attributes with high-bypass engines for use during subsonic flight and then reverts to a less efficient mode for supersonic flight. This could improve engine fuel efficiency by up to 25 percent, translating to greater range. See Bill Carey, "GE, Pratt & Whitney Win Contracts for Next-Generation Engine," *AINonline*, July 1, 2016, http://www.ainonline.com/aviation-news/defense/2016-07-01/ge-pratt-whitney-win-contracts-next-generation-engine (accessed August 1, 2017).

30. Jesus Diaz, "The Secret Engine Technology That Made the SR-71 the Fastest Plane Ever," SPLOID, December 21, 2014, http://sploid.gizmodo.com/the-secret-engine-technology-that-made-the-sr-71-the-fa-1673510951 (accessed July 29, 2017).

31. Above Mach 3.0, surface heating of the air vehicle becomes an issue, so different materials are needed in the hypersonic regime. Traditionally, titanium has been the metal of choice for handling high temperatures in aviation because it is strong and about half the weight of stainless steel. For example, an SR-71's titanium skin reached 500 degrees Fahrenheit during high-speed flight at Mach 3.0. The material limit of titanium, however, is 800 degrees Fahrenheit. See George Tzong, Richard Jacobs, and Salvatore Liguore, *Air Vehicle Integration and Technology Research (AVIATR), Task Order 0015: Predictive Capability for Hypersonic Structural Response and Life Prediction: Phase 1–Identification of Knowledge Gaps, Volume 1–Nonproprietary Version*, Air Force Research Laboratory, Air Vehicles Directorate, Wright-Patterson Air Force Base, Final Report, September 2010, p. 72, www.dtic.mil/get-tr-doc/pdf?AD=ADA535837 (accessed August 1, 2017).

32. Bill Gertz, "China Successfully Tests Hypersonic Missile," *The Washington Free Beacon*, April 27, 2016, http://freebeacon.com/national-security/china-successfully-tests-hypersonic-missile/ (accessed July 21, 2017).

33. This comparison of weight to thrust is called specific impulse. For a comparison of engine performance, see Dora E. Musielak, Aerospace Engineering Consulting, "Propulsion Comparison," in "Fundamentals of Pulse Detonation Engine (PDE) and Related Propulsion Technology," p. 10, https://info.aiaa.org/tac/PEG/HSABPTC/Public%20Documents/Dora%20Musielak%20Publications/Fundamentals%20of%20PDE%20Propulsion_Musielak.pdf (accessed August 1, 2017).

34. Fact Sheet, "Past Projects: X-43A Hypersonic Flight Program," ed. Yvonne Gibbs, National Aeronautics and Space Administration, last updated May 10, 2017, https://www.nasa.gov/centers/dryden/history/pastprojects/HyperX/index.html (accessed July 29, 2017).

35. Kris Osborn, "The World's New Leader in Super Deadly Hypersonic Weapons: China?" *The National Interest*, February 14, 2017, http://nationalinterest.org/blog/the-buzz/the-worlds-leader-super-deadly-hypersonic-weapons-china-19437 (accessed July 24, 2017).

36. Since Vietnam, most air bases and carrier stations have been within 750 nautical miles of the adversary's capital.

37. Single-place aircraft sustained duty day is 12 hours. Multi-place aircraft sustained duty day is 16 hours. The U.S. Air Force limits pilot flying time to 56 hours per seven consecutive days, 130 hours per 30 consecutive days, and 330 hours per 90 consecutive days.

38. Similarly, though to a lesser extent, Russia has improved its existing stock of sea-launched and air-launched cruise missiles and has developed a pair of new intermediate-range cruise and ballistic missiles in violation of the Intermediate Nuclear Forces Treaty. Moreover, both Russia and China are going to some lengths to demonstrate their respective capabilities, with Russia launching long-range cruise missile attacks across Iraq and into Syria in 2016 and China conducting frequent attacks against scale mockups of U.S. facilities on its ballistic missile ranges in the Gobi Desert. See Michaela Dodge, "Russian Intermediate-Range Nuclear Forces: What They Mean for the United States," Heritage Foundation *Backgrounder* No. 3028, July 30, 2015, http://www.heritage.org/europe/report/russian-intermediate-range-nuclear-forces-what-they-mean-the-united-states. For images of these ranges, see Thomas Shugart, "Has China Been Practicing Preemptive Attacks on U.S. Bases?" War on the Rocks, February 6, 2017, https://warontherocks.com/2017/02/has-china-been-practicing-preemptive-missile-strikes-against-u-s-bases/ (accessed July 28, 2017).

39. Congress appropriated $128 million for a single hardened air refueling hanger on Guam in the National Defense Authorization Act for Fiscal Year 2014, Public Law 113–66. This is about one-half the $246 million sticker price of a new KC-46. During the Cold War, tankers were based away from forward areas, and no attempt was made to shelter them. The increased range of the threat, the distances of the Pacific, and the operational requirements of the F-35 are key differences today. See Alan J. Vick, *Air Base Attacks and Defensive Counters: Historical Lessons and Future Challenges* (Santa Monica, CA: RAND, 2015), http://www.rand.org/content/dam/rand/pubs/research_reports/RR900/RR968/RAND_RR968.pdf (accessed July 29, 2017).

Space 201: Thinking About the Space Domain

Dean Cheng

Over the past three decades, the role of outer space in military operations has risen steadily. From the inception of the space age, America's activities in space have included a large national security component. The development of satellites was not only a matter of national prestige in the ideological competition of the Cold War, but also an effort to monitor military and other developments from the strategic high ground of space. Many of the earliest satellites were engaged in the gathering of intelligence.

Due to their sensitive nature and the advanced technologies associated with them, information derived from reconnaissance satellites (sometimes termed national technical means, or NTM) has generally remained highly classified. Rumors have long abounded regarding the capabilities of American reconnaissance satellites, for example, but little of their actual resolution (what they were able to see on the surface of the planet) was revealed during the Cold War. The end of the Cold War and the subsequent use of satellite imagery in 1991 during the first Gulf War pulled back many of the curtains that had obscured the capabilities and nature of reconnaissance satellites as programs were declassified and images were disseminated more broadly.

Space-based capabilities have also evolved from being oriented primarily toward meeting national security requirements to increasingly being part of global commerce. Whereas information from satellites used to be closely held, anyone can now purchase overhead imagery through companies like Digital Globe and Skybox. Similarly, whereas satellite position, navigation, and timing (PNT) used to be employed primarily by military forces to improve weapons accuracy, it is now incorporated as standard equipment in many private cars, and the timing function is employed in myriad activities from precision agriculture to reconciling financial transactions.

It is important to recognize that this massive expansion of the role of space is a relatively recent phenomenon. The space age itself is only a half-century old, having begun on October 4, 1957, with the launch of Sputnik by the USSR.[1] Moreover, because space activities and space-derived information have long been closely held secrets, their full potential for military and civilian applications has yet to be explored. Though information from space systems has been employed in the wars of the past quarter-century, no nations have yet engaged in combat in space. Both the political and technical ramifications of such a conflict are still largely theoretical.

Key Characteristics of Space

Given the growing importance of space in security affairs, it is important to recognize certain key characteristics of the outer space domain.

Characteristic #1: Space is beyond Earth. The outer space region is generally considered to begin somewhere between 100 kilometers (62 miles) and 100 miles above the surface of the Earth and extends from there. At 100 kilometers, aerodynamic forces have minimal impact on reentry vehicles; at 100 miles, the atmosphere is no longer a meaningful presence. While "space" theoretically encompasses the entire vastness of the cosmos, the militarily significant region of space is that bounded by the Earth–Moon area, as well as certain other locations governed by the Earth–Moon relationship. The latter include the Lagrange points, the five points where the gravitational pulls of the Earth, Moon, and Sun balance each other, thus making it possible for an object placed at one of these points to remain there indefinitely with minimal expenditure of fuel.

Because space is literally beyond the Earth, it is not affected by terrestrial borders as is the case with airspace. Whereas the airspace (physical space within the atmosphere above the boundaries of a nation) is considered the equivalent of sovereign territory, the same does not apply once one enters outer space. Instead, spacecraft of all nations are allowed to transit freely overhead and have no obligation to curtail their activities in doing so. (Realistically, such activities as satellite communications and weather forecasting would be virtually impossible if there were a patchwork of sovereignty governing outer space as there is on Earth.) Ironically, this principle of "open skies" was established when the Soviet Union orbited its Sputnik spacecraft. The Soviets argued that Sputnik did not pass over countries; instead, countries rotated underneath the spacecraft.[2]

Because it is beyond Earth, outer space is also not affected by considerations of terrain. There are no features in space (at least within the Earth–Moon system) that provide concealment or otherwise can mask spacecraft operations. Therefore, there is no real ability for spacecraft to hide.

Counterintuitively, this set of considerations actually makes space situational awareness (SSA) a very complicated affair. Because there is no place for satellites to hide, all orbiting objects can be seen, given a suitable suite of sensors. At the same time, however, this means that one must track several tens of thousands of objects in space, ranging from operational and defunct satellites to spent upper stages of rockets, loose nuts and bolts, and other debris from past space missions. Today, the United States Air Force officially keeps track of over 23,000 objects, which is by no means the totality of objects currently orbiting the Earth.[3] To do so, it makes over 400,000 observations (determining where various objects are located) daily.[4]

Undertaking SSA is essential in part because space objects may be mistaken for missiles; in order to prevent false alarms and possible inadvertent escalation, it is vital to track at least the larger objects in orbit so that we can know what is normally in orbit and therefore what new object might warrant closer scrutiny. Almost as important, tracking current objects in space and determining their orbits is critical to preventing collisions between satellites, preventing collisions between orbiting objects and spacecraft that are being launched, and determining whether space objects' orbits are decaying to the point that those objects may reenter the Earth's atmosphere.

To maintain SSA, the United States (like other nations) employs a variety of means. A vital tool is a network of radars. Some are conventional radars, which can track individual targets. Others are large phased-array radars, which can track multiple objects simultaneously and maintain surveillance over large volumes of space. In addition, there are many telescopes that allow imaging of satellites, which in turn allows analysts to determine the likely functions of a given satellite more precisely. All of these are ground-based systems.

Since 2014, the United States has also deployed a series of satellites that allow it to examine satellites from orbit. The Geosynchronous Space Situational Awareness Program (GSSAP) comprises a number of satellites deployed in geosynchronous orbit.[5] These carry electro-optical sensors that provide analysts with up-close pictures of objects in orbit.

Characteristic #2: Space is a hostile environment. The reaches of outer space are some of the most difficult environments in which machines or people operate. Because spacecraft are operating under near-vacuum conditions, gases that are trapped in the material of a spacecraft may be emitted in a process known as outgassing. These gases, in turn, can condense on the surfaces of a spacecraft, damaging components, clouding lenses and sensors, or otherwise adversely affecting the spacecraft.

Because spacecraft operate beyond the protection of Earth's atmosphere, they are exposed to a variety of forms of radiation, including cosmic rays, solar radiation, and even radiation belts that encircle the Earth (for example, the Van Allen radiation belts). Prolonged exposure to ultraviolet radiation can alter the properties of various materials. Spacecraft are also subjected to wild variations in temperature in ranges of hundreds of degrees. This, in turn, can lead to expansion and contraction of materials and even to cold-welding of parts.

Finally, in addition to being potentially vulnerable to collision with other satellites and any objects in orbit, spacecraft may be hit by micrometeoroids.[6] Everything in space is moving at very high speeds. Space debris, for example, typically moves at about 10 kilometers per second on average, which translates to roughly 22,000 mph.[7] Even grains of sand traveling at such speeds can have an abrasive effect, and larger objects can damage solar panels and instrument packages.

In order to operate in such a hostile environment, spacecraft must be manufactured to very high tolerances. Many are practically hand-made, which makes them very expensive. A commercial communications satellite costs at least $200 million.[8] Military communications satellites such as the Wideband Global Satcom satellite cost upwards of $400 million each.[9] Dedicated reconnaissance satellites (spy satellites) can cost over $1 billion. Reportedly, the overall cost for four new U.S. GOES-R weather satellites will be $11 billion.[10]

The steady increase in the cost of satellites is reflected in the American Global Positioning System (GPS) constellation. When fielding of GPS began in the 1990s, each satellite cost approximately $43 million, and launch costs were about $55 million. In 2013, it was reported that the newest GPS III satellites would cost $500 million each and $300 million per launch.[11]

Given the expense, few states can afford to develop, launch, and operate satellites, much less maintain reserve satellites, either in orbit or on the ground. A satellite that is lost due to a malfunction, collision, or other problems therefore cannot be replaced easily. There will likely be gaps in service or coverage until a replacement satellite can be built and launched. Augmenting a constellation is also not something that can be done either easily or inexpensively.

For these reasons, it is in the interest of satellite operators to have satellites last as long as possible. A satellite will typically carry enough fuel to enable orbital maneuvers. These range from station-keeping in order to stay in the proper orbital track and location to altering the orbit in order to avoid collisions. Activities that adversely affect the life span of a satellite (such as extensive maneuvering) are not undertaken lightly. In particular, changing a satellite's orbital plane (angle relative to the Earth's equator) is very expensive in terms of fuel and is usually avoided.

Characteristic #3: Space is difficult to reach. Not only does it take time to build a satellite; it also takes time and a great deal of infrastructure and related expense to launch it. Various capabilities are necessary to place an object into orbit. One must have a satellite and a launch vehicle. That vehicle is launched from some kind of facility that has a launch pad, a mission-control facility, and surveillance equipment with which to monitor and control the launch. There is usually an assembly or mating facility for placing the satellite payload on the rocket. Finally, other tracking sites are necessary to ensure that the payload has reached the proper orbit, has separated from the launching rocket, and is functioning properly after it has entered orbit.

All of these elements combine to make space operations expensive.[12] Until quite recently, only major countries could afford space operations, but private companies have entered the market.

The differences among these major space launch providers are the result of a number of factors, the most important of which is reliability of launch. This is no small affair when satellite payloads cost hundreds of millions or even billions of dollars. ULA has perhaps the longest track record of successful launches. SpaceX, a competing private venture, is the newest entrant and therefore does not yet have an established track record, making its reliability more of an unknown.

Types of Orbits[13]

While there is no terrain in space, there are orbital bands that are loosely defined by their altitude above the Earth's surface. There is no clear demarcation among them, but space experts in general talk about three main orbital bands.

Low Earth Orbit (LEO). This is the part of outer space that begins at about 100 miles above the Earth and extends to 1,200 miles. A variety of satellites populate this band, including various types of reconnaissance and Earth observation satellites, some weather satellites, and various scientific satellites. Because it is closer to Earth, a satellite in LEO can see smaller objects than a comparably equipped satellite at a higher altitude can.

However, satellites in LEO have a more limited field of view. They are essentially viewing a ribbon of the Earth's surface as they orbit around the planet.[14] The closer to Earth, the narrower the ribbon, much as a flashlight's area of illumination shrinks or expands the closer to or farther away it gets from the spot at which it is pointed. Moreover, because of orbital mechanics, an object in LEO cannot hover over a given point unless it uses an enormous amount of fuel to stay in position. Therefore, satellites in this orbital band cannot maintain surveillance over any particular point on Earth. Instead, any individual satellite will pass over a given spot every few hours. Multiple satellites in a constellation can keep a given spot on

FIGURE 3

Types of Earth Orbits

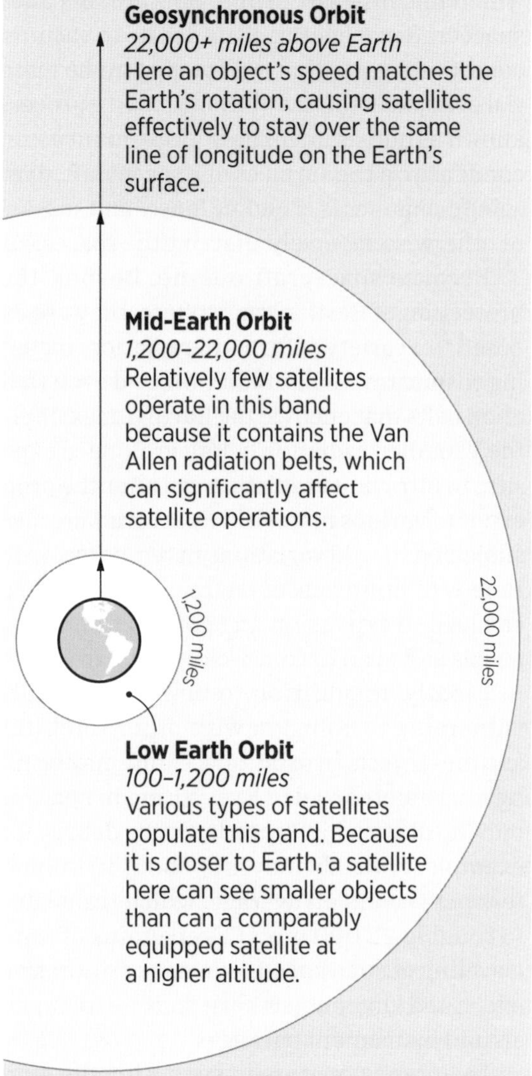

Geosynchronous Orbit
22,000+ miles above Earth
Here an object's speed matches the Earth's rotation, causing satellites effectively to stay over the same line of longitude on the Earth's surface.

Mid-Earth Orbit
1,200–22,000 miles
Relatively few satellites operate in this band because it contains the Van Allen radiation belts, which can significantly affect satellite operations.

1,200 miles

22,000 miles

Low Earth Orbit
100–1,200 miles
Various types of satellites populate this band. Because it is closer to Earth, a satellite here can see smaller objects than can a comparably equipped satellite at a higher altitude.

SOURCE: Heritage Foundation research.

☎ heritage.org

Earth under constant surveillance—but at the cost of fielding multiple satellites.

Objects in LEO also have a more limited life span. Though they are operating above the bulk of Earth's atmosphere, they nonetheless are still operating within its upper reaches. This imposes atmospheric drag so that their orbit drops (or decays) over time. At 150 km altitude, a satellite begins to lose altitude within a day; at 400 km, it could remain in orbit for a year before its orbit began to decay appreciably.[15]

Medium Earth Orbit (MEO). This region stretches from 1,200 miles to 22,000 miles above the Earth's surface. Relatively few satellites operate in this band, partly because it also contains the Van Allen radiation belts, which can affect satellite operations significantly. Within this band, however, is an area where a satellite will revolve around the Earth in 12 hours, going over the same spot twice every day. Satellites orbiting at approximately 12,800 miles above the Earth's surface are said to be in semi-synchronous orbit.

Most of the satellites that operate in semi-synchronous orbits are involved with positioning, navigation, and timing. These include the American GPS satellites and their Russian GLONASS, European Galileo, and Chinese Beidou/Compass counterparts.

Geosynchronous Orbit (GEO). The geosynchronous belt is at approximately 22,000 miles above the Earth's surface. At that altitude, an object in orbit is traveling at a speed that matches the Earth's rotation. Consequently, a satellite will effectively stay over the same line of longitude on the Earth's surface, although it may drift north or south in terms of its footprint on Earth. If a satellite is located at the GEO belt at the Earth's equator, however, it will stay over the same location on the ground and is said to be geostationary.

Theoretically, satellites in a geostationary orbit can keep constant watch over one-third of the Earth's surface. Consequently, this orbital band is considered extremely valuable; GEO slots above the equator are occupied by weather satellites, communications satellites, and missile early warning satellites.

In addition to these three orbital bands, there are several other types of orbits that are militarily useful.

Polar and Sun-Synchronous Orbits. Some satellites are launched into low Earth orbits that are at a very high inclination relative to the Earth's equator, essentially traveling from pole to pole. Polar orbiting satellites will typically see the same spot on Earth twice a day, once in daylight and once at night. A particular type of polar orbit is the sun-synchronous orbit. A satellite in such an orbit will always pass over the same spot on Earth at the same time. If it takes images while passing overhead, the fact that the images are taken at the same time every day facilitates the identification of any changes that may have occurred on the ground in the interval between images.

Lagrange Points. At the five Lagrange points, the Earth, Moon, and Sun's gravitational pulls cancel out each other. As a result, an object located at these points will remain in the same location relative to the Earth even as the Earth–Moon system and the satellite itself revolve around the Sun.

Molniya Orbits. Satellites operating in geosynchronous orbit over the equator stay over the same spot, but their ability to view the extreme northern and southern latitudes is very limited. Russian scientists therefore developed the Molniya orbit, where satellites orbit as high as 24,000 miles at their apogee or highest point while dipping as low as 500 miles above the Earth's surface at their lowest point.

Because the Molniya orbit also has a period of 12 hours, the high-altitude portion of the orbit will occur over the same area of Earth twice each day. Moreover, due to the momentum of the satellite, most of the time when it is moving more slowly will be near the top of its orbit. For most satellites in a Molniya orbit, the top of the orbit will be in the Northern Hemisphere, maximizing the opportunity to observe areas of interest in the high northern latitudes.

Major Satellite Missions

According to the United Nations Office for Outer Space Affairs (UNOOSA), more than 7,600 registered objects (a subset of the more than 23,000 that are tracked) are currently in orbit around the Earth.[16] Of these, only about 1,460 are operational satellites.[17] These satellites are engaged in a number of mission areas.

Intelligence, Surveillance, and Reconnaissance (ISR) Satellites. Satellites tasked

FIGURE 4

Lagrange Points

Lagrange Points are five locations where the gravitational pulls from the Earth, Moon, and Sun cancel each other out. As a result, an object located at any of these points will remain in the same location relative to the Earth, even as the Earth-Moon system and the satellite itself revolve around the Sun.

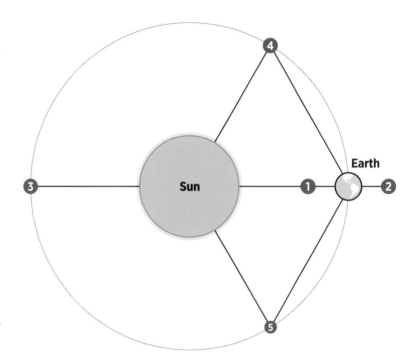

SOURCE: Heritage Foundation research.

☎ heritage.org

---

with monitoring developments in other countries have been a mainstay of space capabilities since the dawn of the space age. Both the United States and the Soviet Union sought to develop spy satellites capable of seeing into the other side's hinterlands. These satellites were initially equipped with cameras that dropped film, but those cameras were later replaced with systems that could beam their images back directly to Earth-based stations. Electro-optical satellites are unable to see through fog and clouds, so some satellites carry radars to overcome the effects of obscuring by clouds; these can often produce very high resolution images.

Imaging satellites of various sorts have been supplemented by satellites that can monitor various types of activities in the electromagnetic spectrum. Some listen to radio traffic, collecting communications intelligence (COMINT). Others are able to detect and record electronic signals, collecting electronic intelligence (ELINT). COMINT and ELINT together are referred to as signals intelligence (SIGINT). SIGINT satellites can provide insight into the types of equipment (such as radars) being

deployed by countries of interest, with the information collected revealing the wavelengths the equipment houses and what types of units (such as anti-aircraft batteries and anti-ship missile forces) are being deployed.

Most ISR satellites operate in LEO.

Earth Observation and Weather Satellites. Not all information collection is necessarily focused on other countries' military and political forces and behavior. Understanding the local environment can also be important.

Earth observation satellites such as the Landsat series have been collecting information about the land and seas for decades. The resulting data are invaluable for creating maps, as well as for understanding, for example, land use and seasonal changes in ground cover like tree foliage and grasses. For both ISR and Earth observation, data from space sensors are combined with information gathered from aircraft and terrestrial sources to give a comprehensive, layered understanding of any spot or vertical column above the ground on the planet.

Of particular security importance among the Earth observation satellites are weather

---

FIGURE 5

Molniya Orbit

500–24,000 miles above Earth's surface

Russian scientists developed the "Molniya" orbit to maximize the opportunity to observe areas of interest in the high northern latitudes.

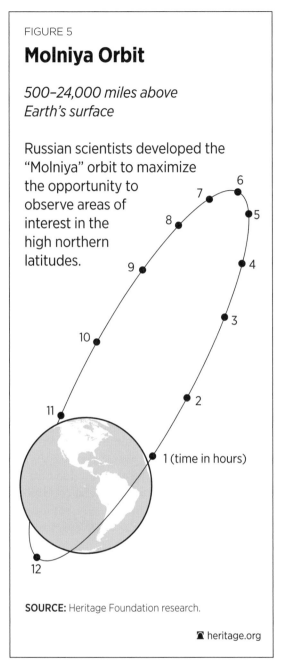

SOURCE: Heritage Foundation research.

☎ heritage.org

destination thousands of miles away. Knowing weather conditions along the route is essential to safe and effective operations, whether they involve military or civilian aircraft. The better one's understanding of weather information is, the lower the risk that one has to accept to carry out a mission.

Possessing better awareness of weather conditions than is possessed by one's opponent can confer important operational advantages. This was the case in June 1944 when Allied meteorologists, unlike their German counterparts, identified an impending lull in storms that were battering the English Channel. Consequently, the Allies landed on the beaches of Normandy on June 6, while the German high command presumed that storms made such an invasion impossible.

Most Earth observation satellites operate in LEO. Some weather satellites operate in LEO, and others are deployed in GEO.

Communications Satellites. One of the earliest commercial types of satellites was the communications satellite (comsat). Because radio, television, and other communications signals travel in straight lines, their ability to connect users on the ground is often limited by the horizon. Comsats essentially serve as relays for the transmission of these signals; a transmitter sends a signal to the communications satellite in orbit, which then transfers the signal to a ground station that may be well beyond the horizon of the original transmitter. Theoretically, a constellation of three comsats at GEO would be sufficient to provide global coverage. In reality, the availability of transponders (which are the actual relays) limits the ability of any given satellite to provide coverage.

Modern communications satellites are an important link in the movement of voice communications, television signals, and data (including Internet traffic). With the growing popularity of satellite television and its potential for entertainment and distance learning, there is a growing demand for comsat services. In addition, communications satellites are a key enabler for military drone operations. From bases

satellites. The ability to forecast weather accurately can have a decisive impact on military operations. Amphibious operations, for example, can be badly disrupted by storms. Similarly, the ability to undertake air operations, whether launched from an aircraft carrier or from a land base, is affected by inclement weather conditions. Aircraft launched from an airbase in the United States may have to fly to a

in the United States, operators can fly drones halfway around the world only because they are able to access comsats that bounce their instruction signals to their drones and relay information gathered by drone aircraft back to controlling or intelligence-processing stations.

Many of the world's communications satellites are run by private companies. Some of the world's largest constellations, for example, are now privately owned by companies such as Intelsat (55 satellites in 2014); Eutelsat (34); and the Canadian company Telesat (10).[18]

Many communications satellites are operated at GEO. However, the Iridium constellation that provides global satellite phone service is largely in LEO. Because of the smaller footprint for satellites operating at that altitude, more are needed to provide global coverage; the Iridium constellation comprises some 66 satellites.

Position, Navigation, and Timing Satellites. Beginning in the 1980s, the United States started to deploy satellites to provide position, navigation, and timing information.

- *Position* provides information about one's location and orientation: "Where am I?"

- *Navigation* provides information linking one's location to a desired destination: "How do I reach my intended location?"

- *Timing* provides precise, accurate time information.[19]

The position and navigation functions are outgrowths of the timing element. Timing functions on the GPS constellation are possible due to the highly accurate atomic clocks that are integrated into each satellite.

Each PNT satellite provides a unique signal indicating which satellite it is and what its orbital parameters are. A receiver (for example, a Garmin receiver in a vehicle) decodes the signal from at least three and usually four satellites to determine its distance from each satellite. This is done by comparing the time stamp signal from each satellite (provided by the onboard atomic clock) with the signals from the others in order to triangulate one's location. The result provides information in three dimensions with accuracy down to a few feet if one is using a cell phone's GPS function to a few inches with dedicated equipment. This is why a navigation application on a phone, in one's car, or aboard a ship far out at sea is able to work.

Because the PNT signal can be reached worldwide and all the clocks in a given constellation are keyed to the same system, the timing function has assumed a growing importance. American military frequency-hopping radios, for example, use the timing signal from GPS to time their jumps from frequency to frequency.

The U.S., Chinese, and European PNT constellations are in MEO, although China's system also includes a component that is based in GEO.

Tracking, Telemetry, and Control

In order to ensure that the various satellites are operating properly, a satellite operator needs a tracking, telemetry, and control (TT&C) network. This network enables the operator to control the satellite's functions.

- *Tracking* refers to the ability to locate a satellite and monitor its orbital condition and situation. This includes the satellite's distance and velocity.

- *Telemetry* is comprised of messages from the satellite that provide the operator with information about how well the satellite is operating. It is typically broken down into information about each of the satellite's subsystems. Telemetry data are distinct from payload data (the missions that the satellite is performing). The former is about the ability of the satellite to perform its mission.

- *Control* refers to the ability of the operator to adjust the satellite's operations. This might involve reorienting onboard instruments such as cameras or the entire satellite (for example, to point the spacecraft's solar panels toward the Sun). It might involve moving the satellite to a different orbit or requests for more telemetry data.

TT&C networks often include stations in foreign countries and may also incorporate dedicated space support ships.

Space and Future Conflicts

Modern warfare is marked by the centrality of information. The ability to conduct joint air, land, and sea operations rests in part on the ability to create a common situational picture. Modern warfare requires the coordination of forces often separated by vast distances: for example, aerial tankers from one airbase, strategic bombers from another, and carrier air wings operating hundreds of miles from the front lines, along with infantry and armored forces. These forces must be able to communicate among themselves, identifying the location not only of the adversary, but also of one's own forces. All of this relies heavily on the ability to access the strategic high ground of space.

For the United States, this dependence is especially acute because American forces typically operate in an expeditionary mode, far from our own shores. By contrast, an Iran, a China, a North Korea, even a Russia is usually operating far closer to its home territory. Consequently, these states can employ a variety of non-space means, ranging from manned and unmanned aerial vehicles to radar networks, and even human observers on land and sea to provide a constant stream of information. Similarly, they have a range of communications options such as microwave, cell phones, and various types of radio systems to link their forces together—options often not available to U.S. forces because of the distances involved when deploying from home to far-flung theaters of operation.

This asymmetric dependence means that adversaries are incentivized to deny the United States easy access to space, which will affect their own operations far less than those of the U.S. armed forces. Conversely, the United States will have to maintain access to space-based systems for a variety of functions if it is to operate as it has operated in various conflicts since the end of the Cold War.

Counter-space operations, however, will not necessarily be anti-satellite systems shooting down satellites, although a number of nations have tested anti-satellite capabilities in recent years. Because space operations depend on ground-based facilities to control the satellites and obtain data from them, there is a significant terrestrial component to space operations. Similarly, both the systems that control satellites and the data that flow over satellite networks are vulnerable to cyber attacks and data manipulation. A hacked satellite that turns off its camera at key moments is as neutralized as a functioning satellite that is intercepted and destroyed by a co-orbital or ground-based anti-satellite system.

In future conflicts, both the outer space and information space domains will be central battlefields, and operations there will have as much impact as traditional activities in the air, on land, and at sea have had.

Endnotes

1. U.S. Central Intelligence Agency, "The Dawn of the Space Age," *News & Information*, updated February 5, 2013, https://www.cia.gov/news-information/featured-story-archive/2007-featured-story-archive/the-dawn-of-the-space-age.html (accessed May 26, 2017).

2. Philip W. Quigg, "Open Skies and Open Space," *Foreign Affairs*, Vol. 37, No. 1 (October 1958), pp. 95–106, https://www.foreignaffairs.com/articles/space/1958-10-01/open-skies-and-open-space (accessed May 26, 2017).

3. U.S. Strategic Command, "USSTRATCOM Space Control and Space Surveillance," October 17, 2016, http://www.stratcom.mil/Media/Factsheets/Factsheet-View/Article/976414/usstratcom-space-control-and-space-surveillance/ (accessed May 26, 2017).

4. European Space Agency, "Space Debris by the Numbers," information correct as of January 2017, http://www.esa.int/Our_Activities/Operations/Space_Debris/Space_debris_by_the_numbers (accessed June 5, 2017).

5. See "Types of Orbits," p. 76.

6. By the European Space Agency's accounting, there are approximately 750,000 man-made objects between 1cm and 10cm in length orbiting the Earth and over 160 million between 1 mm and 1cm in size, all traveling at extraordinary speeds and able to cause varying amounts of damage to functioning satellites. European Space Agency, "Space Debris by the Numbers."

7. Miria M. Finckenor and Kim K. DeGroh, *A Researcher's Guide to: Space Environmental Effects*, National Aeronautics and Space Administration *International Space Station Researcher's Guide Series*, NP-2015-03-015-JSC, p. 15, https://www.nasa.gov/sites/default/files/files/NP-2015-03-015-JSC_Space_Environment-ISS-Mini-Book-2015-508.pdf (accessed June 5, 2017).

8. Tariq Malik, "Launchpad Explosion Destroys SpaceX Falcon 9 Rocket, Satellite in Florida," Space.com, September 1, 2016, http://www.space.com/33929-spacex-falcon-9-rocket-explodes-on-launch-pad.html (accessed June 5, 2017).

9. Irene Klotz, "New US Military Communications Satellite to Launch Saturday," Space.com, March 17, 2017, http://www.space.com/36100-wgs-9-military-communications-satellite-launches-saturday.html (accessed May 26, 2017).

10. Eric Berger, "America's New, Super Expensive Weather Satellite Launches Saturday," *Ars Technica*, November 18, 2016, https://arstechnica.com/science/2016/11/americas-new-super-expensive-weather-satellite-launches-saturday/ (accessed June 5, 2017).

11. George Leopold, "DARPA Seeks to Bring Satellite Costs Back Down to Earth," Defense Systems, December 13, 2013, https://defensesystems.com/articles/2013/12/13/darpa-space-access.aspx (accessed May 26, 2017).

12. Rich Smith, "How Much Does It Cost to Launch a Satellite?" *The Motley Fool*, June 24, 2016, https://www.fool.com/investing/2016/06/24/how-much-does-it-cost-to-launch-a-satellite.aspx (accessed May 26, 2017).

13. Information in this section is drawn from National Aeronautics and Space Administration, Earth Observatory, "Three Classes of Orbit," https://earthobservatory.nasa.gov/Features/OrbitsCatalog/page2.php (accessed June 5, 2017).

14. James E. Oberg, *Space Power Theory* (Colorado Springs: U.S. Air Force Academy, 1999), p. 39, http://www.au.af.mil/au/awc/space/books/oberg/ (accessed June 5, 2017).

15. Ibid.

16. United Nations, Office of Outer Space Affairs, "Online Index of Objects Launched Into Outer Space," http://www.unoosa.org/oosa/osoindex/search-ng.jspx?lf_id (accessed June 5, 2017).

17. Union of Concerned Scientists, "UCS Satellite Database," November 15, 1974–December 31, 2016, http://www.ucsusa.org/nuclear-weapons/space-weapons/satellite-database#.WTWkRkOkv_8 (accessed June 5, 2017).

18. Peter B. de Selding, "The List: 2014 Top Fixed Satellite Service Operators," *Space News*, July 13, 2015, http://spacenews.com/the-list-2014-top-fixed-satellite-service-operators/ (accessed June 5, 2017).

19. U.S. Department of Transportation, "Positioning, Navigation and Timing (PNT) & Spectrum Management," https://www.rita.dot.gov/pnt/about (accessed June 5, 2017).

National Defense and the Cyber Domain

G. Alexander Crowther, PhD

What is "cyberspace," and how does it relate to military affairs? "Cyberspace" is a term that is constantly used but seldom well defined. Its characteristics are poorly understood in the larger public discussion, especially with regard to national security and military matters. This is unfortunate because "cyber" has become profoundly central to nearly everything the military does in defense of U.S. national security interests.

As a domain through which actions can be taken instantaneously, globally, and even anonymously, cyberspace provides opportunities and challenges to countries, groups, and individuals unlike those presented by any other domain or capability. Cyberspace provides someone with the ability to attack anywhere, at any time, with a keystroke. There is no need to deploy a physical force, gain physical access to a region (otherwise done by ship, plane, or overland movement), or be encumbered by mounds of equipment and supplies. An attacker acts in absolute silence, perhaps visible only to the most skilled cyber defender. There is no need to limit one's force to specific ages, physical conditions, or body size, nor is there a need for sprawling bases, expensive facilities (like ports or airfields), square miles of training areas, extensive stockpiles of munitions, or assured access to fuel.

Cyber is generally not affected by environmental concerns or weather conditions. To the extent that cyber operations can be fully automated, they can be undertaken relentlessly, without regard for time, periods of rest, or any other constraint related to the normal use of people and equipment. In short, cyberspace provides a virtually unconstrained sphere through which nearly anyone can act against almost any target without concern for the physical impediments and resources that accompany physical actions.

A wide variety of actors operate in cyberspace. The government of the United States has a variety of responsibilities to the American public, but precisely where the responsibility lies and the extent of that responsibility are currently subjects of debate. Although 90 percent of the Internet traffic in the U.S. is in the private sector,[1] cyberspace is one place for which the U.S. government has acknowledged responsibility. Working mainly through the Department of Defense (DOD), Department of Homeland Security (DHS), and Department of Justice (DOJ):

> The United States will work to promote an **open, interoperable, secure, and reliable** information and communications infrastructure that supports international trade and commerce, strengthens international security, and fosters free expression and innovation. To achieve that goal, [the U.S.] will build and sustain an environment in which **norms of responsible behavior** guide states' actions, sustain partnerships, and support the rule of law in cyberspace.[2]

Cyberspace

Cyberspace has three layers: the physical network, the logical network, and the cyber persona.

- **The physical network** consists of the hardware, such as cables and your computer, and exists all around the world. Because it exists inside states, states have sovereignty over its components, and they must obey the laws of the states in which they reside.

- **The logical network** is the software that operates the network as well as its manifestations, such as a web page. These electrons that make up the logical network bounce around the globe, following the quickest route from one place to another, and route through hardware that is physically located in states. Some states, such as China and Russia, believe that they have sovereignty over this aspect of the cyber domain as well.

- **The cyber persona** is made up of the people who are operating in cyberspace. Like the physical network, they are present within states and subject to their laws and policies.

Colloquially, these three components are known as hardware, software, and wetware.[3]

The cyber domain has effectively penetrated the world's advanced economies and is making headway in the rest of the world. Many places in Africa, for instance, have skipped over the land line and gone straight to smart phones; currently, approximately 3.74 billion people are connected to the Internet.[4]

This connectivity provides a number of opportunities and challenges. It enables actions by both states and individuals across all of the elements of national power: diplomacy, information, the military, and the economy. It makes diplomatic activity more effective, for example, linking embassies and capitals with almost instant communications and allowing for better research. In addition, the opportunities that cyberspace provides for information are almost unlimited. Humankind creates huge amounts of information annually, and individuals and organizations are constantly digitizing old information, making it available to everyone.

Militarily, cyberspace allows for global command and control of forces and operations and the functioning of a globally distributed logistics system without which modern military operations would be impossible. Intelligence communities, commanders, and warfighters alike benefit from the uninterrupted flow of information. Economically, cyberspace has led to a global boom, from the technology giants Google and Amazon to the individual fisherman in India who can now determine where to obtain the best price for his catch.

In short, with its low barrier to entry, cyberspace has provided advantages across the globe and across the elements of national power. And these advantages grow as access to cyberspace spreads.

At the same time, cyberspace creates challenges. Wikileaks has revealed to the world stolen U.S. diplomatic communications, embarrassing the United States, irritating friends, and empowering enemies. Information is harder and harder to secure and easier and easier to steal. Economically, cyberspace has enabled criminals: Cyber crime cost the U.S. $100 billion and the global economy $400 billion in 2015, and the total is projected to reach $2 trillion by 2019.[5] For the U.S. military, compromise of the U.S. global command and control capability can be turned against the Department of Defense, frustrating or even preventing the execution of military operations.

Vulnerabilities and Actors

The U.S. has begun to confront challenges to its major interests in cyberspace: protection and enhancement of the economy, secure command and control of national defense assets, reliable collection of cyber intelligence, and protection of cyber intelligence and information.[6]

Three major groups threaten U.S. national security: people, states, and non-state actors. People include the general population, leaders, workers in nearly all business sectors, and insider threats. States primarily include Russia,

China, Iran, and North Korea. Non-state actors include proxies, hacktivists, and criminals who sometimes work for themselves but also may work in support of others.

The Human Dimension. Humans are the weakest link in the cybersecurity system.[7] Unlike the physical world, in which potential human activity is limited by geographic and space limitations—Israel, for example, uses a barrier to keep out potential terrorists, and people do not own nuclear weapons or aircraft carriers—barriers to entry for cyber are so low that they have democratized cyber activity. Everyone who has a desktop, laptop, or smart phone is an actor and a potential problem. Because the only thing that organizations do well is what their leaders demand of them, leaders can be a key vulnerability, and thus a "threat" to their organizations, by not emphasizing cybersecurity. Workers using poor cyber hygiene are a threat. Gullible people or people with preconceived but flawed notions of safe cyber practices will fall prey to cyber crime or propaganda. Insiders who do not support their organizations are another threat.

The Population. People are the most vulnerable to cyber operations. Because many people engage in commercial transactions online and use social media daily, they are the most exposed to these varied threats. In general, people usually have not received training or education that would enable them to deal with varied cyber threats. Additionally, most people do not see their information as having value.

Leaders. Research supporting the 2014 Chairman of the Joint Chiefs of Staff war game *Iron Crucible* identified "understanding" as the major challenge in the 21st century.[8] Because most senior leaders typically are not involved in the information business, there is a wide variation in their knowledge of or insistence on best practices in the cyber domain.

The U.S. Office of Personnel Management (OPM) hacks of 2015 are a telling example of poor leadership in this area. Although OPM's Assistant Inspector General for Audits indicated that security shortfalls were well known, having been publicly acknowledged since 2007, the OPM Director did not make cybersecurity a priority. By the time the hacks were identified in 2015, nearly a quarter of OPM's information technology (IT) systems, including several of their most critical and sensitive applications, were operating without a valid cyber-certificate authorization.[9] If the Director had understood the implications of basic security shortfalls, perhaps the theft of sensitive personal information on over 22 million Americans could have been prevented.[10]

Senior officials are often the targets of cyber-attacks because they have access to more information, IT bends the rules for them, and the damage and financial payoff for the attacker can be much bigger.[11] Hence, senior leaders need more training and education to understand how to operate their systems, how to lead and manage cyber systems and workers, and how to decrease their own vulnerability. Senior leaders also need to integrate information activities into their day-to-day operations, whether it is in a business, government, or the military. Only when senior leaders understand the implications of cyberspace will they be able to address vulnerabilities and achieve synergies that cyberspace provides.

Workers. In a phishing quiz, 80 percent of participants misidentified at least one phishing e-mail.[12] Workers are a favorite target because the chance of success goes up when more people are targeted. Roughly 20 percent of trained workers will click on a phishing link[13] even if they have been trained not to do so.

Insider Threats. These involve a variety of motivations and are very difficult to identify ahead of time. Edward Snowden and Bradley Manning are well-known cases in the U.S. The Computer Emergency Response Team (CERT) Insider Threat Center at Carnegie Mellon University maintains a database of more than 1,000 insider threat cases and provides analysis and support to organizations working to prevent insider threats.[14] Another type of insider threat is the "Lone Wolf" or "Wolf Pack." These are individuals or groups that have been radicalized, typically through cognition-shaping cyber operations.

State Threats. Included in this category are threats posed by Russia, China, Iran, and North Korea. States can leverage enormous funding, the ability to organize, and the ability to coordinate actions (multi-domain and multi-tool) at levels far above that of an individual or small group. These state actors challenge the U.S. economy with brazen cyber espionage into critical U.S. companies.

In 2014, for example, a grand jury in the Western District of Pennsylvania indicted five officers from the Chinese People's Liberation Army for cyber espionage in support of state-owned enterprises (SOEs).[15] An array of cyber actors also has challenged the ability of the U.S. to secure its command and control of national security networks reliably and to secure its sensitive and personal information data. In 2015, Russians hacked the Joint Staff,[16] and the OPM discovered a Chinese hack of tens of millions of files containing sensitive personal data.[17] Additionally, the Russians have returned to their Cold War practices of aggressive information operations seeking to undermine developed countries[18] as well as international organizations.[19]

Iran and North Korea are second-tier threats for the United States, and both countries are continuously performing cyber operations against economic and government targets in the U.S. In 2016, the DOJ indicted seven Iranian hackers for operating against a dam and banks in the U.S.,[20] and North Korean hackers have been involved in stealing both money and military designs.[21]

Non-State Actors. This category includes threats from proxies, hacktivists, and criminals. Proxies work on behalf of a government that seeks cyber effects without paying a political price, hoping to achieve plausible deniability by outsourcing such work to individuals. The Russians often use criminals as proxies,[22] and the Chinese use other groups that may or may not be affiliated with each other or other similar criminal entities.

Hacktivists will perform a wide range of operations. Much like the difference between terrorists and freedom fighters, hacktivists attack you while patriots attack people you don't like. Ironically, some groups like Anonymous will attack anyone with whom they disagree, regardless of the target's politics.

Criminals operate across the world. As noted, it is estimated that cyber crime cost the U.S. $100 billion and the global economy $400 billion in 2015 and that the total will rise to $2 trillion by 2019.[23]

All of these actors are aided by the fact that it is very difficult to attribute cyber operations to a specific actor. Cyber actors take very specific steps to prevent attribution, typically by manipulating data to pretend to be someone else. This is one of the largest barriers to cybersecurity as it is difficult to deter an actor whose identity you can't prove.

Nature of Competition in Cyberspace

Competition in cyberspace is fierce and ongoing. States seek to undermine the global order to their own advantage. Individual actors and organizations seek to advance their own political agendas. Criminals seek to make illegal financial gains from cyberspace.

All of these can be inimical to the goals of the United States and its allies and partners. Russia seeks to use cyber-enabled information operations to sow discord inside and among the states that are trying to keep Russia at bay in Europe; China uses cyberspace to steal secrets that it can use for economic gain or to avoid the research and development costs (in time and money) for important military systems; Iran seeks to weaken its opponents around the world; and North Korea maneuvers in cyberspace to avoid international sanctions.

Because of the low barrier to entry into cyberspace and the potential gains to be made, the scale of the challenge is large and growing. The U.S. and its allies and partners need to safeguard their own government spaces, their economic activities, and their citizens. Although the U.S. has strengths including a wide variety of resources and a large, educated workforce, these bad actors use cyberspace to challenge the U.S. at every turn. The U.S. is having a hard time using traditional strengths (such as military power) against cyber actors.

The U.S. Government in Cyber

Because the U.S. government has a wide variety of resources and the obligation to safeguard the American population, the executive branch performs many cyber activities to mitigate the foregoing threats. The three main U.S. government actors in cyberspace, as noted, are the Departments of Homeland Security, Justice, and Defense.

- **The DHS** coordinates the national protection against, prevention and mitigation of, and recovery from cyber incidents; disseminates domestic cyber threat and vulnerability analysis; protects critical infrastructure; secures federal civilian systems (the .gov domain); and investigates cyber crimes under its jurisdiction.

- **The DOJ** investigates, attributes, disrupts, and prosecutes cyber crimes; is the lead agency for domestic national security operations; conducts domestic collection, analysis, and dissemination of cyber threat intelligence; supports the national protection against, prevention and mitigation of, and recovery from cyber incidents; and coordinates cyber threat investigations.

- **The DOD** is charged with securing the nation's freedom of action in cyberspace and helping to mitigate risks to national security resulting from America's growing dependence on cyberspace. Specific mission sets include directing, securing, and defending DOD Information Network (DODIN) operations (including the .mil domain); maintaining freedom of maneuver in cyberspace; executing full-spectrum military cyberspace operations; providing shared situational awareness of cyberspace operations, including indications and warning; and providing support to civil authorities and international partners.[24]

Deterrence. Ongoing cyber operations against the United States demonstrate that the country has extremely limited capability to deter cyber operations, that the U.S. cyber deterrence threat is not credible, and that U. S. cyber deterrence is failing.[25]

Deterrence is designed to convince others not to perform certain tasks. In this case, it ideally should prevent other actors from performing all four types of cyber operations. One thing that can make cyber deterrence less effective, as noted, is the difficulty involved in attributing an operation to a specific actor. Additionally, second-order and third-order analysis to predict what ancillary actions would follow certain types of cyber-attacks is very difficult to perform in the cyber realm. Incorrect analysis could cause a deterrence operation to trigger a completely opposite reaction and accidentally escalate rather than deter, which causes second thoughts on allowing offensive cyber operations.[26]

The use of cyber capabilities to deter faces two major barriers: For deterrence to work, opponents must believe that they will pay a price for an action, and the target audience needs to understand who is deterring them. This in turn requires a credible threat. Opponents do not currently believe that they will face retaliation in response to their attacks on U.S. assets. Effective cyber retaliation requires that operators perform an attack and leave behind digital "fingerprints" identifying the originator or an explicit message naming the origin of the attack.

But this presents two further problems: Cyber operators do not want to compromise their capabilities by performing an operation that can be traced to them, and it has been difficult to receive clearance to perform offensive cyber operations (OCOs). Any OCO that has major effects can alert an opponent to the presence of intruders, which allows opponents to defend against the intrusion. It can also reveal cyber capabilities, which is anathema to the community that prizes its ability to work in secret. Moreover, it sometimes takes months to penetrate opposition cyber systems. Executing an attack will announce the operator's presence and "waste" the time required to penetrate and repenetrate target servers.

The Military Cyber Domain

The DOD does not define "domain," but it does define cyberspace as "[a] global domain within the information environment consisting of the interdependent network of information technology infrastructures and resident data, including the Internet, telecommunications networks, computer systems, and embedded processors and controllers."[27] The words "infrastructures and resident data" cover the physical and logical aspects of cyberspace but not the persona aspect. The use of "domain" is meant to indicate that cyberspace is now co-equal with the other conventional domains: sea, air, land, and space.[28] This is intended to communicate to leaders within the DOD that they need to pay as much attention to cyber issues as they would pay to air, sea, land, and space issues.

There are four sets of cyberspace activities that pertain to the military: intelligence, information, crime, and military operations.[29] Although the military has equities in all of these areas, it predominates only in the military operations portion. However, there are aspects of intelligence, information, and criminal activities in cyberspace that do involve the military.

In any of these fields, there is a spectrum of activity that ranges from conventional to cyber-enabled to cyber-centric to pure cyber operations.

Normal intelligence operations like stealing secrets and developing sources would have been the traditional approach before the advent of cyberspace. Cyber-enabled intelligence operations would use cyber capabilities in support of these operations, such as analysis of a terrorist network using data that had been gathered by traditional intelligence means. Cyber intelligence operations would be operations that occur entirely in cyberspace, such as the 2012 operation by Chinese hackers that penetrated Indian Navy computers and compromised sensitive information.[30] Purely cyber operations would consist of information and communications technology, network, and defensive cyber operations.

Conventional criminal operations would be old-school crime, such as entering a bank with a pistol and a bag. Cyber-enabled criminal operations would fuse technology and crime, such as ATM-skimming, where criminals use hidden electronics to steal the personal information stored on bank ATM cards and record PIN numbers in order to access victims' accounts.[31] Cyber crime would be a criminal operation that occurs wholly in cyberspace, such as the use of the SWIFT system to steal $81 million from the Bank of Bangladesh.[32]

Conventional information operations would be old-fashioned propaganda or even advertising via printed text, radio waves, or television. The 2016 hack of the Democratic National Committee would be an example of a cyber-enabled information operation.[33] The information was obtained through cyber operations but released through Wikileaks.[34] Cyber information operations would include Daesh recruiting videos, an information operation that takes place entirely in cyberspace.

Military operations can also be cyber-enabled or executed purely in cyberspace. A normal military operation would be the invasion of Iraq. A normal special operation would be the raid to kill Osama bin Laden. An example of a cyber-enabled conventional military operation would be Russian operations in Georgia in 2008 when Russia conducted cyber operations against Georgian targets to degrade Georgian command and control in support of Russian conventional military operations on the ground and in the air.[35] An example of a cyber-enabled special operation would be the Mumbai attack of 2008. Planners used a Go-Pro camera while walking the route to be used in the attack so everyone could see videos of their routes before the operation. They also used Google Earth during their planning process. The command element monitored Indian social media and traditional media (such as radio and television) to track the response by Indian security forces and steered the ground force away from reacting Indian forces, enabling the operation to continue much longer than it would have normally.[36]

Cyber military operations include conventional and special operations. A conventional cyber operation would be like "dropping cyber bombs on Daesh." Secretary of Defense Ashton Carter explained at an event at NORTHCOM that "[w]e're using these tools to deny the ability of ISIL leadership to command and finance their forces and control their populations; to identify and locate ISIL cyber actors; and to undermine the ability of ISIL recruiters to inspire or direct Homegrown Violent Extremists."[37] This is a conventional operation in that it does not require special techniques or unique modes of employment in a covert nature.

A cyber special operation would be the Stuxnet attacks on Iran. This operation meets many of the criteria for a special operation as defined in the DOD's Joint Publication 3-05, *Special Operations*.[38] It required unique modes of employment, tactics, techniques, procedures, and equipment. It was conducted in a hostile, denied, or politically and/or diplomatically sensitive environment and was characterized by a clandestine or covert nature (no one has yet proved who conducted the operation) and low visibility.

Criminal operations do not usually pertain to militaries in the conventional sense. In cyberspace, however, there are crimes that involve members of the DOD, as well as crimes that involve the Defense Industrial Base. Additionally, members of the DOD participate in several types of activities that pertain to cyber crime and cyber-enabled crime, including cyber security and critical infrastructure protection, law enforcement and counterintelligence, document and media exploitation, and counterterrorism.[39]

Each of these provides examples of how the military would be involved in four areas: crime, intelligence, information operations, and military operations. Although military forces are involved in these areas, they are not involved in all operations in these areas (the DOJ handles most cyber crime). This, then, is the circumscribed area that can be called the military cyber domain. These distinct categories are changing and becoming more integrated with cyber activities. As cyber capabilities expand, more military operations will be enabled by them; eventually all military operations will be enabled by cyber capabilities.

Military Cyber Operations

There are four main types of cyber operations: shaping cognition; cyber surveillance and reconnaissance (CSR); operational preparation of the environment (OPE); and cyberspace attacks. They can be either defensive or offensive in nature. Defensive cyber operations (DCOs) comprise the vast majority of U.S. government (and military) activities. Offensive cyber operations (OCOs) are rarer for the United States. None of these activities is unique to cyberspace. All military operations require reconnaissance and preparation, and shaping cognition through information (for example, through advertising) is ubiquitous in modern society.

Opponents perform shaping-cognition intelligence operations against the United States on a minute-by-minute basis and perform OPE regularly. Large-scale, destructive cyberspace attacks are rare but have the potential to be catastrophic in their effects.

Shaping cognition is using information to cause people to think in a certain way. This can be benign like Facebook or malign like cyber crime. It is perhaps the most significant opportunity and challenge for cyber today. Due to the pervasive nature of information in the 21st century, everyone who connects to the Internet can shape the thoughts of others. Radicalization by state and non-state actors is a significant challenge, especially lone-wolf or wolf-pack radicalization. The Islamic State has successful influence operations running globally 24 hours a day. The fact that volunteers have been to ISIS territory from around the world indicates how successful these operations are. Other actors target populations of other countries (to radicalize); government employees (to create an insider threat); and businesses (to coerce or blackmail them into behavior that the initiator desires). Governments consequently struggle to cope with widespread cognition shaping.

CSR is data gathering. Google gathers data every time one accesses the Internet. States gather data on people in other countries or on their own citizens. States such as China gather economic data and pass it on to their state-owned enterprises who use it to obtain a competitive advantage in the marketplace. Criminals gather data to better execute their criminal activities. Today, everyone is a data-gatherer.

OPE is specific preparation of the environment for follow-on operations by installing "back doors" in targeted computer systems so that they can return at a later time to execute an attack or devising specially designed software that will allow them to achieve an effect, such as opening the gates on a dam. Among recent examples, as noted, are the seven Iranians who were indicted for hacking into banks and a dam in New York.[40]

OCOs are a means by which to achieve an end, another tool that provides additional capabilities to the President and battlefield commanders and relevant forces.

Cyber operations are limited only by the imagination and capability of the attackers, yet there are only two types of cyber-attacks: syntactic and semantic.[41] Syntactic operations involve the actual coding used in a piece of cyber programming (the syntax of the coding), and semantic operations seek to shape thoughts using language or semantics. As an example, a phishing operation begins as a semantic operation, asking the target to "click on this link," and then, once the link is activated, changes to a syntactic attack by which the malicious code enters the target's system and changes the syntax of the code in the targeted platform. Shaping the thoughts of others may be the more important of these two types of attack.

A cyberspace attack produces two forms of effect: manipulation and denial. Manipulation means controlling or changing the adversary's information, information systems, and/or networks in a manner that supports the commander's objectives. Denial attempts to degrade, disrupt, or destroy. Degrading limits the capacity of a target, and disruption completely but temporarily prevents access to a target.[42] Destruction eliminates the target altogether.

Cyber operations are changing the characteristics of warfare. Although the nature of war is constant, the characteristics of warfare can change whenever a new weapon or tactical approach is introduced. Operations in cyberspace now allow for more information to be acquired and shared and better command and control to be exercised on the battlefield, theoretically decreasing the "fog of war" by adding fidelity to the commander's understanding of the battlespace. It allows for more accurate and effective use of the people and logistics capabilities involved, putting the right person or widget at the right place at the right time. It also allows for a significant improvement in the ability to shape cognition.

While it allows all of these to assist friendly forces, however, it also allows our opponents to do the same. They will have a better understanding of—and consequently an opportunity to copy or defeat—our technologies and capabilities. They will be able to access our command and control and logistics networks, potentially modifying orders so that forces or spare parts end up in the wrong place. They also will be able to use patterns in the movement of information to improve their own intelligence, identifying our units and their capabilities.

These capabilities require the U.S. government generally, as well as the U.S. military specifically, to modify its practices. Leaders and organizations need to do a better job of selecting and utilizing new technology. Laws and policies need to be updated to leverage the new technology. Older leaders need to understand how younger followers perceive and use technology.

Implications for Operations. Cyberspace permeates all aspects of our daily lives and therefore all operations whether military, governmental, or commercial. Cyber operations, including information operations, will require attention from leaders from the tactical level to the strategic level.

At the tactical or local level, cyber operations will provide information to the warfighter that previously did not exist or was available only to national-level leaders. Soldiers will carry smart phones, which will require command attention and supervision to prevent the unintentional compromise of militarily relevant information. Units will have access to huge amounts of information, including the position of every friendly vehicle, soldier, airframe, and ship as well as any enemy forces that have been identified. This information will make our forces much more effective and efficient if properly utilized.

At the same time, our opponents will use their similar capabilities as effectively as they can to accomplish their own objectives in keeping with their own integrated information warfare doctrine. It will be difficult for U.S., allied, and partner units to control their own information while exploiting their opponent's information. Units will have to perform DCOs at all levels. Failing to do so will likely result in operational paralysis when their command and control assets are degraded or destroyed. They also will have access to limited OCOs if their particular mission warrants access to that level of support.

Automation and information flows will make day-to-day operations easier. However, while attention to sound DCOs and skillful execution of OCOs will lead to military success, failure in each case will present exploitable opportunities to an enemy.

Implications for the Services. As occurred when airplanes, tanks, and automatic weapons were introduced to war, forces will need to reorganize to integrate robust cyber and particularly information capabilities. Specifically, the services will have to:

- **Modify** training and equipping to ensure that units practice DCO at all times and will have to stand up additional

OCO capabilities as their use becomes more widespread.

- Because cyber operations happen at nearly instantaneous speed and in a wide variety of locations simultaneously, **modify** their doctrine to allow for greater authority to execute cyber operations at much lower and more local levels in order for units to continue to function when command and control are degraded and operate effectively at the speed of information.

- **Purchase** more modern information technology equipment and software, which are inherently more secure.

- **Provide** universal, entertaining, iterative cyber hygiene training to the entire force. Properly equipped and trained units will be able to be much more effective and efficient in information-age combat. According to the Australian Signals Directorate, 85 percent of cyber problems can be mitigated with proper cyber hygiene.[43] This will be expensive in the short term, but once it is fully integrated into the force, it will act as a force multiplier.

U.S. Military Cyber

The Office of the Secretary of Defense articulates three primary cyber missions: "**defend DoD networks, systems, and information**; **defend the nation against cyberattacks of significant consequence**; and **support military operational and contingency plans**."[44]

Because the DOD is a very large, bureaucratic organization that operates around the world, it is proving difficult for it to fully embrace cyberspace operations. First, there are DOD legacy structures. Services such as the Army provide trained and equipped forces, while Combatant Commands (CCMDs) like U.S. European Command (EUCOM) and U.S. Pacific Command (PACOM) use those forces for missions. This means that the DOD, the largest organization in the world, must simultaneously defend every military system that is linked in any way to or affected by "cyber" used by DOD, the Joint Staff, the three military departments, and four services that collectively employ almost 3 million people, more than 450,000 of whom work overseas, both afloat and ashore.

The department's responsibilities also include several hundred thousand individual buildings and structures located at more than 5,000 different locations or sites worldwide.[45] Each person in the DOD needs to communicate and pass information on a daily basis. Many have multiple computers and devices that they operate on different networks. All of this must be secure and reliable, from the Nuclear Command and Control System down to tactical radios that connect soldiers in the field.

Adding further complication, each service is responsible for its own procurement of computers, devices, and components and has its own procedures for doing so.[46] Each service defends itself, at least in part, and the DOD maintains separate organizations to defend the larger organization and defense agencies apart from the individual services and operational commands, all of which makes training and equipping for operations in cyberspace very bureaucratic and cumbersome. This is exacerbated by the overall defensive tone of the three mission sets: The DOD mainly defends their networks and provides defensive assistance to other agencies as required, a set of tasks that must be attended to every second of the day.

The DOD also performs offensive missions when directed to do so by the President. This is a very circumscribed set of missions, for several reasons. First, much as the entire U.S. Marine Corps would be swallowed by a megacity like Lagos, Nigeria, DOD offensive cyber assets would be overwhelmed by being everywhere and helping everyone. Additionally, many aspects of ongoing cyberspace activity do not pertain to the DOD at all. Just as most aviation activity does not concern the Air Force and most maritime activity does not involve the Navy, most cyber activity does not concern

the Defense Department. An example would be an individual using PayPal to make a purchase from the web-retailer Amazon.

Operations in cyberspace as a military domain must therefore be a circumscribed mission set. Nevertheless, militarily relevant information, intelligence, criminal, and military-specific activities occur all over the Internet, so the military must be able to maneuver throughout all of cyberspace.

The Services and Cyber. The service chiefs provide cyber operations capabilities for deployment/support to Combatant Commands as directed by the Secretary of Defense.[47] In addition to joint strategy and doctrine, each service has its own doctrine to deal with cyber issues. This is not just because each service has its own history and culture. Cyber defense of ground forces is different from protecting platform-centric operations like those conducted by the Navy and Air Force. The Army must protect ground units, the Navy must protect groups of ships operating at sea across the globe, and the Air Force must protect individual flying platforms. At the same time, each service must protect its own infrastructure.

Therefore, under their Title 10 role as force providers to the combatant commanders, the services recruit, train, educate, and retain their own military cyber forces. There are four service component commands under U.S. Cyber Command (USCYBERCOM): U.S. Army Cyber Command, U.S. Fleet Cyber Command/U.S. 10th Fleet, 24th Air Force, and U.S. Marine Corps Forces Cyber Command.[48] These service-specific units have several functions: They operate and defend their portion of the DODIN; perform full-spectrum cyber operations, meaning offensive and defensive; provide for cyber training and education; and undertake cyber research and capabilities development for their respective services.

Combatant Commands are responsible for geographic areas (such as European Command) or functional areas (such as Special Operations Command or U.S. Transportation Command) and provide operations instructions and command and control functions to the armed forces. They have a significant impact on how the service component cyber commands are organized, trained, and resourced—areas over which Congress has constitutional authority.[49] CCMDs share cyber information largely through USCYBERCOM and their own joint cyber centers, but various personnel also meet periodically to share information in collaboration sessions.[50]

USCYBERCOM was formed in 2010. It is a subunified command under U.S. Strategic Command (STRATCOM). Congress and the Obama and Trump Administrations have examined the propriety of dividing the two and promoting CYBERCOM to a full Combatant Command. This would allow CYBERCOM to work directly with other commands without having to work through an extra layer of command at STRATCOM. CYBERCOM plans, coordinates, integrates, synchronizes, and conducts activities to direct the operations and defense of specified units and the DODIN. When so directed, it also prepares to conduct full-spectrum military cyberspace operations to enable actions in all domains, ensure U.S. and allied freedom of action in cyberspace and deny the same to adversaries,[51] and counter efforts by opponents to interfere with CCMD operations.

USCYBERCOM's main instrument of power is the Cyber National Mission Force, which conducts cyberspace operations to disrupt and deny adversary attacks against national critical infrastructure. It is the U.S. military's first joint tactical command with a dedicated mission focused on cyberspace operations. It planned to create 133 cyber mission teams by the end of fiscal year 2016;[52] the current plan is for all the teams to be fully functional by 2018.[53] The force eventually will consist of 13 National Mission Teams (NMTs), which are designed to defend the United States and its interests against cyberattacks of significant consequence; 68 Cyber Protection Teams (CPTs), which defend priority DOD networks and systems against priority threats; 27 Combat Mission Teams (CMTs), which aid Combatant Commands by

generating integrated cyberspace effects in support of operational plans and contingency operations; and 25 Cyber Support Teams (CSTs), which provide analytic and planning support to the National Mission and Combat Mission teams.[54]

Put another way, National Mission Teams perform strategic operations, and CMTs conduct cyberspace operations in support of CCMDs. CPTs protect the DODIN, the services, and the CCMDs. CSTs support NMTs and CMTs.

This number of teams and their organizational distribution together ensure that the U.S. military meets the need to conduct offensive and defensive cyber operations around the clock in multiple commands and in multiple areas around the world, something quite unlike conventional military forces outside of active combat engagements. Once the Cyber Mission Force is fully established in 2018, the DOD no doubt will reassess its requirements and modify the force as needed based on experience.

Conclusion

The United States is challenged by a wide variety of state and non-state actors in cyberspace, which is already huge and constantly growing. Additionally, the U.S. has certain societal vulnerabilities at home that make facing these challenges more difficult. The Department of Defense, Department of Homeland Security, and Department of Justice have to operate in this environment as the U.S. government's three principal actors, which also seek partnerships with the private sector that operates almost all of the Internet.

The U.S. government seeks to protect the United States through protection and deterrence. Because of the size and complexity of cyberspace as well as domestic legal and cultural constructs in the United States, the DOD must circumscribe the scope of its operations in cyberspace, operating in the military cyber domain as required in the criminal, informational, intelligence, and operational fields. The DOD must defend itself, assist the President in other areas when directed to do so, and conduct defensive and offensive cyber operations as an integrated part of normal military operations.

In order to conduct these operations, the department has organized cyber forces in each of the services under the command of the Commander, United States Cyber Command, who has the task of training, educating, and building a world-class cyber force while simultaneously conducting cyber operations 24 hours a day around the globe. Conceptually, the DOD has recognized cyber as a domain, making it equal to sea, air, land, and space. "Cyber" promises to provide significant gains in the efficiency and effectiveness of U.S. military units through the full integration of conventional operations, cyber capabilities, and operations in the information environment.

Although military leaders understand the importance of cyber and information, not all understand the scope of the opportunities and challenges that cyber provides. The military services will have to expend more resources on training and equipping not only cyber forces, but all forces that will be serving in an environment where they are under continuous cyber-attack. Defensive cyber operations will protect forces from cyber-attacks while offensive cyber operations enable other conventional and special operations as an integrated whole. The U.S. is ahead of almost all other states in cyber capability, but it must continue to invest time and effort in order to maintain that lead.

Endnotes

1. Author's interview with Brigadier General Greg Touhill, U.S. Air Force (Ret.), March 27, 2015.

2. See *International Strategy for Cyberspace: Prosperity, Security, and Openness in a Networked World*, The White House, May 2011, p. 8, https://obamawhitehouse.archives.gov/sites/default/files/rss_viewer/international_strategy_for_cyberspace.pdf (accessed July 5, 2017). Emphasis in original. Until the Trump Administration develops strategies, we must rely on Obama-era documentation.

3. The Merriam-Webster Dictionary defines wetware as "the human brain or a human being considered especially with respect to human logical and computational capabilities." See "wetware," Merriam-Webster.com, https://www.merriam-webster.com/dictionary/wetware (accessed August 14, 2017).

4. Internet World Stats, "Usage and Population Statistics: World Internet Users and 2017 Population Stats," March 31, 2017–Update, http://www.internetworldstats.com/stats.htm (accessed August 14, 2017).

5. Steve Morgan, "Cyber Crime Costs Projected to Reach $2 Trillion by 2019," *Forbes*, January 17, 2016, https://www.forbes.com/sites/stevemorgan/2016/01/17/cyber-crime-costs-projected-to-reach-2-trillion-by-2019/#3f772b113a91 (accessed June 26, 2017).

6. Among the most recent laws is the Cybersecurity Information Sharing Act of 2015, incorporated into the Consolidated Appropriations Act of 2016, Public Law 114-113, 114th Cong., which was signed into law by President Barack Obama on December 18, 2015. See Brad S. Karp, "Federal Guidance on the Cybersecurity Information Sharing Act of 2015," Harvard Law School Forum on Corporate Governance and Financial Regulation, March 3, 2016, https://corpgov.law.harvard.edu/2016/03/03/federal-guidance-on-the-cybersecurity-information-sharing-act-of-2015/ (accessed July 5, 2017). Policies include a variety of executive orders, and important strategies include the May 2011 White House *International Strategy for Cyberspace* (see note 2, *supra*) and U.S. Department of Defense, *The DoD Cyber Strategy*, April 2015, https://www.defense.gov/Portals/1/features/2015/0415_cyber-strategy/Final_2015_DoD_CYBER_STRATEGY_for_web.pdf (accessed July 5, 2017).

7. Joanna Belbey, "The Weakest Link in Cybersecurity," *Forbes*, February 27, 2015, http://www.forbes.com/sites/joannabelbey/2015/02/27/the-weakest-link-in-cybersecurity/#38c0d3377410 (accessed June 26, 2017).

8. Brigadier General Jon T. Thomas, Deputy Director, Future Joint Force Development, Joint Staff, J7, "Joint Force Development: Moving from Concept to Reality," 2013, p. 10, http://www.dtic.mil/ndia/2013/expwar/WThomas.pdf (accessed July 11, 2017); "Q&A with Rear Adm. Kevin Scott," *CHIPS Magazine*, October–December 2015, http://www.doncio.navy.mil/chips/ArticleDetails.aspx?ID=6918 (accessed July 11, 2017); and U.S. Department of Defense, *Department of Defense Fiscal Year (FY) 2017 President's Budget Submission*, The Joint Staff, *Defense-Wide Justification Book Volume 5 of 5, Research, Development, Test & Evaluation, Defense-Wide*, February 2016, pp. 75–77, http://comptroller.defense.gov/Portals/45/Documents/defbudget/FY2017/budget_justification/pdfs/03_RDT_and_E/RDTE_MasterJustificationBook_Joint_Staff_PB_2017.pdf (accessed July 1, 2017).

9. Eleven out of 47 systems were operating without a valid cyber-certificate authorization. See Evan Perez and Tom LoBianco, "OPM Inspector General Questioned Over Hacking Report," CNN, updated June 17, 2015, http://www.cnn.com/2015/06/16/politics/opm-hack-ig-testimony/index.html (accessed June 26, 2017).

10. Ellen Nakashima, "Hacks of OPM Databases Compromised 22.1 Million People, Federal Authorities Say," *The Washington Post*, July 9, 2015, https://www.washingtonpost.com/news/federal-eye/wp/2015/07/09/hack-of-security-clearance-system-affected-21-5-million-people-federal-authorities-say (accessed June 26, 2017).

11. Kaspersky Lab, "Top 10 Tips for Educating Employees About Cybersecurity," 2015, http://go.kaspersky.com/rs/kaspersky1/images/Top_10_Tips_For_Educating_Employees_About_Cybersecurity_eBook.pdf?mkt_tok=3RkMMJWWfF9wsRonuKXNcO%2FhmjTEU5z16OglWa%2BzlMI%2F0ER3fOvrPUfGjI4ITMZjI%2BSLDwEYGJlv6SgFQrDHMalq1LgPXxE%3D (accessed July 5, 2017).

12. News release, "McAfee Labs Report Highlights Success of Phishing Attacks with 80 Percent of Business Users Unable to Detect Scams," McAfee, September 4, 2014, http://www.mcafee.com/us/about/news/2014/q3/20140904-01.aspx (accessed June 26, 2017).

13. Susan Richardson, "Leaky End Users Star in DBIR 2016," Data on the Edge, May 23, 2016, http://blog.code42.com/leaky-end-users-star-in-dbir-2016/ (accessed June 26, 2017).

14. Computer Emergency Response Team, "CERT Insider Threat Center," Carnegie Mellon University, Software Engineering Institute, 2017, http://www.cert.org/insider-threat/cert-insider-threat-center.cfm (accessed June 26, 2017).

15. News release, "U.S. Charges Five Chinese Military Hackers for Cyber Espionage Against U.S. Corporations and a Labor Organization for Commercial Advantage," U.S. Department of Justice, May 19, 2014, https://www.justice.gov/opa/pr/us-charges-five-chinese-military-hackers-cyber-espionage-against-us-corporations-and-labor (accessed July 5, 2017).

16. Kevin McCaney, "Report: US Suspects Russia in 'Most Sophisticated' Joint Staff Hack," Defense Systems, August 6, 2015, https://defensesystems.com/articles/2015/08/06/joint-staff-email-hack-most-sophisticated.aspx (accessed June 26, 2017).

17. Dominic Rushe, "OPM Hack: China Blamed for Massive Breach of US Government Data," *The Guardian*, June 5, 2015, https://www.theguardian.com/technology/2015/jun/04/us-government-massive-data-breach-employee-records-security-clearances (accessed June 26, 2017).

18. News release, "Joint Statement from the Department of Homeland Security and the Office of the Director of National Intelligence on Election Security," U.S. Department of Homeland Security, October 7, 2016, https://www.dhs.gov/news/2016/10/07/joint-statement-department-homeland-security-and-office-director-national (accessed June 26, 2017).

19. Anthony Cuthbertson, "Russian Cyber Attacks Aim to 'Destabilize' the West and NATO," *Newsweek*, February 3, 2017, http://www.newsweek.com/russian-cyber-attacks-hacking-nato-fallon-putin-destabilize-west-552050 (accessed June 26, 2017).

20. Ellen Nakashima and Matt Zapotosky, "U.S. Charges Iran-Linked Hackers with Targeting Banks, N.Y. Dam," *The Washington Post*, March 24, 2016, https://www.washingtonpost.com/world/national-security/justice-department-to-unseal-indictment-against-hackers-linked-to-iranian-goverment/2016/03/24/9b3797d2-f17b-11e5-a61f-e9c95c06edca_story.html?utm_term=.b0f47016466d (accessed June 26, 2017).

21. Reuters, "North Korean Hackers Were Behind a Recent Major Cyber Attack," *Fortune*, March 15, 2017, http://fortune.com/2017/03/15/north-korea-hackers-cyber-attack/ (accessed June 26, 2017), and Sean Lyngaas, "North Korean Hackers Steal F-15 Design," *FCW: The Business of Federal Technology*, June 13, 2016, https://fcw.com/articles/2016/06/13/north-korea-f15-lyngaas.aspx (accessed June 26, 2017).

22. Timothy Maurer, "Cyber Proxies and the Crisis in Ukraine," Chapter 9 in *Cyber War in Perspective: Russian Aggression Against Ukraine*, ed. Kenneth Geers (Talinn, Estonia: NATO CCD COE Publications, 2015), pp. 79–86, https://ccdcoe.org/sites/default/files/multimedia/pdf/CyberWarinPerspective_Maurer_09.pdf (accessed June 26, 2017).

23. Morgan, "Cyber Crime Costs Projected to Reach $2 Trillion by 2019."

24. G. Alexander Crowther and Shaheen Ghori, "Detangling the Web: A Screenshot of U.S. Government Cyber Activity," *Joint Force Quarterly*, Issue 78 (3rd Quarter 2015), pp. 75–83, http://ndupress.ndu.edu/Portals/68/Documents/jfq/jfq-78/jfq-78.pdf (accessed June 26, 2017).

25. Clorinda Trujillo, "The Limits of Cyberspace Deterrence," *Joint Force Quarterly*, Issue 75 (4th Quarter 2014), pp. 43–52, http://ndupress.ndu.edu/Media/News/News-Article-View/Article/577560/jfq-75-the-limits-of-cyberspace-deterrence/ (accessed June 26, 2017); Gerry Smith, "Stuxnet: U.S. Can Launch Cyberattacks But Not Defend Against Them, Experts Say," *Huffington Post*, June 1, 2012, http://www.huffingtonpost.com/2012/06/01/stuxnet-us-cyberattack_n_1562983.html (accessed June 26, 2017); and Jared Serbu, "Foreign Cyber Weapons 'Far Exceed' US Ability to Defend Critical Infrastructure, Defense Panel Says," Federal News Radio, March 7, 2017, https://federalnewsradio.com/dod-reporters-notebook-jared-serbu/2017/03/foreign-cyber-weapons-far-exceed-u-s-ability-defend-critical-infrastructure-defense-panel-says/ (accessed July 6, 2017).

26. This is not unique to cyber operations; it pertains to all such actions in all domains. An air strike intended to do one thing may generate a response that no one anticipated.

27. "Cyberspace," in U.S. Department of Defense, *DOD Dictionary of Military and Associated Terms*, June 2017, p. 60, http://www.dtic.mil/doctrine/new_pubs/dictionary.pdf (accessed July 6, 2017).

28. David Aucsmith, "Cyberspace Is a Domain of War," War in Cyberspace, May 26, 2012, https://cyberbelli.com/2012/05/26/cyberspace-is-a-domain-of-war/ (accessed July 6, 2017). For another point of view, see Martin C. Libicki, "Cyberspace Is Not a Warfighting Domain," *I/S: A Journal of Law and Policy for the Information Society*, Vol. 8, Issue 2 (2012), pp. 321–336, http://moritzlaw.osu.edu/students/groups/is/files/2012/02/4.Libicki.pdf (accessed June 26, 2017).

29. Military operations as used here include military or paramilitary operations that other security forces (such as the Italian Carabinieri) or intelligence forces (such as the CIA) could perform but are mainly military in nature.

30. Manoj Kumar, "Indian Navy Raises Army for Cyber Front: Recruiting Cadets Against Chinese Hackers," *International Business Times*, July 13, 2012, http://www.ibtimes.co.in/indian-navy-raises-army-for-cyber-front-recruiting-cadets-against-chinese-hackers-362686 (accessed June 26, 2017).

31. Wesley Fenlon, "How Does ATM Skimming Work?" HowStuffWorks, November 8, 2010, http://money.howstuffworks.com/atm-skimming.htm (accessed July 6, 2017).

32. Kim Zetter, "That Insane, $81M Bangladesh Bank Heist? Here's What We Know," *Wired*, May 17, 2016, https://www.wired.com/2016/05/insane-81m-bangladesh-bank-heist-heres-know/ (accessed June 26, 2017).

33. Spencer Ackerman and Sam Thielman, "US Officially Accuses Russia of Hacking DNC and Interfering with Election," *The Guardian*, October 8, 2016, https://www.theguardian.com/technology/2016/oct/07/us-russia-dnc-hack-interfering-presidential-election (accessed June 26, 2017).

34. Tom Hamburger and Karen Tumulty, "WikiLeaks Releases Thousands of Documents About Clinton and Internal Deliberations," *The Washington Post,* July 22, 2016, https://www.washingtonpost.com/news/post-politics/wp/2016/07/22/on-eve-of-democratic-convention-wikileaks-releases-thousands-of-documents-about-clinton-the-campaign-and-internal-deliberations/?utm_term=.c84944ed0527 (accessed June 26, 2017).

35. Andreas Hagen, "The Russo–Georgian War 2008: The Role of the Cyber Attacks in the Conflict," AFCEA Cyber Conflict Case Studies Essay Contest, Second Place Entry, May 24, 2012, http://www.afcea.org/committees/cyber/documents/TheRusso-GeorgianWar2008.pdf (accessed June 26, 2017).

36. Angel Rabasa, Robert D. Blackwill, Peter Chalk, Kim Cragin, C. Christine Fair, Brian A. Jackson, Brian Michael Jenkins, Seth G. Jones, Nathaniel Shestak, and Ashley J. Tellis, *The Lessons of Mumbai*, RAND Corporation, 2009, http://www.rand.org/pubs/occasional_papers/OP249.html (accessed July 6, 2017).

37. Colin Clark, "Carter Details Cyber, Intel Strikes Against Daesh at NORTHCOM Ceremony," *Breaking Defense*, May 13, 2016, http://breakingdefense.com/2016/05/carter-details-cyber-intel-strikes-against-daesh-at-northcom-ceremony/ (accessed June 26, 2017).

38. U.S. Department of Defense, Joint Chiefs of Staff, *Special Operations*, Joint Publication 3-05, July 16, 2014, p. I-1, http://www.dtic.mil/doctrine/new_pubs/jp3_05.pdf (accessed June 26, 2017).

39. U.S. Department of Defense, "Fact Sheet: DoD Cyber Crime Center (DC3)," http://www.dc3.mil/ (accessed July 6, 2017).

40. Nakashima and Zapotosky, "U.S. Charges Iran-Linked Hackers with Targeting Banks, N.Y. Dam."

41. Paul Thompson, "Semantic Hacking and Intelligence and Security Informatics," Conference Paper, International Conference on Intelligence and Security Informatics, Institute for Security Technology Studies, Dartmouth College, May 27, 2003, https://link.springer.com/chapter/10.1007/3-540-44853-5_40 (accessed June 26, 2017).

42. U.S. Department of Defense, Joint Chiefs of Staff, *Cyberspace Operations*, Joint Publication 3-12 (R), February 5, 2013, p. II-5, http://www.dtic.mil/doctrine/new_pubs/jp3_12R.pdf (accessed June 26, 2017).

43. Australian Government, Department of Defence, Australian Signals Directorate, "Strategies to Mitigate Cyber Security Incidents," February 2017, https://www.asd.gov.au/infosec/mitigationstrategies.htm (accessed July 5, 2017).

44. U.S. Department of Defense, *The DoD Cyber Strategy*, p. 3. Emphasis in original.

45. U.S. Department of Defense, "DOD 101: Overview of the Department of Defense," https://www.defense.gov/About/DoD-101/ (accessed June 26, 2017).

46. "The Defense Department procurement process can be confusing and complicated. There are a variety of contract types—each with its own pluses and minuses. The regulations can be daunting since they seem to be the size of the tax code. The competition for contracts can be fierce. There is a lot of paperwork." Michael Bame, "Overview of the DoD Procurement Process," ThoughtCo., updated August 10, 2016, https://www.thoughtco.com/overview-dod-procurement-process-1052245 (accessed June 26, 2017).

47. U.S. Department of Defense, Joint Chiefs of Staff, *Cyberspace Operations*, p. ix.

48. U.S. Department of Defense, *Department of Defense Strategy for Operating in Cyberspace*, July 2011, http://csrc.nist.gov/groups/SMA/ispab/documents/DOD-Strategy-for-Operating-in-Cyberspace.pdf (accessed July 5, 2017).

49. Andrew Feickert, "The Unified Command Plan and Combatant Commanders: Background and Issues for Congress," Congressional Research Service *Report for Congress*, January 3, 2013, http://fas.org/sgp/crs/natsec/R42077.pdf (accessed July 5, 2017).

50. Rita Boland, "Command's Cybersecurity Crosses Domains, Directorates," *Signal*, June 1, 2013, www.acyberstrategufcea.org/content/?q=command%E2%80%99s-cybersecurity%E2%80%A8-crosses-domains-directorates (accessed June 26, 2017).

51. U.S. Strategic Command, "U.S. Cyber Command (USCYBERCOM)," September 30, 2016, http://www.stratcom.mil/Media/Factsheets/Factsheet-View/Article/960492/us-cyber-command-uscybercom/ (accessed June 26, 2017).

52. Crowther and Ghori, "Detangling the Web."

53. U.S. Department of Defense, *The DoD Cyber Strategy*.

54. Ibid.

Global Operating Environment

Assessing the Global Operating Environment

Measuring the "strength" of a military force—the extent to which that force can accomplish missions—requires examination of the environments in which the force operates. Aspects of one environment may facilitate military operations, but aspects of another may work against them. A favorable operating environment presents the U.S. military with obvious advantages; an unfavorable operating environment may limit the effect of U.S. military power. The capabilities and assets of U.S. allies, the strength of foes, the geopolitical environment of the region, and the availability of forward facilities and logistics infrastructure all factor into whether an operating environment is one that can support U.S. military operations.

When assessing an operating environment, one must pay particular attention to any treaty obligations the United States has with countries in the region. A treaty defense obligation ensures that the legal framework is in place for the U.S. to maintain and operate a military presence in a particular country. In addition, a treaty partner usually yields regular training exercises and interoperability as well as political and economic ties.

Additional factors—including the military capabilities of allies that might be useful to U.S. military operations; the degree to which the U.S. and allied militaries in the region are interoperable (e.g., can use common means of command, communication, and other systems); and whether the U.S. maintains key bilateral alliances with nations in the region—also affect the operating environment. Likewise, nations where the U.S. has already stationed assets or permanent bases and countries from which the U.S. has launched military operations in the past may provide needed support to future U.S. military operations. The relationships and knowledge gained through any of these factors would undoubtedly ease future U.S. military operations in a region and contribute greatly to a positive operating environment.

In addition to U.S. defense relations within a region, additional criteria—including the quality of the local infrastructure, the political stability of the area, whether or not a country is embroiled in any conflicts, and the degree to which a nation is economically free—should also be considered.

Each of these factors contributes to the judgment as to whether a particular operating environment is favorable or unfavorable to future U.S. military operations. The operating environment assessment is meant to add critical context to complement the threat environment assessment and U.S. military assessment detailed in subsequent sections of the *Index*.

This *Index* will refer to all disputed territories by the name employed by the United States Department of State and should not be seen as reflecting a position on any of these disputes.

Europe

After nearly a decade of attempted disengagement, the United States is beginning to reinvest military capability and political strength in Europe. The resurgence of Russia, brought into starkest relief in Ukraine, and the continued fight against the (IS) in Iraq, Syria, and Libya brought Europe back into the top tier of U.S. international interests. It is clear why the region matters to the U.S. The 51 countries in the U.S. European Command (EUCOM) area of responsibility include approximately one-fifth of the world's population, 10.7 million square miles of land, and 13 million square miles of ocean.

Additionally, some of America's oldest (France) and closest (the United Kingdom) allies are found in Europe. The U.S. and Europe share a strong commitment to the rule of law, human rights, free markets, and democracy. Many of these ideas, the foundations on which America was built, were brought over by the millions of immigrants from Europe in the 17th, 18th, and 19th centuries. U.S. sacrifice for Europe has been dear. During the 20th century, millions of Americans fought for a free and secure Europe, and hundreds of thousands died.

America's economic ties to the region are likewise important. A stable, secure, and economically viable Europe is in America's economic interest. Regional security means economic viability and prosperity for both Europe and the U.S. For more than 70 years, the U.S. military presence in Europe has contributed to European stability, economically benefiting both Europeans and Americans. The economies of the 28 (soon to be 27[1]) member states of the European Union (EU), along with the United States, account for approximately half of the global economy. The U.S. and the members of the EU are each other's principal trading partners.

Geographical Proximity. Europe is important to the U.S. because of its geographical proximity to some of the world's most dangerous and contested regions. From the eastern Atlantic Ocean to the Middle East and up to the Caucasus through Russia and into the Arctic, Europe is ringed by an arc of instability. The European region also has some of the world's most vital shipping lanes, energy resources, and trade choke points. Thus, European basing for U.S. forces provides the ability to respond robustly and quickly to challenges to U.S. interests in and near the region.

The Arctic. The *2017 Index of U.S. Military Strength* identified the Arctic as an important operating environment in Europe. This has not changed in the 2018 edition. If anything, Russian activity continues to increase tensions, while the U.S. remains poorly positioned to counter Russia's military buildup.

The Arctic region encompasses the lands and territorial waters of eight countries (Canada, Denmark, Finland, Iceland, Norway, Russia, Sweden, and the United States) spread across three continents. The region is home to some of the world's roughest terrain and waters and some of its harshest weather. The Arctic region is rich in minerals, wildlife, fish, and other natural resources and—importantly—hydrocarbons. Estimates that the region contains up to 13 percent of the world's undiscovered oil reserves and almost one-third of its undiscovered natural gas reserves may be low. In April

2017, the Norwegian Petroleum Directorate announced that the amount of undiscovered oil and gas in the Barents Sea is likely to be twice as large as previously estimated.[2]

The region represents one of the world's least populated areas, with sparse nomadic communities and very few large cities and towns. Although official population figures are nonexistent, the Nordic Council of Ministers estimates that the figure in 2013 was slightly in excess of 4 million,[3] making the Arctic's population slightly bigger than Oregon's and slightly smaller than Kentucky's. Approximately half of the Arctic population lives in Russia, which is ranked 114th ("mostly unfree") out of 180 countries in the *2017 Index of Economic Freedom*.[4]

The melting of Arctic ice during the summer months presents challenges for the U.S. in terms of Arctic security, but it also provides new opportunities for economic development. Less ice will mean new shipping lanes, increased tourism, and further exploration for natural resources. Many of the shipping lanes currently used in the Arctic are a considerable distance from search and rescue facilities, and natural resource exploration that would be considered routine in other locations is complex, costly, and dangerous in the Arctic.

The economic incentives for exploiting these shipping lanes are substantial and will drive Arctic nations to press their interests in the region. For example, using the Northern Sea Route (NSR) along the Russian coast cuts the distance between Rotterdam and Shanghai by 22 percent and saves hundreds of thousands of dollars in fuel costs per ship, especially when oil prices are high. Unlike in the Gulf of Aden, no pirates are currently operating in the Arctic, and piracy is unlikely to be a problem in the future.

There is still a long way to go, however, before the NSR becomes a viable option. In 2016, 19 ships made the journey over the top of Russia,[5] compared with the more than 16,833 that transited the Suez Canal,[6] and carried only 214,513 tons of cargo.[7] The NSR did see an increase in ships and cargo tonnage from 2015–2016, but volume remains well below the volume of just a few years ago. In 2013, 71 vessels carrying a total of 1,355,000 tons of cargo shipped along the route, indicating the unpredictability of future shipping trends in the Arctic.[8] While shipments between Asian and European ports across the NSR remain minimal, shipments between ports along the NSR in 2016 were 35 percent higher than they were in 2015.[9]

In June 2015, Russia adopted an Integrated Development Plan for the Northern Sea Route 2015–2030. The plan outlines expectations that NSR shipping volume will reach 80 million tons by 2030.[10] Although the current reality casts doubt on these projections, Russia considers the Arctic to be a region of special value and has accorded it high priority, going so far in 2016 as to give the Federal Security Service (FSB) full control of law enforcement activities along the NSR.[11]

The U.S. has an interest in stability and security in the Arctic because the U.S. is one of the eight Arctic nations. The American commitment to NATO is also relevant because four of the five Arctic littoral powers are in NATO.[12] The U.S., however, is not well positioned in the region. According to Admiral Paul Zukunft, Commandant of the U.S. Coast Guard, "if you look at this Arctic game of chess, if you will, [the Russians have] got us at checkmate, right from the very beginning if it does become a militarized domain."[13] The importance that each country places on operating in the Arctic is illustrated by the fact that Russia maintains a fleet of nearly 40 polar icebreakers, six of which are nuclear powered, while the U.S. Coast Guard sails only two—one of which is over 40 years old.[14]

Threats to Internal Stability. In recent years, Europe has faced turmoil and instability brought about by continued sluggish growth, high government debt, high unemployment, the threat of terrorist attacks, and a massive influx of migrants. Political fragmentation resulting from these pressures and disparate views on how to solve them threaten to erode stability even further.

Russia has sought to seed and inflame discord by weaponizing migrant flows. Former EUCOM Commander General Philip Breedlove said in 2016 that by intentionally targeting civilians in Syria, "Russia and the Assad regime are deliberately weaponizing migration in an attempt to overwhelm European structures and break European resolve."[15] The migrant crisis was partly a result of Russian actions, and the humanitarian, political, security, and societal ripples are only beginning to extend outward. Denmark's Defense Minister has underscored how Russian efforts to sow political fragmentation work: "[The Russians] know about internal relations between different NATO countries and are good at fingering sore points."[16]

Economic freedom in the eurozone is seriously undermined by the excessive government spending needed to support elaborate welfare states. Many eurozone countries pursue economic policies that hinder productivity growth and job creation, causing economic stagnation and rapidly increasing levels of public debt. Underperforming countries have not made the structural reforms needed for long-term adjustment. When asked to judge the current state of their national economies, 56 percent of respondents in the EU and 60 percent of respondents in the eurozone characterized it as "totally bad."[17] Investors are also pessimistic; a recent survey found that "one out of four investors now believes that at least one euro zone member state will quit the single currency in the next 12 months."[18] European leaders are desperately seeking a way to keep the eurozone together without addressing the root causes of the crisis.

Many among Europe's political elite believe that deeper European integration, not prudent economic policies, is the answer to Europe's problem, but there has been a public backlash against deeper political and economic integration across much of Europe. In a June 2016 referendum on EU membership, the United Kingdom voted to leave the European Union. In April 2016, Dutch voters voted against approving an EU–Ukraine Association agreement in a countrywide referendum, largely seen as a protest vote against the EU. Dissatisfaction with the EU is also evident in France where about half of its voters cast their ballots in the first round of presidential elections for candidates espousing anti-EU views. In the second round, 9 percent cast a blank ballot (a protest vote), the highest level in the history of the Fifth Republic.[19] This outcome is hardly surprising; according to a 2016 Eurobarometer Poll, only 29 percent of people in France have a wholly positive view of the EU, and 31 percent have a negative view.[20]

In 2016, the eurozone grew by 1.8 percent,[21] a rate virtually unchanged from 2015's 1.7 percent. As slow recovery has taken hold, the manufacturing sector is performing especially well.[22] Growth and employment disparities, however, remain problematic. Unemployment across the 19-country bloc stands at 9.5 percent, the lowest rate since January 2009 but still very high. Greece has the highest unemployment rate in the EU: 23.1 percent; Spain's is 18.0 percent. And youth unemployment in the eurozone is 19.4 percent but reaches 45.2 percent in Greece, 41.5 percent in Spain, 35.2 percent in Italy, 28.8 percent in Croatia, and 25.4 percent in Portugal.[23]

In addition, Europe's banking sector is burdened by $1.2 trillion in nonperforming loans—three times the amount held by the U.S. banking sector.[24] The Italian banking sector's woes are especially troubling. In February, Italy's Parliament approved a law giving $21 billion in taxpayer money to help prop up troubled banks.[25] The interconnectedness of the global economy and global financial system means that any new economic crisis in Europe will have profound impacts in the U.S. as well.

Since 2015, the continent has also had to deal with a large migrant crisis. Conflicts in Syria and Iraq, as well as open-door policies adopted by several European nations—importantly, Germany and Sweden in 2015—led large numbers of migrants from across Africa, Asia, and the Middle East to travel to Europe in search of safety, economic opportunity, and the benefits of Europe's most generous welfare states. While a tenuous agreement with Turkey in March 2016 has largely capped migrant flows through the Balkans and Greece, arrivals have not stopped altogether. Rather, they have decreased and shifted to a different theater.

In the first three months of 2017, over 20,000 migrants arrived in Europe via the Mediterranean Sea, 80 percent landing in Italy.[26] This represents a significant drop from the first three months of 2016, when over 160,000 migrants arrived via the Mediterranean, yet the numbers are still significant. Instability in Libya, significant flows of migrants traveling from sub-Saharan Africa, and the relative closure of the route to Europe through Turkey mean that flows from North Africa are currently the primary route for migrants arriving in Europe. According to the EU's Frontex border agency, "While the number of migrants from Asia and the Middle East decreased, 2016 was marked with an increase in migratory pressure from Africa, in particular on the route from Libya to Italy." Frontex also notes that although 2016 saw a decrease in illegal border crossings from the previous year, the 511,371 detections of illegal border crossings in 2016 remains well above the 282,933 in 2014, the year before the migrant crisis began in earnest.[27]

The migrant crisis and the response of European governments have led to some increased instability. They have buoyed fringe political parties in some European nations and already have imposed financial, security, and societal costs. In Germany, for example, the Federal Ministry of Finance expects to spend over $86 billion from 2017–2020 "feeding, housing and training refugees as well as helping their home countries to stem the flow."[28] The Swedish government will spend at least €6.1 billion (approximately $7.9 billion) a year on migrants until 2020, well above initial estimates.[29]

The migrant crisis has had a direct impact on NATO resources as well. In February 2016, Germany, Greece, and Turkey requested NATO assistance to deal with illegal trafficking and illegal migration in the Aegean Sea.[30] That month, NATO's Standing Maritime Group 2 deployed to the Aegean to conduct surveillance, monitoring, and reconnaissance of smuggling activities, and the intelligence gathered was sent on to the Greek and Turkish coast guards and to Frontex.[31]

Europe has also faced a series of terrorist attacks over the past year including a Christmas market attack in Berlin and high-profile attacks in London, Nice, and Stockholm. In May, the U.S. Department of State took the rare step of issuing a travel alert for all of Europe, citing the persistent threat from terrorism.[32] Although terrorist attacks may not pose an existential threat to Europe, they do affect security and undermine U.S. allies by increasing instability, forcing nations to spend more financial and military resources on counterterrorism operations, and jeopardizing the safety of U.S. servicemembers, their families, and U.S. facilities overseas. In April 2016, for example, an IS sympathizer was convicted in the United Kingdom of planning to carry out terrorist attacks on U.S. military personnel stationed in the U.K.[33]

U.S. Returning to Europe. Continued Russian aggression in Ukraine and more aggressive air and naval patrolling incidents in the Baltic Sea region have caused the U.S. to turn its attention back to Europe and reinvest military capabilities on the continent. General Curtis M. Scaparrotti, Supreme Allied Commander and EUCOM Commander, has described the change as "returning to our historic role as a warfighting command focused on deterrence and defense."[34] In April 2014, the U.S. launched Operation Atlantic Resolve (OAR), a series of actions meant to reassure U.S. allies in Europe, particularly those bordering Russia. Under OAR, the U.S. returned a rotational armored brigade combat team (BCT) in January 2017. Moving 4,000 soldiers and 90 tanks back to Europe for a scheduled nine-month deployment exposed some logistics shortcomings.[35] Units from the BCT deployed to Bulgaria, Germany, Poland, Romania, and initially to the Baltic States.[36] Major General Timothy McGuire, Deputy Commanding General, U.S. Army Europe, characterized the deployment as "a tangible sign of the United

States' commitment to maintaining peace on this continent."[37] The BCT's training with allies included taking part in the Saber Guardian 17 exercises, which consisted of 40,000 troops from over 20 nations.[38]

It is important to note that basing limitations and the cost of permanently stationing large units overseas (especially when accompanied by families) led the Army to adopt a heel-to-toe rotational policy, according to which an armor brigade will arrive to replace one going back to the U.S. so that there is no break in coverage. The first iterations of this new policy revealed how much had been forgotten about the skills needed to execute such a deployment. Before its anticipated deployment in September 2017, for example, Dagger Brigade reportedly faced both equipment and manpower issues that made preparing for deployment especially challenging.[39]

In addition to back-to-back rotations of armor, the U.S. deployed an Aviation Brigade consisting of 2,200 soldiers and 86 aircraft for a nine-month rotation beginning in February 2017.[40] Based in Germany, the aviation brigade forward deployed five Black Hawks and 50 troops to Lielvarde Air Base in Latvia and five Black Hawks and 50 troops to Mihail Kogalniceanu Air Base in Romania. In April, eight F-35As deployed overseas for the first time to the U.K. for month-long training and maneuvers with British and Dutch forces.[41] At the end of April, two F-35s arrived at Amari airbase in Estonia for exercises.[42] The same month, a training deployment brought two F-35s to Bulgaria.[43] According to General Scaparrotti, the F-35 deployment "shows we are serious about territorial integrity and will defend our interests with the most advanced capabilities our nation has to offer."[44]

The U.S. Army has prepositioned additional equipment across Europe as part of Operation Atlantic Resolve. A prepositioning site in Eygelshoven, Netherlands, opened in December 2016 and will store 1,600 vehicles including "M1 Abrams Tanks, M109 Paladin Self-Propelled Howitzers and other armored and support vehicles."[45] A second site in Dülmen,

Germany, opened in May 2017 and will hold equipment for an artillery brigade.[46] Other prepositioning sites include Zutendaal, Belgium; Miesau, Germany; and Powidz, Poland. The Polish site, which has been selected by the Army for prepositioned armor and artillery, is expected to cost $200 million (funded by NATO) and will open in 2021.[47]

The naval component of OAR has consisted in part of increased deployments of U.S. ships to the Baltic and Black Seas. Additionally, the Navy has taken part in bilateral and NATO exercises. For example, BALTOPS 2016, the 44th iteration of exercises across the Baltic Sea region, involved more than 5,000 personnel, 43 ships, and more than 60 aircraft from Belgium, Denmark, Estonia, Finland, France, Germany, Italy, Latvia, Lithuania, the Netherlands, Norway, Poland, Portugal, Spain, Sweden, the United Kingdom, and the United States.[48]

In June 2014, in an effort to bolster OAR's transatlantic security measures, the U.S. announced a $1 billion European Reassurance Initiative (ERI). For fiscal year (FY) 2017, the Obama Administration proposed that ERI funding be increased to $3.4 billion,[49] but a continuing resolution (CR) for FY 2017 hampered some ERI efforts and fostered uncertainty. A practical example is the addition of a 30mm cannon to Stryker vehicles. The upgraded vehicles for the "dragoons" resulted from a recognition that Russian upgrades have placed U.S. forces at an "unacceptable risk" without the cannon upgrade.[50] However, ammunition for the cannon is considered a new program and cannot be started under a CR. Colonel Glenn Dean, Program Manager for the Army's Stryker brigade combat team at Program Executive Office Ground Combat Systems, warned in April that "if the CR does not lift next month I will not have combat ammunition when I field that vehicle next year."[51] A budget request submitted in May sought $4.8 billion in ERI funds, an increase of $1.4 billion.[52]

Testifying in March 2017, General Scaparrotti was clear about the importance of ERI funding for returning to a posture of deterrence:

Thanks in large measure to ERI, over the last 12 months EUCOM has made demonstrable progress. U.S. tanks have returned to European soil. U.S. F-15s and F-22s have demonstrated air dominance throughout the theater. U.S. naval forces have sailed throughout European waters. EUCOM has operationalized its Joint Cyber Center. With the approval of former Secretary [Ashton] Carter, EUCOM delivered the first new operational plan for the defense of Europe in over 25 years.

ERI also supports high-end exercises and training, improved infrastructure, and enhanced prepositioning of equipment and supplies, while State Department and DOD funds build partner capacity throughout Europe.[53]

EUCOM states that ERI funding in 2017 will expand the scope of the "28 joint and multinational exercises, which annually train more than 18,000 U.S. personnel alongside 45,000 NATO Allies and Partnership for Peace personnel across 40 countries."[54] In 2016, the U.S. Air Force alone took part in 50 exercises and training deployments in the region.[55] In April 2017, U.S. F-22s and F-35s exercised in Virginia with Royal Air Force Typhoons and French Rafales to improve air combat integration involving advanced aircraft.[56] In June, U.S., British, Polish, Lithuanian, and Croatian troops taking part in Saber Strike 17 exercised securing the Suwalki Gap for the first time.[57]

The combat training center at Hohenfels, Germany, is one of a very few located outside of the continental United States at which large-scale combined-arms exercises can be conducted, and more than 60,000 U.S. and allied personnel train there annually. U.S.–European training exercises further advance U.S. interests by developing links between America's allies in Europe and National Guard units back in the U.S. At a time when most American servicemembers do not recall World War II or the Cold War, cementing bonds with allies in Europe is a vital task. Currently, 22 nations in Europe have a state partner in the U.S. National Guard.[58]

In addition to training with fellow NATO member states, the U.S. Joint Multinational Training Group–Ukraine (JMTG–U) will train up to five Ukrainian battalions a year through 2020.[59] Canada, Estonia, Latvia, Lithuania, and the U.K. also participate in JMTG-U.[60] The U.S. also participates in the Ukrainian-hosted peacekeeping exercise Rapid Trident and the naval exercise Sea Breeze, held in the Black Sea.[61]

Nevertheless, U.S. commanders still do not have everything they need for proper deterrence. General Scaparrotti has testified that "I need intelligence, surveillance and reconnaissance in greater numbers than I have now because to deter properly I have to be able to have a good base line of Russia, in particular, so I know when things change and can posture my forces properly."[62] Because Russian exercises could provide cover for a planned invasion, the U.S. increased its presence in the Baltic region during Russia's planned Zapad exercises in September, including taking over air policing, positioning more ships in the Baltic Sea, and potentially deploying a Patriot missile battery temporarily to Lithuania.[63]

There also are nonmilitary threats to the territorial integrity of NATO countries that the alliance has only recently begun to find ways to address. The most likely threat may come not from Russian tanks rolling into a country but from Russian money, propaganda, and establishment of pro-Russia NGOs and other advocacy groups, all of which can be leveraged to undermine a state. Russia's aggressive actions in Ukraine have proven how effective these asymmetrical methods can be in creating instability, especially when coupled with conventional power projection.

U.S. Nuclear Weapons in Europe. The U.S. maintains tactical nuclear weapons in Europe. It is believed that until the end of the Cold War, the U.S. maintained approximately 2,500 nuclear warheads in Europe. Unofficial estimates put the current figure at between 150 and 200 warheads based in Italy, Turkey, Germany, Belgium, and the Netherlands.[64]

All of these weapons are free-fall gravity bombs designed for use with U.S. and allied dual-capable aircraft. The bombs are undergoing a Life Extension Program that it is anticipated will add at least 20 years to their life span.[65] In March 2017, the U.S. carried out a successful test of a new B61-12 gravity bomb, which Paul Waugh, Director of Air-Delivered Capabilities at the Air Force's nuclear division, says "ensures the current capability for the air-delivered leg of the US strategic nuclear triad well into the future for both bombers and dual-capable aircraft supporting North Atlantic Treaty Organization (NATO)."[66]

In addition, NATO is a nuclear alliance. According to its July 2016 Warsaw Summit Communiqué:

> The circumstances in which NATO might have to use nuclear weapons are extremely remote. If the fundamental security of any of its members were to be threatened however, NATO has the capabilities and resolve to impose costs on an adversary that would be unacceptable and far outweigh the benefits that an adversary could hope to achieve.[67]

Important Alliances and Bilateral Relations in Europe

The United States has a number of important multilateral and bilateral relationships in Europe. First and foremost is NATO, the world's most important and arguably most successful defense alliance, but other relationships also have a significant impact on the ability of the U.S. to operate in and through the European region.

The North Atlantic Treaty Organization. NATO is an intergovernmental, multilateral security organization originally designed to defend Western Europe from the Soviet Union. It is the organization that anchored the U.S. firmly in Europe, solidified Western resolve during the Cold War, and rallied European support following the terrorist attacks on 9/11. Since its creation in 1949, NATO has been the bedrock of transatlantic security cooperation, and it is likely to remain so for the foreseeable future.

Beginning in 2002, when alliance operations began in Afghanistan, NATO turned its focus toward out-of-area operations, including counterpiracy operations off the Horn of Africa and an intervention in Libya that led to the toppling of Muammar Qadhafi. More recently, Russian aggression has led to a recent renewed focus within NATO on collective defense alongside moderate increases in defense spending for some European NATO members.

NATO continues to refocus on collective defense, while some voices within the alliance are arguing for a greater focus on counterterrorism.[68] In February 2016, at the request of Germany, Greece, and Turkey, NATO's Standing NATO Maritime Group 2 (SNMG2) deployed to the Aegean Sea to help stop illicit trafficking in people, drugs, weapons, and other contraband in the Mediterranean. In October 2016, NATO's Operation Active Endeavor, created in 2011, was terminated and was succeeded by Operation Sea Guardian, which has a mission of "maritime situational awareness, counterterrorism and capacity building."[69]

Despite the ongoing debate within the alliance over the degree of threat posed by migrant flows and illicit activity in the Mediterranean Sea versus that of Russian aggression, it is clear that NATO continues to view Russia as a threat.[70]

The shift back to collective defense began at the 2014 Wales summit, when the alliance introduced a Readiness Action Plan (RAP) to reassure nervous member states and put in motion "longer-term changes to NATO's forces and command structure so that the Alliance will be better able to react swiftly and decisively to sudden crises."[71] As part of the RAP, following the 2014 Wales summit, NATO announced the creation of a Very High Readiness Joint Task Force (VJTF), "a new Allied joint force that will be able to deploy within a few days to respond to challenges that arise, particularly at the periphery of NATO's territory."[72] A rotational plan for the VJTF's land component was established to maintain this capability through 2023.[73] The VJTF also represents a significant improvement in deployment time. Part of the VJTF can deploy within 48 hours, a marked improvement over the month the VJTF's predecessor, the Immediate Response Force, needed to deploy.[74] According

CHART 1

Few NATO Members Follow Defense Spending Guidelines

NATO members are expected to spend at least 2 percent of their GDP on defense, and at least 20 percent of their defense spending is supposed to go to equipment. Only four of the 28 countries—the U.S., the U.K., Poland, and Romania—do both.

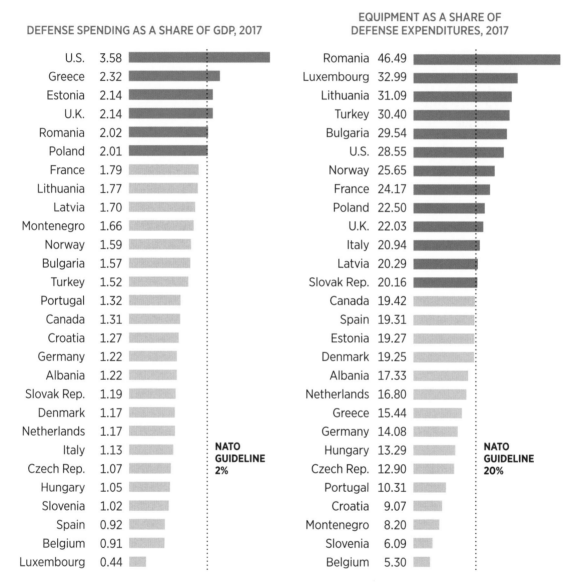

DEFENSE SPENDING AS A SHARE OF GDP, 2017

U.S.	3.58
Greece	2.32
Estonia	2.14
U.K.	2.14
Romania	2.02
Poland	2.01
France	1.79
Lithuania	1.77
Latvia	1.70
Montenegro	1.66
Norway	1.59
Bulgaria	1.57
Turkey	1.52
Portugal	1.32
Canada	1.31
Croatia	1.27
Germany	1.22
Albania	1.22
Slovak Rep.	1.19
Denmark	1.17
Netherlands	1.17
Italy	1.13
Czech Rep.	1.07
Hungary	1.05
Slovenia	1.02
Spain	0.92
Belgium	0.91
Luxembourg	0.44

NATO GUIDELINE 2%

EQUIPMENT AS A SHARE OF DEFENSE EXPENDITURES, 2017

Romania	46.49
Luxembourg	32.99
Lithuania	31.09
Turkey	30.40
Bulgaria	29.54
U.S.	28.55
Norway	25.65
France	24.17
Poland	22.50
U.K.	22.03
Italy	20.94
Latvia	20.29
Slovak Rep.	20.16
Canada	19.42
Spain	19.31
Estonia	19.27
Denmark	19.25
Albania	17.33
Netherlands	16.80
Greece	15.44
Germany	14.08
Hungary	13.29
Czech Rep.	12.90
Portugal	10.31
Croatia	9.07
Montenegro	8.20
Slovenia	6.09
Belgium	5.30

NATO GUIDELINE 20%

NOTES: Figures are estimates for 2017 based on 2010 prices and exchange rates. Iceland is not listed because it has no military.
SOURCE: NATO, "Defence Expenditures of NATO Countries (2010–2017)," June 29, 2017, p. 3, http://www.nato.int/nato_static_fl2014/assets/pdf/pdf_2017_06/20170629_170629-pr2017-111-en.pdf (accessed July 25, 2017).

☏ heritage.org

to an assessment published by the Norwegian Institute of International Affairs, the entire NATO Response Force (NRF), of which the VJTF is a part, will undergo "a much more rigorous and demanding training program than the old NRF. Future NRF rotations will see many more snap-exercises and short notice inspections."[75]

This does not mean, however, that the VJTF and NRF are without their problems. For instance, NATO reportedly believes that the VJTF would be too vulnerable during its deployment phase to be utilized in Poland or the Baltics.[76] Another concern is the 26,000 Initial Follow-on Forces Group (IFFG), which makes up the rest of the NRF and would deploy following the VJTF. The IFFG reportedly would need 30–45 days to deploy in the event of a conflict.[77]

The centerpiece of NATO's renewed focus on collective defense is the four multinational battalions stationed in Poland and the Baltic States as part of the alliance's Enhanced Forward Presence (EFP). In Estonia, the United Kingdom serves as the framework nation, with contributions from France in 2017 and Denmark in 2018. In Latvia, Canada is the framework nation, with Albania, Italy, Poland, Slovenia, Slovakia,[78] and Spain providing contributions. Germany serves as the framework nation in Lithuania, with contributions from Belgium, Luxembourg, the Netherlands, Norway, and Croatia and France beginning in 2018. In Poland, the United States serves as the framework nation, with Romania and the United Kingdom contributing troops.[79] EFP troops are under NATO command and control; a multinational divisional headquarters will be created in Elblag, Poland, to coordinate the battalions.[80] In February, the Baltic States signed an agreement to facilitate the movement of NATO forces among the countries.[81]

At its July 2016 Warsaw Summit, NATO agreed to create a multinational framework brigade based in Craiova, Romania, under the control of Headquarters Multinational Division Southeast.[82] In February 2017, following a defense minister–level meeting of the North Atlantic Council, NATO Secretary General Jens Stoltenberg announced that "[e]ight Allies have committed to provide brigade staff. And five Allies have committed land and air forces for training and air policing." Stoltenberg also announced new maritime measures that include "an increased NATO naval presence in the Black Sea for enhanced training, exercises and situational awareness, and a maritime coordination function for our Standing Naval Forces when operating with other Allied forces in the Black Sea region."[83] In April 2017, four Royal Air Force Typhoons arrived in Romania for a four-month air policing deployment.[84]

Another key area in which NATO is seeking to bolster its capabilities is development of a robust response to increasing cyber threats and threats from space. NATO has expressed plans to spend $3.24 billion "to upgrade its satellite and computer technology over the next three years."[85]

The broad threat that Russia poses to Europe's common interests makes military-to-military cooperation, interoperability, and overall preparedness for joint warfighting especially important in Europe, yet they are not uniformly implemented. For example, day-to-day interaction between U.S. and allied officer corps and joint preparedness exercises have been more regular with Western European militaries than with frontier allies in Central Europe, although the crisis in Ukraine has led to new exercises with eastern NATO nations. In the event of a national security crisis in Europe, first contact with an adversary might still expose America's lack of familiarity with allied warfighting capabilities, doctrines, and operational methods.

Ballistic Missile Defense. At the Warsaw summit, NATO announced the initial operating capability of the Ballistic Missile Defense (BMD) system.[86] An Aegis Ashore site in Deveselu, Romania, became operational in May 2016.[87] Other components include a forward-based early-warning BMD radar at Kürecik, Turkey; BMD-capable U.S. Aegis ships forward deployed at Rota, Spain;[88] and a second Aegis Ashore site in Redzikowo, Poland, which broke

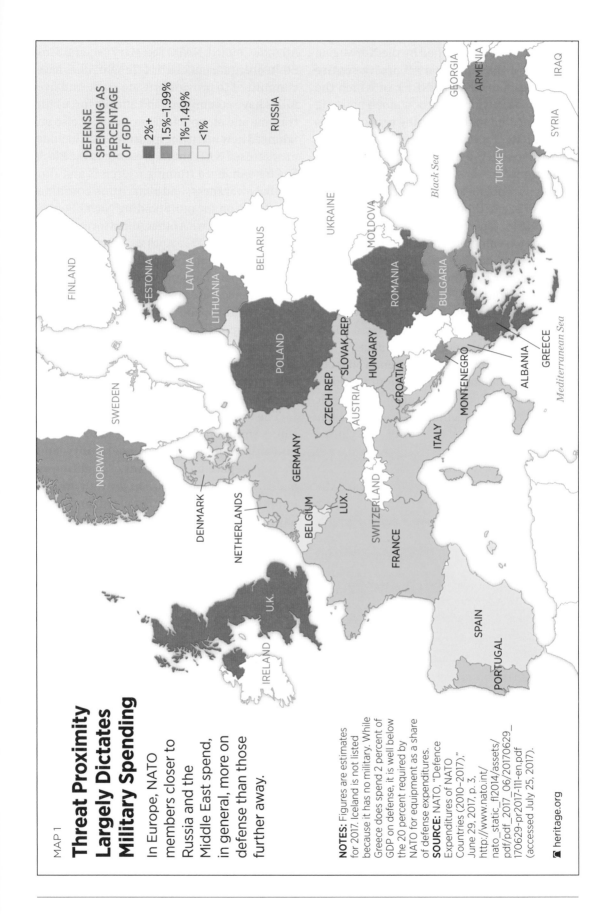

MAP 1

Threat Proximity Largely Dictates Military Spending

In Europe, NATO members closer to Russia and the Middle East spend, in general, more on defense than those further away.

DEFENSE SPENDING AS PERCENTAGE OF GDP

- 2%+
- 1.5%–1.99%
- 1%–1.49%
- <1%

NOTES: Figures are estimates for 2017. Iceland is not listed because it has no military. While Greece does spend 2 percent of GDP on defense, it is well below the 20 percent required by NATO for equipment as a share of defense expenditures.
SOURCE: NATO, "Defence Expenditures of NATO Countries (2010–2017)," June 29, 2017, p. 3, http://www.nato.int/nato_static_fl2014/assets/pdf/pdf_2017_06/20170629_170629-pr2017-111-en.pdf (accessed July 25, 2017).

⬛ heritage.org

ground in May 2016 and is expected to be operational next year.[89] Ramstein Air Base in Germany hosts a command and control center.[90]

In January, the Russian embassy in Norway threatened that if the country contributes ships or radar to NATO BMD, Russia "will have to react to defend our security."[91] Denmark, which agreed in 2014 to equip at least one frigate with radar to contribute to NATO BMD and made further progress in 2016 toward this goal, was threatened by Russia's ambassador in Copenhagen, who stated, "I do not believe that Danish people fully understand the consequences of what may happen if Denmark joins the American-led missile defense system. If Denmark joins, Danish warships become targets for Russian nuclear missiles."[92]

In 2011, the Netherlands announced "plans to upgrade four air-defense frigates with extended long-range missile defense early-warning radars."[93] A decision on a BMD upgrade path for Dutch *Iver Huitfeldt*-class frigates is expected next year according to Chief of the Naval Staff Rear Admiral Frank Trojahn.[94] In December 2016, the German Navy announced plans to upgrade radar on three F124 *Sachsen*-class frigates in order to contribute sea-based radar to NATO BMD.[95] In November 2015, the U.K. stated that it plans to build new ground-based BMD radar as a contribution.[96] It also has been reported that Belgium intends to procure M-class frigates that "will be able to engage ex-atmospheric ballistic missiles."[97] Belgium and the Netherlands are jointly procuring the frigates, although the Dutch position on BMD capabilities is not entirely clear. NATO BMD is expected to be fully operational by 2025.[98]

Quality of Armed Forces in the Region

As an intergovernmental security alliance, NATO is only as strong as its member states. Of NATO's 29 members, 27 are European. European countries collectively have more than 2 million men and women in uniform, yet by some estimates, only 100,000 of them—a mere 5 percent—have the capability to deploy beyond their national borders.[99]

A 2017 RAND report found that France, Germany, and the U.K. would face difficulty in quickly deploying armored brigades to the Baltics in the event of a crisis. The report concludes that getting "deployments up to brigade strength would take...a few weeks in the French case and possibly more than a month in the British or German case" and that "[a] single armored brigade each appears to represent a maximum sustainable effort. There are also questions regarding their ability to operate at the level required for a conflict with the Russians, whether because of training cutbacks, neglected skills, or limited organic support capabilities." The report further states that "the faster British, French, and German forces needed to get to the Baltics, the more direct assistance they would need from the United States in the form of strategic airlift."[100]

Article 3 of the 1949 North Atlantic Treaty, NATO's founding document, states that members at a minimum will "maintain and develop their individual and collective capacity to resist armed attack."[101] Only a handful of NATO members can say that they are living up to their Article 3 commitment. In 2016, only five of 28 NATO member states (Estonia, Greece, Poland, the U.S., and the U.K.) spent the required 2 percent of gross domestic product (GDP) on defense.[102] Recently, NATO total defense expenditures have moved in an upward direction. In 2015, 15 NATO members increased defense spending in real terms; in 2016, 16 NATO allies raised defense spending as a share of GDP. Put another way, in 2016, NATO members collectively increased spending by 3.8 percent, or $10 billion (not including the U.S.).[103] The number of members meeting the 2 percent benchmark is expected to increase to eight by 2018 with Latvia, Lithuania, and Romania meeting the benchmark.

Germany. Germany took a major step forward within NATO by serving as the framework nation for the EFP in Lithuania. Germany has 450 troops and 200 vehicles, including 30 tanks, stationed there.[104] In addition to stationing troops in the Baltics, Germany is the second largest contributor to NATO's Kosovo Force (KFOR) mission and the third largest contributor to the Resolute Support mission in Afghanistan.[105] German troops also contribute to NATO's Very High Readiness Joint Task Force, as well as to Baltic Air Policing, with Germany's air force completing back-to-back deployments out of Amari Air Base in Estonia beginning in August 2016.[106]

In November, the Bundestag approved a yearlong extension of the mandate for Germany to participate in missions against IS in the Middle East. Six German Tornados fly reconnaissance missions out of Incirlik Air Base in Turkey. A German refueling tanker also flies out of Incirlik.[107] In 2016, German Tornadoes flew 692 missions and the tanker aircraft flew 315 missions in support of the anti-IS coalition. Germans also have crewed participating AWACS aircraft and have helped to train and equip Peshmerga forces in Iraq.[108] Despite tensions with Turkey, 240 German soldiers remain based at Incirlik, and a further 15–20 Germans stationed at Konya air base are taking part in NATO AWACS missions.[109] However, German contributions come with caveats. According to one report, "German forces are not authorized for combat missions and the contribution is capped at 1,200 soldiers."[110]

In 2017, Germany increased its defense spending by €2 billion, although overall spending reached only 1.22 percent of GDP; spending on equipment increased from 14.5 percent in 2016 to 16.2 percent in 2017 but was still below the NATO benchmark of 20 percent.[111] The German Bundeswehr plans to have spent €130 billion on armaments by 2030.[112] In May 2017, the government announced an $832 million contract to upgrade 102 Leopard 2 tanks from 2019–2023.[113] According to an inspector general's report, however, only 38 percent of Tornado fighters and 52 percent of Eurofighters are fully operational, only one of three A400M Transport Aircraft and four of 14 Mk 41 Sea King helicopters are fully operational, and the Sea Kings are so outdated that repairs must rely on "unconventional spare parts." Army systems are generally in better condition; 79 percent of Germany's Leopard 2 Main Battle Tanks are fully operational.[114]

Germany's military faces institutional challenges to procurement, including an understaffed procurement office and the need for special approval by a parliamentary budget committee for any expenditure of more than €25 million.[115] In recent years, Germany has put in place a number of joint procurement agreements:

> Joint procurement and maintenance programs with Norway on submarines, Lockheed transport aircraft with France, tanker aircraft with Benelux and Norway and drones with France and Italy are all under way. While not all details on these plans are fixed, the defense spending on aircrafts and submarines alone will amount to several billion euros. In addition, Germany is creating joint military structures together with Romania and the Czech Republic. With the United Kingdom, Berlin is currently working on a defense roadmap to deepen cooperation.[116]

In February, Germany and Norway announced joint development and procurement of naval anti-surface missiles.[117] In October, Germany announced plans to purchase five corvettes for its Navy at a total cost of €1.5 billion.[118]

The Bundeswehr plans to add 5,000 new soldiers to its ranks along with 1,000 civilians and 500 reservists by 2024.[119] In April 2017, the Bundeswehr established a new cyber command, which initially will consist of 260 staff but eventually will number around 13,500 by the time it becomes fully operational in 2021.[120] The Army is a consistent target of cyber-attacks and was subjected to 284,000 such attacks within the first nine weeks of 2017 alone, according to new cyber command head Ludwig Leinhos.[121]

In February, Germany decided to replace its short-range air defense systems, a move that could cost as much as €3.3 billion by 2030; once complete, the upgrade will help to close a gap in Europe's short-range air defense weapons identified in 2016.[122] A report that surfaced in May revealed problems with the procurement of A400M cargo aircraft and has raised questions about whether or not Germany will have replacement transport aircraft ready by 2021, the year its C-160 fleet is due to be retired.[123]

Germany also faces the financial and security challenges associated with a very large influx of migrants. In April, Chancellor Angela Merkel stated there was "no doubt" that some refugees are a security threat to Germany.[124] The country spent €21.7 billion on migrants in 2016, funds that otherwise might have been spent on military capabilities more directly relevant to NATO.[125]

Although Germany is beginning to take on a larger role within NATO and has taken some decisions to strengthen its military capabilities, the military remains underfunded and underequipped. An April 2017 RAND report stated that Germany "has only two battalions with equipment modern enough to serve as a worthy battlefield adversary for Russia."[126] As long as the public appetite for greater investment in defense and a greater role for Germany as a military power remains tepid, the country will continue to punch below its weight in the security realm.

France. France sees itself as a global power, remains one of the most capable militaries within the NATO alliance, and retains an independent nuclear deterrent capability. Although France rejoined NATO's Integrated Command Structure in 2009, it remains outside the alliance's nuclear planning group. Whether current levels of funding will be sustained, however, is not certain. In July, French Chief of Defense General Pierre de Villiers resigned because of President Emmanuel Macron's budget plan, which would cut military spending by $979 million.[127]

France opened a cyber-operational command in December 2016. The Army plans to employ 2,600 cyber soldiers supported by 600 cyber experts, along with 4,400 reservists, as well as to invest €1 billion in this effort, by 2019.[128] French Defense Minister Jean-Yves Le Drian stated in December that "[t]he threats will grow. The frequency and sophistication of attacks is increasing without respite."[129] The French Ministry of Defense faced 24,000 external attacks in 2016, double the number faced in 2015.[130]

France withdrew the last of its troops from Afghanistan at the end of 2014, although all French combat troops had left in 2012. All told, France lost 89 soldiers and had 700 wounded in Afghanistan.[131] In September 2014, France launched Opération Chammal, the name given to the French contribution to the campaign against the so-called Islamic State. France currently has 1,200 soldiers deployed in Opération Chammal.[132] As of the end of January 2017, French planes operating from bases in Jordan and the United Arab Emirates, along with naval aircraft launched from the aircraft carrier *Charles De Gaulle*, had dropped 2,300 bombs against the IS, twice as many as French forces dropped during operations in Libya in 2011.[133] French artillery has taken part in supporting the ground offensive against the IS since September 2016.[134] The pace of the Chammal operation is having a deleterious impact on French forces according to French Air Force Chief of Staff Andre Lanata. In addition to such other problems as a shortage of drones and refueling tankers, Lanata has stated that he is "having a hard time (recruiting and retaining personnel) in a number of positions, from plane mechanics to intelligence officers, image analysts and base defenders."[135]

In Europe, France has deployed 300 troops, along with infantry fighting vehicles and Leclerc main battle tanks, to Estonia,[136] contributing to NATO's Enhanced Forward Presence. French troops will deploy to Lithuania in 2018 as part of the battlegroup stationed in that nation.[137] In addition, the French military is very active in Africa, with over 4,000 troops taking part in anti-terrorism operations in Burkina Faso, Chad, Mali, Mauritania, and Niger as part of Operation Barkhane.[138] France also has over 1,450 troops in Djibouti, along with Mirage fighters, and troops in Côte d'Ivoire, Gabon, and Senegal.[139]

France recently added 11,000 soldiers to its Army.[140] In January 2015, France launched Operation Sentinelle, deploying 11,000 troops to protect the country from terrorist attacks; it is the largest operational commitment for French forces.[141] Operation Sentinelle soldiers helped to foil an attack near the Louvre museum in February 2017 and an attempted attack on a soldier patrolling Orly Airport in March.[142] Along with its successes, however, the operation has placed significant strains on French forces. In a typical year, French soldiers deploy for eight months, two of them as part of Operation Sentinelle. To counteract the strain, the government extended deployment pay to soldiers taking part in Sentinelle and created a new "medal for Protection of the Territory" for troops deployed for 60 days in Sentinelle.[143]

The United Kingdom. America's most important bilateral relationship in Europe is the Special Relationship with the United Kingdom.

In his famous 1946 "Sinews of Peace" speech—now better known as his "Iron Curtain" speech—Winston Churchill described the Anglo–American relationship as one that is based first and foremost on defense and military cooperation. From the sharing of intelligence to the transfer of nuclear technology, a high degree of military cooperation has helped to make the Special Relationship between the U.S. and the U.K. unique. Then-U.K. Prime Minister Margaret Thatcher made clear the essence of the Special Relationship between the U.K. and the U.S. when she first met then-U.S.S.R. President Mikhail Gorbachev in 1984: "I am an ally of the United States. We believe the same things, we believe passionately in the same battle of ideas, we will defend them to the hilt. Never try to separate me from them."[144]

Since the 9/11 terrorist attacks, the United Kingdom has proven itself to be America's number one military partner. For example, Britain provided 46,000 troops for the 2003 invasion of Iraq. At the height of this commitment, the U.K. also deployed 10,000 troops to one of the deadliest parts of Afghanistan—an area that at its peak accounted for 20 percent of the country's total violence—while many other NATO allies operated in the relative safety of the North.

In 2015, the U.K. conducted a defense review, the results of which have driven a modest increase in defense spending and an effort to reverse some of the cuts that had been implemented pursuant to the previous review in 2010. Through 2015, defense spending had dropped to 2.08 percent of GDP,[145] and U.K. forces suffered as a consequence. In 2016, the U.K. moved to repair the damage in capability and capacity by increasing spending to 2.17 percent of GDP, with 22.56 percent of this devoted to equipment purchases.[146] Though its military is small in comparison to the militaries of France and Germany, the U.K. maintains one of the most effective armed forces in European NATO. Defense Secretary Michael Fallon stated in February 2017 that the U.K. will have an expeditionary force of 50,000 troops by 2025.[147] In recent years, it has increased funding for its highly respected Special Forces.

Provided funding is sustained, by 2020, the Royal Air Force (RAF) will operate a fleet of F-35 and Typhoon fighter aircraft, the latter being upgraded to carry out ground attacks. The RAF recently brought into service a new fleet of air-to-air refuelers, which is particularly noteworthy because of the severe shortage of this capability in Europe. With the U.K., the U.S. produced and has jointly operated an intelligence-gathering platform, the RC-135 Rivet Joint aircraft, which has already seen service in Mali, Nigeria, and Iraq and is now part of the RAF fleet.

The U.K. operates seven C-17 cargo planes and has started to bring the European A400M cargo aircraft into service after years of delays. The 2015 defense review recommended keeping 14 C-130Js in service even though they initially were going to be removed from the force structure. The Sentinel R1, an airborne battlefield and ground surveillance aircraft, originally was due to be removed from the force structure in 2015, but its service is being extended to at least 2025, and the U.K. will soon start operating the P-8 Poseidon maritime patrol aircraft. The U.S. and U.K. are in discussions with regard to filling the U.K.'s antisubmarine gap until the new P-8s come into service in 2019.[148] In November 2015, a French maritime patrol aircraft had to assist the Royal Navy in searching for a Russian submarine off the coast of Scotland.[149]

The Royal Navy's surface fleet is based on the new Type-45 Destroyer and the older Type-23 Frigate. The latter will be replaced by the Type-26 Global Combat Ship sometime in the 2020s. In total, the U.K. operates only 19 frigates and destroyers, which most experts agree is dangerously low for the commitment asked of the Royal Navy (in the 1990s, the fleet numbered nearly 60 surface combatants). Nevertheless, the Royal Navy still delivers a formidable capability.

The U.K. will not have an aircraft carrier in service until the first *Queen Elizabeth*-class carrier enters service in the 2020s, although the aircraft meant to operate from them have yet to be acquired. This will be the largest carrier operated in Europe. Two of her class will be built, and both will enter service. Additionally, the Royal Navy is introducing seven *Astute*-class attack submarines as it phases out its older *Trafalgar*-class. Crucially, the U.K. maintains a fleet of 13 Mine Counter Measure Vessels (MCMVs) that deliver world-leading capability and play an important role in Persian Gulf security contingency planning.

Perhaps the Royal Navy's most important contribution is its continuous-at-sea, submarine-based nuclear deterrent based on the *Vanguard*-class ballistic missile submarine and the Trident missile. In July 2016, the House of Commons voted to renew Trident and approved the manufacture of four replacement submarines to carry the missile. However, the replacement submarines are not expected to enter service until 2028 at the earliest.[150]

The U.K. remains a leader inside NATO, taking over temporary responsibility for the VJTF in January and contributing 3,000 troops.[151] In March, 800 British troops arrived in Estonia, where the U.K. is the framework nation for NATO's EFP battalion in that country.[152] U.K. troops also contribute to the American-led battalion in Poland. The Royal Air Force has taken part in Baltic Air Policing four times, including most recently from April–August 2016.[153] In

May 2017, four RAF Typhoons deployed to Romania for a four-month deployment supporting NATO's Southern Air Policing mission.[154]

Turkey. Turkey remains an important U.S. ally and NATO member, but the increasingly autocratic presidency of Recep Tayyip Erdogan and a recent thaw in relations between Turkey and Russia have introduced troubling challenges. Turkey has been an important U.S. ally since the closing days of World War II. During the Korean War, it deployed a total of 15,000 troops and suffered 721 killed in action and more than 2,000 wounded. Turkey joined NATO in 1952, one of only two NATO members (the other was Norway) that had a land border with the Soviet Union. Today, it continues to play an active role in the alliance, but not without difficulties.

Turkey is vitally important to Europe's energy security. It is the gateway to the resource-rich Caucasus and Caspian Basin and controls the Bosporus, one of the world's most important shipping straits. Several major gas and oil pipelines run through Turkey. As new oilfields are developed in the Central Asian states, and given Europe's dependence on Russian oil and gas, Turkey can be expected to play an increasingly important role in Europe's energy security.

On July 15, 2016, elements of the Turkish armed forces attempted a coup d'état against the increasingly Islamist-leaning leadership of President Erdogan. This was the fourth coup attempt since 1960 (the fifth if one counts the so-called postmodern coup in 1997). In each previous case, the military was successful, and democracy was returned to the people; in this case, however, Erdogan immediately enforced a state of emergency and cracked down on many aspects of government, the military, and civil society. In July 2017, it was reported that "about 50,000 people [had] been arrested and 150,000 state workers including teachers, judges and soldiers, [had] been suspended in the crackdown under emergency rule which was imposed soon after the attempted military takeover."[155] As of April, 10,732 police officers, 7,463 members of the military, and 168 generals had been arrested.[156] The post-coup crackdown has had an especially negative effect on the military. Turkey's military is now suffering from a loss of experienced generals and admirals as well as an acute shortage of pilots, and NATO Supreme Allied Commander General Scaparrotti has stated that Erdogan's military purges have "degraded" NATO's capabilities.[157]

Although all opposition parties condemned the coup attempt, the failed plot has enabled Erdogan to consolidate more power. A referendum that was approved by a narrow margin in April granted the president's office further powers—such as eliminating the position of prime minister in the government—most of which will come into effect in 2019 after presidential elections.[158] An interim report by election observers from the Organization for Security and Co-operation in Europe found an "unlevel playing field" and stated that the two sides of the campaign "did not have equal opportunities."[159] Erdogan's response to the coup has further eroded Turkey's democracy, once considered a model for the region. In March, Turkey blocked some cooperation between NATO and partner countries over a controversy with Austria related to the referendum.[160]

Senior government officials' erratic and at times hyperbolic statements alleging U.S. involvement in the coup, combined with Erdogan's rapprochement with Russian President Vladimir Putin, have brought U.S.–Turkish relations to an all-time low. The U.S. decision in May to arm Syrian Kurds of the People's Protection Units (YPG) further angered Turkey, which considers the YPG to be connected to the Kurdistan Workers Party (PKK), which Ankara has long regarded as its primary threat.[161]

Nevertheless, U.S. security interests in the region lend considerable importance to America's relationship with Turkey. Turkey is home to Incirlik Air Base, a major U.S. and NATO air base. Although Turkish officials have threatened to close access to the base, they have not yet done so.[162] One cause for optimism has been NATO's decision to deploy air defense batteries to Turkey and increased AWACS flights in the region after the Turkish government requested them in late 2015.[163] In addition, after an initial period of vacillation in dealing with the threat from the Islamic State, a spate of IS attacks that rocked the country has led Turkey to play a bigger role in attacking the terrorist group.

Turkey's military contribution to international security operations still sets it apart from many of the nations of Western Europe. From August 2016–March 2017, Turkey conducted Operation Euphrates Shield, a military intervention in Syria with the goal of creating secure zones along the border that served primarily to stop YPG militias from gaining territory near the Turkish border.[164] Turkish officials have expressed anger over America's backing of Kurdish rebel forces fighting the IS in Syria, and the objectives of Operation Euphrates Shield and proposed future Turkish military involvement in Syria have been called into question because of their lack of alignment with U.S. and other nations' objectives.[165]

The Turks have deployed thousands of troops to Afghanistan and have commanded the International Security Assistance Force (ISAF) twice since 2002. Turkey continues to maintain more than 500 troops in Afghanistan as part of NATO's Resolute Support mission, making it the sixth-largest troop contributor out of 39 nations.[166] The Turks also have contributed to a number of peacekeeping missions in the Balkans, still maintain 313 troops in Kosovo,[167] and have participated in counter-piracy and counterterrorism missions off the Horn of Africa in addition to deploying planes, frigates, and submarines during the NATO-led operation in Libya.

Turkey has a 355,200-strong active-duty military,[168] making it NATO's second largest after that of the United States. A number of major procurement programs in the works include up to 250 new Altay main battle tanks, 350 T-155 Fırtına 155mm self-propelled howitzers, six Type-214 submarines, and more than 50 T-129 attack helicopters.[169]

With respect to procurement, the biggest area of contention between Turkey and NATO is Turkey's selection of a missile defense system. In September 2013, Turkey selected China Precision Machinery Import–Export Corporation (CPMIEC) for a $3.44 billion deal to provide the system. NATO has said that no Chinese-built system could be integrated into any NATO or American missile defense system. U.S. officials also have warned that any Turkish company that acts as a local subcontractor in the program would face serious U.S. sanctions because CPMIEC has been sanctioned under the Iran, North Korea, and Syria Nonproliferation Act.[170] In November 2015, Turkey cancelled the contract with CPMIEC.[171]

In April 2017, Turkey's Foreign Minister stated that the country had an agreement in principle to purchase Russian-made S-400 systems.[172] However, it remains to be seen whether the sale actually goes through, how many units are purchased, and how the S-400s fit into Turkey's overall air defenses.[173] In April, Turkish Defense Minister Fikri Işık stated that no S-400s would be integrated into the NATO air defense systems.[174]

Geographically and geopolitically, Turkey remains a key U.S. ally and NATO member. It has been a constructive and fruitful security partner for decades, and maintaining the relationship is in America's interest. The challenge for U.S. and NATO policymakers will be to navigate Erdogan's increasingly autocratic leadership and discourage Ankara's warming relations with Russia without alienating Turkey.

The Baltic States. The U.S. has a long history of championing the sovereignty and territorial integrity of the Baltic States that dates back to the interwar period of the 1920s. Since regaining their independence from Russia in the early 1990s, the Baltic States have been staunch supporters of the transatlantic relationship. Although small in absolute terms, the three countries contribute significantly to NATO in relative terms.

Estonia. Estonia has been a leader in the Baltics in terms of defense spending and is one of five NATO members to meet the 2 percent of GDP spending benchmark.[175] Although the Estonian armed forces total only 6,400 active-duty service personnel (including the army, navy,

and air force),[176] they are held in high regard by their NATO partners and punch well above their weight inside the alliance. Since 1996, almost 1,500 Estonian soldiers have served in the Balkans. Between 2003 and 2011, 455 served in Iraq. Perhaps Estonia's most impressive deployment has been to Afghanistan: more than 2,000 troops deployed between 2003 and 2014 and the second-highest number of deaths per capita among all 28 NATO members. In 2015, Estonia reintroduced conscription for men ages 18–27, who must serve eight or 11 months before being added to the reserve rolls.[177]

Estonia has demonstrated that it takes defense and security policy seriously, focusing its defense policy on improving defensive capabilities at home while maintaining the ability to be a strategic actor abroad. Procurements are expected to rise to $210 million by 2020.[178] One recent joint procurement is with neighboring Finland to acquire 12 South Korean–built howitzers by 2021.[179] Over the next few years, Estonia will increase from one to two the number of brigades in its order of battle; it also is making efforts to increase its rapid reaction reserve force from 18,000 to 21,000 troops by 2022.[180] This increase and modernization includes the recently created Cyber Defence League, a reserve force that relies heavily on expertise found in the civilian sector. In 2017, in an explicit step to strengthen their bilateral relationship, Estonia and the U.S. signed a defense cooperation agreement that builds on the NATO–Estonia Status of Forces Agreement to further clarify the legal framework for U.S. troops in Estonia.[181]

Latvia. Latvia's recent military experience also has been centered on operations in Iraq and Afghanistan alongside NATO and U.S. forces. Latvia has deployed more than 3,000 troops to Afghanistan and between 2003 and 2008 deployed 1,165 troops to Iraq. In addition, Latvia has contributed to a number of other international peacekeeping and military missions. These are significant numbers considering that only 5,310 of Latvia's troops are full-time servicemembers; the remainder are reserves.[182]

In July 2016, Latvia's Parliament approved a new National Defense Concept that builds on the 2012 iteration to chart a path to a bright future for the Latvian National Armed Forces. The document clearly defines Russia as a threat to national security and states that "[d]eterrence is enhanced by the presence of the allied forces in Latvia."[183] The concept lays out a plan for the future that is described as "strengthening the operational capability of the National Armed Forces, the further integration of the National Guard within the Armed Forces, strengthening the Special Tasks Unit (special operations forces), as well as boosting early-warning capabilities, airspace surveillance and air defense."[184]

Latvia plans that a minimum of 8 percent of its professional armed forces will be deployed at any one time but will train to ensure that no less than 50 percent will be combat-ready to deploy overseas if required. In 2017, Latvia spent 1.7 percent of GDP on defense, a 22 percent increase over 2016.[185] The government has stated that the NATO benchmark of 2 percent of GDP in defense spending will be met by 2018, and the National Defense Concept lays out a plan to spend no less than 20 percent of the budget on new equipment.[186]

Lithuania. Lithuania is the largest of the three Baltic States, and its armed forces total 17,030 active-duty troops.[187] Lithuania has also shown steadfast commitment to international peacekeeping and military operations. Between 1994 and 2010, more than 1,700 Lithuanian troops were deployed to the Balkans as part of NATO missions in Bosnia, Croatia, and Kosovo. Between 2003 and 2011, Lithuania sent 930 troops to Iraq. Since 2002, just under 3,000 Lithuanian troops have served in Afghanistan, a notable contribution divided between a special operations mission alongside U.S. and Latvian Special Forces and command of a Provisional Reconstruction Team (PRT) in Ghor Province, making Lithuania one of only a handful of NATO members to have commanded a PRT. Lithuania continues to contribute to NATO's KFOR and Resolute Support Missions.[188]

Lithuanian Defense Minister Raimundas Karoblis has stated that Russia's propaganda campaign against Lithuania is a serious threat: "There are real parallels with Crimea's annexation [from Ukraine].... We are speaking of a danger to the territorial integrity of Lithuania."[189] In April 2017, a Lithuanian security services exercise sought to counter a scenario in which Russian special operations forces infiltrated Lithuania after a train traveling through the country broke down and "little green men" disembarked.[190] Also in April, U.S. forces trained with Lithuanian troops with the goal of integrating U.S. forces and capabilities into Lithuanian defense planning.[191] Lithuania's most recent intelligence service threat assessment stated that upgrades to Russia's military in neighboring Kaliningrad mean that an invasion of a Baltic country can be launched in as little as 24 hours, sharpening Baltic State concerns about NATO's Article 5 commitment to member states.[192]

In 2017, Lithuania will spend around 1.8 percent of GDP on defense. In February, the State Defense Council proposed 2.07 percent of GDP for defense in 2018; procurements to modernize its military include howitzers, infantry fighting vehicles, air defense systems, and (potentially) transport helicopters.[193]

In addition, Lithuania's decision to build a liquefied natural gas (LNG) import facility at Klaipėda has begun to pay dividends, breaking Russia's natural gas monopoly in the region. In 2016, Norway overtook Russia as the top exporter of natural gas to Lithuania.[194] In June 2017, a Lithuanian energy company signed an agreement to buy LNG directly from the U.S.[195] In May, the Baltic States agreed to connect their power grids (currently integrated with Belarus and Russia) with Poland's, with the goal of creating a link to the rest of Europe and decreasing dependence on Russian energy.[196]

Poland. Situated in the center of Europe, Poland shares a border with four NATO allies, a long border with Belarus and Ukraine, and a 144-mile border with Russia alongside the Kaliningrad Oblast. Poland also has a 65-mile border with Lithuania, making it the only

NATO member state that borders any of the Baltic States, and NATO's contingency plans for liberating the Baltic States in the event of a Russian invasion are reported to rely heavily on Polish troops and ports.[197]

Poland has an active military force of almost 100,000, including a 48,000-strong army with 985 main battle tanks.[198] In November, Poland's Parliament approved a new 53,000-strong territorial defense force to protect infrastructure and train in "unconventional warfare tactics."[199] The force will cost €800 million (roughly $1.04 billion) over three years. It remains to be seen whether the new force will eventually operate under the existing defense command structure and whether the investment in money and manpower would not be better utilized elsewhere.[200] Ninety percent of General Staff leadership and 80 percent of Army leadership has left or has been replaced following recent military reforms, introducing a measure of volatility into defense planning.[201]

Poland spent 2 percent of GDP on defense in 2016 and nearly 26 percent on equipment, reaching both NATO benchmarks.[202] In April, the defense ministry stated a goal to raise defense spending to the level of 2.5 percent of GDP by 2030.[203] Poland is looking at major equipment purchases including new maritime patrol aircraft and U.S.-made missile defense systems.[204]

Although Poland's focus is territorial defense, it has 192 troops deployed in Afghanistan as part of NATO's Resolute Support Mission.[205] In 2016, Polish F-16s began to fly reconnaissance missions out of Kuwait as part of the anti-IS mission Operation Inherent Resolve.[206] Approximately 60 soldiers deployed to Iraq in 2015 as trainers.[207] Poland's air force has taken part in Baltic Air Policing seven times since 2006, most recently beginning in May 2017 when four F-16s from the Netherlands took over.[208] Poland is part of NATO's EFP in Latvia and has 258 troops taking part in NATO's KFOR mission.[209]

Current U.S. Military Presence in Europe

Former head of U.S. European Command General Philip Breedlove has aptly described the role of U.S. basing in Europe:

The mature network of U.S. operated bases in the EUCOM AOR provides superb training and power projection facilities in support of steady state operations and contingencies in Europe, Eurasia, Africa, and the Middle East. This footprint is essential to TRANSCOM's global distribution mission and also provides critical basing support for intelligence, surveillance, and reconnaissance assets flying sorties in support of AFRICOM, CENTCOM, EUCOM, U.S. Special Operations Command, and NATO operations.[210]

At its peak in 1953, because of the Soviet threat to Western Europe, the U.S. had approximately 450,000 troops in Europe operating across 1,200 sites. During the early 1990s, both in response to a perceived reduction in the threat from Russia and as part of the so-called peace dividend following the end of the Cold War, U.S. troop numbers in Europe were slashed. Today, around 62,000 U.S. forces remain in Europe, an 85 percent decrease in personnel and 75 percent reduction in basing from the height of the Cold War.[211]

Until 2013, the U.S. Army had two heavy brigade combat teams in Europe, the 170th and 172nd BCTs in Germany; one airborne Infantry BCT, the 173rd Airborne Brigade in Italy; and one Stryker BCT, the 2nd Armored Calvary Regiment in Germany, permanently based in Europe. Deactivation of the 170th BCT in October 2012, slightly earlier than the planned date of 2013, marked the end of a 50-year period during which U.S. combat soldiers had been stationed in Baumholder, Germany. Deactivation of the 172nd BCT took place in October 2013. In all, this meant that more than 10,000 soldiers were removed from Europe. The U.S. has returned one armored BCT to Europe as part of continuous rotations; according to General Breedlove, "[t]he challenge EUCOM faces is ensuring it is able to meet its strategic obligations while primarily relying on rotational forces from the continental United States."[212]

The U.S. is on pace to have only 17 main operating bases left in Europe,[213] primarily in Germany, Italy, the United Kingdom, Turkey, and Spain. The number of U.S. installations has declined steadily since the Cold War when

CHART 2

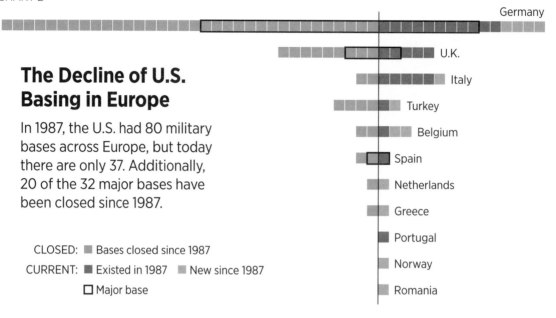

The Decline of U.S. Basing in Europe

In 1987, the U.S. had 80 military bases across Europe, but today there are only 37. Additionally, 20 of the 32 major bases have been closed since 1987.

CLOSED: ■ Bases closed since 1987

CURRENT: ■ Existed in 1987   ■ New since 1987

□ Major base

Germany
U.K.
Italy
Turkey
Belgium
Spain
Netherlands
Greece
Portugal
Norway
Romania

SOURCES: General Accounting Office, "U.S. Personnel in NATO Europe," October 6, 1989, http://www.gao.gov/assets/150/148159.pdf (accessed August 16, 2017); Stockholm International Peace Research Institute, United States Military Forces and Installations in Europe (Oxford: Oxford University Press, 1989), https://www.sipri.org/publications/1989/united-states-military-forces-and-installations-europe (accessed August 16, 2017); and Heritage Foundation research.

☎ heritage.org

in 1990, for example, the U.S. Army alone had more than 850 sites in Europe. Today, the total number for all services is approximately 350. In January 2015, the Department of Defense announced the outcome of its European Infrastructure Consolidation review, under which 15 minor sites across Europe were to be closed.[214] The proposed closures would save $500 million annually, but carrying them out would cost $1.4 billion.[215] In April, EUCOM announced that these base closures were now under review: "Considering the current European security environment, it is a prudent measure to review some of the decisions under the January 2015 European Infrastructure Consolidation effort."[216] Currently, the U.S. Army is scouting sites in lower Saxony in northern Germany for the potential basing of an additional 4,000 troops.[217]

EUCOM's stated mission is to conduct military operations, international military partnering, and interagency partnering to enhance transatlantic security and defend the United States as part of a forward defensive posture. EUCOM is supported by four service component commands and one subordinate unified command: U.S. Naval Forces Europe (NAVEUR); U.S. Army Europe (USAREUR); U.S. Air Forces in Europe (USAFE); U.S. Marine Forces Europe (MARFOREUR); and U.S. Special Operations Command Europe (SOCEUR).

U.S. Naval Forces Europe. NAVEUR is responsible for providing overall command, operational control, and coordination for maritime assets in the EUCOM and Africa Command (AFRICOM) areas of responsibility. This includes more than 20 million square nautical miles of ocean and more than 67 percent of the Earth's coastline.

This command is currently provided by the U.S. Sixth Fleet based in Naples and brings critical U.S. maritime combat capability to an important region of the world. Some of the more notable U.S. naval bases in Europe include the Naval Air Station in Sigonella, Italy; the Naval Support Activity Base in Souda Bay, Greece; and the Naval Station at Rota, Spain. Naval Station Rota is home to four capable Aegis-equipped destroyers.[218] In addition, the USS *Mount Whitney*, a *Blue Ridge*-class command ship, is permanently based in the region.[219] This ship provides a key command-and-control platform that was employed successfully during the early days of the recent Libyan operation.

In 2017, the U.S. allocated over $21 million to upgrade facilities at Keflavik Air Station in Iceland to enable operations of P-8 Poseidon aircraft in the region.[220] With a combat radius of 1,200 nautical miles, the P-8 is capable of flying missions over the entirety of the GIUK (Greenland, Iceland, and United Kingdom) Gap, which has seen an increase in Russian submarine activity. The U.S. Navy expects to complete the replacement of P-3s with P-8s by FY 2019.[221]

The U.S. Navy also keeps a number of submarines in the area that contribute to EUCOM's intelligence, surveillance, and reconnaissance (ISR) capacities, but with increased Russian naval activity, more are needed. In March, General Scaparrotti testified that he did not "have the carrier or the submarine capacity that would best enable me to do my job in EUCOM."[222] Strong U.S.–U.K. military cooperation helps the U.S. to keep submarine assets integrated into the European theater. The British Overseas Territory of Gibraltar, for example, frequently hosts U.S. nuclear-powered submarines. Docking U.S. nuclear-powered submarines in Spain is problematic and bureaucratic, making access to Gibraltar's Z berths vital. Gibraltar is the best place in the Mediterranean to carry out repair work. The U.S. Navy also has a fleet of Maritime Patrol Aircraft and Reconnaissance Aircraft that operate from U.S. bases in Italy, Greece, Spain, and Turkey and complement the ISR capabilities of U.S. submarines. In December, P-8s operating out of Italy searched for Russian subs near NATO's Standing Maritime Group assigned to the Mediterranean.[223]

U.S. Army Europe. USAREUR was established in 1952. Then as today, the U.S. Army formed the bulk of U.S. forces in Europe. At the height of the Cold War, 277,000 soldiers and thousands of tanks, armored personnel carriers, and tactical nuclear weapons were positioned at the Army's European bases. USAREUR also contributed to U.S. operations in the broader region, such as the U.S. intervention in Lebanon in 1985, when it deployed 8,000 soldiers for four months from bases in Europe. In the 1990s, after the fall of the Berlin Wall, USAREUR continued to play a vital role in promoting U.S. interests in the region, especially in the Balkans.

USAREUR is headquartered in Wiesbaden, Germany. The core of USAREUR is formed around the permanent deployment of two BCTs: the 2nd Cavalry Regiment, based in Vilseck, Germany, and the 173rd Airborne Brigade in Italy, with both units supported by the 12th Combat Aviation Brigade out of Ansbach, Germany. In addition, the U.S. Army's 21st Theater Sustainment Command has helped the U.S. military presence in Europe to become an important logistics hub in support of Central Command.

Recently, the 2nd Cavalry Regiment Field Artillery Squadron began training on a Q-53 radar system, described as a "game changer."[224] The unit is the first in the European theater to acquire this system, which is expected to help the Army monitor the border between NATO and Russia more effectively.

Beginning in January, the 3rd Armored Combat Team, 4th Infantry Division from Colorado began rotating into Europe for nine months, raising the number of Army BCTs in Europe to three.[225] In May, an Army battalion of around 600 soldiers took part in an exercise to deploy to Europe on short notice as part of U.S. efforts to practice swift redeployments to Europe.[226]

U.S. Air Forces in Europe. USAFE provides a forward-based air capability that can support a wide range of contingency operations. USAFE originated as the 8th Air Force in 1942 and flew strategic bombing missions over the European continent during World War II.

Headquartered at Ramstein Air Base, US-AFE has seven main operating bases along with 88 geographically separated locations.[227] The main operating bases are the RAF bases at Lakenheath and Mildenhall in the U.K., Ramstein and Spangdahlem Air Bases in Germany, Lajes Field in the Azores, Incirlik Air Base in Turkey, and Aviano Air Base in Italy. These bases provide benefits beyond the European theater. For example, speaking about the "invaluable" importance of Incirlik Air Base to anti-IS operations in Syria and Iraq, USAF Colonel John Dorrian has said that "the entire world has been made safer by the operations that have been conducted there."[228] Approximately 39,000 active-duty, reserve, and civilian personnel are assigned to USAFE along with 200 aircraft.[229]

U.S. Marine Forces Europe. MARFOREUR was established in 1980. It was originally a "designate" component command, meaning that it was only a shell during peacetime but could bolster its forces during wartime. Its initial staff was 40 personnel based in London. By 1989, it had more than 180 Marines in 45 separate locations in 19 countries throughout the European theater. Today, the command is based in Boeblingen, Germany, and 140 of the 1,500 Marines based in Europe are assigned to MARFOREUR.[230] It was also dual-hatted as Marine Corps Forces, Africa (MARFORAF), under U.S. Africa Command in 2008.

In the past, MARFOREUR has supported U.S. Marine units deployed in the Balkans and the Middle East. MARFOREUR also supports the Norway Air Landed Marine Air Ground Task Force, the Marine Corps' only land-based prepositioned stock. The Marine Corps has enough prepositioned stock in Norway to support a force of 13,000 Marines for 30 days, and the Norwegian government covers half of the costs of the prepositioned storage. The prepositioned stock's proximity to the Arctic region makes it of particular geostrategic importance. In 2016, 6,500 pieces of equipment from the stock were utilized for the Cold Response exercise.[231]

Crucially, MARFOREUR provides the U.S. with rapid reaction capability to protect U.S. embassies in North Africa. The Special-Purpose Marine Air-Ground Task Force–Crisis Response–Africa (SPMAGTF) is currently located in Spain, Italy, and Romania and provides a response force of 1,550 Marines. SPMAGTF has KC-130J Hercules and V-22 Osprey aircraft, but six of the 12 Ospreys were sent back to the U.S. in 2016 as a result of defense budget cuts. Marine Corps General Joseph Dunford, current Chairman of the Joints Chief of Staff, said that this reduction in strength "does reduce the [unit's] flexibility, it reduces the depth."[232]

In July 2015, Spain and the United States signed the Third Protocol of Amendment to the U.S.–Spanish Agreement for Defense and Cooperation, which allows the U.S. Marine Corps to station up to 2,200 military personnel, 21 aircraft, and 500 non-military employees permanently at Morón Air Base. The Defense Department stated that "a surge capability was included in the amendment of another 800 dedicated military crisis-response task force personnel and 14 aircraft at Moron, for a total of 3,500 U.S. military and civilian personnel and 35 aircraft."[233] In January 2017, 285 Marines began a rotational deployment to Vaernes, Norway, to train and exercise with Norwegian forces.[234] The presence of the Marines led some Russian officials to threaten that Norway could become a target for Russian strategic weapons.[235]

The Marine Corps maintains a Black Sea Rotational Force (BSRF) composed of approximately 400 Marines that rotate to the Black Sea region (based in Romania) to conduct training events with regional partners.[236]

U.S. Special Operations Command Europe. SOCEUR is the only subordinate unified command under EUCOM. Its origins are in the Support Operations Command Europe, and it was initially based in Paris. This headquarters provided peacetime planning and operational control of special operations forces during unconventional warfare in EUCOM's area of responsibility. In 1955, the headquarters was reconfigured as a joint task force and renamed Support Operations Task Force Europe (SOTFE) and later Special Operations Task Force

Europe. When French President Charles de Gaulle forced American troops out of France in 1966, SOTFE relocated to its current headquarters in Panzer Kaserne near Stuttgart, Germany, in 1967. It also operates out of RAF Mildenhall. In 1982, it was redesignated for a fourth time as U.S. Special Operations Command Europe.

Due to the sensitive nature of special operations, publicly available information is scarce. However, it has been documented that SOCEUR elements participated in various capacity-building missions and civilian evacuation operations in Africa; took an active role in the Balkans in the mid-1990s and in combat operations in the Iraq and Afghanistan wars; and most recently supported AFRICOM's Operation Odyssey Dawn in Libya. SOCEUR also plays an important role in joint training with European allies; since June 2014, it has maintained an almost continuous presence in the Baltic States and Poland in order to train special operations forces in those countries.[237]

The FY 2018 DOD budget request included over $105 million for various special operations programs and functions through ERI. This funding is intended to go to such projects as enhancement of special operations forces' staging capabilities and prepositioning in Europe, exercise support, enhancement of intelligence capabilities, and partnership activities with Eastern and Central European allies' special operations forces.[238]

EUCOM has played an important role in supporting other combatant commands, such as CENTCOM and AFRICOM. Of the 65,000 U.S. troops based in Europe, almost 10,000 are there to support other combatant commands. The facilities available in EUCOM allowed the U.S. to play a leading role in combating Ebola in western Africa during the 2014 outbreak.

In addition to CENTCOM and AFRICOM, U.S. troops in Europe have worked closely with U.S. Cyber Command (CYBERCOM) to implement Department of Defense cyber policy in Europe and to bolster the cyber defense capabilities of America's European partners. This work has included hosting a number of cyber-related conferences and joint exercises with European partners.

In the past year, there have been significant improvements in cyber security in Europe. This improvement includes operationalization of EUCOM's Joint Cyber Center.[239] EUCOM has also supported CYBERCOM's work inside NATO by becoming a full member of the NATO Cooperative Cyber Defense Center of Excellence in Tallinn, Estonia.

Key Infrastructure and Warfighting Capabilities

One of the major advantages of having U.S. forces in Europe is the access it provides to logistical infrastructure. For example, EUCOM supports the U.S. Transportation Command (TRANSCOM) with its array of airbases and access to ports throughout Europe. EUCOM supported TRANSCOM with work on the Northern Distribution Network (NDN), which supplied U.S. troops in Afghanistan during major combat operations there. Today, Mihail Kogalniceanu Air Base in Romania is a major logistics and supply hub for U.S. equipment and personnel traveling to the Middle East region.[240]

Europe is a mature and advanced operating environment. America's decades-long presence there means that the U.S. has tried and tested systems that involve moving large numbers of matériel and personnel into, inside, and out of the continent. This offers an operating environment second to none in terms of logistical capability. For example, there are more than 166,000 miles of rail line in Europe (not including Russia), and an estimated 90 percent of roads in Europe are paved. The U.S. enjoys access to a wide array of airfields and ports across the continent.

ERI has supported infrastructure improvements across the region. Two major projects funded include a replacement hospital at Landstuhl in Germany. When completed in 2022, the new permanent facility "will provide state-of-the-art combat and contingency medical support to service members from EUCOM, AFRICOM and CENTCOM."[241] ERI funds are also contributing to creation of the Joint Intelligence Analysis Center, which will consolidate intelligence functions formerly spread across multiple bases and "strengthen EUCOM, NATO and UK intelligence relationships."[242]

Some of the world's most important shipping lanes are also in the European region. In fact, the world's busiest shipping lane is the English Channel, through which pass 500 ships a day, not including small boats and pleasure craft. Approximately 90 percent of the world's trade travels by sea. Given the high volume of maritime traffic in the European region, no U.S. or NATO military operation can be undertaken without consideration of how these shipping lanes offer opportunity—and risk—to America and her allies. In addition to the English Channel, other important shipping routes in Europe include the Strait of Gibraltar; the Turkish Straits (including the Dardanelles and the Bosporus); the Northern Sea Route; and the Danish Straits.

Strait of Gibraltar. The Strait of Gibraltar connects the Mediterranean Sea with the Atlantic Ocean and separates North Africa from Gibraltar and Spain on the southernmost point of the Iberian Peninsula. The strait is about 40 miles long and approximately eight miles wide at its narrowest point. More than 200 cargo vessels pass through the Strait of Gibraltar every day, carrying cargoes to Asia, Europe, Africa, and the Americas.

The strait's proximity to North Africa, combined with its narrowness, has presented security challenges for U.S. and allied warships. In 2002, Moroccan security forces foiled an al-Qaeda plot to attack U.S. and U.K. naval ships in the Strait of Gibraltar using the same tactics that had been used in the attack on the USS *Cole*. A 2014 article in the al-Qaeda English-language publication *Resurgence* urged attacks on oil tankers and cargo ships crossing the Strait of Gibraltar as a way to cause "phenomenal" damage to the world economy.[243]

The Turkish Straits (Including the Dardanelles and the Bosporus). These straits are long and narrow: 40 and 16 miles long, respectively, with the narrowest point in the Bosporus, which connects the Black Sea with the Sea of Marmara, only 765 yards wide. Approximately 46,000 ships each year transit the straits, including more than 5,600 tankers.[244]

The 1936 Montreux Convention gave Turkey control of the Bosporus and placed limitations on the number, transit time, and tonnage of naval ships from non–Black Sea countries that can use the straits and operate in the Black Sea.[245] This places limitations on U.S. Navy operation in the Black Sea. The U.S. Navy spent 207 days in the Black Sea in 2014, 150 days in 2015, and only 58 days in 2016.[246]

GIUK Gap. This North Atlantic naval corridor between Greenland, Iceland, and the United Kingdom is strategically vital. During the Cold War, Soviet submarines, bombers, and reconnaissance aircraft traversed the GIUK Gap to gain access to the Atlantic Ocean from the northern Russian coast. Recent increased Russian activity through and near the GIUK Gap has led the U.S. to return military assets to Keflavik in southwest Iceland.

The Danish Straits. Consisting of three channels connecting the Baltic Sea to the North Sea via the Kattegat and Skagerrak seas, the Danish Straits are particularly important to the Baltic Sea nations as a way to import and export goods. This is especially true for Russia, which increasingly has been shipping its crude oil exports to Europe through its Baltic ports.[247] Russian oil companies have announced plans to stop the use of foreign ports on the Baltic Sea to export crude by 2018, saying that they will focus instead on increased use of Russian ports.[248] More than 125,000 ships per year transit these straits.[249]

Geostrategic Islands in the Baltic Sea. Three other critically important locations are the Åland Islands (Finnish); Gotland Island (Swedish); and Borholm Island (Danish). The Åland Islands have been demilitarized since the 1856 Treaty of Paris ending the Crimean War and have always been considered the most important geostrategic piece of real estate in the Baltic Sea. Gotland Island is strategically located halfway between Sweden and Latvia in the middle of the Baltic Sea. Sweden maintained a permanent military garrison on the island for hundreds of years until 2005. At the height of the Cold War, 15,000–20,000 Swedish military personnel were stationed on Gotland.[250] Today, Sweden is standing up a 300-strong Battle Group Gotland, to be fully established on the island by 2018. In 2017, Sweden will spend $45 million to improve the battlegroup's preparedness and anti-aircraft capabilities.[251] The military facilities will need to be reconstituted, as most were sold for civilian use after 2005. In September 2017, around 1,000 U.S. forces will take part in the Aurora exercise in and around Gotland.[252] Bornholm Island is strategically located at the mouth of the Baltic Sea.

In March 2015, Russia carried out a large-scale training exercise with up to 33,000 soldiers, which included the capture of the Åland, Gotland, and Borholm islands as part of its scenario. Reinforcing the Baltic region would be nearly impossible without control of these islands.

The biggest danger to infrastructure assets in Europe pertains to any potential NATO conflict with Russia in one or more of NATO's eastern states. In such a scenario, infrastructure would be heavily targeted in order to deny or delay the alliance's ability to move the significant numbers of manpower, matériel, and equipment that would be needed to retake any territory lost during an initial attack. In such a scenario, the shortcomings of NATO's force posture would become obvious.

Conclusion

Overall, the European region remains a stable, mature, and friendly operating environment. Russia remains the preeminent threat to the region, both conventionally and nonconventionally, and the impact of the migrant crisis, continued economic sluggishness, threat from terrorism, and political fragmentation increase the potential for internal instability. The threats emanating from the previously noted arc of instability that stretches from the eastern Atlantic Ocean to the Middle East and up to the Caucasus through Russia and into the Arctic have spilled over into Europe itself in the form of terrorism and migrants arriving on the continent's shores.

America's closest and oldest allies are located in Europe. The region is incredibly important to the U.S. for economic, military, and political reasons. Perhaps most important, the U.S. has treaty obligations through NATO to defend the European members of that alliance. If the U.S. needs to act in the European region or nearby, there is a history of interoperability with allies and access to key logistical infrastructure that makes the operating environment in Europe more favorable than the environment in other regions in which U.S. forces might have to operate.

The past year saw continued U.S. reengagement with the continent both militarily and politically along with modest increases in European allies' defense budgets and capability investment. NATO continued its steady progression toward strengthening its deterrence posture in the East and reaffirmed that it remains a nuclear alliance. NATO's biggest challenges pertain to continued underinvestment from European members, a tempestuous Turkey, and a return to collective defense that is undermined by disparate threat perceptions within the alliance.

Scoring the European Operating Environment

As noted at the beginning of this section, various considerations must be taken into account in assessing the regions within which the U.S. may have to conduct military operations to defend its vital national interests against threats. Our assessment of the operating environment utilized a five-point scale, ranging from "very poor" to "excellent" conditions and covering four regional characteristics of greatest relevance to the conduct of military operations:

1. **Very Poor.** Significant hurdles exist for military operations. Physical infrastructure is insufficient or nonexistent, and the region is politically unstable. The U.S. military is poorly placed or absent, and alliances are nonexistent or diffuse.

2. **Unfavorable.** A challenging operating environment for military operations is marked by inadequate infrastructure, weak alliances, and recurring political instability. The U.S. military is inadequately placed in the region.

3. **Moderate.** A neutral to moderately favorable operating environment is characterized by adequate infrastructure, a moderate alliance structure, and acceptable levels of regional political stability. The U.S. military is adequately placed.

4. **Favorable.** A favorable operating environment includes good infrastructure, strong alliances, and a stable political environment. The U.S. military is well placed in the region for future operations.

5. **Excellent.** An extremely favorable operating environment includes well-established and well-maintained infrastructure, strong capable allies, and a stable political environment. The U.S. military is exceptionally well placed to defend U.S. interests.

The key regional characteristics consist of:

a. **Alliances.** Alliances are important for interoperability and collective defense, as allies would be more likely to lend support to U.S. military operations. Various indicators provide insight into the strength or health of an alliance. These include whether the U.S. trains regularly with countries in the region, has good interoperability with the forces of an ally, and shares intelligence with nations in the region.

b. **Political Stability.** Political stability brings predictability for military planners when considering such things as transit, basing, and overflight rights for U.S. military operations. The overall degree of political stability indicates whether U.S. military actions would be hindered or enabled and considers, for example, whether transfers of power in the region are generally peaceful and whether there have been any recent instances of political instability in the region.

c. **U.S. Military Positioning.** Having military forces based or equipment and supplies staged in a region greatly facilitates the United States' ability to respond to crises and, presumably, achieve successes in critical "first battles" more quickly. Being routinely present in a region also assists in maintaining familiarity with its characteristics and the various actors that might try to assist or thwart U.S. actions. With this in mind, we assessed whether or not the U.S. military was well positioned in the region. Again, indicators included bases, troop presence, prepositioned equipment, and recent examples of military operations (including training and humanitarian) launched from the region.

d. **Infrastructure.** Modern, reliable, and suitable infrastructure is essential to military operations. Airfields, ports, rail lines, canals, and paved roads enable the U.S. to stage, launch operations from, and logistically sustain combat operations. We combined expert knowledge of regions with publicly available information on critical infrastructure to arrive at our overall assessment of this metric.

For Europe, scores this year remained steady, with no substantial changes in any individual categories or average scores. The *2018 Index* again assesses the European Operating Environment as "favorable":

- Alliances: **4—Favorable**

- Political Stability: **4—Favorable**

- U.S. Military Positioning: **3—Moderate**

- Infrastructure: **4—Favorable**

Leading to a regional score of: **Favorable**

Operating Environment: Europe

	VERY POOR	UNFAVORABLE	MODERATE	FAVORABLE	EXCELLENT
Alliances				✔	
Political Stability				✔	
U.S. Military Posture			✔		
Infrastructure				✔	
OVERALL				✔	

Endnotes

1. On March 29, 2017, Great Britain began a two-year process of formal withdrawal from the EU by invoking Article 50 of the Treaty on European Union.

2. Norwegian Petroleum Directorate, "Doubling the Resource Estimate for the Barents Sea," April 25, 2017, http://www.npd.no/en/news/News/2017/Doubling-the-resource-estimate-for-the-Barents-Sea/ (accessed June 1, 2017).

3. Nordic Council of Ministers, *The Arctic Human Development Report: Regional Processes and Global Linkages*, ed. Joan Nymand Larsen and Gail Fondahl, 2014, p. 53, http://norden.diva-portal.org/smash/get/diva2:788965/FULLTEXT03.pdf (accessed June 1, 2017).

4. Terry Miller and Anthony B. Kim, *2017 Index of Economic Freedom* (Washington: The Heritage Foundation, 2017), p. 276.

5. Northern Sea Route Information Office, Transit Statistics, "Vessels Transited NSR in Y2016," http://www.arctic-lio.com/docs/nsr/transits/Transits_2016.pdf (accessed June 1, 2017).

6. Suez Canal Authority, Navigation Statistics, 2016, http://www.suezcanal.gov.eg/English/Navigation/Pages/NavigationStatistics.aspx (accessed June 1, 2017).

7. Atle Staalesen, "Moscow Boasts Potential, But Arctic Transit Shipments Between Europe–Asia Remain Poor," *The Independent Barents Observer*, March 2, 2017, https://thebarentsobserver.com/en/arctic/2017/03/moscow-boasts-potential-arctic-transit-shipments-between-europe-asia-remain-poor#.WLrh6AdarJo.twitter (accessed June 1, 2017).

8. Trude Pettersen, "Northern Sea Route Traffic Plummeted," *Barents Observer*, December 16, 2014, http://barentsobserver.com/en/arctic/2014/12/northern-sea-route-traffic-plummeted-16-12 (accessed June 1, 2017).

9. Staalesen, "Moscow Boasts Potential."

10. Atle Staalesen, "Russia's Northern Sea Route Saw Downturn in Cargo Transits in 2015," *Alaska Dispatch News*, updated September 28, 2016, http://www.adn.com/article/20160216/russias-northern-sea-route-saw-downturn-cargo-transits-2015 (accessed June 1, 2017).

11. Atle Staalesen, "FSB Takes Control on Northern Sea Route," *The Independent Barents Observer*, June 27, 2016, https://thebarentsobserver.com/en/security/2016/06/fsb-takes-control-northern-sea-route (accessed June 1, 2017).

12. The four NATO military members are the United States, Canada, Norway, and Denmark (Greenland). The non-NATO Arctic sea power is Russia.

13. Joel Gehrke, "Trump Team Weighs Arming Coast Guard Icebreakers," *The Washington Examiner*, May 3, 2017, http://www.washingtonexaminer.com/trump-team-weighs-arming-coast-guard-icebreakers/article/2621998 (accessed June 1, 2017).

14. U.S. Department of Homeland Security, U.S. Coast Guard, Office of Waterways and Ocean Policy, "Major Icebreakers of the World," updated May 1, 2017, http://www.dco.uscg.mil/Portals/9/DCO%20Documents/Office%20of%20Waterways%20and%20Ocean%20Policy/20170501%20major%20icebreaker%20chart.pdf?ver=2017-06-08-091723-907 (accessed July 12, 2017).

15. Deutsche Welle, "NATO Commander: Russia Uses Syrian Refugees as 'Weapon' Against West," March 2, 2016, http://www.dw.com/en/nato-commander-russia-uses-syrian-refugees-as-weapon-against-west/a-19086285 (accessed June 23, 2017).

16. Bruce Jones, "Danish Defence Intelligence Service Warns of Russia's Plans to Cause Trouble Between NATO Troops," *Jane's 360*, April 26, 2017, http://www.janes.com/article/69831/danish-defence-intelligence-service-warns-of-russia-s-plans-to-cause-trouble-between-nato-troops (accessed July 12, 2017).

17. News release, "Autumn 2016 Standard Eurobarometer: Immigration and Terrorism Continue to Be Seen as the Most Important Issues Facing the EU," European Commission, December 22, 2016, http://europa.eu/rapid/press-release_IP-16-4493_en.htm (accessed June 1, 2017).

18. Reuters, "Daily Briefing: Euro Break-up; Nerves Rising," February 28, 2017, http://uk.reuters.com/article/uk-europe-view-tuesday-idUKKBN1670W3?utm_source=Twitter&utm_medium=Social (accessed July 12, 2017).

19. Eliza Mackintosh and Judith Vonberg, "A Record Number of French Voters Cast Their Ballots for Nobody," CNN, May 8, 2017, http://www.cnn.com/2017/05/08/europe/french-voters-spoiled-ballots-abstained/index.html?sr=twCNN050817french-voters-spoiled-ballots-abstained0442PMVODtopLink&linkId=37346306 (accessed June 1, 2017).

20. European Commission, Standard Director-General for Communication, "Public Opinion in the European Union, First Results," Standard Eurobarometer 86, December 2016, p. 17, http://ec.europa.eu/commfrontoffice/publicopinion/index.cfm/ResultDoc/download/Documentky/76422 (accessed September 13, 2017).

21. Claire Jones, "Eurozone Annual GDP Hits 1.8%," *Financial Times*, January 31, 2017, https://www.ft.com/content/242578a0-8ad4-32b2-87ae-5bc01ea3d508 (accessed May 8, 2017).

22. "Manufacturing Across Europe Continues Steady Growth," *The Irish Times*, May 2, 2017, http://www.irishtimes.com/business/manufacturing/manufacturing-across-europe-continues-steady-growth-1.3068581 (accessed June 1, 2017).

23. News release, "February 2017: Euro Area Unemployment at 9.5%, EU28 at 8.0%," European Commission–EUROSTAT, April 3, 2017, http://ec.europa.eu/eurostat/documents/2995521/7963741/3-03042017-BP-EN.pdf/d77023a5-64cb-4bf5-8181-8f4d3a0ee292 (accessed June 1, 2017).

24. Silvia Amaro, "Potential New Banking Crises Are a Concern in Europe: Analyst," CNBC, January 2, 2017, http://www.cnbc.com/2017/01/02/potential-new-banking-crises-are-a-concern-in-europe-analyst.html (accessed June 1, 2017).

25. Sonia Sirletti and Chiara Vasarri, "Italy Approves $21 Billion Fund to Shore Up Its Troubled Banks," Bloomberg, February 16, 2017, https://www.bloomberg.com/news/articles/2017-02-16/italy-approves-21-billion-fund-to-shore-up-its-troubled-banks (accessed June 1, 2017).

26. News release, "Mediterranean Migrant Arrivals Reach 20,484, Deaths: 525," United Nations, International Organization for Migration, March 21, 2017, http://www.iom.int/news/mediterranean-migrant-arrivals-reach-20484-deaths-525 (accessed June 1, 2017).

27. Frontex, *Risk Analysis for 2017*, February 2017, p. 6, http://frontex.europa.eu/assets/Publications/Risk_Analysis/Annual_Risk_Analysis_2017.pdf (accessed July 12, 2017).

28. Andrea Thomas, "Germany Puts Migration-Related Costs at Over $86 Billion Over Next Four Years," *The Wall Street Journal*, June 1, 2016, https://www.wsj.com/articles/germany-puts-migration-related-costs-at-over-86-billion-over-next-four-years-1467392402 (accessed June 1, 2017).

29. Henriette Jacobsen, "Sweden Sees Costs of Migration Crisis Almost Quadruple," Euractiv, April 13, 2017, http://www.euractiv.com/section/global-europe/news/sweden-sees-costs-of-migration-crisis-almost-quadruple/ (accessed July 12, 2017).

30. North Atlantic Treaty Organization, "Assistance for the Refugee and Migrant Crisis in the Aegean Sea," last updated June 27, 2016, http://www.nato.int/cps/en/natohq/topics_128746.htm (accessed July 10, 2017).

31. News release, "Statement by the NATO Secretary General on NATO Support to Assist with the Refugee and Migrant Crisis," North Atlantic Treaty Organization, February 25, 2016, http://www.nato.int/cps/en/natohq/opinions_128372.htm?selectedLocale=en (accessed June 1, 2017).

32. U.S. Department of State, Bureau of Consular Affairs, U.S. Passports and International Travel, "Europe Travel Alert: The Department of State Alerts U.S. Citizens to the Continued Threat of Terrorist Attacks Throughout Europe," updated May 1, 2017, https://travel.state.gov/content/passports/en/alertswarnings/Europe.html (accessed July 12, 2017).

33. Alexis Flynn, "ISIS Sympathizer Found Guilty of Planning Attack Against U.S. Military in U.K.," *The Wall Street Journal*, April 1, 2016, http://www.wsj.com/articles/isis-sympathizer-found-guilty-of-planning-attack-against-u-s-military-in-u-k-1459514064 (accessed June 1, 2017).

34. Stenographic transcript of *Hearing to Receive Testimony on United States European Command*, Committee on Armed Services, U.S. Senate, March 23, 2017, p. 14, https://www.armed-services.senate.gov/imo/media/doc/17-24_03-23-17.pdf (accessed August 8, 2017).

35. Robert Wall, "U.S. Army Deployment to Europe Encounters Logistical Challenges," *The Wall Street Journal*, January 24, 2017, https://www.wsj.com/articles/u-s-army-deployment-to-europe-encounters-logistical-challenges-1485203221 (accessed June 1, 2017).

36. Fact Sheet, "3rd Army Brigade Combat Team, 4th Infantry Division" U.S. Army Europe, January 4, 2017, http://www.eur.army.mil/organization/factsheets/Factsheet_3-4ID.pdf (accessed July 12, 2017).

37. Sgt. 1st Class Jacob A. McDonald, "Tanks Arrive in Germany to Begin Armor Rotations," U.S. Army, January 6, 2017, https://www.army.mil/article/180361 (accessed July 12, 2017).

38. Meghann Myers, "Back to Europe: The Army Is Sending More Troops, Tanks and Helicopters to Deter Russia," *Army Times*, March 19, 2017, https://www.armytimes.com/articles/back-to-europe-the-army-is-sending-more-troops-tanks-and-helicopters-to-deter-russia (accessed June 1, 2017).

39. Thomas Donnelly and James Cunningham, "The Troops Train to Reassure Europe," *The Wall Street Journal*, May 3, 2017, https://www.wsj.com/articles/the-troops-train-to-reassure-europe-1493852663 (accessed June 1, 2017).

40. Fact Sheet, "10th Combat Aviation Brigade, 10th Mountain Division," U.S. Army Europe, February 3, 2017, http://www.eur.army.mil/organization/factsheets/Factsheet_10thCAB.pdf (accessed July 12, 2017).

41. Oriana Pawlyk, "2 More F-35s to Join Fleet in Europe After Fuel Valve Glitch," *DoD Buzz*, April 19, 2017, https://www.dodbuzz.com/2017/04/19/2-more-f-35s-to-join-fleet-in-europe-after-fuel-valve-glitch/ (accessed July 12, 2017).

42. Associated Press, "US F-35 Stealth Fighters Arrive in Estonia for NATO Drills," Fox News, April 25, 2017, http://www.foxnews.com/us/2017/04/25/us-f-35-stealth-fighters-arrive-in-estonia-for-nato-drills.html (accessed June 2, 2017).

43. News release, "F-35A Lightning IIs Arrive in Bulgaria," United States European Command, April 28, 2017, http://www.eucom.mil/media-library/pressrelease/35660/f-35a-lightning-iis-arrive-in-bulgaria (accessed July 12, 2017).

44. Ibid.

45. Sgt. 1st Class Jacob McDonald, "Prepositioned Equipment Site Officially Opens in Netherlands," U.S. Army, December 16, 2016, https://www.army.mil/article/179831/prepositioned_equipment_site_officially_opens_in_netherlands (accessed June 5, 2017).

46. Sgt. 1st Class Jacob A. McDonald, "Ribbon Cut on Second Prepositioned Equipment Site," U.S. Army, May 11, 2017, https://www.army.mil/article/187565/ (accessed July 12, 2017).

47. Dan Stoutamire, "Army to Move Brigade's Worth of Firepower into Poland," *Stars and Stripes*, April 26, 2017, https://www.stripes.com/news/army-to-move-brigade-s-worth-of-firepower-into-poland-1.465372#.WQyodoWcHcv (accessed July 12, 2017).

48. Megan Eckstein, "Foggo: BALTOPS 2016 Includes More Anti-Sub, More Challenging Amphibious Operations," USNI News, June 15, 2016, https://news.usni.org/2016/06/15/baltops_amphibious_challenges (accessed July 12, 2017); Karen E. Rybarczyk, "BALTOPS 2016 Comes to a Close in Kiel, Germany," U.S. Naval Forces Europe–Africa/U.S. 6th Fleet, June 17, 2016, http://www.c6f.navy.mil/news/baltops-2016-comes-close-kiel-germany (accessed August 8, 2017).

49. Yasmin Tadjdeh, "Budget Impasse Could Damage Army's Part in European Reassurance Initiative," *National Defense*, April 27, 2017, http://www.nationaldefensemagazine.org/articles/2017/4/27/continuing-resolution-could-hurt-armys-european-reassurance-initiative-effort (accessed June 5, 2017).

50. Defence Blog, "US Military Will Send New Strykers with 30mm Cannon to Europe in 2018," October 31, 2016, http://defence-blog.com/army/us-military-will-send-new-strykers-with-30mm-cannon-to-europe-in-2018.html (accessed July 12, 2017).

51. Tadjdeh, "Budget Impasse Could Damage Army's Part in European Reassurance Initiative."

52. News release, "U.S. Commitment 'Galvanized' in ERI Implementation Plans," United States European Command, May 24, 2017, http://www.eucom.mil/media-library/pressrelease/35714/u-s-commitment-galvanized-in-eri-implementation-plans (accessed June 5, 2017).

53. General Curtis M. Scaparrotti, U.S Army, Commander, United States European Command, statement before the Committee on Armed Services, U.S. Senate, March 23, 2017, p. 2, https://www.armed-services.senate.gov/imo/media/doc/Scaparrotti_03-23-17.pdf (accessed July 12, 2017).

54. "Fact Sheet: U.S. Assurance and Deterrence Efforts in Support of NATO Allies," The White House, July 8, 2016, https://obamawhitehouse.archives.gov/the-press-office/2016/07/08/fact-sheet-us-assurance-and-deterrence-efforts-support-nato-allies (accessed August 8, 2017).

55. Scaparrotti, statement before Senate Committee on Armed Services, March 23, 2017, p. 12.

56. Todd Miller, "The West's Best Fighter Jets, Together in Virginia," War is Boring, May 3, 2017, http://warisboring.com/the-wests-best-fighter-jets-together-in-virginia/ (accessed June 5, 2017).

57. Andrius Sytas, "NATO War Game Defends Baltic Weak Spot for First Time," Reuters, June 18, 2017, http://www.reuters.com/article/us-nato-russia-suwalki-gap-idUSKBN1990L2 (accessed June 29, 2017).

58. U.S. Department of Defense, National Guard Bureau, "State Partnership Program," January 1, 2017, http://www.nationalguard.mil/Portals/31/Documents/J-5/InternationalAffairs/StatePartnershipProgram/SPP%20Partnership%20Map.pdf (accessed July 12, 2017).

59. United States Army Europe, Joint Multinational Training Group–Ukraine, "What Is Joint Multinational Training Group–Ukraine?" http://www.eur.army.mil/jmtg-u/ (accessed July 12, 2017).

60. Scaparrotti, statement before Senate Committee on Armed Services, March 23, 2017, p. 17.

61. Vincent L. Morelli, "Ukraine: Current Issues and U.S. Policy," Congressional Research Service *Report for Members and Committees of Congress*, January 3, 2017, p. 39, https://fas.org/sgp/crs/row/RL33460.pdf (accessed June 5, 2017).

62. Jamie McIntyre, "NATO Commander Calls for More US Troops in Europe to Deter Russia," *Washington Examiner*, March 28, 2017, http://www.washingtonexaminer.com/nato-commander-calls-for-more-u.s.-troops-in-europe-to-deter-russia/article/2618636?custom_click=rss (accessed June 5, 2017).

63. Julian E. Barnes, "U.S. to Boost Surveillance for Russian Exercise," *The Wall Street Journal*, May 10, 2017, https://www.wsj.com/articles/u-s-to-boost-surveillance-for-russian-exercise-1494415602 (accessed June 5, 2017).

64. Malcolm Chalmers and Simon Lunn, "NATO's Tactical Nuclear Dilemma," Royal United Services Institute *Occasional Paper*, March 2010, p. 1, https://rusi.org/sites/default/files/201003_op_natos_tactical_nuclear_dilemma.pdf (accessed September 6, 2016).

65. Geoff Ziezulewicz, "B61-12 Life Extension Program Receives NNSA Approval," UPI, August 2, 2016, http://www.upi.com/Business_News/Security-Industry/2016/08/02/B61-12-life-extension-program-receives-NNSA-approval/3261470147434/ (accessed August 18, 2016).

66. Tom O'Connor, "The U.S. Is Building a Nuclear Bomb That's More Accurate Than Ever," *Newsweek*, April 18, 2017, http://www.newsweek.com/us-build-better-nuclear-missile-585686 (accessed June 5, 2017).

67. News release, "Warsaw Summit Communiqué Issued by the Heads of State and Government Participating in the Meeting of the North Atlantic Council in Warsaw 8–9 July 2016," North Atlantic Treaty Organization, July 9, 2016, http://www.nato.int/cps/en/natohq/official_texts_133169.htm (accessed July 11, 2017).

68. Julian E. Barnes, "NATO Considers New Counterterrorism Post Following Trump Demands," *The Wall Street Journal*, May 1, 2017, https://www.wsj.com/articles/nato-considers-new-counterterrorism-post-following-trump-demands-1493638028 (accessed July 12, 2017).

69. North Atlantic Treaty Organization, "Operation Active Endeavour," last updated October 27, 2016, http://www.nato.int/cps/en/natohq/topics_7932.htm (accessed July 12, 2017); "NATO Kicks Off New Operation Sea Guardian," *Naval Today*, November 9, 2016, http://navaltoday.com/2016/11/09/nato-kicks-off-new-operation-sea-guardian/ (accessed June 6, 2017).

70. "Russia's destabilising actions and policies include: the ongoing illegal and illegitimate annexation of Crimea, which we do not and will not recognise and which we call on Russia to reverse; the violation of sovereign borders by force; the deliberate destabilisation of eastern Ukraine; large-scale snap exercises contrary to the spirit of the Vienna Document, and provocative military activities near NATO borders, including in the Baltic and Black Sea regions and the Eastern Mediterranean; its irresponsible and aggressive nuclear rhetoric, military concept and underlying posture; and its repeated violations of NATO Allied airspace. In addition, Russia's military intervention, significant military presence and support for the regime in Syria, and its use of its military presence in the Black Sea to project power into the Eastern Mediterranean have posed further risks and challenges for the security of Allies and others." News release, "Warsaw Summit Communiqué."

71. North Atlantic Treaty Organization, "Readiness Action Plan," last updated January 25, 2017, http://www.nato.int/cps/on/natohq/topics_119353.htm (accessed July 12, 2017).

72. News release, "Wales Summit Declaration," North Atlantic Treaty Organization, September 5, 2014, http://www.nato.int/cps/en/natohq/official_texts_112964.htm (accessed June 6, 2016).

73. North Atlantic Treaty Organization, *The Secretary General's Annual Report: 2016*, p. 14, http://www.nato.int/nato_static_fl2014/assets/pdf/pdf_2017_03/20170313_SG_AnnualReport_2016_en.pdf#page=13 (accessed July 12, 2017).

74. Jens Ringsmose and Sten Rynning, "Can NATO's New Very High Readiness Joint Task Force Deter?" Norwegian Institute of International Affairs *Policy Brief* No. 15/2016, 2016, p. 2, https://brage.bibsys.no/xmlui/bitstream/handle/11250/2392132/NUPI_Policy_Brief_15_16_Ringmose_Rynning.pdf ?sequence=3&isAllowed=y (accessed July 14, 2017).

75. Ibid.

76. Sam Jones, "NATO Rapid Unit Not Fit for Eastern Europe Deployment, Say Generals," *Financial Times*, May 15, 2016, https://www.ft.com/content/7ac5075c-1a96-11e6-b286-cddde55ca122 (accessed June 6, 2016).

77. Ringsmose and Rynning, "Can NATO's New Very High Readiness Joint Task Force Deter?" p. 2.

78. Tatiana Jancarikova and Gareth Jones, "Slovakia to Buy APCs for 1.2 Billion Euros, Send Troops to NATO Missions," Reuters, May 17, 2017, http://www.reuters.com/article/us-slovakia-defence-idUSKCN18D1OZ (accessed June 6, 2017).

79. North Atlantic Treaty Organization, *The Secretary General's Annual Report: 2016*, p. 15.

80. Ibid. and Republic of Poland, Ministry of Foreign Affairs, "Poland's 18 Years in the North Atlantic Alliance," March 12, 2017, http://www.msz.gov.pl/en/news/poland_s_18_years_in_the_north_atlantic_alliance (accessed July 13, 2017).

81. Baltic News Service, "Baltic Countries Sign Agreement on Fast Movement of NATO Forces," Latvian Information Agency, February 15, 2017, http://www.leta.lv/eng/defence_matters_eng/defence_matters_eng/news/CEB6CED4-EA2D-404C-8814-A8765D6BA915/ (accessed July 12, 2017).

82. Boris Toucas, "NATO and Russia in the Black Sea: A New Confrontation?" Center for Strategic and International Studies, March 6, 2017, https://www.csis.org/analysis/nato-and-russia-black-sea-new-confrontation (accessed June 6, 2017); news release, "Warsaw Summit Communiqué."

83. Transcript, "Press Conference by NATO Secretary General Jens Stoltenberg Following the Meeting of the North Atlantic Council at the Level of Defence Ministers," Brussels, Belgium, February 16, 2017, http://www.nato.int/cps/en/natohq/opinions_141340.htm (accessed July 12, 2017).

84. North Atlantic Treaty Organization, "NATO Jets Start Air Patrols over Romania," last updated April 25, 2017, http://www.nato.int/cps/en/natohq/news_143268.htm?selectedLocale=en (accessed July 11, 2017).

85. Robin Emmott, "NATO to Spend 3 Billion Euros on Satellite, Cyber Defenses," Reuters, March 27, 2017, http://mobile.reuters.com/article/idUSKBN16Y0P5 (accessed June 6, 2017).

86. News release, "Warsaw Summit Communiqué."

87. Robin Emmott, "U.S. Activates Romanian Missile Defense Site, Angering Russians," Reuters, May 12, 2016, http://www.reuters.com/article/us-nato-shield-idUSKCN0Y30JX (accessed June 6, 2017).

88. Fact Sheet, "NATO Ballistic Missile Defence," North Atlantic Treaty Organization, July 2016, http://www.nato.int/nato_static_fl2014/assets/pdf/pdf_2016_07/20160630_1607-factsheet-bmd-en.pdf (accessed June 6, 2017).

89. Lisa Ferdinando, "Work Joins Groundbreaking for Ballistic Missile Defense Site in Poland," U.S. Department of Defense, May 13, 2016, https://www.defense.gov/News/Article/Article/759662/work-joins-groundbreaking-for-ballistic-missile-defense-site-in-poland/ (accessed August 8, 2017).

90. Fact Sheet, "NATO Ballistic Missile Defence."

91. Russian Embassy in Norway and Norway Today, "Russia Threatens Norway to Stay Out of NATO Missile Defense," Atlantic Council, March 21, 2017, http://www.atlanticcouncil.org/blogs/natosource/russia-threatens-norway-to-stay-out-of-nato-missile-defense (accessed June 6, 2017).

92. Gerard O'Dwyer, "Denmark Progresses in NATO Ballistic Missile Defense Role," *Defense News*, April 22, 2016, http://www.defensenews.com/story/defense/air-space/strike/2016/04/22/denmark-progresses-nato-ballistic-missile-defense-role/83391868/ (accessed June 6, 2017).

93. "Fact Sheet: NATO Ballistic Missile Defence."

94. Daniel Wasserbly and Richard Scott, "Royal Danish Navy Sets SM-2 Buy as Priority, Mulls Frigate BMD Upgrade," *Jane's 360*, November 23, 2016, http://www.janes.com/article/65700/royal-danish-navy-sets-sm-2-buy-as-priority-mulls-frigate-bmd-upgrade (accessed July 11, 2017).

95. "German Navy to Modernize Its Sachsen-Class Frigates with New Radar to Join NATO BMD," *Navy Recognition*, December 23, 2016, http://www.navyrecognition.com/index.php/news/defence-news/2016/december-2016-navy-naval-forces-defense-industry-technology-maritime-security-global-news/4719-german-navy-to-modernize-its-f124-sachsen-class-frigates-with-new-radar-to-join-nato-bmd.html (accessed July 12, 2017).

96. "Fact Sheet: NATO Ballistic Missile Defence."

97. "Future Belgian Navy Frigates May Have Ballistic Missile Capabilities," *Navy Recognition*, January 5, 2017, http://www.navyrecognition.com/index.php/news/defence-news/2017/january-2017-navy-naval-forces-defense-industry-technology-maritime-security-global-news/4766-future-belgian-navy-frigates-may-have-ballistic-missile-defense-capabilities.html (accessed June 6, 2017).

98. O'Dwyer, "Denmark Progresses in NATO Ballistic Missile Defense Role."

99. Nick Witney, "Re-Energising Europe's Security and Defence Policy," European Council on Foreign Relations *Policy Paper*, July 2008, p. 20, http://www.feelingeurope.eu/Pages/Re%20energising%20Europe%20Security%20and%20Defence%20Policy%20july%202008.pdf (accessed June 6, 2017).

100. Michael Shurkin, "The Abilities of the British, French, and German Armies to Generate and Sustain Armored Brigades in the Baltics," RAND Corporation *Research Report* No. 1629-A, 2017, pp. 1 and 9, https://www.rand.org/content/dam/rand/pubs/research_reports/RR1600/RR1629/RAND_RR1629.pdf (accessed July 11, 2017).

101. The North Atlantic Treaty, Article 3, April 4, 1949, last updated March 21, 2016, http://www.nato.int/cps/en/SID-857936BB-66246E10/natolive/official_texts_17120.htm (accessed June 6, 2017).

102. News release, "Defence Expenditure of NATO Countries (2009–2016)," North Atlantic Treaty Organization, March 13, 2017, http://www.nato.int/nato_static_fl2014/assets/pdf/pdf_2017_03/20170313_170313-pr2017-045.pdf (accessed July 11, 2017).

103. North Atlantic Treaty Organization, *The Secretary General's Annual Report: 2016*, pp. 29–31.

104. Michael Dalder, "Germany Sends Tanks to Lithuania for NATO Mission," Reuters, January 31, 2017, http://www.reuters.com/article/us-nato-russia-germany-idUSKBN15F1IH (accessed June 6, 2017).

105. North Atlantic Treaty Organization, *The Secretary General's Annual Report: 2016*, pp. 100–101.

106. North Atlantic Treaty Organization, Allied Air Command, "Germany Continues Augmenting Baltic Air Policing," January 6, 2017, http://www.ac.nato.int/archive/2017/germany-continues-augmenting-baltic-air-policing (accessed July 12, 2017).

107. Deutsche Welle, "German Military Flew Nearly 700 Missions Against 'Islamic State' in 2016," December 29, 2016, http://www.dw.com/en/german-military-flew-nearly-700-missions-against-islamic-state-in-2016/a-36936076 (accessed June 6, 2017).

108. Ibid.

109. Deutsche Welle, "German Lawmakers Call for Withdrawal of Bundeswehr Troops from Turkey," March 12, 2016, http://www.dw.com/en/german-lawmakers-call-for-withdrawal-of-bundeswehr-troops-from-turkey/a-37911461 (accessed July 12, 2017); Deutsche Welle, "AWACS to Be Added to German Anti-IS Operations," October 12, 2016, http://www.dw.com/en/awacs-to-be-added-to-german-anti-is-operations/a-36027493 (accessed July 12, 2017).

110. Deutsche Welle, "German Parliament Approves Extension of Anti-IS Mission from Turkish Base," November 10, 2016, http://www.dw.com/en/german-parliament-approves-extension-of-anti-is-mission-from-turkish-base/a-36351109 (accessed June 6, 2017).

111. Reuters, "Germany Says Boosting Defense Spending, Demands Clear U.S. Agenda," January 18, 2017, http://www.reuters.com/article/us-germany-military-idUSKBN1522UG (accessed July 11, 2017).

112. Jochen Bittner and Peter Dausend, "A Military Upgrade for America?" *Zeit Online*, February 28, 2017, http://www.zeit.de/politik/ausland/2017-02/nato-defense-germany-armament-donald-trump (accessed June 6, 2017).

113. Sebastian Sprenger, "Germany Beefs Up Tank Fleet with $832M Acquisition," *Defense News*, May 9, 2017, http://www.defensenews.com/articles/germany-beefs-up-tank-fleet-with-832m-acquisition (accessed June 6, 2017).

114. Kai Biermann and Julian Stahnke, "Kaputte Truppe," *Zeit Online*, April 20, 2017, http://www.zeit.de/politik/deutschland/2017-04/bundeswehr-bestand-ausruestung-panzer (accessed July 10, 2017).

115. Konstantin von Hammerstein and Peter Müller, "Germany's Self-Imposed Obstacles to Increasing Defense Spending," Atlantic Council, February 21, 2017, http://www.atlanticcouncil.org/blogs/natosource/germany-s-self-imposed-obstacles-to-increasing-defense-spending (accessed July 11, 2017).

116. Niklas Helwig, "Germany's New Defense Pragmatism Is Not Measured in Euros," War on the Rocks, March 13, 2017, https://warontherocks.com/2017/03/germanys-new-defense-pragmatism-is-not-measured-in-euros/ (accessed July 12, 2017).

117. Stefan Rentzsch, "Germany and Norway to Extend Naval Cooperation from Submarines to Antisurface Missiles," Federal Republic of Germany, Federal Ministry of Defence, February 13, 2017, https://www.bmvg.de/portal/a/bmvg/start/journal/sicherheitspolitik/!ut/p/z1/hY_RC4IwEMb_l2-bWPbolGBiYimVe4mhwwzbZCzpoT--SeCbdA8f3Pfd_Y4DDlfgSkx9J2yvlRhcX_PNjYZZIZEdIVURJ4gdfErxkbCw8OEMI38j3MVopSIEpVRQO8Z2jUGYDyVw4K30Gq2kndVKZXunnRFWG2_Uxg5z8jLGJV7fQo1wQhFeTuFPIKZxXAV-kDB6moEPMYn3siua-Wmo70K1gyx0E_2M8bkP8zzovt1RqTA!/dz/d5/L2dBISEvZ0FBIS9nQSEh/#Z7_B8LTL2922TPCD0IM3BB1Q2I2I3 (accessed July 13, 2017).

118. Reuters, "Germany to Spend 1.5 Bln Euros for More Navy Ships–Navy," October 14, 2016, http://www.reuters.com/article/german-navy-idUSL8N1CK4QI (accessed June 6, 2017).

119. Reuters, "Germany to Increase Army to 198,000 by 2024 Amid NATO Spending Row," February 21, 2017, http://www.reuters.com/article/germany-army-idUSL8N1G65BZ (accessed June 6, 2017).

120. Nina Werkhäuser, "German Army Launches New Cyber Command," Deutsche Welle, April 1, 2017, http://www.dw.com/en/german-army-launches-new-cyber-command/a-38246517 (accessed July 11, 2017).

121. Saim Saeed, "German Cybersecurity Chief: Army Attacked over 284,000 Times This Year," *Politico*, April 3, 2017, http://www.politico.eu/pro/german-cybersecurity-chief-army-attacked-over-284000-times-this-year/?utm_content=bufferf1c8c&utm_medium=social&utm_source=twitter.com&utm_campaign=buffer (accessed June 6, 2017).

122. Andrea Shalal, "Germany to Move Ahead on New Short-Range Air Defense System," Reuters, February 2, 2017, http://www.reuters.com/article/us-germany-military-idUSKBN15H1Z9 (accessed June 6, 2017).

123. Sabine Siebold, "Exclusive: German Report Raises Concerns Over A400M Military Readiness," Reuters, May 8, 2017, http://www.reuters.com/article/us-germany-airbus-a400m-exclusive-idUSKBN1841NY?utm_source=twitter&utm_medium=Social (accessed June 6, 2017).

124. Cynthia Kroet, "Angela Merkel: 'No Doubt' Some Refugees Are a Security Threat," *Politico*, April 13, 2017, http://www.politico.eu/article/angela-merkel-no-doubt-some-refugees-are-a-security-threat/ (accessed June 6, 2017).

125. Cynthia Kroet, "Refugee Crisis Cost Germany Over €20 Billion in 2016," *Politico*, January 27, 2017, http://www.politico.eu/article/refugee-crisis-cost-germany-over-e20-billion-in-2016/ (accessed June 8, 2017).

126. John Vandiver, "Report: Europe's Armies Too Slow for a Baltic Clash," *Stars and Stripes*, April 13, 2017, http://www.military.com/daily-news/2017/04/13/report-europes-armies-too-slow-baltic-clash.html (accessed June 6, 2017).

127. Alissa J. Rubin, "France's Top General Resigns in Dispute Over Military Spending," *The New York Times*, July 19, 2017, https://www.nytimes.com/2017/07/19/world/europe/france-general-pierre-de-villiers-macron-military-budget.html (accessed July 20, 2017).

128. Reuters, "FEATURE–Under Threat, France Grooms Army Hackers for Cyberwarfare," April 5, 2017, http://uk.reuters.com/article/france-cyber-idUKL5N1HC2XQ (accessed June 6, 2017).

129. Ibid.

130. Geert De Clercq, "French Military to Boost Defenses Against Cyber Attacks: Minister," Reuters, January 7, 2017, http://www.reuters.com/article/us-france-cyber-idUSKBN14R0OD (accessed June 6, 2017).

131. RFI, "Last French Troops Handover in Afghanistan," December 31, 2014, http://www.english.rfi.fr/asia-pacific/20141231-last-french-troops-handover-afghanistan (accessed June 7, 2017).

132. French Republic, Ministry of Defense, "Carte des Opérations et Mission Militaires," updated June 28, 2016, http://www.defense.gouv.fr/english/operations/rubriques_complementaires/carte-des-operations-et-missions-militaires (accessed July 13, 2017).

133. i24NEWS, "France Has Dropped Twice as Many Bombs on ISIS as in Libya: Airforce Chief," January 30, 2017, https://www.i24news.tv/en/news/international/136413-170130-france-has-dropped-twice-as-many-bombs-on-is-as-in-libya-airforce-chief (accessed June 7, 2017).

134. Chris Church, "Anti-Islamic State Coalition Losing French Flattop," *Stars and Stripes,* November 30, 2016, https://www.stripes.com/news/anti-islamic-state-coalition-losing-french-flattop-1.441857#.WO5qGYjyvcs (accessed June 7, 2017).

135. i24NEWS, "France Has Dropped Twice as Many Bombs on ISIS as in Libya."

136. Defence Blog, "Heavy Equipment for French Troops Arrive in Estonia for Major NATO Deployment," March 28, 2017, http://defence-blog.com/army/heavy-equipment-for-french-troops-arrive-in-estonia-for-major-nato-deployment.html (accessed June 7, 2017).

137. North Atlantic Treaty Organization, *The Secretary General's Annual Report: 2016*, p. 15.

138. French Republic, Ministry of Defence, "Carte des Opérations et Mission Militaires."

139. Ibid.; French Republic, Ministry of Defense, "Les forces françaises stationnées à Djibouti," September 20, 2016, http://www.defense.gouv.fr/ema/forces-prepositionnees/djibouti/dossier/les-forces-francaises-stationnees-a-djibouti (accessed July 13, 2017); Reuters, "France Starts Pulling Troops from Central African Republic," December 4, 2014, http://www.voanews.com/content/france-starts-pulling-troops-from-central-african-republic/2545843.html (accessed July 13, 2017).

140. Jim Garamone, "France Deploys Globally in Counter-Extremism Fight," U.S. Department of Defense, January 17, 2017, https://www.defense.gov/News/Article/Article/1050644/france-deploys-troops-globally-in-counter-extremism-fight (accessed June 7, 2017).

141. International Institute for Strategic Studies, *The Military Balance 2017: The Annual Assessment of Global Military Capabilities and Defence Economics* (London: Routledge, 2017), p. 78.

142. Laura Smith-Spark and Laura Goehler, "Louvre Knife Attack: Soldier Shoots Assailant Near Paris Museum," CNN, February 3, 2017, http://www.cnn.com/2017/02/03/europe/france-paris-louvre-incident/ (accessed July 13, 2017); Alissa J. Rubin and Benoît Morenne, "Gunman Is Killed in Orly Airport in France After Attacking a Soldier," *The New York Times*, March 18, 2017, https://www.nytimes.com/2017/03/18/world/europe/orly-airport-france-shooting.html (accessed July 13, 2017).

143. "On the Frontline with Operation Sentinelle," *Politico*, December 29, 2016, http://www.politico.eu/interactive/french-soldiers-deployed-operation-sentinelle-paris-terror-attacks/ (accessed June 7, 2017).

144. Transcript of Geoffrey Smith interview with Margaret Thatcher, Margaret Thatcher Foundation, January 8, 1990, http://www.margaretthatcher.org/document/109324 (accessed June 7, 2017).

145. News release, "Defence Expenditure of NATO Countries (2010-2017)," North Atlantic Treaty Organization, June 29, 2017, p. 8, http://www.nato.int/nato_static_fl2014/assets/pdf/pdf_2017_06/20170629_170629-pr2017-111-en.pdf (accessed August 8, 2018).

146. News release, "Defence Expenditures of NATO Countries (2009–2016)."

147. Steve McCarthy, "Britain's Defense Capabilities and the Future of Transatlantic Security," Atlantic Council, February 28, 2017, http://www.atlanticcouncil.org/blogs/natosource/britain-s-defense-capabilities-and-the-future-of-transatlantic-security (accessed June 7, 2017).

148. Aaron Mehta, "US, UK Still Discussing Anti-Sub Gap Options," *Defense News*, April 19, 2016, http://www.defensenews.com/story/defense/naval/naval-aviation/2016/04/19/us-uk-asw-antisub-russia-p8/83224392/ (accessed June 7, 2017).

149. Ben Farmer, "Britain Calls in French to Hunt Russian Sub Lurking off Scotland," *The Telegraph*, November 22, 2015, http://www.telegraph.co.uk/news/uknews/defence/12010438/Britain-calls-in-French-to-hunt-Russian-sub-lurking-off-Scotland.html (accessed June 7, 2017).

150. Reuters, "Trident: UK Parliament Backs Nuclear-Armed Submarine Fleet Renewal," July 18, 2016, http://www.abc.net.au/news/2016-07-19/uk-parliament-backs-trident-nuclear-submarine-renewal/7640160 (accessed June 7, 2017).

151. "UK to Lead NATO's Very High Readiness Joint Task Force," Army-technology.com, January 4, 2017, http://www.army-technology.com/news/newsuk-assumes-responsibility-to-lead-natos-vjtf-5708989 (accessed July 13, 2017); United Kingdom, Army, "British Forces Lead NATO Spearhead Force," January 1, 2017, http://www.army.mod.uk/news/28881.aspx (accessed July 13, 2017).

152. BBC, "UK Troops in Estonia to deter 'Russian Aggression,'" March 18, 2017, http://www.bbc.com/news/uk-39311670 (accessed June 7, 2017).

153. North Atlantic Treaty Organization, Allied Air Command, "Baltic Air Policing Augmenting Nations Pass Baton at Ämari, Estonia," August 31, 2016, https://ac.nato.int/archive/2016/baltic-air-policing-augmenting-nations-pass-baton-at-amari--estonia (accessed July 13, 2017).

154. News release, "UK's NATO Southern Air Policing Mission to Begin in May," United Kingdom, March 27, 2017, https://www.gov.uk/government/news/uks-nato-southern-air-policing-mission-to-begin-in-may (accessed July 13, 2017).

155. Reuters, "Turkey Orders 72 University Staff Detained in Coup-Related Probe: Anadolu," July 10, 2017, https://www.reuters.com/article/us-turkey-security-detentions-idUSKBN19V0RT (accessed July 13, 2017).

156. Reuters, "Turkey Formally Arrests Newspaper Staff over Suspected Coup Links: Paper," May 27, 2017, http://www.reuters.com/article/us-turkey-security-newspaper-idUSKBN18N08Y (accessed July 13, 2017).

157. Peter Müller and Maximilian Popp, "Purges Have Weakened Once Mighty Turkish Military," *Spiegel Online*, January 18, 2017, http://www.spiegel.de/international/world/purges-have-weakened-once-mighty-turkish-military-a-1130494.html (accessed July 13, 2017).

158. Tuvan Gumrukcu and Humeyra Pamuk, "Turkey's Erdogan Declares Referendum Victory, Opponents Plan Challenge," Reuters, April 17, 2017, http://www.reuters.com/article/us-turkey-referendum-idUSKBN17H0CU (accessed June 7, 2017).

159. Organization for Security and Co-operation in Europe, Office for Democratic Institutions and Human Rights, and Council of Europe, Parliamentary Assembly, "International Referendum Observation Mission, Republic of Turkey–Constitutional Referendum, 16 April 2017: Statement of Preliminary Findings and Conclusions," p. 1, http://www.osce.org/odihr/elections/turkey/311721?download=true (accessed July 13, 2017).

160. Tom Körkemeier and Shadia Nasralla, "Turkey Blocks Some Cooperation with NATO Partners as EU Row Escalates," Reuters, March 15, 2017, http://www.reuters.com/article/us-turkey-referendum-nato-idUSKBN16M2OR (accessed June 7, 2017).

161. Radio Free Europe/Radio Liberty, "Erdogan Urges U.S. to Reverse Decision on Arming Syrian Kurds," last updated May 10, 2017, https://www.rferl.org/a/turkey-protests-us-arming-syria-kurds/28477965.html (accessed July 13, 2017).

162. Richard Sisk, "Turkey Hints at Shuttering Incirlik to US Air Operations," Military.com, January 4, 2017, http://www.military.com/daily-news/2017/01/04/turkey-hints-shuttering-incirlik-us-air-operations.html (accessed June 7, 2017).

163. North Atlantic Treaty Organization, *The Secretary General's Annual Report: 2016*, p. 14; Deutsche Welle, "NATO Discussing Request for AWACS Surveillance Aircraft in Syrian Anti-'IS' Fight," January 22, 2016, http://www.dw.com/en/nato-discussing-request-for-awacs-surveillance-aircraft-in-syrian-anti-is-fight/a-18998325 (accessed June 7, 2017).

164. Al Jazeera, "Turkey Ends 'Euphrates Shield' Operation in Syria," March 29, 2017, http://www.aljazeera.com/news/2017/03/turkey-ends-euphrates-shield-operation-syria-170329211428970.html (accessed July 13, 2017).

165. BBC, "Turkey 'Ends' Euphrates Shield Campaign in Syria," March 30, 2017, http://www.bbc.com/news/world-middle-east-39439593 (accessed July 10, 2017).

166. North Atlantic Treaty Organization, "Resolute Support Mission (RSM): Key Facts and Figures," February 2017, http://www.nato.int/nato_static_fl2014/assets/pdf/pdf_2017_02/20170209_2017-02-RSM-Placemat.pdf (accessed July 13, 2017).

167. North Atlantic Treaty Organization, *The Secretary General's Annual Report: 2016*, p. 101.

168. International Institute for Strategic Studies, *The Military Balance 2017*, p. 166.

169. International Institute for Strategic Studies, *The Military Balance 2016: The Annual Assessment of Global Military Capabilities and Defence Economics* (London: Routledge, 2016), pp. 147–148.

170. Tulay Karadeniz, "Turkey Eyes Deal with China on Missile Defense Despite NATO Concern," Reuters, February 18, 2015, http://www.reuters.com/article/2015/02/19/us-turkey-china-defence-idUSKBN0LN0W220150219 (accessed June 7, 2017).

171. Burak Ege Bekdil, "Turkey Scraps $3.4B Air Defense Contract," *Defense News*, November 15, 2015, http://www.defensenews.com/story/defense/2015/11/15/turkey-cancels-missile-deal-china/75826180/ (accessed June 7, 2017).

172. Emanuele Scimia, "Shadows Over Turkey's Possible Purchase of the Russian S-400," *Asia Times*, May 5, 2017, http://www.atimes.com/shadows-turkeys-possible-purchase-russian-s-400/ (accessed June 7, 2017).

173. Reuters, "Turkey Needs to Sort Out Price Issues with Russia on S-400 Missiles, Defense Minister Says," May 10, 2017, https://www.usnews.com/news/world/articles/2017-05-10/turkey-needs-to-sort-out-price-issues-with-russia-on-s-400-missiles-defense-minister-says (accessed June 7, 2017); Scimia, "Shadows Over Turkey's Possible Purchase of the Russian S-400."

174. "S-400 Missile System Purchase at Final Stage: Turkish Defense Minister," *Daily Sabah*, April 13, 2017, https://www.dailysabah.com/diplomacy/2017/04/13/s-400-missile-system-purchase-at-final-stage-turkish-defense-minister (accessed June 7, 2017).

175. Press release, "Defence Expenditures of NATO Countries (2010–2017)," p. 3.

176. International Institute for Strategic Studies, *The Military Balance 2017*, p. 107.

177. Simon Newton, "Why NATO's Military Might Is Focused on Estonia," Forces Network, November 5, 2015, http://forces.tv/54579182 (accessed July 13, 2017).

178. Richard Tomkins, "Estonia Consolidates Military Procurement Process," UPI, January 3, 2017, http://www.upi.com/Defense-News/2017/01/03/Estonia-consolidates-military-procurement-process/9171483458417/ (accessed June 7, 2017).

179. Jarolsław Adamowski, "Estonia Joins Finland in Howitzer Procurement," *Defense News*, February 6, 2017, http://www.defensenews.com/articles/estonia-joins-finland-in-howitzer-procurement (accessed June 7, 2017).

180. Republic of Estonia, Defence Forces, *National Defence Development Plan 2013–2022*, 2013, http://www.kaitseministeerium.ee/riigikaitse2022/riigikaitse-arengukava/index-en.html (accessed July 13, 2017).

181. U.S. Embassy in Estonia, "Signing of Defense Cooperation Agreement–Remarks by Ambassador James D. Melville," Talinn, Estonia, January 17, 2017, https://ee.usembassy.gov/signing-defense-cooperation-agreement-remarks-ambassador-james-d-melville/ (accessed July 13, 2017).

182. International Institute for Strategic Studies, *The Military Balance 2016*, p. 91, and *The Military Balance 2017*, p. 132.

183. Raimonds Bergmanis, Minister of Defence, "The National Defence Concept," Republic of Latvia, Ministry of Defence, June 16, 2016, p. 8, http://mepoforum.sk/wp-content/uploads/2017/01/Latvia-national-defence-concept-2016-en.pdf (accessed July 13, 2017).

184. Olevs Nikers, "Inside Latvia's New State Defense Concept: Riga Declares Its Military Ambitions Ahead of NATO Summit," Jamestown Foundation, *Eurasia Daily Monitor*, Vol. 13, Issue 104 (May 28, 2016), https://jamestown.org/program/inside-latvias-new-state-defense-concept-riga-declares-its-military-ambitions-ahead-of-nato-summit/ (accessed June 7, 2017).

185. "Latvian Defence Budget Is One of the Fastest Growing in the World," sargs.lv, December 14, 2016, http://www.sargs.lv/Zinas/Military_News/2016/12/14-01.aspx#lastcomment (accessed July 13, 2017).

186. Latvian Information Agency, "Saeima Passes Latvia's 2017 Budget," November 24, 2016, http://leta.lv/eng/home/important/133A2642-865F-C4C7-590E-B2C707E6826F/ (accessed June 7, 2017); Bergmanis, "The National Defence Concept," p. 14.

187. International Institute for Strategic Studies, *The Military Balance 2017*, p. 133.

188. North Atlantic Treaty Organization, *The Secretary Generals' Annual Report: 2016*, pp. 100–101.

189. Christopher Woody, "Baltic States Think Russia Is Laying the Groundwork for Looming 'Kinetic Operations,'" *Business Insider*, April 3, 2017, http://www.businessinsider.com/russia-propaganda-in-lithuania-attack-on-the-baltics-2017-4 (accessed June 7, 2017).

190. UaPosition, "Lithuania Stages Drills Against 'Little Green Men,'" April 12, 2017, http://uaposition.com/latest-news/lithuania-stages-drills-against-little-green-men/?utm_source=dlvr.it&utm_medium=twitter (accessed June 7, 2017).

191. Christopher Diamond, "US Partners with Lithuania in Savage Wolf Exercise," *Defense News*, April 7, 2017, http://www.defensenews.com/articles/us-partners-with-lithuania-in-savage-wolf-exercise (accessed June 7, 2017).

192. Andrius Sytas, "Lithuania Says Russia Has Ability to Launch Baltic Attack in 24 Hours," Reuters, April 3, 2017, http://www.reuters.com/article/us-lithuania-russia-idUSKBN1750Z0?utm_campaign=trueAnthem:+Trending+Content&utm_content=58e2336704d30161eb0192e8&utm_medium=trueAnthem&utm_source=twitter (accessed June 7, 2017).

193. Jaroslaw Adamowski, "Lithuania Mulls Transport, Combat Helo Acquisitions," *Defense News*, April 13, 2017, http://www.defensenews.com/articles/lithuania-mulls-transport-combat-helo-acquisitions (accessed June 7, 2017).

194. Reuters, "Norway to Surpass Russia as Lithuania's Top Gas Supplier in 2016," February 8, 2016, http://mobile.reuters.com/article/idUSL8N15N1UF (accessed June 9, 2017).

195. Reuters, "Lithuania Signs First Deal for U.S. LNG," June 26, 2017, http://mobile.reuters.com/article/amp/idUSKBN19H14M (accessed June 29, 2017).

196. Reuters, "Baltic States Agree to Link Their Power Grids to EU via Poland," May 8, 2017, http://www.voanews.com/a/baltic-states-to-link-power-grids-to-eu-via-poland/3843362.html?utm_source=dlvr.it&utm_medium=twitter (accessed June 9, 2017).

197. Daniel Kochis, "Poland: The Lynchpin of Security on NATO's Front Lines," Heritage Foundation *Issue Brief* No. 4455, August 17, 2015, http://www.heritage.org/research/reports/2015/08/poland-the-lynchpin-of-security-on-natos-front-lines.

198. International Institute for Strategic Studies, *The Military Balance 2017*, p. 145.

199. Christian Davies, "New Polish Military Force Worries Political Opposition," *Politico*, November 16, 2016, http://www.politico.eu/article/new-polish-military-force-worries-political-opposition/ (accessed June 9, 2017);

200. Davies, "New Polish Military Force Worries Political Opposition."

201. Marek Strzelecki, "Poland Guts Military Command on NATO Front Line," *Stars and Stripes*, February 23, 2017, https://www.stripes.com/news/europe/poland-guts-military-command-on-nato-front-line-1.455528#.WRHPh4WcHcs (accessed June 9, 2017).

202. News release, "Defence Expenditures of NATO Countries (2009–2016)," pp. 9 and 12.

203. Radio Poland, "Poland to Increase Defence Spending," April 25, 2017, http://www.thenews.pl/1/9/Artykul/304138,Poland-to-increase-defence-spending (accessed June 9, 2017).

204. Jaroslaw Adamowski, "Poland Initiates Maritime Patrol Aircraft Tender," *Defense News*, May 5, 2017, http://www.defensenews.com/articles/poland-initiates-maritime-patrol-aircraft-tender (accessed June 9, 2017); Lidia Kelly, "Poland Expects to Ink $7.6 Billion Deal for Patriot Systems by End-2017," Reuters, March 31, 2017, http://www.reuters.com/article/us-poland-defence-raytheon-patriots-idUSKBN1720X3 (accessed June 9, 2017).

205. North Atlantic Treaty Organization, "Resolute Support Mission (RSM): Key Facts and Figures."

206. Master Sgt. Benjamin Wilson, "Weather Station Supports Intelligence, Surveillance, Reconnaissance Mission," U.S. Central Command, May 1, 2017, http://www.centcom.mil/MEDIA/NEWS-ARTICLES/News-Article-View/Article/1168329/weather-station-supports-intelligence-surveillance-reconnaissance-mission/ (accessed August 8, 2017).

207. Kurdistan Regional Government, Representation in Poland, "Poland Sent F-16 Fighter Aircraft, 200 Soldiers to Iraq and Kuwait," June 19, 2015, http://poland.gov.krd/polski-polska-wysyla-sily-zbrojne-do-walki-z-isis/ (accessed July 13, 2017).

208. BNS/TBT Staff, "Poland Taking Over NATO Air-Policing Mission at Lithuanian Air Base from Netherlands," *The Baltic Times*, May 2, 2017, http://www.baltictimes.com/poland_taking_over_nato_air-policing_mission_at_lithuanian_air_base_from_netherlands/ (accessed June 9, 2017).

209. North Atlantic Treaty Organization, *The Secretary General's Annual Report: 2016*, pp. 16 and 101.

210. General Philip Breedlove, Commander, U.S. Forces Europe, statement before the Committee on Armed Services, U.S. Senate, March 1, 2016, pp. 18–19, https://www.armed-services.senate.gov/imo/media/doc/Breedlove_03-01-16.pdf (accessed July 13, 2017).

211. U.S. European Command, Communication and Engagement Directorate, "U.S. Military Presence in Europe (1945–2016)," May 26, 2016, http://www.eucom.mil/doc/35220/u-s-forces-in-europe (accessed August 8, 2017).

212. Breedlove, statement before the Committee on Armed Services, U.S. Senate, p. 20.

213. General Philip Breedlove, Commander, U.S. Forces Europe, statement prepared for the Committees on Armed Services, U.S. Senate and U.S. House of Representatives, April 1, 2014, p. 25, http://www.eucom.mil/Tags/posture-statement (accessed July 12, 2017).

214. News release, "DoD Announces European Infrastructure Consolidation Actions and F-35 Basing in Europe," U.S. Department of Defense, January 8, 2015, http://www.defense.gov/Releases/Release.aspx?ReleaseID=17097 (accessed June 12, 2017).

215. John Vandiver, "EUCOM Gives 'Another Look' at Planned Base Closures," *Stars and Stripes*, April 17, 2017, http://www.military.com/daily-news/2017/04/17/eucom-gives-another-look-planned-base-closures.html (accessed June 12, 2017).

216. Ibid.

217. "US Army Considers New Base in Northern Germany," *The Local*, March 10, 2017, https://www.thelocal.de/20170310/us-army-to-deploy-more-soldiers-to-germany?utm_content=buffer59ce7&utm_medium=social&utm_source=twitter.com&utm_campaign=buffer (accessed June 12, 2017).

218. "US Destroyer Begins Third Forward Deployed Patrol from Spain," *Naval Today*, March 17, 2017, http://navaltoday.com/2017/03/17/us-destroyer-begins-third-forward-deployed-patrol-from-spain/ (accessed June 12, 2017).

219. U.S. Naval Forces Europe–Africa/U.S. 6th Fleet, "USS Mount Whitney (LCC 20)," http://www.c6f.navy.mil/ships/uss-mount-whitney (accessed July 12, 2017).

220. Deutsche Welle, "Iceland Agrees to the Return of American Troops," June 30, 2016, http://www.dw.com/en/iceland-agrees-to-the-return-of-american-troops/a-19369461 (accessed July 12, 2017).

221. "U.S. Navy Receives 50th P-8A Poseidon," *Naval Today*, January 6, 2017, http://navaltoday.com/2017/01/06/u-s-navy-receives-50th-p-8a-poseidon/ (accessed June 12, 2017).

222. *Hearing to Receive Testimony on United States European Command*, p. 41.

223. David Cenciotti, "NATO Hunting at Least One Russian Navy Oscar II Class Submarine That Is Chasing Aircraft Carriers in the Mediterranean Sea," The Aviationist, December 9, 2016, https://theaviationist.com/tag/boeing-p-8-poseidon/ (accessed July 12, 2017).

224. Martin Egnash, "New Radar Extends Army's Vision in Europe as Eyes Turn to Russia," *Stars and Stripes*, April 7, 2017, https://www.stripes.com/news/new-radar-extends-army-s-vision-in-europe-as-eyes-turn-to-russia-1.462469#.WQyaeYWcHct (accessed June 12, 2017).

225. U.S. Army Europe, "U.S. Army Europe to Increase Presence Across Eastern Europe," November 4, 2016, https://www.army.mil/article/177819/us_army_europe_to_increase_presence_across_eastern_europe (accessed July 12, 2017).

226. Tom Roeder, "Like Their Fathers and Grandfathers, Fort Carson Troops Head for Training in Germany," *Colorado Springs Gazette*, May 15, 2017, http://gazette.com/like-their-fathers-and-grandfathers-fort-carson-troops-head-for-training-in-germany/article/1603196 (accessed July 12, 2017); Alexa Maye Asperin, "Soldiers from Fort Carson to Deploy to Germany on Short-Notice Orders," Fox 21 News, http://fox21news.com/2017/05/02/soldiers-from-fort-carson-to-deploy-to-germany-on-short-notice-orders/ (accessed June 12, 2017).

227. United States Air Force, "U.S. Air Forces in Europe & Air Forces Africa, Units," http://www.usafe.af.mil/units/ (accessed July 10, 2017).

228. Sisk, "Turkey Hints at Shuttering Incirlik to US Air Operations."

229. United States European Command, "Our Forces: U.S. Air Forces in Europe," http://www.eucom.mil/about/organization/our-forces/u-s-air-forces-in-europe (accessed July 10, 2017).

230. United States European Command, "Our Forces: U.S. Marine Forces Europe," http://www.eucom.mil/about/organization/our-forces/u-s-marine-forces-europe (accessed July 12, 2017).

231. Ryan Browne, "U.S. Stationing Tanks and Artillery in Classified Norwegian Caves," CNN, updated February 19, 2016, http://edition.cnn.com/2016/02/18/politics/u-s-tanks-artillery-norwegian-caves/ (accessed July 12, 2017).

232. Michael S. Darnell, "Marines Cutting 6 Ospreys from Crisis Response Task Force," *Stars and Stripes*, May 4, 2016, https://www.stripes.com/news/marines-cutting-6-ospreys-from-crisis-response-task-force-1.407781#.WRs8CmgrLcs (accessed June 12, 2017).

233. Cheryl Pellerin, "U.S., Spain Agree to Make U.S. Crisis Force Deployment Permanent," U.S. Department of Defense, June 18, 2015, http://www.defense.gov/News/Article/Article/604842 (accessed June 12, 2017).

234. Hope Hodge Seck, "For Marine Corps Force in Norway, 'Russia' Is a Four-Letter Word," Military.com, May 16, 2017, http://www.military.com/daily-news/2017/05/16/for-marine-corps-force-in-norway-russia-is-a-four-letter-word.html (accessed June 12, 2017).

235. "'Norway Will Suffer': Russia Makes Nuclear Threat over US Marines," *The Local*, October 31, 2016, https://www.thelocal.no/20161031/norway-will-suffer-russia-makes-nuclear-threat-over-us-marines (accessed June 12, 2017).

236. Jeff Schogol, "Mud Is No Problem for Marines Training in Romania," *Marine Corps Times*, March 3, 2017, https://www.marinecorpstimes.com/articles/marines-train-in-romania (accessed July 12, 2017).

237. General Philip Breedlove, Commander, U.S. Forces Europe, statement before the Committee on Armed Services, U.S. House of Representatives, February 25, 2015, p. 12, http://www.google.com/url?sa=t&rct=j&q=&esrc=s&source=web&cd=1&ved=0ahUKEwin6OWsrITVAhWDbD4KHaqgCxgQFggiMAA&url=http%3A%2F%2Fwww.eucom.mil%2Fmedia-library%2Fdocument%2F31979%2Fu-s-european-command-posture-statement-2015&usg=AFQjCNF3-qnKiFUmMC4FamE_ZjIcFThk3g (accessed July 12, 2017).

238. U.S. Department of Defense, Office of the Under Secretary of Defense (Comptroller), *Department of Defense Budget, Fiscal Year (FY) 2018: European Reassurance Initiative*, May 2017, pp. 22–25, http://comptroller.defense.gov/Portals/45/Documents/defbudget/fy2018/fy2018_ERI_J-Book.pdf (accessed July 12, 2017).

239. General Curtis M. Scaparrotti, Commander, United States European Command, statement before the Military Construction, Veterans Affairs, and Related Agencies Subcommittee, Committee on Appropriations, U.S. Senate, May 2, 2017, p. 2, https://www.appropriations.senate.gov/imo/media/doc/050217-Scaparrotti-Testimony.pdf (accessed July 12, 2017).

240. Dan Stoutamire, "Romanian Air Base Proving Crucial as US Hub Ahead of Major Exercises," *Stars and Stripes*, April 18, 2017, https://www.stripes.com/news/romanian-air-base-proving-crucial-as-us-hub-ahead-of-major-exercises-1.464105#.WPZirOR1rcs (accessed June 12, 2017).

241. Scaparrotti, statement before Military Construction, Veterans Affairs, and Related Agencies Subcommittee, May 2, 2017, p. 2.

242. Ibid.

243. James Fielding, "EXCLUSIVE: Al Qaeda Targets Oil Tankers in Gibraltar," *Express*, October 26, 2014, http://www.express.co.uk/news/uk/527524/EXCLUSIVE-Al-Qaeda-targets-oil-tankers-Gibraltar (accessed June 12, 2017).

244. Bosphorus Strait News, "Yearly Ship Statistics of Bosphorus Strait—2013," March 13, 2014, http://www.bosphorusstrait.com/2014/03/13/yearly-ship-statistics-of-bosphorus-strait-2013/ (accessed June 12, 2017).

245. U.S. Department of Energy, Energy Information Administration, "World Oil Transit Chokepoints," last updated August 22, 2012, http://www.marsecreview.com/wp-content/uploads/2012/08/World-Oil-Transit-Chokepoints.pdf (accessed June 12, 2017).

246. Information collected from *Bosphorus Naval News*, https://turkishnavy.net/ (accessed June 12, 2017).

247. U.S. Department of Energy, "World Oil Transit Chokepoints."

248. Reuters, "Russia to Stop Oil Product Export via Foreign Baltic Ports by 2018," September 12, 2016, http://www.reuters.com/article/us-russia-oil-exporst-baltic-idUSKCN11I1RR (accessed June 23, 2017).

249. Defence Command Denmark, "Facts & Figures," last updated April 14, 2016, http://www2.forsvaret.dk/eng/About/Facts/Pages/FactsFigures.aspx (accessed July 10, 2017).

250. Paul Adams, "Russian Menace Pushes Sweden Towards Nato," BBC, February 4, 2016, http://www.bbc.com/news/world-europe-35456535 (accessed July 10, 2017).

251. Richard Tomkins, "Swedish Government to Increase Defense Spending by $55B," UPI, April 19, 2017, http://www.upi.com/Defense-News/2017/04/19/Swedish-government-to-increase-defense-spending-by-55B/6881492614059/ (accessed June 12, 2017).

252. Malcolm Brabant, "Long-Neutral Sweden Beefs Up Military Defenses to Face Russia Threat," *PBS NewsHour*, May 25, 2017, http://www.pbs.org/newshour/bb/long-neutral-sweden-beefs-military-defenses-face-russia-threat/ (accessed June 13, 2017).

Middle East

Strategically situated at the intersection of Europe, Asia, and Africa, the Middle East has long been an important focus of United States foreign policy. U.S. security relationships in the region are built on pragmatism, shared security concerns, and economic interests, including large sales of U.S. arms to countries in the region that are seeking to defend themselves. The U.S. also maintains a long-term interest in the Middle East that is related to the region's economic importance as the world's primary source of oil and gas.

The region is home to a wide array of cultures, religions, and ethnic groups, including Arabs, Jews, Kurds, Persians, and Turks, among others. It also is home to the three Abrahamic religions of Judaism, Christianity, and Islam, in addition to many smaller religions like the Bahá'í, Druze, Yazidi, and Zoroastrian faiths. The region contains many predominantly Muslim countries as well as the world's only Jewish state.

The Middle East is deeply sectarian, and these long-standing divisions, exacerbated by religious extremists vying for power, are central to many of the challenges that the region faces today. In some cases, these sectarian divides go back centuries. Contemporary conflicts, however, have less to do with these histories than they do with modern extremist ideologies and the fact that modern-day borders often do not reflect the region's cultural, ethnic, or religious realities. Today's borders are often the results of decisions taken by the British, French, and other powers during and soon after World War I as they dismantled the Ottoman Empire.[1]

In a way not understood by many in the West, religion remains a prominent fact of daily life in the modern Middle East. At the heart of many of the region's conflicts is the friction within Islam between Sunnis and Shias. This friction dates back to the death of the Prophet Muhammad in 632 AD.[2] Sunni Muslims, who form the majority of the world's Muslim population, hold power in most of the Arab countries in the Middle East.

Viewing the current instability in the Middle East through the lens of a Sunni–Shia conflict, however, does not show the full picture. The cultural and historical division between Persians and Arabs has reinforced the Sunni–Shia split. The mutual distrust of many Arab/Sunni powers and the Persian/Shia power (Iran), compounded by clashing national and ideological interests, has fueled instability, including in Bahrain, Iraq, Lebanon, Syria, and Yemen. Sunni extremist organizations such as al-Qaeda and the Islamic State have exploited sectarian and ethnic tensions to gain support by posing as champions of Sunni Arabs against Iran, Syria's Alawite-dominated regime, and other non-Sunni governments and movements.

Current regional demographic trends also are destabilizing factors. The Middle East contains one of the world's youngest and fastest-growing populations. In most of the West, this would be viewed as an advantage, but not in the Middle East. Known as "youth bulges," these demographic tsunamis have overwhelmed the inadequate political, economic, and educational infrastructures in many countries, and the lack of access to education, jobs, and meaningful political participation fuels discontent.

Because more than 60 percent of the region's inhabitants are less than 25 years old, this demographic bulge will continue to have a substantial effect on political stability across the region.

The Middle East contains more than half of the world's oil reserves and is the world's chief oil-exporting region. As the world's biggest oil consumer, the U.S. has a vested interest in maintaining the free flow of oil and gas from the region. This is true even though the U.S. actually imports relatively little of its oil from the Middle East.[3] Oil is a fungible commodity, and the U.S. economy remains vulnerable to sudden spikes in world oil prices.

Because many U.S. allies depend on Middle East oil and gas, there is also a second-order effect for the U.S. if supply from the Middle East is reduced or compromised. For example, Japan (the world's third largest economy) is the world's largest liquefied natural gas (LNG) importer, accounting for 32 percent of the global market share of LNG demand.[4] Qatar is the second largest supplier of LNG to Japan. In 2016, another U.S. ally in Asia—South Korea, the world's 15th largest economy[5]—depended on the Middle East for 82 percent of its imports of crude oil.[6] The U.S. itself might not be dependent on Middle East oil or LNG, but the economic consequences arising from a major disruption of supplies would ripple across the globe.

Financial and logistics hubs are also growing along some of the world's busiest transcontinental trade routes. One of the region's economic bright spots in terms of trade and commerce is found in the Persian Gulf. The emirates of Dubai and Abu Dhabi in the United Arab Emirates (UAE), along with Qatar, are competing to become the region's top financial center. Although many oil-exporting countries recovered from the 2008 financial crisis and subsequent recession, they have since experienced the deepest economic downturn since the 1990s as a result of falling oil prices.[7] Various factors such as weak demand, infighting within the Organization of the Petroleum Exporting Countries (OPEC), and increased U.S.

domestic oil production have contributed to these plunging oil prices.[8]

Nevertheless, the Middle East is full of economic extremes. For example:

- Qatar is the world's wealthiest country in terms of gross domestic product (GDP) per capita; Yemen, a mere 700 miles away, ranks 198th.[9]

- Saudi Arabia has 265 billion barrels of proven oil reserves. It shares a nearly 500-mile border with Jordan, which has just 1 million barrels of proven oil reserves.

- According to the *2017 Index of Economic Freedom*, published by The Heritage Foundation, the UAE ranks 8th in the world in terms of economic freedom; Iran, located just across the Persian Gulf, ranks 155th.[10]

These disparities are made worse by government corruption across most of the region, which not only squanders economic and human resources, but also restricts economic competition and hinders the development of free enterprise.

The economic situation is part of what drives the Middle East's political environment. The lack of economic freedom was an important factor leading to the Arab Spring uprisings, which disrupted economic activity, depressed foreign and domestic investment, and slowed economic growth.

The political environment has a direct bearing on how easily the U.S. military can operate in a region. In many Middle Eastern countries, the political situation remains fraught with uncertainty. The Arab Spring uprisings that began in early 2011 formed a regional sandstorm that eroded the foundations of many authoritarian regimes, erased borders, and destabilized many countries in the region. Even so, the popular uprisings in Tunisia, Libya, Egypt, Bahrain, Syria, and Yemen did not usher in a new era of democracy and liberal rule, as many in the West were hoping. At best, these uprisings made slow progress toward democratic reform. At worst, they added to political instability, exacerbated economic problems, and contributed to the rise of Islamist extremists. Six years later, the economic and political outlooks remain bleak.[11]

There is no shortage of security challenges for the U.S. and its allies in this region. Iran has exacerbated Shia–Sunni tensions to increase its influence on embattled regimes and undermine adversaries in Sunni-led states. Tehran attempts to run an unconventional empire by exerting great influence on sub-state entities like Hamas (Palestinian territories); Hezbollah (Lebanon); the Mahdi movement (Iraq); and the Houthi insurgents (Yemen). In Afghanistan, Tehran's influence on some Shiite groups is such that many have even volunteered to fight for Basher al-Assad in Syria.[12] Iran also provided arms to the Taliban after it was ousted from power by a U.S.-led coalition[13] and has long considered the Afghan city of Herat, near the Afghan–Iranian border, to be within its sphere of influence.

The Iran nuclear agreement has strengthened Tehran's ability to establish regional hegemony. Tehran has recovered approximately $100 billion in frozen assets that will boost its economy and enhance its strategic position, military capabilities, and support for surrogate networks and terrorist groups.[14] This economic transfusion will enable Tehran to tilt the regional balance of power even further in its favor.

Iran already looms large over weak and divided Arab rivals. Iraq and Syria have been destabilized by insurgencies and civil war and may never fully recover. Egypt is distracted by its own internal problems, economic imbalances, and the Islamist extremist insurgency in the Sinai Peninsula. Jordan has been inundated by a flood of Syrian refugees and is threatened by the spillover of Islamist extremist groups from Syria. Meanwhile, Tehran has continued to build up its missile arsenal (now the largest in the Middle East) and has increased its naval provocations in the Persian Gulf, intervened to prop up the Assad regime in Syria, and

reinforced Shiite Islamist revolutionaries in Yemen and Bahrain.[15]

In Syria, the Assad regime's brutal repression of peaceful demonstrations in early 2011 ignited a fierce civil war that has led to the deaths of more than half a million people[16] and displaced about 4.8 million refugees in Turkey, Lebanon, Jordan, Iraq, and Egypt.[17] More than 6.3 million people are internally displaced within Syria.[18] The destabilizing spillover effects of this civil war include the creation of large refugee populations that could become a reservoir of potential recruits for extremist groups. In Jordan, where King Abdullah's regime has been buffeted by Arab Spring protests and adverse economic trends, Syrian refugees now account for more than 10 percent of the population. This has placed even more strain on Jordan's small economy, scarce water resources, and limited social services, creating rising resentment among the local population.

In 2015, more than 1 million migrants and refugees from across the Middle East crossed into Europe—the largest numbers of migrating people that Europe has seen since World War II.[19] This has sparked a crisis as countries struggle to cope with the massive influx and its social, economic, and political ramifications.

Thanks to the power vacuum created by the ongoing civil war in Syria, Islamist extremist groups, including the al-Qaeda–affiliated Jabhat Fateh al-Sham (formally known as al-Nusra Front) and the self-styled Islamic State (IS), formerly known as ISIS or ISIL and before that as al-Qaeda in Iraq, have carved out extensive sanctuaries where they are building proto-states and training militants from a wide variety of other Arab countries, Central Asia, Russia, Europe, Australia, and the United States. With a sophisticated Internet and social media presence and by capitalizing on the civil war in Syria and sectarian divisions in Iraq, the IS has been able to recruit over 25,000 fighters from outside the region to join its ranks in Iraq and Syria. These foreign fighters include over 4,500 citizens from Western nations, including approximately 250 U.S. citizens.[20]

In late 2013, the IS exploited the Shia-dominated Iraqi government's heavy-handed alienation, marginalization, and repression of the Sunni Arab minority in Iraq to reinvigorate its insurgency and seize territory. In the summer of 2014, the IS spearheaded a broad Sunni uprising against Baghdad. The assault was incredibly effective, and by the end of the year, the IS controlled one-third of Iraq and one-third of Syria—a land mass roughly equal to the area of Great Britain—where the extremist group ruled upward of 9 million people. The self-proclaimed caliphate lost its final major redoubt in Iraq's second largest city, Mosul, and its so-called capital city located in Raqqa, Syria, is currently under siege by Syrian Democratic Forces. The Peshmerga militia of the Kurdistan Regional Government, an autonomous area in northeastern Iraq, took advantage of the chaos caused by the collapse of the Iraqi security forces and occupied the city of Kirkuk, which Kurds have long considered to be rightfully theirs—a claim rejected by the central government in Baghdad. The IS continues to attack the Shia-dominated government in Baghdad, massacre Shia civilians and Sunnis who disagree with it, and terrorize religious and ethnic minorities in northern Iraq including the Christian community, Kurds, Turkmen, and Yazidis. In early 2016, Iraq's military and militia forces, backed by air power from the U.S.-led coalition and by Peshmerga forces, launched an offensive to retake Mosul.

On September 10, 2014, the U.S. announced the formation of a broad international coalition to defeat the Islamic State. Today, this coalition has 69 members including non-state organizations like NATO and INTERPOL. However, many of these members merely provide political support: Today, 9,000 troops contributed by 23 of the coalition's 69 member countries are on the ground in Iraq and Syria, and the bulk of these are from the U.S. (There are approximately 5,000 U.S. troops in Iraq and another 1,000 in Syria.) The U.S.-led air campaign has played a significant role in degrading IS capabilities, especially in support of the Mosul offensive, but even though the list of participants in this campaign (Australia, Bahrain, Belgium, Canada, Denmark, France, Jordan, Saudi Arabia, the Netherlands, Turkey, the United Arab Emirates, and the United Kingdom) is impressive, the U.S. conducts the vast majority of air strikes in Iraq and almost all of them in Syria.

Arab–Israeli tensions are another source of instability. The repeated breakdown of Israeli–Palestinian peace negotiations and the rise of the Hamas regime in Gaza in a 2007 coup have created an even more antagonistic situation. Hamas, the Palestinian branch of the Muslim Brotherhood, seeks to transform the conflict from a national struggle over sovereignty and territory into a religious conflict in which compromise is denounced as blasphemy. Hamas invokes jihad in its struggle against Israel and seeks to destroy the Jewish state and replace it with an Islamic state.

Although elected to power with only 44 percent of the vote in the 2006 elections (elections were due to be held in 2014 but have since been suspended indefinitely), Hamas has since forced its radical agenda on the people of Gaza. This has led in turn to diminished public support and a high degree of needless suffering. Hamas provoked wars with Israel in 2008, 2009, 2012, and 2014 and continues to threaten Israel and representatives of Egypt, Jordan, and the Palestinian Authority who have signed peace agreements with Israel. As long as Hamas remains imbued with its Islamist extremist ideology that advocates the destruction of Israel and retains a stranglehold over Gaza, achieving a sustainable Israeli–Palestinian peace agreement appears to be impossible.[21]

Important Alliances and Bilateral Relations in the Middle East

The U.S. has strong military, security, intelligence, and diplomatic ties with several Middle Eastern nations, including Israel, Egypt, Jordan, and the members of the Gulf Cooperation Council (GCC).[22] Since the historical and political circumstances that led to the creation of NATO have largely been absent in the Middle East, the region lacks a similarly strong collective security organization. Middle Eastern countries traditionally have preferred to maintain bilateral relationships with the U.S. and generally have shunned multilateral arrangements because of the lack of trust among Arab states.

This lack of trust manifested itself in June 2017 when the Kingdom of Saudi Arabia, the United Arab Emirates, Bahrain, Egypt, and several other Muslim-majority countries cut or downgraded diplomatic ties with Qatar. All commercial land, air, and sea travel between Qatar and these nations has been severed, and Qatari diplomats and citizens have been evicted.

This is the best example of how regional tensions can transcend the Arab–Iranian or Israeli–Palestinian debate. Qatar has long supported Muslim Brotherhood groups, as well as questionable Islamist factions in Syria and Libya, and has often been seen as being too close for comfort with Iran, a major adversary of Sunni Arab states in the Gulf.

This is not the first time that something like this has happened, albeit on a much smaller scale. In 2014, a number of Arab states recalled their ambassadors to Qatar to protest Doha's support for Egypt's Muslim Brotherhood movement. It took eight months to resolve this dispute before relations could be fully restored.

Bilateral and multilateral relations in the region, especially with the U.S. and other Western countries, are often made more difficult by their secretive nature. The opaqueness of these relationships sometimes creates problems for the U.S. when trying to coordinate defense and security cooperation with European allies active in the region (mainly the U.K. and France).

Military training is an important part of these relationships. The main motivation behind these exercises is to ensure close and effective coordination with key regional partners, demonstrate an enduring U.S. security commitment to regional allies, and train Arab armed forces so that they can assume a larger share of responsibility for regional security. Last year, the U.S. Naval Forces Central Command launched the world's largest maritime exercise across the Middle East to demonstrate global resolve in maintaining freedom of navigation and the free flow of maritime commerce.[23] This has been followed by subsequent, albeit smaller, maritime exercises.

Kuwait, Bahrain, the UAE, Saudi Arabia, and Qatar have participated in, and in some cases have commanded, Combined Task Force-152, formed in 2004 to maintain maritime security in the Persian Gulf. The commander of the U.S. Central Command (CENTCOM) noted that Middle Eastern partners have begun to take the threat from transnational Islamist extremist groups more seriously as ISIS has gained momentum, increased in strength, and expanded its international influence.[24] Middle Eastern countries have also participated further afield in Afghanistan; since 2001, Jordan, Egypt, Bahrain, and the UAE have supplied troops to the U.S.-led mission there. During the 2011 NATO-led operation in Libya, U.S. allies Qatar, Jordan, and the UAE participated to varying degrees.

In addition to military training, U.S. defense relations are underpinned by huge defense equipment deals. U.S. military hardware (and, to a lesser extent, British and French hardware) is preferred across the region because of its effectiveness and symbolic value as a sign of a close security relationship, and much of it has been combat tested. For example, Kuwait, the UAE, Jordan, and Saudi Arabia combined have more than 400 F-15, F-16, and F/A-18 jet fighter aircraft. Following the Iran nuclear deal, threatened Arab states undertook military buildups and a flood of arms purchases. The U.S. approved $33 billion worth of weapons sales to its Gulf Cooperation Council allies between May 2015 and March 2016. During his first overseas visit, President Trump announced a new $110 billion arms deal with Saudi Arabia.[25] U.S. arms deals with GCC countries include ballistic missile defense systems, attack helicopters, advanced frigates, and anti-armor missiles. The use of U.S.-made hardware helps with interoperability and lays the foundation for longer-term regional engagement and cooperation.

Iran continues to incite violence against Israel by providing thousands of increasingly long-range rockets to Hamas, Palestine Islamic Jihad, and Hezbollah, all of which are committed to destroying Israel. Additionally, Iran has escalated its threats against Arab neighbors in the Persian Gulf by funding, training, equipping, and supporting anti-government militant groups in an attempt to undermine various Arab regimes.

Israel. America's most important bilateral relationship in the Middle East is with Israel. Both countries are democracies, value free-market economies, and believe in human rights at a time when many countries in the Middle East reject those values. Israel has been designated as a Major Non-NATO ally (MNNA)[26] because of its close ties to the U.S. With support from the United States, Israel has developed one of the world's most sophisticated air and missile defense networks.[27] No significant progress on peace negotiations with the Palestinians or on stabilizing Israel's volatile neighborhood is possible without a strong and effective Israeli–American partnership.[28]

In March 2015, incumbent Prime Minister Benjamin Netanyahu soundly defeated his chief rival faction, the center-left Zionist Union. Netanyahu's reelection enabled him to criticize the July 2015 U.S. nuclear agreement with Iran from a position of strength and further strained political relations with the Obama Administration. However, with the election of President Trump, U.S.–Israeli relations are as strong as they have been in years if not decades.

Saudi Arabia. After Israel, the U.S. military relationship is deepest with the Gulf states, including Saudi Arabia, which serves as de facto leader of the GCC. The United States started to play a more active role in the Persian Gulf after the U.K. completed the withdrawal of its military presence from bases "east of Suez" in 1971. The U.S. is also the largest provider of arms to Saudi Arabia and regularly, if not controversially, sells munitions needed to re-supply stockpiles expended in the Saudi-led

campaign against the Houthis in Yemen. As noted, President Trump recently approved a $110 billion arms sale to the Saudis.

America's relationship with Saudi Arabia is based on pragmatism and is important for both security and economic reasons. The Saudis enjoy huge influence across the Muslim world. Roughly 2 million Muslims participate in the annual Hajj pilgrimage to the holy city of Mecca. Saudi Arabia owns the world's second largest oil reserves and is the world's foremost oil exporter. The uninterrupted flow of Saudi oil exports is crucial for fueling the global economy.

Riyadh has been a key partner in efforts to counterbalance Iran. Saudi Arabia also has played a growing role in countering the al-Qaeda terrorist network. Until 2003, Riyadh was in denial about Saudi connections to the 9/11 attacks. However, after Saudi Arabia was targeted by al-Qaeda terrorist attacks on its own soil, the government began to cooperate more closely in combating al-Qaeda.[29] After the death of King Abdullah, his half-brother, Crown Prince Salman, ascended to the throne in late January 2015.

Gulf Cooperation Council. The countries of the GCC (Bahrain, Kuwait, Oman, Qatar, Saudi Arabia, and the UAE) are located close to the Arab–Persian fault line, making them strategically important to the U.S.[30] The root of the Arab–Iranian tensions in the Gulf is Tehran's ideological drive to export its Islamist revolution and overthrow the traditional rulers of the Arab kingdoms. This ideological clash has further amplified long-standing sectarian tensions between Shia Islam and Sunni Islam. Tehran has sought to radicalize Shia Arab minority groups to undermine Sunni Arab regimes in Saudi Arabia, Kuwait, and Bahrain. It also sought to incite revolts by the Shia majorities in Iraq against Saddam Hussein's regime and in Bahrain against the Sunni al-Khalifa dynasty.

Culturally, many Iranians look down on the Gulf states, many of which they see as artificial states carved out of the former Persian Empire and propped up by Western powers.

Long-standing Iranian territorial claims in the Gulf add to Arab–Persian tensions.[31] For example, Iran has long considered Bahrain to be part of its territory, a claim that has strained bilateral relations and contributed to Bahrain's decision to break diplomatic ties after the attack on the Saudi embassy in Tehran in early 2016.[32] Iran also occupies the small but strategically important islands of Abu Musa, Greater Tunb, and Lesser Tunb (also claimed by the UAE) near the Strait of Hormuz.

The GCC often has problems agreeing on a common policy on matters of security. This reflects both the organization's intergovernmental nature and the desire of its members to place national interests above those of the GCC. The recent events regarding Qatar illustrate this difficulty. Another source of disagreement involves the question of how best to deal with Iran. On one end of the spectrum, Saudi Arabia, Bahrain, and the UAE take a hawkish view of the threat from Iran. Oman and Qatar, both of which share natural gas fields with Iran, view Iran's activities in the region as less of a threat and maintain good relations with Tehran. Kuwait tends to fall somewhere in the middle. Inter–GCC relations also can be problematic. The UAE, Bahrain, and Saudi Arabia have been at odds with Qatar over Qatar's support for the Muslim Brotherhood, which they see as a threat to internal security, and Qatar has recently decreased its overt support for the organization in order to strengthen relations with its GCC partners.

Apart from Bahrain, the GCC countries have weathered the political turbulence of the Arab Spring relatively well. Many of their citizens enjoy a high standard of living (made possible by millions of foreign workers and the export of oil and gas), which makes it easier for them to tolerate authoritarian rule. Of the six GCC states, Bahrain fared the worst during the 2011 popular uprisings due to persistent Sunni–Shia sectarian tensions worsened by Iranian antagonism and the increased willingness of Shiite youths to protest what they see as discrimination by the al-Khalifa monarchy.

Egypt. Egypt is another important U.S. military ally. As one of only two Arab countries (the other being Jordan) that have diplomatic relations with Israel, Egypt is closely enmeshed in the Israeli–Palestinian conflict and remains a leading political, diplomatic, and military power in the region.

Relations between the U.S. and Egypt have been problematic since the 2011 downfall of President Hosni Mubarak after 30 years of rule. The Muslim Brotherhood's Mohamed Morsi was elected president in 2012 and used the Islamist-dominated parliament to pass a constitution that advanced an Islamist agenda. Morsi's authoritarian rule, combined with rising popular dissatisfaction with falling living standards, rampant crime, and high unemployment, led to a massive wave of protests in June 2013 that prompted a military coup in July. The leader of the coup, Field Marshal Abdel Fattah el-Sisi, pledged to restore democracy and was elected president in 2014. His government faces major political, economic, and security challenges. Egypt's limping economy has been badly damaged by more than five years of political turbulence and violence that has reduced tourism revenues, deterred foreign investment, and raised the national debt. The new regime also faces an emboldened ISIS, which launched waves of attacks in North Sinai including the destruction of a Russian airliner over the Sinai Peninsula in October 2015.[33] Occasional attacks continue today.

The July 2013 coup led by el-Sisi against the Muslim Brotherhood–backed Morsi regime strained relations with the Obama Administration and resulted in a temporary hold on U.S. military assistance to Egypt. U.S. assistance was eventually restored in 2015, but diplomatic relations remain strained. Cairo demonstrated its initial displeasure by buying Russian arms financed by Saudi Arabia in late 2013. Bilateral relations with the U.S. slowly started to improve after Egypt's military made good on its promises to hold elections in 2014. President Trump's willingness to work with el-Sisi has further improved U.S.–Egyptian relations.

Lebanon and Yemen. The United States has developed cooperative defense arrangements with Lebanon and Yemen, two states that face substantial threats from Iranian-supported terrorist groups as well as from al-Qaeda and the Islamic State. The United States has provided arms, equipment, and training for the Lebanese Armed Forces (LAF), which has found itself increasingly challenged by Sunni Islamist extremist groups, including the IS, in addition to the long-term threat posed by Hezbollah. Hezbollah has emerged as Lebanon's most powerful military force, adding to GCC fears about growing Iranian influence in Lebanon. In early 2016, Saudi Arabia cut off its funding for $4 billion worth of military aid to Lebanon because the country did not condemn attacks on Saudi diplomatic missions in Iran, thereby intensifying the proxy war with Iran.[34]

Washington's security relationship with Yemen has grown since the 9/11 attacks. Yemen, Osama bin Laden's ancestral homeland, faces major security threats from al-Qaeda in the Arabian Peninsula (AQAP), one of the most dangerous al-Qaeda affiliates.

The overall political and security situation in Yemen deteriorated further in 2014–2016. In January 2015, the Houthis, a militant Shiite group based in northern Yemen and backed by Iran,[35] overran the capital city of Sana'a and forced the internationally recognized government led by President Abd Rabbu Mansour Hadi to resign. The Houthis solidified their control throughout the North and West of Yemen, and President Hadi fled to Riyadh. Backed by the U.S., the U.K., and France, Saudi Arabia formed a coalition of 10 Sunni countries and led an air campaign against Houthi forces that began in March 2015. The coalition has rolled back the Houthis but is no closer to reinstating the internationally recognized government in Sana'a.

The Yemeni conflict has become a proxy war between Saudi Arabia and Iran. Riyadh supports the Yemeni government, and Iran has provided money, arms, and training to the Houthi rebels, who belong to the Zaidi sect of Shia Islam. The unstable political situation in Yemen caused the United States to evacuate its embassy and withdraw its special operations forces in 2015, severely undermining U.S. counterterrorism and intelligence capabilities in the country. The growing chaos enabled AQAP to expand its presence and establish a "mini-state" spanning more than 350 miles of coastline.[36] The IS entered Yemen in March 2015; however, estimates suggest that the number of IS personnel in Yemen is in the hundreds, while al-Qaeda numbers in the thousands.[37] Under President Trump, the U.S. has taken a more robust role in Yemen with its counterterrorism operations. For example, in March 2017 alone, the U.S. conducted more than 70 strikes in Yemen—double the total number of U.S. strikes in all of 2016.[38]

Quality of Armed Forces in the Middle East

The quality and capabilities of the region's armed forces are mixed. Some countries spend billions of dollars each year on advanced Western military hardware, and others spend very little. Due to the drop in global oil prices, defense spending decreased in 2016 for oil-producing countries in the region while increasing for the non–oil-producing countries. Saudi Arabia was by far the region's largest military spender despite dropping from $81.9 billion in 2015 to $56.9 billion in 2016—a decrease of 30 percent. By 2015, Iraq's defense spending had increased by 536 percent when compared to 2006. However, like other oil-producing countries in the region, Iraq decreased its defense spending by 14.1 percent in 2016 even though large parts of the country remain under IS control.[39] It is too early to tell how the lifting of European Union and U.S. sanctions will affect Iran's military expenditure, but Tehran is expected to increase spending.

Historically, figures on defense spending for the Middle East have been very unreliable, but the lack of data has worsened. For 2016, there were no available data for Kuwait, Qatar, Syria, the United Arab Emirates, and Yemen according to a report by the Stockholm International Peace Research Institute.[40]

Different security factors drive the degree to which Middle Eastern countries fund, train, and arm their militaries. For Israel, which defeated Arab coalitions in wars in 1948, 1956, 1967, 1973, and 1982, the chief potential threats to its existence are now posed by an Iranian regime that has called for Israel to be "wiped from the map."[41] As a result of Israel's military dominance, states and non-state actors in the region have invested in asymmetric and unconventional capabilities to offset Israel's military superiority.[42] For the Gulf states, the main driver of defense policy is the Iranian military threat combined with internal security challenges. For Iraq, the internal threat posed by insurgents and terrorists drives defense policy. In many ways, the Obama Administration's engagement with Tehran united Israel and its Arab neighbors against the shared threat of Iran.

The Israel Defense Forces (IDF) are widely considered the most capable military force in the Middle East. On a conventional level, the IDF consistently surpasses other regional military forces.[43] Other countries, such as Iran, have developed asymmetric tactics and have built up the military capabilities of proxy groups to close the gap in recent years,[44] but the IDF's quality and effectiveness remain unparalleled with regard to both technical capacity and personnel.[45] This was demonstrated by Israel's 2014 military operations against Hamas in the Gaza Strip: After weeks of conflict, the IDF mobilized over 80,000 reservists, demonstrating the depth and flexibility of the Israeli armed forces.[46]

Israel funds its military sector heavily and has a strong national industrial capacity supported by significant funding from the U.S. Combined, these factors give Israel a regional advantage despite limitations of manpower and size.[47] In particular, the IDF has focused on maintaining its superiority in missile defense, intelligence collection, precision weapons, and cyber technologies.[48] The Israelis regard their cyber capabilities as especially important. In early 2016, the IDF unveiled a new five-year plan, worth roughly $78.6 billion, to enhance cyber-protected and networked combat capabilities in order to augment the IDF's capacity to fight in multiple theaters.[49] Cyber technologies are used for a number of purposes, including defending Israeli cyberspace, gathering intelligence, and carrying out attacks.[50] Israel maintains its qualitative superiority in medium-range and long-range missile capabilities.[51] It also fields effective missile defense systems, including Iron Dome and Arrow, both of which the U.S. helped to finance.[52] U.S. spending on Israel's air and missile defense has soared in the past decade, from $133 million in 2006 to $488 million in 2016.[53]

Israel also has a nuclear weapons capability (which it does not publicly acknowledge) that increases its strength relative to other powers in the region. Israel's nuclear weapons capability has helped to deter adversaries as the gap in conventional capabilities has been reduced.[54]

After Israel, the most technologically advanced and best-equipped armed forces are found in the Gulf Cooperation Council. Previously, the export of oil and gas meant that there was no shortage of resources to devote to defense spending, but the collapse of crude oil prices may force oil-exporting countries to adjust their defense spending patterns. At present, however, GCC nations still have the best-funded, although not necessarily the most effective, Arab armed forces in the region.

The GCC established a joint expeditionary force called the Peninsula Shield Force (PSF), which has had only modest operational success and has never met its stated ambition of deploying tens of thousands of soldiers. Created in 1984, its main purpose today is to counter Iran's military buildup and help maintain internal security. The PSF first deployed a modest force of 3,000 troops to help liberate Kuwait during the first Gulf War. Its most recent deployment was to Bahrain in 2011 to help restore order after Iranian-backed Shiite protests brought the country to a standstill and threatened the monarchy.[55] Internal divisions inside the GCC, especially among Qatar, UAE, and Saudi Arabia, have prevented the PSF from playing a more active role in the region.

All GCC members boast advanced defense hardware with a preference for U.S., U.K., and

French equipment. Saudi Arabia maintains the most capable military force in the GCC. It has an army of 75,000 soldiers and a National Guard of 100,000 personnel reporting directly to the king. The army operates 900 main battle tanks including 370 U.S.-made M1A2s. Its air force is built around American and British-built aircraft and consists of more than 338 combat-capable aircraft including F-15s, Tornados, and Typhoons.[56] These aircraft flew missions over Yemen against Houthi rebels in 2009–2010, during Operation Decisive Storm in Yemen beginning in March 2015, and most recently over Syria as part of the U.S.-led fight against ISIS.[57] Both Saudi Arabia[58] and the UAE[59] have hundreds of Storm Shadow air-launched cruise missiles (known as Black Shaheen in the UAE) in their inventories. These weapons proved highly effective when the British and French used them during the air campaign over Libya in 2011.

In fact, air power is the strong suit of most GCC members. Oman operates F-16s and has purchased 12 Typhoons, on track to be delivered in 2017. According to *Defense Industry Daily*, "The UAE operates the F-16E/F Desert Falcon, which holds more advanced avionics than any F-16 variant in the US inventory."[60] Qatar operates French-made Mirage fighters. The UAE and Qatar deployed fighters to participate in NATO-led operations over Libya in 2011 (although they did not participate in strike operations). Beginning in early fall 2014, all six GCC members joined the U.S.-led anti-ISIS coalition, with the UAE contributing the most in terms of air power.[61] However, air strikes in Syria by members of the GCC decreased substantially in 2017. The navies of the GCC members rarely deploy beyond their Exclusive Economic Zones, but all members (other than Oman) have participated in regional combined task forces led by the U.S.[62] In 2016, Oman and Britain launched a multimillion-dollar joint venture to develop Duqm as a strategic Middle Eastern port in the Indian Ocean to improve defense security and prosperity agendas.[63]

Even with the billions of dollars invested each year by members of the GCC, most see security ties with the United States as crucial for their security. As former U.S. Defense Secretary Robert Gates once noted, the Saudis will "fight the Iranians to the last American."[64]

Egypt has the largest Arab military force in the Middle East, with 438,500 active personnel and 479,000 reserve personnel in its armed forces.[65] It possesses a fully operational military with an army, air force, air defense, navy, and special operations forces. Until 1979, when the U.S. began to supply Egypt with military equipment, Cairo relied primarily on less capable Soviet military technology.[66] Since then, its army and air force have been significantly upgraded with U.S. military weapons, equipment, and warplanes.

Egypt substantially increased troop deployments and military operations in 2015 following the onslaught of Islamist and insurgent activity at its borders. This has been the case especially with respect to Libya, where the Egyptian air force has conducted a number of air strikes in the past two years aimed at terrorist targets there.[67] It has also sought closer security cooperation with other North African states to improve border and internal security.[68]

The most visible expression of U.S. influence in Cairo is military aid, which was withheld in some areas after the 2013 military coup but reinstated in 2015. Since 1948, the U.S. has provided Egypt with more than $77 billion in foreign aid.[69] Recently, this support has helped Egypt to procure Apache attack helicopters, F-16s, Harpoon ship-to-ship missile systems, and M1A1 tank kits.

Egypt has struggled with increased terrorist activity in the Sinai Peninsula, including attacks on Egyptian soldiers, attacks on foreign tourists, and the October 2015 bombing of a Russian airliner departing from the Sinai, for all of which the Islamic State's "Sinai Province" terrorist group has claimed responsibility. The government's response to the uptick of violence has been severe: arrests of thousands of suspected Islamist extremists and restrictive measures such as a law criminalizing media reporting that contradicts official reports.[70]

Jordan is a close U.S. ally with small but effective military forces. Its principal security threats include ISIS, turbulence in Syria and Iraq, and the resulting flow of refugees. Jordan is currently home to more than 1.4 million registered and unregistered Syrian refugees. In January 2016, King Abdullah announced that Jordan had reached the saturation point in its ability to take in more Syrian refugees.[71] While Jordan faces few conventional threats from its neighbors, its internal security is threatened by Islamist extremists returning from fighting in the region who have been emboldened by the growing influence of al-Qaeda and other Islamist militants. As a result, Jordan's highly professional armed forces have been focused in recent years on border and internal security. Nevertheless, Jordan's conventional capability is significant considering its size.

Jordan's ground forces total 74,000 soldiers and include 390 British-made Challenger 1 tanks. The backbone of its air force is comprised of 43 F-16 Fighting Falcons.[72] Jordan's special operations forces are highly capable, having benefitted from extensive U.S. and U.K. training. Jordanian forces have served in Afghanistan and in numerous U.N.-led peacekeeping operations.

Iraq has fielded one of the region's most dysfunctional military forces. After the 2011 withdrawal of U.S. troops, Iraq's government selected and promoted military leaders according to political criteria. Shiite army officers were favored over their Sunni, Christian, and Kurdish counterparts. Then-Prime Minister Nouri al-Maliki chose top officers according to their political loyalties. Politicization of the armed forces also exacerbated corruption within many units, with some commanders siphoning off funds allocated for "ghost soldiers" who never existed or had been separated from the army for various reasons.

The promotion of incompetent military leaders, poor logistical support due to corruption and other problems, limited operational mobility, and weaknesses in intelligence, reconnaissance, medical support, and air force capabilities have combined to weaken the effectiveness of the Iraqi armed forces. In June 2014, for example, the collapse of up to four divisions, which were routed by vastly smaller numbers of Islamic State fighters, led to the fall of Mosul. Although security and stability operations continue, Iraqi Prime Minister Haider al-Abadi announced the liberation of Mosul on July 9, 2017.[73]

Current U.S. Military Presence in the Middle East

The United States maintained a limited military presence in the Middle East before 1980, chiefly a small naval force based at Bahrain since 1958. The U.S. "twin pillar" strategy relied on prerevolutionary Iran and Saudi Arabia to take the lead in defending the Persian Gulf from the Soviet Union and its client regimes in Iraq, Syria, and South Yemen,[74] but the 1979 Iranian revolution demolished one pillar, and the December 1979 Soviet invasion of Afghanistan increased the Soviet threat to the Gulf. President Jimmy Carter proclaimed in January 1980 that the United States would take military action to defend oil-rich Persian Gulf states from external aggression, a commitment known as the Carter Doctrine. In 1980, he ordered the creation of the Rapid Deployment Joint Task Force (RDJTF), the precursor to USCENTCOM, established in January 1983.[75]

Up until the late 1980s, a possible Soviet invasion of Iran was considered to be the most significant threat facing the U.S. in the Middle East.[76] After the collapse of the Soviet Union, Saddam Hussein's Iraqi regime became the chief threat to regional stability. Iraq invaded Kuwait in August 1990, and the United States responded in January 1991 by leading an international coalition of more than 30 nations to expel Iraqi forces from Kuwait. CENTCOM commanded the U.S. contribution of more than 532,000 military personnel to the coalition armed forces, which totaled at least 737,000.[77] This marked the peak U.S. force deployment in the Middle East.

Confrontations with Iraq continued throughout the 1990s as a result of Iraqi violations of the 1991 Gulf War cease-fire. Baghdad's failure to cooperate with U.N. arms inspectors to verify the destruction of its weapons of mass destruction and its links to terrorism led to the U.S. invasion of Iraq in 2003. During the initial invasion, U.S. forces reached nearly 150,000, joined by military personnel from coalition forces. Apart from the "surge" in 2007, when President George W. Bush deployed an additional 30,000 personnel, American combat forces in Iraq fluctuated between 100,000 and 150,000.[78] In December 2011, the U.S. officially completed its withdrawal of troops, leaving only 150 personnel attached to the U.S. embassy in Iraq.[79] In the aftermath of IS territorial gains in Iraq, the U.S. has redeployed thousands of troops to Iraq. Today, approximately 5,000 troops are helping with the anti-IS effort in that country.

In addition, the U.S. continues to maintain a limited number of forces in other locations in the Middle East, primarily in GCC countries. Currently, tens of thousands of U.S. troops are serving in the region. Their exact disposition is not made public because of political sensitivities,[80] but information gleaned from open sources reveals the following:

- **Kuwait.** Approximately 17,500 U.S. personnel are based in Kuwait. (The U.S. routinely maintains 15,000 troops in Kuwait but recently added another 2,500 in support of the anti-IS campaign in Iraq.[81]) These forces are spread among Camp Arifjan, Ahmed Al Jaber Air Base, and Ali Al Salem Air Base. A large depot of prepositioned equipment and a squadron of fighters and Patriot missile systems are also deployed to Kuwait.

- **UAE.** According to CENTCOM, about 4,000 U.S. personnel,[82] mainly from the U.S. Air Force, are stationed in the UAE, primarily at Al Dhafra Air Base. Their main mission in the UAE is to operate fighters, unmanned aerial vehicles (UAVs), refueling aircraft, and surveillance aircraft. The United States also has regularly deployed F-22 Raptor combat aircraft to Al Dhafra.[83] Patriot missile systems are deployed for air and missile defense.

- **Oman.** Since 2004, Omani facilities reportedly have not been used for air support operations in either Afghanistan or Iraq, and the number of U.S. military personnel in Oman has fallen to about 200, mostly from the U.S. Air Force. According to the Congressional Research Service, "the United States reportedly can use—with advance notice and for specified purposes—Oman's military airfields in Muscat (the capital), Thumrait, and Masirah Island."[84]

- **Bahrain.** The oldest U.S. military presence in the Middle East is found in Bahrain. Today, some 8,000 U.S. military personnel are based there.[85] Bahrain is home to the Naval Support Activity Bahrain and the U.S. Fifth Fleet, so most U.S. military personnel there belong to the U.S. Navy. A significant number of U.S. Air Force personnel operate out of Shaykh Isa Air Base, where F-16s, F/A-18s, and P-3 surveillance aircraft are stationed.[86] U.S. Patriot missile systems also are deployed to Bahrain. The deep-water port of Khalifa bin Salman is one of the few facilities in the Gulf that can accommodate U.S. aircraft carriers.

- **Saudi Arabia.** The U.S. withdrew the bulk of its forces from Saudi Arabia in 2003. Little information on the number of U.S. military personnel currently based there is available. However, the six-decade-old United States Military Training Mission to the Kingdom of Saudi Arabia, the four-decade-old Office of the Program Manager of the Saudi Arabian National Guard Modernization Program, and the Office of the Program Manager–Facilities Security Force are based in Eskan Village Air Base approximately 13 miles south of the capital city of Riyadh.[87]

- **Qatar.** Approximately 10,000 U.S. personnel, mainly from the U.S. Air Force, are deployed in Qatar.[88] The U.S. operates its Combined Air Operations Center at Al

Udeid Air Base, which is one of the most important U.S. air bases in the world. It is also the base from which the anti-ISIS campaign is headquartered. Heavy bombers, tankers, transports, and ISR aircraft operate from there. Al Udeid Air Base also serves as the forward headquarters of CENTCOM. The base also houses prepositioned U.S. military equipment and is defended by U.S. Patriot missile systems.

It is too soon to say how recent diplomatic moves by Saudi Arabia and other Arab states against Doha will affect the United States' relationship with Qatar, if at all. U.S. military relationships in the region have been known for their flexibility and pragmatism. In the short term, the Saudi-led GCC ban on commercial travel and shipping to Qatar might adversely affect America's ability to keep the base supplied with food and other essentials. The U.S. will be able to overcome this challenge, but at a cost. If the travel restrictions continue, the U.S. will eventually have to weigh the benefits of maintaining the base against the cost of doing so.

- **Jordan.** According to CENTCOM, Jordan "is one of our strongest and most reliable partners in the Levant sub-region."[89] Although there are no U.S. military bases in Jordan, the U.S. has a long history of conducting training exercises in the country. Due to recent events in neighboring Syria, approximately 2000 troops, a squadron of F-16s, a Patriot missile battery, and M142 High Mobility Artillery Rocket Systems have been deployed in Jordan.[90]

In addition, there have been media reports that the U.S. government operates a secret UAV base in Saudi Arabia from which drone attacks against militants in Yemen are launched.[91] There also are reports of an American base on Yemen's Socotra Island, which is located near the coast of Somalia, being used for counterterrorism operations off the Horn of Africa and Yemen.[92]

CENTCOM's stated mission is to promote cooperation among nations; respond to crises; deter or defeat state and non-state aggression; support economic development; and, when necessary, perform reconstruction in order to establish the conditions for regional security, stability, and prosperity.

CENTCOM is supported by four service component commands and one subordinate unified command: U.S. Naval Forces Middle East (USNAVCENT); U.S. Army Forces Middle East (USARCENT); U.S. Air Forces Middle East (USAFCENT); U.S. Marine Forces Middle East (MARCENT); and U.S. Special Operations Command Middle East (SOCCENT).

- **U.S. Naval Forces Central Command.** USNAVCENT is the maritime component of USCENTCOM. With its forward headquarters in Bahrain, it is responsible for commanding the afloat units that rotationally deploy or surge from the United States, in addition to other ships that are based in the Gulf for longer periods. USNAVCENT conducts persistent maritime operations to advance U.S. interests, deter and counter disruptive countries, defeat violent extremism, and strengthen partner nations' maritime capabilities in order to promote a secure maritime environment in an area encompassing about 2.5 million square miles of water.

- **U.S. Army Forces Central Command.** USARCENT is the land component of USCENTCOM. Based in Kuwait, it is responsible for land operations in an area encompassing 4.6 million square miles (1.5 times larger than the continental United States).

- **U.S. Air Forces Central Command.** USAFCENT is the air component of USCENTCOM. Based in Qatar, it is responsible for air operations and for working with the air forces of partner countries in the region. Additionally, USAFCENT manages an extensive supply and equipment prepositioning program at several regional sites.

- **U.S. Marine Forces Central Command.** USMARCENT is the designated Marine Corps service component for USCENT-COM. Based in Bahrain, it is responsible for all Marine Corps forces in the region.

- **U.S. Special Operations Command Central.** SOCCENT is a subordinate USCENTCOM unified command. Based in Qatar, it is responsible for planning special operations throughout the USCENT-COM region, planning and conducting peacetime joint/combined special operations training exercises, and orchestrating command and control of peacetime and wartime special operations.

In addition to the American military presence in the region, two U.S. allies—the United Kingdom and France—play an important role that should not be overlooked.

The U.K.'s presence in the Middle East is a legacy of British imperial rule. The U.K. has maintained close ties with many countries over which it once ruled and has conducted military operations in the region for decades. Approximately 1,200 British service personnel are based throughout the Gulf.

The British presence in the region is dominated by the Royal Navy. In terms of permanently based naval assets, there are four mine hunters and one Royal Fleet Auxiliary supply ship. Generally, there also are frigates or destroyers in the Gulf or Arabian Sea performing maritime security duties. Although such matters are not the subject of public discussion, U.K. attack submarines also operate in the area. As a sign of its long-term maritime presence in the region, the U.K. broke ground on an $11 million headquarters for its Maritime Component Command at Bahrain's Salman Naval Base in 2014[93] and recently announced a multimillion-dollar investment to modernize the Duqm Port complex in Oman to accommodate the U.K.s new *Queen Elizabeth*-class aircraft carriers.[94]

The U.K. also has a sizeable Royal Air Force (RAF) presence in the region, mainly in the UAE and Oman. A short drive from Dubai, Al-Minhad Air Base is home to a small contingent of U.K. personnel. The U.K. also operates small RAF detachments in Oman that support U.K. and coalition operations in the region. Although considered to be in Europe, the U.K.'s Sovereign Base Areas of Akrotiri and Dhekelia in Cyprus have supported U.S. military and intelligence operations in the past and will continue to do so in the future.

The British presence in the region extends beyond soldiers, ships, and planes. A British-run staff college operates in Qatar, and Kuwait chose the U.K. to help run its own equivalent of the Royal Military Academy at Sandhurst.[95] The U.K. also plays a very active role in training the Saudi Arabian and Jordanian militaries.

The French presence in the Gulf is smaller than the U.K.'s but is still significant. France opened its first military base in the Gulf in 2009 in Abu Dhabi in the UAE. This was the first foreign military installation built by the French in 50 years.[96] In total, the French have 650 personnel based in the country along with eight Rafale fighter jets.[97] French ships have access to the Zayed Port, which is big enough to handle every ship in the French Navy except the aircraft carrier *Charles De Gaulle*.

Another important actor in Middle East security is the small East African country of Djibouti. It sits on the Bab el-Mandeb Strait, through which nearly 4.7 million barrels of oil a day transit and which is a choke point on the route to the Suez Canal. An increasing number of countries recognize Djibouti's value as a base from which to project maritime power and launch counterterrorism operations. It is home to the U.S.'s only permanent military base in Africa, Camp Lemonnier, with its approximately 4,000 personnel. In 2016, Djibouti granted China a 10-year lease on land to build China's first permanent overseas base, which will have the capacity to house 10,000 troops and is just across a bay from Camp Lemonnier. Saudi Arabia also announced in 2016 that it would build a base in Djibouti. France, Italy, Germany, and Japan already have presences of varying strength there.

Key Infrastructure and Warfighting Capabilities

The Middle East is geographically situated in a critical location. Two-thirds of the world's population lives within an eight-hour flight from the Gulf region, making it accessible from most of the globe. The Middle East also contains some of the world's most critical maritime choke points, such as the Suez Canal and the Strait of Hormuz.

While infrastructure is not as developed in the Middle East as it is in North America or Europe, a decades-long presence means that the U.S. has tried and tested systems that involve moving large numbers of matériel and personnel into and out of the region. For example, according to the Department of Defense, at the height of U.S. combat operations in Iraq during the Second Gulf War, there were 165,000 servicemembers and 505 bases. Moving personnel and equipment out of the country was an enormous undertaking—"the largest logistical drawdown since World War II"[98]—and included the redeployment of "the 60,000 troops who remained in Iraq at the time and more than 1 million pieces of equipment ahead of their deadline."[99]

The condition of roads in the region varies from country to country. For example, 100 percent of the roads in Israel, Jordan, and the UAE are paved. Other nations, such as Oman (49 percent), Saudi Arabia (21.5 percent), and Yemen (8.7 percent), have poor paved road coverage according to the most recent information available.[100] Rail coverage is also poor. For instance, Saudi Arabia has only 563 miles of railroads.[101] By comparison, New Hampshire, which is roughly 1 percent the size of Saudi Arabia, has about the same amount in freight rail miles alone.[102] In Syria, six years of civil war has wreaked havoc on the rail system.[103]

The U.S. has access to several airfields in the region. The primary air hub for U.S. forces is at Al Udeid Air Base in Qatar. Other airfields include Ali Al Salem Air Base, Kuwait; Al Dhafra, UAE; Al Minhad, UAE; Isa, Bahrain; Eskan Village Air Base, Saudi Arabia; Muscat, Oman; Thumrait, Oman; Masirah Island, Oman; and use of the commercial airport at Seeb, Oman.

In the past, the U.S. has used major airfields in Iraq, including Baghdad International Airport and Balad Air Base, as well as Prince Sultan Air Base in Saudi Arabia. Just because the U.S. has access to a particular air base today does not mean that it will be made available for a particular operation in the future. For example, it is highly unlikely that Qatar and Oman would allow the U.S. to use air bases in their territory for strikes against Iran.

The U.S. has access to ports in the region, perhaps most importantly in Bahrain. The Naval Support Activity Bahrain has undertaken a $260 million expansion project that will enable the homeporting of littoral combat ships by 2018 in one of the world's busiest waterways.[104] The U.S. also has access to a deep-water port, Khalifa bin Salman, in Bahrain and naval facilities at Fujairah, UAE.[105] The UAE's commercial port of Jebel Ali is open for visits from U.S. warships and prepositioning of equipment for operations in theater.[106]

Approximately 90 percent of the world's trade travels by sea, and some of the busiest and most important shipping lanes are located in the Middle East. For example, the Strait of Hormuz and the Bab el-Mandeb Strait combined have over 65,000 cargo ships travelling through them each year.[107] Given the high volume of maritime traffic in the region, no U.S. military operation can be undertaken without consideration of how these shipping lanes offer opportunity and risk to America and her allies. The major shipping routes include:

- **The Suez Canal.** In 2016, 974 million tons of cargo transited the canal, averaging 46 ships each day.[108] Considering that the canal itself is 120 miles long but only 670 feet wide, this is an impressive amount of traffic. The Suez Canal is important for Europe in terms of oil transportation. The canal also serves as an important strategic asset, as it is used routinely by the U.S. Navy to move surface combatants between the Mediterranean Sea and the Red Sea.

MAP 2

Middle East Oil Transit Choke Points

Almost 20 percent of the world's traded oil passes through the Strait of Hormuz, making it the busiest passageway for oil tankers in the world.

The Bab el-Mandeb Strait is an important route for Persian Gulf exports to Europe and was the site of a anti-ship missile attack by Houthi rebels in Yemen on the HSV-2 *Swift* in 2016.

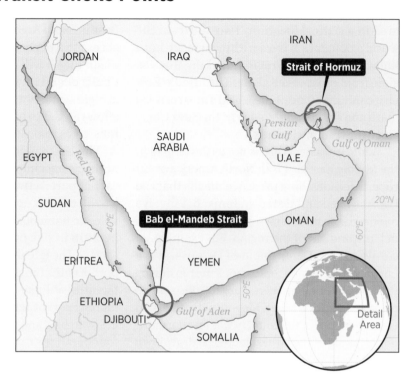

SOURCE: Heritage Foundation research and media reports.

☎ heritage.org

Thanks to a bilateral arrangement between Egypt and the United States, the U.S. Navy enjoys priority access to the canal. However, the journey through the narrow waterway is no easy task for large surface combatants. The canal was not constructed with the aim of accommodating 90,000-ton aircraft carriers and therefore exposes a larger ship to attack. For this reason, different types of security protocols are followed, including the provision of air support by the Egyptian military.[109]

- **Strait of Hormuz.** The Strait of Hormuz is a critical oil-supply bottleneck and the world's busiest passageway for oil tankers. The strait links the Persian Gulf with the Arabian Sea and the Gulf of Oman. Nearly 17 million barrels of oil per day, "about 30% of all seaborne-traded oil," pass through the strait for an annual total of more than 6 billion barrels of oil. Most of these crude oil exports go to Asian markets, particularly Japan, India, South Korea, and China.[110]

The shipping routes through the Strait of Hormuz are particularly vulnerable to disruption, given the extremely narrow passage and its proximity to Iran. Tehran has repeatedly threatened to close the strategic strait if Iran is attacked. While attacking shipping in the strait would drive up oil prices, Iran would also lose, both because it depends on the Strait of Hormuz to export its own crude oil and because such an attack would undermine Tehran's relations with such oil importers as China, Japan, and India. Tehran

---

also would pay a heavy military price if it provoked a U.S. military response.

- **Bab el-Mandeb Strait.** The Bab el-Mandeb strait is a strategic waterway located between the Horn of Africa and Yemen that links the Red Sea to the Indian Ocean. Exports from the Persian Gulf and Asia destined for Western markets must pass through the strait en route to the Suez Canal. Oil tankers transport approximately 4.7 million barrels of oil per day through the strait.[111] The Bab el-Mandeb Strait is 18 miles wide at its narrowest point, limiting passage to two channels for inbound and outbound shipments.[112]

Over the past decade, piracy off the coast of Somalia has dominated the focus of international maritime security efforts. Recently, however, the frequency of pirate attacks in the region has reached its lowest point since 2006, according to the International Maritime Bureau's global piracy report. Pirate activity, however, continues to threaten international trade and the safety of the international commons.[113]

Maritime Prepositioning of Equipment and Supplies. The U.S. military has deployed non-combatant maritime prepositioning ships (MPS) containing large amounts of military equipment and supplies in strategic locations from which they can reach areas of conflict relatively quickly as associated U.S. Army or Marine Corps units located elsewhere arrive in the areas. The British Indian Ocean Territory of Diego Garcia, an island atoll, hosts the U.S. Naval Support Facility Diego Garcia, which supports prepositioning ships that can supply Army or Marine Corps units deployed for contingency operations in the Middle East.

Conclusion

For the foreseeable future, the Middle East region will remain a key focus for U.S. military planners. An area that was once considered relatively stable, mainly due to the ironfisted rule of authoritarian regimes, is now highly unstable and a breeding ground for terrorism. Overall security in the region has deteriorated in recent years. Conflicts in Iraq, Libya, Syria, and Yemen have worsened, with Islamic State or al-Qaeda fighters playing major roles. The regional dispute with Qatar has made U.S. relations in the region even more complex and difficult to manage. The Russian and Iranian interventions in Syria have greatly complicated the fighting there. Egypt faces a growing insurgency in the Sinai that is gradually spreading. Iraq has managed to stem the advance of and actually to push back the Islamic State but needs substantial help to defeat it.

Many of the borders created after World War I are under significant stress. In countries like Iraq, Libya, Syria, and Yemen, the supremacy of the nation-state is being challenged by non-state actors that wield influence, power, and resources comparable to those of small states. The main security and political challenges in the region are linked inextricably to the unrealized aspirations of the Arab Spring, surging transnational terrorism, and the potential threat of Iran. These challenges are made more difficult by the Arab–Israeli conflict, Sunni–Shia sectarian divides, the rise of Iran's Islamist revolutionary nationalism, and the proliferation of Sunni Islamist revolutionary groups.

Thanks to decades of U.S. military operations in the Middle East, the U.S. has tried and tested procedures for operating in the region. Bases and infrastructure are well established. The logistical processes for maintaining a large force forward deployed thousands of miles away from the homeland are well in place. Unlike in Europe, all of these processes have recently been tested in combat. The personal links between allied armed forces are also present. Joint training exercises improve interoperability, and U.S. military educational courses, which officers (and often royals) from the Middle East regularly attend, allow the U.S. to influence some of the region's future leaders.

America's relationships in the region are based pragmatically on shared security and economic concerns. As long as these issues remain relevant to both sides, the U.S. is likely to have an open door to operate in the Middle East when its national interests require it to do so.

Scoring the Middle East Operating Environment

As noted at the beginning of this section, various aspects of the region facilitate or inhibit the ability of the U.S. to conduct military operations to defend its vital national interests against threats. Our assessment of the operating environment utilizes a five-point scale, ranging from "very poor" to "excellent" conditions and covering four regional characteristics of greatest relevance to the conduct of military operations:

1. **Very Poor.** Significant hurdles exist for military operations. Physical infrastructure is insufficient or nonexistent, and the region is politically unstable. In addition, the U.S. military is poorly placed or absent, and alliances are nonexistent or diffuse.

2. **Unfavorable.** A challenging operating environment for military operations is marked by inadequate infrastructure, weak alliances, and recurring political instability. The U.S. military is inadequately placed in the region.

3. **Moderate.** A neutral to moderately favorable operating environment is characterized by adequate infrastructure, a moderate alliance structure, and acceptable levels of regional political stability. The U.S. military is adequately placed.

4. **Favorable.** A favorable operating environment includes good infrastructure, strong alliances, and a stable political environment. The U.S. military is well placed in the region for future operations.

5. **Excellent.** An extremely favorable operating environment includes well-established and well-maintained infrastructure, strong and capable allies, and a stable political environment. The U.S. military is exceptionally well placed to defend U.S. interests.

The key regional characteristics consist of:

a. **Alliances.** Alliances are important for interoperability and collective defense, as allies would be more likely to lend support to U.S. military operations. Various indicators provide insight into the strength or health of an alliance. These include whether the U.S. trains regularly with countries in the region, has good interoperability with the forces of an ally, and shares intelligence with nations in the region.

b. **Political Stability.** Political stability brings predictability for military planners when considering such things as transit, basing, and overflight rights for U.S. military operations. The overall degree of political stability indicates whether U.S. military actions would be hindered or enabled and considers, for example, whether transfers of power in the region are generally peaceful and whether there have been any recent instances of political instability.

c. **U.S. Military Positioning.** Having military forces based or equipment and supplies staged in a region greatly facilitates the ability if the United States to respond to crises and, presumably, achieve success in critical "first battles" more quickly. Being routinely present in a region also assists in maintaining familiarity with its characteristics and the various actors who might assist or thwart U.S. actions. With this in mind, we assessed whether or not the U.S. military was well positioned in the region. Again, indicators included bases, troop presence, prepositioned equipment, and recent examples of military operations (including training and humanitarian) launched from the region.

d. **Infrastructure.** Modern, reliable, and suitable infrastructure is essential to military operations. Airfields, ports, rail lines, canals, and paved roads enable the U.S. to stage, launch, and logistically sustain combat operations. We combined expert knowledge of regions with publicly available information on critical infrastructure to arrive at our overall assessment of this metric.[114]

In summary, the U.S. has developed an extensive network of bases in the region and has acquired substantial operational experience in combatting regional threats, but many of its allies are hobbled by political instability, economic problems, internal security threats, and mushrooming transnational threats. Although the overall score remains "moderate," as it was last year, it has fallen lower and is in danger of falling to "poor" because of increasing political instability and growing bilateral tensions with allies over the security implications of the nuclear agreement with Iran and how best to fight the Islamic State.

With this in mind, we arrived at these average scores for the Middle East (rounded to the nearest whole number):

- Alliances: **3—Moderate**

- Political Stability: **1—Very Poor**

- U.S. Military Positioning: **3—Moderate**

- Infrastructure: **3—Moderate**

Leading to a regional score of: **Moderate**

Operating Environment: Middle East

	VERY POOR	UNFAVORABLE	MODERATE	FAVORABLE	EXCELLENT
Alliances			✔		
Political Stability	✔				
U.S. Military Posture			✔		
Infrastructure			✔		
OVERALL			✔		

Endnotes

1. For example, Sir Mark Sykes, Britain's lead negotiator with the French on carving up the Ottoman Empire in the Middle East, during a 1916 meeting in Downing Street pointed to the map and told the Prime Minister that for Britain's sphere of influence in the Middle East, "I should like to draw a line from the *e* in Acre [modern-day Israel] to the last *k* in Kirkuk [modern-day Iraq]." See James Barr, *A Line in the Sand: Britain, France, and the Struggle That Shaped the Middle East* (London: Simon & Schuster U.K., 2011), pp. 7–20. See also Margaret McMillan, *Paris 1919: Six Months That Changed the World* (New York: Random House, 2003).

2. "What Is the Difference Between Sunni and Shia Muslims?" *The Economist*, May 28, 2013, http://www.economist.com/blogs/economist-explains/2013/05/economist-explains-19/ (accessed June 22, 2017).

3. U.S. net imports of oil equaled roughly 25 percent of U.S. consumption in 2016. Of this, 18 percent came from Persian Gulf countries. Since 2005, U.S. oil imports have decreased year on year. See U.S. Department of Energy, Energy Information Administration, "Oil: Crude and Petroleum Products Explained: Oil Imports and Exports," last updated May 8, 2017, https://www.eia.gov/energyexplained/index.cfm?page=oil_imports (accessed June 22, 2017).

4. U.S. Department of Energy, Energy Information Administration, "Country Analysis Brief: Japan," last updated February 2, 2017, https://www.eia.gov/beta/international/analysis_includes/countries_long/Japan/japan.pdf (accessed June 26, 2017).

5. World Bank, "Republic of Korea: Overview," last updated April 14, 2017, http://www.worldbank.org/en/country/korea/overview (accessed June 26, 2017).

6. U.S. Department of Energy, Energy Information Administration, "Country Analysis Brief: South Korea," last updated January 19, 2017, https://www.eia.gov/beta/international/analysis_includes/countries_long/Korea_South/south_korea.pdf (accessed June 26, 2017).

7. Clifford Krauss, "Oil Prices: What to Make of the Volatility," *The New York Times*, updated June 14, 2017, http://www.nytimes.com/interactive/2016/business/energy-environment/oil-prices.html?_r=0 (accessed June 22, 2017).

8. Tim Bowler, "Falling Oil Prices: Who Are the Winners and Losers?" BBC News, January 19, 2015, http://www.bbc.com/news/business-29643612 (accessed June 22, 2017).

9. U.S. Central Intelligence Agency, *The World Factbook 2017*, https://www.cia.gov/library/publications/the-world-factbook/index.html (accessed May 30, 2017).

10. "Country Rankings," in Ambassador Terry Miller and Anthony B. Kim, *2017 Index of Economic Freedom* (Washington: The Heritage Foundation, 2017), http://www.heritage.org/index/ranking.

11. "The Arab Winter." *The Economist*, January 9, 2016, http://www.economist.com/news/middle-east-and-africa/21685503-five-years-after-wave-uprisings-arab-world-worse-ever (accessed June 22, 2017).

12. Sune Engel Rasmussen and Zahra Nader, "Iran Covertly Recruits Afghan Shias to Fight in Syria," *The Guardian*, June 30, 2016, https://www.theguardian.com/world/2016/jun/30/iran-covertly-recruits-afghan-soldiers-to-fight-in-syria (accessed June 22, 2017).

13. BBC News, "Hague Fury as 'Iranian Arms' Bound for Taliban Seized," March 9, 2011, http://www.bbc.com/news/uk-12694266 (accessed June 22, 2017).

14. James Phillips, "The Dangerous Regional Implications of the Iran Nuclear Agreement," Heritage Foundation *Backgrounder* No. 3124, May 9, 2016, http://www.heritage.org/middle-east/report/the-dangerous-regional-implications-the-iran-nuclear-agreement.

15. Ibid.

16. Bethan Mckernan, "Past Month 'Deadliest on Record' for Syrian Civilians Killed in US-Led Air Strikes," *Independent*, May 23, 2017, http://www.independent.co.uk/news/world/middle-east/syria-war-us-air-strikes-civilian-death-toll-deadliest-on-record-isis-donald-trump-a7751911.html (accessed June 22, 2017).

17. Mercy Corps, "Quick Facts: What You Need to Know About the Syria Crisis," March 9, 2017, https://www.mercycorps.org/articles/iraq-jordan-lebanon-syria-turkey/quick-facts-what-you-need-know-about-syria-crisis (accessed June 22, 2017).

18. Ibid.

19. BBC News, "Migrant Crisis: Migration to Europe Explained in Seven Charts," March 4, 2016, http://www.bbc.com/news/world-europe-34131911 (accessed June 22, 2017).

20. Lisa Curtis, ed., "Combatting the ISIS Foreign Fighter Pipeline: A Global Approach," Heritage Foundation *Special Report* No. 180, January 6, 2016, http://www.heritage.org/middle-east/report/combatting-the-isis-foreign-fighter-pipeline-global-approach (accessed June 22, 2017).

21.   James Phillips, "Gaza Crisis Illuminates a Grave New World," Heritage Foundation *Commentary*, July 17, 2014, http://www.heritage.org/middle-east/commentary/gaza-crisis-illuminates-grave-new-world.

22.   Bahrain, Kuwait, Oman, Qatar, Saudi Arabia, and the United Arab Emirates.

23.   U.S. Naval Forces Central Command, "World's Largest Maritime Exercise Underway in Middle East," April 4, 2016, http://www.navy.mil/submit/display.asp?story_id=93996 (accessed June 22, 2017).

24.   General Lloyd J. Austin III, Commander, U.S. Central Command, statement on "The Posture of U.S. Central Command" before the Committee on Armed Services, U.S. Senate, March 8, 2016, https://www.armed-services.senate.gov/imo/media/doc/Austin_03-08-16.pdf (accessed June 22, 2017).

25.   Patricia Zengerle, "U.S. Lawmakers to Fight Massive Trump Saudi Arms Deal," Reuters, May 25, 2017, http://www.reuters.com/article/us-usa-saudi-arms-congress-idUSKBN18L2XN (accessed June 22, 2017).

26.   The MNNA designation was established during the dying days of the Cold War in 1989 to acknowledge American partners that contribute to U.S. security, defense, and broader geopolitical goals but are not members of NATO. The first tranche of countries to become MNNAs included South Korea, Israel, Egypt, Australia, and Japan. The country most recently awarded this title is Afghanistan, designated in 2012 by President Barack Obama.

27.   Pieter D. Wezeman, "Conventional Strategic Military Capabilities in the Middle East," EU Non-Proliferation Consortium *Background Paper*, July 2011, https://www.sipri.org/sites/default/files/2016-03/Conventional-strategic-military-capabilities-in-the-Middle-East.pdf (accessed June 22, 2017).

28.   James Phillips, "Threats Demand U.S., Israeli Partnership," Heritage Foundation *Commentary*, July 7, 2010, http://www.heritage.org/middle-east/commentary/threats-demand-us-israeli-partnership.

29.   Ibid.

30.   Created in 1981, the GCC was founded to offset the threat from Iran, which became hostile to Sunni-led Arab states after its 1979 revolution.

31.   "US Embassy Cables: Bahrain's Relations with Iran," *The Guardian*, February 15, 2011, http://www.theguardian.com/world/us-embassy-cables-documents/164906 (accessed June 22, 2017).

32.   BBC News, "Saudi Arabia's Allies Bahrain, Sudan and UAE Act Against Iran," January 4, 2016, http://www.bbc.com/news/world-middle-east-35222365 (accessed June 22, 2017).

33.   BBC News, "Russia Plane Crash: 'Terror Act' Downed A321 over Egypt's Sinai," November 17, 2015, http://www.bbc.com/news/world-europe-34840943 (accessed June 22, 2017).

34.   Ben Hubbard, "Saudis Cut Off Funding for Military Aid to Lebanon," *The New York Times*, February 23, 2016, http://www.nytimes.com/2016/02/20/world/middleeast/saudis-cut-off-funding-for-military-aid-to-lebanon.html (accessed June 22, 2017).

35.   Zachary Laub, "Yemen in Crisis," Council on Foreign Relations *Backgrounder*, last updated April 19, 2016, http://www.cfr.org/yemen/yemen-crisis/p36488 (accessed August 2, 2016).

36.   Ibid.

37.   Asa Fitch and Saleh Al Batati, "ISIS Fails to Gain Much Traction in Yemen," *The Wall Street Journal*, March 28, 2016, http://www.wsj.com/articles/isis-fails-to-gain-much-traction-in-yemen-1459203675 (accessed June 22, 2017).

38.   Andrew Buncombe, "Donald Trump Administration Orders 70 Airstrikes on Yemen in a Month—Twice as Many as 2016 Total," *Independent*, April 4, 2017, http://www.independent.co.uk/news/world/americas/us-politics/donald-trump-yemen-airstrikes-monthly-double-2016-obama-a7666676.html (accessed June 22, 2017).

39.   International Institute for Strategic Studies, *The Military Balance 2017: The Annual Assessment of Global Military Capabilities and Defence Economics* (London: Routledge, 2017), pp. 358–359.

40.   Stockholm International Peace Research Institute, "Trends in World Military Expenditure, 2016," Fact Sheet, April 2017, https://www.sipri.org/sites/default/files/Trends-world-military-expenditure-2016.pdf (accessed May 31, 2017).

41.   Nazila Fathi, "Wipe Israel 'Off the Map' Iranian Says," *The New York Times*, October 27, 2005, http://www.nytimes.com/2005/10/26/world/africa/26iht-iran.html?_r=0 (accessed June 22, 2017).

42.   Ibid.

43.   International Institute for Strategic Studies, *The Military Balance 2017*, p. 382.

44.   Zach Pontz, "New Military Index Ranking World's Top Armies Places Israel Just Three Ahead of Iran," *The Algemeiner*, June 14, 2013, http://www.algemeiner.com/2013/06/14/new-military-index-ranking-worlds-top-armies-places-israel-just-three-ahead-of-iran/ (accessed June 22, 2017).

45. Fareed Zakaria, "Israel Dominates the Middle East," *The Washington Post*, November 21, 2012, http://www.washingtonpost.com/opinions/fareed-zakaria-israel-dominates-the-middle-east/2012/11/21/d310dc7c-3428-11e2-bfd5-e202b6d7b501_story.html (accessed June 22, 2017).

46. Voice of America News, "Israel Calls Up 16,000 More Reservists," GlobalSecurity.org, July 31, 2014, http://www.globalsecurity.org/military/library/news/2014/07/mil-140731-voa01.htm (accessed June 22, 2017).

47. Anthony H. Cordesman and Aram Nerguizian, "The Arab–Israeli Military Balance: Conventional Realities and Asymmetric Challenges," Center for Strategic and International Studies, revised June 29, 2010, p. 4, http://csis.org/files/publication/100629_Arab-IsraeliMilBal.pdf (accessed June 22, 2017).

48. Ibid.

49. Barbara Opall-Rome, "Israel's 5-Year Plan Bulks Up Combat Capabilities; Cuts Manpower," *Defense News*, January 7, 2016, http://www.defensenews.com/story/defense/policy-budget/policy/2016/01/07/israels-5-year-plan-bulks-up-combat-capabilities-cuts-manpower/78421050/ (accessed June 22, 2017).

50. Cordesman and Nerguizian, "The Arab–Israeli Military Balance," p. 4.

51. Ruth Eglash and William Booth, "Israel to Launch One of the Most Advanced Missile Defense Systems in the World, with U.S. Help," *The Washington Post*, March 3, 2016, https://www.washingtonpost.com/world/middle_east/israel-to-launch-one-of-the-most-advanced-missile-defense-systems-in-the-world-with-us-help/2016/03/03/6383cb88-dfd5-11e5-8c00-8aa03741dced_story.html (accessed June 22, 2017).

52. GlobalSecurity.org, "Iron Dome," July 23, 2014, http://www.globalsecurity.org/military/world/israel/iron-dome.htm (accessed July 31, 2014).

53. Jeremy M. Sharp, "U.S. Foreign Aid to Israel," Congressional Research Service *Report for Members and Committees of Congress*, December 22, 2016, https://fas.org/sgp/crs/mideast/RL33222.pdf (accessed May 31, 2017).

54. William Wunderle and Andre Briere, "Augmenting Israel's Qualitative Military Edge," *Middle East Quarterly*, Vol. 15, No. 1 (Winter 2008), pp. 49–58, http://www.meforum.org/1824/augmenting-israels-qualitative-military-edge (accessed June 22, 2017).

55. "GCC Forces Are 'Protecting Key Installations,'" *Gulf Digital News*, January 5, 2014, http://www.gulf-daily-news.com/NewsDetails.aspx?storyid=368082 (accessed June 22, 2017).

56. International Institute for Strategic Studies, *The Military Balance 2017*, p. 402.

57. Brian Kalman and Edwin Watson, "Military Analysis: Saudi Arabia Deploys Combat Aircraft to Turkey," SouthFront, February 24, 2016, https://southfront.org/military-analysis-saudi-arabia-deploys-combat-aircraft-to-turkey/ (accessed July 3, 2017).

58. Andrew Chuter, "BAE Plans First Powered Flight Tests of Storm Shadow Missile on Typhoon," *Defense News*, July 10, 2016, http://www.defensenews.com/story/defense/air-space/strike/2016/06/10/bae-storm-shadow-cruise-missile/85688780/ (accessed June 22, 2017).

59. Center for Strategic and International Studies, Missile Defense Project, "Missile Threat: Apache AP/SCALP EG/Storm Shadow/SCALP Naval/Black Shaheen," last updated December 2, 2016, https://missilethreat.csis.org/missile/apache-ap/ (accessed June 22, 2017).

60. *Defense Industry Daily* Staff, "Top Falcons: The UAE's F-16 Block 60/61 Fighters," *Defense Industry Daily*, January 26, 2014, http://www.defenseindustrydaily.com/the-uaes-f-16-block-60-desert-falcon-fleet-04538/ (accessed June 22, 2017).

61. Helene Cooper and Anne Barnard, "Jordan and Emirates Carry Out Airstrikes in Syria Against ISIS," *The New York Times*, February 10, 2015, www.nytimes.com/2015/02/11/world/middleeast/united-arab-emirates-resume-airstrikes-against-isis.html (accessed June 22, 2017).

62. Combined Maritime Forces, "CTF-152: Gulf Maritime Security," http://combinedmaritimeforces.com/ctf-152-gulf-security-cooperation/ (accessed May 10, 2016).

63. U.K. Ministry of Defence and The Rt. Hon. Michael Fallon, MP, "Multi-million Pound Joint Venture Announced Between Britain and Oman," March 30, 2016, https://www.gov.uk/government/news/multi-million-pound-joint-venture-announced-between-britain-and-oman (accessed June 22, 2017).

64. Quoted in editorial, "More Complaints from the Saudis," *Chicago Tribune*, December 17, 2013, http://articles.chicagotribune.com/2013-12-17/opinion/ct-saudis-versus-obama-edit-1217-20131217_1_saudis-president-barack-obama-riyadh (accessed June 22, 2017).

65. International Institute for Strategic Studies, *The Military Balance 2017*, p. 372.

66. GlobalSecurity.org, "Egypt: Introduction," April 4, 2012, http://www.globalsecurity.org/military/world/egypt/intro.htm (accessed June 22, 2017).

67. Giles Elgood, "Egyptian Warplanes Bomb Targets in Libya After Attack on Christians," Reuters, May 26, 2017, http://www.reuters.com/article/us-egypt-security-strikes-idUSKBN18M2G4 (accessed June 22, 2017).

68. International Institute for Strategic Studies, *The Military Balance 2017*, p. 372.

69. Muhammad Mansour, "US Aid to Egypt: Wrong but Inevitable," Middle East Eye, May 15, 2017, http://www.middleeasteye.net/columns/us-aid-egypt-wrong-inevitable-1572718623 (accessed June 26, 2017).

70. Jared Malsin, "Egypt Is Struggling to Cope With Its ISIS Insurgency," *Time*, July 23, 2015, http://time.com/3969596/egypt-isis-sinai/ (accessed June 22, 2017).

71. Rana F. Sweis, "Jordan Struggles Under a Wave of Syrian Refugees," *The New York Times*, February 13, 2016, http://www.nytimes.com/2016/02/14/world/middleeast/jordan-syria-refugees.html?_r=0 (accessed June 22, 2017).

72. International Institute for Strategic Studies, *The Military Balance 2017*, pp. 385–386.

73. Tim Arango and Michael R. Gordon, "Iraqi Prime Minister Arrives in Mosul to Declare Victory over ISIS," *The New York Times*, July 9, 2017, https://www.nytimes.com/2017/07/09/world/middleeast/mosul-isis-liberated.html?mcubz=0 (accessed September 8, 2017).

74. During 1967 and 1990, South Yemen, officially known as the People's Democratic Republic of Yemen, was a socialist state in the southeastern provinces of the present-day Republic of Yemen.

75. U.S. Central Command, "U.S. Central Command History," http://www.centcom.mil/ABOUT-US/HISTORY/ (accessed June 22, 2017).

76. Ibid.

77. Lieutenant Colonel Joseph P. Englehardt, *Desert Shield and Desert Storm: A Chronology and Troop List for the 1990–1991 Persian Gulf Crisis*, U.S. Army War College, Strategic Studies Institute *Special Report*, March 25, 1991, p. 5, http://www.dtic.mil/dtic/tr/fulltext/u2/a234743.pdf (accessed June 26, 2017).

78. BBC News, "Iraq War in Figures," December 14, 2011, http://www.bbc.com/news/world-middle-east-11107739 (accessed July 28, 2014).

79. Reuters, "Timeline: Invasion, Surge, Withdrawal; U.S. Forces in Iraq," December 18, 2011, http://www.reuters.com/article/2011/12/18/us-iraq-usa-pullout-idUSTRE7BH08E20111218 (accessed June 22, 2017).

80. Julia Zorthian and Heather Jones, "This Graphic Shows Where U.S. Troops Are Stationed Around the World," *Time*, October 16, 2015, http://time.com/4075458/afghanistan-drawdown-obama-troops/ (accessed August 2, 2016).

81. Charlsy Panzino and Andrew deGrandre, "The U.S. Is Sending 2,500 Troops to Kuwait, Ready to Step Up the Fight in Syria and Iraq," *Army Times*, March 9, 2017, https://www.armytimes.com/articles/82nd-airborne-syria-iraq-kuwait-islamic-state (accessed June 22, 2017).

82. General Joseph L. Votel, Commander, U.S. Central Command, statement on "The Posture of U.S. Central Command" before the Committee on Armed Services, U.S. Senate, March 9, 2017, https://www.armed-services.senate.gov/imo/media/doc/Votel_03-09-17.pdf (accessed June 22, 2017).

83. Kenneth Katzman, "The United Arab Emirates (UAE): Issues for U.S. Policy," Congressional Research Service *Report for Members and Committees of Congress*, February 28, 2017, p. 19, https://fas.org/sgp/crs/mideast/RS21852.pdf (accessed June 22, 2017).

84. Kenneth Katzman, "Oman: Reform, Security, and U.S. Policy," Congressional Research Service *Report for Members and Committees of Congress*, April 26, 2016, p14, https://fas.org/sgp/crs/mideast/RS21534.pdf (accessed June 26, 2017).

85. Kenneth Katzman, "Bahrain: Reform, Security, and U.S. Policy," Congressional Research Service *Report for Members and Committees of Congress*, April 13, 2017, p. 17, https://fas.org/sgp/crs/mideast/95-1013.pdf (accessed June 1, 2017).

86. Ibid., pp. 17–18.

87. U.S. Air Forces Central Command, "Wing Leadership Visits Eskan Village," July 5, 2013, http://www.afcent.af.mil/Units/379thAirExpeditionaryWing/News/Display/tabid/5382/Article/350180/wing-leadership-visits-eskan-village.aspx (accessed June 22, 2017).

88. Votel, statement on "The Posture of U.S. Central Command."

89. Ibid.

90. "Officials Say Three U.S. Service Members Killed in Jordan Attack," *Military Times*, November 4, 2016, http://www.militarytimes.com/articles/jordan-american-trainer-air-base-shootout (accessed June 26, 2017).

91. BBC News, "CIA Operating Drone Base in Saudi Arabia, US Media Reveal," February 6, 2013, http://www.bbc.com/news/world-middle-east-21350437 (accessed June 22, 2017).

92. "Israel and Iran: Closer to Takeoff," *The Economist*, February 11, 2012, http://www.economist.com/node/21547297 (accessed June 22, 2017).

93. U.K. Royal Navy, "UK Minister Breaks Ground on Royal Navy HQ in Bahrain," April 28, 2014, http://www.royalnavy.mod.uk/news-and-latest-activity/news/2014/april/28/140428-hq-in-bahrain (accessed June 22, 2017).

94. U.K. Ministry of Defence, "Multi-Million Pound Joint Venture Announced Between Britain and Oman," March 30, 2016, https://www.gov.uk/government/news/multi-million-pound-joint-venture-announced-between-britain-and-oman (accessed June 22, 2017).

95. Frank Gardner, "'East of Suez': Are UK Forces Returning?" BBC News, April 29, 2013, http://www.bbc.com/news/uk-22333555 (accessed June 22, 2017).

96. Harriet Alexander, "Where Are the World's Major Military Bases?" *The Telegraph*, July 11, 2013, http://www.telegraph.co.uk/news/uknews/defence/10173740/Where-are-the-worlds-major-military-bases.html (accessed June 22, 2017).

97. International Institute for Strategic Studies, *The Military Balance 2017*, p. 412.

98. Donna Miles, "Centcom Undertakes Massive Logistical Drawdown in Afghanistan," Armed Forces Press Service, June 21, 2013, http://archive.defense.gov/news/newsarticle.aspx?id=120348 (accessed June 22, 2017).

99. Ibid.

100. U.S. Central Intelligence Agency, *The World Factbook 2017*, "Field Listing: Roadways: Country Comparison to the World," https://www.cia.gov/library/publications/the-world-factbook/fields/2085.html (accessed June 22, 2017).

101. World Bank, "Rail Lines (Total Route-km)," 1980–2015, http://data.worldbank.org/indicator/IS.RRS.TOTL.KM/countries?display=default (accessed June 26, 2017).

102. Association of American Railroads, "U.S. Freight Railroad Industry Snapshot," updated 2015, https://www.aar.org/data-center/railroads-states#state/NH (accessed June 22, 2017).

103. Anne Barnard, "Once Bustling, Syria's Fractured Railroad Is a Testament to Shattered Ambitions," *The New York Times*, May 25, 2014, http://www.nytimes.com/2014/05/26/world/middleeast/damascus-syria-hejaz-railway-station.html (accessed June 22, 2017).

104. Hendrick Simoes, "Work in Progress to Upgrade Facilities at Navy Base in Bahrain," *Stars and Stripes*, April 11, 2014, http://www.stripes.com/news/work-in-progress-to-upgrade-facilities-at-navy-base-in-bahrain-1.277483 (accessed June 22, 2017).

105. Katzman, "Bahrain: Reform, Security, and U.S. Policy."

106. Ibid.

107. Combined Maritime Forces, "CMF Commanders Speak on Maritime Security at Doha Maritime Defence Exhibition," April 1, 2014, http://combinedmaritimeforces.com/2014/04/01/cmf-commanders-speak-on-maritime-security-at-doha-maritime-defence-exhibition/ (accessed June 22, 2017).

108. Suez Canal Authority, "Navigation Statistics," http://www.suezcanal.gov.eg/English/Navigation/Pages/NavigationStatistics.aspx (accessed June 22, 2017).

109. Associated Press, "US Carrier Crosses Suez Canal into Red Sea," *The Times of Israel*, November 8, 2013, http://www.timesofisrael.com/us-carrier-crosses-suez-canal-into-red-sea/ (accessed June 26, 2017).

110. U.S. Department of Energy, Energy Information Administration, "World Oil Transit Chokepoints," last updated November 10, 2014, p. 4, http://www.eia.gov/beta/international/analysis_includes/special_topics/World_Oil_Transit_Chokepoints/wotc.pdf (accessed June 22, 2017).

111. U.S. Department of Energy, Energy Information Administration, "Oil Trade off Yemen Coast Grew by 20% to 4.7 Million Barrels per Day in 2014," *Today in Energy*, April 23, 2015, http://www.eia.gov/todayinenergy/detail.cfm?id=20932 (accessed June 22, 2017).

112. Reuters, "Factbox—Some Facts on the Bab Al-Mandab Shipping Lane," June 4, 2011, http://uk.reuters.com/article/2011/06/04/uk-yemen-shipping-bab-al-mandab-idUKTRE75241G20110604 (accessed June 22, 2017).

113. International Chamber of Commerce, Commercial Crime Services, "IMB Piracy Report Highlights Violence in West Africa," July 15, 2013, https://www.icc-ccs.org/news/865-imb-piracy-report-highlights-violence-in-west-africa (accessed June 22, 2017).

114. See, for example, World Bank, "Logistics Performance Index: Quality of Trade and Transport-Related Infrastructure (1=Low to 5=High)," 2007–2016, http://data.worldbank.org/indicator/LP.LPI.INFR.XQ (accessed June 26, 2017).

Asia

Since the founding of the American republic, Asia has been a key area of interest for the United States for both economic and security reasons. One of the first ships to sail under an American flag was the aptly named *Empress of China*, which inaugurated America's participation in the lucrative China trade in 1784. In the more than 200 years since then, the United States has worked under the strategic assumption that it was inimical to American interests to allow any single nation to dominate Asia. Asia constituted too important a market and was too great a source of key resources for the United States to be denied access. Thus, beginning with U.S. Secretary of State John Hay's "Open Door" policy toward China in the 19th century, the United States has worked to prevent the rise of a regional hegemon, whether it was imperial Japan in Asia or the Soviet Union in Europe.

In the 21st century, Asia's importance to the United States will continue to grow. Already, 40 percent of U.S. trade in goods is in Asian markets. Asia is a key source of vital natural resources and a crucial part of the global value chain in areas like electronic components. It is America's second largest trading partner in services.[1] Disruption in Asia, as occurred with the March 2011 earthquake in Japan, affects the production of things like cars, aircraft, and computers around the world, as well as the global financial system.

Asia is of more than just economic concern, however. Several of the world's largest militaries are in Asia, including those of China, India, North and South Korea, Pakistan, Russia, and Vietnam. The United States also maintains a network of treaty alliances and security partnerships, as well as a significant military presence, in Asia. Five Asian states (China, North Korea, India, Pakistan, and Russia) possess nuclear weapons.

The region is a focus of American security concerns both because of the presence of substantial military forces and because of the legacy of conflict. Both of the two major "hot" wars fought by the United States during the Cold War were in Asia: Korea and Vietnam. Moreover, the Asian security environment is unstable. For one thing, the Cold War has not ended in Asia. Of the four states divided between Communism and democracy by the Cold War, three (China, Korea, and Vietnam) were in Asia. Neither the Korean situation nor the China–Taiwan situation was resolved despite the fall of the Berlin Wall and the collapse of the Soviet Union.

The Cold War itself was an ideological conflict layered atop long-standing—and still lingering—historical animosities. Asia is home to several major territorial disputes, among them:

- Northern Territories/Southern Kuriles (Japan and Russia);

- Senkakus/Diaoyutai/Diaoyu Dao (Japan, China, and Taiwan);

- Dok-do/Takeshima (Korea and Japan);

- Paracels/Xisha Islands (Vietnam, China, and Taiwan);

- Spratlys/Nansha Islands (China, Taiwan, Vietnam, Brunei, Malaysia, and the Philippines);

- Kashmir (India and Pakistan); and

- Aksai Chin and parts of the Indian state of Arunachal Pradesh (India and China).

Even the various names applied to the disputed territories reflect the fundamental differences in point of view, as each state refers to the disputed areas under a different name. Similarly, different names are applied to the various major bodies of water: for example, "East Sea" or "Sea of Japan" and "Yellow Sea" or "West Sea." China and India do not even agree on the length of their disputed border, with Chinse estimates as low as 2,000 kilometers and Indian estimates generally in the mid-3,000s.

These disputes over names also reflect the broader tensions rooted in historical animosities—enmities that still scar the region. Most notably, Japan's actions leading up to and during World War II remain a major source of controversy, particularly in China and South Korea, where debates over issues such as what is incorporated in textbooks and governmental statements prevent old wounds from completely healing. Similarly, a Chinese claim that much of the Korean Peninsula was once Chinese territory aroused reactions in both Koreas. The end of the Cold War did little to resolve any of these underlying disagreements.

It is in this light that one should consider the lack of a political–security architecture, or even much of an economic one, undergirding East Asia. Despite substantial trade and expanding value chains among the various Asian states, as well as with the rest of the world, formal economic integration is limited. There is no counterpart to the European Union or even to the European Economic Community, just as there is no parallel with the European Coal and Steel Community, the precursor to European economic integration.

The Association of Southeast Asian Nations (ASEAN) is a far looser agglomeration of disparate states, although they have succeeded in expanding economic linkages among themselves over the past 50 years through a range of economic agreements like the ASEAN Free Trade Area (AFTA). Less important to regional stability has been the South Asia Association of Regional Cooperation (SAARC), which includes Afghanistan, Bangladesh, Bhutan, India, Maldives, Nepal, Pakistan, and Sri Lanka. The SAARC is largely ineffective, both because of the lack of regional economic integration and because of the historical rivalry between India and Pakistan. Also, despite attempts, there is still no Asia-wide free trade agreement, although the Trans-Pacific Partnership, if it proceeds without the U.S., and the Regional Comprehensive Economic Partnership would help to remedy this gap to some extent.

Similarly, there is no equivalent of NATO, despite an ultimately failed mid-20th century effort to forge a parallel multilateral security architecture through the Southeast Asia Treaty Organization (SEATO). Regional security entities like the Five Power Defence Arrangement (involving the United Kingdom, Australia, New Zealand, Malaysia, and Singapore in an "arrangement," not an alliance) or discussion forums like the ASEAN Regional Forum and the ASEAN Defense Ministers-Plus Meeting have been far weaker. Nor did an Asian equivalent of the Warsaw Pact arise. Instead, Asian security has been marked by a combination of bilateral alliances, mostly centered on the United States, and individual nations' efforts to maintain their own security.

Important Alliances and Bilateral Relations in Asia

For the United States, the keys to its position in the Western Pacific are its alliances with Japan, the Republic of Korea (ROK), the Philippines, Thailand, and Australia. These five alliances are supplemented by very close security relationships with New Zealand, Afghanistan, Pakistan, and Singapore and evolving relationships with other nations in the region like India, Vietnam, Malaysia, and Indonesia. The U.S. also has a robust unofficial relationship with Taiwan.

The United States enjoys the benefit of sharing common weapons and systems with many of its allies, which facilitates interoperability. Many nations, for example, have equipped their ground forces with M-16/M-4–based infantry weapons (and share the 5.56mm caliber); field F-15 and F-16 combat aircraft; and employ LINK-16 data links. Australia, Japan, and South Korea are partners in the production of the F-35 Joint Strike Fighter; Australia and Japan have already taken delivery of aircraft, and South Korea is due to take delivery next year. Consequently, in the event of conflict, the various air, naval, and even land forces will be capable of sharing information in such key areas as air defense and maritime domain awareness. This advantage is further expanded by the constant ongoing range of both bilateral and multilateral exercises, which acclimates various forces to operating together and familiarizes both American and local commanders with each other's standard operating procedures (SOPs), as well as training and tactics.

Japan. The U.S.–Japan defense relationship is the linchpin in the American network of relations in the Western Pacific. The U.S.–Japan Treaty of Mutual Cooperation and Security, signed in 1960, provided for a deep alliance between two of the world's largest economies and most sophisticated military establishments, and changes in Japanese defense policies are now enabling an even greater level of cooperation on security issues between the two allies and others in the region.

Since the end of World War II, Japan's defense policy has been distinguished by Article 9 of its constitution. This article, which states in part that "the Japanese people forever renounce war as a sovereign right of the nation and the threat or use of force as means of settling international disputes,"[2] in effect prohibits the use of force by Japan's governments as an instrument of national policy. It also has led to several other associated policies.

One such policy is a prohibition on "collective self-defense." Japan recognized that nations have a right to employ their armed forces to help other states defend themselves (i.e., to engage in collective defensive operations) but rejected that policy for itself: Japan would employ its forces only in defense of Japan. In 2015, this changed. The U.S. and Japan revised their defense cooperation guidelines, and the Japanese passed legislation needed to allow Japan to exercise limited collective self-defense in certain cases involving threats to both the U.S. and Japan, as well as in multilateral peacekeeping operations.

A similar policy decision was made regarding Japanese arms exports in 2014. For a variety of economic and political reasons, Tokyo had chosen until then to rely on domestic or licensed production to meet most of its military requirements while essentially banning defense-related exports. The relaxation of these export rules in 2014 enabled Japan, among other things, to pursue (ultimately unsuccessfully) an opportunity to build new state-of-the-art submarines in Australia, for Australia, and possible sales of amphibious search and rescue aircraft to the Indian navy. Japan has also sold multiple patrol vessels to the Philippine and Vietnamese Coast Guards and is exploring various joint development opportunities with the U.S. and a few other nations.

Tokyo relies heavily on the United States for its security. In particular, it depends on the United States to deter nuclear attacks on the home islands. The combination of the pacifist constitution and Japan's past (i.e., the atomic bombings of Hiroshima and Nagasaki) has forestalled much public interest in obtaining an independent nuclear deterrent. Similarly, throughout the Cold War, Japan relied on the American conventional and nuclear commitment to deter Soviet and Chinese aggression.

As part of its relationship with Japan, the United States maintains some 54,000 military personnel and another 8,000 Department of Defense civilian employees in Japan under the rubric of U.S. Forces Japan (USFJ).[3] These forces include a forward-deployed carrier battle group centered on the USS *Ronald Reagan*; a submarine tender; an amphibious assault ship at Yokosuka; and the bulk of the Third Marine Expeditionary Force (III MEF) on Okinawa. U.S. forces exercise regularly with their Japanese counterparts; in recent years, this collaboration has expanded from air and naval exercises to practicing amphibious operations together.

The American presence is supported by a substantial American defense infrastructure throughout Japan, including Okinawa. The array of major bases provides key logistical and communications support for U.S. operations throughout the Western Pacific, cutting travel time substantially compared with deployments from Hawaii or the West Coast of the United States. They also provide key listening posts on Russian, Chinese, and North Korean military operations. This is supplemented by Japan's growing array of space systems, including new reconnaissance satellites.

The Japanese government currently provides some $2 billion annually to support the cost of USFJ.[4] These funds cover a variety of expenses, including utility and labor costs at U.S. bases, improvements to U.S. facilities in Japan, and the cost of relocating training exercises away from populated areas in Japan. Japan is also covering nearly all of the expenses related to relocation of the Futenma Marine Corps Air Station from its crowded urban location to a less densely populated part of the island and facilities in Guam to accommodate some Marines being moved off the island.

At least since the 1990 Gulf War, the United States had sought to expand Japanese participation in international security affairs. Japan's political system, based on the view that Japan's constitution, legal decisions, and popular attitudes all forbid such a shift, generally resisted this effort. Attempts to expand Japan's range of defense activities, especially away from the home islands, have often been vehemently opposed by Japan's neighbors, especially China and South Korea, due to unresolved differences on issues ranging from territorial claims and boundaries to historical grievances and Japanese visits to the Yasukuni Shrine. Even with the incremental changes allowing for broader Japanese defense contributions, these issues will doubtless continue to constrain Japan's contributions to the alliance.

These historical issues have been sufficient to torpedo efforts to improve defense cooperation between Seoul and Tokyo, a fact highlighted in 2012 by South Korea's last-minute decision not to sign an agreement to share sensitive military data, including details about the North Korean threat to both countries.[5] In December 2014, the U.S., South Korea, and Japan signed a military data-sharing agreement limited to information on the North Korean military threat and requiring both allies to pass information through the United States military. This was supplemented in 2016 by a Japan–ROK bilateral agreement on sharing military intelligence. Similar controversies, rooted in history as well as in contemporary politics, have also affected Sino–Japanese relations and, to a lesser extent, Japanese ties to some Southeast Asian states.

Republic of Korea. The United States and the Republic of Korea signed their Mutual Defense Treaty in 1953. That treaty codified the relationship that had grown from the Korean War, when the United States dispatched troops to help South Korea defend itself against invasion by Communist North Korea. Since then, the two states have forged an enduring alliance supplemented by a substantial trade and economic relationship that includes a free trade agreement.

As of March 2017, the United States maintained some 23,411 troops in Korea,[6] the largest concentration of American forces on the Asian mainland. This presence is centered mainly on the U.S. 2nd Infantry Division, rotating brigade combat teams, and a significant number of combat aircraft.

The U.S.–ROK defense relationship involves one of the more integrated and complex command-and-control structures. A United Nations Command (UNC) established in 1950 was the basis for the American intervention and remained in place after the armistice was signed in 1953. UNC has access to a number of bases in Japan in order to support U.N. forces in Korea. In concrete terms, however, it only oversaw South Korean and American forces as other nations' contributions were gradually withdrawn or reduced to token elements.

In 1978, operational control of frontline South Korean and American military forces passed from UNC to Combined Forces Command (CFC). Headed by an American officer who is also Commander, U.N. Command, CFC reflects an unparalleled degree of U.S.–South Korean military integration. Similarly, the system of Korean Augmentees to the United States Army (KATUSA), which places South Korean soldiers into American units assigned to Korea, allows for an atypical degree of tactical-level integration and cooperation.

Current command arrangements for the U.S. and ROK militaries are for CFC to exercise operational control (OPCON) of all forces on the peninsula in time of war, while peacetime control rests with respective national authorities, although the U.S. exercises peacetime OPCON over non-U.S., non-ROK forces located on the peninsula. In 2003, South Korean President Roh Moo-hyun, as agreed with the U.S., began the process of transferring wartime operational control from CFC to South Korean commanders, thereby establishing the ROK military as fully independent of the United States. This decision engendered significant opposition within South Korea and raised serious military questions about the impact on unity of command. Faced with various North Korean provocations, including a spate of missile tests as well as attacks on South Korean military forces and territory in 2010, Washington and Seoul agreed in late 2014 to postpone wartime OPCON transfer.[7]

The domestic political constraints under which South Korea's military operates are less stringent than those that govern the operations of the Japanese military. Thus, South Korea rotated several divisions to fight alongside Americans in Vietnam. In the first Gulf War, the Iraq War, and Afghanistan, South Korea limited its contributions to non-combatant forces and monetary aid. The focus of South Korean defense planning remains on North Korea, especially as Pyongyang has deployed its forces in ways that optimize a southward advance and has carried out several penetrations of ROK territory over the years by ship, submarine, commandos, and drones. The sinking of the South Korean frigate *Cheonan* and shelling of Yongpyeong-do in 2010, which together killed 48 military personnel, wounded 16, and killed two civilians, have only heightened concerns about North Korea.

Over the past several decades, the American presence on the peninsula has slowly declined. In the early 1970s, President Richard Nixon withdrew the 7th Infantry Division, leaving only the 2nd Infantry Division on the peninsula. Those forces have been positioned farther back so that there are now few Americans deployed on the Demilitarized Zone (DMZ).

Washington generally maintains "more than 28,000 American troops" in the ROK.[8] These forces regularly engage in major exercises with their ROK counterparts, including the Key Resolve and Foal Eagle series, both of which involve the actual deployment of a substantial number of forces and are partly intended to deter Pyongyang, as well as to give U.S. and ROK forces a chance to practice operating together. The ROK government also provides substantial resources to defray the costs of U.S. Forces–Korea. It pays approximately half of all non-personnel costs for U.S. forces stationed in South Korea, amounting to $821 million in 2016, and "is paying $9.74 billion for the relocation of several U.S. bases within the country and construction of new military facilities."[9]

With new governments in place in both the U.S. and South Korea, the health of the alliance at the political level will need to be monitored closely for impact on the operational levels. The two could diverge on issues such as North Korea sanctions policy, the timing of engagement with North Korea, deployment of THAAD, and ROK–Japan relations.

The Philippines. America's oldest defense relationship in Asia is with the Philippines. The United States seized the Philippines from the Spanish over a century ago as a result of the Spanish–American War and a subsequent conflict with Philippine indigenous forces. Unlike other colonial states, however, the U.S. also put in place a mechanism for the Philippines to gain its independence, transitioning through a period as a commonwealth until the archipelago was granted full independence in 1946. Just as important, substantial numbers of Filipinos fought alongside the United States against Japan in World War II, establishing a bond between the two peoples. Following World War II and after assisting the newly independent Filipino government against the Communist Hukbalahap movement in the 1940s, the United States and the Philippines signed a mutual security treaty.

For much of the period between 1898 and the end of the Cold War, the largest American bases in the Pacific were in the Philippines, centered around the U.S. Navy base in Subic Bay and the complex of airfields that developed around Clark Field (later Clark Air Base). While the Philippines have never had the ability to provide substantial financial support for the American presence, the unparalleled base infrastructure provided replenishment and repair facilities and substantially extended deployment periods throughout the East Asian littoral.

These bases were often centers of controversy, as they were reminders of the colonial era. In 1991, a successor to the Military Bases Agreement between the U.S. and the Philippines was submitted to the Philippine Senate for ratification. The Philippines, after a lengthy debate, rejected the treaty, compelling American withdrawal from Philippine bases. Coupled with the effects of the 1991 eruption of Mount Pinatubo, which devastated Clark Air Base and damaged many Subic Bay facilities, and the end of the Cold War, closure of the bases was not seen as fundamentally damaging to America's posture in the region.

Moreover, despite the closing of the American bases and consequent slashing of American military assistance, U.S.–Philippine military relations remained close, and assistance began to increase again after 9/11 as U.S. forces assisted the Philippines in countering Islamic terrorist groups, including the Abu Sayyaf Group (ASG), in the south of the archipelago. From 2002–2015, the U.S. rotated 500–600 special

operations forces regularly through the Philippines to assist in counterterrorism operations. That operation, Joint Special Operations Task Force–Philippines (JSOTF–P), closed in the first part of 2015, but the U.S. presence in Mindanao continues at reduced levels.

The Philippines continues to have serious problems with Islamist insurgencies and terrorists in its South. This affects the government's priorities and, potentially, its stability. Although not a direct threat to the American homeland, it also bears on the U.S. military footprint in the Philippines and the type of cooperation the two militaries undertake. In addition to the current threat from ISIS-affiliated groups like the ASG, trained ISIS fighters returning to the Philippines could pose a threat similar to that of the "mujahedeen" who returned from Afghanistan after the Soviet war there in the 1980s.

Thousands of U.S. troops participate in combined exercises with Philippine troops, most notably as a part of the annual Balikatan exercises. In all, 258 activities with the Philippines are planned for 2017, including other "joint and service-to-service exercises."[10]

In 2014, the United States and the Philippines announced a new Enhanced Defense Cooperation Agreement (EDCA), which allows for an expanded American presence in the archipelago,[11] and in early 2016, they agreed on five specific bases subject to the agreement. Subsequent agreement has been reached to begin with Basa Air Base in Pampanga, central Luzon, the main Philippine island.[12] Under the EDCA, U.S. forces will rotate through these locations on an expanded basis, allowing for a more regular presence (but not new, permanent bases) in the islands and more joint training with the Armed Forces of the Philippines (AFP) forces. The agreement also facilitates the provision of humanitarian assistance and disaster relief. The United States also agreed to improve the facilities it uses and to transfer and sell more military equipment to the AFP to help it modernize. This is an important step, as the Philippine military has long been one of the region's weakest despite the need to defend an incredibly large expanse of ocean, shoreline, and territory.

One long-standing difference between the U.S. and the Philippines has been application of the U.S.–Philippine Mutual Defense Treaty to disputed islands in the South China Sea. The U.S. has long maintained that the treaty does not extend American obligations to disputed areas and territories, but Filipino officials occasionally have held otherwise.[13] The EDCA does not settle this question, but tensions in the South China Sea, including in recent years at Scarborough Shoal, have highlighted Manila's need for greater support from and cooperation with Washington. Moreover, the U.S. government has long been explicit that any attack on Philippine government ships or aircraft, or on the Philippine armed forces, would be covered under the treaty, "thus separating the issue of territorial sovereignty from attack on Philippine military and public vessels."[14]

In 2016, the Philippines elected a very unconventional President, Rodrigo Duterte, to a six-year term. His rhetorical challenges to current priorities in the U.S.–Philippines alliance have raised questions about the trajectory of the alliance and initiatives that are important to it. With the support of the Philippine government at various levels, however, the two militaries continue to work together with some adjustment in the size and purpose of their cooperation.[15]

Thailand. The U.S.–Thai security relationship is built on the 1954 Manila Pact, which established the now-defunct SEATO, and the 1962 Thanat–Rusk agreement. These were supplemented by the 2012 Joint Vision statement for U.S.–Thai relations. In 2003, Thailand was designated a "major, non-NATO ally," giving it improved access to American arms sales.

Thailand's central location has made it an important component of the network of U.S. alliances in Asia. During the Vietnam War, a variety of American aircraft were based in Thailand, ranging from fighter-bombers and B-52s to reconnaissance aircraft. In the first Gulf War and again in the Iraq War, some of those same air bases were essential for the rapid deployment of American forces to the Persian Gulf.

U.S. and Thai forces exercise together regularly, most notably in the annual Cobra Gold exercises, first begun in 1982. This builds on a partnership that began with the dispatch of Thai forces to the Korean War, where over 1,200 Thai troops died out of some 6,000 deployed. The Cobra Gold exercises are among the world's largest multilateral military exercises.

U.S.–Thai relations have been strained in recent years as a result of domestic unrest and two coups in Thailand. This strife has limited the extent of U.S.–Thai military cooperation, as U.S. law prohibits U.S. funding for many kinds of assistance to a foreign country in which a military coup deposes a duly elected head of government. Nonetheless, the two states continue to cooperate, including in joint military exercises and counterterrorism. The Counter Terrorism Information Center (CTIC) continues to allow the two states to share vital information about terrorist activities in Asia. Among other things, the CTIC reportedly played a key role in the capture of the leader of Jemaah Islamiyah, Hambali, in 2003.[16]

Thailand has also been drawing closer to the People's Republic of China (PRC). This process, underway since the end of the Vietnam War, is accelerating because of expanding economic relations between the two states. Between 2005 and 2010, the value of trade between the two states doubled. Today, China is Thailand's second leading trading partner.[17]

Relations between the Thai and Chinese militaries also have improved over the years. Intelligence officers began formal meetings in 1988. Thai and Chinese military forces have engaged in joint naval exercises since 2005, joint counterterrorism exercises since 2007, and joint marine exercises since 2010[18] and conducted their first joint air force exercises in 2015. The Thais have been buying Chinese military equipment for many years. Recent purchases include two significant buys of battle tanks[19] as well as armored personnel carriers. In 2017, Thailand made the first of three planned submarine purchases in one of the most expensive arms deals in its history.[20] Submarines could be particularly critical to Sino–Thai relations because the training and maintenance required will entail greater Chinese military presence at Thai military facilities. Thai–Chinese military relations may have accelerated as a result of the U.S. restrictions imposed in the wake of Thailand's political instability.

Australia. Australia is one of America's most important allies in the Asia–Pacific. U.S.–Australia security ties date back to World War I, when U.S. forces fought under Australian command on the Western Front in Europe. These ties deepened during World War II when, after Japan commenced hostilities in the Western Pacific, Australian forces committed to the North Africa campaign were not returned to defend the continent—despite British promises to do so. As Japanese forces attacked the East Indies and secured Singapore, Australia turned to the United States to bolster its defenses, and American and Australian forces subsequently cooperated closely in the Pacific War. Those ties and America's role as the main external supporter for Australian security were codified in the Australia–New Zealand–U.S. (ANZUS) pact of 1951.

A key part of the Obama Administration's "Asia pivot" was to rotate additional United States Air Force units and Marines through Northern Australia.[21] Eventually expected to total some 2,500 troops, the initial deployments of 1,250 Marines and their equipment, including up to 13 aircraft, have been based near the northern city of Darwin.[22] The two sides concluded negotiations over the terms of the full deployment late in 2016, and it is now estimated that deployment will be complete by 2020.[23] The Air Force has deployed F-22 fighter aircraft to northern Australia for joint training exercises, and there have been discussions about rotational deployments of other assets to that part of the country as well.[24] Meanwhile, the two nations engage in a variety of security cooperation efforts, including joint space surveillance activities. These were codified in 2014 with an agreement that allows sharing of space information data among the U.S., Australia, the U.K., and Canada.[25]

The two nations' chief defense and foreign policy officials meet annually in the Australia–United States Ministerial (AUSMIN) process to address such issues of mutual concern as security developments in the Asia–Pacific region, global security and development, and bilateral security cooperation.[26] Australia has also granted the United States access to a number of joint facilities, including space surveillance facilities at Pine Gap and naval communications facilities on the North West Cape of Australia.[27]

Australia and the United Kingdom are two of America's closest partners in the defense industrial sector. In 2010, the United States approved Defense Trade Cooperation Treaties with Australia and the U.K. that allow for the expedited and simplified export or transfer of certain defense services and items between the U.S. and its two key partners without the need for export licenses or other approvals under the International Traffic in Arms Regulations. This also allows for much greater integration among the American, Australian, and British defense industrial establishments.[28]

Singapore. Although Singapore is not a security treaty ally of the United States, it is a key security partner in the region. Their close defense relationship was formalized in 2005 with the Strategic Framework Agreement (SFA) and expanded in 2015 with the U.S.–Singapore Defense Cooperation Agreement (DCA).

The 2005 SFA was the first agreement of its kind since the end of the Cold War. It built on the 1990 Memorandum of Understanding Regarding United States Use of Facilities in Singapore, as amended, which allows for U.S. access to Singaporean military facilities.[29] The 2015 DCA establishes "high-level dialogues between the countries' defense establishments" and a "broad framework for defense cooperation in five key areas, namely in the military, policy, strategic and technology spheres, as well as cooperation against non-conventional security challenges, such as piracy and transnational terrorism."[30]

New Zealand. For much of the Cold War, U.S. defense ties with New Zealand were similar to those between America and Australia. As a result of controversies over U.S. Navy employment of nuclear power and the possible deployment of U.S. naval vessels with nuclear weapons, the U.S. suspended its obligations to New Zealand under the 1951 ANZUS Treaty. Defense relations improved, however, in the early 21st century as New Zealand committed forces to Afghanistan and dispatched an engineering detachment to Iraq. The 2010 Wellington Declaration and the 2012 Washington Declaration, while not restoring full security ties, allowed the two nations to resume high-level defense dialogues.

In 2013, U.S. Secretary of Defense Chuck Hagel and New Zealand Defense Minister Jonathan Coleman announced the resumption of military-to-military cooperation,[31] and in July 2016, the U.S. accepted an invitation from New Zealand to make a single port call, reportedly with no change in U.S. policy to confirm or deny the presence of nuclear weapons on the ship.[32] At the time of the visit in November 2016,[33] both sides claimed to have satisfied their respective legal requirements. The Prime Minister of New Zealand expressed confidence that the vessel was not nuclear-powered and did not possess nuclear armaments, and the U.S. neither confirmed nor denied this. The visit occurred in a unique context, including an international naval review and relief response to the Kaikoura earthquake, but the arrangement may portend a longer-term solution to the nuclear impasse between the two nations.

Taiwan. When the United States shifted its recognition of the government of China from the Republic of China (on Taiwan) to the People's Republic of China (the mainland), it declared certain commitments concerning the security of Taiwan. These commitments are embodied in the Taiwan Relations Act (TRA) and the subsequent "Six Assurances."

The TRA is an American law and not a treaty. Under the TRA, the United States maintains programs, transactions, and other relations with Taiwan through the American Institute in Taiwan (AIT). Except for the Sino–U.S. Mutual Defense Treaty, which had governed U.S.

security relations with Taiwan, all other treaties and international agreements made between the Republic of China and the United States remain in force. (President Jimmy Carter terminated the Sino–U.S. Mutual Defense Treaty following the shift in recognition to the PRC.)

Under the TRA, it is the policy of the United States "to provide Taiwan with arms of a defensive character." The TRA also states that the U.S. will "make available to Taiwan such defense articles and services in such quantity as may be necessary to enable Taiwan to maintain a sufficient self-defense capability." The U.S. has implemented these provisions of the TRA through sales of weapons to Taiwan.

The TRA states that it is U.S. policy to "consider any effort to determine the future of Taiwan by other than peaceful means, including by boycotts or embargoes, a threat to the peace and security of the Western Pacific area and of grave concern to the United States." It also states that it is U.S. policy to "maintain the capacity of the United States to resist any resort to force or other forms of coercion that would jeopardize the security, or the social or economic system, of the people on Taiwan."[34]

The TRA requires the President to inform Congress promptly of "any threat to the security or the social or economic system of the people on Taiwan and any danger to the interests of the United States arising therefrom." It then states: "The President and the Congress shall determine, in accordance with constitutional processes, appropriate action by the United States in response to any such danger."

Supplementing the TRA are the "Six Assurances" issued by President Ronald Reagan in a secret July 1982 memo, subsequently publicly released and the subject of a Senate hearing. These assurances were intended to moderate the third Sino–American communiqué, itself generally seen as one of the "Three Communiqués" that form the foundation of U.S.–PRC relations. These assurances of July 14, 1982, were that:

[I]n negotiating the third Joint Communiqué with the PRC, the United States:

---

1. has not agreed to set a date for ending arms sales to Taiwan;

2. has not agreed to hold prior consultations with the PRC on arms sales to Taiwan;

3. will not play any mediation role between Taipei and Beijing;

4. has not agreed to revise the Taiwan Relations Act;

5. has not altered its position regarding sovereignty over Taiwan;

6. will not exert pressure on Taiwan to negotiate with the PRC.[35]

Although the United States sells Taiwan a variety of military equipment, it does not engage in joint exercises with the Taiwan armed forces. Some Taiwan military officers, however, attend professional military education institutions in the United States. There also are regular high-level meetings between senior U.S. and Taiwan defense officials, both uniformed and civilian. The United States does not maintain any bases in Taiwan or its territories.

Vietnam, Malaysia, and Indonesia. The U.S. has security relationships with several key Southeast Asian countries. None of these relationships is as extensive and formal as its relationship with Singapore and its treaty allies, but all are of growing significance. The U.S. "rebalance" to the Pacific incorporated a policy of "rebalance within the rebalance" that included efforts to expand relations with this second tier of American security partners and diversify the geographical spread of its forward-deployed forces.

Since shortly after the normalization of diplomatic relations between the two countries in 1995, the U.S. and Vietnam also have normalized their defense relationship, albeit very slowly. The relationship was codified in 2011 with a Memorandum of Understanding "advancing bilateral defense cooperation" that covers five areas of operations, including maritime security, and was updated with the 2015 Joint Vision Statement on Defense Cooperation, which includes a reference to "cooperation in the production of new technologies and equipment."[36]

The most significant development in security ties over the past several years has been the relaxation of the ban on sales of arms to Vietnam. The U.S. lifted the embargo on maritime security–related equipment in the fall of 2014 and then lifted the ban completely when President Barack Obama visited Hanoi in 2016. This full embargo had long served as a psychological obstacle to Vietnamese cooperation on security issues, but lifting it does not necessarily change the nature of the articles likely to be sold. The only transfer to have been announced is the provision under the Foreign Assistance Act of a decommissioned *Hamilton*-class Coast Guard cutter.[37] Others, including P-3 maritime patrol aircraft, discussed since the relaxation of the embargo three years ago have yet to be concluded. Lifting the embargo does, however, expand the potential of the relationship and better positions the U.S. to compete with Chinese and Russian positions there.

The Joint Statement from President Obama's visit also memorialized a number of other improvements in the U.S.–Vietnam relationship, including the Cooperative Humanitarian and Medical Storage Initiative (CHAMSI), which will advance cooperation on humanitarian assistance and disaster relief by, among other things, prepositioning related American equipment in Danang, Vietnam.[38] During Vietnamese Prime Minister Nguyen Xuan Phuc's visit to Washington in 2017, the U.S. and Vietnam recommitted to this initiative and pledged to implement it expeditiously. President Trump and Prime Minister Phuc also pledged to strengthen defense ties under the 2011 and 2015 foundational documents.[39]

There remain significant limits on the U.S.–Vietnam security relationship, including a Vietnamese defense establishment that is very cautious in its selection of defense partners, party-to-party ties between the Communist parties of Vietnam and China, and a foreign policy that seeks to balance relationships with all major powers. The U.S. remains, like others among Vietnam's security partners, officially limited to one port call a year with an additional one to two calls on Vietnamese bases negotiable. The U.S. has not docked a warship at the Vietnamese military base at Cam Ranh Bay since the end of the Vietnam War, but it has used the international port there a number of times since it was opened in 2016.[40]

The U.S. and Malaysia "have maintained steady defense cooperation since the 1990s" despite occasional political differences. Each year, they participate jointly in dozens of bilateral and multilateral exercises to promote effective cooperation across a range of missions.[41] The U.S. occasionally flies P-3 and/or P-8 patrol aircraft out of Malaysian bases in Borneo.

The U.S.–Indonesia defense relationship was revived in 2005 following a period of estrangement caused by American human rights concerns. It now includes regular joint exercises, port calls, and sales of weaponry. The U.S. is also working closely with Indonesia's defense establishment to institute reforms in Indonesia's strategic defense planning processes. Because of their impact on the operating environment in and around Indonesia, as well as the setting of priorities in the U.S.–Indonesia relationship, Islamist extremism and terrorism need to be carefully monitored. Similar to the case with the Philippines, the return of ISIS fighters to their homes in Indonesia (and Malaysia) could further complicate operating environments.

The U.S. is working across the board at modest levels of investment to help build Southeast Asia's maritime security capacity.[42] Most notable in this regard is the Maritime Security Initiative (MSI) announced by Secretary of Defense Ashton Carter in 2015.[43]

Afghanistan. On October 7, 2001, U.S. forces invaded Afghanistan in response to the September 11, 2001, attacks on the United States. This marked the beginning of Operation Enduring Freedom to combat al-Qaeda and its Taliban supporters. The U.S., in alliance with the U.K. and the anti-Taliban Afghan Northern Alliance forces, ousted the Taliban from power in December 2001. Most Taliban and al-Qaeda leaders fled across the border into Pakistan's Federally Administered Tribal Areas (FATA),

where they regrouped and started an insurgency in Afghanistan in 2003.

In August 2003, NATO joined the war in Afghanistan and assumed control of the International Security Assistance Force (ISAF). At the height of the war in 2011, there were 50 troop-contributing nations and nearly 150,000 NATO and U.S. forces on the ground in Afghanistan.

On December 28, 2014, NATO formally ended combat operations and relinquished responsibility to the Afghan security forces, which currently number around 352,000 (including army and police).[44] After Afghan President Ashraf Ghani signed a bilateral security agreement with the U.S. and a Status of Forces Agreement with NATO, the international coalition launched Operation Resolute Support to train and support Afghan security forces. As of February 2017, more than 13,400 U.S. and NATO forces were stationed in Afghanistan. Most U.S. and NATO forces are stationed at bases in Kabul and Bagram, with tactical advise-and-assist teams located there, in Mazar-i-Sharif, Herat, Kandahar, and Laghman.[45]

In 2014, President Obama pledged to cut U.S. force levels to around 5,500 by the end of 2015 and then to zero by the end of 2016, but he reversed himself the following year, announcing that the U.S. instead would maintain this force level when he departed office. He revised his pledge again in 2016 to say that he would keep 8,400 in place, leaving any further reductions up to his successor. In August 2017, while declining to announce specific troop levels, President Trump announced that "conditions on the ground" would guide the new strategy for Afghanistan.[46]

Pakistan. During the war in Afghanistan, the U.S. and NATO relied heavily on logistical supply lines running through Pakistan to resupply coalition forces in Afghanistan. Supplies and fuel were carried on transportation routes from the port at Karachi to Afghan–Pakistani border crossing points at Torkham in the Khyber Pass and Chaman in Baluchistan province. During the initial years of the Afghan war, about 80 percent of U.S. and NATO supplies traveled through Pakistani territory. This amount decreased to around 50 percent–60 percent as the U.S. shifted to northern routes and when U.S.–Pakistan relations significantly deteriorated because of U.S. drone strikes, continued Pakistani support to Taliban militants, and the fallout surrounding the U.S. raid on Osama bin Laden's hideout in Abbottabad on May 2, 2011.

From October 2001 until December 2011, the U.S. leased Pakistan's Shamsi airfield southwest of Quetta in Baluchistan province and used it as a base from which to conduct surveillance and drone operations against terrorist targets in Pakistan's tribal border areas. Pakistan ordered the U.S. to vacate the base shortly after NATO forces attacked Pakistani positions along the Afghanistan border, killing 24 Pakistani soldiers, on November 26, 2011.

Escalation of the U.S. drone strike campaign in Pakistan's border areas from 2009–2012 led to the significant degradation of al-Qaeda's ability to plot, plan, and train for terrorist attacks. The U.S. began to curtail drone strikes in 2013, largely as a result of Pakistan's growing complaints that the drone campaign infringed on its sovereignty and criticism from international human rights organizations about the number of civilian casualties. All told, there have been over 400 drone strikes since January 2008, including the strike that killed Taliban leader Mullah Akhtar Mansour in Baluchistan province in May 2016.

The U.S. provides significant amounts of military aid to Pakistan and "reimbursements" in the form of coalition support funds (CSF) for Pakistan's military deployments and operations along the border with Afghanistan. Pakistan has some 150,000 troops stationed in regions bordering Afghanistan and recently conducted a robust military campaign against Pakistani militants in North Waziristan. From FY 2002–FY 2018, the U.S. has provided almost $8 billion in security-related assistance and more than $14 billion in CSF funds to Pakistan.[47] While $1 billion in CSF reimbursements was authorized for Pakistan in 2015, the U.S. withheld $300 million because of Pakistan's failure to crack down on the Haqqani network.

In 2016, reflecting a trend of growing congressional resistance to military assistance for Pakistan, Congress blocked funds for the provision of eight F-16s to Pakistan.

India. During the Cold War, U.S.–Indian military cooperation was minimal, except for a brief period during the Sino–Indian border war in 1962 when the U.S. sided with India and supplied it with arms and ammunition. The rapprochement was short-lived, however, and mutual suspicion continued to mark the Indo–U.S. relationship because of India's robust relationship with Russia and the U.S. provision of military aid to Pakistan, especially during the 1970s under the Nixon Administration. America's ties with India hit a nadir during the 1971 Indo–Pakistani war when the U.S. deployed the aircraft carrier USS *Enterprise* toward the Bay of Bengal in a show of support for Pakistani forces.

Military ties between the U.S. and India have improved significantly over the past decade as the two sides have moved toward establishment of a strategic partnership based on their mutual concern about rising Chinese military and economic influence and converging interests in countering regional terrorism. The U.S. and India have completed contracts worth approximately $14 billion for the supply of U.S. military equipment to India, including C-130J and C-17 transport aircraft and P-8 maritime surveillance aircraft.

Defense ties between the two countries are poised to expand further as India moves forward with an ambitious military modernization program and following three successful summit-level meetings between President Obama and Indian Prime Minister Narendra Modi. During President Obama's January 2015 visit to India, the two sides agreed to renew and upgrade their 10-year Defense Framework Agreement. Under the Defense Trade and Technology Initiative (DTTI) launched in 2012, the U.S. and India are cooperating on development of six very specific "pathfinder" technology projects.[48] During Prime Minister Modi's visit to the U.S. in June 2016, the two sides welcomed finalization of the text of a logistics-sharing agreement that would allow each country to access the other's military supplies and refueling capabilities through ports and military bases. The signing of the logistics agreement, formally called the Logistics Exchange Memorandum of Agreement (LEMOA), marks a milestone in the Indo–U.S. defense partnership. During that visit, the U.S. also designated India a "major defense partner," a designation unique to India that is intended to ease its access to American defense technology. The Trump Administration subsequently reaffirmed this status.[49] New Delhi and Washington regularly hold joint exercises across all services, including an annual naval exercise in which Japan will now participate on an annual basis and in which Australia and Singapore have also participated in the past.

Quality of Allied Armed Forces in Asia

Because of the lack of an integrated, regional security architecture along the lines of NATO, the United States partners with most of the nations in the region on a bilateral basis. This means that there is no single standard to which all of the local militaries aspire; instead, there is a wide range of capabilities that are influenced by local threat perceptions, institutional interests, physical conditions, historical factors, and budgetary considerations.

Moreover, the lack of recent major conflicts in the region makes assessing the quality of Asian armed forces difficult. Most Asian militaries have limited combat experience; some (e.g., Malaysia) have never fought an external war since gaining independence in the mid-20th century. The Indochina wars, the most recent high-intensity conflicts, are now 30 years in the past. It is therefore unclear how well Asian militaries have trained for future warfare and whether their doctrine will meet the exigencies of wartime realities. In particular, no Asian militaries have engaged in high-intensity air or naval combat, so the quality of their personnel, training, or equipment is likewise unclear.

Based on examinations of equipment, however, it is assessed that several Asian allies and

friends have substantial military capabilities supported by robust defense industries and significant defense spending. Japan's, South Korea's, and Australia's defense budgets are estimated to be among the world's 15 largest. Each of their military forces fields some of the world's most advanced weapons, including F-15s in the Japan Air Self Defense Force and ROK Air Force; airborne early warning (AEW) platforms; AEGIS-capable surface combatants and modern diesel-electric submarines; and third-generation main battle tanks. As noted, all three nations are involved in the production and purchase of F-35 fighters.

At this point, both the Japanese and Korean militaries are arguably more capable than most European militaries, at least in terms of conventional forces. Japan's Self Defense Forces, for example, field more tanks, principal surface combatants, and combat-capable aircraft (690, 47, and 556, respectively) than their British opposite numbers (227, 19, and 267, respectively).[50] Similarly, South Korea fields a larger military of tanks, principal surface combatants, and combat-capable aircraft (more than 2,434, 23, and 567, respectively) than their German counterparts (306, 15, and 209, respectively).[51]

Both the ROK and Japan are also increasingly interested in developing missile defense capabilities, including joint development and coproduction in the case of Japan. After much negotiation and indecision, Seoul and Washington began to deploy America's Terminal High-Altitude Area Defense (THAAD) missile defense system on the peninsula in 2017, but newly elected liberal South Korean President Moon Jae-in demanded a halt pending a lengthy environmental impact assessment. Moon subsequently reversed himself after North Korea's second ICBM test in July 2017, deciding to allow temporary deployment. South Korea also continues to pursue an indigenous missile defense capability.

Singapore's small population and physical borders limit the size of its military, but in terms of equipment and training, it has the largest defense budget among Southeast Asia's countries[52] and fields some of the region's highest-quality forces. For example, Singapore's ground forces can deploy third-generation Leopard II main battle tanks, and its fleet includes five conventional submarines (including one with air-independent propulsion systems), six frigates, and six missile-armed corvettes. In addition, its air force not only has F-15E Strike Eagles and F-16s, but also has one of Southeast Asia's largest fleets of airborne early warning and control aircraft (six G550 aircraft) and a tanker fleet of KC-130s that can help to extend range or time on station.

At the other extreme, the Armed Forces of the Philippines (AFP) are among the region's weakest military forces. Having long focused on waging counterinsurgency campaigns while relying on the United States for its external security, the AFP has one of the lowest budgets in the region—and one of the most extensive coastlines to defend. With a base defense budget of only $2.7 billion[53] and forced to deal with a number of insurgencies, including the Islamist Abu Sayyaf and New People's Army, Philippine defense resources have long been stretched thin. The last squadron of fighter aircraft (1960s-vintage F-5 fighters) was decommissioned in 2005; the Philippine Air Force (PAF) has had to employ its S-211 trainers as fighters and ground attack aircraft. The most modern ships in the Philippine navy are three former U.S. *Hamilton*-class Coast Guard cutters; its other main combatant is a World War II destroyer escort, one of the world's oldest serving warships.

Current U.S. Presence in Asia

U.S. Pacific Command. PACOM is the oldest and largest of American unified commands. Established on January 1, 1947, PACOM, "together with other U.S. government agencies, protects and defends the United States, its territories, allies, and interests."[54] To this end, the U.S. seeks to preserve a "geographically distributed, operationally resilient, and politically sustainable" regional force posture within the PACOM area of responsibility that can effectively deter any potential adversaries.[55]

PACOM's area of responsibility includes not only the expanses of the Pacific, but also Alaska and portions of the Arctic, South Asia, and the Indian Ocean. It includes 36 nations holding more than 50 percent of the world's population, two of the three largest economies, and nine of the 10 smallest; the most populous nation (China); the largest democracy (India); the largest Muslim-majority nation (Indonesia); and the world's smallest republic (Nauru). The region is a vital driver of the global economy and includes the world's busiest international sea-lanes and nine of its 10 largest ports. By any meaningful measure, the Asia–Pacific is also the most militarized region in the world, with seven of its 10 largest standing militaries and five of its declared nuclear nations.[56]

Under PACOM are a number of component commands, including:

- **U.S. Army Pacific.** USARPAC is the Army's component command in the Pacific. It is comprised of 80,000 soldiers and supplies Army forces as necessary for various global contingencies. Among others, it administers the 25th Infantry Division headquartered in Hawaii, U.S. Army Japan, and U.S. Army Alaska.[57]

- **U.S. Pacific Air Force.** PACAF is responsible for planning and conducting defensive and offensive air operations in the Asia–Pacific region. It has three numbered air forces under its command: 5th Air Force (in Japan); 7th Air Force (in Korea); and 11th Air Force (headquartered in Alaska). These field two squadrons of F-15s, two squadrons of F-22s, five squadrons of F-16s, and a single squadron of A-10 ground attack aircraft, as well as two squadrons of E-3 early-warning aircraft, tankers, and transports.[58] Other forces that regularly come under PACAF command include B-52, B-1, and B-2 bombers.

- **U.S. Pacific Fleet.** PACFLT normally controls all U.S. naval forces committed to the Pacific, which usually represents 60 percent of the Navy's fleet. It is organized into Seventh Fleet, headquartered in Japan, and Third Fleet, headquartered in California. Seventh Fleet comprises the forward-deployed element of PACFLT and includes the only American carrier strike group (CTF-70) and amphibious group (CTF-76) home-ported abroad, ported at Yokosuka and Sasebo, Japan, respectively. The Third Fleet's area of responsibility (AOR) spans the West Coast of the United States to the International Date Line and includes the Alaskan coastline and parts of the Arctic. In recent years, this boundary between the two fleets' areas of operation have been blurred under a concept called "Third Fleet Forward." This has eased the involvement of the Third Fleet's five carrier strike groups in the Western Pacific. Since 2015, the conduct of Freedom of Navigation Operations (FONOPS) that challenge excessive maritime claims, a part of the Navy's mission since 1979, has assumed a very high profile as a result of five well-publicized operations in the South China Sea.

- **U.S. Marine Forces Pacific.** MARFOR-PAC controls elements of the U.S. Marine Corps operating in the Asia–Pacific region. Its headquarters are in Hawaii. Because of its extensive responsibilities and physical span, MARFORPAC controls two-thirds of Marine Corps forces: the I Marine Expeditionary Force (MEF), centered on the 1st Marine Division, 3rd Marine Air Wing, and 1st Marine Logistics Group, and the III Marine Expeditionary Force, centered on the 3rd Marine Division, 1st Marine Air Wing, and 3rd Marine Logistics Group. The I MEF is headquartered at Camp Pendleton, California, and the III MEF is headquartered on Okinawa, although each has various subordinate elements deployed at any time throughout the Pacific on exercises, maintaining presence, or engaged in other activities. MARFORPAC is responsible for supporting three different commands: It is the U.S. Marine Corps component of PACOM, provides the Fleet Marine Forces to PACFLT, and provides Marine forces for U.S. Forces Korea (USFK).[59]

- **U.S. Special Operations Command Pacific.** SOCPAC has operational control of various special operations forces, including Navy SEALs; Naval Special Warfare units; Army Special Forces (Green Berets); and Special Operations Aviation units in the Pacific region, including elements in Japan and South Korea. It supports the Pacific Command's Theater Security Cooperation Program as well as other plans and contingency responses. Until 2015, this included Joint Special Operations Task Force–Philippines (JSOTF–P), 500–600 soldiers assisting Manila in combatting Islamist insurgencies in the southern Philippines such as Abu Sayyaf. SOCPAC forces also support various operations in the region other than warfighting, such as counterdrug operations, counterterrorism training, humanitarian assistance, and demining activities.

- **U.S. Forces Korea and U.S. Eighth Army.** Because of the unique situation on the Korean Peninsula, two subcomponents of PACOM, U.S. Forces Korea (USFK) and U.S. Eighth Army, are based in Korea. USFK, a joint headquarters led by a four-star U.S. general, is in charge of the various U.S. military elements on the peninsula. U.S. Eighth Army operates in conjunction with USFK as well as with the United Nations presence in the form of United Nations Command.

Other forces, including space capabilities, cyber capabilities, air and sealift assets, and additional combat forces, may be made available to PACOM depending on requirements and availability.

U.S. Central Command—Afghanistan. Unlike the U.S. forces deployed in Japan and

South Korea, there is no permanent force structure committed to Afghanistan; instead, forces rotate through the theater under the direction of PACOM's counterpart in that region of the world, U.S. Central Command (CENTCOM). As of May 2016, these forces included:

- **Resolute Support Mission,** including U.S. Forces Afghanistan.[60]

- **Special Operations Joint Task Force—Afghanistan.** This includes a Special Forces battalion, based out of Bagram Airfield, and additional allied special operations forces at Kabul.

- **9th Air and Space Expeditionary Task Force.** This includes the 155th Air Expeditionary Wing, providing air support from Bagram airfield; the 451st Air Expeditionary Group and 455th Expeditionary Operations Group, operating from Kandahar and Bagram airfields, respectively, providing air support and surveillance operations over various parts of Afghanistan; and the 421st Expeditionary Fighter Squadron, providing close air support from Bagram airfield.

- **Combined Joint Task Force 10/10th Mountain Division,** centered on Bagram airfield. This is the main U.S. national support element. It includes seven battalions of infantry, air defense artillery for counter-artillery missions, and explosive ordnance disposal across Afghanistan. It also includes three Army aviation battalions, a combat aviation brigade headquarters, and two additional joint task forces to provide nationwide surveillance support.[61]

- **Five Train, Advise, Assist Commands** in Afghanistan, each of which is a multi-national force tasked with improving local capabilities to conduct operations.[62]

Key Infrastructure That Enables Expeditionary Warfighting Capabilities

Any planning for operations in the Pacific will be dominated by the "tyranny of distance." Because of the extensive distances that must be traversed in order to deploy forces, even Air Force units will take one or more days to deploy, and ships measure steaming time in weeks. For instance, a ship sailing at 20 knots requires nearly five days to get from San Diego to Hawaii. From there, it takes a further seven days to get to Guam, seven days to Yokosuka, Japan, and eight days to Okinawa—if ships encounter no interference along the journey.[63]

China's growing anti-access/area denial (A2/AD) capabilities, ranging from an expanding fleet of modern submarines to anti-ship ballistic and cruise missiles, increase the operational risk for deployment of U.S. forces in the event of conflict. China's capabilities not only jeopardize American combat forces that would flow into the theater for initial combat, but also would continue to threaten the logistical support needed to sustain American combat power for the subsequent days, weeks, and months.

American basing structure in the Indo–Pacific region, including access to key allied facilities, is therefore both necessary and increasingly at risk.

American Facilities

Much as in the 20th century, Hawaii remains the linchpin of America's ability to support its position in the Western Pacific. If the United States cannot preserve its facilities in Hawaii, both combat power and sustainability become moot. The United States maintains air and naval bases, communications infrastructure, and logistical support on Oahu and elsewhere in the Hawaiian Islands. Hawaii is also a key site for undersea cables that carry much of the world's communications and data, as well as satellite ground stations.

The American territory of Guam is located 4,600 miles farther west. Obtained from Spain as a result of the Spanish–American War, Guam became a key coaling station for U.S. Navy ships. Seized by Japan in World War II, it was

MAP 3

The Tyranny of Distance

Steam times are in parentheses.

Arctic Ocean

RUSSIA

Alaska

Bering Sea

Gulf of Alaska

U.S.

CHINA

JAPAN

San Diego
6,700 miles
(13–21 days)

40°N

Tokyo
1,700 miles

Okinawa
1,000 miles (2–3 days)

South China Sea

160°W

140°W

180°

160°E

20°N

Hawaii
5,000 miles
(10–16 days)

Guam
1,700 miles
(3–5 days)

0°

Pacific Ocean

1,900 miles *Darwin*

20°S

AUSTRALIA

SOURCE: Heritage Foundation estimates based on data from Shirley A. Kan, "Guam: U.S. Defense Deployments," Congressional Research Service, April 29, 2014, Table 1, https://www.hsdl.org/?view&did=752725 (accessed January 13, 2015).

☎ heritage.org

---

liberated by U.S. forces in 1944 and after the war became an unincorporated, organized territory of the United States. Key U.S. military facilities on Guam include U.S. Naval Base Guam, which houses several attack submarines and possibly a new aircraft carrier berth, and Andersen Air Force Base, one of a handful of facilities that can house B-2 bombers. U.S. task forces can stage out of Apra Harbor, drawing weapons from the

Ordnance Annex in the island's South Central Highlands. There is also a communications and data relay facility on the island.

Guam's facilities have improved steadily over the past 20 years. B-2 bombers, for example, began operating from Andersen Air Force Base in 2005.[64] These improvements have been accelerated and expanded even as China's A2/AD capabilities have raised doubts about the ability of the U.S. to sustain operations in the Asian littoral. The concentration of air and naval assets as well as logistical infrastructure, however, makes the island an attractive potential target in the event of conflict. The increasing reach of Chinese and North Korean ballistic missiles reflects this growing vulnerability.

The U.S. military has noncombatant maritime prepositioning ships (MPS), which contain large amounts of military equipment and supplies, in strategic locations from which they can reach areas of conflict relatively quickly as associated U.S. Army or Marine Corps units located elsewhere arrive in the areas. U.S. Navy units on Guam and in Saipan, Commonwealth of the Northern Marianas, support prepositioning ships that can supply Army or Marine Corps units deployed for contingency operations in Asia.

Allied and Friendly Facilities

For the United States, access to bases in Asia has long been a vital part of its ability to support military operations in the region. Even with the extensive aerial refueling and replenishment skills of the U.S. Air Force and U.S. Navy, it is still essential for the United States to retain access to resupply and replenishment facilities, at least in peacetime. The ability of those facilities to survive and function will directly influence the course of any conflict in the Western Pacific region. Moreover, a variety of support functions, including communications, intelligence, and space support, cannot be accomplished without facilities in the region.

At the present time, it would be extraordinarily difficult to maintain maritime domain awareness or space situational awareness without access to facilities in the Asia–Pacific region. The American alliance network is therefore a matter both of political partnership and of access to key facilities on allied soil.

Japan. In Japan, the United States has access to over 100 different facilities, including communications stations, military and dependent housing, fuel and ammunition depots, and weapons and training ranges, in addition to major bases such as air bases at Misawa,

Yokota, and Kadena and naval facilities at Yokosuka, Atsugi, and Sasebo. The naval facilities support the USS *Ronald Reagan* carrier strike group (CSG), which is home-ported in Yokosuka, as well as a Marine Expeditionary Strike Group (ESG) centered on the USS *Bonhomme Richard*, home-ported at Sasebo. Additionally, the skilled workforce at places like Yokosuka is needed to maintain American forces and repair equipment in time of conflict. Replacing them would take years, if not decades. This combination of facilities and workforce, in addition to physical location and political support, makes Japan an essential part of any American military response to contingencies in the Western Pacific. Japanese financial support for the American presence also makes these facilities some of the most cost-effective in the world.

The status of one critical U.S. base has been a matter of public debate in Japan for many years. The U.S. Marine Corps' Third Marine Expeditionary Force, based on Okinawa, is the U.S. rapid reaction force in the Pacific. The Marine Air-Ground Task Force, comprised of air, ground, and logistics elements, enables quick and effective response to crises or humanitarian disasters. To improve the political sustainability of U.S. forces by reducing the impact on the local population in that densely populated area, the Marines are relocating some units to Guam and less-populated areas of Okinawa. The latter includes moving a helicopter unit from Futenma to a new facility in a more remote location in northeastern Okinawa. Because of local resistance, construction of the Futenma Replacement Facility at Camp Schwab will not be complete until 2025, but the U.S. and Japanese governments have affirmed their support for the project.

South Korea. The United States also maintains an array of facilities in South Korea, with a larger Army footprint than in Japan, as the United States and South Korea remain focused on deterring North Korean aggression and preparing for any possible North Korean contingencies. The Army maintains four major facilities (which in turn control a number of smaller sites) at Daegu, Yongsan in Seoul, and Camps

Red Cloud/Casey and Humphreys. These facilities support the U.S. 2nd Infantry Division, which is based in South Korea. Other key facilities include air bases at Osan and Kunsan and a naval facility at Chinhae near Pusan.

The Philippines. In 1992, The United States ended nearly a century-long presence in the Philippines when it withdrew from its base in Subic Bay as its lease there ended. Clark Air Base had been closed earlier due to the eruption of Mount Pinatubo; the costs of repairing the facility were deemed too high to be worthwhile. In 2014, however, with the growing Chinese assertiveness in the South China Sea, including against Philippine claims such as Mischief Reef (seized in 1995) and Scarborough Shoal (2012), the U.S. and the Philippines negotiated the Enhanced Defense Cooperation Agreement, which will allow for the rotation of American forces through Philippine military bases.

In 2016, the two sides agreed on an initial list of five bases in the Philippines that will be involved. Geographically distributed across the country, they are Antonio Bautista Air Base in Palawaan closest to the Spratlys; Basa Air Base on the main island of Luzon and closest to the hotly contested Scarborough Shoal; Fort Magsaysay, also on Luzon and the only facility on the list that is not an air base; Lumbia Air Base in Mindanao, where Manila remains in low-intensity combat with Islamist insurgents; and Mactan-Benito Ebuen Air Base in the central Philippines.[65]

It remains unclear precisely which forces would be rotated through the Philippines as a part of this agreement, which in turn affects the kinds of facilities that would be most needed. However, outside the context of the EDCA, the U.S. deployed E/A-18G Growler electronic attack, A-10 Warthog close air support aircraft, and Pavehawk helicopters to the Philippines in 2016.[66] The base upgrades and deployments pursuant to the EDCA are part of a broader expansion of U.S.–Philippines defense ties, which most recently included the U.S. leaving behind men and matériel at Clark Air Base following annual exercises,[67] as well as joint naval patrols and increased levels of assistance under the Maritime Security Initiative (MSI). Since July 2016, the Duterte government has shed doubt on the future of U.S.–Philippines military cooperation, but it continues to be robust at the operational level.

Singapore. The United States does not have bases in Singapore, but it is allowed access to several key facilities that are essential for supporting American forward presence. Since the closure of its facilities at Subic Bay, the United States has been allowed to operate the principal logistics command for the Seventh Fleet out of the Port of Singapore Authority's Sembawang Terminal. The U.S. Navy also has access to Changi Naval Base, one of the few docks in the world that can handle a 100,000-ton American aircraft carrier. In addition, a small U.S. Air Force contingent operates out of Paya Lebar Air Base to support U.S. Air Force combat units visiting Singapore and Southeast Asia, and Singapore hosts two new Littoral Combat Ships (LCS) (with the option of hosting two more) and a rotating squadron of F-16 fighter aircraft.[68]

Australia. A much-discussed element of the "Asia pivot" has been the 2011 agreement to deploy U.S. Marines to Darwin in northern Australia. While planned to amount to 2,500 Marines, the rotations fluctuate and have not yet reached that number. "In its mature state," according to the Australian Department of Defence, "the Marine Rotational Force–Darwin (MRF–D) will be a Marine Air-Ground Task Force...with a variety of aircraft, vehicles and equipment."[69] The Marines do not constitute a permanent presence in Australia, in keeping with Australian sensitivities about permanent American bases on Australian soil.[70] Similarly, the United States jointly staffs the Joint Defence Facility Pine Gap and the Joint Geological and Geophysical Research Station at Alice Springs and has access to the Harold E. Holt Naval Communication Station in Western Australia, including the space surveillance radar system there.[71]

Finally, the United States is granted access to a number of facilities in Asian states on a contingency or crisis basis. Thus, U.S. Air Force units transited Thailand's U-Tapao Air Base and Sattahip Naval Base during the first Gulf War and during the Iraq War, but they do not maintain a permanent presence there. Additionally, the U.S. Navy conducts hundreds of port calls throughout the region.

Diego Garcia. The American facilities on the British territory of Diego Garcia are vital to U.S. operations in the Indian Ocean and Afghanistan and provide essential support for operations in the Middle East and East Asia. The island is home to the 12 ships of Maritime Prepositioning Squadron-2 (MPS-2), which can support a Marine brigade and associated Navy elements for 30 days. There are also several elements of the U.S. global space surveillance and communications infrastructure on the island, as well as basing facilities for the B-2 bomber.

Conclusion

The Asian strategic environment is extremely expansive, as it spans half the globe, with a variety of political relationships among states that have wildly varying capabilities. The region includes long-standing American allies with relationships dating back to the beginning of the Cold War as well as recently established states and some long-standing adversaries such as North Korea.

American conceptions of the region must therefore start from the physical limitations imposed by the tyranny of distance. Moving forces within the region (never mind to it) will take time and require extensive strategic lift assets as well as sufficient infrastructure, such as sea and aerial ports of debarkation that can handle American strategic lift assets, and political support. At the same time, the complicated nature of intra-Asian relations, especially unresolved historical and territorial issues, means that the United States, unlike Europe, cannot necessarily count on support from all of its regional allies in responding to any given contingency.

Scoring the Asia Operating Environment

As with the operating environments of Europe and the Middle East, we assessed the characteristics of Asia as they would pertain to supporting U.S. military operations. Various aspects of the region facilitate or inhibit America's ability to conduct military operations to defend its vital national interests against threats. Our assessment of the operating environment utilized a five-point scale, ranging from "very poor" to "excellent" conditions and covering four regional characteristics of greatest relevance to the conduct of military operations:

1. **Very Poor.** Significant hurdles exist for military operations. Physical infrastructure is insufficient or nonexistent, and the region is politically unstable. The U.S. military is poorly placed or absent, and alliances are nonexistent or diffuse.

2. **Unfavorable.** A challenging operating environment for military operations is

marked by inadequate infrastructure, weak alliances, and recurring political instability. The U.S. military is inadequately placed in the region.

3. **Moderate.** A neutral to moderately favorable operating environment is characterized by adequate infrastructure, a moderate alliance structure, and acceptable levels of regional political stability. The U.S. military is adequately placed.

4. **Favorable.** A favorable operating environment includes good infrastructure, strong alliances, and a stable political environment. The U.S. military is well placed in the region for future operations.

5. **Excellent.** An extremely favorable operating environment includes well-established and well-maintained infrastructure, strong and capable allies, and a stable political

environment. The U.S. military is exceptionally well placed to defend U.S. interests.

The key regional characteristics consisted of:

a. **Alliances.** Alliances are important for interoperability and collective defense as allies would be more likely to lend support to U.S. military operations. Various indicators provide insight into the strength or health of an alliance. These include whether the U.S. trains regularly with countries in the region, has good interoperability with the forces of an ally, and shares intelligence with nations in the region.

b. **Political Stability.** Political stability brings predictability for military planners when considering such things as transit, basing, and overflight rights for U.S. military operations. The overall degree of political stability indicates whether U.S. military actions would be hindered or enabled and considers, for example, whether transfers of power in the region are generally peaceful and whether there have been any recent instances of political instability in the region.

c. **U.S. Military Positioning.** Having military forces based or equipment and supplies staged in a region greatly facilitates the ability of the United States to respond to crises and, presumably, more quickly achieve successes in critical "first battles."

Being routinely present in a region also assists in maintaining familiarity with its characteristics and the various actors who might act to assist or thwart U.S. actions. With this in mind, we assessed whether or not the U.S. military was well positioned in the region. Again, indicators included bases, troop presence, prepositioned equipment, and recent examples of military operations (including training and humanitarian) launched from the region.

d. **Infrastructure.** Modern, reliable, and suitable infrastructure is essential to military operations. Airfields, ports, rail lines, canals, and paved roads enable the U.S. to stage, launch operations from, and logistically sustain combat operations. We combined expert knowledge of regions with publicly available information on critical infrastructure to arrive at our overall assessment of this metric.[72]

For Asia, we arrived at these average scores:

- Alliances: **4—Favorable**

- Political Stability: **3—Moderate**

- U.S. Military Positioning: **4—Favorable**

- Infrastructure: **4—Favorable**

Aggregating to a regional score of: **Favorable**

Operating Environment: Asia

	VERY POOR	UNFAVORABLE	MODERATE	FAVORABLE	EXCELLENT
Alliances				✔	
Political Stability			✔		
U.S. Military Posture				✔	
Infrastructure				✔	
OVERALL				✔	

Endnotes

1. Alexis N. Grimm and Maya Ortiz, "U.S. International Services: Trade in Services in 2015 and Services Supplied Through Affiliates in 2014," U.S. Department of Commerce, Bureau of Economic Analysis, December 2016, p. 5, https://www.bea.gov/scb/pdf/2016/12%20December/1216_international_services.pdf (accessed August 10, 2016).

2. "Aspiring sincerely to an international peace based on justice and order, the Japanese people forever renounce war as a sovereign right of the nation and the threat or use of force as means of settling international disputes. In order to accomplish the aim of the preceding paragraph, land, sea, and air forces, as well as other war potential, will never be maintained. The right of belligerency of the state will not be recognized." Constitution of Japan, Article 9, promulgated November 3, 1946, came into effect May 3, 1947, http://japan.kantei.go.jp/constitution_and_government_of_japan/constitution_e.html (accessed August 10, 2017).

3. U.S. Forces, Japan, "About USFJ," http://www.usfj.mil/AboutUSFJ.aspx (accessed April 12, 2016).

4. Emma Chanlett-Avery, William H. Cooper, Mark E. Manyin, and Ian E. Rinehart, "Japan–U.S. Relations: Issues for Congress," Congressional Research Service *Report for Members and Committees of Congress*, February 20, 2014, http://mansfieldfdn.org/mfdn2011/wp-content/uploads/2014/02/USJ.Feb14.RL33436.pdf (accessed August 10, 2017).

5. K. J. Kwon, "South Korea and Japan Put Military Intelligence Pact on Hold After Outcry," CNN, updated June 29, 2012, http://www.cnn.com/2012/06/29/world/asia/south-korea-japan-pact/index.html (accessed August 10, 2017).

6. U.S. Department of Defense, Defense Manpower Data Center, DoD Personnel, Workforce Reports and Publications, Military and Civilian Personnel by Service/Agency by State/Country (Updated Quarterly), "Counts of Active Duty and Reserve Service Members and APF Civilians by Location Country, Personnel Category, and Service and Component as of March 31, 2017," https://www.dmdc.osd.mil/appj/dwp/dwp_reports.jsp (accessed August 10, 2017). The total includes 23,114 "Active Duty" and 297 "National Guard/Reserve" personnel. If the 3,136 in the "APF DOD Civilian" category are added, the total comes to 26,547.

7. For further details, see Bruce Klingner, "The U.S. and South Korea Should Focus on Improving Alliance Capabilities Rather Than the OPCON Transfer," Heritage Foundation *Backgrounder* No. 2935, August 7, 2014, http://www.heritage.org/research/reports/2014/08/the-us-and-south-korea-should-focus-on-improving-alliance-capabilities-rather-than-the-opcon-transition.

8. News release, "President Donald J. Trump Proclaims July 27, 2017, as National Korean War Veterans Armistice Day," The White House, July 26, 2017, https://www.whitehouse.gov/the-press-office/2017/07/26/president-donald-j-trump-proclaims-july-27-2017-national-korean-war (accessed August 10, 2017).

9. Mark E. Manyin, Emma Chanlett-Avery, Mary Beth D. Nikitin, Brock R. Williams, and Jonathan R. Corrado, "U.S.–South Korea Relations," Congressional Research Service *Report for Members and Committees of Congress*, May 23, 2017, p. 23, https://fas.org/sgp/crs/row/R41481.pdf (accessed August 14, 2017).

10. Admiral Harry B. Harris Jr., U.S. Navy, Commander, U.S. Pacific Command, statement "On U.S. Pacific Command Posture" before the Committee on Armed Services, U.S. Senate, April 27, 2017, p. 26, https://www.armed-services.senate.gov/imo/media/doc/Harris_04-27-17.pdf (accessed August 10, 2017).

11. "Fact Sheet: United States–Philippines Bilateral Relations," The White House, April 28, 2014, http://www.whitehouse.gov/the-press-office/2014/04/28/fact-sheet-united-states-philippines-bilateral-relations (accessed August 10, 2017).

12. Frances Mangosing, "US to Start Constructing Facilities for EDCA in 2017—Lorenzana," Inquirer.net, January 26, 2017, http://globalnation.inquirer.net/152092/us-start-constructing-facilities-edca-2017-lorenzana (accessed August 10, 2017).

13. Ben Dolven, Mark E. Manyin, and Shirley A. Kan, "Maritime Territorial Disputes in East Asia: Issues for Congress," Congressional Research Service *Report for Members and Committees of Congress*, May 14, 2014, p. 31, https://fas.org/sgp/crs/row/R42930.pdf (accessed August 10, 2017).

14. Walter Lohman, "Scarborough Shoal and Safeguarding American Interests," Heritage Foundation *Issue Brief* No. 3603, May 14, 2012, p. 2, http://www.heritage.org/research/reports/2012/05/south-china-sea-dispute-between-china-and-the-philippines-safeguarding-americas-interests.

15. Seth Robson, "US–Philippines Relations on an Uptick Ahead of Annual Balikatan Drills," *Stars and Stripes*, April 24, 2017, https://www.stripes.com/news/us-philippines-relations-on-an-uptick-ahead-of-annual-balikatan-drills-1.465104#.WSXN72jyu70 (accessed August 10, 2017).

16. Emma Chanlett-Avery, Ben Dolven, and Wil Mackey, "Thailand: Background and U.S. Relations," Congressional Research Service *Report for Members and Committees of Congress*, July 29, 2015, pp. 8–9, http://fas.org/sgp/crs/row/RL32593.pdf (accessed August 25, 2016).

17. Association of Southeast Asian Nations, *ASEAN Community in Figures (ACIF) 2016*, p. 18, http://www.aseanstats.org/wp-content/uploads/2017/01/25Content-ACIF.pdf (accessed August 10, 2017).

18. Phuong Nguyen and Brittany Billingsley, "China's Growing Military-to-Military Engagement with Thailand & Myanmar," Center for Strategic and International Studies, Asia Program, cogitASIA blog, September 12, 2013, http://cogitasia.com/chinas-growing-military-to-military-engagement-with-thailand-and-myanmar/ (accessed August 10, 2017).

19. Mike Yeo, "Thailand to Buy More Chinese Tanks, Reportedly for $58M," *Defense News*, April 4, 2017, http://www.defensenews.com/articles/thailand-to-buy-more-chinese-tanks-reportedly-for-58m (accessed August 10, 2017).

20. Reuters, "Thailand Approves $393-Mln Purchase of Chinese Submarines," April 24, 2017, http://in.reuters.com/article/thailand-china-idINKBN17Q150 (accessed August 10, 2017); Prashanth Parameswaran, "When Will Thailand's First China Submarine Arrive?" *The Diplomat*, January 31, 2017, http://thediplomat.com/2017/01/will-thailand-seal-its-china-submarine-deal-this-year/ (accessed August 10, 2017).

21. Australian Government, Department of Defence, "United States Force Posture Initiatives in Australia," http://defence.gov.au/usfpi/ (accessed August 25, 2016).

22. Australian Government, Department of Defence, "United States Force Posture Initiatives: United States Marine Corps Initiative," http://www.defence.gov.au/Initiatives/USFPI/Marines.asp (accessed August 10, 2017).

23. Jeff Schogol, "Sending 2,500 Marines to Australia Is Taking a Long Time—and It's Not Donald Trump's Fault," *Marine Corps Times*, February 2, 2017, https://www.marinecorpstimes.com/articles/disagreement-on-darwin-rotations (accessed August 10, 2017).

24. Australian Aviation, "USAF F-22s Arrive in Australia for Joint Training Exercises with the RAAF," February 10, 2017, http://australianaviation.com.au/2017/02/usaf-f-22s-head-to-australia-for-joint-training-exercises-with-the-raaf/ (accessed August 10, 2017); Andrew Greene, "Long-Range Heavy Bombers Could Be Based in Australia, US General Reveals," ABC News, updated March 8, 2016, http://www.abc.net.au/news/2016-03-08/long-range-bombers-could-rotate-through-nt-general-says/7231098 (accessed August 10, 2017).

25. Aaron Mehta, "US, UK, Australia and Canada Announce Combined Space Ops," vBulletin, May 20, 2014, http://www.w54.biz/showthread.php?1083-Space-Warfare/page28 (accessed August 29, 2016).

26. Bruce Vaughn, "Australia: Background and U.S. Relations," Congressional Research Service *Report for Congress*, August 15, 2013, pp. 4–5, https://www.hsdl.org/?view&did=744342 (accessed August 10, 2017).

27. Stephen Smith, Minister of Defence and Deputy Leader of the House, Ministerial Statement on "Full Knowledge and Concurrence," Commonwealth of Australia, Parliamentary Debates, House of Representatives, June 26, 2013, pp. 7071–7075, http://parlinfo.aph.gov.au/parlInfo/genpdf/chamber/hansardr/4d60a662-a538-4e48-b2d8-9a97b8276c77/0016/hansard_frag.pdf;fileType=application%2Fpdf (accessed August 10, 2017).

28. "Fact Sheet: U.S. Defense Trade Cooperation Treaties with the United Kingdom and Australia," U.S. Department of State, September 30, 2010, https://2009-2017.state.gov/r/pa/prs/ps/2010/09/148478.htm (accessed August 11, 2017).

29. Emma Chanlett-Avery, "Singapore: Background and U.S. Relations," Congressional Research Service *Report for Congress*, July 26, 2013, pp. 3–4, https://www.fas.org/sgp/crs/row/RS20490.pdf (accessed May 15, 2015).

30. DOD News, "Carter, Singapore Defense Minister Sign Enhanced Defense Cooperation Agreement," U.S. Department of Defense, December 7, 2015, http://www.defense.gov/News-Article-View/Article/633243/carter-singapore-defense-minister-sign-enhanced-defense-cooperation-agreement (accessed August 11, 2017).

31. Nick Simeone, "U.S., New Zealand Announce Expanded Defense Cooperation," U.S. Department of Defense, October 28, 2013, http://archive.defense.gov/news/newsarticle.aspx?id=121016 (accessed August 10, 2017).

32. David B. Larter, "In Port Visit, New Zealand and U.S. Seek to Bolster Military Ties," *Navy Times*, July 22, 2016, http://www.navytimes.com/story/military/2016/07/22/port-visit-new-zealand-and-us-seek-bolster-military-ties/87450022/ (accessed August 10, 2017).

33. Associated Press, "US Warship to Visit New Zealand as USS Sampson's Arrival Ends Stalemate on Nuclear Vessels," ABC News, October 18, 2016, http://www.abc.net.au/news/2016-10-18/new-zealand-to-end-stalemate-on-us-warships/7943252 (accessed August 10, 2017).

34. Taiwan Relations Act, Public Law 96-8, 96th Cong., January 1, 1979, 22 U.S.C. §§ 3301–3316, https://www.ait.org.tw/our-relationship/policy-history/key-u-s-foreign-policy-documents-region/taiwan-relations-act/ (accessed August 10, 2017).

35. Shirley A. Kan, "China/Taiwan: Evolution of the 'One China' Policy—Key Statements from Washington, Beijing, and Taipei," Congressional Research Service *Report for Members and Committees of Congress*, October 10, 2014, pp. 43–44, https://www.fas.org/sgp/crs/row/RL30341.pdf (accessed August 10, 2017).

36. Aaron Mehta, "New US–Vietnam Agreement Shows Growth, Challenges," *Defense News*, June 1, 2015, http://www.defensenews.com/story/defense/policy-budget/budget/2015/06/01/us-vietnam-joint-vision-statement-signed-in-hanoi/28291963/ (accessed August 10, 2017).

37. Jon Grevatt, "Vietnam to Acquire USCG Cutter," *Jane's 360*, April 21, 2017, http://www.janes.com/article/69742/vietnam-to-acquire-uscg-cutter (accessed August 10, 2017).

38. U.S. Pacific Command, "Joint Statement: Between the United States of America and the Socialist Republic of Vietnam," May 23, 2016, http://www.pacom.mil/Media/News/News-Article-View/Article/779376/joint-statement-between-the-united-states-of-america-and-the-socialist-republic/ (accessed August 27, 2016).

39. News release, "Joint Statement for Enhancing the Comprehensive Partnership Between the United States of America and the Socialist Republic of Vietnam," The White House, May 31, 2017, https://www.whitehouse.gov/the-press-office/2017/05/31/joint-statement-enhancing-comprehensive-partnership-between-united (accessed August 10, 2017).

40. Prashanth Parameswaran, "Third US Warship Visits Vietnam's Cam Ranh International Port," *The Diplomat*, December 16, 2016, http://thediplomat.com/2016/12/third-us-warship-visits-vietnams-cam-ranh-international-port/ (accessed August 10, 2017).

41. Ian E. Rinehart, "Malaysia: Background and U.S. Relations," Congressional Research Service *Report for Members and Committees of Congress*, November 19, 2015, p. 15, https://www.fas.org/sgp/crs/row/R43505.pdf (accessed August 10, 2017).

42. "Fact Sheet: U.S. Building Maritime Capacity in Southeast Asia," The White House, November 17, 2015, https://www.whitehouse.gov/the-press-office/2015/11/17/fact-sheet-us-building-maritime-capacity-southeast-asia (accessed August 10, 2017).

43. Prashanth Parameswaran, "US Kicks Off New Maritime Security Initiative for Southeast Asia," *The Diplomat*, April 10, 2016, http://thediplomat.com/2016/04/us-kicks-off-new-maritime-security-initiative-for-southeast-asia/ (accessed August 26, 2016).

44. U.S. Department of Defense, *Enhancing Security and Stability in Afghanistan*, December 2016, p. 33, https://www.defense.gov/Portals/1/Documents/pubs/Afghanistan-1225-Report-December-2016.pdf (accessed August 10, 2017).

45. North Atlantic Treaty Organization, "Resolute Support Mission: Key Facts and Figures," February 2017, http://www.nato.int/nato_static_fl2014/assets/pdf/pdf_2017_02/20170209_2017-02-RSM-Placemat.pdf (accessed August 10, 2017).

46. "Remarks by President [Donald] Trump on the Strategy in Afghanistan and South Asia," Fort Myer, Arlington, Virginia, August 21, 2017, https://www.whitehouse.gov/the-press-office/2017/08/21/remarks-president-trump-strategy-afghanistan-and-south-asia (accessed September 8, 2017).

47. Congressional Research Service, "Direct Overt U.S. Aid Appropriations for and Military Reimbursements to Pakistan, FY2002–FY2018," May 23, 2017, https://www.fas.org/sgp/crs/row/pakaid.pdf (accessed August 10, 2017).

48. Press Trust of India, "Ind[ia], US Agree on 2 New Pathfinder Projects," *India Today*, April 12, 2016, http://indiatoday.intoday.in/story/ind-us-agree-on-2-new-pathfinder-projects/1/641257.html (accessed August 27, 2016).

49. Vivek Raghuvanshi, "Trump Administration Reaffirms India as Major Defense Partner," *Defense News*, April 19, 2017, http://www.defensenews.com/articles/trump-administration-reaffirms-india-as-major-defense-partner (accessed August 10, 2017).

50. International Institute for Strategic Studies, *The Military Balance 2017: The Annual Assessment of Global Military Capabilities and Defence Economics* (London: Routledge, 2017), pp. 170–175 and 299–305.

51. Ibid., pp. 116–120 and 306–310.

52. Stockholm International Peace Research Institute, "Military Expenditure by Country, in Constant (2015) US\$ m., 1988–1996," 2017, https://www.sipri.org/sites/default/files/Milex-constant-2015-USD.pdf (accessed August 10, 2017).

53. Jon Grevatt, "Philippines Settles 2017 Defence Budget," *Jane's 360*, December 27, 2016, http://www.janes.com/article/66547/philippines-settles-2017-defence-budget (accessed August 10, 2017).

54. Donna Miles, "Pacom: Asia–Pacific Focus Represents 'Whole of Government' Rebalance," U.S. Department of Defense, August 3, 2012, http://archive.defense.gov/news/newsarticle.aspx?id=117399 (accessed August 10, 2017).

55. News release, "Joint Statement of the Security Consultative Committee," U.S. Department of Defense, April 26, 2012, http://archive.defense.gov/releases/release.aspx?releaseid=15220 (accessed August 11, 2017).

56. U.S. Pacific Command, "USPACOM Strategy," https://jsou.blackboard.com/bbcswebdav/library/Library%20Content/JSOU%20References/SOPC/USPACOM%20Strategy.pdf (accessed August 27, 2016).

57. United States Army, U.S. Army Pacific, "About Us," https://www.usarpac.army.mil/about.asp (accessed August 10, 2017).

58. International Institute for Strategic Studies, *The Military Balance 2016: The Annual Assessment of Global Military Capabilities and Defence Economics* (London: Routledge, 2016), p. 46.

59. U.S. Marine Corps, "U.S. Marine Corps Forces, Pacific (MARFORPAC)," last revised March 10, 2015, https://marinecorpsconceptsandprograms.com/organizations/operating-forces/us-marine-corps-forces-pacific-marforpac (accessed August 27, 2016).

60. Wesley Morgan, "Afghanistan Order of Battle: Coalition Combat and Advisory Forces in Afghanistan," Institute for the Study of War, May 1, 2016, p. 1, http://www.understandingwar.org/sites/default/files/ORBAT%20May%202016.pdf (accessed July 6, 2016).

61. Ibid.

62. U.S. Central Command, "Resolute Support," http://www.centcom.mil/OPERATIONS-AND-EXERCISES/RESOLUTE-SUPPORT/ (accessed August 11, 2017).

63. These steaming times were calculated using Marine Vessel Traffic, "Sea Distance Calculator," 2016, http://www.marinevesseltraffic.com/2013/07/distance-calculator.html (accessed August 27, 2016).

64. Airforce-Technology.com, "B-2 Spirit Stealth Bomber, United States of America," http://www.airforce-technology.com/projects/b2/ (accessed August 11, 2017).

65. News release, "Sixth United States–Philippines Bilateral Strategic Dialogue Joint Statement," U.S. Department of State, March 18, 2016, https://2009-2017.state.gov/r/pa/prs/ps/2016/03/254833.htm (accessed July 27, 2016).

66. Phillip Swarts, "Navy Growlers Replace A-10s, Pavehawks in Philippine Rotation," *Air Force Times*, July 4, 2016, https://www.airforcetimes.com/news/your-air-force/2016/07/04/navy-growlers-replace-a-10s-pavehawks-in-philippine-rotation/ (accessed August 11, 2017).

67. Eric Haun, "US Ramps up Military Presence in the Philippines," Marine Link, April 14, 2016, http://www.marinelink.com/news/military-presence-ramps408137.aspx (accessed July 27, 2016).

68. Sam LaGrone, "Two Littoral Combat Ships to Deploy to Singapore Next Year, Four by 2017," USNI News, April 24, 2015, https://news.usni.org/2015/04/24/two-littoral-combat-ships-to-deploy-to-singapore-next-year-four-by-2017 (accessed August 11, 2017).

69. Australian Government, Department of Defence, "United States Force Posture Initiatives in Australia."

70. Wyatt Olson, "Deal to Bring More US Assets to Australia," *Stars and Stripes*, June 21, 2014, http://www.military.com/daily-news/2014/06/21/deal-likely-to-bring-more-us-military-assets-to-australia.html (accessed August 23, 2016).

71. Smith, Ministerial Statement on "Full Knowledge and Concurrence."

72. For an example of a very accessible database, see World Bank, "Logistics Performance Index: Quality of Trade and Transport-Related Infrastructure (1=Low to 5=High)," http://data.worldbank.org/indicator/LP.LPI.INFR.XQ (accessed August 11, 2017).

Conclusion: Scoring the Global Operating Environment

The U.S. is a global power with global security interests, and threats to those interests can emerge from any region. Consequently, the U.S. military must be ready to operate in any region when called upon to do so, and it must account for the range of conditions it might encounter when planning for potential military operations. This informs its decisions about the type and amount of equipment it purchases (especially to transport and sustain the force); where it might operate from; and how easy (or not) it will be to project and sustain combat power when engaged with the enemy.

Aggregating the three regional scores provides a Global Operating Environment score.

Global Operating Environment: **FAVORABLE**

Global Operating Environment

	VERY POOR	UNFAVORABLE	MODERATE	FAVORABLE	EXCELLENT
Europe				✔	
Middle East			✔		
Asia				✔	
OVERALL				✔	

Scoring of the Global Security Environment remained "favorable" for the *2018 Index of U.S. Military Strength*, despite significant shifts in the scoring of the Asia Operating Environment.

Global Operating Environment

VERY POOR	UNFAVORABLE	MODERATE	**FAVORABLE**	EXCELLENT

The Middle East Operating Environment remained "moderate" in 2018. The region remains plagued by instability, substantial internal security challenges, and spreading, extremely violent transnational threats.

The Europe Operating Environment also did not see categorical changes in any of its scores, remaining "favorable." The migrant crisis, economic sluggishness, and political fragmentation increase the potential for instability, but the region remains generally stable and friendly to U.S. interests.

Although overall scoring for the Asia Operating Environment remained at "favorable" from the *2017 Index* to the *2018 Index,* political instability in Thailand and a new government in South Korea caused the political stability score to drop from "favorable" to "moderate." Uncertainty regarding the future of U.S. alliances in the region also prompted a decrease from "excellent" to "favorable" in that category.

Threats to U.S. Vital Interests

Assessing Threats to U.S. Vital Interests

The United States is a global power with global interests. Scaling its military power to threats requires judgments with regard to the importance and priority of those interests, whether the use of force is the most appropriate and effective way to address the threats to those interests, and how much and what types of force are needed to defeat such threats.

This *Index* focuses on three fundamental, vital national interests:

- Defense of the homeland;

- Successful conclusion of a major war that has the potential to destabilize a region of critical interest to the U.S.; and

- Preservation of freedom of movement within the global commons: the sea, air, and outer space domains through which the world conducts business.

The geographical focus of the threats in these areas is further divided into three broad regions: Asia, Europe, and the Middle East.

This is not to say that these are America's only interests. Among many others, the U.S. has an interest in the growth of economic freedom in trade and investment, the observance of internationally recognized human rights, and the alleviation of human suffering beyond our borders. None of these interests, however, can be addressed principally and effectively by the use of military force, nor would threats to these interests result in material damage to the foregoing vital national interests. These additional American interests, however important

they may be, therefore are not used in this assessment of the adequacy of current U.S. military power.

Throughout this *Index,* we reference two public sources as a mechanism to check our work against that of other recognized professional organizations in the field of threat analysis: *The Military Balance,* published annually by the London-based International Institute for Strategic Studies,[1] and the annual *Worldwide Threat Assessment of the US Intelligence Community* (WWTA).[2] The latter serves as a reference point produced by the U.S. government against which each threat assessment in this *Index* was compared. We note any differences between assessments in this *Index* and the work of the two primary references in summary comments.

The juxtaposition of our detailed, reviewed analysis against both *The Military Balance* and the WWTA revealed two stark limitations in these external sources.

- *First, The Military Balance* is an excellent, widely consulted source, but it is only a count of military hardware without context in terms of equipment capability, maintenance and readiness, training, manpower, integration of services, doctrine, or the behavior of competitors— those that threaten the national interests— of the U.S. as defined in this *Index.*

- *Second,* the WWTA omits many threats, and its analysis of those it does address is limited. Moreover, it does not reference underlying strategic dynamics that are

Threat Categories

Behavior	HOSTILE	AGGRESSIVE	TESTING	ASSERTIVE	BENIGN
Capability	FORMIDABLE	GATHERING	CAPABLE	ASPIRATIONAL	MARGINAL

key to the evaluation of threats and that may be more predictive of future threats than is a simple extrapolation of current events.

We suspect that this is a consequence of the U.S. intelligence community's withholding from public view its very sensitive assessments, which are derived from classified sources. Given the need to avoid compromising sources and methods of collection, such a policy is understandable, but it also causes the WWTA's threat assessments to be of limited value to policymakers, the public, and analysts working outside of the government. Perhaps surprisingly, The Heritage Foundation's *Index of U.S. Military Strength* may actually serve as a useful correction to the systemic deficiencies we found in these open sources.

Measuring or categorizing a threat is problematic because there is no absolute reference that can be used in assigning a quantitative score. Two fundamental aspects of threats, however, are germane to this *Index*: the threatening entity's desire or intent to achieve its objective and its physical ability to do so. Physical ability is the easier of the two to assess, but intent is quite difficult. A useful surrogate for intent is observed behavior, because this is where intent becomes manifest through action. Thus, a provocative, belligerent pattern of behavior that seriously threatens U.S. vital interests would be very worrisome. Similarly, a comprehensive ability to accomplish objectives even in the face of U.S. military power would cause serious concern for U.S. policymakers, while weak or very limited abilities would lessen U.S. concerns even if an entity behaved provocatively vis-à-vis U.S. interests.

Each categorization used in the *Index* conveys a word picture of how troubling a threat's behavior and set of capabilities have been during the assessed year. The five ascending categories for observed behavior are:

- Benign,
- Assertive,
- Testing,
- Aggressive, and
- Hostile.

The five ascending categories for physical capability are:

- Marginal,
- Aspirational,
- Capable,
- Gathering, and
- Formidable.

These characterizations—behavior and capability—form two halves of an overall assessment of the threats to U.S. vital interests.

As noted, the following assessments are arranged by region (Europe, Middle East, and Asia) to correspond with the flow of the chapter on operating environments and then by U.S. vital interest (threat posed by an actor to the U.S. homeland, potential for regional war, and freedom of global commons) within each region. Each actor is then discussed in terms of how and to what extent its behavior and physical capabilities posed a challenge to U.S. interests in the assessed year.

Endnotes:

1. International Institute for Strategic Studies, *The Military Balance 2014: The Annual Assessment of Global Military Capabilities and Defence Economics* (London: Routledge, 2014); *The Military Balance 2015: The Annual Assessment of Global Military Capabilities and Defence Economics* (London: Routledge, 2015); *The Military Balance 2016: The Annual Assessment of Global Military Capabilities and Defence Economics* (London: Routledge, 2016); and *The Military Balance 2017: The Annual Assessment of Global Military Capabilities and Defence Economics* (London: Routledge, 2017).

2. James R. Clapper, Director of National Intelligence, "Statement for the Record: Worldwide Threat Assessment of the US Intelligence Community," Select Committee on Intelligence, U.S. Senate, January 29, 2014, http://www.dni.gov/files/documents/Intelligence%20Reports/2014%20WWTA%20%20SFR_SSCI_29_Jan.pdf; James R. Clapper, Director of National Intelligence, "Statement for the Record: Worldwide Threat Assessment of the US Intelligence Community," Select Committee on Intelligence, U.S. Senate, February 26, 2015, http://www.armed-services.senate.gov/imo/media/doc/Clapper_02-26-15.pdf; James R. Clapper, Director of National Intelligence, "Statement for the Record: Worldwide Threat Assessment of the US Intelligence Community," Committee on Armed Services, U.S. Senate, February 9, 2016, https://www.armed-services.senate.gov/imo/media/doc/Clapper_02-09-16.pdf; Daniel R. Coats, Director of National Intelligence, "Statement for the Record: Worldwide Threat Assessment of the US Intelligence Community," Select Committee on Intelligence, U.S. Senate, May 11, 2017, https://www.dni.gov/files/documents/Newsroom/Testimonies/SSCI%20Unclassified%20SFR%20-%20Final.pdf.

Europe

The resurgence of an aggressive, belligerent Russia has thrown conventional post–Cold War thinking into the waste bin. Russian President Vladimir Putin's decision to invade Ukraine and annex Crimea has changed post–Cold War norms. From the Arctic to the Baltics, Ukraine, and the South Caucasus, Russia has proven to be the source of much instability in Europe. Despite economic problems, Russia continues to prioritize the rebuilding of its military and funding for its military operations abroad. Russia's military and political antagonism toward the United States continues unabated, and its efforts to undermine U.S. institutions and the NATO alliance are serious and troubling. Russia's aggressive stance in a number of theaters, including the Balkans, Georgia, Syria, and Ukraine, continues to contribute to destabilization and run counter to U.S. interests.

Russian Military Capabilities. According to the International Institute for Strategic Studies (IISS), among the key weapons in Russia's inventory are 324 intercontinental ballistic missiles; 2,700 main battle tanks; and more than 4,900 armored infantry fighting vehicles, 6,100 armored personnel carriers, and 4,316 pieces of artillery. The navy has one aircraft carrier; 62 submarines (including 13 ballistic missile submarines); five cruisers; 15 destroyers; 12 frigates; and 95 patrol and coastal combatants. The air force has 1,046 combat-capable aircraft. The IISS counts 270,000 members of the army. Russia also has a total reserve force of 2,000,000 for all armed forces.[1]

To avoid political blowback from military deaths abroad, Russia has increasingly deployed paid private volunteer troops trained at Special Forces bases and often under the command of Russian Special Forces. Russia has used such volunteers in Libya, Syria, and Ukraine because "[t]hey not only provide the Kremlin with plausible political deniability but also apparently take casualties the Russian authorities do not report."[2]

Another key development in Russian force structure occurred in July 2016 when Vladimir Putin signed a law creating a 340,000-strong (both civilian and military) National Guard over which he will have direct control[3] and which will be responsible for "enforcing emergency-situation regimes, combating terrorism, defending Russian territory, and protecting state facilities and assets."[4] According to reports, the National Guard was crafted by amalgamating "several different domestic security forces" under presidential control. Although Putin could issue a directive to deploy the force abroad,[5] forces are more likely to be used to stifle domestic dissent.

Hamstrung by low oil prices, economic sanctions, and deep structural issues, Russia's economy is projected to produce only tepid growth of 1.4 percent in 2017.[6] The combined impact of Western sanctions and Ukraine's decision to end delivery of military products and components to Russia in 2014 have hurt the ability of Russia's defense industries to access certain technology and components.[7] Overall, Russia's industrial capacity and capability remain problematic. In 2017, Russia's defense budget was cut 25.5 percent. "Despite the cut," however, "the 2017 budget will remain about 14.4% higher than the level of defence spending seen in 2014 in nominal terms."[8] Nevertheless, the macroeconomic situation in Russia has had an impact on defense: "In real terms, projected total military expenditure is estimated to fall by 9.5% in 2017 and by 7.1% in 2018, and then by a more modest 1.7% in 2019."[9] Russia continues to seek cuts elsewhere to safeguard its procurement and modernization plans.[10]

Russia has been investing heavily in modernization of its armed forces, especially its nuclear arsenal and navy. As of December 2016, 60 percent of Russia's nuclear forces had been modernized.[11] According to the IISS:

> Upgrades to Russia's land- and sea-based strategic nuclear forces continue with plans to update 40 missiles a year. In 2015, 21 Yars intercontinental ballistic missiles (ICBMs) were delivered to the Strategic Missile Troops, along with about ten Bulava submarine-launched ballistic missiles (SLBMs) and the same number of Liner (upgraded Sineva) SLBMs.[12]

Russia has announced that the new RS-28 ballistic missile, commissioned in 2011, will come into service in 2018 as planned.[13] The armed forces also continue to undergo process modernization begun by Defense Minister Anatoly Serdyukov in 2008.[14] Russia projects that by the end of 2017, 62 percent of Russian military equipment in service will be modern.[15] In March 2017, Russia announced life extension programs for its *Akula*-class and *Oscar II*-class nuclear-powered submarines, which operate in both the Northern and Pacific Fleets.[16] However, problems remain:

> The naval shipbuilding industry has suffered from years of neglect and under investment; while the Ukraine crisis and the imposition of sanctions is starting to have an effect. The refurbishment of existing naval vessels is progressing, albeit at a slower, and more expensive, pace than originally envisaged. Although several new frigates, corvettes and submarines have already entered service, delivery of new vessels is behind schedule.[17]

After years of delays, the Russian Navy expects to commission two stealth guided missile frigates and a logistic ship in 2017.[18] However, according to some analysts, tight budgets and an inability to procure parts from Ukrainian industry make it unlikely that Russia will procure the 16 guided missile frigates in keeping with its stated intention.[19] The buildup of Russia's Northern Fleet has implications beyond the immediate theater. "In 2016," according to one report, "the aircraft carrier Kuznetsov transited from the Kola Peninsula and into the Mediterranean Sea to conduct strikes against targets in Syria in support of the Assad regime."[20] The carrier was joined in the Mediterranean by the "Pyotr Veliky nuclear-powered battle cruiser, anti-submarine destroyer Severomorsk, the destroyer Vice-Admiral Kulakov, a tug, a surveillance vessel and a tanker," all based out of the Kola peninsula.[21]

Transport remains a nagging problem, and Russia's Defense Minister has stressed the paucity of Russian transport vessels. In March, Russia reportedly needed to purchase civilian cargo vessels and use icebreakers to transport troops and equipment to Syria at the beginning of major operations in support of the Assad regime.[22]

Russian officials have announced a follow-on modernization program, the State Armament Program 2018–2025. Though budget shortfalls have hampered modernization efforts overall, analysts believe that Russia will continue to focus on developing high-end systems such as the S-500 surface-to-air missile system and T-50 fighter jet[23] and that, although "the new State Armaments Program to 2025 will be less well funded on the whole than its earlier version," it "will continue to support the modernization of the force structure with a special emphasis on high-technology assets."[24] Russia's new armaments program prioritizes nuclear modernization, submarine development, and fighter aircraft at the expense of procuring a new aircraft carrier and nuclear-powered destroyers, acquisition of which has been postponed.[25]

Russian Exercises. Russian military exercises, especially snap exercises, are a source of serious concern because they have masked real military operations in the past. In 2013, Russia reintroduced snap exercises, which are conducted with little or no warning and often involve thousands of troops and pieces of equipment.[26] In February 2017, for example, Russia ordered snap exercises involving 45,000 troops, 150 aircraft, and 200 anti-aircraft pieces.[27]

Snap exercises have been used for military campaigns as well. According to General Curtis Scaparrotti, NATO Supreme Allied Commander and Commander, U.S. European Command (EUCOM), "the annexation of Crimea took place in connection with a snap exercise by Russia."[28] Snap exercises have practiced additional aggression against Ukraine. According to the IISS:

> The largest of these took place in August 2016, with three military districts—Southern, Western and Central—simultaneously put on alert, along with the Northern Fleet and the airborne troops. The aim of this inspection was to practise the concentration of forces in the southwestern part of Russia for potential contingencies in the Caucasus and against Ukraine.[29]

Snap exercises also provide Russian leadership with a hedge against unpreparedness or corruption. "In addition to affording combat-training benefits," the IISS reports, "snap inspections appear to be of increasing importance as a measure against corruption or deception. As a result of a snap inspection in the Baltic Fleet in June 2016, the fleet's commander, chief of staff and dozens of high-ranking officers were dismissed."[30]

In September, Russia and Belarus will conduct Zapad 2017, a massive exercise in Russia's Western military district, Kaliningrad, and Belarus, the last iteration of which took place in 2013. Former NATO Supreme Allied Commander General Philip Breedlove has estimated that 100,000 troops will take place in Zapad 17.[31] Russia has claimed that only 13,000 troops will participate and that only 3,000 of those troops and 280 pieces of equipment will be Russian.[32] Yet it plans to use around 4,000

train cars to transport troops to Belarus for the exercises—enough for around 30,000 troops—and additional forces are likely to be moved by air transport.[33] Russia reportedly "plans to involve chemical, biological, radiological and nuclear (CBKN) military units in the exercise."[34] Estonian Defence Minister Margus Tsahkna believes that Russia may plan to leave significant forces in Belarus following the exercises: "For Russian troops going to Belarus, it is a one-way ticket."[35]

Zapad 17 will take part while Swedish exercises are concurrently ongoing with 19,000 troops, including American troops. According to Lieutenant General Ben Hodges, Commander of U.S. Army Europe, "We will be alert, we will be very vigilant. But we don't want it to turn into a face-off during their biggest exercise of the year."[36]

Threats to the Homeland

Russia is the only state adversary in the region that possesses the capability to threaten the U.S. homeland with both conventional and nonconventional means. Although there is no indication that Russia plans to use its capabilities against the United States absent a broader conflict involving America's NATO allies, the plausible potential for such a scenario serves to sustain the strategic importance of those capabilities. Russia's explicitly belligerent behavior during the past year further adds to the need for the U.S. to give due consideration to Russia's ability to place the security of the U.S. at risk.[37]

Russia's National Security Strategy, released in December 2015, describes NATO as a threat to the national security of the Russian Federation:

> The buildup of the military potential of the North Atlantic Treaty Organization (NATO) and the endowment of it with global functions pursued in violation of the norms of international law, the galvanization of the bloc countries' military activity, the further expansion of the alliance, and the location of its military infrastructure closer to Russian borders are creating a threat to national security.[38]

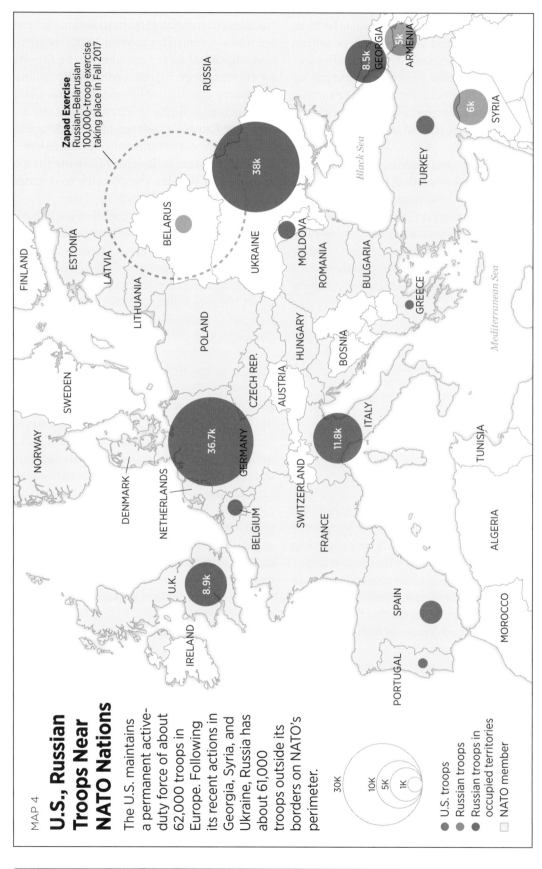

MAP 4

U.S., Russian Troops Near NATO Nations

The U.S. maintains a permanent active-duty force of about 62,000 troops in Europe. Following its recent actions in Georgia, Syria, and Ukraine, Russia has about 61,000 troops outside its borders on NATO's perimeter.

Zapad Exercise
Russian-Belarusian 100,000-troop exercise taking place in Fall 2017

30K
10K
5K
1K

● U.S. troops
● Russian troops
● Russian troops in occupied territories
☐ NATO member

heritage.org

SOURCES: U.S. Department of Defense, Defense Manpower Data Center, September 2015, and Heritage Foundation research.

The document also clearly states that Russia will use every means at its disposal to achieve its strategic goals: "Interrelated political, military, military-technical, diplomatic, economic, informational, and other measures are being developed and implemented in order to ensure strategic deterrence and the prevention of armed conflicts."[39] In December 2014, Putin signed a new version of Russia's military doctrine emphasizing the claimed threat of NATO and global strike systems to Russia.[40]

Russian Strategic Nuclear Threat. Russia possesses the largest arsenal of nuclear weapons among the nuclear powers (when short-range nuclear weapons are included). It is one of the few nations with the capability to destroy many targets in the U.S. homeland and in U.S.-allied nations and to threaten and prevent free access to the commons by other nations. Russia has both intercontinental-range and short-range ballistic missiles and a varied nuclear weapons arsenal that can be delivered by sea, land, and air. It also is investing significant resources in modernizing its arsenal and maintaining the skills of its workforce.

Russia is currently relying on its nuclear arsenal to ensure its invincibility against any enemy, intimidate European powers, and deter counters to its predatory behavior in its "near abroad," primarily in Ukraine but also concerning the Baltic States.[41] This arsenal serves as a protective umbrella under which Russia can modernize its conventional forces at a deliberate pace. While its nuclear deterrent protects Russia from a large-scale attack, Russia also needs a modern and flexible military to fight local wars such as those against Georgia in 2008 and the ongoing war against Ukraine that began in 2014. Under Russian military doctrine, the use of nuclear weapons in conventional local and regional wars is seen as de-escalatory because it would cause an enemy to concede defeat. In May, for example, a Russian parliamentarian threatened that nuclear weapons might be used if the U.S. or NATO were to move to retake Crimea or defend eastern Ukraine.[42]

General Scaparrotti discussed the risks of Russian use of tactical nuclear weapons in his March 23, 2017, EUCOM posture statement: "Most concerning...is Moscow's substantial inventory of non-strategic nuclear weapons in the EUCOM AOR [Area of Responsibility] and its troubling doctrine that calls on the potential use of these weapons to escalate its way out of a failing conflict."[43]

Particularly worrisome are Moscow's plans for rail-based nuclear-armed missiles, which are very difficult to detect. The missiles are scheduled to begin testing in 2019 and to become operational in 2020. Russia reportedly plans to deploy five regiments with a total of 30 railroad ICBMs: six missiles per regiment.[44] The Defense Ministry states that the new armed forces structure is being created with the goal of increased flexibility, mobility, and readiness for combat in limited-scale conflicts. Strategic Rocket Forces are the first line of defense (and offense) against Russia's great-power counterparts.[45]

Russia has two strategies for nuclear deterrence. The first is based on a threat of massive launch-on-warning and retaliatory strikes to deter a nuclear attack; the second is based on a threat of limited demonstration and "de-escalation" nuclear strikes to deter or terminate a large-scale conventional war.[46] Russia's reliance on nuclear weapons is based partly on their small cost relative to conventional weapons (especially in terms of their effect) and on Russia's inability to attract sufficient numbers of high-quality servicemembers. Thus, Russia sees its nuclear weapons as a way to offset the lower quantity and quality of its conventional forces.

Moscow has repeatedly threatened U.S. allies in Europe with nuclear deployments and even preemptive nuclear strikes.[47] The Russians justify their aggressive behavior by pointing to deployments of U.S. missile defense systems in Europe even though these systems are not scaled or postured to mitigate Russia's advantage in ballistic missiles and nuclear weapons to any significant degree.

Russia continues to violate the Intermediate-Range Nuclear Forces (INF) Treaty, which bans the testing, production, and possession of intermediate-range missiles.[48] In early 2017, Russia fully deployed the SSC-X-8 Cruise Missile in violation of the INF treaty. One battalion with the cruise missile remains at a missile test site in southern Russia, and another battalion with the missile deployed to an operational base in December 2016. U.S. officials acknowledge that the banned cruise missiles are no longer in the testing phase and now consider them to be fully operational.[49] In March, General Paul Selva, Vice Chairman of the Joint Chiefs of Staff, testified that Russia's cruise missile deployment "violates the spirit and intent of the Intermediate Nuclear Forces Treaty" and "presents a risk to most of our facilities in Europe."[50]

WWTA: The 2017 WWTA states that "Russia has developed a ground-launched cruise missile (GLCM) that the United States has declared is in violation of the Intermediate-Range Nuclear Forces (INF) Treaty." Moreover, "[d]espite Russia's ongoing development of other Treaty-compliant missiles with intermediate ranges, Moscow probably believes that the new GLCM provides sufficient military advantages that make it worth risking the political repercussions of violating the INF Treaty."[51]

Summary: The sizable Russian nuclear arsenal remains the only threat to the existence of the U.S. homeland emanating from Europe and Eurasia. While the potential for use of this arsenal remains low, the fact that Russia continues to threaten Europe with nuclear attack demonstrates that it will continue to play a central strategic role in shaping both Russia's military and political thinking and its level of aggressive behavior beyond its borders.

Threat of Regional War

To many U.S. allies, Russia does pose a threat. At times, this threat is of a military nature. At other times, Russia uses less conventional tactics such as cyber-attacks, utilization of energy resources, and propaganda. Today as in Imperial times, Russia's influence is exerted by both the pen and the sword. Organizations like the Collective Security Treaty Organization (CSTO) or Eurasia Economic Union attempt to bind regional capitals to Moscow through a series of agreements and treaties.

Espionage is another tool that Russia uses in ways that are damaging to U.S. interests. In May 2016, a Russian spy was sentenced to prison for gathering intelligence for the Russian SVR intelligence agency while working as a banker in New York. The spy specifically transmitted intelligence on "potential U.S. sanctions against Russian banks and the United States' efforts to develop alternative energy resources."[52] In May 2016, a senior intelligence official from Portugal working for the Portuguese Security Intelligence Service was arrested for passing secrets to the Russian Federation, especially classified NATO intelligence and material.

Russian intelligence operatives are reportedly mapping U.S. telecommunications infrastructure around the United States near fiber optic cables.[53] In March 2017, the U.S. charged four people including two Russian intelligence officials with directing hacks of user data for Yahoo and Google accounts.[54] In December 2016, the U.S. expelled 35 Russian intelligence operatives, closed two compounds in Maryland and New York that were used for espionage, and levied additional economic sanctions against individuals who took part in interfering in the U.S. election.[55] Russia has also used its relations with friendly nations for espionage purposes. In April, Nicaragua began using a Russian-provided satellite station at Managua that the Nicaraguan government denies is for spying but is still of concern to the U.S.[56]

There are four areas of critical interest to the U.S. in the European region where Russia poses a direct threat: Central and Eastern Europe, the Arctic or High North, the Balkans, and the South Caucasus.

Russian Pressure on Central and Eastern Europe. Moscow poses a security challenge to members of NATO that border Russia. Although the likelihood of a conventional Russian attack against the Baltic States is low, primarily because it would trigger a NATO response, Russia has used nonconventional means to apply pressure to and sow discord among these countries. The Baltic States continue to view Russia as a significant threat. Lithuania's 2017 National Security Threat Assessment states that Russia is currently "capable to conduct combat activities against the Baltic States with 24–48 hrs. notice."[57]

After World War I, the three Baltic nations of Estonia, Latvia, and Lithuania proclaimed their independence, and by 1923, the U.S. had granted full recognition to all three. In June 1940, as part of the Molotov–Ribbentrop Pact between Nazi Germany and Stalinist Russia, Soviet troops entered and occupied the three Baltic countries. A month later, acting U.S. Secretary of State Sumner Welles issued what was later to be known as the Welles Declaration, condemning Russia's occupation and stating America's refusal to recognize the legitimacy of Soviet control of these three states. The three states regained their independence with the end of the Cold War.

Due to decades of Russian domination, the Baltic States factor Russia into their military planning and foreign policy formulation in a way that is simply unimaginable in many Western European countries and North America. Estonia and Latvia have sizable ethnic Russian populations, and there is concern that Russia might exploit the situation as a pretext for aggression. This view is not without merit, considering Moscow's irredentist rhetoric and Russia's use of this technique to annex Crimea.

Russia has also demonstrated a willingness to use military force to change the borders of modern Europe. When Kremlin-backed Ukrainian President Viktor Yanukovych failed to sign an Association Agreement with the European Union (EU) in 2013, months of street demonstrations led to his ouster early in 2014. Russia responded by violating Ukraine's territorial integrity, sending troops, aided by pro-Russian local militia, to occupy the Crimean Peninsula under the pretext of "protecting Russian people." This led to Russia's eventual annexation of Crimea, the first such forcible annexation of territory in Europe since the Second World War.[58]

Russia's annexation of Crimea has de facto halved Ukraine's coastline, and Russia has claimed rights to underwater resources off the Crimean Peninsula.[59] Russia currently can supply Crimea only by air and sea. Construction has begun on a planned 11.8-mile bridge to connect the Crimean Peninsula with Russia by road and rail at a cost of $3.2 billion to $4.3 billion,[60] but there are significant doubts about the project's economic viability and timeline to completion, as well as the suitability of the strait as a site for a bridge.[61] Russia has deployed 28,000 troops to Crimea and has embarked on a major program to build housing, restore airfields, and install new radars there.[62] In addition, control of Crimea has allowed Russia to use the Black Sea as a platform to launch and support naval operations in the Gulf of Aden and the Eastern Mediterranean.[63] Russia has allocated $1 billion to modernize the Black Sea fleet by 2020 and has stationed additional warships there including two equipped with Caliber-NK long-range cruise missiles.[64] Caliber cruise missiles have a range of at least 2,500km, placing cities from Rome to Vilnius within range of Black Sea–based cruise missiles.[65] In August 2016, Russia deployed S-400 air defense systems with a potential range of around 250 miles to Crimea.[66]

In eastern Ukraine, Russia has helped to foment and sustain a separatist movement. Backed, armed, and trained by Russia, separatist leaders in eastern Ukraine have declared the so-called Lugansk People's Republic and Donetsk People's Republic. Russia has backed separatist factions in the Donbas region of eastern Ukraine with advanced weapons, technical and financial assistance, and Russian conventional and special operations forces. Russian-backed separatists daily violate the September 2014 and February 2015 cease-fire agreements, known respectively as Minsk I and Minsk II.[67] Of the 10,000 deaths produced by the war, approximately a third have occurred since the signing of Minsk II.[68] Alexander Hug, chief of the Organization for Security and Co-operation in Europe (OSCE) Special Monitoring Mission (SMM) to Ukraine, described the fighting in and around Avdiivka in January 2017 as "the worst fighting we've seen in Ukraine since 2014 and early 2015."[69] Ukrainian troops have been on the receiving end of Russian propaganda. In February, for instance, Ukrainian troops received text messages with such threats as "You are just meat to your commanders," "Your body will be found when the snow melts," and "You're like the Germans in Stalingrad."[70]

The Minsk cease-fire agreements have led to the de facto partition of Ukraine and have created a frozen conflict that remains both deadly and advantageous for Russia. General Scaparrotti described the seriousness of the situation in his 2017 EUCOM posture statement:

> Recently in eastern Ukraine, Russia controls the battle tempo, again ratcheting up the number of daily violations of the cease fire and—even more concerning—directing combined Russian-separatist forces to target civilian infrastructure and threaten and intimidate OSCE monitors in order to turn up the pressure on Ukraine. Furthermore, Moscow's support for so-called "separatists" in eastern Ukraine destabilizes Kyiv's political structures....[71]

Extensive Russian cyber-attacks against Ukraine (more than 6,500 in the last two months of 2016 alone) have targeted government ministries, as well as the energy grid and industrial processes such as the monitoring of oil and gas pipelines.[72] Russia is also employing espionage and misinformation to derail Ukraine. In October 2016, for example, Ukraine announced that it had arrested a Ukrainian on charges of spying for Russian military intelligence.[73] Moscow's poor track record in implementing cease-fires should raise doubts among those who expected that Russia would not use its influence to control the separatists in eastern Ukraine.

Russia is still in violation of the 2008 peace agreement signed to end the war against Georgia. Russian troops are still based in areas where they are not supposed to be, and Moscow continues to prevent international observers from crossing into South Ossetia and Abkhazia even though they patrol freely in the rest of Georgia.

In Moldova, Russia supports the breakaway enclave of Transnistria, where yet another frozen conflict festers to Moscow's liking. According to EUCOM's 2017 posture statement:

> Russia has employed a decades-long strategy of indirect action to coerce, destabilize, and otherwise exercise a malign influence over other nations. In neighboring states, Russia continues to fuel "protracted conflicts." In Moldova, for example, Russia has yet to follow through on its 1999 Istanbul summit commitments to withdraw an estimated 1,500 troops—whose presence has no mandate—from the Moldovan breakaway region of Transnistria. Russia asserts that it will remove its force once a comprehensive settlement to the Transnistrian conflict has been reached. However, Russia continued to undermine the discussion of a comprehensive settlement to the Transnistrian conflict at the 5+2 negotiations.[74]

Whether in Georgia, eastern Ukraine, or Moldova, it is in Russia's interests to keep these conflicts frozen. Russia derives much of its regional influence from these conflicts, and bringing them to a peaceful conclusion would decrease Russia's influence in the region.

The other countries in Central and Eastern Europe also see Russia as a threat, although to varying degrees. Most tend to rely almost completely on Russia for their energy resources, some have felt the sharp end of Russian aggression in the past, and all were once in the Warsaw Pact and fear being forced back into a similar arrangement. Such historical experiences inevitably have shaped Russia's image throughout Central and Eastern Europe.

In November 2016, Russia announced that deployments of advanced mobile S-400 air defense systems and mobile short-range ballistic missile systems including Iskander missiles in the Kaliningrad Oblast exclave would be permanent.[75] There have been reports that it has deployed tactical nuclear weapons in Kaliningrad.[76] Russia also has outfitted a missile brigade in Luga, Russia, a mere 74 miles from the Estonian city of Narva, with Iskander missiles.[77] Recently, Russian military officials have reportedly asked manufacturers to increase the range of the Iskander missiles and improve their accuracy.[78] Moreover, Russia is not deploying missiles only in Europe. In November 2016, Russia announced that it had stationed Bal and Bastion missile systems on the Kurile islands of Iturup and Kunashir, which are also claimed by Japan.[79]

Russia has deployed additional troops and capabilities near its western borders. Bruno Kahl, head of the German Federal Intelligence Service, stated in March 2017 that "Russia has doubled its fighting power on its Western border, which cannot be considered as defensive against the West."[80] In January, Russia's defense ministry announced that four S-400 air defense systems would be deployed to the Western Military District in 2017.[81] In January 2016, Commander in Chief of Russian Ground Forces General Oleg Salyukov announced that four new ground divisions would be formed in 2016, three of which would be based in the Western Military District, allegedly in response to "intensified exercises of NATO countries."[82] According to an assessment published by the Carnegie Endowment for International Peace, "The overall effect is to produce a line of substantial Russian combat forces along the western border, including opposite Belarus. By contrast with the ad hoc arrangements of the early stages of the conflict with Ukraine, these new forces are permanently established."[83]

WWTA: The WWTA states that Russian "strategic objectives in Ukraine—maintaining long-term influence over Kyiv and frustrating Ukraine's attempts to integrate into Western institutions—will remain unchanged in 2017" and that Vladimir Putin "is likely to maintain pressure on Kyiv through multiple channels, including through Russia's actions in eastern Ukraine, where Russia arms so-called 'separatists.'" In addition, Moscow "seeks to undermine Ukraine's fragile economic system and divided political situation to create opportunities to rebuild and consolidate Russian influence in Ukrainian decision making." The WWTA also states that "[s]ettlement talks over the breakaway region of Transnistria will continue, but any progress is likely to be limited to smaller issues."[84]

Summary: NATO members in Eastern and Central Europe view Russia as a threat, a fear that is not unfounded considering Russian aggression against Ukraine and Georgia. The threat of conventional attack against a NATO member by Russia remains low but cannot be ruled out entirely. Russia's grasp and use of unconventional warfare against neighboring countries should remain a top issue for U.S. and NATO planners.

Militarization of the High North. The Arctic region is home to some of the roughest terrain and harshest weather found anywhere in the world. Increasingly, the melting of Arctic ice during the summer months is causing new challenges for the U.S. in terms of Arctic security. Many of the shipping lanes currently used in the Arctic are a considerable distance from search and rescue (SAR) facilities, and natural resource exploration that would be considered routine in other locations is complex, costly, and dangerous in the Arctic.

The U.S. is one of five littoral Arctic powers and one of only eight countries with territory located above the Arctic Circle, the area just north of 66 degrees north latitude that includes portions of Norway, Sweden, Finland, Russia, Canada, Greenland, Iceland, and the United States.

Arctic actors take different approaches to military activity in the region. Although the security challenges currently faced in the Arctic are not yet military in nature, there is still a requirement for military capability in the region that can support civilian authorities. For example, civilian SAR and response to natural disasters in such an unforgiving environment can be augmented by the military.

Russia has taken steps to militarize its presence in the region. In March, a decree signed by Russian President Putin gave the Federal Security Service (FSB) additional powers to confiscate land "in areas with special objects for land use, and in the border areas."[85] Russia's

MAP 5

Russia Maintains Strong Base Presence in Arctic Region

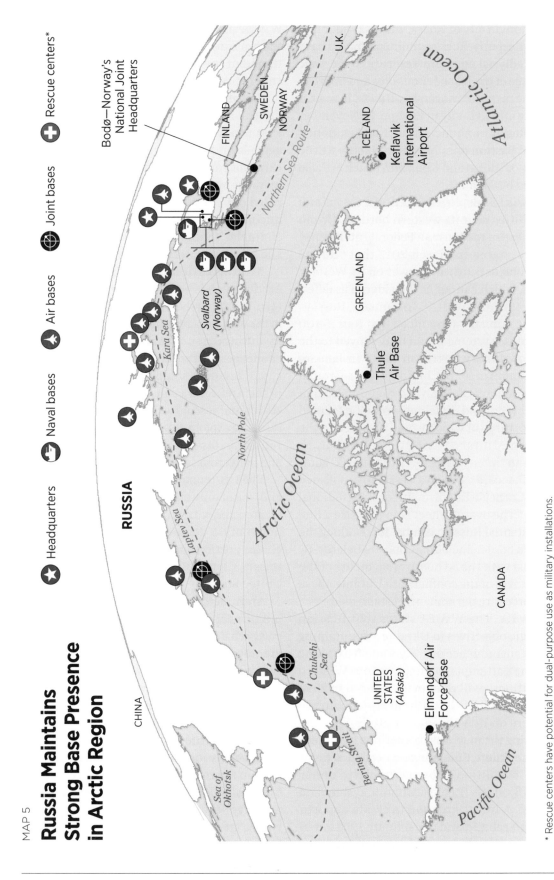

Bodø—Norway's National Joint Headquarters

Northern Sea Route

FINLAND

SWEDEN

NORWAY

U.K.

ICELAND

Keflavik International Airport

Atlantic Ocean

GREENLAND

Thule Air Base

Svalbard (Norway)

Kara Sea

North Pole

Arctic Ocean

RUSSIA

Laptev Sea

CANADA

Chukchi Sea

UNITED STATES (Alaska)

Elmendorf Air Force Base

Bering Strait

CHINA

Sea of Okhotsk

Pacific Ocean

Legend:
- Headquarters
- Naval bases
- Air bases
- Joint bases
- Rescue centers*

* Rescue centers have potential for dual-purpose use as military installations.

SOURCE: Heritage Foundation research.

heritage.org

Arctic territory is included within this FSB-controlled border zone. In a parade on May 9, 2017, Russia showcased its Pantsir-SA SAM system, which is designed to operate in the Arctic. The system began firing trials in June.[86] In addition, the Arctic-based Northern Fleet accounts for two-thirds of the Russian Navy. A new Arctic command was established in 2015 to coordinate all Russian military activities in the Arctic region.[87] Two Arctic brigades have been formed, and Russia is planning to form Arctic Coastal Defense divisions,[88] which will be under the command of the Northern Fleet and stationed in the Kola Peninsula and in Russia's eastern Arctic.[89]

Russia is also investing in Arctic bases. Its base on Alexandra Land, which will be commissioned in 2017,[90] can house 150 soldiers autonomously for up to 18 months.[91] In addition, old Soviet-era facilities have been reopened. The airfield on Kotelny Island, for example, has been put into use for the first time in almost 30 years.[92] The base will house 250 people and will have air defense missiles.[93]

In fact, air power in the Arctic is increasingly important to Russia, which has 14 operational airfields in the Arctic along with 16 deep-water ports.[94] The 45th Air Force and Air Defense Army of the Northern Fleet was formed in December 2015, and Russia reportedly has placed radar and S-300 missiles on the Arctic bases at Franz Joseph Land, New Siberian Islands, Novaya Zemlya, and Severnaya Zemlya.[95]

Russia's ultimate goal is to have a combined Russian armed force deployed in the Arctic by 2020, and it appears that Moscow is on track to accomplish this.[96] Russia is developing equipment optimized for Arctic conditions like the Mi-38 helicopter[97] and three new nuclear icebreakers to add to the 40 icebreakers already in service (six of which are nuclear).[98] Admiral Paul F. Zukunft, Commandant of the U.S. Coast Guard, has expressed concern that "Russia probably is going to launch two icebreaking corvettes with cruise missiles on them over the course of the next several years."[99] Russia's Northern Fleet is also building newly refitted

submarines including "a newly converted Belgorod nuclear submarine in 2018 to carry out "special missions."[100] Construction on the vessel had been suspended in 2000 when the *Kursk*, its sister submarine, sank. According to Russian media reports, the submarine "will be engaged in studying the bottom of the Russian Arctic shelf, searching for minerals at great depths, and also laying underwater communications."[101] In May, Russia announced that its buildup of the Northern Fleet's nuclear capacity is intended "to phase 'NATO out of [the] Arctic.'"[102]

Russia's Maritime Doctrine of Russian Federation 2020, adopted in July 2015, lists the Arctic as one of two focal points along with the Atlantic, a point emphasized by Deputy Prime Minister Dmitry Rogozin.[103] In April 2016, a Russian Severodvinsk submarine participated in Arctic exercises that involved 20 vessels and fired a Kalibr cruise missile that reportedly hit a target on land.[104]

Also in April 2016, Russian and Chechen paratroopers took part in separate military exercises in the Arctic. It was not the first time that these exercises had taken place. In 2014, 90 paratroopers landed on Barneo ice camp in the Arctic; in 2015, 100 paratroopers from Russia, Belarus, and Tajikistan took part in exercises on Barneo.[105] In advance of the April 2016 exercises, personnel and equipment were transferred through Longyearbyen airport on Svalbard, over which Norway has sovereignty. The use of the airport likely violated the Svalbard Treaty, which demilitarized the islands.[106]

WWTA: The WWTA assesses that "as the Arctic becomes more open to shipping and commercial exploitation," the "risk of competition over access to sea routes and resources, including fish, will include countries traditionally active in the Arctic as well as other countries that do not border on the region but increasingly look to advance their economic interests there."[107]

Summary: While NATO has been slow to turn its attention to the Arctic, Russia continues to develop and increase its military capabilities in the region. The likelihood of armed conflict remains low, but physical changes in the region mean that the posture of players in the Arctic will continue to evolve. It is clear that Russia intends to exert a dominant influence. In the words of EUCOM's 2017 posture statement, "Russia is reasserting its military prowess and positioning itself for strategic advantage in the Arctic."[108]

Threat from Russian Propaganda. Russia has consistently used propaganda to garner support for its foreign policies. The 2016 Concept of the Foreign Policy of the Russian Federation makes clear the Russian government's aims in using mass media to further its foreign policy objectives:

> Russia seeks to ensure that the world has an objective image of the country, develops its own effective ways to influence foreign audiences, promotes Russian and Russian-language media in the global information space, providing them with necessary government support, is proactive in international information cooperation, and takes necessary steps to counter threats to its information security. New information and communication technology is used to this end.[109]

Russian media are hardly independent. Russia ranked 148th out of 180 countries in Reporters Without Borders' *2017 World Press Freedom Index*, the same as its ranking in the 2016 edition.[110] Specifically:

> What with draconian laws and website blocking, the pressure on independent media has grown steadily since Vladimir Putin's return to the Kremlin in 2012. Leading independent news outlets have either been brought under control or throttled out of existence. As TV channels continue to inundate viewers with propaganda, the climate has become increasingly oppressive for those who try to maintain quality journalism or question the new patriotic and neo-conservative. More and more bloggers are receiving prisons sentences for their activity on online social networks. The leading human rights NGOs have been declared "foreign agents." The oppressive climate at the national level encourages powerful provincial officials far from Moscow to crack down even harder on their media critics.[111]

Much of Moscow's propaganda is meant for domestic Russian audiences, who still rely widely on television for their news. Russia's leaders are reportedly looking to overhaul TV to improve its ability to attract young audiences who have been turning increasingly to social media and online news for information.[112] Widespread demonstrations against corruption in March were striking not only because they occurred in over 100 cities and towns across Russia, but also because they were heavily attended by young Russians, who are not as affected by TV-based propaganda.[113]

In addition to retaining power internally, Russia's leaders are working actively to influence audiences abroad. In 2016, Russia allocated $900 million toward propaganda efforts.[114] Russian propaganda TV network RT received around $310 million in state funding in 2016.[115] While its overall budget is expected to stay the same in 2017, RT will receive an extra $19 million to start a French-language TV channel to complement an existing French-language website.[116]

In EUCOM's 2016 posture statement, General Breedlove described how Russian propaganda works: "Russia overwhelms the information space with a barrage of lies that must be addressed by the United States more aggressively in both public and private sectors to effectively expose the false narratives pushed daily by Russian-owned media outlets and their proxies."[117] British Defence Secretary Michael Fallon sees Russia as "a country that in weaponizing misinformation has created what we might now see as the post-truth age."[118]

In Ukraine, examples abound. For instance, Russian media have promoted the false claims that Russia is simply defending ethnic Russians in Ukraine from far-right thugs, that the government in Kyiv is to blame for the violence that has enveloped parts of the country, and that the U.S. has instigated unrest in Ukraine.[119] In 2014, after a civilian airliner was shot down by Russian-backed separatists, Russian propaganda put out stories alleging that the plane was shot down by the Ukrainian government.[120]

Nor are Russian propaganda efforts limited only to TV channels. There are widespread reports that the Russian government has paid people to post comments to Internet articles that parrot the government's propaganda.[121] People working in so-called troll factories with English-language skills are reportedly paid more.[122] Twitter has been used in Ukraine to disseminate false or exaggerated Russian government claims. The 2017 EUCOM posture statement includes several instructive examples of Russian propaganda efforts:

> Examples include Russia's outright denial of involvement in the lead up to Russia's occupation and attempted annexation in Crimea; attempts to influence elections in the United States, France and elsewhere; its aggressive propaganda campaigns targeting ethnic Russian populations among its neighbors; and cyber activities directed against infrastructure in the Baltic nations and Ukraine.[123]

Russian propaganda poses its greatest threat to NATO allies that have a significant ethnic Russian population: the Baltic States, especially Estonia and Latvia. Many ethnic Russians in these countries get their news through Russian-language media (especially TV channels) that parrot the official Russian state line, often interspersed with entertainment shows, making it more appealing to viewers. In 2014, Lithuania and Latvia temporarily banned certain Russian TV stations such as RTR Rossiya in light of Russian aggression in Ukraine,[124] and in March 2016, Latvia banned the Russian "news agency" and propaganda website Sputnik from operating in the country.[125] Lithuanian Defense Minister Raimundas Karoblis stated in April 2017 that he believed Russian disinformation, especially propaganda stating that the capital city of Vilnius never belonged to Lithuania, are meant to lay the groundwork for future "kinetic operations."[126]

The inability to reach ethnic Russians in their vernacular remains a glaring vulnerability for planners when thinking about Baltic security. In an effort to provide an independent, alternative Russian-language media outlet, Estonia, Latvia, and Lithuania are in various stages of planning and creating their own Russian-language programming to counter Russian propaganda efforts.[127] In September 2015, Estonia launched ETV+, a Russian-language TV channel.[128] Lithuania announced a temporary ban on the Russian state TV channel RTR Planeta in November 2016 and has limited the amount of Russian-language TV in the country.[129] Latvia has imposed similar temporary bans, including on Russian channel Rossiya RTR in April 2016, and has sought to help journalists counter Russian propaganda through workshops.[130]

Outside of the Baltics, in May 2016, Ukraine announced a long-term ban on a number of Russian TV channels, websites, and Russian media personnel.[131] The U.S., albeit belatedly, has also begun efforts to produce Russian-language programming. Current Time, a Russian-language network that is the result of collaboration between the Voice of America and Radio Free Europe/Radio Liberty, began broadcasting in February 2017. Its 24-hour broadcasts are "an eclectic mix of documentaries, human interest programming and traditional news shows."[132]

As General Scaparrotti testified in March, Russian propaganda and disinformation should be viewed as an extension of Russia's military capabilities: "The Russians see this as part of that spectrum of warfare, it's their asymmetric approach."[133] Russia has also sought to use misinformation to undermine NATO's Enhanced Forward Presence in the Baltics. In April, Russian hackers planted a false story about U.S. troops being poisoned by mustard gas in Latvia on the Baltic News Service's website.[134] Similarly, Lithuanian parliamentarians and media outlets began receiving e-mails in February containing a false story that German soldiers had sexually assaulted an underage Lithuanian girl.[135] U.S. troops stationed in Poland for NATO's EFP have been the target of similar Russian misinformation campaigns.[136]

WWTA: The WWTA states that "Russia is likely to sustain or increase its propaganda campaigns."[137] It also makes clear the link between cyber operations and information operations: "Information from cyber espionage can be leaked indiscriminately or selectively to shape perceptions. Furthermore, even a technically secure Internet can serve as a platform for the delivery of manipulative content crafted by foes seeking to gain influence or foment distrust."[138]

Summary: Russia has used propaganda consistently and aggressively to advance its foreign policy aims. This is likely to remain an essential element of Russian aggression and planning. The potential for its use to stir up agitation in the Baltic States, to undermine NATO, and to expose fissures between Western states makes Russian propaganda a continued threat to regional stability and a possible threat to the NATO alliance.

Russian Destabilization in the South Caucasus. The South Caucasus sits at a crucial geographical and cultural crossroads and has proven to be strategically important, both militarily and economically, for centuries. Although the countries in the region (Armenia, Georgia, and Azerbaijan) are not part of NATO and therefore do not receive a security guarantee from the United States, they have participated to varying degrees in NATO and U.S.-led operations. This is especially true of Georgia, which aspires to join NATO.

Russia views the South Caucasus as part of its natural sphere of influence and stands ready to exert its influence in the region by force if necessary. In August 2008, Russia invaded Georgia, coming as close as 15 miles to the capital city of Tbilisi. Seven years later, several thousand Russian troops occupied the two Georgian provinces of South Ossetia and Abkhazia.

In 2015, Russia signed so-called integration treaties with South Ossetia and Abkhazia. Among other things, these treaties call for a coordinated foreign policy, creation of a common security and defense space, and implementation of a streamlined process for Abkhazians and South Ossetians to receive Russian citizenship.[139] The Georgian Foreign Ministry criticized the treaties as a step toward "annexation of Georgia's occupied territories,"[140] both of which are still internationally recognized as part of Georgia. In March 2017, Putin approved an agreement with South Ossetia to incorporate "some military units" into the Russian Army, a development that Georgian authorities denounced as "yet another Russian provocation aimed at destabilizing the region."[141] In January, Russia announced tank drills in Abkhazia with over 2,000 troops, armored personnel carriers, and Russian T-72B3 tanks.[142] Russia has based 7,000 soldiers in Abkhazia and South Ossetia[143] and is regularly expanding its "creeping annexation" of Georgia.[144] In July 2015, Russian troops expanded the border of the occupied territories to include a piece of the Baku–Supsa pipeline, which carries oil from Azerbaijan to Supsa, Georgia, with a capacity of 100,000 barrels a day and is owned by British Petroleum.[145]

Towns are split in two and families are separated as a result of Russia's occupation and imposition of an internal border. In 2016 alone, 134 people were detained by Russian border guards for illegal crossings into South Ossetia.[146] In April 2017, South Ossetia held a referendum to change its name to the "Republic of South Ossetia-Alania." The referendum, along with elections in Abkhazia in March and South Ossetia in April, was widely unrecognized including by the U.S., Georgia, and NATO.[147]

Today, Moscow continues to exploit ethnic divisions and tensions in the South Caucasus to advance pro-Russian policies that are often at odds with America's or NATO's goals in the region, but Russia's influence is not restricted to soft power. In the South Caucasus, the coin of the realm is military might. It is a rough neighborhood surrounded by instability and insecurity reflected in terrorism, religious fanaticism, centuries-old sectarian divides, and competition for natural resources.

Russia maintains a sizable military presence in Armenia based on an agreement giving Moscow access to bases in that country for 49 years.[148] The bulk of Russia's forces, consisting of approximately 5,000 soldiers, dozens of fighter planes and attack helicopters, and approximately 100 T-72 tanks, as well as S-300 and Buk M01 air defense systems, are based around the 102nd Military Base.[149] In 2015, Russia and Armenia signed a Combined Regional Air Defense System agreement. This past year, Armenia acquired Russian Iskander missiles, although there is "a lack of consensus among defense experts on who really controls these Armenian Iskander missiles—Moscow or Yerevan."[150] In addition to a joint air defense zone, Russia and Armenia signed a joint forces agreement in December 2016. Under this agreement, the initial term of which is five years, leadership of the combined force transfers to Russia's Southern Military District Commander during periods of hostility.[151]

Another source of regional instability is the Nagorno–Karabakh conflict, which began in 1988 when Armenia made territorial claims to Azerbaijan's Nagorno–Karabakh Autonomous Oblast.[152] By 1992, Armenian forces and Armenian-backed militias occupied 20 percent of Azerbaijan, including the Nagorno–Karabakh region and seven surrounding districts. A cease-fire agreement was signed in 1994, and the conflict has been described as frozen since then. Since August 2014, violence has increased noticeably along the Line of Contact between Armenian and Azerbaijani forces. Intense fighting in April 2016 left 200 dead.[153] In addition, Azerbaijani forces recaptured some of the territory lost to Armenia in the early 1990s, the first changes in the Line of Contact since 1994.[154] Recently, tensions have simmered, and smaller-scale fighting has continued to prove deadly. In June 2017, the International Crisis Group reported that "[a] year after Nagorno–Karabakh's April 2016 violent flare-up, Armenia and Azerbaijan are closer to war than at any point since the 1994 ceasefire."[155]

This conflict offers another opportunity for Russia to exert malign influence and consolidate power in the region. While its sympathies lie with Armenia, Russia is the largest supplier of weapons to both Armenia and Azerbaijan.[156] As noted by the late Dr. Alexandros Petersen, a highly respected expert on Eurasian security, it

is no secret "that the Nagorno–Karabakh dispute is a Russian proxy conflict, maintained in simmering stasis by Russian arms sales to both sides so that Moscow can sustain leverage over Armenia, Azerbaijan and by its geographic proximity Georgia."[157]

Following the outbreak of fighting, Russia expanded its influence in the region by brokering a shaky cease-fire that has largely held. By the time the OSCE Minsk Group, created in 1995 to find a peaceful solution to the Nagorno–Karabakh conflict, met, the Russian-brokered cease-fire was already in place.[158]

The South Caucasus might seem distant to many American policymakers, but the spillover effect of ongoing conflict in the region can have a direct impact on both U.S. interests and the security of America's partners, as well as on Turkey and other countries that are dependent on oil and gas transiting the region.

WWTA: The WWTA predicts that the "potential for large-scale hostilities [in the Nagorno–Karabakh region] will remain in 2017" and that the Georgian government will continue on the path of Euro-Atlantic integration.[159]

Summary: Russia views the South Caucasus as a vital theater and uses a multitude of tools that include military aggression, economic pressure, and the stoking of ethnic tensions to exert influence and control, usually to promote outcomes that are at odds with U.S. interests.

Russia's Actions in Syria. Although Russia has had a military presence in Syria for decades, in September 2015, it became the decisive actor in Syria's ongoing civil war, having saved Bashar al-Assad from being overthrown and having strengthened his hand militarily, thus enabling government forces to retake territory lost during the war. In January 2017, Russia signed an agreement with the Assad regime to expand the naval facility at Tartus (Russia's only naval base on the Mediterranean) "under a 49-year lease that could automatically renew for a further 25 years." The planned expansion reportedly would "provide simultaneous berthing for up to 11 warships, including nuclear-powered vessels, more than doubling its present known capacity."[160]

The agreement also includes upgrades to the Hmeymim air base at Latakia, including repairs to a second runway.[161] Russia deployed the S-400 anti-aircraft missile system to Hmeymim in late 2015.[162]

Russia's actions in Syria provide a useful propaganda tool. In May 2016, for example, one hundred journalists toured Palmyra, a city that Russia had helped Assad's forces retake with air strikes and Special Forces troops.[163] In addition, Russia is using Syria as a testing ground for new weapons systems while obtaining valuable combat experience for its troops. According to Lieutenant General Ben Hodges, Commander, U.S. Army Europe, Russia has used its intervention in Syria as a "live-fire training opportunity."[164] In February 2017, Russian Defense Minister Sergei Shoigu claimed that Russia had tested 162 weapons systems in Syria.[165] Despite this display of Russian arms in Syria, however, Russian weapons exports have remained flat, in part because India and China are developing more weapons systems domestically.[166] In 2016, Russian arms exports rose slightly to $15 billion, up from $14.5 billion in 2015 but still lower than $15.7 billion in 2013.[167]

Russia's activities in Syria have allowed Assad to stay in power and have made achievement of a peaceful political settlement with rebel groups nearly impossible. They also have undermined American policy in the Middle East, including by frequently targeting forces backed by the U.S. As summarized in EUCOM's 2017 posture statement:

> Russia's military intervention has changed the dynamics of the conflict, bolstered the Bashar al-Assad regime, targeted moderate opposition elements, and compounded human suffering in Syria, and complicated U.S. and coalition operations against the Islamic State of Iraq and Syria (ISIS). Russia has used this chaos to establish a permanent presence in the Middle East and eastern Mediterranean.[168]

The Putin regime will likely seek to link cooperation in Syria with a softening of U.S. policy in Europe, especially with regard to economic sanctions.

Russian pilots have occasionally acted dangerously in the skies over Syria. In one incident in May 2017, a Russian fighter jet intercepted a U.S. KC-10 tanker, performing a barrel roll over the top of the KC-10.[169] That same month, Russia stated that U.S. and allied aircraft would be banned from flying over large areas of Syria because of a deal agreed to by Russia, Iran, and Turkey. The U.S. responded that the deal does not "preclude anyone from going after terrorists wherever they may be in Syria."[170] The U.S. and Russia have a deconfliction hotline to avoid mid-air collisions and incidents. In April, Russia threatened to cut the line following U.S. cruise missile strikes against a Syrian airbase.[171] In May, Lieutenant General Jeffrey Harrigian, Commander of U.S. Air Forces Central Command, reported increased use of the line as a result of stepped up operations near Raqqa.[172]

WWTA: The WWTA concludes that "Moscow's deployment of combat assets to Syria in late 2015 helped change the momentum of the conflict."[173] It further concludes that "Russia will continue to look to leverage its military support to the Asad regime to drive a political settlement process in Syria on its terms"; that "Moscow has demonstrated that it can sustain a modest force at a high-operations tempo in a permissive, expeditionary setting while minimizing Russian casualties and economic costs"; and that "Moscow is also likely to use Russia's military intervention in Syria, in conjunction with efforts to capitalize on fears of a growing ISIS and extremist threat, to expand its role in the Middle East."[174]

Summary: While not an existential threat to the U.S., Russia's intervention in Syria ensures that any future settlement will be run through Moscow and will include terms consistent with Russian strategic interests. Russia's intervention in Syria has helped to keep Assad in power, has further entrenched Russia's military position in the region, and has greatly degraded the impact of U.S. policy in Syria, often seeking to counteract U.S. actions and targeting U.S.-backed forces on the ground.

The Balkans. Security has improved dramatically in the Balkans since the 1990s, but violence based on religious and ethnic differences remains an ongoing possibility. These tensions are exacerbated by sluggish economies, high unemployment, and political corruption. According to the 2017 EUCOM posture statement, "[t]he Balkans' stability since the late 90's masks political and socio-economic fragility," and Russia's influence in the region has led to further destabilization: "In the Balkans, Russia exploits ethnic tensions to slow progress on European and transatlantic integration. In 2016, Russia overtly interfered in the political processes of both Bosnia–Herzegovina and Montenegro."[175]

Senior members of the Russian government have cited NATO enlargement in the Balkans as one of the biggest threats to Russia.[176] In June 2017, Montenegro became NATO's 29th member state, joining Albania and Croatia as NATO member states in the Balkans. Russia stands accused of being behind a failed plot to break into Montenegro's parliament on election day in 2016, assassinate its former prime minister, and install a pro-Russian government. Russia has denied involvement in the plot, but Montenegro's chief prosecutor has named two Russian citizens as the alleged organizers and has characterized the plot as the work of "nationalists from Russia."[177]

After Russia annexed Crimea, the Montenegrin government backed European sanctions against Moscow and even implemented its own sanctions. Nevertheless, Russia has significant economic influence in Montenegro and in 2015 sought unsuccessfully to gain access to Montenegrin ports for the Russian navy to refuel and perform maintenance.

Serbia in particular has long served as Russia's foothold in the Balkans. Both Russia and Serbia are Orthodox countries, and Russia wields huge political influence in Serbia. Moscow backed Serbian opposition to Kosovo's independence in 2008 and continues to use Kosovo's independence to justify its own actions in Crimea, South Ossetia, and Abkhazia. Russian media are active in the country, broadcasting in Serbian.[178]

Serbia and Russia have signed a strategic partnership agreement focused on economic issues. Russia's inward investment is focused on the transport and energy sectors. Except for those in the Commonwealth of Independent States, Serbia is the only country in Europe that has a free trade deal with Russia. It therefore seemed odd when Russia decided to scrap the South Stream gas pipeline, likely costing Serbia billions of euros of inward investment and thousands of local jobs. Even with the negative impact of the South Stream cancellation, however, Serbia will likely continue to consider Russia its closest ally.

Serbia's current president is trying to walk a fine line, promising closer ties with Russia, after speaking out against sanctions imposed on Russia because of its actions in Ukraine,[179] while also promising to continue on the path to EU integration.[180] In October, the Russian ambassador to Serbia warned of damage to bilateral economic relations if Serbia were to join the EU.[181] With 80 percent of its gas coming from Russia, Serbia remains dependent on Russian energy. In January, seeking to diversify its energy supply, Serbia signed a memorandum of understanding with Bulgaria to develop an energy link between the two nations.[182]

The Russian–Serbian military relationship is similarly close. Russia signed an agreement with Serbia to allow Russian soldiers to be based at Niš airport, which Serbia has used to meddle in northern Kosovo.[183] Serbia has observer status in the Collective Security Treaty Organization, Russia's answer to NATO, and has signed a 15-year military cooperation agreement with Russia that includes the sharing of intelligence, military officer exchanges, and joint military exercises. The situation in Ukraine has not changed Serbian attitudes regarding military cooperation with Russia. During a state visit in October 2014, Putin was honored with the largest Serbian military parade since the days of Yugoslavia.[184] The two countries have also carried out military training exercises, and Serbia has inquired about obtaining Russia's S-300 surface-to-air missile system.[185] Following a May 2017 visit to Russia, Serbian Defense Minister Zoran Djordjevic stated that Russia had agreed to deliver six MiG-29s, 30 T-72 tanks, and 30 BRDM-2 armored vehicles to Serbia.[186]

In November 2016, Serbia hosted a joint exercise named Slavic Brotherhood with Belarus and Russia that consisted of 700 troops. However, Serbia still exercises far more without Russia than with Russia: "In 2016, out of 26 training exercises only two are with Russia. Out of 21 multinational training drills in 2015, the Serbian military participated in only two with Russia."[187] Like Russia, Serbia is a member of NATO's Partnership for Peace program. Additionally, Serbia has been part of the U.S. National Guard's State Partnership Program, partnering with the State of Ohio since 2006.

Russia is also active in Bosnia and Herzegovina—specifically, the ethnically Serb Republika Srpska, one of two substate entities inside Bosnia and Herzegovina that emerged from that country's civil war in the 1990s.

Bosnia and Herzegovina is on the path to joining the transatlantic community but has a long way to go. It negotiated a Stabilization and Association Agreement with the EU, but the agreement is not in force because key economic and political reforms have not been implemented. In 2010, NATO offered Bosnia and Herzegovina a Membership Action Plan, but progress on full membership has been stalled because immovable defense properties are still not controlled by the Ministry of Defense. Moscow knows that exploiting internal ethnic and religious divisions among the Serb, Bosniak, and Croat populations is the easiest way to prevent Bosnia and Herzegovina from entering the transatlantic community.

Republika Srpska's leader, Milorad Dodik, has long advocated independence for the region and has enjoyed a very close relationship with the Kremlin. Recent events in Ukraine, especially the annexation of Crimea, have inspired more separatist rhetoric in Republika Srpska. In many ways, Russia's relationship with Republika Srpska is akin to its relationship with Georgia's South Ossetia and Abkhazia autonomous regions: more like a relationship with another sovereign state than a relationship with a semiautonomous region inside Bosnia

and Herzegovina. When Putin visited Serbia in October 2014, Dodik was treated like a head of state and invited to Belgrade to meet with him. More recently, in September 2016, Dodik was treated as a head of state on a visit to Moscow just days before a referendum that chose January 9 as Republika Srpska's "statehood day," a date filled with religious and ethnic symbolism for the Serbs.[188] Republika Srpska hosted its "statehood day" in defiance of a ruling by Bosnia's federal constitutional court that both the celebration and the referendum establishing it were illegal.[189] The U.S. sanctioned Dodik in January 2017, saying that "by obstructing the Dayton accords, Milorad Dodik poses a significant threat to the sovereignty and territorial integrity of Bosnia–Herzegovina."[190] Dodik has further promised to hold a referendum on independence by the end of 2018.[191]

Russia has also cast doubt on the future of the European-led peacekeeping operations in Bosnia and Herzegovina. Russian Foreign Minister Sergei Lavrov said in January that "We have reminded our Western partners multiple times that it's getting indecent to retain in Bosnia and Herzegovina, which is considered to be an independent state, the so-called Office of the High representative" that was created by the Dayton accords.[192] Russia, which holds veto power in the U.N. Security Council, abstained in November 2015 during the annual vote on extending the peacekeeping mission.[193] This was the first time in 14 years that it failed to vote for this resolution. When a U.N. resolution extending the mandate of the EUFOR ALTHEA mission to Bosnia and Herzegovina was adopted unanimously in 2016, Russia's U.N. representative condemned alleged "anti-Serbian bias" and again urged that international monitors be removed from the country.[194]

The situation with Kosovo remains fragile, but an EU-led rapprochement between Kosovo and Serbia has shown signs of modest success. In January, a train traveling from Belgrade to Mitrovica, a heavily Serb town in Kosovo, was stopped at the Kosovar border. The Russian-made train was "painted in the colors of the Serbian flag and feature[d] pictures of churches, monasteries, and medieval towns, as well as the words 'Kosovo is Serbian' in 21 languages."[195] The incident raised tensions in the region significantly.

Macedonia has made great progress toward joining NATO but has been blocked by Greece because of a name dispute. Macedonia faced six months of unrest and massive protests after elections in December produced a hung Parliament. Tensions remain high. A coalition government took office in May. It includes two ethnic Albanian parties that are seeking concessions, including that Albanian be made a second language, as a condition of their continued support.[196]

Another challenge for the region is the increasing presence of the Islamic State and the rise of extremism. Thankfully, the region has not suffered a major attack from ISIS, but it has served as a fertile recruiting ground for the Islamic State. Several hundred fighters from the Balkans are in Iraq and Syria.[197] Most of these foreign fighters, who have formed a so-called Balkans Battalion for Islamic State, have come from Kosovo, but others can be traced back to Albania, Bosnia, and the Republic of Macedonia.

The closing of the Balkan route for migrants means that Islamist transit through the region no longer poses the threat that it once did. Some of the terrorists who perpetrated attacks in Paris in November 2015 and Brussels in 2016 are known to have transited through the Balkan Peninsula. However, the region remains fertile ground for Islamist ideology,[198] which is spread in part by Salafists operating in the region who are backed by countries like Saudi Arabia.[199]

The U.S. has invested heavily in the Balkans since the end of the Cold War. Tens of thousands of U.S. servicemembers have served in the Balkans, and the U.S. has spent billions of dollars in aid there, all in the hope of creating a secure and prosperous region that will someday be part of the transatlantic community.

WWTA: The WWTA notes that the tightening of border controls in the Balkans has led to a limitation of migration to Europe.[200]

Summary: The Balkans are being squeezed from three sides: by increased Russian involvement in internal affairs, ISIS using the region as a transit and recruiting ground, and continued economic sluggishness and unemployment. The region faced greater turmoil over the past year than it has for some time. Russia continues to inflame historic religious and ethnic tensions to maximize its influence and destabilize the region.

Threats to the Commons

Other than cyberspace and (to some extent) airspace, the commons are relatively secure in the European region. Despite periodic Russian aggressive maneuvers near U.S. and NATO vessels, this remains largely true with respect to the security of and free passage through shipping lanes in the region. The maritime domain is heavily patrolled by the navies and coast guards of NATO and NATO partner countries; except in remote areas in the Arctic Sea, search and rescue capabilities are readily available; maritime-launched terrorism is not a significant problem; and piracy is virtually nonexistent in the European region.

Sea. In May 2017, three Russian corvettes sailed four nautical miles off the Latvian coast within the Exclusive Economic Zone (EEZ) of Latvia; in April, a *Kilo*-class Russian submarine was detected near Latvian sea space.[201] Altogether, 209 Russian aircraft or naval vessels were detected near Latvian air or sea space in 2016.[202] Also in May, two Russian Su-24 fighters flew within 200 meters of a Dutch frigate, the HNLMS *Evertsen*.[203] On February 10, the USS *Porter*, a destroyer operating in international waters in the Black Sea, was buzzed by two Russian Su-24 fighters, followed by a solo Su-24 and finally by a Russian IL-38. The aircraft were flying with their transponders switched off and did not respond to radio requests to stop. A spokesperson for EUCOM said that such buzzing incidents are "always concerning because they could result in miscalculation or accident."[204]

Moreover, Russian aggressive actions in the sea-lanes extend beyond European waters. In

April, Russian surveillance ships followed the Carl Vinson Strike Group, which the U.S. had deployed near the Korean Peninsula in the Pacific.[205]

Russian threats to the maritime theater are not limited to surface vessels. In October 2015, news reports of Russian vessels operating aggressively near undersea communications cables raised concerns that Russia might be laying the groundwork for severing the cables in the event of a future conflict.[206] According to Admiral Michelle Howard, Commander, U.S. Naval Forces Europe, "We're seeing activity [by Russia] that we didn't even see when it was the Soviet Union."[207]

In July, Russia sailed its last remaining Typhoon-class nuclear submarine, the *Dmitry Donskoy*, from Severodvinsk across the entire length of Norway into the North Sea, past Denmark and Sweden, and into the Baltic Sea before sailing on to St. Petersburg. This was the first time a Typhoon-class submarine had sailed into the Baltic Sea. A Russian nuclear-powered cruiser armed with cruise missiles, surface-to-air missiles, torpedoes, and rocket launchers from the Northern Fleet joined the *Dmitry Donskoy* in St. Petersburg.[208]

Russian advances in submarine activity are likewise worrisome. Haga Lunde, the head of Norway's Intelligence Service, stated in February that "[w]e are seeing an increase in Russian submarine activity; also that their vessels are moving further west. Meanwhile, the submarine's technology has been so well developed that it is becoming increasingly difficult to detect them."[209]

Closer to the United States, Russia's naval vessels are being used for espionage. In March, a Russian spy ship was tracked 20 miles off the U.S. coast near the naval base at Kings Bay, Georgia. In February, the same vessel had sailed 30 miles off the coast of Connecticut, potentially near the U.S. submarine base at Groton.[210]

Airspace. Russia has continued its provocative military flights near U.S. and European airspace over the past year. In October 2016, two Russian TU-160 Blackjack bombers flew north of Norway, then northwest of Scotland, and on west of Ireland before flying into the Bay of Biscay off French and Spanish territory and then turning around and flying a similar route back to Russia. France, Norway, Spain, and the U.K. scrambled jets to intercept the bombers. Iceland's foreign ministry stated that the bombers had flown between 6,000 and 9,000 feet under a commercial aircraft flying from Reykjavik, Iceland, to Stockholm, Sweden.[211]

Aggressive Russian flying has also occurred near U.S. airspace. Over the course of four days in April 2017, Russian aircraft flew near the Alaskan coast in four separate incidents. In the first incident, two-F-22s and an E-3 AWAC intercepted two Russian Tu-95 bombers. The next day, two Tu-95 bombers were tracked by a U.S. AWACS while a Russian IL-38 flew into Alaska's Air Defense Identification Zone and then left. In the third incident, two IL-38s identified by NORAD and a maritime patrol flew halfway up the Aleutian Islands. In the final incident, two Russian Tu-95s flew near Alaska and Canada before being intercepted by U.S. F-22s and Canadian CF-18s.[212] Soon afterward, on May 3, U.S. F-22s intercepted two Russian Tu-95 bombers and Su-35 fighter escorts flying within 50 miles of Alaska. This was the first time since 2015 that Russian bombers had flown near the U.S. escorted by fighter jets.[213]

Russian flights have also targeted U.S. ally Japan. In April, three Russian Tu-95 Bear Bombers and an IL-20 surveillance aircraft flew within 36 miles of the Japanese coast, and 14 Japanese fighters were scrambled to intercept them.[214] A similar incident occurred in January when three Russian Bear bombers, three refueling IL-78 aircraft, and two radar and communications A-50 AWACS flew near Japan. The bombers flew around Japan, and the incident caused NORAD to increase its threat posture from 5 to 4.[215]

The main threat from Russian airspace incursions, however, remains near NATO territory in Eastern Europe, specifically the Black Sea and Baltic regions. In May 2017, a Russian

Su-27 flew within 20 feet of a U.S. P-8A plane flying in international airspace over the Black Sea.[216] In the Baltics, NATO aircraft intercepted Russian military aircraft 110 times in 2016, down from a high of 160 intercepts in 2015 but far above the 43 recorded in 2013; NATO officials believe the decrease in 2016 could be due to Russia's shifting resources to the Syrian theater.[217] In May 2017, a plane carrying Russian Foreign Minister Lavrov, flying without a filed flight plan and without establishing radio contact, briefly violated Estonian airspace, very likely to send a political message.

That the provocative and hazardous behavior of the Russian armed forces or Russian-sponsored groups poses a threat to civilian aircraft in Europe was demonstrated by the downing of Malaysia Airlines Flight MH17, killing all 283 passengers and 15 crewmembers, over the skies of southeastern Ukraine. In addition, there have been several incidents involving Russian military aircraft flying in Europe without using their transponders. In February 2015, for example, civilian aircraft in Ireland had to be diverted or were prevented from taking off when Russian bombers flying with their transponders turned off flew across civilian air lanes.[218] Similarly, in March 2014, an Scandinavian Airlines (SAS) plane almost collided with a Russian signals intelligence (SIGINT) plane, the two coming within 90 meters of each other.[219] In a December 2014 incident, a Cimber Airlines flight from Copenhagen to Poznan nearly collided with a Russian intelligence plane that was flying with its transponder turned off.[220]

WWTA: The WWTA does not specifically mention threats to sea-lanes or airspace, but it does emphasize global displacement as an ongoing challenge: "Europe and other host countries will face accommodation and integration challenges in 2017, and refugees and economic migrants will probably continue to seek to transit to Europe."[221]

Summary: Russia's violation of the sovereign airspace of NATO member states is a probing and antagonistic policy that is designed both to test the defense of the alliance and as practice for potential future conflicts.

Similarly, Russian antagonistic behavior in international waters is a threat to freedom of the seas. Russia's reckless aerial activity in the region remains a threat to civilian aircraft flying in European airspace.

Space. Admiral Cecil Haney, head of U.S. Strategic Command, said in March 2015 that "[t]he threat in space, I fundamentally believe, is a real one."[222] Russia's space capabilities are robust, but Moscow "has not recently demonstrated intent to direct malicious and destabilizing actions toward U.S. space assets."[223] However, Admiral Haney testified in March 2015 that "Russian leaders openly maintain that they possess anti-satellite weapons and conduct anti-satellite research."[224]

In December 2016, Russia carried out the fifth test of its PL-19 Nudol anti-satellite missile. In March 2016, Air Force Lieutenant General David J. Buck, Commander, Joint Functional Component Command for Space, stated that "Russia views U.S. dependency on space as an exploitable vulnerability, and [the Russians] are taking deliberate actions to strengthen their counter-space capabilities."[225] Air Force Lieutenant General John "Jay" Raymond, Commander, Air Force Space Command, has testified that Russia's anti-satellite capabilities have progressed to the extent that "we are quickly approaching the point where every satellite in every orbit can be threatened."[226]

WWTA: According to the WWTA, "Russian military strategists likely view counterspace weapons as an integral part of broader aerospace defense rearmament and are very likely pursuing a diverse suite of capabilities to affect satellites in all orbital regimes." In addition, "Russian lawmakers have promoted military pursuit of ASAT missiles to strike low-Earth orbiting satellites, and Russia is testing such a weapon for eventual deployment. A Russian official also acknowledged development of an aircraft-launched missile capable of destroying satellites in low-Earth orbit."[227] The assessment notes Russia's interest in electronic warfare for use against U.S. space systems and states that Russia "intends to modernize its EW forces and field a new generation of EW weapons by 2020."[228] Russia is also developing an airborne laser weapon and will "continue to conduct sophisticated on-orbit satellite activities, such as rendezvous and proximity operations, at least some of which are likely intended to test dual-use technologies with inherent counterspace functionality."[229]

Summary: Despite some interruption of cooperation in space because of Russia's invasion of Ukraine, cooperation on the International Space Station and commercial transactions involving space-related technology have continued unabated. Russia also continues the aggressive building out of its counterspace capabilities.

Cyber. Russian cyber capabilities are incredibly advanced. Over the past year, Russia engaged in high-profile cyber aggression targeted at Europe and the United States. Russian cyber-attacks and intrusions were a critical element in a larger effort to undermine Americans' confidence in their elections. A report released by the Office of the Director of National Intelligence in January 2017, which took into account assessments by the Central Intelligence Agency, Federal Bureau of Investigation, and National Security Agency, stated that "Russia's intelligence services conducted cyber operations against targets associated with the 2016 US presidential election, including targets associated with both major US political parties."[230] In addition, "We assess with high confidence that Russian military intelligence (General Staff Main Intelligence Directorate or GRU) used the Guccifer 2.0 persona and DCLeaks.com to release US victim data obtained in cyber operations publicly and in exclusives to media outlets and relayed material to WikiLeaks."[231] The Russian cyber operations also "accessed elements of multiple state or local electoral boards," but not systems involved in vote tallying.[232]

Russian hackers also targeted other democratic electoral or government systems, including in France, Germany, Italy, and the Netherlands, over the past year. Hans-Georg Maassen, President of Germany's Federal Office for the Protection of the Constitution, a domestic security agency, said that "large amounts of data" were stolen in cyber-attacks against the Bundestag in May 2015.[233] The theft, reportedly involving 16 gigabytes, has been attributed to Russia.[234] Germany's Parliament and political parties, among them Chancellor Angela Merkel's Christian Democratic Union, have been targeted in subsequent cyber-attacks,[235] including attempted attacks in January 2017.[236] Over the course of four months in 2016, Italy's foreign ministry was subjected to a Russian cyber-attack that involved non-encrypted communications.[237]

In March, the head of the Netherlands' General Intelligence and Security Service, Rob Bertholee, stated that Russian hackers had tried to gain access to more than 100 Dutch government e-mail accounts. Russia is widely believed to be behind a May cyber-attack against then-candidate for the French presidency Emmanuel Macron. E-mails and documents stolen in the attacks were released along with a mix of fake documents.[238] National Security Agency Director Admiral Mike Rogers testified in May that the U.S. warned French authorities about the cyber-attacks: "[W]e gave them a heads up: 'Look, we are watching the Russians. We are seeing them penetrate some of your infrastructure. Here's what we've seen.... [W]hat can we do to assist?"[239] Frequent cyber-attacks against French defense targets included 24,000 attacks in 2016, according to French Defense Minister Jean-Yves Le Drian.[240]

U.S. defense targets are also in the sights of Russian hackers, who reportedly sought to hack into the Twitter accounts of more than 10,000 people working at the Pentagon.[241] NATO is another frequent target, with Russian cyber-attacks up 60 percent in 2016 over the previous year.[242]

Nor do Russian cyber-attacks focus solely on government targets. In May 2017, Ukrainian authorities closed two Russian social media platforms, citing concerns that they were being used for cyber-attacks.[243] A sophisticated Russian cyber-attack on Ukrainian power companies in December 2015 resulted in power outages that affected 225,000 Ukrainians for several hours. The cyber-attack has been linked to a Russian-based hacking group.[244] Subsequent investigations by Ukrainian and U.S. cyber officials found that it was "synchronized and coordinated, probably following extensive reconnaissance," and that efforts were taken to "attempt to interfere with expected restoration efforts."[245] A year later, in December 2016, a new cyber-attack against Ukraine's electricity grid left 100,000–200,000 people without power.[246] In February, the former U.S. Deputy Secretary of Energy stated that she believed Russia was behind the 2016 attack.[247] The Ukrainian attacks represent an escalation, moving beyond crippling communications or mere infiltration of critical systems to taking down critical infrastructure with widespread physical effects.

In the Baltic theater, Russian hackers have launched multiple cyber-attacks against the energy infrastructure of the Baltic States, including two attacks against the electricity grid, as well as attacks targeting a gas distribution system.[248] In early 2016, the U.S. Defense Intelligence Agency warned that Russian hackers using software from Russian-origin companies could gain access to industrial systems in the U.S., including electrical and water systems.[249] Russia is also thought to be behind five days of cyber-attacks against Sweden's Air Traffic Control system in November 2015, which led to flight delays and groundings.[250] Swedish authorities reportedly believe that the attack was the work of Russian military intelligence, the GRU.[251]

The Russian hacking group APT28 or Fancy Bear, believed to be linked to Russia's GRU military intelligence, is believed to have hacked Denmark's Defence Ministry across 2015 and 2016 and to have gained access to nonclassified information.[252] The group is also thought to be responsible for cyber-attacks against the Democratic National Committee in the United States and the French TV station TV5Monde, which was taken off the air following an April 2015 cyber-attack.[253] General Yuri Baluyevsky, former chief of Russia's General Staff, has characterized Russia's use of cyber-attacks as "much more important than victory in a classical military conflict, because it is bloodless, yet the impact is overwhelming and can paralyze all of the enemy state's power structures."[254]

Russia continues to use allied criminal organizations (so-called patriotic hackers) to help it engage in cyber aggression. Cyber-attacks against Estonia in 2007 and Georgia in 2008 and the December 2015 attack against Ukraine's power grid were conducted by these "patriotic hackers" and likely coordinated or sponsored by Russian security forces.[255] Using these hackers gives the Russians greater resources and can help to shield their true capabilities. Patriotic hackers also give the Russian government deniability. In June, for example, Putin stated that "[i]f they (hackers) are patriotically-minded, they start to make their own contribution to what they believe is the good fight against those who speak badly about Russia. Is that possible? Theoretically it is possible."[256]

WWTA: The WWTA states that "Russia is a full-scope cyber actor that will remain a major threat to US Government, military, diplomatic, commercial, and critical infrastructure. Moscow has a highly advanced offensive cyber program, and in recent years, the Kremlin has assumed a more aggressive cyber posture." This aggressive posture "was evident in Russia's efforts to influence the 2016 US election, and we assess that only Russia's senior-most officials could have authorized the 2016 US election-focused data thefts and disclosures, based on the scope and sensitivity of the targets." Russian actors also "have conducted damaging and disruptive cyber attacks" outside the United States, "including on critical infrastructure networks," and in some cases "have masqueraded as third parties, hiding behind false online personas designed to cause the victim to misattribute the source of the attack. Russia has also leveraged cyberspace to seek to influence public opinion across Europe and Eurasia." The WWTA concludes "that Russian cyber operations will continue to target the United States and its allies to gather intelligence, support Russian decision making, conduct influence operations to support Russian military and political objectives, and prepare the cyber environment for future contingencies."[257]

Summary: Russia's cyber capabilities are advanced and are a key tool in realizing the state's strategic aims. Russia has used cyber-attacks to further the reach and effectiveness of its propaganda and disinformation campaigns, and its recent cyber-attacks against election processes in the U.S. and European countries have been designed to undermine citizens' belief in the veracity of electoral outcomes and erode support for democratic institutions in the longer term. Russia also has used cyber-attacks to target physical infrastructure, including electrical grids, air traffic control, and gas distribution systems. Russia's increasingly bold use of cyber capabilities, coupled with their sophistication and Moscow's willingness to use them aggressively, presents a challenge for the U.S. and its interests abroad.

Conclusion

Overall, the threat to the U.S. homeland originating from Europe remains low, but the threat to American interests and allies in the region remains significant. Behind this threat lies Russia. Although Russia has the military capability to harm and (in the case of its nuclear arsenal) to pose an existential threat to the U.S., it has not conclusively demonstrated the intent to do so.

The situation is different when it comes to America's allies in the region. Through NATO, the U.S. is obliged by treaty to come to the aid of the alliance's European members. Russia continues to seek to undermine the NATO alliance and presents an existential threat to U.S. allies in Eastern Europe. NATO has been the cornerstone of European security and stability since its creation in 1949, and it is in America's interest to ensure that it maintains both the military capability and political will to fulfill its treaty obligations.

While Russia is not the threat to U.S. global interests that the Soviet Union was during the Cold War, it does pose challenges to a range of America's interests and those of its allies and friends closest to Russia's borders. Russia possesses a full range of capabilities from ground forces to air, naval, space, and cyber. It still maintains the world's largest nuclear arsenal, and although a strike on the U.S. is highly unlikely, the latent potential for such a strike still gives these weapons enough strategic value vis-à-vis America's NATO allies and interests in Europe to keep them relevant.

Russian provocations far below any scenario involving a nuclear exchange pose the most serious challenge to American interests, particularly in Central and Eastern Europe, the Arctic, the Balkans, and the South Caucasus. It is with respect to these contingencies that Russia's military capabilities are most relevant.

Threat Scores by Country

Russia. Russia seeks to maximize its strategic position in the world at the expense of the United States. It also seeks to undermine U.S. influence and moral standing, harasses U.S. and NATO forces, and is working to sabotage U.S. and Western policy in Syria. In addition, Russia has sought to increase its influence in the Western Balkans while maintaining robust information warfare and propaganda campaigns across Europe and even in the U.S. Moscow's continued aggression and willingness to use every tool at its disposal in pursuit of its aims leads this *Index* to assess the overall threat from Russia as "aggressive" and "formidable." This level is consistent with the threat assessment of Russia in the *2017 Index.*

Threats: Russia

	HOSTILE	AGGRESSIVE	TESTING	ASSERTIVE	BENIGN
Behavior		✓			

	FORMIDABLE	GATHERING	CAPABLE	ASPIRATIONAL	MARGINAL
Capability	✓				

Endnotes

1. International Institute for Strategic Studies, *The Military Balance 2017*: *The Annual Assessment of Global Military Capabilities and Defence Economics* (London: Routledge, 2017) pp. 210–224.

2. Pavel Felgenhauer, "Private Military Companies Forming Vanguard of Russian Foreign Operations," Jamestown Foundation, *Eurasia Daily Monitor*, Vol. 14, Issue 36 (March 16, 2017), https://jamestown.org/program/private-military-companies-forming-vanguard-russian-foreign-operations/ (accessed July 17, 2017).

3. International Institute for Strategic Studies, *The Military Balance 2017*, p. 186.

4. Radio Free Europe/Radio Liberty, "Putin Creates National Guard Force," July 4, 2016, https://www.rferl.org/a/putin-national-guard-dissent-riots/27836301.html (accessed July 10, 2017).

5. International Institute for Strategic Studies, *The Military Balance 2017*, p. 186.

6. Alanna Petroff, "Russia's Economy Is Recovering Well," CNN, May 19, 2017, http://money.cnn.com/2017/05/19/news/economy/russia-economy-imf/ (accessed July 17, 2017).

7. Julian Cooper, *Russia's State Armament Programme to 2020: A Quantitative Assessment of Implementation 2011–2015*, Swedish Defence Research Agency, FOI-R-4239-SE, March 2016, p. 35, https://www.researchgate.net/publication/299338379_Russia%27s_state_armament_programme_to_2020_a_quantitative_assessment_of_implementation_2011-2015_FOI_Report (accessed July 17, 2017).

8. Craig Caffrey, "Russia Announces Deepest Defence Budget Cuts Since 1990s," *Jane's 360*, March 16, 2017, http://www.janes.com/article/68766/russia-announces-deepest-defence-budget-cuts-since-1990s (accessed July 17, 2017).

9. Lucie Béraud-Sudreau and Douglas Barrie, "Russia's Defence Spending: The Impact of Economic Contraction," International Institute for Strategic Studies *Military Balance Blog*, March 6, 2017, http://www.iiss.org/en/militarybalanceblog/blogsections/2017-edcc/march-f0a5/russias-defence-spending-7de6 (accessed July 10, 2017).

10. Ibid.

11. Claire Mills, "Russia's Rearmament Programme," House of Commons Library *Briefing Paper* No. 7877, January 24, 2017, p. 6, http://researchbriefings.parliament.uk/ResearchBriefing/Summary/CBP-7877#fullreport (accessed July 17, 2017).

12. International Institute for Strategic Studies, *The Military Balance 2017*, p. 191.

13. David Lawler, "Russia Unveils 'Satan 2' Missile Powerful Enough to 'Wipe Out UK, France or Texas,'" *The Telegraph*, October 25, 2016, http://www.telegraph.co.uk/news/2016/10/25/russia-unveils-satan-2-missile-powerful-enough-to-wipe-out-uk-fr/ (accessed July 17, 2017).

14. International Institute for Strategic Studies, *The Military Balance 2017*, p. 159.

15. Nikolai Novichkov, "State Armament Programme for 2018–2025 to Beef Up Combat Capabilities of Russian Armed Forces," *Jane's 360*, May 19, 2017, http://www.janes.com/article/70599/state-armament-programme-for-2018-2025-to-beef-up-combat-capabilities-of-russian-armed-forces (accessed July 10, 2017).

16. Thomas Nilsen, "Russian Navy Upgrades Multi-Purpose Submarines," *The Independent Barents Observer*, March 20, 2017, https://thebarentsobserver.com/en/security/2017/03/russian-navy-upgrades-multi-purpose-submarines (accessed July 10, 2017).

17. Mills, "Russia's Rearmament Programme," p. 6. Punctuation as in original.

18. Franz-Stefan Gady, "Russia's New Stealth Frigate to Be Commissioned in November 2017," *The Diplomat*, May 18, 2017, http://thediplomat.com/2017/05/russias-new-stealth-frigate-to-be-commissioned-in-november-2017/ (accessed July 10, 2017).

19. Ibid.

20. Magnus Nordenman, "The Russian Challenge in the Arctic Isn't About Icebreakers [Commentary]," *Defense News*, February 24, 2017, http://www.defensenews.com/articles/the-russian-challenge-in-the-arctic-isnt-about-icebreakers-commentary (accessed July 10, 2017).

21. Thomas Nilsen, "Two Nuclear Submarines from Kola Sail into Mediterranean," *The Independent Barents Observer*, October 30, 2016, https://thebarentsobserver.com/en/security/2016/10/two-nuclear-submarines-kola-sails-mediterranean (accessed July 10, 2017).

22. Reuters, "Russia Expands Military Transport Fleet to Move Troops Long Distances," March 7, 2017, http://www.reuters.com/article/russia-navy-expansion-idUSL5N1GK470 (accessed July 10, 2017).

23. Roger McDermott, "Russia's State Armaments Program to 2025 Promises High-Technology Procurement," Jamestown Foundation, *Eurasia Daily Monitor*, Vol. 14, Issue 34 (March 14, 2017), https://jamestown.org/program/russias-state-armaments-program-2025-promises-high-technology-procurement/ (accessed July 17, 2017).

24. Ibid.

25. Matthew Bodner, "Russia's Putin Drafts New Rearmament Program," *Defense News*, May 26, 2017, http://www.defensenews.com/articles/russias-putin-drafts-new-rearmament-program (accessed July 10, 2017).

26. Colonel Tomasz K. Kowalik and Dominik P. Janikowski, "The Dangerous Tool of Russian Military Exercises," Center for European Policy Analysis, May 9, 2017, http://cepa.org/EuropesEdge/The-dangerous-tool-of-Russian-military-exercises (accessed July 10, 2017).

27. Damien Sharkov, "Putin Calls 45,000 Troops to Snap Air Drill," *Newsweek*, February 8, 2017, http://www.newsweek.com/putin-called-45000-troops-snap-air-drill-554312 (accessed July 10, 2017).

28. U.S. Strategic Command, "Remarks by Gen. Curtis M. Scaparrotti at the 2016 Deterrence Symposium," La Vista, Nebraska, July 27, 2016, http://www.stratcom.mil/Media/Speeches/Article/986470/2016-deterrence-symposium/ (accessed July 17, 2017).

29. International Institute for Strategic Studies, *The Military Balance 2017*, p. 187.

30. Ibid.

31. Julian E. Barnes, "Planned Russian Exercises in September Sow NATO Worries," *The Wall Street Journal*, updated March 28, 2017, https://www.wsj.com/articles/planned-russian-exercises-in-september-sow-nato-worries-1490715830 (accessed July 17, 2017).

32. Piotr Kosiński, "Russia Rolls Out New Disinformation on Zapad," Center for European Security Analysis *Brief*, March 20, 2017, http://infowar.cepa.org/Briefs/Bl_20_March17 (accessed July 10, 2017).

33. Ihor Kabanenko, "Rekindled Train Wagon Debate Calls into Question Planned Size for 'Zapad 2017' Exercise," Jamestown Foundation, *Eurasia Daily Monitor*, Vol. 14, Issue 22 (February 22, 2017), https://jamestown.org/program/rekindled-train-wagon-debate-calls-question-planned-size-zapad-2017-exercise/ (accessed July 17, 2017).

34. Ibid.

35. Robin Emmott, "Estonia Says Russia May Put Troops in Belarus to Challenge NATO," *U.S. News & World Report*, April 27, 2017, https://www.usnews.com/news/world/articles/2017-04-27/estonia-says-russia-may-put-troops-in-belarus-to-challenge-nato (accessed July 11, 2017).

36. Barnes, "Planned Russian Exercises in September Sow NATO Worries."

37. See, for example, Damien Sharkov, "Russia Has Threatened Nuclear Attack, Says Ukraine Defence Minister," *Newsweek*, September 1, 2014, http://www.newsweek.com/russia-has-threatened-nuclear-attack-says-ukraine-defence-minister-267842 (accessed July 11, 2017).

38. Vladimir Putin, "On the Russian Federation's National Security Strategy," Presidential Edict 683, December 31, 2015, http://www.ieee.es/Galerias/fichero/OtrasPublicaciones/Internacional/2016/Russian-National-Security-Strategy-31Dec2015.pdf (accessed July 11, 2017).

39. Ibid.

40. Pavel Podvig, "New Version of the Military Doctrine," *Russian Strategic Nuclear Forces* blog, December 26, 2014, http://russianforces.org/blog/2014/12/new_version_of_the_military_do.shtml (accessed July 17, 2017).

41. Ibid.

42. Tom O'Connor, "Russia Conflict with NATO and U.S. Would Immediately Result in Nuclear War, Russian Lawmaker Warns," *Newsweek*, May 30, 2017, http://www.newsweek.com/russia-politician-nuclear-weapons-us-nato-crimea-617613 (accessed July 11, 2017).

43. General Curtis M. Scaparrotti, Commander, United States European Command, statement before the Committee on Armed Services, U.S. Senate, March 23, 2017, p. 5, https://www.appropriations.senate.gov/imo/media/doc/050217-Scaparrotti-Testimony.pdf (accessed July 17, 2017). Cited hereafter as Scaparrotti, "2107 EUCOM Posture Statement." (Note: This statement follows a brief "Resource Requirements" addendum to General Scaparrotti's statement before the Subcommittee on Military Construction, Veterans Affairs, and Related Agencies of the Committee on Appropriations, U.S. Senate, May 2, 2017.)

44. Kyle Mizokami, "All Aboard Russia's Nuclear Weapon Apocalypse Train," *Popular Mechanics*, February 27, 2017, http://www.popularmechanics.com/military/weapons/a25423/all-aboard-russias-apocalypse-train/ (accessed July 11, 2017).

45. Mikhail Barabanov, Konstantin Makienko, and Ruslan Pukhov, "Military Reform: Toward the New Look of the Russian Army," Valdai Discussion Club *Analytical Report*, July 2012, p. 14, http://vid1.rian.ru/ig/valdai/Military_reform_eng.pdf (accessed July 11, 2017).

46. Barry D. Watts, *Nuclear-Conventional Firebreaks and the Nuclear Taboo*, Center for Strategic and Budgetary Assessments, 2013, http://csbaonline.org/publications/2013/04/nuclear-conventional-firebreaks-and-the-nuclear-taboo/ (accessed July 11, 2017).

47. Shaun Waterman, "Russia Threatens to Strike NATO Missile Defense Sites," *The Washington Times*, May 3, 2012, http://www.washingtontimes.com/news/2012/may/3/russia-threatens-strike-nato-missile-defense-sites/?page=all (accessed July 11, 2017).

48. Michael R. Gordon, "U.S. Says Russia Tested Missile, Despite Treaty," *The New York Times*, January 29, 2014, http://www.nytimes.com/2014/01/30/world/europe/us-says-russia-tested-missile-despite-treaty.html (accessed July 11, 2017).

49. Michael R. Gordon, "Russia Deploys Missile, Violating Treaty and Challenging Trump," *The New York Times*, February 14, 2017, https://www.nytimes.com/2017/02/14/world/europe/russia-cruise-missile-arms-control-treaty.html?_r=1 (accessed May 23, 2017).

50. Michael R. Gordon, "Russia Has Deployed Missiles Barred by Treaty, U.S. General Tells Congress," *The New York Times*, March 8, 2017, https://www.nytimes.com/2017/03/08/us/politics/russia-inf-missile-treaty.html?smid=tw-nytimesworld&smtyp=cur (accessed July 13, 2017).

51. Daniel R. Coats, Director of National Intelligence, "Statement for the Record: Worldwide Threat Assessment of the US Intelligence Community," Select Committee on Intelligence, U.S. Senate, May 11, 2017, p. 6, https://www.dni.gov/files/documents/Newsroom/Testimonies/SSCI%20Unclassified%20SFR%20-%20Final.pdf (accessed July 15, 2017). Cited hereafter as Coats, "2017 Worldwide Threat Assessment."

52. News release, "Russian Banker Sentenced in Connection with Conspiracy to Work for Russian Intelligence," U.S. Department of Justice, May 25, 2016, https://www.justice.gov/opa/pr/russian-banker-sentenced-connection-conspiracy-work-russian-intelligence (accessed July 13, 2017).

53. Ali Watkins, "Russia Escalates Spy Games After Years of U.S. Neglect," *Politico*, June 1, 2017, http://www.politico.com/story/2017/06/01/russia-spies-espionage-trump-239003 (accessed July 13, 2017).

54. BBC, "US Charges Russian Spies over Yahoo Breach," March 15, 2017, http://www.bbc.com/news/technology-39281063 (accessed July 13, 2017).

55. Katie Bo Williams, "US Sanctions Russia over Hacking, Expels 35 Officials," *The Hill*, December 29, 2016, http://thehill.com/policy/national-security/312119-us-announces-sanctions-on-russia (accessed July 13, 2017).

56. Cristina Silva, "New Cold War: Is Russia Spying on the U.S. from a Nicaragua Military Compound?" *Newsweek*, May 22, 2017, http://www.newsweek.com/new-cold-war-russia-spying-us-nicaragua-military-compound-613427 (accessed July 13, 2017).

57. Republic of Latvia, State Security Department and Ministry of National Defence, Second Investigation Department, *National Security Threat Assessment*, 2017, p. 7, https://www.vsd.lt/wp-content/uploads/2017/03/AKATSKT_DRAFT-3-31-EN-HQ.pdf (accessed July 17, 2017).

58. Kathrin Hille, Neil Buckley, Courtney Weaver, and Guy Chazan, "Vladimir Putin Signs Treaty to Annex Crimea," *Financial Times*, March 18, 2014, http://www.ft.com/cms/s/0/d93e4c7c-ae6d-11e3-8e41-00144feab7de.html (accessed July 13, 2017).

59. Janusz Bugajski and Peter B. Doran, "BLACK SEA RISING: Russia's Strategy in Southeast Europe," Center for European Policy Analysis *Black Sea Strategic Report* No. 1, February 2016, p. 8, http://cepa.org/files/?id_plik=2096 (accessed July 13, 2017).

60. David Choi, "'Putin's Bridge' Connecting Russia to Crimea Might Be Having Issues," *Business Insider*, September 26, 2016, http://www.businessinsider.com/putins-bridge-russia-crimea-problems-2016-9 (accessed July 13, 2017).

61. Halya Coynash, "Putin's Bridge to Crimea Is Doomed to Collapse," *Newsweek*, January 13, 2017, http://www.newsweek.com/putin-bridge-crimea-doomed-collapse-541578 (accessed July 13, 2017).

62. International Institute for Strategic Studies, *The Military Balance 2017*, p. 224; Reuters, "In Crimea, Russia Signals Military Resolve with New and Revamped Bases," November 1, 2016, http://www.reuters.com/investigates/special-report/russia-crimea/ (accessed July 13, 2017).

63. Bugajski and Doran, "BLACK SEA RISING: Russia's Strategy in Southeast Europe," p. 3.

64. Sam Jones and Kathrin Hille, "Russia's Military Ambitions Make Waves in the Black Sea," *Financial Times*, May 13, 2016, https://next.ft.com/content/1b9c24d8-1819-11e6-b197-a4af20d5575e (accessed July 13, 2017); Radio Free Europe/Radio Liberty, "Russia Adds Cruise-Missile Ships to Black Sea Force," December 12, 2015, http://www.rferl.org/content/russia-black-sea-fleet-cruise-missile-ships/27422679.html (accessed July 13, 2017).

65. "Russia: SSGN Severodvinsk to Get Caliber Cruise Missiles," *Naval Today*, August 16, 2012, http://navaltoday.com/2012/08/16/russia-ssgn-severodvinsk-to-get-caliber-cruise-missiles/ (accessed July 13, 2017); Jones and Hille, "Russia's Military Ambitions Make Waves in the Black Sea."

66. Reuters, "Russia Deploys Advanced S-400 Air Missile System to Crimea: Agencies," August 12, 2016, http://www.reuters.com/article/us-ukraine-crisis-crimea-missiles-idUSKCN10N1H4 (accessed July 17, 2017); Sebastien Roblin, "Syria and the S-400: The Most Dangerous Game of Cat and Mouse on Earth," *The National Interest*, April 15, 2017, http://nationalinterest.org/blog/the-buzz/syria-the-s-400-the-most-dangerous-game-cat-mouse-earth-20200 (accessed July 17, 2017).

67. Meetings coverage, "Situation in Eastern Ukraine Remains 'Tense and Volatile' Despite Post-Ceasefire Reduction in Fighting, Security Council Told During Briefing," U.N. Security Council, December 11, 2015, https://www.un.org/press/en/2015/sc12154.doc.htm (accessed July 14, 2017).

68. Nolan Peterson, "Paris and Washington Send a Message to Moscow: No Sanctions Relief Until Russian Troops Leave Ukraine," The Daily Signal, May 12, 2017, http://dailysignal.com/2017/05/12/paris-and-washington-send-a-message-to-moscow-no-sanctions-relief-until-russian-troops-leave-ukraine/.

69. Christian Borys, "Everything Is Destroyed: A Deadly Surge of Violence Strikes Eastern Ukraine," The Washington Post, February 3, 2017, https://www.washingtonpost.com/world/europe/an-on-the-ground-look-at-the-deadly-surge-of-violence-in-eastern-ukraine/2017/02/03/29d1c37c-ea1a-11e6-903d-9b11ed7d8d2a_story.html?utm_term=.dd277190ce10 (accessed July 14, 2017).

70. Christopher Miller, "'Our Tanks Are Ready': Ukraine Braces for Escalation in Easter War," Radio Free Europe / Radio Liberty, February 3, 2017, https://www.rferl.org/a/ukraine-avdiyivka-fighting-escalation/28276963.html (accessed July 17, 2017).

71. Scaparrotti, "2017 EUCOM Posture Statement," p. 8.

72. Natalia Zinets, "Ukraine Charges Russia with New Cyber Attacks on Infrastructure," Reuters, February 15, 2017, http://www.reuters.com/article/us-ukraine-crisis-cyber-idUSKBN15U2CN (accessed July 17, 2017).

73. Reuters, "Ukraine Catches Russian Spy," October 10, 2016, http://www.skynews.com.au/news/world/europe/2016/10/10/ukraine-catches-russian-spy.html (accessed July 17, 2017).

74. Scaparrotti, "2017 EUCOM Posture Statement," pp. 5–6.

75. Brendan Cole, "Russia Will Keep Nuclear-Armed Missiles on NATO Border to Counter 'Alliance Expansion,'" International Business Times, November 22, 2016, http://www.ibtimes.co.uk/russia-will-keep-nuclear-armed-missiles-nato-border-counter-alliances-expansion-1592733 (accessed July 14, 2017).

76. Michael Krepon and Joe Kendall, "Beef Up Conventional Forces; Don't Worry About a Tactical Nuke Gap," Breaking Defense, March 28, 2016, http://breakingdefense.com/2016/03/beef-up-conventional-forces-dont-worry-about-a-tactical-nuke-gap/ (accessed July 14, 2017).

77. Kalev Stoicescu and Henrik Praks, "Strengthening the Strategic Balance in the Baltic Sea Area," International Centre for Defence and Security Report, March 2016, p. 14, https://www.icds.ee/fileadmin/media/icds.ee/failid/Kalev_Stoicescu__Henrik_Praks_-_Strengthening_the_Strategic_Balance_in_the_Baltic_Sea_Area.pdf (accessed July 17, 2017).

78. Damien Sharkov, "Russian Military Asks Weapons Makers to Extend Range and Precision of Nuclear-Capable Iskander Missiles," Newsweek, May 19, 2017, http://www.newsweek.com/russia-military-weapons-maker-nato-arms-missiles-iskander-nuclear-capable-612409 (accessed July 14, 2017).

79. Radio Free Europe/Radio Liberty, "Russia Deploys Coastal Missile Systems on Disputed Kurile Islands," November 22, 2016, https://www.rferl.org/a/russia-deploys-coastal-missile-systems-on-disputed-kurile-islands/28133041.html (accessed July 17, 2017).

80. Roland Oliphant, "British Troops Arrive in Estonia as German Spy Chief Warns of Russian Troop Build Up," The Telegraph, March 18, 2017, http://www.telegraph.co.uk/news/2017/03/18/british-troops-arrive-estonia-german-spy-chief-warns-russian/ (accessed July 14, 2017).

81. TASS Russian News Agency, "Russia's Western Military District to Get Four S-400 Missile Systems This Year," January 13, 2017, http://tass.com/defense/924840 (accessed July 17, 2017).

82. Radio Free Europe/Radio Liberty, "Russia to Create New Military Divisions in Response to NATO," January 22, 2016, http://www.rferl.org/content/russia-new-military-divisions-nato/27503176.html (accessed June 27, 2016).

83. Keir Giles, "Assessing Russia's Reorganized and Rearmed Military," Carnegie Endowment for International Peace, Task Force on U.S. Policy Toward Russia, Ukraine, and Eurasia, May 3, 2017, p. 9, http://carnegieendowment.org/files/5.4.2017_Keir_Giles_RussiaMilitary.pdf (accessed July 14, 2017).

84. Coats, "2017 Worldwide Threat Assessment," p. 18.

85. Thomas Nilsen, "FSB Gets Right to Confiscate Land from People," The Independent Barents Observer, May 16, 2017, https://thebarentsobserver.com/en/security/2017/05/fsb-gets-right-confiscate-land-people#.WR3YvGBXtZy.twitter (accessed July 14, 2017).

86. Nikolai Novichkov, "Pantsir-SA Firing Tests to Start in June," Jane's 360, May 10, 2017, http://www.janes.com/article/70235/pantsir-sa-firing-tests-to-start-in-june (accessed July 14, 2017).

87. Dave Majumdar, "Russia to Standup New Arctic Command," USNI News, February 18, 2014, http://news.usni.org/2014/02/18/russia-standup-new-arctic-command (accessed July 14, 2017).

88. Reuters, "Putin Instigating Biggest Russian Arctic Military Buildup Since Soviet Fall," The Japan Times, January 31, 2017, http://www.japantimes.co.jp/news/2017/01/31/world/putin-instigating-biggest-russian-arctic-military-buildup-since-soviet-fall/#.WSMOIoWcHcs (accessed July 14, 2017).

89. MarEx, "New Forces to Guard Northern Sea Route," *The Maritime Executive*, January 20, 2017, http://www.maritime-executive.com/article/new-forces-to-guard-northern-sea-route (accessed July 14, 2017).

90. Elizabeth McLaughlin, "The Race for the Arctic: As New Frontier Opens, Russia Leaves US in Its Wake," ABC News, May 10, 2017, http://abcnews.go.com/International/race-arctic-frontier-opens-russia-leaves-us-wake/story?id=47304875 (accessed July 14, 2017).

91. Andrew Osborn, "Putin's Russia in Biggest Arctic Military Push Since Soviet Fall," Reuters, January 30, 2017, http://mobile.reuters.com/article/idUSKBN15E0W0 (accessed July 14, 2017).

92. Trude Pettersen, "Russia Re-opens Arctic Cold War Era Air Base," *Barents Observer*, October 30, 2013, http://barentsobserver.com/en/security/2013/10/russia-re-opens-arctic-cold-war-era-air-base-30-10 (accessed July 14, 2017).

93. Osborn, "Putin's Russia in Biggest Arctic Military Push Since Soviet Fall."

94. Robbie Gramer, "Here's What Russia's Military Build-Up in the Arctic Looks Like," *Foreign Policy*, January 25, 2017, http://foreignpolicy.com/2017/01/25/heres-what-russias-military-build-up-in-the-arctic-looks-like-trump-oil-military-high-north-infographic-map/?utm_content=buffer12641&utm_medium=social&utm_source=twitter.com&utm_campaign=buffer (accessed June 2, 2017).

95. Trude Pettersen, "Northern Fleet Gets Own Air Force, Air Defense Forces," *The Independent Barents Observer*, February 1, 2016, https://thebarentsobserver.com/en/security/2016/02/northern-fleet-gets-own-air-force-air-defense-forces (accessed July 14, 2017).

96. RIA Novosti, "Russian Commandos Train for Arctic Combat," Sputnik, October 14, 2013, https://sputniknews.com/military/20131014/184143129/Russian-Commandos-Train-for-Arctic-Combat.html (accessed July 14, 2017).

97. Stephen Blank, "Russia's New Arctic Base Continue[s] the Militarization of the High North," Jamestown Foundation, *Eurasia Daily Monitor*, Vol. 12, Issue 202 (November 6, 2015), http://www.jamestown.org/single/?tx_ttnews%5Btt_news%5D=44572&no_cache=1#.VxqCwfkrJph (accessed July 14, 2017).

98. Osborn, "Putin's Russia in Biggest Arctic Military Push Since Soviet Fall."

99. Richard R. Burgess, "Russia Developing Missile-Armed Icebreakers, Coast Guard Commandant Says," *Seapower*, May 3, 2017, http://seapowermagazine.org/stories/20170503-Russia.html (accessed July 14, 2017).

100. Sputnik, "Russia to Convert Belgorod Submarine for Special Missions," February 9, 2012, https://sputniknews.com/military/20120209171227695/ (accessed July 14, 2017).

101. Sputnik, "Russian Navy to Receive Biggest and Most Unique Nuclear Submarine in the World," April 23, 2017, https://sputniknews.com/military/201704231052905471-russia-navy-biggest-sub/ (accessed July 14, 2017).

102. Daniel Brown, "Russia's NATO Northern Fleet Beefs Up Its Nuclear Capabilities to Phase 'NATO Out of Arctic,'" *Business Insider*, June 1, 2017, http://www.businessinsider.com/russias-northern-fleet-beefs-up-its-nuclear-capabilities-phase-nato-out-arctic-2017-6 (accessed July 14, 2017).

103. Agence France-Presse, "Russia Revises Navy Doctrine," *Defense News*, July 26, 2015, http://www.defensenews.com/story/defense/international/europe/2015/07/26/russia-revises-navy-doctrine/30705553 (accessed July 14, 2017).

104. Russian Times, "Submerged Russian Nuclear Sub Fires Kalibr Cruise Missile in Arctic Drills," April 30, 2016, https://www.rt.com/news/341440-kalibr-submarine-drills-arctic/ (accessed June 27, 2016).

105. Trude Pettersen, "Russian Military Instructors Plan to Land on Svalbard," *The Independent Barents Observer*, April 7, 2016, https://thebarentsobserver.com/en/security/2016/04/russian-military-instructors-plan-land-svalbard (accessed June 30, 2016).

106. Samia Madwar, "Ice Cracks and Tensions Rise at a North Pole Camp," Arctic Deeply, July 14, 2016, https://www.newsdeeply.com/arctic/articles/2016/07/14/ice-cracks-and-tensions-rise-at-a-north-pole-camp (accessed July 17, 2017).

107. Coats, "2017 Worldwide Threat Assessment," p. 13.

108. Scaparrotti, "2017 EUCOM Posture Statement," p. 2.

109. Russian Federation, Ministry of Foreign Affairs, *Foreign Policy Concept of the Russian Federation (Approved by President of the Russian Federation Vladimir Putin on November 30, 2016)*, December 1, 2016, http://www.mid.ru/en/foreign_policy/official_documents/-/asset_publisher/CptICkB6BZ29/content/id/2542248 (accessed July 14, 2017).

110. Reporters Without Borders, *2017 World Press Freedom Index: Russia*, https://rsf.org/en/russia (accessed July 14, 2017).

111. Ibid.

112. Alexander Zemlianichenko, "Kremlin Reportedly Considers Overhauling State TV to Compete Better Against the Internet," *The Moscow Times*, April 5, 2017, https://themoscowtimes.com/news/kremlin-reportedly-considers-overhauling-state-tv-to-compete-better-against-the-internet-57646 (accessed July 14, 2017).

113. Andrew Higgins and Andrew E. Kramer, "In Protests, Kremlin Fears a Young Generation Stirring," *The New York Times*, March 27, 2017, https://www.nytimes.com/2017/03/27/world/europe/in-protests-kremlin-fears-a-young-generation-stirring.html (accessed July 14, 2017).

114. UAWire, "Russia Allocated Nearly $1 Billion for Propaganda in 2016," August 4, 2016, http://www.uawire.org/news/russia-allocated-nearly-1-billion-on-propaganda-in-2016# (accessed July 17, 2017).

115. Fred Weir, "Inside the Belly of Russia's 'Propaganda Machine': A Visit to RT News Channel," *The Christian Science Monitor*, January 17, 2017, http://www.csmonitor.com/World/Europe/2017/0117/Inside-the-belly-of-Russia-s-propaganda-machine-A-visit-to-RT-news-channel (accessed July 14, 2017).

116. Maxim Stulov, "RT Gets 1.22 Bln Rubles to Start French Channel," December 8, 2016, https://themoscowtimes.com/news/rt-gets-122-bln-rubles-to-start-french-channel-56468?utm_source=newsletter&utm_medium=email&utm_campaign=kremlin_watch_monitor&utm_term=2016-12-12 (accessed July 14, 2017).

117. General Philip Breedlove, Commander, U.S. Forces Europe, statement before the Committee on Armed Services, U.S. Senate, March 1, 2016, p. 12, https://www.armed-services.senate.gov/imo/media/doc/Breedlove_03-01-16.pdf, p. 12 (accessed July 17, 2017).

118. Reuters, "Britain Says Russia Is Trying to Undermine West by 'Weaponizing Information,'" February 3, 2017, http://mobile.reuters.com/article/idUSKBN15I0U0?feedType=RSS&feedName=worldNews&rpc=69 (accessed July 14, 2017).

119. Djurdja Jovanovic Padejski, "Russian Disinformation Campaign in Ukraine," Stanford University, Freeman Spogli Institute for International Studies, June 29, 2017, https://fsi.stanford.edu/news/russian-disinformation-campaign-ukraine (accessed July 17, 2017).

120. "Russia Today Tells the 'Untold Story' of MH-17—But Other Kremlin Propaganda Already Debunked the Theory," *Business Insider*, October 26, 2014, http://www.businessinsider.com/rt-mh-17-propaganda-2014-10 (accessed July 17, 2017).

121. Olga Khazan, "Russia's Online-Comment Propaganda Army," *The Atlantic*, October 9, 2013, http://www.theatlantic.com/international/archive/2013/10/russias-online-comment-propaganda-army/280432/ (accessed July 14, 2017).

122. Shaun Walker, "Salutin' Putin: Inside a Russian Troll House," *The Guardian*, April 2, 2015, http://www.theguardian.com/world/2015/apr/02/putin-kremlin-inside-russian-troll-house (accessed July 14, 2017).

123. Scaparrotti, "2017 EUCOM Posture Statement," p. 6.

124. Associated Press, "Latvia Joins Lithuania in Temporary Ban Against Russian TV Broadcasts for 'Biased' Reporting," April 7, 2014, http://www.foxnews.com/world/2014/04/07/latvia-joins-lithuania-in-temporary-ban-against-russian-tv-broadcasts-for/ (accessed July 14, 2017).

125. Sputnik, "Russia to Press for Latvia's Explanations over Sputnik's Website Ban," April 1, 2016, http://sputniknews.com/europe/20160401/1037350082/russia-media-latvia-oscee.html (accessed July 14, 2017).

126. Christopher Woody, "Baltic States Think Russia Is Laying the Groundwork for Looming 'Kinetic Operations,'" *Business Insider*, April 3, 2017, http://www.businessinsider.com/russia-propaganda-in-lithuania-attack-on-the-baltics-2017-4 (accessed July 14, 2017).

127. Estonian Public Broadcasting, "Latvian Public Broadcasting to Launch Russian-Language Channel," March 20, 2015, http://news.err.ee/v/International/81f7c8a3-f90a-4a67-8bfd-24ba1f8bf7ad (accessed July 14, 2017).

128. Associated Press, "Estonia Launches Russian-Language TV Channel, Seeks Balance," September 28, 2015, https://apnews.com/e9a79e320ff047e68bca0e11eb4c5734/estonia-launches-russian-language-tv-channel-seeks-balance (accessed July 14, 2017).

129. Associated Press, "Lithuania to Suspend State-Run Russian TV Over Anti-US Comments Inciting 'War, Discord, and Hatred,'" *Business Insider*, November 16, 2017, http://www.businessinsider.com/ap-russian-tv-suspended-after-harsh-anti-us-comments-2016-11 (accessed July 14, 2017); Gene Zolotarev, "The Baltic Times and Media Developments in the Baltic States," *The Baltic Times*, January 11, 2017, http://www.baltictimes.com/the_baltic_times_and_media_development_in_the_baltic_states/ (accessed July 14, 2017).

130. BNS/TBT-Staff/Riga, "Russia Questions Latvia's Ban on Rossiya RTR Channel," *The Baltic Times*, April 8, 2016, http://www.baltictimes.com/russia_questions_latvia_s_ban_on_rossiya_rtr_channel/ (accessed July 19, 2017); Zolotarev, "The Baltic Times and Media Developments in the Baltic States."

131. Zolotarev, "The Baltic Times and Media Developments in the Baltic States."

132. CBS/AP, "U.S. Launches TV Network as Alternative to Russian Propaganda," February 9, 2017, http://www.cbsnews.com/news/us-current-time-tv-network-rfe-russia-russian-propaganda-misinformation-rt/ (accessed July 19, 2017).

133. Bill Gertz, "Russia Waging Information Warfare, General Says," *The Washington Free Beacon*, March 24, 2017, http://freebeacon.com/national-security/russia-waging-information-warfare-general-says/ (accessed July 14, 2017).

134. BNS/TBT Staff, "Fake News About US Troops Posted on BNS Website and Cyber Attack Suspected," *The Baltic Times*, April 13, 2017, http://www.baltictimes.com/fake_news_about_us_troops_posted_on_bns_website_and_cyber_attack_suspected/ (accessed July 14, 2017).

135. Deutsche Welle, "NATO: Russia Targeted German Army with Fake News Campaign," February 16, 2017, http://www.dw.com/en/nato-russia-targeted-german-army-with-fake-news-campaign/a-37591978 (accessed July 14, 2017).

136. Bill Gertz, "Russia Steps Up Anti-U.S. Military Propaganda," *The Washington Free Beacon*, April 27, 2017, http://freebeacon.com/national-security/russia-steps-anti-u-s-military-propaganda/ (accessed July 14, 2017).

137. Coats, "2017 Worldwide Threat Assessment," p. 18.

138. Ibid., pp. 2–3.

139. Civil Georgia, "Moscow, Sokhumi Endorse Final Text of New Treaty," November 22, 2014, http://www.civil.ge/eng/article.php?id=27841 (accessed July 14, 2017).

140. Civil Georgia, "Tbilisi Condemns Russia's Move to Sign New Treaty with Sokhumi," November 22, 2014, http://www.civil.ge/eng/article.php?id=27842 (accessed July 14, 2017).

141. Liz Fuller, "Putin Gives Green Light for Incorporating Some South Ossetian Units into Russian Army," Radio Free Europe/Radio Liberty, March 20, 2017, https://www.rferl.org/a/russia-south-ossetia-army-incorportation/28379998.html (accessed July 19, 2017).

142. Damien Sharkov, "2,000 Russian Troops to Practice Tank Fire in Georgian Breakaway Region," *Newsweek*, January 17, 2017, http://www.newsweek.com/2000-russian-troops-practice-tank-fire-georgian-breakaway-region-543265 (accessed July 19, 2017).

143. International Institute for Strategic Studies, "The Military Balance," p. 206.

144. Adrian Croft, "Georgia Says Russia Bent on 'Creeping Annexation' of Breakaway Regions," Reuters, February 26, 2015, http://www.reuters.com/article/us-georgia-russia-idUSKBN0LU2M020150226 (accessed July 27, 2017).

145. Radio Free Europe/Radio Liberty Georgian Service, "Russian Troops Demarcate Part of Georgian Oil Pipeline," July 14, 2015, http://www.rferl.org/content/russian-troops-demarcate-georgian-oil-pipeline/27126985.html (accessed July 14, 2017).

146. Stephanie Joyce, "Along a Shifting Border, Georgia and Russia Maintain an Uneasy Peace," National Public Radio, March 13, 2017, http://www.npr.org/sections/parallels/2017/03/13/519471110/along-a-shifting-border-georgia-and-russia-maintain-an-uneasy-peace (accessed July 14, 2017).

147. News release, "United States Condemns Illegitimate Elections and Referenda in Georgia's Occupied Territories," U.S. Department of State, April 7, 2017, https://www.state.gov/r/pa/prs/ps/2017/04/269629.htm (accessed July 14, 2017); Giorgi Kvirikashvili, Prime Minister of Georgia, "Georgian Prime Minister's Statement on the So-Called Elections and Referendum in Occupied Tskhinvali Region," April 9, 2017, http://gov.ge/index.php?lang_id=ENG&sec_id=463&info_id=60646 (accessed July 19, 2017); News release, "NATO Condemns Illegitimate Elections and Referendum in Georgia's Occupied Territories–Statement by the NATO Spokesperson Oana Lungescu," April 10, 2017, http://nato.int/cps/en/natohq/news_143120.htm (accessed July 19, 2017).

148. Andrew Osborn, "Russia to Beef Up Military Presence in Former Soviet Space," *The Telegraph*, August 18, 2010, http://www.telegraph.co.uk/news/worldnews/europe/russia/7952433/Russia-to-beef-up-military-presence-in-former-Soviet-space.html (accessed July 14, 2017).

149. Nikolai Litovkin, "Russia and Armenia to Create Joint Defense Force in Caucasus," United Press International, November 16, 2016, http://www.upi.com/Russia-and-Armenia-to-create-joint-defense-force-in-Caucasus/1461479301074/ (accessed July 19, 2017).

150. Zaur Shiriyev, "Azerbaijan's Possible Reactions to Armenia's Iskanders: Defense Versus Offense," Jamestown Foundation, *Eurasia Daily Monitor*, Vol. 13, Issue 160 (October 5, 2016), https://jamestown.org/program/azerbaijans-possible-reactions-armenias-iskanders-defense-versus-offense/ (accessed July 19, 2017).

151. Litovkin, "Russia and Armenia to Create Joint Defense Force in Caucasus."

152. In 1991, the Azerbaijan SSR Parliament dissolved the Nagorno–Karabakh Autonomous Oblast and divided the area among five rayons (administrative regions) in Azerbaijan.

153. Reuters, "Armenia, Azerbaijan Closer to War over Nagorno-Karabakh Than at Any Time Since 1994–ICG," June 1, 2017, http://www.reuters.com/article/armenia-azerbaijan-conflict-idUSL8N1IY402 (accessed July 14, 2017).

154. Deutsche Welle, "Ceasefire Holds in Contested Armenia–Azerbaijan Border Region," April 6, 2016, http://www.dw.com/en/ceasefire-holds-in-contested-armenia-azerbaijan-border-region/a-19170371 (accessed July 14, 2017).

155. Reuters, "Armenia, Azerbaijan Closer to War over Nagorno-Karabakh Than at Any Time Since 1994."

156. Jack Farchy, "Russia Senses Opportunity in Nagorno–Karabakh Conflict," *Financial Times*, April 19, 2016, https://next.ft.com/content/3d485610-0572-11e6-9b51-0fb5e65703ce (accessed July 14, 2017).

157. Alexandros Petersen, "Russia Shows Its Hand on Karabakh," *EUObserver*, November 8, 2013, https://euobserver.com/opinion/122032 (accessed July 19, 2017).

158. Farchy, "Russia Senses Opportunity in Nagorno–Karabakh Conflict."

159. Coats, "2017 Worldwide Threat Assessment," p. 19.

160. Rod Nordland, "Russia Signs Deal for Syria Bases; Turkey Appears to Accept Assad," *The New York Times*, January 20, 2017, https://mobile.nytimes.com/2017/01/20/world/middleeast/russia-turkey-syria-deal.html?_r=1&referer=https://t.co/T1Cwr3UdJi (accessed July 14, 2017).

161. Reuters, "Russia to Upgrade Its Naval, Air Bases in Syria: Interfax," January 15, 2017, http://www.reuters.com/article/us-mideast-crisis-syria-russia-base-idUSKBN14Z0FQ (accessed July 14, 2017).

162. Jonathan Marcus, "Russia S-400 Syria Missile Deployment Sends Robust Signal," BBC, December 1, 2015, http://www.bbc.com/news/world-europe-34976537 (accessed July 14, 2017).

163. Thomas Gibbons-Neff, "How Russian Special Forces Are Shaping the Fight in Syria," *The Washington Post*, March 29, 2016, https://www.washingtonpost.com/news/checkpoint/wp/2016/03/29/how-russian-special-forces-are-shaping-the-fight-in-syria/ (accessed July 14, 2017); Frederik Pleitgen, "Russia's Military in Syria: Bigger Than You Think and Not Going Anywhere," CNN, May 9, 2016, http://www.cnn.com/2016/05/09/middleeast/russia-military-syria/ (accessed July 14, 2017).

164. BBC, "Russia Used Syria as Live-Fire Training–US General," December 22, 2016, http://www.bbc.com/news/world-europe-38402506 (accessed July 14, 2017).

165. Lucian Kim, "Russian Defense Minister Says His Military Has Tested 162 Weapons in Syria," National Public Radio, February 23, 2017, http://www.npr.org/sections/parallels/2017/02/23/516895124/russian-defense-minister-says-his-military-has-tested-162-weapons-in-syria (accessed July 14, 2017).

166. Tobin Harshaw, "Putin's Arms Bazaar Is in a Serious Sales Slump," Bloomberg, April 25, 2017, https://www.bloomberg.com/view/articles/2017-04-25/putin-s-arms-bazaar-is-in-a-serious-sales-slump (accessed July 14, 2017).

167. Marcus Weisgerber, "Russia's Arms Export Boom Stalls; Wisconsin Shipbuilding and Trump; Mattis Meets Industry Leaders; and a Lot More," *Defense One*, April 20, 2017, http://www.defenseone.com/business/2017/04/global-business-brief-april-20-2017/137185/ (accessed July 19, 2017).

168. Scaparrotti, "2017 EUCOM Posture Statement," p. 4.

169. Ryan Browne, "US Official: Russia Apologized After Russian Jet Performed Barrel Roll over US Plane," CNN, May 25, 2017, http://www.cnn.com/2017/05/25/politics/russia-us-aircraft-barrel-roll/ (accessed July 19, 2017).

170. Anne Barnard, "Russia Says Deal Bars American Jets from Much of Syria's Skies. U.S. Says No," *The New York Times*, May 5, 2017, https://www.nytimes.com/2017/05/05/world/middleeast/syria-deescalation-zones-russia-iran-turkey.html (accessed July 14, 2017).

171. CBS/AP, "Russia Cuts 'Deconfliction' Hotline with U.S. Following Syrian Strikes," last updated April 7, 2017, http://www.cbsnews.com/news/russia-agrees-maintain-deconfliction-channel-us-syria-strikes/ (accessed July 19, 2017).

172. Shawn Snow, "US Increases Use of Deconfliction Hotline with Russia Amid Pending Operation to Liberate Raqqa," *Military Times*, May 24, 2017, http://www.militarytimes.com/articles/deconfliction-tanf-russia-syria-kurds (accessed July 19, 2017).

173. Coats, "2017 Worldwide Threat Assessment," p. 21.

174. Ibid., p. 18.

175. Scaparrotti, "2017 EUCOM Posture Statement," pp. 9 and 6.

176. Leonid Bershidsky, "Russia Re-Enacts the Great Game in the Balkans," Bloomberg, January 19, 2017, https://www.bloomberg.com/view/articles/2017-01-19/russia-re-enacts-the-great-game-in-the-balkans (accessed July 14, 2017).

177. Associated Press, "Montenegro Prosecutor: Russian Nationalists Behind Alleged Coup Attempt," *The Wall Street Journal*, updated November 6, 2016, http://www.wsj.com/articles/montenegro-prosecutor-russian-nationalists-behind-alleged-coup-attempt-1478473032 (accessed July 19, 2017).

178. "In the Balkans, NATO Has Outmuscled Russia," *The Economist*, December 11, 2015, http://www.economist.com/news/europe/21683967-montenegros-accession-fills-one-few-remaining-gaps-western-alliance (accessed July 14, 2017).

179. Radio Free Europe/Radio Liberty Balkan Service, "Vucic Sworn in as Serbian President Amid Protests," last updated May 31, 2017, https://www.rferl.org/a/serbia-vucic-inauguration-protests/28520253.html (accessed July 19, 2017).

180. Aleksandar Vasovic, "Serbia's Conservative Leader Sworn in as President," Reuters, May 31, 2017, http://www.reuters.com/article/us-serbia-president-idUSKBN18R1QI (accessed July 14, 2017).

181. Snezana Bjelotomic, "CHEPURIN: Serbia's EU Accession Will Negatively Impact Economic Relations with Russia," *Serbian Monitor*, October 18, 2016, http://serbianmonitor.com/en/politics/25988/chepurin-serbias-eu-accession-will-negatively-impact-economic-relations-with-russia/ (accessed July 14, 2017).

182. Reuters, "Bulgaria, Serbia Agree to Work on Pipeline to Cut Reliance on Russian Gas," January 19, 2017, http://www.reuters.com/article/bulgaria-serbia-energy-idUSL5N1F84F2 (accessed July 19, 2017).

183. Julian Borger, "Vladimir Putin Warns over Rise of Neo-Nazism Before Serbia Visit," *The Guardian*, October 15, 2014, http://www.theguardian.com/world/2014/oct/15/vladimir-putin-nazism-warning-serbia-visit (accessed July 14, 2017).

184. BBC, "Putin Guest of Honour at Serbia Military Parade," October 16, 2014, http://www.bbc.com/news/world-europe-29641642 (accessed July 14, 2017).

185. Bruce Jones, "Serbian President Lobbies Russia, Belarus for Supply of S-300s," *Jane's 360*, April 21, 2017, http://www.janes.com/article/69723/serbian-president-lobbies-russia-belarus-for-supply-of-s-300s (accessed July 14, 2017).

186. Associated Press, "Serbia: Putin Agrees to Large Weapons Delivery to Balkans," March 29, 2017, http://www.voanews.com/a/serbia-putin-agrees-to-large-weapons-delivery-to-balkans/3786287.html (accessed July 14, 2017).

187. Aleksandar Vasovic, "Serbia Hosts Joint Military Exercises with Russia," Reuters, November 3, 2016, http://www.reuters.com/article/us-serbia-defence-russia-idUSKBN12Y1JX (accessed July 14, 2017).

188. Radio Free Europe/Radio Liberty, "Tensions Rise as Bosnian Serbs Vote in Banned Referendum," last updated September 25, 2016, https://www.rferl.org/a/balkan-tensions-rise-as-bosnian-serbs-push-ahead-with-banned-referendum/28010813.html (accessed July 19, 2017); Gordana Knezevic, "Russia's Fingers in Bosnia's Pie," Radio Free Europe/Radio Liberty, September 28, 2016, https://www.rferl.org/a/russia-putin-republika-srpska-bosnia-dodik-referendum-statehood-day/28018362.html (accessed July 19, 2017).

189. Andrew Byrne, "Bosnian Serb Forces Take Part in Illegal 'Statehood Day' Parade," *Financial Times*, January 9, 2017, https://www.ft.com/content/5ffff694-d66f-11e6-944b-e7eb37a6aa8e (accessed July 14, 2017).

190. Radio Free Europe/Radio Liberty, "U.S. Imposes Sanctions on Republika Srpska's President Dodik," January 17, 2017, https://www.rferl.org/a/dodik-republika-srpska-united-states-sanctions/28239895.html (accessed July 19, 2017).

191. Matthew Brunwasser, "Bosnian Serbs Challenge Dayton Order in Referendum," *Politico*, September 25, 2016, http://www.politico.eu/article/bosnian-serbs-challange-dayton-order-in-referendum-milorad-dodik-the-president-of-republika-srpska/ (accessed July 14, 2017).

192. Bershidsky, "Russia Re-Enacts the Great Game in the Balkans."

193. Deutsche Welle, "Russia Snubs UN Support for EU Troops in Bosnia Amid Ukraine Crisis," November 12, 2014, http://www.dw.com/en/russia-snubs-un-support-for-eu-troops-in-bosnia-amid-ukraine-crisis/a-18057557 (accessed July 14, 2017).

194. Meetings coverage, "Security Council Renews Authorization of Multinational Stabilization Force in Bosnia and Herzegovina, Adopting Resolution 2315 (2016)," U.N. Security Council, November 8, 2016, https://www.un.org/press/en/2016/sc12580.doc.htm (accessed July 19, 2017).

195. Radio Free Europe/Radio Liberty Balkan Service, "Serbia Stops 'Promo Train' to Kosovo's North," last updated January 14, 2017, https://www.rferl.org/a/28233304.html (accessed July 14, 2017).

196. Konstantin Testorides, "Macedonian Lawmakers Face Vote That Could End Stalemate," *The Journal Gazette*, May 31, 2017, http://www.journalgazette.net/news/world/20170531/macedonian-lawmakers-face-vote-that-could-end-stalemate (accessed July 19, 2017).

197. Ali Weinberg, "ISIS in Iraq, Syria Recruiting Foreign Fighters from Balkans," ABC News, October 22, 2014, http://abcnews.go.com/International/isis-iraq-syria-recruiting-foreign-fighters-balkans/story?id=26358320 (accessed July 14, 2017).

198. Carlotta Gall, "How Kosovo Was Turned into Fertile Ground for ISIS," *The New York Times*, May 21, 2016, https://www.nytimes.com/2016/05/22/world/europe/how-the-saudis-turned-kosovo-into-fertile-ground-for-isis.html (accessed July 19, 2017).

199. Boris Georgievski, "Could Balkan Nations Become the New Hotbeds of Islamist Extremism?" Deutsche Welle, May 30, 2017, http://www.dw.com/en/could-balkan-nations-become-the-new-hotbeds-of-islamist-extremism/a-39045256 (accessed July 14, 2017).

200. Coats, "2017 Worldwide Threat Assessment," p. 20.

201. UNIAN Information Agency, "Russia Puts Europe on Alert as Putin's Warships Enter Waters After U.S. Destroyer Swoops–Media," May 8, 2017, https://www.unian.info/world/1912091-russia-puts-europe-on-alert-as-putins-warships-enter-waters-after-us-destroyer-swoops-media.html (accessed July 14, 2017).

202. Ibid.

203. Alex Lockie, "Watch 2 Russian Attack Jets Harass a Dutch Navy Frigate in the Baltic Sea," *Business Insider*, May 17, 2017, http://www.businessinsider.com/russian-su-23-hnlms-evertsen-buzz-nato-baltic-2017-5 (accessed July 14, 2017).

204. Bill Gertz, "Russian Jets Buzzed U.S. Destroyer," *The Washington Free Beacon*, February 14, 2017, http://freebeacon.com/national-security/russian-jets-buzzed-u-s-destroyer/ (accessed July 14, 2017).

205. Conor Gaffey, "Russia and China Are 'Tailing' U.S. Warship En Route to North Korea Region," *Newsweek*, April 17, 2017, http://www.newsweek.com/russia-china-north-korea-carl-vinson-585048 (accessed July 20, 2017).

206. David E. Sanger and Eric Schmitt, "Russian Ships Near Data Cables Are Too Close for U.S. Comfort," *The New York Times*, October 25, 2015, http://www.nytimes.com/2015/10/26/world/europe/russian-presence-near-undersea-cables-concerns-us.html?hp&action=click&pgtype=Homepage&module=first-column-region&region=top-news&WT.nav=top-news&_r=1 (accessed July 14, 2017); Daniel Kochis, "Undersea Cables: How Concerned Should You Be?" The Daily Signal, October 27, 2015, http://dailysignal.com/2015/10/27/undersea-cables-how-concerned-should-you-be/.

207. Alexander Smith, "Russian Navy Activity in Europe Now at Cold-War Levels: Admiral," NBC News, April 10, 2017, http://www.nbcnews.com/news/world/russian-navy-activity-europe-now-cold-war-levels-admiral-n744516?cid=sm_npd_nn_tw_ma (accessed July 14, 2017).

208. Thomas Nilsen, "World's Biggest Nuclear Sub to Show Off in the Baltic," *The Independent Barents Observer*, April 4, 2017, https://thebarentsobserver.com/en/security/2017/04/worlds-biggest-nuclear-submarine-show-off-baltic-sea (accessed July 14, 2017).

209. Gerard Taylor, "Russia's New Submarines Are More Difficult to Detect," *Norway Today*, February 6, 2017, http://norwaytoday.info/news/russias-new-submarines-difficult-detect/ (accessed July 14, 2017).

210. Zachary Cohen, "Russian Spy Ship Again Spotted Off East Coast," CNN, March 16, 2017, http://www.cnn.com/2017/03/15/us/russian-spy-ship-georgia-coast/ (accessed July 14, 2017).

211. BBC, "NATO Jets Scrambled as Russian Bombers Fly South," October 5, 2016, http://www.bbc.com/news/world-europe-37562499 (accessed July 20, 2017).

212. Luis Martinez, "Russian Aircraft Fly Close to Alaska for 4th Time in 4 Days," ABC News, April 21, 2017, http://abcnews.go.com/International/russian-aircraft-close-alaska-4th-time-days/story?id=46939351 (accessed July 14, 2017).

213. Barbara Starr, Ryan Browne, and Zachary Cohen, "US F-22s Intercept Russian Bombers, Fighters Near Alaska," CNN, http://www.cnn.com/2017/05/04/politics/us-f-22-intercept-russian-aircraft-alaska/index.html (accessed July 20, 2017).

214. Lucas Tomlinson, "Russian Nuclear-Capable Bombers Fly Near Japan, US Officials Say," Fox News, April 12, 2017, http://www.foxnews.com/world/2017/04/12/russian-nuclear-capable-bombers-fly-near-japan-us-officials-say.html (accessed July 20, 2017).

215. Lucas Tomlinson, "NORAD Responds After Russian Bombers Zoom Around Japan," Fox News, January 25, 2017, http://www.foxnews.com/us/2017/01/25/norad-responds-after-russian-bombers-zoom-around-japan.html (accessed July 20, 2017).

216. CNN, "Russian Fighter Jet Flies Near US Navy Plane, Says Official," updated May 12, 2017, http://www.ksbw.com/article/russian-fighter-jet-flies-near-us-navy-plane-says-official/9643526 (accessed July 20, 2017).

217. Damien Sharkov, "NATO: Russian Aircraft Intercepted 110 Times Above Baltic in 2016," *Newsweek*, January 4, 2017, http://www.newsweek.com/nato-intercepted-110-russian-aircraft-around-baltic-2016-538444 (accessed July 14, 2017).

218. Sean O'Riordan, "Passenger Planes Dodged Russian Bombers," *Irish Examiner*, March 3, 2015, http://www.irishexaminer.com/ireland/passenger-planes-dodged-russian-bombers-315623.html (accessed July 14, 2017).

219. "SAS Flight in Russian Spy Plane Near Miss," *The Local*, May 8, 2014, http://www.thelocal.se/20140508/sas-plane-in-russian-spy-plane-near-miss (accessed July 20, 2017).

220. David Cenciotti, "Russian Spy Plane Nearly Collided with Airliner off Sweden. Again," The Aviationist, December 14, 2014, http://theaviationist.com/2014/12/14/near-collision-off-sweden/ (accessed July 14, 2017).

221. Coats, "2017 Worldwide Threat Assessment," p. 15.

222. News Transcript, "Department of Defense Press Briefing by Adm. Haney in the Pentagon Briefing Room," U.S. Department of Defense, March 24, 2015, http://www.defense.gov/transcripts/transcript.aspx?source=GovDelivery&transcriptid=5605 (accessed July 14, 2017).

223. Micah Zenko, "Dangerous Space Incidents," Council on Foreign Relations, Center for Preventive Action *Contingency Planning Memorandum* No. 21, April 2014, http://www.cfr.org/space/dangerous-space-incidents/p32790 (accessed July 14, 2017).

224. Admiral C. D. Haney, Commander, United States Strategic Command, statement before the Committee on Armed Services, U.S. Senate, March 19, 2015, http://www.armed-services.senate.gov/hearings/15-03-19-us-strategic-command-us-transportation-command-and-us-cyber-command (accessed July 14, 2017).

225. Bill Gertz, "Russia Conducts Fifth Test of New-Anti-Satellite Missile," *The Washington Free Beacon*, December 21, 2016, http://freebeacon.com/national-security/russia-conducts-fifth-test-new-anti-satellite-missile/ (accessed July 14, 2017).

226. Bill Gertz, "Military Gears Up for Space Warfare," *The Washington Free Beacon*, March 26, 2015, http://freebeacon.com/national-security/military-gears-up-for-space-warfare/ (accessed July 14, 2017).

227. Coats, "2017 Worldwide Threat Assessment," p. 9.

228. Ibid., p. 8.

229. Ibid., p. 9.

230. Office of the Director of National Intelligence, *Assessing Russian Activities and Intentions in Recent US Elections*, Intelligence Community Assessment 2017-01D, January 6, 2017, p. ii, https://assets.documentcloud.org/documents/3254237/Russia-Hack-Report.pdf (accessed July 28, 2017). (Note: This report follows a two-page explanatory document, "Background to 'Assessing Russian Activities and Intentions in Recent US Elections': The Analytic Process and Cyber Incident Attribution," also released by the Office of the Director of National Intelligence and dated January 6, 2017.)

231. Ibid., pp. ii–iii.

232. Ibid., p. 3.

233. Radio Free Europe/Radio Liberty, "German Intelligence Agency Expects More Cyberattacks Before Election," May 4, 2017, https://www.rferl.org/a/germany-russia-cyberattacks-election/28468137.html (accessed July 20, 2017).

234. Reuters, "German Parliament Foiled Cyber Attack by Hackers Via Israeli Website," March 29, 2017, http://www.reuters.com/article/us-germany-cyber-idUSKBN1701V3 (accessed July 20, 2017); BBC, Russia 'Was Behind German Parliament Hack,'" May 13, 2016, http://www.bbc.com/news/technology-36284447 (accessed July 20, 2017).

235. Andrea Shalal, "Germany Challenges Russia Over Alleged Cyberattacks," Reuters, May 4, 2017, http://www.reuters.com/article/us-germany-security-cyber-russia-idUSKBN1801CA (accessed July 20, 2017).

236. Reuters, "German Parliament Foiled Cyber Attack by Hackers Via Israeli Website."

237. Stephanie Kirchgaessner, "Russia Suspected Over Hacking Attack on Italian Foreign Ministry," *The Guardian*, February 10, 2017, https://www.theguardian.com/world/2017/feb/10/russia-suspected-over-hacking-attack-on-italian-foreign-ministry (accessed July 14, 2017).

238. Reuters, "Macron Campaign Says It Is the Victim of Massive, Coordinated Hacking Campaign," May 5, 2017, http://www.cnbc.com/2017/05/05/macron-campaign-says-it-is-the-victim-of-massive-coordinated-hacking-campaign-reuters.html (accessed July 20, 2017).

239. Zachary Cohen, "Rogers: US Warned France of Russian Cyberactivity," CNN, updated May 9, 2017, http://www.cnn.com/2017/05/09/politics/mike-rogers-hearing-french-election-hacks/ (accessed July 20, 2017).

240. BBC, "France Thwarts 24,000 Cyber-Attacks Against Defence Targets," January 8, 2017, http://www.bbc.com/news/world-europe-38546415 (accessed July 20, 2017).

241. Morgan Chalfant, "Russia Tried to Take Over Pentagon Twitter Accounts: Report," *The Hill*, May 18, 2017, http://thehill.com/policy/cybersecurity/334045-russia-tried-to-gain-access-to-pentagon-twitter-accounts-report (accessed July 14, 2017).

242. Sam Jones, "Russia Mobilises an Elite Band of Cyber Warriors," *The Financial Times*, February 23, 2017, https://www.ft.com/content/f41e1dc4-ef83-11e6-ba01-119a44939bb6 (accessed July 14, 2017).

243. Thomas Grove, "Russian Social Media Seen as Threat to Ukraine and to Cybersecurity," *The Wall Street Journal*, May 29, 2017, https://www.wsj.com/articles/russian-social-media-seen-as-threat-to-ukraine-and-to-cybersecurity-1496055606?utm_content=buffer3e5d2&utm_medium=social&utm_source=twitter.com&utm_campaign=buffer (accessed July 14, 2017).

244. Dustin Volz, "U.S. Government Concludes Cyber Attack Caused Ukraine Power Outage," Reuters, February 25, 2016, http://www.reuters.com/article/us-ukraine-cybersecurity-idUSKCN0VY30K (accessed July 14, 2017).

245. U.S. Department of Homeland Security, International Control Systems Cyber Emergency Response Team (ICS-CERT), "Cyber-Attack Against Ukrainian Critical Infrastructure," IR-Alert-H-16-056-01, February 25, 2016, https://ics-cert.us-cert.gov/alerts/IR-ALERT-H-16-056-01 (accessed September 9, 2016).

246. Patrick Tucker, "Ukrainian Power Company '99% Certain' Blackout Result of Cyber Attack," *Defense One*, December 21, 2016, http://www.defenseone.com/technology/2016/12/ukrainian-power-company-99-certain-blackout-result-cyber-attack/134099/ (accessed July 14, 2017).

247. Evan Perez, "U.S. Official Blames Russia for Power Grid Attack in Ukraine," CNN, updated February 11, 2017, http://www.cnn.com/2016/02/11/politics/ukraine-power-grid-attack-russia-us/index.html (accessed July 20, 2017).

248. Stephen Jewkes and Oleg Vukmanovic, "Suspected Russia-Backed Hackers Target Baltic Energy Networks," Reuters, May 11, 2017, http://mobile.reuters.com/article/idUSKBN1871W5 (accessed July 14, 2017).

249. Bill Gertz, "DIA: Russian Software Could Threaten U.S. Industrial Control Systems," *The Washington Free Beacon*, March 1, 2016, http://freebeacon.com/national-security/dia-russian-software-could-threaten-u-s-industrial-control-systems/ (accessed July 14, 2017).

250. Mary-Ann Russon, "Russia Blamed for Crashing Swedish Air Traffic Control to Test Electronic Warfare Capabilities," *International Business Times*, April 14, 2016, http://www.ibtimes.co.uk/russia-blamed-bringing-down-swedish-air-traffic-control-test-electronic-warfare-capabilities-1554895 (accessed July 14, 2017).

251. Kjetil Stormark, "Sweden Issued Cyber Attack Alert," Aldrimer, April 12, 2016, https://www.aldrimer.no/sweden-issued-cyber-attack-alert-as-its-air-traffic-reeled/ (accessed June 27, 2016).

252. Reuters and Copenhagen Post, "Denmark: Russia Hacked Our Defense Ministry for Two Years," Atlantic Council NATOSource, April 24, 2017, http://www.atlanticcouncil.org/blogs/natosource/denmark-russia-hacked-our-defense-ministry-for-two-years (accessed July 14, 2017).

253. Gordon Corera, "How France's TV5 Was Almost Destroyed by 'Russian Hackers,'" BBC, October 10, 2016, http://www.bbc.com/news/technology-37590375 (accessed July 15, 2017).

254. BBC, "Russian Military Admits Significant Cyber-War Efforts," February 23, 2017, http://www.bbc.com/news/world-europe-39062663 (accessed July 15, 2017).

255. Matthew Dean and Catherine Herridge, "'Patriotic Hackers' Attacking on Behalf of Mother Russia," Fox News, January 16, 2016, http://www.foxnews.com/politics/2016/01/16/patriotic-hackers-attacking-on-behalf-mother-russia.html (accessed July 15, 2017).

256. Denis Pinchuk, "Patriotic Russians May Have Staged Cyber Attacks on Own Initiative: Putin," Reuters, June 1, 2017, http://www.reuters.com/article/us-russia-economic-forum-putin-cyber-idUSKBN18S56Y (accessed July 14, 2017).

257. Coats, "2017 Worldwide Threat Assessment," p. 1.

Middle East

Threats to the Homeland

Radical Islamist terrorism in its many forms remains the most immediate global threat to the safety and security of U.S. citizens at home and abroad, and most of the actors posing terrorist threats originate in the greater Middle East. More broadly, threats to the U.S. homeland and to Americans abroad include terrorist threats from non-state actors such as al-Qaeda that use the ungoverned areas of the Middle East as bases from which to plan, train, equip, and launch attacks; terrorist threats from state-supported groups such as Hezbollah; and the developing ballistic missile threat from Iran.

Terrorism Originating from al-Qaeda, Its Affiliates, and the Islamic State (IS). Although al-Qaeda has been damaged by targeted strikes that have killed key leaders in Pakistan, including Osama bin Laden, the terrorist network has evolved in a decentralized fashion, and regional affiliates continue to pose potent threats to the U.S. homeland. The regional al-Qaeda groups share the same long-term goals as the parent organization, but some have developed different priorities related to their local conflict environments.

Al-Qaeda in the Arabian Peninsula (AQAP) has emerged as one of the leading terrorist threats to homeland security since the al-Qaeda high command was forced into hiding in Pakistan.

Yemen has long been a bastion of support for militant Islamism in general and al-Qaeda in particular. Many Yemenis who migrated to Saudi Arabia to find work during the 1970s oil boom were exposed to radicalization there. Yemenis made up a disproportionate number of the estimated 25,000 foreign Muslims who flocked to Afghanistan to join the war against the Soviet occupation in the 1980s. They also make up a large segment of al-Qaeda, which was founded by foreign veterans of that war to expand the struggle into a global revolutionary campaign.

Al-Qaeda's first terrorist attack against Americans occurred in Yemen in December 1992, when a bomb was detonated in a hotel used by U.S. military personnel involved in supporting the humanitarian food relief flights to Somalia. Al-Qaeda launched a much deadlier attack in Yemen in October 2000 when it attacked the USS *Cole* in the port of Aden with a boat filled with explosives, killing 17 American sailors.[1]

Yemen was a site for the radicalization of American Muslims such as John Walker Lindh, who traveled there to study Islam before being recruited to fight in Afghanistan. Seven Yemeni Americans from Lackawanna, New York, were recruited by al-Qaeda before 9/11. Six were convicted of supporting terrorism and sent to prison, and the seventh became a fugitive who later surfaced in Yemen.

Yemen has become increasingly important as a base of operations for al-Qaeda in recent years after crackdowns in other countries. In September 2008, al-Qaeda launched a complex attack on the U.S. embassy in Yemen that killed 19 people, including an American woman. Yemen's importance to al-Qaeda increased further in January 2009 when al-Qaeda members who had been pushed out of Saudi Arabia merged with the Yemeni branch to form Al-Qaeda in the Arabian Peninsula.

AQAP's Anwar al-Aulaqi, a charismatic American-born Yemeni cleric, reportedly incited several terrorist attacks on U.S. targets before being killed in a drone air strike in 2011. He inspired Major Nidal Hassan, who perpetrated the 2009 Fort Hood shootings that killed 13 soldiers,[2] and Umar Farouk Abdulmutallab, the failed suicide bomber who sought to destroy an airliner bound for Detroit on Christmas Day 2009.[3] Aulaqi is also suspected of playing a role in the November 2010 AQAP plot to dispatch parcel bombs to the U.S. in cargo planes. After Aulaqi's death, his videos on the Internet continued to radicalize and recruit young Muslims, including the perpetrators of the April 2013 bombing of the Boston Marathon that killed three people; the July 2015 fatal shootings of four Marines and a Navy sailor at a military recruiting office in Chattanooga, Tennessee; the December 2015 terrorist attack in San Bernardino, California, that killed 14 people; and the June 2016 shootings of 49 people in a nightclub in Orlando, Florida.[4]

AQAP, estimated to have had as many as 4,000 members in 2015,[5] has greatly expanded in the chaos of Yemen's civil war, particularly since the overthrow of Yemen's government by Iran-backed Houthi rebels in 2015. AQAP has exploited alliances with powerful, well-armed Yemeni tribes (including the Aulaq tribe from which Osama bin Laden and the radical cleric Aulaqi claimed descent) to establish sanctuaries and training bases in Yemen's rugged mountains. This is similar to al-Qaeda's *modus operandi* in Afghanistan before 9/11 and in Pakistan today. In April 2015, AQAP seized the city of al Mukalla and expanded its control of rural areas in southern Yemen. After AQAP withdrew in April 2016, the city was recaptured by pro-government Yemeni troops and troops from the United Arab Emirates (UAE), a member of the Saudi-led coalition that intervened in March 2015 in support of the Yemeni government. Nevertheless, AQAP remains a potent force that could capitalize on the anarchy of Yemen's multi-sided civil war to seize new territory.

The Islamic State (IS), formerly known as the Islamic State of Iraq and Syria (ISIS) or the Islamic State in Iraq and the Levant (ISIL), and before that as the Islamic State of Iraq and Al-Qaeda in Iraq, emerged as an al-Qaeda splinter group but has outstripped its parent organization in terms of the immediate threats it poses to U.S. national interests. It seeks to overthrow the governments of Iraq, Syria, Lebanon, and Jordan and establish a nominal Islamic state governed by a harsh and brutal interpretation of Islamic law that is an existential threat to Christians, Shiite Muslims, Yazidis, and other religious minorities. Its long-term goals are to launch what it considers a jihad (holy war) to drive Western influence out of the Middle East; destroy Israel; diminish and discredit Shia Islam, which it considers apostasy; and become the nucleus of a global Sunni Islamic empire.

The Islamic State is composed of Sunni Muslims drawn to radical Islamist ideology. U.S. intelligence officials estimated in May 2016 that it commanded between 19,000 and 25,000 fighters in Iraq and Syria even after suffering extensive losses.[6] By June 2017, according to an Iraqi expert, the Islamic State had been reduced to about 8,000 fighters, including about 2,000 foreign fighters, in Iraq and Syria.[7] Most of its members are Iraqi and Syrian Arabs, although it also has attracted more than 25,000 foreign fighters who have joined its ranks on a temporary or permanent basis, including at least 6,000 from Tunisia, 2,275 from Saudi Arabia, 2,000 from Jordan, 1,700 from Russia, 1,550 from France, 1,400 from Turkey, and 1,200 from Lebanon.[8] Many of the foreign fighters have been killed or have fled from Iraq and Syria as IS has been pushed back on several fronts.

The group was established as Al-Qaeda in Iraq (AQI) in 2004 by Abu Musab al-Zarqawi, a Palestinian Islamist extremist born in Jordan who fought in Afghanistan against the Soviet invasion. He was a close associate of Osama bin Laden, although he did not formally join al-Qaeda until 2004 when he was recognized as the leader of AQI. His organization has always taken a harder line against Shiites, whom it denigrates as apostates who deserve death, than have other franchises of the al-Qaeda network.

Zarqawi was killed in a U.S. air strike in 2006, and his organization was decimated by a U.S.-led counterterrorism campaign. The group made a comeback in Iraq after the withdrawal of U.S. troops in 2011 reduced the pressure on it and Iraqi Prime Minister Nouri al-Maliki's Shia-dominated government alienated Sunni Iraqis, driving many of them to see ISIS as the lesser evil.

The IS began as a branch of al-Qaeda before it broke away from the core al-Qaeda leadership in 2013 in a dispute over leadership of the jihad in Syria. The IS shares a common ideology with its al-Qaeda parent organization but differs with respect to how to apply that ideology. It now rejects the leadership of bin Laden's successor, Ayman al-Zawahiri, who criticized its extreme brutality, which has alienated many Muslims. This is a dispute about tactics and strategies, however, not long-term goals. The schism also was fueled by a personal rivalry between Zawahiri and IS leader Abu Bakr al-Baghdadi, who sees himself as bin Laden's true successor and the leader of a new generation of jihadists. Baghdadi also declared the formation of a caliphate with himself as the leader in June 2014, a claim that al-Qaeda rejects as illegitimate.

In 2014, the IS greatly expanded its control of a wide swath of western Iraq and eastern Syria, territory that it sought to use as a launching pad for operations in the heart of the Arab world and beyond. By May 2016, the United States and its allies had reduced the territory controlled by the Islamic State at its zenith by 45 percent in Iraq and 20 percent in Syria,[9] but the IS continued to expand elsewhere, particularly in Afghanistan, Bangladesh, Egypt, Libya, Pakistan, the Philippines, and Yemen. Boko Haram, the Nigeria-based Islamist terrorist group, also pledged allegiance to the IS in March 2015.

The Islamic State primarily poses a regional threat. It has launched terrorist attacks inside Afghanistan, Egypt, Jordan, Kuwait, Lebanon, Libya, Saudi Arabia, Tunisia, Turkey, and Yemen, among other countries. It also claimed responsibility for the October 31, 2015, downing of a Russian passenger jet over Egypt's Sinai Peninsula that killed 224 people.

The Islamic State's early success in attracting the support of foreign militants, including at least 4,500 from Western countries and at least 250 from the United States, has amplified its potential threat as these foreign volunteers, many of whom received military training, return home.[10] IS foreign fighters teamed with local Islamist militants to launch terrorist attacks that killed 130 people in Paris, France, in November 2015 and 32 people in Brussels, Belgium, in March 2016, as well as a string of smaller attacks. The IS also has inspired self-radicalized individuals to use vehicles as battering rams in terrorist attacks. A terrorist in a truck killed 86 people at a Bastille Day celebration in July 2016 in Nice, France; another truck attack killed 12 people at a Christmas market in Berlin, Germany, in December 2016; and in June 2017, three men in a van killed eight people on or near London Bridge in London, England, by running them over or stabbing them. In May 2017, a terrorist with proven links to the Islamic State killed 22 people in a suicide bombing at a concert in Manchester, England.

IS leader al-Baghdadi threatened to strike "in the heart" of America in July 2012.[11] The IS reportedly has tried to recruit Americans who have joined the fighting in Syria and would be in a position to carry out this threat after returning to the United States.[12] It also has inspired several terrorist attacks by self-radicalized "stray dogs" or "lone wolves" who have acted in its name, such as the foiled May 3, 2015, attack by two Islamist extremists who were fatally shot by police before they could commit mass murder in Garland, Texas; the July 16, 2015, shootings that killed four Marines and a sailor in Chattanooga, Tennessee; the December 2, 2015, shootings that killed 14 people in San Bernardino, California; and the June 12, 2016, shootings at a nightclub in Orlando, Florida, that killed 49 people. Such terrorist attacks, incited but not directed by the IS, are likely to continue for the foreseeable future.

Hayat Tahrir al-Sham (HTS—Organization for the Liberation of the Levant), al-Qaeda's official affiliate in Syria, is a front organization formed in January 2017 in a merger between Jabhat Fateh al-Sham (Front for the Conquest of Syria), formerly known as the al-Nusra Front, and several other Islamist extremist movements. HTS was estimated to have 12,000 to 14,000 fighters in March 2017.[13] Before the merger, al-Nusra had an estimated 5,000 to 10,000 members and had emerged as one of the top two or three rebel groups fighting Syria's Assad dictatorship.[14] Al-Nusra was established as an offshoot of Al-Qaeda in Iraq (now renamed the Islamic State) in late 2011 by Abu Muhammad al-Julani, a lieutenant of AQI leader Abu Bakr al-Baghdadi.[15] It has adopted a more pragmatic course than its extremist parent organization and has cooperated with moderate Syrian rebel groups against the Assad regime, as well as against the Islamic State.

When Baghdadi unilaterally proclaimed the merger of his organization and al-Nusra in April 2013 to form the Islamic State of Iraq and Syria, Julani rejected the merger and renewed his pledge to al-Qaeda leader Ayman al-Zawahiri. The two groups have clashed repeatedly, causing an estimated 3,000 deaths by March 2014.[16]

Al-Nusra has focused its attention on overthrowing the Syrian regime and has not emphasized its hostility to the United States, but that will change if it consolidates power within Syria. It already poses a potential threat because of its recruitment of foreign Islamist militants, including some from Europe and the United States. According to U.S. officials, al-Qaeda leader al-Zawahiri dispatched a cadre of experienced al-Qaeda operatives to Syria, where they were embedded with al-Nusra and charged with organizing terrorist attacks against Western targets. Many members of the group, estimated to number in the dozens, were veterans of al-Qaeda's operations in Afghanistan and Pakistan (part of what was called Khorasan in ancient times) and were referred to as the "Khorasan group" by U.S. officials.[17]

An American Muslim recruited by al-Nusra, Moner Mohammad Abusalha, conducted a suicide truck bombing in northern Syria on May 25, 2014, the first reported suicide attack by an American in Syria.[18] At least five men have been arrested inside the United States for providing material assistance to al-Nusra, including Abdirahman Sheik Mohamud, a naturalized U.S. citizen born in Somalia who was arrested in April 2015 after returning from training in Syria, possibly to launch a terrorist attack inside the United States.[19] The Khorasan group was targeted by a series of U.S. air strikes in 2014–2015 that degraded its capacity to organize terrorist attacks in Western countries. By mid-2015, the FBI assessed that the Islamic State had eclipsed al-Nusra as a threat to the U.S. homeland.[20]

Then-FBI Director James Comey stated in 2014 that tracking Americans who have returned from Syria is one of the FBI's top counterterrorism priorities.[21] Then-Attorney General Eric Holder urged his international counterparts to block the flow of thousands of foreign fighters to Syria, which he termed "a cradle of violent extremism." Speaking at a conference in Norway in July 2014, Holder warned:

> We have a mutual and compelling interest in developing shared strategies for confronting the influx of U.S.-[born] and European-born violent extremists into Syria. And because our citizens can freely travel, visa free, from the U.S. to Norway and other European states— and vice versa—the problem of fighters in Syria returning home to any of our countries is a problem for all of our countries.[22]

Al-Qaeda in the Islamic Maghreb (AQIM), one of al-Qaeda's weaker franchises before the Arab Spring uprisings began in 2011, has flourished in recent years in North Africa and is now one of al-Qaeda's best-financed and most heavily armed elements. The overthrow of Libyan dictator Muammar Qadhafi in 2011 pried open a Pandora's box of problems that AQIM has exploited to bolster its presence in Algeria, Libya, Mali, Morocco, and Tunisia. AQIM accumulated large quantities of arms, including man-portable air defense systems (MANPADS), looted from Qadhafi's huge arms depots.

The fall of Qadhafi also led hundreds of heavily armed Tuareg mercenaries formerly employed by his regime to cross into Mali, where they joined a Tuareg separatist insurgency against Mali's weak central government. In November 2011, they formed the separatist National Movement for the Liberation of Azawad (MNLA) and sought to carve out an independent state. In cooperation with AQIM and the Islamist movement Ansar Dine, they gained control of northern Mali, a territory as big as Texas and the world's largest terrorist sanctuary until the January 2013 French military intervention dealt a major setback to AQIM and its allies.

AQIM is estimated to have several hundred militants operating in Algeria, Libya, Mali, Niger, and Tunisia.[23] Many AQIM cadres pushed out of Mali by the French intervention have regrouped in southwestern Libya and remain committed to advancing AQIM's self-declared long-term goal of transforming the Sahel "into one vast, seething, chaotic Somalia."[24]

The September 11, 2012, attack on the U.S. diplomatic mission in Benghazi underscored the extent to which Islamist extremists have grown stronger in the region, particularly in eastern Libya, a longtime bastion of Islamic fervor. The radical Islamist group that launched the attack, Ansar al-Sharia, has links to AQIM and shares its violent ideology. Ansar al-Sharia and scores of other Islamist militias have flourished in post-Qadhafi Libya because the weak central government has been unable to tame fractious militias, curb tribal and political clashes, or dampen rising tensions between Arabs and Berbers in the West and between Arabs and the Toubou tribe in the South.

AQIM does not pose as much of a threat to the U.S. homeland as other al-Qaeda offshoots pose, but it does threaten regional stability and U.S. allies in North Africa and Europe, where it has gained supporters and operates extensive networks for the smuggling of arms, drugs, and people.

WWTA: The WWTA assesses that "US-based homegrown violent extremists (HVEs) will remain the most frequent and unpredictable Sunni violent extremist threat to the US homeland," that they "will be spurred on by terrorist groups' public calls to carry out attacks in the West," and that "some attacks will probably occur with little or no warning." Continuing:

> In 2016, 16 HVEs were arrested, and three died in attacks against civilian soft targets. Those detained were arrested for a variety of reasons, including attempting travel overseas for jihad and plotting attacks in the United States. In addition to the HVE threat, a small number of foreign-based Sunni violent extremist groups will also pose a threat to the US homeland and continue publishing multilingual propaganda that calls for attacks against US and Western interests in the US homeland and abroad.

The WWTA further reports that ISIS "continues to pose an active terrorist threat to the United States and its allies because of its ideological appeal, media presence, control of territory in Iraq and Syria, its branches and networks in other countries, and its proven ability to direct and inspire attacks against a wide range of targets around the world" but that "territorial losses in Iraq and Syria and persistent counterterrorism operations against parts of its global network are degrading its strength and ability to exploit instability and societal discontent."

The WWTA also concludes that "[d]uring the past 16 years, US and global counterterrorism (CT) partners have significantly reduced al-Qa'ida's ability to carry out large-scale, mass casualty attacks, particularly against the US homeland," but that "al-Qa'ida and its affiliates remain a significant CT threat overseas as they remain focused on exploiting local and regional conflicts."[25]

Summary: Although the al-Qaeda core group has been weakened, the Islamic State and al-Qaeda franchises based in the Middle East pose a growing threat to the U.S. homeland as a result of the recruitment of Muslim militants from Western countries, including the United States, and their efforts to inspire terrorist attacks by homegrown Islamist extremists.

Hezbollah Terrorism. Hezbollah (Party of God), the radical Lebanon-based Shiite revolutionary movement, poses a clear terrorist threat to international security. Hezbollah terrorists have murdered Americans, Israelis, Lebanese, Europeans, and citizens of many other nations. Originally founded in 1982, this Lebanese group has evolved from a local menace into a global terrorist network that is strongly backed by regimes in Iran and Syria, assisted by a political wing that has dominated Lebanese politics and funded by Iran and a web of charitable organizations, criminal activities, and front companies.

Hezbollah regards terrorism not only as a useful tool for advancing its revolutionary agenda, but also as a religious duty as part of a "global jihad." It helped to introduce and popularize the tactic of suicide bombings in Lebanon in the 1980s; developed a strong guerrilla force and a political apparatus in the 1990s; provoked a war with Israel in 2006; intervened in the Syrian civil war after 2011 at Iran's direction; and has become a major destabilizing influence in the ongoing Arab–Israeli conflict.

Hezbollah murdered more Americans than any other terrorist group before September 11, 2001. Despite al-Qaeda's increased visibility since then, Hezbollah remains a bigger, better equipped, better organized, and potentially more dangerous terrorist organization, in part because it enjoys the support of the two chief state sponsors of terrorism in the world today: Iran and Syria. Hezbollah's demonstrated capabilities led former Deputy Secretary of State Richard Armitage to dub it "the A-Team of Terrorists."[26]

Hezbollah has expanded its operations from Lebanon to regional targets in the Middle East and then far beyond. It now is a global terrorist threat that draws financial and logistical support from its Iranian patrons as well as from the Lebanese Shiite diaspora in the Middle East, Europe, Africa, Southeast Asia, North America, and South America. Hezbollah fundraising and equipment procurement cells have been detected and broken up in the United States and Canada. Europe is believed to contain many more of these cells.

Hezbollah has been implicated in numerous terrorist attacks against Americans, including:

- The April 18, 1983, bombing of the U.S. embassy in Beirut, which killed 63 people, including 17 Americans;

- The October 23, 1983, suicide truck bombing of the Marine barracks at Beirut Airport, which killed 241 Marines and other personnel deployed as part of the multinational peacekeeping force in Lebanon;

- The September 20, 1984, suicide truck bombing of the U.S. embassy annex in Lebanon, which killed 23 people, including two Americans; and

- The June 25, 1996, Khobar Towers bombing, which killed 19 American servicemen stationed in Saudi Arabia.

Hezbollah also was involved in the kidnapping of several dozen Westerners, including 14 Americans, who were held as hostages in Lebanon in the 1980s. The American hostages eventually became pawns that Iran used as leverage in the secret negotiations that led to the Iran–Contra affair in the mid-1980s.

Hezbollah has launched numerous attacks outside of the Middle East. It perpetrated the two deadliest terrorist attacks in the history of South America: the March 1992 bombing of the Israeli embassy in Buenos Aires, Argentina, which killed 29 people, and the July 1994 bombing of a Jewish community center in Buenos Aires that killed 96 people. The trial of those who were implicated in the 1994 bombing revealed an extensive Hezbollah presence in Argentina and other countries in South America.

Hezbollah has escalated its terrorist attacks against Israeli targets in recent years as part of Iran's intensifying shadow war against Israel. In 2012, Hezbollah killed five Israeli tourists and a Bulgarian bus driver in a suicide bombing near Burgas, Bulgaria. Hezbollah terrorist plots against Israelis were foiled in Thailand and Cyprus during that same year.

In 2013, Hezbollah admitted that it had deployed several thousand militia members to fight in Syria on behalf of the Assad regime. By 2015, Hezbollah forces had become crucial in propping up the Assad regime after the Syrian army was hamstrung by casualties, defections, and low morale. Hezbollah also deployed personnel to Iraq after the 2003 U.S. intervention to assist pro-Iranian Iraqi Shia militias that were battling the U.S.-led coalition. In addition, Hezbollah has deployed personnel in Yemen to train and assist the Iran-backed Houthi rebels.

Although Hezbollah operates mostly in the Middle East, it has a global reach and has established a presence inside the United States. Hezbollah cells in the United States generally are focused on fundraising, including criminal activities such as those perpetrated by over 70 used-car dealerships identified as part of a scheme to launder hundreds of millions of dollars of cocaine-generated revenue that flowed back to Hezbollah.[27]

Covert Hezbollah cells could morph into other forms and launch terrorist operations inside the United States. Given Hezbollah's close ties to Iran and its past record of executing terrorist attacks on Iran's behalf, there is a real danger that Hezbollah terrorist cells could be activated inside the United States in the event of a conflict between Iran and the U.S. or Israel. On June 1, 2016, two naturalized U.S. citizens were arrested and charged with providing material support to Hezbollah and conducting preoperational surveillance of military and law enforcement sites in New York City and at Kennedy Airport, the Panama Canal, and the American and Israeli embassies in Panama.[28]

WWTA: The WWTA concludes that "Iran continues to be the foremost state sponsor of terrorism and, with its primary terrorism partner, Lebanese Hizballah, will pose a continuing threat to US interests and partners worldwide."[29]

Summary: Hezbollah operates mostly in the Middle East, but it has established cells inside the United States that could be activated, particularly in the event of a military conflict with Iran, Hezbollah's creator and chief backer.

Palestinian Terrorist Threats. A wide spectrum of Palestinian terrorist groups threaten Israel, including Fatah (al-Aqsa Martyrs Brigade); Hamas; Palestinian Islamic Jihad; the Popular Front for the Liberation of Palestine (PFLP); the Popular Front for the Liberation of Palestine–General Command (PFLP–GC); the Palestine Liberation Front; and the Army of Islam. Most of these groups are also hostile to the United States, which they denounce as Israel's primary source of foreign support.

Although they are focused more on Israel and regional targets, these groups also pose a limited potential threat to the U.S. homeland, particularly should the Israeli–Palestinian peace process break down completely and the Palestinian Authority be dissolved. In the event of a military confrontation with Iran, Tehran also might seek to use Palestinian Islamic Jihad, the PFLP–GC, or Hamas as surrogates to strike the United States. Jihadist groups based in Gaza, such as the Army of Islam, also could threaten the U.S. homeland even if a terrorist attack there would set back Palestinian national interests. In general, however, Palestinian groups present a much bigger threat to Israel, Jordan, Egypt, and other regional targets than they do to the United States.

WWTA: The WWTA does not reference the potential threat of Palestinian terrorist attacks on the U.S. homeland.

Summary: Palestinian terrorist groups are focused primarily on Israeli targets and potentially on Egypt and Jordan, which are perceived as collaborating with Israel. They also, however, pose a limited potential threat to the U.S. homeland because of the possibility that if the Israeli–Palestinian peace process broke down completely or Iran became involved in a military conflict with the U.S., Palestinian surrogates could be used to target the U.S. homeland.

Iran's Ballistic Missile Threat. Iran has an extensive missile development program that has received key assistance from North Korea and more limited support from Russia and China before sanctions were imposed by

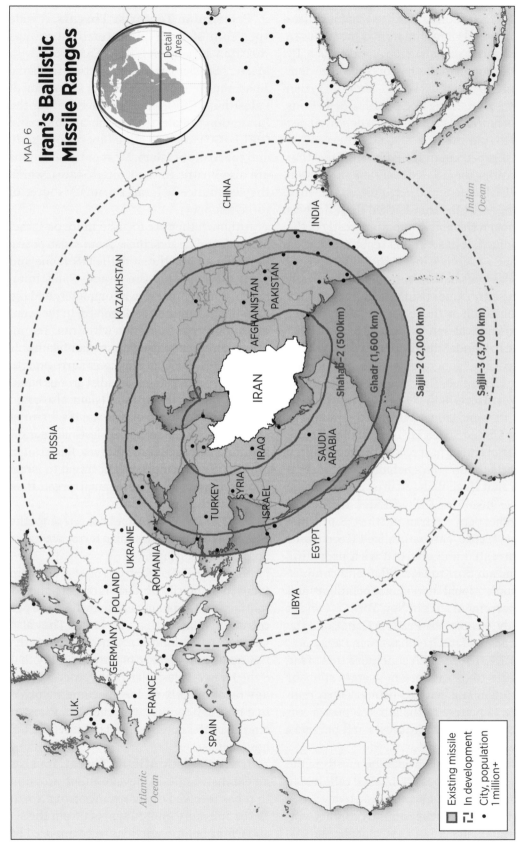

MAP 6

Iran's Ballistic Missile Ranges

CHINA

KAZAKHSTAN

RUSSIA

AFGHANISTAN

PAKISTAN

INDIA

Indian Ocean

IRAN

IRAQ

SAUDI ARABIA

Shahab-2 (500km)

Ghadr (1,600 km)

Sajjil-2 (2,000 km)

Sajjil-3 (3,700 km)

TURKEY

SYRIA

ISRAEL

UKRAINE

GERMANY

POLAND

ROMANIA

FRANCE

EGYPT

LIBYA

U.K.

SPAIN

Atlantic Ocean

Detail Area

Existing missile

In development

City, population
1 million+

SOURCES: International Institute for Strategic Studies, *The Military Balance 2014* (London: Routledge, 2014), and Michael Elleman, "Iran's Ballistic Missile Program,"

the U.N. Security Council. The National Air and Space Intelligence Center noted in 2013 that:

Iran could develop and test an ICBM capable of reaching the United States by 2015. Since 2008, Iran has conducted multiple successful launches of the two-stage Safir space launch vehicle and has also revealed the larger two-stage Simorgh space launch vehicle, which could serve as a test bed for developing ICBM technologies.[30]

Although Tehran's missile arsenal primarily threatens U.S. bases and allies in the region, Iran eventually could expand the range of its missiles to include the continental United States. In its January 2014 report on Iran's military power, the Pentagon assessed that "Iran continues to develop technological capabilities that could be applicable to nuclear weapons and long-range missiles, which could be adapted to deliver nuclear weapons, should Iran's leadership decide to do so."[31]

WWTA: The WWTA assesses that "Tehran would choose ballistic missiles as its preferred method of delivering nuclear weapons, if it builds them. Iran's ballistic missiles are inherently capable of delivering WMD, and Tehran already has the largest inventory of ballistic missiles in the Middle East." In addition, "Tehran's desire to deter the United States might drive it to field an intercontinental ballistic missile (ICBM). Progress on Iran's space program could shorten a pathway to an ICBM because space launch vehicles use similar technologies."[32]

Summary: Iran's ballistic missile force poses a regional threat to the U.S. and its allies, but Tehran eventually could expand the range of its missiles to threaten the continental United States.

Threat of Regional War

The Middle East region is one of the most complex and volatile threat environments faced by the United States and its allies. Iran, various al-Qaeda offshoots, Hezbollah, Arab–Israeli clashes, and a growing number of radical Islamist militias and revolutionary groups

in Egypt, Iraq, Jordan, Lebanon, Libya, Syria, and Yemen pose actual or potential threats to the U.S. and its allies.

Iranian Threats in the Middle East. Iran is an anti-Western revolutionary state that seeks to tilt the regional balance of power in its favor by driving out the Western presence, undermining and overthrowing opposing governments, and establishing its hegemony over the oil-rich Persian Gulf region. It also seeks to radicalize Shiite communities and advance their interests against Sunni rivals. Iran has a long record of sponsoring terrorist attacks against American allies and other interests in the region. With regard to conventional threats, Iran's ground forces dwarf the relatively small armies of the other Gulf states, and its formidable ballistic missile forces pose significant threats to its neighbors.

The July 14, 2015, Iran nuclear agreement, which lifted nuclear-related sanctions on Iran in January 2016, gave Tehran access to about $100 billion in restricted assets and allowed it to expand its oil and gas exports, its chief source of state revenues. This sanctions relief boosted Iran's economy and enabled Iran to enhance its strategic position, military capabilities, and support for surrogate networks and terrorist groups. Tehran announced in May 2016 that it was increasing its military budget for 2016–2017 to $19 billion—a 90 percent increase over the previous year.[33]

The lifting of sanctions also has allowed Tehran to emerge from diplomatic isolation and strengthen strategic ties with Russia that will allow it to purchase advanced arms and modernize its military forces. Russian President Vladimir Putin traveled to Iran in November 2015 to meet with Ayatollah Khamenei, Iran's Supreme Leader, and other officials. Both regimes called for enhanced military cooperation. During President Hassan Rouhani's visit to Russia in March 2017, Putin proclaimed his intention to raise bilateral relations to the level of a "strategic partnership."[34]

This growing strategic relationship could result in Iran's largest arms imports since the 1979 revolution. Tehran announced in April

2016 that Russia had started deliveries of up to five S-300 *Favorit* long-range surface-to-air missile systems, which can track up to 100 aircraft and engage six of them simultaneously at a range of 200 kilometers.[35] Moscow also began negotiations to sell Iran T-90 tanks and advanced Sukhoi Su-30 *Flanker* fighter jets.[36] The warplanes will significantly improve Iran's air defense and long-range strike capabilities.

After the nuclear agreement, Iran and Russia escalated their strategic cooperation in propping up Syria's embattled Assad regime. Iran's growing military intervention in Syria was partly eclipsed by Russia's military intervention and launching of an air campaign against Assad's enemies in September 2015, but Iran's Islamic Revolutionary Guard Corps (IRGC) and surrogate groups have played the leading role in spearheading the ground offensives that have clawed back territory from Syrian rebel groups and tilted the military balance in favor of the Assad regime. By October 2015, Iran had deployed an estimated 7,000 IRGC troops and paramilitary forces in Syria, along with an estimated 20,000 foreign fighters from Iran-backed Shiite militias from Lebanon, Iraq, Afghanistan, and Pakistan.[37]

Terrorist Attacks. Iran has adopted a political warfare strategy that emphasizes irregular warfare, asymmetric tactics, and the extensive use of proxy forces. The Islamic Revolutionary Guard Corps has trained, armed, supported, and collaborated with a wide variety of radical Shia and Sunni militant groups, as well as Arab, Palestinian, Kurdish, and Afghan groups that do not share its radical Islamist ideology. The IRGC's elite Quds (Jerusalem) Force has cultivated, trained, armed, and supported numerous proxies, particularly the Lebanon-based Hezbollah; Iraqi Shia militant groups; Palestinian groups such as Hamas and Palestinian Islamic Jihad; and groups that have fought against the governments of Afghanistan, Bahrain, Egypt, Israel, Iraq, Jordan, Kuwait, Saudi Arabia, Turkey, and Yemen.

Iran is the world's foremost state sponsor of terrorism and has made extensive efforts to export its radical Shia brand of Islamist revolution. It has found success in establishing a network of powerful Shia revolutionary groups in Lebanon and Iraq; has cultivated links with Afghan Shia and Taliban militants; and has stirred Shia unrest in Bahrain, Iraq, Lebanon, Saudi Arabia, and Yemen. In recent years, Iranian arms shipments have been intercepted regularly by naval forces off the coasts of Bahrain and Yemen, and Israel has repeatedly intercepted arms shipments, including long-range rockets, bound for Palestinian militants in Gaza.

Mounting Missile Threat. Iran possesses the largest number of deployed missiles in the Middle East.[38] In June 2017, Iran launched mid-range missiles from its territory that struck opposition targets in Syria. This was the first such operational use of mid-range missiles by Iran for almost 30 years, but it was not as successful as Tehran would have hoped. It was reported that of the five missiles launched, three missed Syria altogether and landed in Iraq, and the remaining two landed in Syria but missed their intended targets by miles.[39] The backbone of the Iranian ballistic missile force is formed by the Shahab series of road-mobile surface-to-surface missiles, which are based on Soviet-designed Scud missiles. The Shahab missiles are potentially capable of carrying nuclear, chemical, or biological warheads in addition to conventional high-explosive warheads. Their relative inaccuracy (compared to NATO ballistic missiles) limits their effectiveness unless they are employed against large, soft targets such as cities.

Iran's heavy investment in such weapons has fueled speculation that the Iranians intend eventually to replace the conventional warheads in their longer-range missiles with nuclear warheads. The Nuclear Threat Initiative has concluded that "[r]egardless of the veracity of these assertions, Tehran indisputably possesses a formidable weapons delivery capability, and its ongoing missile program poses serious challenges to regional stability."[40]

Iran is not a member of the Missile Technology Control Regime, and it has sought aggressively to acquire, develop, and deploy a wide spectrum of ballistic missile, cruise missile, and space launch capabilities. During the 1980–1988 Iran–Iraq war, Iran acquired Soviet-made Scud-B missiles from Libya and later acquired North Korean–designed Scud-C and No-dong missiles, which it renamed the Shahab-2 (with an estimated range of 500 kilometers or 310 miles) and Shahab-3 (with an estimated range of 900 kilometers or 560 miles). It now can produce its own variants of these missiles as well as longer-range Ghadr-1 and Qiam missiles.

Iran's Shahab-3 and Ghadr-1, which is a modified version of the Shahab-3 with a smaller warhead but greater range (about 1,600 kilometers or 1,000 miles), are considered more reliable and advanced than the North Korean No-dong missile from which they are derived. In 2014, then-Director of the Defense Intelligence Agency Lieutenant General Michael T. Flynn warned that:

> Iran can strike targets throughout the region and into Eastern Europe. In addition to its growing missile and rocket inventories, Iran is seeking to enhance lethality and effectiveness of existing systems with improvements in accuracy and warhead designs. Iran is developing the Khalij Fars, an anti-ship ballistic missile which could threaten maritime activity throughout the Persian Gulf and Strait of Hormuz.[41]

Iran's ballistic missiles pose a major threat to U.S. bases and allies from Turkey, Israel, and Egypt in the west to Saudi Arabia and the other Gulf states to the south and Afghanistan and Pakistan to the east. However, it is Israel, which has fought a shadow war with Iran and its terrorist proxies, that is most at risk from an Iranian missile attack. In case the Israeli government had any doubt about Iran's implacable hostility, the Revolutionary Guards displayed a message written in Hebrew on the side of one of the Iranian missiles tested in March 2016: "Israel must be wiped off the earth."[42] The development of nuclear warheads for Iran's ballistic missiles would seriously degrade Israel's ability to deter attacks, an ability

that the existing (but not officially acknowledged) Israeli monopoly on nuclear weapons in the Middle East currently provides.

For Iran's radical regime, hostility to Israel, which Iran sometimes calls the "little Satan," is second only to hostility to the United States, which the leader of Iran's 1979 revolution, Ayatollah Khomeini, dubbed the "great Satan." But Iran poses a greater immediate threat to Israel than it does to the United States, since Israel is a smaller country with fewer military capabilities and is located much closer to Iran. It already is within range of Iran's Shahab-3 missiles. Moreover, all of Israel can be hit with the thousands of shorter-range rockets that Iran has provided to Hezbollah in Lebanon and to Hamas and Palestinian Islamic Jihad in Gaza.

Weapons of Mass Destruction. Tehran has invested tens of billions of dollars since the 1980s in a nuclear weapons program that was masked within its civilian nuclear power program. It built clandestine underground uranium-enrichment facilities, which were subsequently discovered near Natanz and Fordow, and is building a heavy-water reactor near Arak that will give it a second potential route to nuclear weapons.[43]

Before the 2015 nuclear deal, Iran had accumulated enough low-enriched uranium to build eight nuclear bombs if enriched to weapons-grade levels, and it could enrich enough uranium to arm one bomb in less than two months.[44] Clearly, the development of an Iranian nuclear bomb would greatly amplify the threat posed by Iran. Even if Iran did not use a nuclear weapon or pass it on to one of its terrorist surrogates to use, the regime in Tehran could become emboldened to expand its support for terrorism, subversion, and intimidation, assuming that its nuclear arsenal would protect it from retaliation as has been the case with North Korea.

On July 14, 2015, President Barack Obama announced that the United States and Iran, along with China, France, Germany, Russia, the United Kingdom, and the European Union High Representative for Foreign Affairs and Security Policy, had reached a "comprehensive, long-term deal with Iran that will prevent it from obtaining a nuclear weapon."[45] The agreement, however, did a much better job of dismantling sanctions against Iran than it did of dismantling Iran's nuclear infrastructure.

In fact, the agreement did not require that any of the illicit facilities that Iran covertly built had to be dismantled. Tehran was allowed to continue use of its uranium enrichment facilities at Natanz and Fordow, although the latter facility is to be repurposed at least temporarily as a research site. The heavy-water reactor at Arak was also retained with modifications that will reduce its yield of plutonium. All of these facilities, built covertly and housing operations prohibited by multiple U.N. Security Council Resolutions, have been legitimized by the agreement.

Under the agreement, Tehran not only gets to keep all of its illicit nuclear facilities, but also merely has to mothball—not destroy—centrifuges used to enrich uranium. This means that Iran can quickly expand its enrichment activities and rapidly shorten its nuclear breakout timeline when restrictions on the number of centrifuges and uranium enrichment levels expire in 10 to 15 years.

Iran can quickly reverse all of its concessions if it decides to renege on the deal in the future. Sanctions on Iran, however, especially at the U.N., will not "snap back" into place, but rather will take considerable time to reimpose and take effect—assuming that they can be reimposed at all. Any objections by the Russians or Chinese would further delay the inherent time lag before sanctions could have any significant effect and might even derail U.N. sanctions completely.

The Iran nuclear agreement marked a risky departure from more than five decades of U.S. nonproliferation efforts under which Washington opposed the spread of sensitive nuclear technologies, such as uranium enrichment, even for allies. Iran got a better deal on uranium enrichment under the agreement than such U.S. allies as the United Arab Emirates, South Korea, and Taiwan have received from Washington in the past. In fact, the Obama Administration gave Iran better terms on uranium enrichment than the Ford Administration gave to the Shah of Iran, a close U.S. ally before the 1979 revolution.

Although the Obama Administration downplayed the risks inherent in the nuclear agreement, worried governments in the region are bound to take out insurance policies against a nuclear Iran in the form of their own nuclear programs. This could spur a cascade of nuclear proliferation from threatened states such as Saudi Arabia, Egypt, Turkey, and the UAE. Saudi officials already have announced plans to build as many as 16 nuclear power plants by 2040. The Saudi government signed agreements with Rosatom, Russia's state-run nuclear company, in June 2015 and with China in January 2016 that will significantly advance the Saudi nuclear program,[46] and Egypt signed a November 2015 agreement with Russia to build four nuclear reactors. Although these are civilian nuclear programs, they could be used to mask a push for nuclear weapons, as happened in Iran.

Iran is a declared chemical weapons power that claims to have destroyed all of its chemical weapons stockpiles. U.S. intelligence agencies assess that Iran maintains the capability to produce chemical warfare agents and "probably" has the capability to produce some biological warfare agents for offensive purposes if it should decide to do so.[47] Iran also has threatened to disrupt the flow of Persian Gulf oil exports by closing the Strait of Hormuz in the event of a conflict with the U.S. or its allies.

WWTA: The WWTA assesses that "The Islamic Republic of Iran remains an enduring threat to US national interests because of Iranian support to anti-US terrorist groups and militants, the Asad regime, Huthi rebels in Yemen, and because of Iran's development of advanced military capabilities." Iran "continues to develop a range of new military capabilities to monitor and target US and allied military assets in the region, including armed UAVs, ballistic missiles, advanced naval mines, unmanned explosive boats, submarines and advanced torpedoes, and anti-ship and land-attack cruise missiles," and "has the largest ballistic missile force in the Middle East and can strike targets up to 2,000 kilometers from [its] borders." In addition, "Russia's delivery of the SA-20c surface-to-air missile system in 2016 provides Iran with its most advanced long-range air defense system," and "IRGC Navy forces operating aggressively in the Persian Gulf and Strait of Hormuz pose a risk to the US Navy." The WWTA concludes "that limited aggressive interactions will continue and are probably intended to project an image of strength and possibly to gauge US responses."[48]

Summary: Iran poses a major potential threat to U.S. bases, interests, and allies in the Middle East by virtue of its ballistic missile capabilities, continued nuclear ambitions, longstanding support for terrorism, and extensive support for Islamist revolutionary groups.

Arab Attack on Israel. In addition to threats from Iran, Israel faces the constant threat of attack from Palestinian, Lebanese, Egyptian, Syrian, and other Arab terrorist groups. The threat posed by Arab states, which lost four wars against Israel in 1948, 1956, 1967, and 1973 (Syria and the PLO lost a fifth war in 1982 in Lebanon), has gradually declined. Egypt and Jordan have signed peace treaties with Israel, and Iraq, Libya, Syria, and Yemen have increasingly brutal civil wars. Although the conventional military threat to Israel from Arab states has declined, the unconventional military and terrorist threats, especially from an expanding number of sub-state actors, have risen substantially.

Iran has systematically bolstered many of these groups, even when it did not necessarily share their ideology. Today, Iran's surrogates, Hezbollah and Palestinian Islamic Jihad, along with Hamas, a more distant ally, pose the chief immediate threats to Israel. After Israel's May 2000 withdrawal from southern Lebanon and the September 2000 outbreak of fighting between Israelis and Palestinians, Hezbollah stepped up its support for such Palestinian extremist groups as Hamas, Palestinian Islamic Jihad, the al-Aqsa Martyrs' Brigades, and the Popular Front for the Liberation of Palestine.

It also expanded its own operations in the West Bank and Gaza and provided funding for specific attacks launched by other groups.

In July 2006, Hezbollah forces crossed the Lebanese border in an effort to kidnap Israeli soldiers inside Israel, igniting a military clash that claimed hundreds of lives and severely damaged the economies on both sides of the border. Hezbollah has since rebuilt its depleted arsenal with help from Iran and Syria. Israeli officials estimate that Hezbollah has amassed around 150,000 rockets, including a number of long-range Iranian-made missiles capable of striking cities throughout Israel.[49]

Since Israel's withdrawal from the Gaza Strip in 2005, Hamas, Palestinian Islamic Jihad, and other terrorist groups have fired more than 11,000 rockets into Israel, sparking wars in 2008–2009, 2012, and 2014.[50] Over 5 million Israelis out of a total population of 8.1 million live within range of rocket attacks from Gaza, although the successful operation of the Iron Dome anti-missile system greatly mitigated this threat during the Gaza conflict in 2014. In that war, Hamas also unveiled a sophisticated tunnel network that it used to infiltrate Israel to launch attacks on Israeli civilians and military personnel.

Israel also faces a growing threat of terrorist attacks from Syria. Islamist extremist groups fighting the Syrian government, including the al-Qaeda–affiliated Hayat Tahrir al-Sham (formerly al-Nusra Front), have attacked Israeli positions in the Golan Heights, which Israel captured in the 1967 Arab–Israeli war.

WWTA: The WWTA does not reference Arab threats to Israel.

Summary: The threat posed to Israel by Arab states has declined in recent years as a result of the overthrow or weakening of hostile Arab regimes in Iraq and Syria. However, there is a growing threat from sub-state actors such as Hamas, Hezbollah, the Islamic State, and other terrorist groups in Egypt, Gaza, Lebanon, and Syria. Given the region's inherent volatility, the general destabilization that has occurred as a consequence of Syria's civil war, the growth of the Islamic State as a major threat actor, and the United States' long-standing support for

Israel, any concerted attack on Israel would be a major concern for the U.S.

Terrorist Threats from Hezbollah. Hezbollah is a close ally of, frequent surrogate for, and terrorist subcontractor for Iran's revolutionary Islamist regime. Iran played a crucial role in creating Hezbollah in 1982 as a vehicle for exporting its revolution, mobilizing Lebanese Shia, and developing a terrorist surrogate for attacks on its enemies.

Tehran provides the bulk of Hezbollah's foreign support: arms, training, logistical support, and money. The Pentagon estimates that Iran provides up to $200 million in annual financial support for Hezbollah; other estimates run as high as $350 million annually.[51] Tehran has lavishly stocked Hezbollah's expensive and extensive arsenal of rockets, sophisticated land mines, small arms, ammunition, explosives, anti-ship missiles, anti-aircraft missiles, and even unmanned aerial vehicles that Hezbollah can use for aerial surveillance or remotely piloted terrorist attacks. Iranian Revolutionary Guards have trained Hezbollah terrorists in Lebanon's Bekaa Valley and in Iran.

Iran has used Hezbollah as a club to hit not only Israel and Tehran's Western enemies, but also many Arab countries. Iran's revolutionary ideology has fueled its hostility to other Middle Eastern states, many of which it seeks to overthrow and replace with radical allies. During the Iran–Iraq war, Iran used Hezbollah to launch terrorist attacks against Iraqi targets and against Arab states that sided with Iraq. Hezbollah launched numerous terrorist attacks against Saudi Arabia and Kuwait, which extended strong financial support to Iraq's war effort, and participated in several other terrorist operations in Bahrain and the United Arab Emirates.

Iranian Revolutionary Guards conspired with the branch of Hezbollah in Saudi Arabia to conduct the 1996 Khobar Towers bombing in Saudi Arabia. Hezbollah collaborated with the IRGC's Quds Force to destabilize Iraq after the 2003 U.S. occupation and helped to train and advise the Mahdi Army, the radical anti-Western Shiite militia led by militant Iraqi cleric Moqtada al-Sadr. Hezbollah detachments also have cooperated with IRGC forces in Yemen to train and assist the Houthi rebel movement.

Hezbollah threatens the security and stability of the Middle East and Western interests in the Middle East on a number of fronts. In addition to its murderous actions against Israel, Hezbollah has used violence to impose its radical Islamist agenda and subvert democracy in Lebanon. Although some experts believed that Hezbollah's participation in the 1992 Lebanese elections and subsequent inclusion in Lebanon's parliament and coalition governments would moderate its behavior, its political inclusion did not lead it to renounce terrorism.

Hezbollah also poses a potential threat in Europe to America's NATO allies. Hezbollah established a presence inside European countries in the 1980s amid the influx of Lebanese citizens seeking to escape Lebanon's civil war. It took root among Lebanese Shiite immigrant communities throughout Europe. German intelligence officials estimate that roughly 900 Hezbollah members live in Germany alone. Hezbollah also has developed an extensive web of fundraising and logistical support cells throughout Europe.[52]

France and Britain have been the principal European targets of Hezbollah terrorism, in part because both countries opposed Hezbollah's agenda in Lebanon and were perceived as enemies of Iran, Hezbollah's chief patron. Hezbollah has been involved in many terrorist attacks against Europeans, including:

- The October 1983 bombing of the French contingent of the multinational peacekeeping force in Lebanon (on the same day as the U.S. Marine barracks bombing), which killed 58 French soldiers;

- The December 1983 bombing of the French embassy in Kuwait;

- The April 1985 bombing of a restaurant near a U.S. base in Madrid, Spain, which killed 18 Spanish citizens;

- A campaign of 13 bombings in France in 1986 that targeted shopping centers and railroad facilities, killing 13 people and wounding more than 250; and

- A March 1989 attempt to assassinate British novelist Salman Rushdie that failed when a bomb exploded prematurely, killing a terrorist in London.

Hezbollah attacks in Europe trailed off in the 1990s after Hezbollah's Iranian sponsors accepted a truce in their bloody 1980–1988 war with Iraq and no longer needed a surrogate to punish states that Tehran perceived as supporting Iraq. Significantly, the participation of European troops in Lebanese peacekeeping operations, which became a lightning rod for Hezbollah terrorist attacks in the 1980s, could become an issue again if Hezbollah attempts to revive its aggressive operations in southern Lebanon. Troops from European Union member states may someday find themselves attacked by Hezbollah with weapons financed by Hezbollah supporters in their home countries.

As of 2015, Hezbollah operatives were deployed in countries throughout Europe, including Belgium, Bulgaria, Cyprus, France, Germany, and Greece.[53]

WWTA: The WWTA assesses that Iran remains "the foremost state sponsor of terrorism and, with its primary terrorism partner, Lebanese Hizballah, will pose a continuing threat to US interests and partners worldwide. The Syrian, Iraqi, and Yemeni conflicts will continue to aggravate the rising Sunni-Shia sectarian conflict, threatening regional stability."[54]

Summary: Hezbollah poses a major potential terrorist threat to the U.S. and its allies in the Middle East and Europe.

Al-Qaeda: A Continuing Regional Threat. The Arab Spring uprisings that began in 2011 have created power vacuums that al-Qaeda, the Islamic State, and other Islamist extremist groups have exploited to advance their hostile agendas. The al-Qaeda network has taken advantage of failed or failing states in Iraq, Libya, Mali, Syria, and Yemen. The fall of autocratic Arab regimes and the subsequent factional infighting within the ad hoc coalitions that ousted them created anarchic conditions that have enabled al-Qaeda franchises to expand the territories that they control. Rising sectarian tensions resulting from conflicts in Iraq, Syria, and Yemen also have presented al-Qaeda and other Sunni extremist groups with major opportunities to expand their activities.

Jonathan Evans, Director General of the British Security Service (MI5), has warned that "parts of the Arab world have once more become a permissive environment for al-Qaeda."[55] In Egypt, Libya, Syria, Tunisia, and Yemen, the collapse or purge of intelligence and counterterrorism organizations removed important constraints on the growth of al-Qaeda and similar Islamist terrorist groups. Many dangerous terrorists were released or escaped from prison. Al-Qaeda and other revolutionary groups were handed new opportunities to recruit, organize, attract funding for, train, and arm a new wave of followers and to consolidate safe havens from which to mount future attacks.

The Arab Spring uprisings were a golden opportunity for al-Qaeda, coming at a time when its sanctuaries in Pakistan were increasingly threatened by U.S. drone strikes. Given al-Qaeda's Arab roots, the Middle East and North Africa provide much better access to potential Arab recruits than is provided by the more distant and remote regions along the Afghanistan-Pakistan border, where many al-Qaeda cadres fled after the fall of Afghanistan's Taliban regime in 2001. The countries destabilized by the Arab uprisings also could provide easier access to al-Qaeda's Europe-based recruits, who pose dangerous threats to the U.S. homeland by virtue of their European passports and greater ability to blend into Western societies.

WWTA: The WWTA assesses that "US and global counterterrorism (CT) partners have significantly reduced al-Qa'ida's ability to carry out large-scale, mass casualty attacks, particularly against the US homeland," but that "al-Qa'ida and its affiliates remain a significant CT threat overseas as they remain focused on exploiting local and regional conflicts." Both "al-Nusrah Front and al-Qa'ida in the Arabian Peninsula (AQAP) faced CT pressure in Syria and Yemen, respectively," in 2016 "but have preserved the resources, manpower, safe haven, local influence, and operational capabilities to continue to pose a threat."[56]

Summary: The al-Qaeda network and the Islamic State have exploited the political turbulence of the Arab Spring to expand their strength and control of territory in the Middle East. Although the Islamic State has been rolled back in Iraq and Syria, it continues to pose regional threats to the U.S. and its allies.

Growing Threats to Jordan. Jordan, a key U.S. ally, faces external threats from Syria's Assad regime and from Islamist extremists, including the Islamic State, who have carved out sanctuaries in Syria and Iraq. Jordan's cooperation with the United States, Saudi Arabia, and other countries in the air campaign against the IS in Syria and in supporting moderate elements of the Syrian opposition has angered both the Assad regime and Islamist extremist rebels. Damascus could retaliate for Jordanian support for Syrian rebels with cross-border attacks, air strikes, ballistic missile strikes, or the use of terrorist attacks by such surrogates as Hezbollah or the PFLP–GC.

The Islamic State is committed to overthrowing the government of Jordan and replacing it with an Islamist dictatorship. In its previous incarnation as al-Qaeda in Iraq, the IS mounted attacks against targets in Jordan that included the November 2005 suicide bombings at three hotels in Amman that killed 57 people.[57] The IS also burned to death a Jordanian Air Force pilot captured in Syria after his plane crashed and released a video of his grisly murder in February 2015. Jordan also faces threats from Hamas and from Jordanian Islamist extremists, particularly some based in the southern city of Maan who organized pro-IS demonstrations in 2014. Although Jordanian security forces have foiled several IS terrorist plots, six Jordanian border guards were killed by a car bomb on June 21, 2016, prompting Jordan to close the border.

WWTA: The WWTA does not reference threats to Jordan.

Summary: Jordan faces significant security threats from the Islamic State, based in neighboring Syria and Iraq. Because Jordan is one of the very few Arab states that maintain a peaceful relationship with Israel and has been a key regional partner in fighting Islamist terrorism, its destabilization would be a troubling development.

Terrorist Attacks on and Possible Destabilization of Egypt. The 2011 ouster of President Hosni Mubarak's regime undermined the authority of Egypt's central government and allowed disgruntled Bedouin tribes, Islamist militants, and smuggling networks to grow stronger and bolder in Egypt's Sinai Peninsula. President Mohamed Morsi's Muslim Brotherhood–backed government, elected to power in 2012, took a relaxed attitude toward Hamas and other Gaza-based Islamist extremists, enabling Islamist militants in the Sinai to grow even stronger with support from Gaza. They carved out a staging area in the remote mountains of the Sinai that they have used as a springboard for attacks on Israel, Egyptian security forces, tourists, the Suez Canal, and a pipeline carrying Egyptian natural gas to Israel and Jordan.

The July 2013 coup against Morsi resulted in a military government that took a much harder line against the Sinai militants, but it also raised the ire of more moderate Islamists, who could turn to terrorism to avenge Morsi's fall. Terrorist attacks, which had been limited to the Sinai, expanded in lethality and intensity to include bomb attacks in Cairo and other cities by early 2014. In November 2014, the Sinai-based terrorist group Ansar Bayt al-Maqdis (Supporters of Jerusalem) declared its allegiance to the Islamic State and renamed itself the Sinai Province of the Islamic State. It has launched a growing terrorist campaign against Egypt's army, police, and other government institutions, as well as the country's Christian minority, and has claimed responsibility for the October 31, 2015, bombing of a Russian passenger plane flying to Saint Petersburg from Sharm-el-Sheikh that killed 224 people.

Egypt also faces potential threats from Islamist militants and al-Qaeda affiliates based in Libya. The Egyptian air force bombed Islamic State targets in Libya on February 16, 2015, the day after the terrorist organization released a video showing the decapitation of 21 Egyptian Christians who had been working in Libya. Egypt has stepped up security operations along the border with Libya to block the smuggling of arms and militants into Egypt. Cairo also has supported Libyans fighting Islamist extremists in eastern Libya.

During the 2014 conflict between Hamas and Israel, Egypt closed tunnels along the Gaza–Sinai border that have been used to smuggle goods, supplies, and weapons into Gaza. It has continued to uncover and destroy tunnels to disrupt an important source of external support for Sinai Province terrorists. Egypt has continued to uphold its peace treaty with Israel and remains an important ally against Islamist terrorist groups.

WWTA: The WWTA does not reference threats to Egypt.

Summary: Egypt is threatened by Islamist extremist groups that have established bases in the Sinai Peninsula, Gaza, and Libya. Left unchecked, these groups could foment greater instability not only in Egypt, but also in neighboring countries.

Threats to Saudi Arabia and Other Members of the Gulf Cooperation Council. Saudi Arabia and the five other Arab Gulf states—Bahrain, Kuwait, Oman, Qatar, and the United Arab Emirates—formed the Gulf Cooperation Council (GCC) in 1981 to deter and defend against Iranian aggression. Iran remains the primary external threat to their security. Tehran has supported groups that launched terrorist attacks against Bahrain, Kuwait, Saudi Arabia, and Yemen. It sponsored the Islamic Front for the Liberation of Bahrain, a surrogate group that plotted a failed 1981 coup against Bahrain's ruling Al Khalifa family, the Sunni rulers of the predominantly Shia country. Iran also has long backed Bahraini branches of Hezbollah and the Dawa Party. However, in recent years, some members of the GCC, led mainly by Saudi Arabia, have shown concern over Qatar's perceived coziness with Iran, with which Doha shares a

major gas field in the Gulf. This led to the breakdown of diplomatic relations between many Arab states and Qatar in June 2017.[58]

When Bahrain was engulfed in a wave of Arab Spring protests in 2011, its government charged that Iran again exploited the protests to back the efforts of Shia radicals to overthrow the royal family. Saudi Arabia, fearing that a Shia revolution in Bahrain would incite its own restive Shia minority, led a March 2011 GCC intervention that backed Bahrain's government with about 1,000 Saudi troops and 500 police from the United Arab Emirates.

Bahrain has repeatedly intercepted shipments of Iranian arms, including sophisticated bombs employing explosively formed penetrators (EFPs). The government withdrew its ambassador to Tehran when two Bahrainis with ties to the IRGC were arrested after their arms shipment was intercepted off Bahrain's coast in July 2015. Iranian hardliners have steadily escalated pressure on Bahrain. In March 2016, a former IRGC general who is a close adviser to Ayatollah Khamenei stated that "Bahrain is a province of Iran that should be annexed to the Islamic Republic of Iran."[59] After Bahrain stripped a senior Shiite cleric, Sheikh Isa Qassim, of his citizenship, General Qassim Suleimani, commander of the IRGC's Quds Force, threatened to make Bahrain's royal family "pay the price and disappear."[60]

Saudi Arabia also has criticized Iran for supporting radical Saudi Shiites, intervening in Syria, and supporting Shiite Islamists in Lebanon, Iraq, and Yemen. In January 2016, Saudi Arabia executed a Shiite cleric charged with sparking anti-government protests and cut diplomatic ties with Iran after Iranian mobs enraged by the execution attacked and set fire to the Saudi embassy in Tehran.

Saudi Arabia also faces threats from Islamist extremists, including al-Qaeda offshoots in Iraq and Yemen that have attracted many Saudi recruits. Al-Qaeda launched a series of bombings and terrorist attacks inside the kingdom in 2003 and a major attack on the vital Saudi oil facility in Abqaiq in 2006, but a security crackdown drove many of its members out of the country by the end of the decade. Many of them joined

Al-Qaeda in the Arabian Peninsula in neighboring Yemen. AQAP has flourished, aided by the instability fostered by Arab Spring protests and the ouster of the Yemeni government by Iran-backed Houthi rebels in early 2015.

In addition to terrorist threats and possible rebellions by Shia or other disaffected internal groups, Saudi Arabia and the other GCC states face possible military threats from Iran. Because of their close security ties with the United States, Tehran is unlikely to launch direct military attacks against these countries, but it has backed Shiite terrorist groups within GCC states such as Saudi Hezbollah and has supported the Shiite Houthi rebels in Yemen. In March 2015, Saudi Arabia led a 10-country coalition that launched a military campaign against Houthi forces and provided support for ousted Yemeni President Abdu Rabu Mansour Hadi, who took refuge in Saudi Arabia. The Saudi Navy also established a blockade of Yemeni ports to prevent Iran from aiding the rebels.

WWTA: The WWTA assesses that "Iran's leaders remain focused on thwarting US and Israeli influence and countering what they perceive as a Saudi-led effort to fuel Sunni extremism and terrorism against Iran and Shia communities throughout the region."[61]

Summary: Saudi Arabia and other members of the Gulf Cooperation Council face continued threats from Iran as well as rising threats from Islamist extremist groups such as al-Qaeda, the Islamic State, and Houthi militias in Yemen. Saudi citizens and Islamic charities have supported Islamist extremist groups, and the Saudi government promulgates the religious views of the fundamentalist Wahhabi sect of Sunni Islam, but the Saudi government also serves to check radical Islamist groups like the Islamic State and is a regional counterbalance to Iran.

Threats to the Commons

The United States has critical interests at stake in the Middle Eastern commons: sea, air, space, and cyber. The U.S. has long provided the security backbone in these areas, which in turn has supported the region's economic development and political stability.

Maritime. Maintaining the security of the sea lines of communication in the Persian Gulf, Arabian Sea, Red Sea, and Mediterranean Sea is a high priority for strategic, economic, and energy security purposes. The Persian Gulf region contains approximately 50 percent of the world's oil reserves and is a crucial source of oil and gas for energy-importing states, particularly China, India, Japan, South Korea, and many European countries. The flow of that oil could be interrupted by interstate conflict or terrorist attacks.

Bottlenecks such as the Strait of Hormuz, the Suez Canal, and the Bab el-Mandeb Strait are potential choke points for restricting the flow of oil, international trade, and the deployment of U.S. Navy warships. The chief potential threat to the free passage of ships through the Strait of Hormuz, one of the world's most important maritime choke points, is Iran. Approximately 17 million barrels of oil a day—roughly 30 percent of the seaborne oil traded worldwide—flowed through the strait in 2016.[62]

Iran has trumpeted the threat that it could pose to the free flow of oil exports from the Gulf if it is attacked or threatened with a cutoff of its own oil exports. Iran's leaders have threatened to close the Strait of Hormuz, the jugular vein through which most Gulf oil exports flow to Asia and Europe. Although the United States has greatly reduced its dependence on oil exports from the Gulf, it still would sustain economic damage in the event of a spike in world oil prices, and many of its European and Asian allies and trading partners import a substantial portion of their oil needs from the region. Iran's Supreme Leader, Ayatollah Ali Khamenei, has repeatedly played up Iran's threat to international energy security, proclaiming in 2006 that "[i]f the Americans make a wrong move toward Iran, the shipment of energy will definitely face danger, and the Americans would not be able to protect energy supply in the region."[63]

Iran has established a precedent for attacking oil shipments in the Gulf. During the Iran–Iraq war, each side targeted the other's oil facilities, ports, and oil exports. Iran escalated attacks to include neutral Kuwaiti oil tankers and terminals and clandestinely laid mines in

Persian Gulf shipping lanes while its ally Libya clandestinely laid mines in the Red Sea. The United States defeated Iran's tactics by reflagging Kuwaiti oil tankers, clearing the mines, and escorting ships through the Persian Gulf, but a large number of commercial vessels were damaged during the "Tanker War" from 1984 to 1987.

Iran's demonstrated willingness to disrupt oil traffic through the Persian Gulf in the past to place economic pressure on Iraq is a red flag to U.S. military planners. During the 1980s Tanker War, Iran's ability to strike at Gulf shipping was limited by its aging and outdated weapons systems and the U.S. arms embargo imposed after the 1979 revolution. However, since the 1990s, Iran has been upgrading its military with new weapons from North Korea, China, and Russia, as well as with weapons manufactured domestically.

Today, Iran boasts an arsenal of Iranian-built missiles based on Russian and Chinese designs that pose significant threats to oil tankers as well as warships. Iran is well stocked with Chinese-designed anti-ship cruise missiles, including the older HY-2 Seersucker and the more modern CSS-N-4 Sardine and CSS-N-8 Saccade models. Iran also has reverse engineered Chinese missiles to produce its own anti-ship cruise missiles, the Ra'ad and Noor.[64] Shore-based missiles deployed along Iran's coast would be augmented by aircraft-delivered laser-guided bombs and missiles, as well as by television-guided bombs.

Iran has a large supply of anti-ship mines, including modern mines that are far superior to the simple World War I–style contact mines that it used in the 1980s. They include the Chinese-designed EM-52 "rocket" mine, which remains stationary on the sea floor and fires a homing rocket when a ship passes overhead. In addition, Iran can deploy mines or torpedoes from its three Kilo-class submarines, which would be effectively immune to detection for brief periods when running silent and remaining stationary on a shallow bottom just outside the Strait of Hormuz,[65] and also could deploy mines by mini-submarines, helicopters, or small boats disguised as fishing vessels.

Iran's Revolutionary Guard naval forces have developed swarming tactics using fast attack boats and could deploy naval commandos trained to attack using small boats, mini-submarines, and even jet skis. The Revolutionary Guards also have underwater demolition teams that could attack offshore oil platforms and other facilities.

On April 28, 2015, the Revolutionary Guard naval force seized the Maersk Tigris, a container ship registered in the Marshall Islands, near the Strait of Hormuz. Tehran claimed that it seized the ship because of a previous court ruling ordering the Maersk Line, which charters the ship, to make a payment to settle a dispute with a private Iranian company. The ship was later released after being held for more than a week.[66] An oil tanker flagged in Singapore, the Alpine Eternity, was surrounded and attacked by Revolutionary Guard gunboats in the strait on May 14, 2015, when it refused to be boarded. Iranian authorities alleged that it had damaged an Iranian oil platform in March, although the ship's owners maintained that it had hit an uncharted submerged structure.[67] The Revolutionary Guard's aggressive tactics in using commercial disputes as pretexts for the illegal seizures of transiting vessels prompted the U.S. Navy to escort American and British-flagged ships through the Strait of Hormuz for several weeks in May before tensions eased.

The July 2015 nuclear agreement has not altered the confrontational tactics of the Revolutionary Guards in the Gulf.[68] IRGC naval forces have frequently challenged U.S. naval forces in a series of incidents in recent years. IRGC missile boats launched rockets within 1,500 yards of the carrier Harry S. Truman near the Strait of Hormuz in late December 2015, flew drones over U.S. warships, and detained and humiliated 10 American sailors in a provocative January 12, 2016, incident. Despite the fact that the two U.S. Navy boats carrying the sailors had drifted inadvertently into Iranian territorial waters, the vessels had the right of innocent passage, and their crews should not have been subjected to being disarmed, forced onto their knees, filmed, and exploited in propaganda videos.

Finally, Tehran could use its extensive client network in the region to sabotage oil pipelines and other infrastructure or to strike oil tankers in port or at sea. Iranian Revolutionary Guards deployed in Yemen reportedly played a role in the unsuccessful October 9 and 12, 2016, missile attacks launched by Houthi rebels against the USS *Mason*, a U.S. Navy warship, near the Bab el-Mandeb Strait in the Red Sea.[69] The Houthis denied that they launched the missiles, but they did claim responsibility for an October 1, 2016, attack on a UAE naval vessel and the suicide bombing of a Saudi warship in February 2017.

Terrorists also pose a potential threat to oil tankers and other ships. Al-Qaeda strategist Abu Mus'ab al-Suri identified four strategic choke points that should be targeted for disruption: the Strait of Hormuz, the Suez Canal, the Bab el-Mandeb Strait, and the Strait of Gibraltar.[70] In 2002, al-Qaeda terrorists attacked and damaged the French oil tanker *Limbourg* off the coast of Yemen. Al-Qaeda also almost sank the USS *Cole*, a guided-missile destroyer, in the port of Aden, killing 17 American sailors with a suicide boat bomb in 2000. An Egyptian patrol boat was attacked in November 2014 by the crews of small boats suspected of smuggling arms to Islamist terrorists in Gaza. In July 2015, the Islamic State–Sinai Province claimed responsibility for a missile attack on an Egyptian coast guard vessel.

Terrorists also have targeted the Suez Canal. In two incidents on July 29 and August 31, 2013, ships in the waterway were attacked with rocket-propelled grenades. The attacks were claimed by a shadowy Islamist extremist group called the Furqan Brigades, which operated in Egypt's Sinai Peninsula.[71] The vessels reportedly escaped major damage. More important, the canal was not forced to close, which would have disrupted global shipping operations, ratcheted up oil prices, and complicated the deployment of U.S. and NATO naval vessels responding to potential crises in the Middle East, Persian Gulf, and Horn of Africa.

Over the past decade, piracy off the coast of Somalia has threatened shipping near the Bab el-Mandeb Strait and the Gulf of Aden. After more than 230 pirate attacks off the coast of Somalia in 2011, the number of attacks fell off steeply because of security precautions such as the deployment of armed guards on cargo ships and increased patrols by the U.S. Navy and other navies.[72] Then, after a four-year lull, pirate attacks surged in 2016 with 27 incidents, although no ships were hijacked. Between January and May 2017, three commercial vessels were hijacked, the first to be taken since 2012.[73] Somali criminal networks apparently have exploited a decline in international naval patrols and the complacency of some shipping operators who have failed to deploy armed guards on ships in vulnerable shipping lanes.

WWTA: The WWTA does not reference maritime threats in the Middle East region.

Summary: Iran poses the chief potential threat to shipping in the Strait of Hormuz and a growing threat in the Red Sea, and various terrorist groups pose the chief threats to shipping in the Suez Canal and the Bab el-Mandeb Strait. Although pirate attacks off the coast of Somalia declined steeply between 2011 and 2016, there was a spike in attacks in early 2017.

Airspace. The Middle East is particularly vulnerable to attacks on civilian aircraft. Large quantities of arms, including man-portable air defense systems (MANPADS), were looted from Libyan arms depots after the fall of Muammar Qadhafi's regime in 2011. Although Libya is estimated to have had up to 20,000 MANPADS, mostly old Soviet models, only about 10,000 have been accounted for, and an unknown number may have been smuggled out of Libya, which is a hotbed of Islamist radicalism.[74]

U.S. intelligence sources have estimated that at least 800 MANPADS fell into the hands of foreign insurgent groups after being moved out of Libya.[75] Libyan MANPADS have turned up in the hands of AQIM, the Nigerian Boko Haram terrorist group, and Hamas in Gaza. At some point, one or more could be used in a terrorist attack against a civilian airliner. Insurgents or terrorists also could use anti-aircraft missile systems captured from regime forces in Iraq, Syria, and Yemen. In January 2015, a commercial airliner landing at Baghdad International Airport was hit by gunfire that injured a passenger and prompted a temporary suspension of flights to Baghdad.

Al-Qaeda also has used MANPADS in several terrorist attacks. In 2002, it launched two SA-7 MANPADS in a failed attempt to bring down an Israeli civilian aircraft in Kenya. In 2007, the al-Qaeda affiliate al-Shabaab shot down a Belarusian cargo plane in Somalia, killing 11 people.[76] Al-Qaeda's al-Nusra Front and the Islamic State have acquired substantial numbers of MANPADS from government arms depots in Iraq and Syria. Although such weapons may pose only a limited threat to modern warplanes equipped with countermeasures, they pose a growing threat to civilian aircraft in the Middle East and could be smuggled into the United States and Europe to threaten aircraft there.

The Islamic State–Sinai Province claimed responsibility for a bomb that destroyed Metrojet Flight 9268, a Russian passenger jet en route from Sharm el-Sheikh, Egypt, to Saint Petersburg, Russia, on October 31, 2015. The incident claimed the lives of 224 people on the plane, one of the biggest death tolls in a terrorist attack in recent years. The May 19, 2016, crash of EgyptAir flight MS804, which killed 66 people flying from Paris, France, to Cairo, Egypt, has been attributed to a fire, but the cause of that onboard fire has not been determined.

WWTA: The WWTA makes no mention of the terrorist threat to airspace in the Middle East.

Summary: Al-Qaeda, the Islamic State, and other terrorists have seized substantial numbers of anti-aircraft missiles from military bases in Iraq, Libya, and Syria that pose potential threats to safe transit of airspace in the Middle East, North Africa, and elsewhere.

Space. Iran has launched satellites into orbit, but there is no evidence that it has an offensive space capability. Tehran successfully launched three satellites in February 2009, June 2011, and February 2012 using the Safir space launch vehicle, which uses a modified Ghadr-1 missile for its first stage and has a second stage that is based on an obsolete Soviet submarine-launched ballistic missile, the

R-27.[77] The technology probably was transferred by North Korea, which built its BM-25 missiles using the R-27 as a model.[78] Safir technology could be used as a basis to develop long-range ballistic missiles.

Iran claimed that it launched a monkey into space and returned it safely to Earth twice in 2013.[79] Tehran also announced in June 2013 that it had established its first space tracking center to monitor objects in "very remote space" and to help manage the "activities of satellites."[80]

WWTA: The WWTA assesses that "[p]rogress on Iran's space program could shorten a pathway to an ICBM because space launch vehicles use similar technologies."[81]

Summary: Iran has launched satellites into orbit successfully, but there is no evidence that it has developed an offensive space capability that could deny others the use of space or exploit space as a base for offensive weaponry.

Cyber Threats. Iranian cyber capabilities present a significant threat to the U.S. and its allies. Iran has developed offensive cyber capabilities as a tool of espionage and sabotage and claims to have the world's fourth largest cyber force, "a broad network of quasi-official elements, as well as regime-aligned 'hacktivists,' who engage in cyber activities broadly consistent with the Islamic Republic's interests and views."[82]

The creation of the "Iranian Cyber Army" in 2009 marked the beginning of a cyber offensive against those whom the Iranian government regards as enemies. A hacking group dubbed the Ajax Security Team, believed to be operating out of Iran, has used malware-based attacks to target U.S. defense organizations and has successfully breached the Navy Marine Corps Intranet. In addition, the group has targeted dissidents within Iran, seeding versions of anti-censorship tools with malware and gathering information about users of those programs.[83] Iran has invested heavily in cyber capabilities, with an annual budget reported to be almost $1 billion in 2012.[84]

Hostile Iranian cyber activity has increased significantly since the beginning of 2014 and could threaten U.S. critical infrastructure, according to an April 2015 report released by the American Enterprise Institute. The Islamic Revolutionary Guard Corps and Sharif University of Technology are two Iranian institutions that investigators have linked to efforts to infiltrate U.S. computer networks, according to the report.[85]

Iran allegedly has used cyber weapons to engage in economic warfare, most notably the sophisticated and debilitating denial-of-service attacks against a number of U.S. financial institutions, including the Bank of America, JPMorgan Chase, and Citigroup.[86] In February 2014, Iran launched a crippling cyber attack against the Sands Casino in Las Vegas, owned by Sheldon Adelson, a leading supporter of Israel who is known to be critical of the Iranian regime.[87] In 2012, Tehran was suspected of launching the "Shamoon" virus attack on Saudi Aramco, the national oil company that produces more than 10 percent of the world's oil, which destroyed around 30,000 computers, as well as an attack on Qatari natural gas company Rasgas's computer networks.[88]

U.S. officials warned of a surge of sophisticated computer espionage by Iran in the fall of 2015 that included a series of cyber attacks against State Department officials.[89] In March 2016, the Justice Department indicted seven Iranian hackers for penetrating the computer system that controlled a dam in the State of New York.[90]

The sophistication of these and other Iranian cyber attacks, together with Iran's willingness to use these weapons, has led various experts to name Iran as one of America's most cyber-capable opponents. Iranian cyber forces have gone so far as to create fake online personas in order to extract information from U.S. officials through accounts such as LinkedIn, YouTube, Facebook, and Twitter.[91]

WWTA: The WWTA assessed that "Tehran continues to leverage cyber espionage, propaganda, and attacks to support its security priorities, influence events and foreign perceptions, and counter threats—including against US allies in the region." It also has "used its cyber capabilities directly against the United States. For example, in 2013, an Iranian hacker

conducted an intrusion into the industrial control system of a US dam, and in 2014, Iranian actors conducted a data deletion attack against the network of a US-based casino."[92]

Summary: Iranian cyber capabilities present significant espionage and sabotage threats to the U.S. and its allies, and Tehran has shown willingness and skill in using them.

Threat Scores

Iran. Iran represents by far the most significant security challenge to the United States, its allies, and its interests in the greater Middle East. Its open hostility to the United States and Israel, sponsorship of terrorist groups like Hezbollah, and history of threatening the commons underscore the problem it could pose. Today, Iran's provocations are mostly a concern for the region and America's allies, friends, and assets there. Iran relies heavily on irregular (to include political) warfare against others in the region and fields more ballistic missiles than any of its neighbors. The development of its ballistic missiles and potential nuclear capability also mean that it poses a long-term threat to the security of the U.S. homeland.

According to the International Institute for Strategic Studies' *Military Balance 2017*, among the key weapons in Iran's inventory are 22-plus MRBMs, 18-plus SRBMs, 333 combat-capable aircraft, 1,513 main battle tanks, 640-plus APCs, 21 tactical submarines, seven corvettes, and 13 amphibious landing ships. There are 523,000 personnel in the armed forces, including 350,000 in the Army, 125,000 in the Islamic Revolutionary Guard Corps, and 18,000 in the Navy. With regard to these capabilities, the IISS assesses that:

> Iran continues to rely on a mix of ageing combat equipment, reasonably well-trained regular and Islamic Revolutionary Guard Corps (IRGC) forces, and its ballistic-missile inventory to underpin the security of the state. The IRGC, including senior military leaders, has been increasingly involved in the civil war in Syria, supporting President Bashar al-Assad's regular and irregular forces; it was first deployed to Syria in an "advisory" role in 2012....

The military continues to struggle with an ageing inventory of primary combat equipment that ingenuity and asymmetric warfare techniques can only partially offset....

The nuclear agreement with the P5+1 and the European Union also begins to open the way for Iran to revamp its equipment inventory, with China and Russia potentially major suppliers, though sales of conventional systems remain embargoed for five years.[93]

This *Index* assesses the overall threat from Iran, considering the range of contingencies, as "aggressive" and "gathering." Iran's capability score holds at "gathering" from 2017 to 2018.

Threats: Iran

	HOSTILE	AGGRESSIVE	TESTING	ASSERTIVE	BENIGN
Behavior		✓			

	FORMIDABLE	GATHERING	CAPABLE	ASPIRATIONAL	MARGINAL
Capability		✓			

Greater Middle East–Based Terrorism

Collectively, the varied non-state actors in the Middle East that are vocally and actively opposed to the United States are the closest to being rated "aggressive" with regard to the degree of provocation they exhibit. These groups, from the Islamic State to al-Qaeda and its affiliates, Hezbollah, and the range of Palestinian terrorist organizations in the region, are primarily a threat to America's allies, friends, and interests in the Middle East. Their impact on the American homeland is mostly a concern for American domestic security agencies, but they pose a challenge to the stability of the region that could result in the emergence of more dangerous threats to the United States.

The IISS *Military Balance* addresses only the military capabilities of states. Consequently, it does not provide any accounting of such entities as Hezbollah, Hamas, al-Qaeda, or the Islamic State.

This *Index* assesses the overall threat from greater Middle East–based terrorism, considering the range of contingencies, as "aggressive" and "capable." The decrease from "hostile" to "aggressive" reflects significant losses in territorial control and subsequent need to focus their efforts on defending and maintaining regional holds.[94]

Threats: Middle East Terrorism

	HOSTILE	AGGRESSIVE	TESTING	ASSERTIVE	BENIGN
Behavior		✓			

	FORMIDABLE	GATHERING	CAPABLE	ASPIRATIONAL	MARGINAL
Capability			✓		

Endnotes

1. James Phillips, "The Yemen Bombing: Another Wake-up Call in the Terrorist Shadow War," Heritage Foundation *Executive Memorandum* No. 773, October 25, 2000, http://www.heritage.org/middle-east/report/the-yemen-bombing-another-wake-call-the-terrorist-shadow-war.

2. Stephen F. Hayes and Thomas Joscelyn, "Connecting the Dots," *The Weekly Standard*, November 23, 2009, http://www.weeklystandard.com/Content/Public/Articles/000/000/017/225edzea.asp (accessed June 22, 2017).

3. Peter Finn, "Al-Awlaki Directed Christmas 'Underwear Bomber' Plot, Justice Department Memo Says," *The Washington Post*, February 10, 2012, http://www.washingtonpost.com/world/national-security/al-awlaki-directed-christmas-underwear-bomber-plot-justice-department-memo-says/2012/02/10/gIQArDOt4Q_story.html (accessed June 22, 2017).

4. Scott Shane, "The Enduring Influence of Anwar al-Awlaki in the Age of the Islamic State," Combating Terrorism Center at West Point, *CTC Sentinel*, Vol. 9, Issue 7 (July 2016), pp. 15–19, https://www.ctc.usma.edu/v2/wp-content/uploads/2016/08/CTC-SENTINEL_Vol9Iss710.pdf (accessed June 26, 2017).

5. U.S. Department of State, Bureau of Counterterrorism, "Foreign Terrorist Organizations," Chapter 6 in *Country Reports on Terrorism 2015*, June 2016, http://www.state.gov/j/ct/rls/crt/2015/257523.htm (accessed June 22, 2017).

6. Eric Schmitt, "Al Qaeda Turns to Syria, With a Plan to Challenge ISIS," *The New York Times*, May 15, 2016, http://www.nytimes.com/2016/05/16/world/middleeast/al-qaeda-turns-to-syria-with-a-plan-to-challenge-isis.html?_r=0 (accessed June 22, 2017).

7. Michael Georgy and Maher Chmaytelli, "From 'Caliph' to Fugitive: IS Leader Baghdadi's New Life on the Run," Reuters, June 14, 2017, http://www.reuters.com/article/mideast-crisis-iraq-baghdadi-idUSKBN1931KL (accessed June 26, 2017).

8. Lisa Curtis, ed., "Combatting the ISIS Foreign Fighter Pipeline: A Global Approach," Heritage Foundation *Special Report* No. 180, January 6, 2016, p. 3, http://thf-reports.s3.amazonaws.com/2015/SR180.pdf.

9. Eric Schmitt, "U.S. Says Its Strikes Are Hitting More Significant ISIS Targets," *The New York Times*, May 25, 2016, http://www.nytimes.com/2016/05/26/us/politics/us-strikes-isis-targets.html?_r=0 (accessed June 22, 2017).

10. Curtis, ed., "Combatting the ISIS Foreign Fighter Pipeline," p. 5.

11. Brian Bennett, "Al-Qaeda in Iraq Threatens Attacks in U.S.," *Los Angeles Times*, July 25, 2012, http://articles.latimes.com/2012/jul/25/nation/la-na-qaeda-us-20120726 (accessed June 22, 2017).

12. James Phillips and Cassandra Lucaccioni, "Al-Qaeda Recruits Americans in Syria," The Daily Signal, January 10, 2014, http://dailysignal.com/2014/01/10/al-qaeda-seeks-american-recruits-syria/.

13. Charles Lister, "Al-Qaeda Is Starting to Swallow the Syrian Opposition," *Foreign Policy*, March 15, 2017, http://foreignpolicy.com/2017/03/15/al-qaeda-is-swallowing-the-syrian-opposition/ (accessed June 22, 2017).

14. Schmitt, "Al Qaeda Turns to Syria."

15. U.S. Department of State, Bureau of Counterterrorism, "Foreign Terrorist Organizations," Chapter 6 in *Country Reports on Terrorism 2012*, May 2013, http://www.state.gov/j/ct/rls/crt/2012/209989.htm (accessed June 22, 2017).

16. Associated Press, "ISIL Says It Faces War with Nusra in Syria," Al Jazeera, March 8, 2014, http://www.aljazeera.com/news/middleeast/2014/03/isil-says-it-faces-war-with-nusra-syria-20143719484991740.html (accessed June 22, 2017).

17. James Phillips, "The Rise of Al-Qaeda's Khorasan Group: What It Means for U.S. National Security," Heritage Foundation *Issue Brief* No. 4281, October 6, 2014, http://www.heritage.org/middle-east/report/the-rise-al-qaedas-khorasan-group-what-it-means-us-national-security.

18. Adam Goldman, Greg Miller, and Nicole Rodriquez, "American Who Killed Himself in Syria Suicide Attack Was from South Florida," *The Washington Post*, May 31, 2014, http://www.washingtonpost.com/world/national-security/american-who-killed-himself-in-syria-suicide-attack-was-from-south-florida-official-says/2014/05/30/03869b6e-e7f4-11e3-a86b-362fd5443d19_story.html (accessed June 22, 2017).

19. Adam Goldman, "Ohio Man Who Trained with Jabhat al-Nusra Is Indicted on Terrorism Charges," *The Washington Post*, April 16, 2015, http://www.washingtonpost.com/world/national-security/ohio-man-who-trained-with-jabhat-al-nusra-is-indicted-on-terrorism-charges/2015/04/16/8e8ded08-e455-11e4-b510-962fcfabc310_story.html (accessed June 22, 2017).

20. Evan Perez and Tom LoBianco, "FBI Head: Khorasan Group Diminished; ISIS Bigger Threat than al Qaeda," CNN, July 23, 2015, http://www.cnn.com/2015/07/22/politics/fbi-james-comey-isis-khorasan-group/ (accessed June 22, 2017).

21. Eric Schmitt and Ben Hubbard, "Suicide Bomber in Syria Was U.S. Citizen, Officials Say," *The New York Times*, May 28, 2014, http://www.nytimes.com/2014/05/29/world/middleeast/us-citizen-in-suicide-act-in-syria-officials-say.html (accessed June 22, 2017).

22. Sari Horwitz, "Eric Holder Urges European Countries to Help Stop Flow of Radicals to Syria," *The Washington Post*, July 8, 2014, http://www.washingtonpost.com/world/national-security/eric-holder-urges-european-states-to-help-stop-flow-of-radicals-to-syria/2014/07/08/b50d01ae-0692-11e4-8a6a-19355c7e870a_story.html (accessed June 22, 2017).

23. U.S. Department of State, *Country Reports on Terrorism 2015.*

24. William Maclean, "Local Wars Blur al-Qaeda's Threat to West," Reuters, July 5, 2012, http://uk.reuters.com/article/2012/07/05/uk-security-qaeda-idUKBRE86408B20120705 (accessed June 22, 2017).

25. Daniel R. Coats, Director of National Intelligence, "Statement for the Record: Worldwide Threat Assessment of the US Intelligence Community," Select Committee on Intelligence, U.S. Senate, May 11, 2017, p. 5, https://www.dni.gov/files/documents/Newsroom/Testimonies/SSCI%20Unclassified%20SFR%20-%20Final.pdf (accessed June 26, 2017). Cited hereafter as Coats, "2017 Worldwide Threat Assessment."

26. Rebecca Leung, "Hezbollah: 'A-Team of Terrorists,'" CBS News, April 18, 2003, http://www.cbsnews.com/news/hezbollah-a-team-of-terrorists/ (accessed June 22, 2017).

27. Suzanne Kelly, "Experts: Hezbollah Positioned for Attack in U.S.," CNN, March 21, 2012, http://security.blogs.cnn.com/2012/03/21/house-panel-hears-testimony-on-hezbollah-in-u-s/ (accessed June 22, 2017).

28. Ellie Kaufman, "Two Americans Led Double Lives as Hezbollah Agents, Officials Say," CNN, June 9, 2017, http://www.cnn.com/2017/06/08/us/americans-accused-hezbollah-agents/ (accessed June 22, 2017).

29. Coats, "2017 Worldwide Threat Assessment," p. 5.

30. National Air and Space Intelligence Center, "Ballistic and Cruise Missile Threat," July 11, 2013, p. 3, https://fas.org/programs/ssp/nukes/nuclearweapons/NASIC2013_050813.pdf (accessed June 22, 2017).

31. U.S. Department of Defense, unclassified "Annual Report on Military Power of Iran: Executive Summary," January 2014, http://freebeacon.com/wp-content/uploads/2014/07/Iranmilitary.pdf (accessed June 22, 2017).

32. Coats, "2017 Worldwide Threat Assessment," p. 7.

33. Saeed Ghasseminejad, "Iran Doubles Down on Its Military Budget," Foundation for Defense of Democracies *Policy Brief,* June 3, 2016, http://www.defenddemocracy.org/media-hit/saeed-ghasseminejad-iran-doubles-down-on-its-military-budget/ (accessed June 22, 2017).

34. Sima Shine and Zvi Magen, "President Rouhani's Visit to Russia: A New Level of Relations?" Tel Aviv University, Institute for National Security Studies, *INSS Insight* No. 914, April 5, 2017, http://www.inss.org.il/publication/president-rouhanis-visit-russia-new-level-relations/ (accessed June 22, 2017).

35. Reuters, "Iran Says Russia Delivers First Part of S-300 Defense System," April 11, 2016, http://www.reuters.com/article/us-russia-iran-arms-idUSKCN0X80MM?elqTrackId=e02d5aca6d48418984d902ced0c33d77&elq=39fecef381094e0cbc6de535feb74a3c&elqaid=17334&elqat=1&elqCampaignId=10743 (accessed June 22, 2017).

36. Farzin Nadimi, "Iran and Russia's Growing Defense Ties," Washington Institute for Near East Policy *PolicyWatch* No. 2563, February 18, 2016, http://www.washingtoninstitute.org/policy-analysis/view/iran-and-russias-growing-defense-ties (accessed June 22, 2017).

37. Sam Dagher and Asa Fitch, "Iran Expands Role in Syria in Conjunction with Russia's Airstrikes," *The Wall Street Journal*, October 2, 2015, http://www.wsj.com/articles/iran-expands-role-in-syria-in-conjunction-with-russias-airstrikes-1443811030 (accessed June 22, 2017).

38. Nuclear Threat Initiative, Country Profiles, "Iran: Missile," last updated October 2015, http://www.nti.org/country-profiles/iran/delivery-systems/ (accessed June 22, 2017).

39. Amos Harel, "Iran's Missile Attack on Syria Failed: 5 Missed, 3 Landed in Iraq," *Haaretz*, June 21, 2017, http://www.haaretz.com/middle-east-news/1.796836 (accessed June 22, 2017).

40. Nuclear Threat Initiative, "Iran: Missile."

41. Lieutenant General Michael T. Flynn, U.S. Army, Director, Defense Intelligence Agency, "Annual Threat Assessment," statement before the Committee on Armed Services, U.S. Senate, February 11, 2014, p. 20, http://www.dia.mil/Portals/27/Documents/News/2014_DIA_SFR_SASC_ATA_FINAL.pdf (accessed June 26, 2017).

42. Tim Hume and Alireza Hajihosseini, "Iran Fires Ballistic Missiles a Day After Test; U.S. Officials Hint at Violation," CNN, March 9, 2016, http://www.cnn.com/2016/03/09/middleeast/iran-missile-test/ (accessed June 22, 2017).

43. James Phillips, "Iran's Nuclear Program: What Is Known and Unknown," Heritage Foundation *Backgrounder* No. 2393, March 26, 2010, http://www.heritage.org/research/reports/2010/03/iran-s-nuclear-program-what-is-known-and-unknown.

44. Valerie Lincy and Gary Milhollin, "Iran's Nuclear Timetable," Wisconsin Project for Nuclear Arms Control, *Iran Watch*, June 17, 2015, http://www.iranwatch.org/our-publications/articles-reports/irans-nuclear-timetable (accessed June 22, 2017).

45. News release, "Statement by the President on Iran," The White House, July 14, 2015, https://www.whitehouse.gov/the-press-office/2015/07/14/statement-president-iran (accessed June 22, 2017).

46. Christopher M. Blanchard, "Saudi Arabia: Background and U.S. Relations," Congressional Research Service *Report for Members and Committees of Congress*, April 22, 2016, p. 20, https://www.fas.org/sgp/crs/mideast/RL33533.pdf (accessed June 22, 2017).

47. Kenneth Katzman, "Iran, Gulf Security, and U.S. Policy," Congressional Research Service *Report for Members and Committees of Congress*, March 30, 2016, p. 24, https://www.fas.org/sgp/crs/mideast/RL32048.pdf (accessed June 22, 2017).

48. Coats, "2017 Worldwide Threat Assessment," p. 23.

49. Avi Issacharoff, "Israel Raises Hezbollah Rocket Estimate to 150,000," *The Times of Israel*, November 12, 2015, http://www.timesofisrael.com/israel-raises-hezbollah-rocket-estimate-to-150000/ (accessed June 22, 2017).

50. Israel Defense Forces, "Rocket Attacks on Israel from Gaza," IDF Blog, http://www.idfblog.com/facts-figures/rocket-attacks-toward-israel/ (accessed June 22, 2017).

51. Matthew Levitt, "A Proxy for Iran," Washington Institute for Near East Policy, *Cipher Brief*, July 14, 2016, http://www.washingtoninstitute.org/policy-analysis/view/a-proxy-for-iran (accessed June 26, 2017).

52. James Phillips, "Hezbollah's Terrorist Threat to the European Union," testimony before the Subcommittee on Europe, Committee on Foreign Affairs, U.S. House of Representatives, June 20, 2007, http://www.heritage.org/research/testimony/hezbollahs-terrorist-threat-to-the-european-union.

53. Matthew Levitt, "Inside Hezbollah's European Plots," Washington Institute for Near East Policy, July 20, 2015, https://www.washingtoninstitute.org/policy-analysis/view/inside-hezbollahs-european-plots (accessed June 22, 2017).

54. Coats, "2017 Worldwide Threat Assessment," p. 5.

55. "Address at the Lord Mayor's Annual Defence and Security Lecture by the Director General of the Security Service, Jonathan Evans," London, MI5 Security Service, June 25, 2012, https://www.mi5.gov.uk/home/about-us/who-we-are/staff-and-management/director-general/speeches-by-the-director-general/the-olympics-and-beyond.html (accessed June 22, 2017).

56. Coats, "2017 Worldwide Threat Assessment," p. 5.

57. James Phillips, "Zarqawi's Amman Bombings: Jordan's 9/11," Heritage Foundation *WebMemo* No. 919, November 18, 2005, http://www.heritage.org/research/reports/2005/11/zarqawis-amman-bombings-jordans-9-11.

58. For more information on the inter-Arab dispute with Qatar, see "Assessing the Global Operating Environment," p. 145ff.

59. Middle East Media Research Institute, "Former IRGC General Close to Supreme Leader Khamenei: 'Bahrain Is a Province of Iran That Should Be Annexed to [It],'" *Special Dispatch* No. 6358, March 23, 2016, http://www.memri.org/report/en/0/0/0/0/0/0/9090.htm (accessed June 26, 2017).

60. Maayan Groisman, "Iranian Commander Threatens to Make Bahrain's Royal Family 'Disappear'," *The Jerusalem Post*, June 21, 2016, http://www.jpost.com/Middle-East/Iran-News/Iranian-Quds-Force-commander-threatens-to-make-Bahrains-royal-family-disappear-457354 (accessed June 22, 2017).

61. Coats, "2017 Worldwide Threat Assessment," p. 23.

62. Tyler Durden, "World Oil and Its Seven Biggest Chokepoints," November 10, 2016, http://www.zerohedge.com/news/2016-11-10/world-oil-and-its-seven-biggest-chokepoints (accessed June 26, 2017).

63. Thom Shanker, "Rice Dismisses Iranian Cleric's Warning on Oil," *The New York Times*, June 5, 2006, http://www.nytimes.com/2006/06/05/world/middleeast/05diplo.html?_r=0 (accessed June 22, 2017).

64. Robert Hewson, "Iran Ready to Field Maritime Cruise Missile," *Jane's Defence Weekly*, February 25, 2004, http://www.network54.com/Forum/242875/thread/1086131208/Iran+Ready+To+Field+New+Maritime+Cruise+Missile (accessed June 26, 2017).

65. Michael Knights, *Troubled Waters: Future U.S. Security Assistance in the Persian Gulf* (Washington: Washington Institute for Near East Policy, 2006), p. 71, http://www.washingtoninstitute.org/uploads/Documents/pubs/TroubledWaters.pdf.pdf (accessed June 22, 2017).

66. Asa Fitch, "Iranian Authorities Release Maersk Tigris," *The Wall Street Journal*, May 7, 2015, http://www.wsj.com/articles/iranian-authorities-release-maersk-tigris-1430991500 (accessed June 22, 2017).

67. ASC Staff, "Iran Attack: Alpine Eternity Moved to Dubai Drydocks," Arabian Supply Chain.com, May 26, 2015, http://www.arabiansupplychain.com/article-11359-iran-attack-alpine-eternity-moved-to-dubai-drydocks/ (accessed June 22, 2017).

68. James Phillips, "The Dangerous Regional Implications of the Iran Nuclear Agreement," Heritage Foundation *Backgrounder* No. 3124, May 9, 2016, http://www.heritage.org/middle-east/report/the-dangerous-regional-implications-the-iran-nuclear-agreement.

69. Paul Bucala, Caitlin Shayda Pendleton, Christopher Harmer, Emily Estelle, and Marie Donovan, "Iranian Involvement in Missile Attacks on the USS Mason," American Enterprise Institute, October 19, 2016, https://www.criticalthreats.org/analysis/iranian-involvement-in-missile-attacks-on-the-uss-mason (accessed June 22, 2017).

70. Niklas Anziger, "Jihad at Sea—Al Qaeda's Maritime Front in Yemen," Center for International Maritime Security, February 25, 2014, http://cimsec.org/jihad-sea-yemen-al-qaedas-new-frontier (accessed June 22, 2017).

71. Steven Starr, "Attacks in the Suez: Security of the Canal at Risk?" Combating Terrorism Center at West Point, *CTC Sentinel*, Vol. 7, Issue 1 (January 15, 2014), https://www.ctc.usma.edu/posts/attacks-in-the-suez-security-of-the-canal-at-risk (accessed June 22, 2017).

72. Thomas Gibbons-Neff, "Piracy Back on the Rise off Somalia, U.S. Military Says," *Chicago Tribune*, April 23, 2017, http://www.chicagotribune.com/news/nationworld/ct-piracy-somali-waters-20170423-story.html (accessed June 22, 2017).

73. Lisa Otto, "Has Somali Piracy Returned?" *The Maritime Executive*, May 22, 2017, http://maritime-executive.com/editorials/has-somali-piracy-returned (accessed June 22, 2017).

74. Scott Stewart, "The Continuing Threat of Libyan Missiles," Stratfor Global Intelligence, *Security Weekly*, May 3, 2012, http://www.stratfor.com/weekly/continuing-threat-libyan-missiles#axzz39ABWqV00 (accessed June 22, 2017).

75. David Ignatius, "Libyan Missiles on the Loose," *The Washington Post*, May 8, 2012, http://www.washingtonpost.com/opinions/libyan-missiles-on-the-loose/2012/05/08/gIQA1FCUBU_story.html (accessed June 22, 2017).

76. Matt Schroeder, "New Information on Somali MANPADS," Federation of American Scientists, July 27, 2007, https://fas.org/blogs/security/2007/07/new_information_on_somali_manp/ (accessed June 22, 2017).

77. Nuclear Threat Initiative, "Iran: Missile," p. 4.

78. Viola Gienger and Tony Capaccio, "Iran May Have Missiles from North Korea, Cables Posted by Wikileaks Show," Bloomberg, November 29, 2010, https://www.youtube.com/watch?v=3ukx2EJgh1c (accessed June 22, 2017).

79. Lateef Mungin, "Iran Claims 2nd Launch of Monkey into Space and Back," CNN, December 14, 2013, http://www.cnn.com/2013/12/14/world/meast/iran-monkey-space/ (accessed September 17, 2014).

80. Nasser Karimi, "Iran Says It Sets up Space Monitoring Center," Associated Press, June 9, 2013, http://news.yahoo.com/iran-says-sets-space-monitoring-center-072742942.html (accessed June 27, 2017).

81. Coats, "2017 Worldwide Threat Assessment," p. 7.

82. Ilan Berman, "The Iranian Cyber Threat, Revisited," statement before the Subcommittee on Cybersecurity, Infrastructure Protection, and Security Technologies, Committee on Homeland Security, U.S. House of Representatives, March 20, 2013, https://homeland.house.gov/hearing/subcommittee-hearing-cyber-threats-china-russia-and-iran-protecting-american-critical/ (accessed June 22, 2017).

83. Nart Villeneuve, Ned Moran, Thoufique Haq, and Mike Scott, "Operation Saffron Rose 2013," FireEye *Special Report*, 2014, https://www.fireeye.com/content/dam/fireeye-www/global/en/current-threats/pdfs/rpt-operation-saffron-rose.pdf (accessed June 22, 2017).

84. Siobhan Gorman and Julian E. Barnes, "Iran Blamed for Cyberattacks," *The Wall Street Journal*, October 12, 2012, http://online.wsj.com/news/articles/SB10000872396390444657804578052931555576700?mg=reno64-wsj (accessed June 22, 2017).

85. Frederick W. Kagan and Tommy Stiansen, *The Growing Cyberthreat from Iran: The Initial Report of Project Pistachio Harvest*, American Enterprise Institute Critical Threats Project and Norse Corporation, April 2015, https://www.aei.org/publication/growing-cyberthreat-from-iran/ (accessed June 27, 2017).

86. Berman, "The Iranian Cyber Threat, Revisited," p. 3.

87. Anthony Capaccio, David Lerman, and Chris Strohm, "Iran Behind Cyber-Attack on Adelson's Sands Corp., Clapper Says," Bloomberg Business, February 26, 2015, http://www.bloomberg.com/news/articles/2015-02-26/iran-behind-cyber-attack-on-adelson-s-sands-corp-clapper-says (accessed June 22, 2017).

88. Christopher Bronk and Eneken Tikk-Ringas, "The Cyber Attack on Saudi Aramco," International Institute for Strategic Studies, *Survival: Global Politics and Strategy*, Vol. 55, No. 2 (April/May 2013), pp. 81–96, http://www.iiss.org/en/publications/survival/sections/2013-94b0/survival--global-politics-and-strategy-april-may-2013-b2cc/55-2-08-bronk-and-tikk-ringas-e272 (accessed June 22, 2017); Saudi Aramco, "Oil Production," http://www.saudiaramco.com/en/home/our-business/upstream/oil-production.html (accessed June 22, 2017).

89. David E. Sanger and Nicole Perlroth, "Iranian Hackers Attack State Dept. via Social Media Accounts," *The New York Times*, November 24, 2015, http://www.nytimes.com/2015/11/25/world/middleeast/iran-hackers-cyberespionage-state-department-social-media.html?_r=0 (accessed June 22, 2017).

90. Ellen Nakashima and Matt Zapotosky, "U.S. Charges Iran-Linked Hackers with Targeting Banks, N.Y. Dam," *The Washington Post*, March 24, 2016, https://www.washingtonpost.com/world/national-security/justice-department-to-unseal-indictment-against-hackers-linked-to-iranian-goverment/2016/03/24/9b3797d2-f17b-11e5-a61f-e9c95c06edca_story.html (accessed June 22, 2017).

91. David E. Sanger, "Iran Hackers Dangle a Familiar Name to Fish for Data," *The New York Times*, May 30, 2014, http://www.nytimes.com/2014/05/31/world/middleeast/iran-hackers-dangle-a-familiar-name-to-fish-for-data.html?_r=2 (accessed June 22, 2017).

92. Coats, "2017 Worldwide Threat Assessment," pp. 1–2.

93. International Institute for Strategic Studies, *The Military Balance 2017: The Annual Assessment of Global Military Capabilities and Defence Economics* (London: Routledge, 2017), pp. 376–380.

94. This *Index* scores threat capability as it relates to the vital national interests of the U.S. and the role and utility of U.S. military forces. Terrorist groups clearly have the ability to conduct attacks using improvised explosive devices (IEDs), firearms, and even hijacked airplanes. The bombing of the Boston Marathon in April 2013, an attempted car bomb attack in New York City's Times Square in May 2010, and al-Qaeda's attacks on September 11, 2001, are stark examples. Often, the U.S. has handled terrorism as a law enforcement and intelligence collection matter, especially within the United States and when it presents a threat to particular U.S. interests in other countries. Compared to the types of threats posed by states such as China or Russia, terrorism is a lesser sort of threat to the security and viability of the U.S. as a global power. This *Index* does not dismiss the deaths, injuries, and damage that terrorists can inflict on Americans at home and abroad; it places the threat posed by terrorism in context with substantial threats to the U.S. homeland, the potential for major regional conflict, and the potential to deny U.S. access to the global commons. With this in mind, terrorist groups seldom have the physical ability either to accomplish the extreme objectives they state or to present a physical threat that rises to a level that threatens U.S. vital security interests. Of course, terrorist organizations can commit acts of war on a continuing basis, as reflected in their conduct in the war against al-Qaeda and its associates in which the United States has been engaged for more than a decade.

Asia

Threats to the Homeland

Threats to the U.S. homeland include terrorist threats from non-state actors resident in ungoverned areas of South Asia, an active and growing North Korean ballistic missile capability, and a credible Chinese nuclear missile capability that supports other elements of China's national power.

Terrorism Originating from Afghanistan and Pakistan (AfPak). Terrorist groups operating from Pakistan and Afghanistan continue to pose a direct threat to the U.S. homeland. Pakistan is home to a host of terrorist groups that keep the region unstable and contribute to the spread of global terrorism. The killing of Osama bin Laden at his hideout in Abbottabad, Pakistan, in May 2011 and an intensive drone campaign in Pakistan's tribal areas bordering Afghanistan from 2010–2012 have helped to degrade the al-Qaeda threat. However, the presence of a major al-Qaeda training camp in southern Afghanistan that U.S. and Afghan forces destroyed last October demonstrates that the international terrorist organization has the ability to regenerate, particularly in areas where the Taliban is influential. A joint U.S.–Afghan military operation involving 200 U.S. Special Operations Forces destroyed the al-Qaeda camp located in Kandahar province, killing 160 terrorists.[1]

In addition to al-Qaeda, several other like-minded terrorist groups still thrive along the Afghanistan–Pakistan border, carry out regular attacks in Pakistan and Afghanistan, and target U.S. interests in the region and beyond. The Afghan Taliban and its allies, headquartered in Pakistan, have stepped up attacks against the Afghan National Security Forces (ANSF) over the past year and are making a push to regain territory in Afghanistan as international forces depart. As of April 2016, around 13,200 U.S. and NATO troops were in Afghanistan as part of Operation Resolute Support to train and advise the Afghan forces.

The Afghan Taliban controls more territory now than at any other time in the past 15 years and was able to capture the northern city of Kunduz temporarily last October. A Taliban resurgence in Afghanistan could allow al-Qaeda to regain ground in the region and pave the way for terrorist groups of all stripes to reestablish bases there.[2] Shortly after the fall of Kunduz, President Barack Obama reversed his earlier pledge to withdraw nearly all troops by the end of his term and said that the U.S. would instead keep a force level of 5,500 U.S. troops in the country when he departed office in January 2017. He later revised this further to say that he would keep 8,400 troops in place, leaving any further reductions up to his successor.[3] In June 2017, President Donald Trump gave his Secretary of Defense authority to set troop levels,[4] leading to reports that as many as 5,000 additional troops would be deployed. With that authorization, Secretary James Mattis has reportedly ordered the deployment of approximately 3,500 troops to expand air and ground capabilities.[5]

ISIS also is seeking to make inroads into Pakistan and Afghanistan, but its efforts have met with only limited success. This is most likely due to al-Qaeda's well-established roots in the region, ability to maintain the loyalty of the various South Asian terrorist groups, and careful nurturing of its relationship with the

Afghan Taliban. The Afghan Taliban views ISIS as a direct competitor, vying for financial resources, recruits, and ideological influence. This competition was evident in a letter sent by the Taliban to ISIS leader al-Baghdadi in June of 2015, urging the group not to take actions that could lead to "division of the Mujahideen's command." There also have been reports of clashes between ISIS militants and the Taliban in eastern and southern Afghanistan.

A spokesman for the U.S.-led coalition in Afghanistan said in April 2016 that ISIS has the potential to be an "enormous" threat in Afghanistan, but its presence has declined since the beginning of 2016.[6] According to this official, the U.S. carried out between 70 and 80 air strikes against ISIS targets in Afghanistan from January–March 2016. He also attributed ISIS's waning footprint to Taliban attacks, local uprisings, and Afghan security force operations.

Pakistan's continued support for terrorist groups that have links to al-Qaeda undermines U.S. counterterrorism goals in the region. Pakistan's military and intelligence leaders maintain a short-term tactical approach of fighting some terrorist groups that are deemed to be a threat to the state while supporting others that are aligned with Pakistan's goal of extending its influence and curbing India's.

A terrorist attack on a school in Peshawar on December 16, 2014, that killed over 150 people, mostly children, shocked the Pakistani public and prompted the government led by Prime Minister Nawaz Sharif to introduce a National Action Plan (NAP) to reinvigorate the country's fight against terrorism. The action plan includes steps like lifting the moratorium on the death penalty for terrorists, establishing special military courts to try terrorists, curbing the spread of extremist literature and propaganda on social media, freezing the assets of terrorist organizations, and forming special committees of army and political leaders in the provinces to implement the NAP.

Implementation of the NAP and the Pakistani military's operations against TTP (Pakistani Taliban) hideouts in North Waziristan have helped to reduce Pakistan's internal terrorist threat to some degree. Over three years, from 2013–2016, terrorist attacks in Pakistan plummeted.[7] However, the first part of 2017 featured a series of attacks that claimed hundreds of casualties.

There are few signs that Pakistan's crackdown on terrorism extends to groups that target India, such as the Lashkar-e-Taiba (LeT), which was responsible for the 2008 Mumbai attacks, and the Jaish-e-Mohammed (JeM), which carried out an attack on the Indian airbase at Pathankot on January 2, 2016. In early April 2015, Pakistan released on bail the mastermind of the Mumbai attacks, Zakiur Rehman Lakhvi, who had been in Pakistani custody since 2009. The day before Lakhvi's release, the U.S. Department of State had announced approval of nearly $1 billion in U.S. military sales to Pakistan.

In April 2012, the U.S. issued a $10 million reward for information leading to the arrest or conviction of LeT founder Hafez Muhammad Saeed. The LeT has engaged in recruitment and fundraising activities in the U.S. In September 2011, for instance, U.S. authorities arrested Jubair Ahmad, an American permanent resident born in Pakistan, for providing material support to the LeT by producing LeT propaganda and uploading it to the Internet. Ahmad reportedly attended an LeT training camp in Pakistan before moving to the U.S. in 2007.[8]

The U.S. trial of Pakistani American David Coleman Headley, who was arrested in Chicago in 2009 for his involvement in the 2008 Mumbai attacks, led to striking revelations about the LeT's international reach and close connections to Pakistani intelligence. Headley had traveled frequently to Pakistan, where he received terrorist training from the LeT, and to India, where he scouted the sites of the Mumbai attacks. In four days of testimony and cross-examination, Headley provided details about his meetings with a Pakistani intelligence officer, a former army major, and a navy frogman who were among the key players in orchestrating the Mumbai assault.[9]

The possibility that terrorists could gain effective access to Pakistani nuclear weapons is contingent on a complex chain of circumstances. In terms of consequence, however, it is the most dangerous regional threat scenario. Concern about the safety and security of Pakistan's nuclear weapons increases when Indo–Pakistani tensions increase. For example, during the 1999 Kargil crisis, U.S. intelligence indicated that Pakistan had made "nuclear preparations," which spurred greater U.S. diplomatic involvement in defusing the crisis.[10]

If Pakistan were to move around its nuclear assets or, worse, take steps to mate weapons with delivery systems, the likelihood of terrorist theft or infiltration would increase. Increased reliance on tactical nuclear weapons (TNWs) is of particular concern because launch authorities for TNWs are typically delegated to lower-tier field commanders far from the central authority in Islamabad. Another concern is the possibility that miscalculations could lead to regional nuclear war if top Indian leaders were to lose confidence that nuclear weapons in Pakistan are under government control or, conversely, were to assume that they were under Pakistani government control after they ceased to be.

There is concern that Islamist extremist groups with links to the Pakistan security establishment could exploit those links to gain access to nuclear weapons technology, facilities, and/or materials. The realization that Osama bin Laden stayed for six years within a half-mile of Pakistan's premier defense academy has fueled concern that al-Qaeda can operate relatively freely in parts of Pakistan and might eventually gain access to Pakistan's nuclear arsenal. The Nuclear Threat Initiative (NTI) *Nuclear Security Index* ranks 24 countries with "one kilogram or more of weapons-usable nuclear materials" for their susceptibility to theft. Pakistan's weapons-grade materials are the 22nd least secure, with only Iran's and North Korea's ranking lower. In the NTI's broader survey of 44 countries with nuclear power and related facilities, Pakistan ranks 38th least secure against sabotage.[11]

There is the additional, though less likely, scenario of extremists gaining access through a collapse of the state. While Pakistan remains unstable because of its weak economy, regular terrorist attacks, sectarian violence, civil–military tensions, and the growing influence of religious extremist groups, it is unlikely that the Pakistani state will collapse altogether. The country's most powerful institution, the 550,000-strong army that has ruled Pakistan for almost half of its existence, would almost certainly intervene and take charge once again if the political situation began to unravel.[12] The potential breakup of the Pakistani state would have to be preceded by the disintegration of the army, which currently is not plausible.[13]

WWTA: Although the WWTA assesses that "fighting will continue to threaten US personnel, allies, and partners, particularly in Kabul and urban population centers," it does not reference any threat to the homeland from AfPak-based terrorism. The 2016 assessment noted that, despite the degradation of al-Qaeda's leadership in Afghanistan and Pakistan, al-Qaeda "nodes" there are "dedicating resources to planning attacks," and both the 2016 and 2017 assessments include references to a low-level threat to U.S. and Western interests from the Khorasan branch of ISIS.[14]

Summary: The threat to the American homeland emanating from Afghanistan and Pakistan is diverse, complex, and mostly indirect and largely involves non-state actors. The intentions of non-state terrorist groups like the TTP, al-Qaeda, and ISIS toward the U.S. are demonstrably hostile. Despite the broad and deep U.S. relationships with Pakistan's governing elites and military, however, it is likely that the political–military interplay in Pakistan and instability in Afghanistan will continue to result in an active threat to the American homeland.

Missile Threat: North Korea and China. The two sources of the ballistic missile threat to the U.S. are very different in terms of their sophistication and integration into broader strategies for achieving national goals. The threats from North Korea and China are therefore very different in nature.

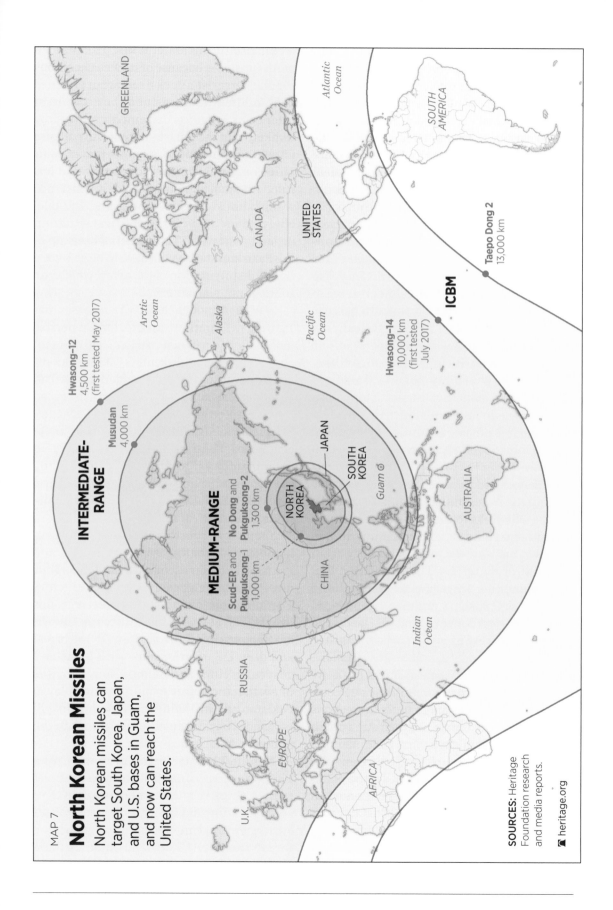

MAP 7

North Korean Missiles

North Korean missiles can target South Korea, Japan, and U.S. bases in Guam, and now can reach the United States.

INTERMEDIATE-RANGE

MEDIUM-RANGE

Scud-ER and **Pukguksong-1**
1,000 km

No Dong and **Pukguksong-2**
1,300 km

Musudan
4,000 km

Hwasong-12
4,500 km
(first tested May 2017)

Hwasong-14
10,000 km
(first tested July 2017)

ICBM

Taepo Dong 2
13,000 km

NORTH KOREA

SOUTH KOREA

JAPAN

Guam ⌀

CHINA

RUSSIA

AUSTRALIA

Indian Ocean

EUROPE

AFRICA

U.K.

Arctic Ocean

Atlantic Ocean

Pacific Ocean

GREENLAND

CANADA

UNITED STATES

Alaska

SOUTH AMERICA

SOURCES: Heritage Foundation research and media reports.

 heritage.org

North Korea. In July 2017, North Korea conducted two successful tests of a road-mobile ICBM. Both launches were flown in an elevated trajectory so as not to fly over Japan and to allow testing of a reentry vehicle to protect a nuclear warhead during an attack. Experts assess that the intercontinental ballistic missile (ICBM) has the capability to fly 10,000 or perhaps 11,000 kilometers. At that range, Los Angeles, Denver, and Chicago (and possibly New York City, Boston, and Washington, D.C.) are within range.[15] In December 2012 and February 2016, North Korea successfully put a satellite into orbit. The same technology that launches satellites can be used to build ICBMs. North Korea conducted its fourth and fifth nuclear tests in 2016 and its sixth nuclear test—the first of a much more powerful hydrogen bomb—in 2017. These events clearly signaled that new leader Kim Jong-un had no intention either of resuming North Korea's Six-Party Talks pledge to denuclearize or of abiding by U.N. resolutions that require a cessation of Pyongyang's nuclear and missile programs. North Korean officials told a Heritage Foundation expert that "denuclearization is totally off the table" and that there is nothing that the U.S. or South Korea could offer to induce denuclearization.[16]

North Korea has declared that it already has a full nuclear strike capability, even altering its constitution to enshrine itself as a nuclear-armed state.[17] Among North Korea's many direct verbal threats to the U.S., the regime warned in March 2016 that it would "reduce all bases and strongholds of the U.S. and south Korean warmongers for provocation and aggression into ashes in a moment, without giving them any breathing spell."[18]

The United States and South Korea have revised their estimates and now see a direr North Korean threat. In June 2017, Vice Admiral James Syring, head of the U.S. Missile Defense Agency, testified that "[i]t is incumbent on us to assume that North Korea today can range the United States with an ICBM carrying a nuclear warhead."[19] In April 2016, Admiral William Gortney, head of U.S. Northern Command, stated that "[i]t's the prudent decision on my part to assume that North Korea has the capability to miniaturize a nuclear weapon and put it on an ICBM."[20]

In 2016 and 2017, North Korea had breakthrough successes with many missiles in development. It successfully test-launched the Hwasong 12 intermediate-range ballistic missile, which can target critical U.S. bases in Guam, and both the Pukguksong-2 road-mobile medium-range ballistic missile and the Pukguksong-1 submarine-launched ballistic missile. In June 2017, in written testimony before the House Armed Services Committee, Secretary of Defense James Mattis called North Korea "the most urgent and dangerous threat to peace and security."[21]

China. Chinese nuclear forces are the responsibility of the People's Liberation Army Rocket Forces (PLARF), one of the three new services created on December 31, 2015. China's nuclear ballistic missile forces include land-based missiles with a range of 13,000 kilometers that can reach the U.S. (CSS-4) and submarine-based missiles that can reach the U.S. when the submarine is deployed within missile range.

The PRC became a nuclear power in 1964 when it exploded its first atomic bomb as part of its "two bombs, one satellite" effort. In quick succession, China then exploded its first thermonuclear bomb in 1967 and orbited its first satellite in 1970, demonstrating the capability to build a delivery system that can reach the ends of the Earth. China chose to rely primarily on a land-based nuclear deterrent instead of developing two or three different basing systems as the United States did.

Furthermore, unlike the United States or the Soviet Union, China chose to pursue only a minimal nuclear deterrent. The PRC fielded only a small number of nuclear weapons, with estimates of about 100–150 weapons on medium-range ballistic missiles and about 60 ICBMs. Its only ballistic missile submarine (SSBN) conducted relatively few deterrence patrols (perhaps none),[22] and its first-generation SLBM, the JL-1, if it ever attained full operational capability had limited reach. The

JL-1's 1,700-kilometer range makes it comparable to the first-generation Polaris A1 missile fielded by the U.S. in the 1960s.

While China's nuclear force remained stable for several decades, it has been part of the modernization effort of the past 20 years. The result has been modernization and some expansion of the Chinese nuclear deterrent. The core of China's ICBM force is the DF-31 series, a solid-fueled, road-mobile system, along with a growing number of longer-range DF-41 missiles (also rail mobile) that may be in the PLA operational inventory. The DF-41 may be deployed with multiple independently targetable reentry vehicles (MIRVs). China's medium-range nuclear forces have similarly shifted to mobile, solid-rocket systems so that they are both more survivable and more easily maintained.

Notably, the Chinese are expanding their ballistic missile submarine fleet. Replacing the one Type 092 *Xia*-class SSBN are several Type 094 *Jin*-class SSBNs, four of which are already operational. These are expected to be equipped with the new, longer-range JL-2 SLBM. Such a system would provide the PRC with a "secure second-strike" capability, substantially enhancing its nuclear deterrent. There is also some possibility that the Chinese nuclear arsenal now contains land-attack cruise missiles. The CJ-20, a long-range, air-launched cruise missile carried on China's H-6 bomber, may be nuclear tipped, although there is not much evidence that China has pursued such a capability at this time. China is also believed to be working on a cruise missile submarine, which, if equipped with nuclear cruise missiles, would further expand the range of its nuclear attack options.[23]

As a result of its modernization efforts, China's nuclear forces appear to be shifting from a minimal deterrent posture (one suited only to responding to an attack and even then with only limited numbers) to a more robust but still limited deterrent posture. While the PRC will still likely field fewer nuclear weapons than either the United States or Russia, it will field a more modern and diverse set of capabilities than India or Pakistan (or North Korea), its nuclear-armed neighbors. If there

are corresponding changes in doctrine, modernization will enable China to engage in limited nuclear options in the event of a conflict.

WWTA: The WWTA's assessment of the Chinese nuclear missile threat is unchanged from 2016: China "continues to modernize its nuclear missile force by adding more survivable road-mobile systems and enhancing its silo-based systems. This new generation of missiles is intended to ensure the viability of China's strategic deterrent by providing a second-strike capability."[24] The 2015 WWTA noted that China was likely to begin seaborne nuclear deterrence patrols in the near future but offered no judgment on the degree of threat that this poses to the U.S. The 2016 and 2017 WWTAs have not included this observation.

The WWTA continues to classify North Korea's nuclear weapons and missile programs as a "serious threat to US interests and to the security environment in East Asia" and again reports that North Korea is "committed to developing a long-range, nuclear-armed missile that is capable of posing a direct threat to the United States."[25] The report correctly points out that although North Korea had not yet flight-tested an ICBM, it was "poised" to do so in 2017.[26] For the first time, the report also uses the words "increasingly grave" to describe the broader national security threat from North Korea's "weapons of mass destruction program, public threats, defiance of the international community, confrontational military posturing, cyber activities, and potential for internal instability."[27]

Summary: The respective missile threats to the American homeland from North Korea and China are very different. China has many more nuclear weapons, multiple demonstrated and tested means of delivery, and more mature systems, but it is a more stable actor with a variety of interests, including relations with the United States and the international system. North Korea has fewer weapons and questionable means of delivery, but it is less stable and less predictable, with a vastly lower stake in the international system. There is also a widely acknowledged difference in intentions: China seeks a stable second-strike capability and, unlike North Korea, is not actively and directly threatening the United States.

Threat of Regional War

America's forward-deployed military at bases throughout the Western Pacific, five treaty allies, security partners in Taiwan and Singapore, and growing security partnership with India are keys to the U.S. strategic footprint in Asia. One of its critical allies, South Korea, is under active threat of invasion from the North, and Japan faces both intimidation attacks intended to deny the U.S. its base access to Japan and nuclear attacks on U.S. bases in the case of conflict on the Korean Peninsula.[28] Taiwan is under a long-standing, well-equipped, and purposely positioned military threat from China. Japan and the Philippines, by virtue of maritime territorial disputes, are under growing paramilitary, military, and political pressure from China.

In South Asia, India is geographically positioned between two major security threats: Pakistan to its west and China to its northeast. From Pakistan, India faces the additional threat of terrorism, whether state-enabled or carried out without state knowledge or control.

North Korean Attack on American Bases and Allies. North Korea's conventional and nuclear missile forces threaten U.S. bases in South Korea, Japan, and Guam.

Beyond its nuclear weapons programs, North Korea poses additional risks to its neighbors. North Korea has an extensive ballistic missile force. Pyongyang has deployed approximately 800 Scud short-range tactical ballistic missiles, 300 No-dong medium-range missiles, and 50 Musudan intermediate-range ballistic missiles. The Scud missiles threaten South Korea, the No-dong can target all of Japan and South Korea, and the Musudan and Hwasong-12 intermediate-range ballistic missiles can hit U.S. bases on Okinawa and Guam. Pyongyang continues its development of several different ICBMs with enough range to hit the continental U.S.[29]

North Korea has approximately 1 million people in its military, with reserves numbering several million more. Pyongyang has forward-deployed 70 percent of its ground forces within 90 miles of the Demilitarized Zone (DMZ), making it possible to attack with little or no warning, which is of particular concern because South Korea's capital, Seoul, is only 30 miles south of the DMZ.[30] In addition to three conventional corps alongside the DMZ, Pyongyang has deployed two mechanized corps, an armor corps, and an artillery corps.[31]

South Korea remains North Korea's principal target. In 2005, South Korea initiated a comprehensive defense reform strategy to transform its military into a smaller but more capable force to deal with the North Korean threat. Overall, South Korean military manpower would be reduced approximately 25 percent, from 681,000 to 500,000. The army would face the largest cuts, disbanding four corps and 23 divisions and cutting troops from 560,000 in 2004 to 370,000 in 2020. Seoul planned to compensate for decreased troop levels by procuring advanced fighter and surveillance aircraft, naval platforms, and ground combat vehicles.[32]

That North Korea's conventional forces are a very real threat to South Korea was clearly demonstrated by two deadly attacks on South Korea in 2010. In March, a North Korean submarine sank the South Korean naval corvette *Cheonan* in South Korean waters, killing 46 sailors. In November, North Korean artillery shelled Yeonpyeong Island, killing four South Koreans.

Since the North Korean military is predominantly equipped with older ground force equipment, Pyongyang has prioritized deployment of strong asymmetric capabilities, including special operations forces, long-range artillery, and missiles. As noted, North Korea has deployed hundreds of Scud short-range ballistic missiles that can target all of South Korea with explosive, chemical, and biological warheads. The land and sea borders between North and South Korea remain unsettled, heavily armed, and actively subject to occasional, limited armed conflict.

MAP 8

U.S. and Allied Military Bases Align Geographically

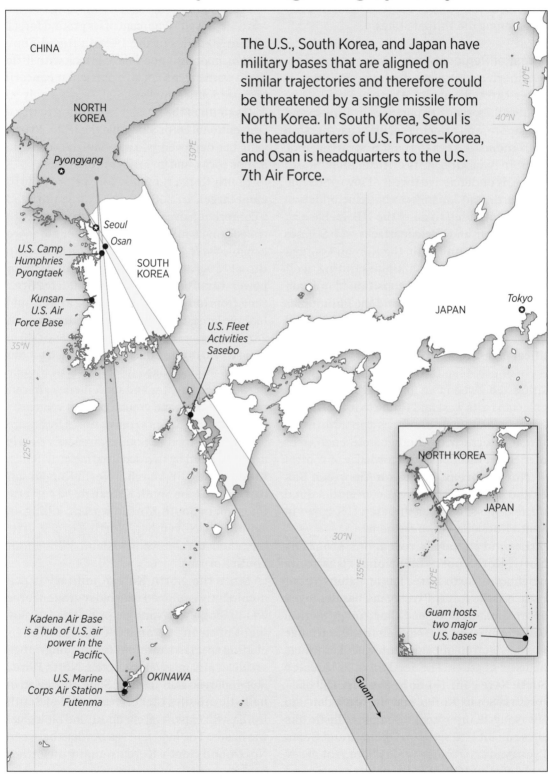

The U.S., South Korea, and Japan have military bases that are aligned on similar trajectories and therefore could be threatened by a single missile from North Korea. In South Korea, Seoul is the headquarters of U.S. Forces–Korea, and Osan is headquarters to the U.S. 7th Air Force.

CHINA

NORTH KOREA

Pyongyang

Seoul
Osan

U.S. Camp Humphries Pyongtaek

SOUTH KOREA

Kunsan U.S. Air Force Base

U.S. Fleet Activities Sasebo

JAPAN

Tokyo

NORTH KOREA

JAPAN

Guam hosts two major U.S. bases

Kadena Air Base is a hub of U.S. air power in the Pacific

U.S. Marine Corps Air Station Futenma

OKINAWA

Guam →

SOURCE: Heritage Foundation research.

heritage.org

Most non-government experts assess that North Korea has perhaps 16–20 nuclear weapons. However, an April 2017 assessment by David Albright of the Institute for Science and International Security concluded that Pyongyang could have as many as 33 nuclear weapons,[33] and a study by Albright that was published in February 2013 by the Korea Institute at Johns Hopkins University's Nitze School of Advanced International Studies predicted a worst-case scenario of Pyongyang's having 100 nuclear weapons by 2020.[34] North Korea's September 2017 hydrogen bomb test—in excess of 100 kilotons—demonstrated a technical achievement far beyond what most experts assessed that the regime was capable of achieving. It is unknown whether the warhead has been miniaturized for a missile.

In any event, enough information is available to conclude that North Korea has likely already achieved the ability to deliver nuclear weapons by means of its No-dong medium-range missile.[35] Factors for such an assessment include the decades-long duration of North Korea's nuclear and missile programs; the technology, expertise, and components acquired from collaborative involvement with Pakistan, the A. Q. Khan network, and Iran; repeated instances of experts underestimating North Korean nuclear and missile capabilities; North Korea's declarations of its ability to hit the U.S. and its allies with nuclear weapons; and U.S. and South Korean government assessments of North Korean breakthroughs.

In March 2016, the Korean Central News Agency declared that Pyongyang has a "military operation plan...to liberate south Korea and strike the U.S. mainland" and that "offensive means have been deployed to put major strike targets in the operation theaters of south Korea within the firing range and the powerful nuclear strike targeting the U.S. imperialist aggressor forces bases in the Asia-Pacific region and the U.S. mainland...."[36] In April 2016, General Vincent Brooks, Commander, U.S. Forces Korea, stated that the U.S. should assume that North Korea "has the technical capability to mount and deliver a nuclear warhead using ballistic missiles."[37]

WWTA: As noted, the WWTA references the "serious threat to...the security environment in East Asia" that is posed by North Korea.[38] It also specifically cites Pyongyang's "credible and evolving military threats" to South Korea and Japan and its expanded strike options that "can reach more U.S. and allied targets in South Korea."[39]

Summary: North Korean forces arrayed against American allies in South Korea and Japan are substantial, and North Korea's history of provocation is a consistent indicator of its intent to achieve its political objectives by threat of force.

Chinese Threat to Taiwan. China's long-standing threat to end the de facto independence of Taiwan and ultimately to bring it under the authority of Beijing—if necessary, by force—is both a threat to a major American security partner and a threat to the American interest in peace and stability in the Western Pacific.

After easing for eight years, tensions across the Taiwan Strait have resumed as a result of Beijing's reaction to the outcome of Taiwan's 2016 presidential election. Regardless of the state of the relationship at any given time, however, Chinese leaders from Deng Xiaoping and Mao Zedong to Xi Jinping have consistently emphasized the importance of ultimately reclaiming Taiwan. The island—along with Tibet—is the clearest example of a geographical "core interest" in Chinese policy. China has never renounced the use of force, and it continues to employ political warfare against Taiwan's political and military leadership.

For the Chinese leadership, the failure to effect unification, whether peacefully or through the use of force, would reflect fundamental political weakness in the PRC. For this reason, there is no realistic means by which any Chinese leadership can back away from the stance of having to unify the island with the mainland. As a result, the island remains an essential part of the People's Liberation Army's "new historic missions," shaping PLA acquisitions and military planning.

Two decades of double-digit increases in China's announced defense budget have produced a significantly more modern PLA, much of which remains focused on a Taiwan contingency. This modernized force includes more than 1,000 ballistic missiles, a modernized air force, and growing numbers of modern surface combatants and diesel-electric submarines capable of mounting a blockade. As the 1995–1996 Taiwan Strait crisis demonstrated, Beijing is prepared at least to use open displays of force—and might have been willing to go further in the absence of a strong American presence.

It is widely posited that China's anti-access/area-denial (A2/AD) strategy—the deployment of an array of overlapping capabilities, including anti-ship ballistic missiles (ASBMs), submarines, and long-range cruise missiles, satellites, and cyber weapons—is aimed largely at forestalling American intervention in support of friends and allies in the Western Pacific, including Taiwan. By holding at risk key American platforms and systems (e.g., aircraft carriers), the Chinese seek to delay or even deter American intervention in support of key friends and allies, allowing the PRC to achieve a fait accompli. The growth of China's military capabilities is specifically oriented toward countering America's ability to assist in the defense of Taiwan.

Chinese efforts to reclaim Taiwan are not limited to overt military means. The "three warfares" highlight Chinese political warfare methods, including legal warfare/lawfare, public opinion warfare, and psychological warfare. The PRC employs such approaches to undermine both Taiwan's will to resist and America's willingness to support Taiwan. The Chinese goal would be to "win without fighting"—to take Taiwan without firing a shot or with only minimal resistance before the United States could organize an effective response.

WWTA: The WWTA does not reference the threat that China poses to Taiwan but does mention Beijing's "firm stance" with regard to Taipei.[40]

Summary: The Chinese threat to Taiwan is long-standing. After an extended lull in apparent tensions, the change in government in Taipei has once again brought the threat to the fore. China's ability to execute a military action against Taiwan, albeit at high economic, political, and military cost, is improving. Its intent to unify Taiwan with the mainland under the full authority of the PRC central government and to end the island's de facto independence has been consistent over time.

Major Pakistan-Backed Terrorist Attack on India Leading to Open Warfare Between India and Pakistan. An Indo–Pakistani conflict would jeopardize multiple U.S. interests in the region and increase the threat of global terrorism. Pakistan would rely on militant non-state actors to help it fight India and thus create a more permissive environment in which various terrorist groups could operate freely. The threat of conflict going nuclear would force U.S. businesses to exit the region and disrupt investment and trade flows, mainly between the U.S. and India, whose bilateral trade currently totals around $100 billion. The effects of an actual nuclear exchange—both the human lives lost and the long-term economic damage—would be devastating.

India and Pakistan are engaged in a nuclear arms race that threatens stability throughout the subcontinent. Both countries tested nuclear weapons in 1998, establishing themselves as overtly nuclear weapons states. Both countries also are developing naval nuclear weapons and already possess ballistic missile and aircraft-delivery platforms.[41]

Pakistan has the fastest-growing nuclear weapons arsenal in the world today. Islamabad currently has an estimated 140 nuclear weapons and "has lowered the threshold for nuclear weapons use by developing tactical nuclear weapons capabilities to counter perceived Indian conventional military threats."[42] This, in turn, affects India's nuclear use threshold, which could affect China and then possibly others.

The broader military and strategic dynamic between India and Pakistan is essentially unstable. As noted, Pakistan continues to harbor terrorist groups like Lashkar-e-Taiba and Jaish-e-Mohammed, which carried out the January 2, 2016, attack on the Indian airbase at Pathankot. JeM had been less visible for several years, but JeM leader Masood Azhar resurfaced in 2014 in Pakistan to address a large public rally where he called on suicide attackers to resume jihad against India. Media reports indicate that some JeM leaders were detained in Pakistan following the Pathankot attack, but no charges have been filed.

Hafez Muhammed Saeed, LeT's founder and leader of its front organization, Jamaat-ud-Dawa (JuD), earlier this year was placed under house arrest, where he remained as of the time this edition of the *Index* was published. Previously, he had operated freely in Pakistan, often holding press conferences and inciting violence against India during large-scale public rallies. In December 2014, Saeed held a two-day conclave in Lahore that received support from the Pakistani government, including security from 4,000 police officers and government assistance in transporting attendees to the gathering of more than 400,000. India condemned the Pakistani government's support for the gathering as "blatant disregard" of global norms against terrorism.[43]

The possibility of armed conflict between India and Pakistan seemed to heighten slightly following the May 2014 election of Bharatiya Janata Party (BJP) leader Narendra Modi as India's Prime Minister. While Modi initially sought to reach out to Pakistan by inviting Pakistani Prime Minister Nawaz Sharif to his swearing-in ceremony, he subsequently called off foreign secretary–level talks that were scheduled for August 2014 to express anger over a Pakistani official's meeting with Kashmiri separatist leaders. Modi's cancellation of the talks signaled that his government is likely to take a harder line toward Islamabad than the one taken by his predecessor, Manmohan Singh, and tie progress in dialogue to Pakistani steps to crack down on anti-India terrorists. Before it took power last year, the BJP often criticized Singh for being too soft on Pakistan. Another obstacle to improved Indo–Pakistani ties is the political weakness of Pakistani Prime Minister Sharif, whose government barely survived month-long street protests led by the opposition in August 2014.

Adding to the tension has been an increase in cross-border firing between the Indian and Pakistani militaries, raising questions about whether a cease-fire that has been in place since 2003 may be breaking down. In August 2014, the two sides engaged in intense firing and shelling along their international border (called the working boundary) and across the Line of Control (LoC) that divides Kashmir. India's Border Security Force Director noted that the firing across the international border was the worst it had been since India and Pakistan fought a war in 1971.[44] Tensions were defused following a phone call between the Directors General of Military Operations in which they mutually agreed to stop the firing. A similar escalation in border tensions occurred again in December 2014 when a series of firing incidents over a one-week period resulted in the deaths of at least five Pakistani soldiers and one Indian soldier.

On December 25, 2015, Prime Minister Modi made an impromptu visit to Lahore to meet with Nawaz Sharif. The visit created enormous goodwill between the two countries and raised hope that official dialogue would soon resume. However, six days later, JeM militants attacked the Indian airbase at Pathankot, killing seven Indian security personnel. India has provided information on the attackers to Pakistan and demanded action against JeM. Official Indo–Pakistani dialogue thus remains deadlocked even though the two sides are reportedly communicating quietly through their foreign secretaries and national security advisers.

There is some concern about the impact on Indo–Pakistani relations of the international troop drawdown in Afghanistan. The vacuum created by the departing international forces will allow the Taliban and other extremists to strengthen their grip in the region, potentially reinvigorating the insurgency in Kashmir and raising the chances of a major terrorist attack against India. Afghan security forces thwarted an attack on the Indian consulate in Herat, Afghanistan, in May 2014. A successful future attack on Indian interests in Afghanistan along the lines of the bombing of the Indian embassy in Kabul in 2008 would sharpen tensions between New Delhi and Islamabad.

With terrorist groups operating relatively freely in Pakistan and maintaining links to the country's military and intelligence services, there is a moderate risk that the two countries might climb the military escalation ladder and eventually engage in all-out conflict. Pakistan's nuclear weapons capability appears to have acted as a deterrent against Indian military escalation both during the 2001–2002 military crisis and following the 2008 Mumbai attacks, but the Indian government would be under great pressure to react strongly in the face of a terrorist provocation. Pakistan's recent focus on incorporating tactical nuclear weapons into its warfighting doctrine has also raised concern that if conflict does break out, there is now a higher risk of nuclear exchange.[45]

WWTA: The WWTA does not reference the threat to American interests from a Pakistani attack on India and potential escalation. It does, however, refer to "tense" relations between the two countries and notes that they "might deteriorate further in 2017, especially in the event of another high-profile terrorist attack in India that New Delhi attributes to originating in or receiving assistance from Pakistan." It further notes that "increasing numbers of firefights along the Line of Control, including the use of artillery and mortars, might exacerbate the risk of unintended escalation between these nuclear-armed neighbors."[46]

Summary: Indian military retaliation against a Pakistan-backed terrorist strike against India could include targeted air strikes on terrorist training camps inside Pakistan. This would likely lead to broader military conflict with some prospect of escalating to a nuclear exchange. Neither side desires another general war. Both countries have limited objectives and have demonstrated their intent to avoid escalation, but this is a delicate calculation.

Major Chinese Border Incursion into India. The possibility of armed conflict between India and China, while currently remote, poses an indirect threat to U.S. interests because it could disrupt the territorial status quo and raise nuclear tensions in the region. A border conflict between India and China could also prompt Pakistan to try to take advantage of the situation, further contributing to regional instability.

Long-standing border disputes that led to a Sino–Indian War in 1962 have been heating up again in recent years. In April 2013, the most serious border incident between India and China in over two decades occurred when Chinese troops settled for three weeks several miles inside northern Indian territory on the Depsang Plains in Ladakh. A visit to India by Chinese President Xi Jinping in September 2014 was overshadowed by another flare-up in border tensions when hundreds of Chinese PLA forces reportedly set up camps in the mountainous regions of Ladakh, prompting Indian forces to deploy to forward positions in the region. The border standoff lasted three weeks and was defused when both sides agreed to pull their troops back to previous positions. India claims that China occupies more than 14,000 square miles of Indian territory in the Aksai Chin along its northern border in Kashmir, and China lays claim to more than 34,000 square miles of India's northeastern state of Arunachal Pradesh. The issue is also closely related to China's concern for its control of Tibet and the presence in India of the Tibetan government in exile and Tibet's spiritual leader, the Dalai Lama.

The Chinese are building up military infrastructure and expanding a network of road, rail, and air links in the border areas. To meet these challenges, the BJP government has also committed to expanding infrastructure development along India's disputed border with China, especially in the Indian states of Arunachal Pradesh and Sikkim. Although China currently holds a decisive military edge over India, New Delhi is engaged in an ambitious military modernization program.

The Border Defense and Cooperation Agreement (BDCA) signed during then-Prime Minister Singh's visit to China in October 2013 is unlikely to reduce border tensions significantly or

MAP 9

Areas of Dispute Along the India-China Border

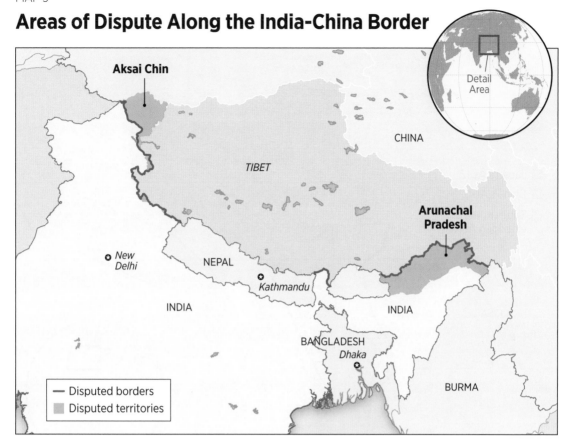

SOURCE: Alyssa Ayres, "China's Mixed Messages to India," Council on Foreign Relations, September 17, 2014, http://blogs.cfr.org/asia/2014/09/17/chinas-mixed-messages-to-india/ (accessed January 5, 2014).

🚩 heritage.org

lead to a broader settlement in the near future. The accord is aimed at putting into place institutional mechanisms for maintaining peace along the border, but several Indian analysts worry that it is part of China's effort to keep in place the status quo, which favors the Chinese. Some have even contended that the Chinese intend to buy time on their border disputes with India through the BDCA while focusing on other territorial claims in the Asia–Pacific.[47]

The BDCA affirms that neither side will use its military capability against the other and proposes opening a hotline between the two countries' military headquarters, instituting meetings between border personnel in all sectors, and ensuring that neither side tails the other's patrols along the Line of Actual Control (LAC).[48] The agreement also includes language stipulating that in the event the two sides come face-to-face, they "shall exercise maximum self-restraint, refrain from any provocative actions, not use force or threaten to use force against the other side, treat each other with courtesy, and prevent exchange of armed conflict."[49]

WWTA: Unlike the 2015 WWTA, which referenced both the likely pursuit of better economic relations and tensions along the border,[50] the 2016 and 2017 WWTAs have been silent with respect to India–China relations.

Summary: American interest in India's security is substantial and expanding. The threat

MAP 10

Overlapping Air Defense Identification Zones

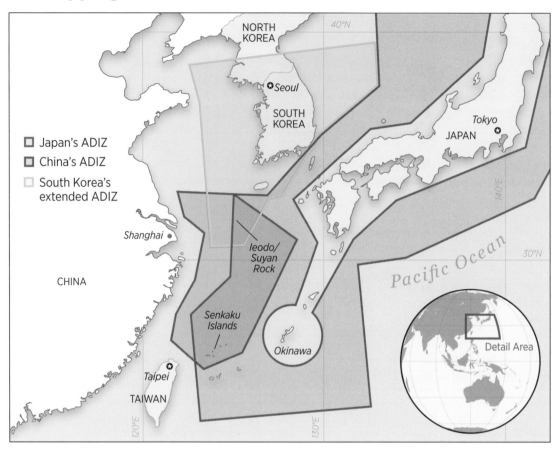

- ☐ Japan's ADIZ
- ☐ China's ADIZ
- ☐ South Korea's extended ADIZ

NORTH KOREA

Seoul

SOUTH KOREA

Tokyo

JAPAN

Shanghai

Ieodo/ Suyan Rock

CHINA

Pacific Ocean

Senkaku Islands

Okinawa

Detail Area

Taipei

TAIWAN

SOURCE: Mark J. Valencia, "Troubled Skies: China's New Air Zone and the East China Sea Disputes," *Global Asia*, Vol. 8, No. 4 (Winter 2013), http://www.globalasia.org/article/troubled-skies-chinas-new-air-zone-and-the-east-china-sea-disputes/ (accessed January 5, 2015).

☎ heritage.org

to this interest from China is active, albeit part of a broader, multifaceted bilateral relationship that includes many cooperative dimensions. Both India and China apparently want to avoid allowing minor incidents to escalate into a more general war. The Chinese seem to use border tensions for limited diplomatic and political gain vis-à-vis India, and India responds in ways intended to contain minor incursions and maximize reputational damage to China. Despite limited aims, however, the unsettled situation and gamesmanship along the border could result in miscalculation, accidents, or overreaction.

Threats to the Commons

The U.S. has critical direct interests at stake in the East Asia and South Asia commons that include sea, air, space, and cyber interests. These interests include an economic interest in the free flow of commerce and the military use of the commons to safeguard America's own security and contribute to the security of its allies and partners.

Washington has long provided the security backbone in these areas, which in turn has supported the region's remarkable economic development. However, China is taking increasingly assertive steps to secure its own interests in these areas independent of U.S. efforts to maintain freedom of the commons for all in the region. It cannot be assumed that China shares a common conception of international space with the United States or an interest in perpetuating American predominance in securing the commons.

In addition, as China expands its naval capabilities, it will be operating farther and farther away from Chinese shores. China has now established its first formal overseas military base, having initialed an agreement with the government of Djibouti in January 2017.[51] Chinese officials appear also to be in discussions with Pakistan about allowing military access to the port of Gwadar.

Maritime and Airspace Commons. The aggressiveness of the Chinese navy, maritime law enforcement forces, and air forces in and over the waters of the East China Sea and South China Sea, coupled with ambiguous, extralegal territorial claims and assertion of control there, poses an incipient threat to American and overlapping allied interests. Chinese military writings emphasize the importance of establishing dominance of the air and maritime domains in any future conflict.

East China Sea. Since 2010, China has intensified its efforts to assert claims of sovereignty over the Senkaku Islands of Japan in the East China Sea. Beijing asserts not only exclusive economic rights within the disputed waters, but also recognition of "historic" rights to dominate and control those areas as part of its territory.

Chinese and Japanese maritime law enforcement and coast guard vessels regularly operate in waters surrounding the Senkakus that are administered by Japan, raising the potential for miscalculation and escalation into a military clash. In the summer of 2016, China began to deploy naval units into the area.

In November 2013, China declared an Air Defense Identification Zone (ADIZ) in the East China Sea that largely aligned with its claimed maritime Exclusive Economic Zone (EEZ). The People's Liberation Army declared that it would "take defense emergency measures to respond to aircraft that do not cooperate in identification or refuse to follow orders."[52] The announcement was a provocative act and another Chinese attempt to change the status quo unilaterally. The ADIZ declaration is part of a broader Chinese pattern of using intimidation and coercion to assert expansive extralegal claims of sovereignty and/or control incrementally. In June 2016, a Chinese fighter made an "unsafe" pass near a U.S. RC-135 reconnaissance aircraft in the East China Sea area. In March 2017, Chinese authorities warned the crew of an American B-1B bomber operating in the area of the ADIZ that they were flying illegally in PRC airspace. In response to the incident, the Chinese Foreign Ministry called for the U.S. to respect the ADIZ.[53] In May, the Chinese intercepted an American WC-135, also over the East China Sea.[54]

South China Sea. Roughly half of global trade in goods, a third of trade in oil, and over half of global liquefied natural gas shipments pass through the South China Sea, which also accounts for approximately 10 percent of global fish catch and may contain massive potential reserves of oil and natural gas. The U.S. Navy also operates in the area and requires access to meet its security and treaty obligations in the region most effectively.

The South China Sea is hotly contested by six countries, including Taiwan and the Philippines. Incidents between Chinese law enforcement vessels and other claimants' fishing boats occur on a regular basis there, as do other Chinese assertions of administrative authority. The U.S. presence also has become an object of Chinese attention, from confrontations with the ocean surveillance ship USNS *Impeccable* and the destroyer USS *John McCain* in 2009 to the confrontation with the guided-missile cruiser USS *Cowpens* in December 2013 and a dangerous intercept of a U.S. Navy P-8 aircraft in August 2014. In May 2016, there was another unsafe intercept of an American aircraft, an EP-3, and in December, the crew of a PLA Navy vessel seized an American unmanned underwater vehicle as it was being recovered by the USNS *Bowditch*. There were several similar incidents involving U.S. aircraft during the first half of 2017.

MAP 11

Areas of Dispute in the East China Sea

KOREAN MARITIME BOUNDARIES
South Korea's claim constitutes the Northern Limit Line, which serves as an operational maritime border between North and South. However, sovereignty over the area is in dispute.

LIANCOURT ROCKS
Known as "Dokdo" in South Korea and "Takeshima" in Japan, the two disputed islands—better measured in acres than in square kilometers—evoke considerable emotion.

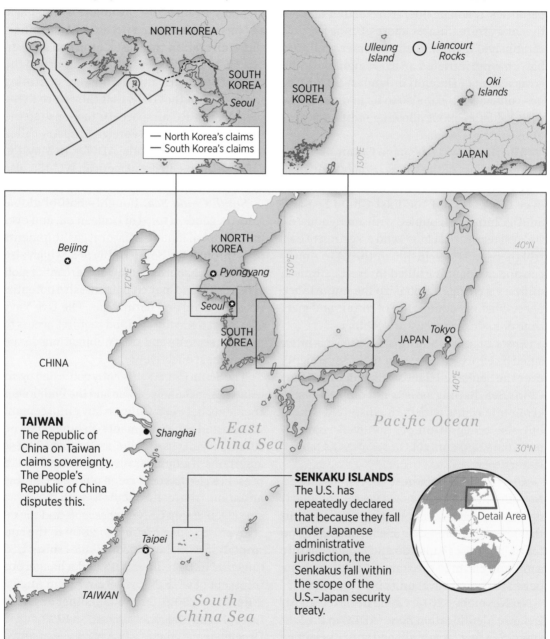

SENKAKU ISLANDS
The U.S. has repeatedly declared that because they fall under Japanese administrative jurisdiction, the Senkakus fall within the scope of the U.S.–Japan security treaty.

TAIWAN
The Republic of China on Taiwan claims sovereignty. The People's Republic of China disputes this.

SOURCE: Heritage Foundation research. Korean maritime boundaries are from Political Geography Now, "What Is North Korea?" April 11, 2013, http://www.polgeonow.com/2013/04/what-is-north-korea.html (accessed January 5, 2015).

☎ heritage.org

MAP 12

Areas of Dispute in the South China Sea

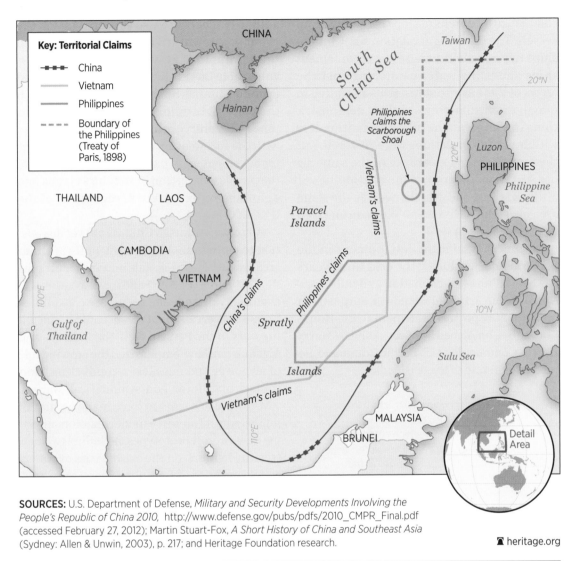

SOURCES: U.S. Department of Defense, *Military and Security Developments Involving the People's Republic of China 2010,* http://www.defense.gov/pubs/pdfs/2010_CMPR_Final.pdf (accessed February 27, 2012); Martin Stuart-Fox, *A Short History of China and Southeast Asia* (Sydney: Allen & Unwin, 2003), p. 217; and Heritage Foundation research.

🅗 heritage.org

The most serious intraregional incidents in the South China Sea have occurred between China and the Philippines and China and Vietnam. In 2012, a Philippine naval ship operating on behalf of the country's coast guard challenged private Chinese poachers in waters around Scarborough Shoal. The resulting escalation left Chinese government ships in control of the shoal. In 2016, there were reports that the Chinese intend to consolidate their gains in the area by reclaiming the sea around the shoal, but there is as yet no indication that this has happened.

Furthermore, with the election of Philippine President Rodrigo Duterte in 2016, there has been a general warming in China–Philippines relations. Duterte has sought to set aside the dispute over the South China Sea, and the Chinese, while not accepting the authority of a 2016 ruling by the Permanent Court of Arbitration (PCA) that favored a range of the Philippines' positions, have allowed Filipino fishermen access to Scarborough Shoal in accordance with it.

China–Vietnam tensions in the South China Sea were on starkest display in 2014 when state-owned China National Offshore Oil Corporation (CNOOC) deployed an oil rig inside Vietnam's EEZ. The Chinese platform was accompanied by dozens of ships including naval vessels. The resulting escalation saw Chinese ships ramming Vietnamese law enforcement ships and using water cannon against the crews of Vietnamese ships. It also resulted in massive and sometimes violent demonstrations in Vietnam. The oil rig was ultimately withdrawn, and relations were restored, but the occasional reappearance of the same rig has served to underscore the continuing volatility of this issue, which involves the same area over which China and Vietnam engaged in armed battle in 1974.

The most significant development in the South China Sea during the past three years has been Chinese reclamation and militarization of seven artificial islands or outposts. In his April 2017 posture statement to the House Committee on Armed Services, Admiral Harry Harris, Commander, U.S. Pacific Command, described the state of these islands:

> China's military-specific construction in the Spratly islands includes the construction of 72 fighter aircraft hangars—which could support three fighter regiments—and about ten larger hangars that could support larger airframes, such as bombers or special mission aircraft. All of these hangars should be completed this year. During the initial phases of construction China emplaced tank farms, presumably for fuel and water, at Fiery Cross, Mischief and Subi reefs. These could support substantial numbers of personnel as well as deployed aircraft and/or ships. All seven outposts are armed with a large number of artillery and gun systems, ostensibly for defensive missions. The recent identification of buildings that appear to have been built specifically to house long-rang surface-to-air missiles is the latest indication China intends to deploy military systems to the Spratlys.[55]

The 2016 PCA award invalidated China's sweeping claims to waters in the South China Sea and found its "island" reclamation to be in violation of Beijing's commitments under the U.N. Convention on the Law of the Sea (UNCLOS). There is the possibility that China will ultimately declare an ADIZ above the South China Sea in an effort to assert its authority. There are also concerns that in the event of a downturn in its relationship with the Philippines, it will take action against vulnerable targets like Philippines-occupied Second Thomas Shoal or Reed Bank, which the panel determined are part of the Philippines EEZ and continental shelf, or proceed with the reclamation at Scarborough. The latter development in particular would facilitate the physical assertion of Beijing's claims and enforcement of an ADIZ, regardless of the UNCLOS award.

Airpower. Although China is not yet in a position to enforce an ADIZ consistently in either area, the steady two-decade improvement of the PLA Air Force (PLAAF) and naval aviation will eventually provide the necessary capabilities. Chinese observations of recent conflicts, including wars in the Persian Gulf, the Balkans, and Afghanistan, have emphasized the growing role of airpower and missiles in conducting "non-contact, non-linear, non-symmetrical" warfare.

China also seems to have made a point of publicizing its air force modernization, unveiling new aircraft prototypes, including two new stealthy fighters, on the eve of visits by American Secretaries of Defense. (Secretary Chuck Hagel's visit in 2014 was preceded by the unveiling of the J-15 naval fighter.) Those aircraft have been flown much more aggressively, with Chinese fighters flying very close to Japanese aircraft in China's East China Sea ADIZ and conducting armed combat air patrols in the skies over Tibet.[56]

The PLA has shed most of its 1960s-era aircraft, replacing them with much more modern systems. Today's PLAAF is dominated by fourth-generation and 4.5th-generation fighter aircraft. These include the domestically designed and produced J-10, as well as the Su-27/Su-30/J-11 system, comparable to the F-15 or F-18, that dominates both the fighter and strike missions.[57] Older airframes such as the J-7 are steadily being retired from the fighter inventory. China is also believed to be preparing to field two stealthy fifth-generation fighter designs. The J-20 is the larger aircraft, resembling the American F-22 fighter. The J-31 appears to resemble the F-35 but with two engines rather than one. The production of advanced combat aircraft engines remains one of the greatest challenges to Chinese fighter design.

China fields some long-range strike aircraft, largely the H-6 bomber based on the Soviet-era Tu-16 Badger. While this aircraft has little prospect of penetrating advanced air defenses, it is suitable as a cruise missile carrier. China also has used the H-6 as the basis for initial efforts to develop an aerial tanker fleet and seems to be examining other options as well. As China deploys more tankers, this will extend the range and loiter time of its fighter aircraft. China will then be better equipped to enforce its newly declared East China Sea Air Defense Identification Zone and any possible future South China Sea ADIZ.

A variety of modern support aircraft have also entered the PLAAF inventory, including airborne early warning (AEW), command and control (C2), and electronic warfare (EW) aircraft. At the Zhuhai Air Show, Chinese companies have displayed a variety of unmanned aerial vehicles (UAVs), reflecting substantial investments and research and development efforts. The surveillance and armed UAV systems include the Xianglong (Soaring Dragon) and Sky Saber systems. The 2014 DOD report on Chinese capabilities also reports that China has tested a stealthy flying-wing UAV, the Lijian.[58]

China's air defenses, which are under the control of the PLAAF, have also been steadily modernizing. China has acquired the advanced S-300 surface-to-air missile (SAM) system (SA-10B/SA-20), which is roughly analogous to the American Patriot SAM system, and is developing its own advanced SAM, the HQ-9, which is deployed both on land and at sea. In early 2014, Russia announced that it would sell China the S-400 SAM system. This would mark a substantial improvement in PLAAF air defense capabilities, as the S-400 has anti-aircraft and anti-missile

capabilities.[59] China has deployed these SAM systems in a dense, overlapping belt along its coast, protecting the nation's economic center of gravity. Key industrial and military centers such as Beijing are also heavily defended by SAM systems. Some of these systems have reportedly been deployed to the Paracel islands in the South China Sea.

A third component of the PLAAF is China's airborne forces. The 15th Airborne Army is part of the PLAAF, with three divisions of 10,000–15,000 personnel each. These are not believed to be assigned to any of the Chinese military regions but are instead a strategic reserve as well as a rapid reaction force. In 2009, in the military review associated with the 60th anniversary of the founding of the PRC, Chinese airborne units paraded through Tiananmen Square with ZBD-03 mechanized airborne combat vehicles. These vehicles provide Chinese airborne forces with tactical mobility as well as some degree of protected fire support from their 30mm autocannon and HJ-73 anti-tank missile (a domestic version of the AT-3 Sagger)—something American airborne forces continue to lack.

One shortcoming of the Chinese airborne forces is the lack of military transport aircraft, although the PLAAF undoubtedly can call on China's substantial civilian fleet of airliners in time of crisis or war.

Sea power. As the world's foremost trading state, China depends on the seas for its economic well-being. China's factories are increasingly powered by imported oil, and Chinese diets contain a growing percentage of imported food. Chinese products rely on the seas to be moved to markets. At the same time, because China's economic center of gravity is now in the coastal region, it has had to emphasize maritime power to defend key assets and areas. Consequently, China has steadily expanded its maritime power, including its merchant marine and maritime law enforcement capabilities, but especially the People's Liberation Army Navy (PLAN).

The PLAN is no longer an unsophisticated coastal defense force. Instead, since the end of the Cold War, China's navy has moved away from reliance on mass toward incorporating advanced platforms and weapons. Most notably, the Chinese navy is the first in East Asia to deploy its own aircraft carrier since World War II. The *Liaoning* carries a mixed air group of J-15 fighters (based on the navalized Su-27) and helicopters and is believed to be fully operational.

Meanwhile, many obsolete vessels have been decommissioned, including scores of older, missile-armed, fast attack craft. In their place, China has produced a range of more capable combatants and is building each class in significant numbers. These range from the Type 022 *Houbei* missile-armed catamaran, armed with sea-skimming supersonic anti-ship cruise missiles, to the Type-052C *Luyang-II* destroyer, equipped with a phased-array radar for its HQ-9 SAM system. The HQ-9, with its ability to combat most air-breathing systems and a limited anti–ballistic missile capability, is believed to be comparable to early model Patriot missiles. Although these new ships are not replacing older Chinese surface combatants on a one-for-one basis, the overall capability of the PLAN surface force is steadily improving.

The PLAN has similarly been modernizing its submarine force. Since 2000, the PLAN has consistently fielded between 50 and 60 diesel-electric submarines, but the age and capability of the force has been improving as older boats, especially 1950s-vintage *Romeo*-class boats, are replaced with newer designs. These include a dozen *Kilo*-class submarines purchased from Russia and domestically designed and manufactured *Song* and *Yuan* classes. All of these are believed to be capable of firing not only torpedoes, but also anti-ship cruise missiles. The Chinese have also developed variants of the *Yuan*, with an air-independent propulsion (AIP) system that reduces the boats' vulnerability by removing the need to use noisy diesel engines to recharge batteries.

The PLAN also has been augmenting its aerial maritime strike capability. In addition to more modern versions of the H-6 twin-engine bombers (a version of the Soviet/Russian Tu-16 Badger), the PLAN's Naval Aviation force has added a range of other strike aircraft to its inventory. These include the JH-7/FBC-1 Flying Leopard, which can carry between two and four YJ-82 anti-ship cruise missiles, and the Su-30 strike fighter. Within Chinese littoral waters, the PLAN Air Force can bring a significant amount of firepower to bear.

The PLAN also has been working to improve its "fleet train." The 2010 PRC defense white paper notes the accelerated construction of "large support vessels." It also specifically notes that the navy is exploring "new methods of logistics support for sustaining long-time maritime missions."[60]

As with other aspects of PLA modernization, even as the PLAN is upgrading its weapons, it is also improving its doctrine and training, including increased emphasis on joint operations and the incorporation of electronic warfare into its training regimen. Such improvements suggest that PLA Air Force assets, space and cyber operations, and even PLA Rocket Force units might support naval aviation strikes. The new anti-ship ballistic missile forces, centered on the DF-21D anti-ship ballistic missile (now reportedly at initial operational capability), should be seen as part of joint Chinese efforts to control the seas, complementing PLAAF and PLAN air, surface, and sub-surface forces.

Escalation of Territorial Disputes or Incidents at Sea. Because the PRC and other countries in the region see active disputes over the East and South China Seas not as differences regarding the administration of the commons, but rather as matters of territorial sovereignty, there exists the threat of armed conflict between China and American allies who are also claimants, particularly Japan and the Philippines.

Beijing prefers to accomplish its objectives quietly and through nonmilitary means. In both the East and South China Seas, China has sought to exploit "gray zones," gaining control incrementally and deterring others without resort to the lethal use of force. It uses military and economic threats, bombastic language, and enforcement through military bullying. Chinese paramilitary-implemented, military-backed encroachment in support of expansive extralegal claims could lead to an unplanned armed clash.

Rising nationalism is exacerbating tensions, making geostrategic relations in Asia increasingly complex and volatile. In the face of persistent economic challenges, nationalist themes are becoming an increasingly strong undercurrent, affecting policymaking. Although the nationalist phenomenon is not new, it is gaining force and complicating efforts to maintain regional stability.

Governments may choose to exploit nationalism for domestic political purposes, but they also run the risk of being unable to control the genie that they have released. Nationalist rhetoric is mutually reinforcing, which makes countries less likely to back down than in the past. The increasing power that the Internet and social media provide to the populace, largely outside of government control, add elements of unpredictability to future clashes.

In case of armed conflict between China and the Philippines or between China and Japan, either by intention or as a result of an accidental incident at sea, the U.S. could be required to exercise its treaty commitments.[61] Escalation of a direct U.S.–China incident is itself not unthinkable. Keeping an inadvertent incident from escalating into a broader military confrontation would be difficult. This is particularly true in the East and South China Seas, where naval as well as civilian law enforcement vessels from both China and the U.S. operate in what the U.S. considers to be international waters.

WWTA: The WWTA does not address threats to the maritime and airspace commons, but it does say that "China will continue to pursue an active foreign policy" in the region, "highlighted by [among other things] a firm stance on competing territorial claims in the East China Sea (ECS) and South China Sea (SCS)." It also predicts continuing regional tensions "as China completes construction

at its expanded outposts in the SCS."[62] It offers no judgment either on the threat that this poses to American interests or on the prospect for large-scale conventional conflict in the region.

Summary: In both the air and maritime domains, China is ever more capable of challenging American dominance and disrupting the freedom of the commons that benefits the entire region. Both territorial disputes related to what the U.S. and its allies consider the commons and accidental incidents could draw the U.S. into conflict. China likely does not intend to engage in armed conflict with its neighbors, particularly American treaty allies, or with the U.S. itself. However, it will continue to press its territorial claims at sea in ways that, even if inadvertent, cause incidents that could escalate into broader conflict.

Space. One of the key force multipliers for the United States is its extensive array of space-based assets. Through its various satellite constellations, the U.S. military can track opponents, coordinate friendly forces, engage in precision strikes against enemy forces, and conduct battle-damage assessments so that its munitions are expended efficiently.

The American military is more reliant than many others on space-based systems because it is also an expeditionary military (i.e., its wars are conducted far distant from the homeland). Consequently, it requires global rather than regional reconnaissance, communications and data transmission, and meteorological information and support. At this point, only space-based systems can provide this sort of information on a real-time basis. The U.S. can leverage space in ways that no other country can, and this is a major advantage, but this heavy reliance on space systems is also a key American vulnerability.

China fields an array of space capabilities, including its own navigation and timing satellites, the Beidou/Compass system, and has claimed a capacity to refuel satellites.[63] It has three satellite launch centers, and a fourth is under construction. China's interest in space dominance includes not only accessing space, but also denying opponents the ability to do the same. As one Chinese assessment notes, space capabilities provided 70 percent of battlefield communications, over 80 percent of battlefield reconnaissance and surveillance, and 100 percent of meteorological information for American operations in Kosovo. Moreover, 98 percent of precision munitions relied on space for guidance information. In fact, "It may be said that America's victory in the Kosovo War could not be achieved without fully exploiting space."[64]

To this end, the PLA has been developing a range of anti-satellite capabilities that include both hard-kill and soft-kill systems. The former include direct-ascent kinetic-kill vehicles (DA-KKV), such as the system tested in 2007, but also more advanced systems that are believed to be capable of reaching targets in mid-Earth orbit and even geosynchronous orbit.[65] The latter include anti-satellite lasers for either dazzling or blinding purposes.[66] This is consistent with PLA doctrinal writings, which emphasize the need to control space in future conflicts. "Securing space dominance has already become the prerequisite for establishing information, air, and maritime dominance," says one Chinese teaching manual, "and will directly affect the course and outcome of wars."[67]

Soft-kill attacks need not come only from dedicated weapons, however. The case of Galaxy-15, a communications satellite owned by Intelsat Corporation, showed how a satellite could effectively disrupt communications simply by being in "switched on" mode all of the time.[68] Before it was finally brought under control, it had drifted through a portion of the geosynchronous belt, forcing other satellite owners to move their assets and juggle frequencies. A deliberate such attempt by China (or any other country) could prove far harder to handle, especially if conducted in conjunction with attacks by kinetic systems or directed-energy weapons.

China has created a single service, the PLA Strategic Support Force (PLASSF), with authority over its space, electronic warfare, and network warfare capabilities. In essence, this is a service that is focused on fighting in the information domain, striving to secure what the PLA terms "information dominance" for themselves while denying it to others. This service will probably combine electronic warfare, cyber warfare, and physical attacks against adversary space and information systems in order to deny them the ability to gather, transmit, and exploit information.

WWTA: The WWTA assesses that China "perceive[s] a need to offset any US military advantage derived from military, civil, or commercial space systems and [is] increasingly considering attacks against satellite systems as part of [its] future warfare doctrine." China will "continue to pursue a full range of anti-satellite (ASAT) weapons as a means to reduce US military effectiveness" and to develop "capabilities to challenge" the U.S. in space. The report also references discussions by Chinese researchers concerning "methods to enhance robust jamming capabilities with new systems to jam commonly used frequencies." Some of China's "ASAT weapons, including destructive systems, will probably complete development in the next several years," and its "ground-launched ASAT missiles might be nearing operational service within the PLA."[69]

Summary: The PRC poses a challenge to the United States that is qualitatively different from the challenge posed by any other potential adversary in the post–Cold War environment. It is the first nation to be capable of accessing space on its own while also jeopardizing America's ability to do the same. This appears to be its intent.

Cyber. Threats in this area derive primarily from China and North Korea, and the threats posed by both countries are serious.

China. In 2013, the Verizon Risk Center identified China as the "top external actor from which [computer] breaches emanated, representing 30 percent of cases where country-of-origin could be determined."[70] Given the difficulties of attribution, country of origin should not necessarily be conflated with the perpetrator, but forensic efforts have identified at least one Chinese military unit with cyber intrusions.[71] Similarly, the Verizon report concluded that China was the source of 95 percent of state-sponsored cyber-espionage attacks. Since the 2015 Xi–Obama summit where the two sides reached an understanding to reduce cyber economic espionage, Chinese cyber actions have shifted. While the overall level of activity appears to be unabated, the Chinese appear to have moved toward more focused attacks mounted from new sites.

China's cyber-espionage efforts are often aimed at economic targets, reflecting the much more holistic Chinese view of both security and information. Rather than creating an artificial dividing line between military security and civilian security, much less information, the PLA plays a role in supporting both aspects and seeks to obtain economic intellectual property as well as military electronic information.

This is not to suggest, however, that the PLA has not emphasized the military importance of cyber warfare. Chinese military writings since the 1990s have emphasized a fundamental transformation in global military affairs (*shijie junshi gaige*). Future wars will be conducted through joint operations involving multiple services rather than through combined operations focused on multiple branches within a single service. These future wars will span not only the traditional land, sea, and air domains, but also outer space and cyberspace. The latter two arenas will be of special importance because warfare has shifted from an effort to establish material dominance (characteristic of Industrial Age warfare) to establishing information dominance (*zhi xinxi quan*). This is due to the rise of the information age and the resulting introduction of information technology into all areas of military operations.

Consequently, according to PLA analysis, future wars will most likely be "local wars under informationized conditions." That is, they will be wars in which information and information technology not only will be widely applied, but also will be a key basis of victory. The ability to gather, transmit, analyze, manage, and exploit information will be central to winning such wars: The side that is able to do these things more accurately and more quickly will be the side that wins. This means that future conflicts will no longer be determined by platform-versus-platform performance and not even by system against system (*xitong*). Rather, conflicts are now clashes between rival arrays of systems of systems (*tixi*).[72]

Chinese military writings suggest that a great deal of attention has been focused on developing an integrated computer network and electronic warfare (INEW) capability. This would allow the PLA to reconnoiter a potential adversary's computer systems in peacetime, influence opponent decision-makers by threatening those same systems in times of crisis, and disrupt or destroy information networks and systems by cyber and electronic warfare means in the event of conflict. INEW capabilities would complement psychological warfare and physical attack efforts to secure "information dominance," which Chinese military writings emphasize as essential for fighting and winning future wars.

Attacks on computer networks in particular have the potential to be extremely disruptive. The recent indictment of five serving PLA officers on the grounds of cyber espionage highlights how active the Chinese military is in this realm.[73]

It is essential to recognize, however, that the PLA views computer network operations as part of information operations (*xinxi zuozhan*), or information combat. Information operations are specific operational activities that are associated with striving to establish information dominance. They are conducted in both peacetime and wartime, with the peacetime focus on collecting information, improving its flow and application, influencing opposing decision-making, and effecting information deterrence.

Information operations involve four mission areas:

- **Command and Control Missions.** An essential part of information operations is the ability of commanders to control joint operations by disparate forces. Thus, command, control, communications, computers, intelligence, surveillance, and reconnaissance structures constitute a key part of information operations, providing the means for collecting, transmitting, and managing information.

- **Offensive Information Missions.** These are intended to disrupt the enemy's battlefield command and control systems and communications networks, as well as to strike the enemy's psychological defenses.

- **Defensive Information Missions.** Such missions are aimed at ensuring the survival and continued operation of information systems. They include deterring an opponent from attacking one's own information systems, concealing information, and combating attacks when they do occur.

- **Information Support and Information-Safeguarding Missions.** The ability to provide the myriad types of information necessary to support extensive joint operations and to do so on a continuous basis is essential to their success.[74]

Computer network operations are integral to all four of these overall mission areas. They can include both strategic and battlefield network operations and can incorporate both offensive and defensive measures. They also include protection not only of data, but also of information hardware and operating software.

Computer network operations will not stand alone, however, but will be integrated with electronic warfare operations, as reflected in the phrase "network and electronics unified [*wangdian yiti*]." Electronic warfare operations are aimed at weakening or destroying enemy electronic facilities and systems while defending one's own.[75] The combination of electronic and computer network attacks will produce synergies that affect everything from finding and assessing the adversary to locating one's own forces to weapons guidance to logistical support and command and control. The creation of the PLASSF is intended to integrate these forces and make them more complementary and effective in future "local wars under informationized conditions."

North Korea. In February 2016, North Korea conducted the first government-sponsored digital bank robbery. North Korean hackers gained access to the Society for Worldwide Interbank Financial Telecommunication (SWIFT), the system used by central banks to authorize monetary transfers, to steal $81 million. The regime had attempted to send money transfer requests of $951 million from the Central Bank of Bangladesh to banks in the Philippines, Sri Lanka, and other parts of Asia.[76] North Korean hackers also targeted the World Bank, the European Central Bank, 20 Polish banks, and large American banks such as BankAmerica,[77] as well as financial institutions in Costa Rica, Ecuador, Ethiopia, Gabon, India, Indonesia, Iraq, Kenya, Malaysia, Nigeria, Poland, Taiwan, Thailand, and Uruguay.[78]

In 2014, North Korea conducted a cyberattack on Sony Pictures in retaliation for the studio's release of a satirical film depicting the assassination of Kim Jong-un. The cyberattack was accompanied by physical threats against U.S. theaters and citizens. Contrary to the perception of North Korea as a technologically backward nation, the regime has an active cyber warfare capability. In 2009, North Korea declared that it was "fully ready for any form of high-tech war."[79] According to South Korea's National Intelligence Service, North Korean leader Kim Jong-un has described cyber warfare as "a magic weapon" that empowers Pyongyang to launch "ruthless strikes" against South Korea.[80]

The Reconnaissance General Bureau, North Korea's intelligence agency, oversees Unit 121 with almost 6,000 "cyber-warriors" dedicated to attacking Pyongyang's enemies, up from 3,000 just two years ago. Defectors from the unit have told South Korean intelligence officials that hackers are sent to other countries for training as well as to conduct undercover operations. The unit's hackers never operate primarily within North Korea, because the country's limited computer network would make it too easy to identify the source of the attack.[81]

Seoul concluded that North Korea was behind cyber-attacks using viruses or distributed denial-of-service tactics against South Korean government agencies, businesses, banks, and media organizations in 2009, 2011, 2012, and 2013. The most devastating attack, launched in 2013 against South Korean banks and media outlets, deleted the essential Master Boot Record from 48,000 computers.[82] North Korea also jammed GPS signals in 2012, posing a risk to hundreds of airplanes transiting Seoul's Incheon airport. Lieutenant General Bae Deag-sig, head of South Korea's Defense Security Command, stated that "North Korea is attempting to use hackers to infiltrate our military's information system to steal military secrets and to incapacitate the defense information system."[83]

WWTA: The WWTA assesses that "Beijing will continue actively targeting the US Government, its allies, and US companies for cyber espionage" and references Beijing's selective use of cyberattacks "against foreign targets that it probably believes threaten Chinese domestic stability or regime legitimacy."[84] The 2016 WWTA assessed that North Korea "probably remains capable and willing to launch disruptive or destructive cyberattacks to support its political objectives."[85] This year, there is no such modifier concerning this capability. The 2017 WWTA also has added a reference to "Pyongyang's cyber threat to US allies."[86]

Summary: With obvious implications for the U.S., the PLA emphasizes the need to suppress and destroy an enemy's information systems while preserving one's own, as well as the importance of computer and electronic warfare in both the offensive and defensive roles. Methods to secure information dominance would include establishing an information blockade; deception (including through electronic means); information contamination; and information paralysis.[87] China sees cyber as part of an integrated capability for achieving strategic dominance in the Western Pacific region. For North Korea, cyber security is an area in which even its limited resources can directly support discrete political objectives.

Threat Scores

AfPak-Based Terrorism. A great deal of uncertainty surrounds the threat from AfPak. For the U.S., Pakistan is both a security partner and a security challenge. Pakistan provides a home and support to terrorist groups that are hostile to the U.S., other U.S. partners in South Asia like India, and the fledgling government of Afghanistan. Afghanistan is particularly vulnerable to destabilization efforts. Both Pakistan and Afghanistan are already among the world's most unstable states. The instability of the former, given its nuclear arsenal, has a direct bearing on U.S. security.

The IISS *Military Balance* largely addresses the military capabilities of states. Its limited section on the capabilities of non-state actors does not include those in the AfPak region. The 2017 edition contains no reference to the possibility that Pakistani nuclear weapons might fall into hands that would threaten the American homeland or interests more broadly. The 2014 edition stated that Pakistan's "nuclear weapons are currently believed to be well-secured against terrorist attack."[88] Pakistan's Army Strategic Forces Command has 30 medium-range ballistic missiles, 30 short-range ballistic missiles, and land-attack cruise missiles.[89] Previous editions of the *Military Balance* have also cited development of "likely nuclear capable" artillery. Pakistan also has "1–2 squadrons of F-16A/B or Mirage 5 attack aircraft that may be assigned a nuclear strike role."[90]

This *Index* assesses the overall threat from AfPak-based terrorists, considering the range of contingencies, as "aggressive" for level of provocation of behavior and "capable" for level of capability.

Threats: Af-Pak Terrorism

	HOSTILE	AGGRESSIVE	TESTING	ASSERTIVE	BENIGN
Behavior		✓			

	FORMIDABLE	GATHERING	CAPABLE	ASPIRATIONAL	MARGINAL
Capability			✓		

China. China presents the United States with the most comprehensive security challenge in the region. It poses various threat contingencies across all three areas of vital American national interests: homeland; regional war (extending from attacks on overseas U.S. bases or against allies and friends); and the global commons. China's provocative behavior is well documented. It is challenging the U.S. and U.S. allies like Japan at sea and in cyberspace. It has raised concerns on its border with India and is a standing threat to Taiwan. While there may be a lack of official transparency, publicly available sources shed considerable light on China's fast-growing military capabilities.

According to the IISS *Military Balance*, among the key weapons in China's inventory are 62 Chinese ICBMs; 405 shorter-range ballistic missiles;[91] four SSBNs with up to 12 missiles; 72 satellites; 6,740 main battle tanks; 57 tactical submarines; 79 principal surface combatants (including one aircraft carrier and 21 destroyers); and 2,307 combat-capable aircraft in its air force. There are 1,150,000 members of the People's Liberation Army,[92] down 450,000 from last year.

With regard to these capabilities, the 2014 *Military Balance* stated that because of "a lack of war-fighting experience, questions over training and morale, and key capability weaknesses in areas such as C4ISTAR and ASW," the PLA "remains qualitatively inferior, in some respects, to more technologically advanced armed forces in the region—such as South Korea and Japan—and it lags far behind the U.S."[93] Subsequent editions have not included this caveat. The 2017 *Military Balance* cites "significant amounts of old equipment [remaining in] service" and questions about the quality of domestically produced equipment.[94]

This *Index* assesses the overall threat from China, considering the range of contingencies, as "testing" for level of provocation of behavior and "formidable" for level of capability.

Threats: China

	HOSTILE	AGGRESSIVE	TESTING	ASSERTIVE	BENIGN
Behavior			✓		

	FORMIDABLE	GATHERING	CAPABLE	ASPIRATIONAL	MARGINAL
Capability	✓				

North Korea. In the first instance, North Korea poses the most acute security challenge for American allies and bases in South Korea. However, it is also a significant challenge to U.S. allies in Japan and American bases there and in Guam.

North Korean authorities are very actively and vocally provocative toward the United States. While North Korea has used its missile and nuclear tests to enhance its prestige and importance—domestically, regionally, and globally—and to extract various concessions from the United States in negotiations over its nuclear program and various aid packages, such developments also improve North Korea's military posture. North Korea likely has already achieved warhead miniaturization, the ability to place nuclear weapons on its medium-range missiles, and an ability to reach the continental United States with a missile.

According to the IISS *Military Balance*, key weapons in North Korea's inventory include 3,500-plus main battle tanks, 560-plus light tanks, and 21,100 pieces of artillery. The navy has 73 tactical submarines, three frigates, and 383 patrol and coastal combatants.[95] The air force has 545 combat-capable aircraft (58 fewer than 2014), including 80 H-5 bombers. The IISS counts 1,020,000 active-duty members of the North Korean army, a reserve of 600,000, and 5,700,000 paramilitary personnel. Regarding the missile threat in particular, the 2017 *Military Balance* restates that the Hwasong-13 (KN-08) road-mobile ICBM, while assessed as operational, remains untested.[96] With respect to conventional forces, the 2017 *Military Balance* includes a caveat that they "remain reliant on increasingly obsolete equipment with little evidence of widespread modernization across the armed services."[97]

This *Index* assesses the overall threat from North Korea, considering the range of contingencies, as "aggressive" for level of provocation of behavior and "gathering" for level of capability.

Threats: North Korea

	HOSTILE	AGGRESSIVE	TESTING	ASSERTIVE	BENIGN
Behavior		✓			

	FORMIDABLE	GATHERING	CAPABLE	ASPIRATIONAL	MARGINAL
Capability		✓			

Endnotes

1. Dan Lamothe, "'Probably the Largest' al-Qaeda Training Camp Ever Destroyed in Afghanistan," *The Washington Post*, October 30, 2015, https://www.washingtonpost.com/news/checkpoint/wp/2015/10/30/probably-the-largest-al-qaeda-training-camp-ever-destroyed-in-afghanistan/ (accessed June 29, 2017).

2. James R. Clapper, Director of National Intelligence, "Statement for the Record: Worldwide Threat Assessment of the US Intelligence Community," Committee on Armed Services, U.S. Senate, February 11, 2014, http://www.dni.gov/files/documents/2014%20WWTA%20SFR_SASC_11_Feb.pdf (accessed July 3, 2017).

3. Mark Landler, "Obama Says He Will Keep More Troops in Afghanistan Than Planned," *The New York Times*, July 6, 2016, http://www.nytimes.com/2016/07/07/world/asia/obama-afghanistan-troops.html (accessed June 29, 2017).

4. Joe Gould, "Mattis: Trump Authorized Military to Set Troop Levels in Afghanistan," *Defense News,* June 14, 2017, http://www.defensenews.com/articles/mattis-trump-authorized-military-to-set-troop-levels-in-afghanistan (accessed June 29, 2017).

5. Tara Copp, "Mattis Signs Orders to Send About 3,500 More US Troops to Afghanistan," *Military Times*, September 11, 2017, https://www.militarytimes.com/news/your-military/2017/09/11/mattis-signs-orders-to-send-about-3500-more-us-troops-to-afghanistan/ (accessed September 11, 2017).

6. Rebecca Kheel, "General: ISIS in Afghanistan Potentially an 'Enormous' Threat," *The Hill*, April 14, 2016, http://thehill.com/policy/defense/276325-general-isis-in-afghanistan-potentially-enormous-threat (accessed June 29, 2017).

7. Peter Oborne and Sabin Agha, "Pakistan Is Winning Its War on Terror," *The Spectator*, December 31, 2016, https://www.spectator.co.uk/2016/12/pakistan-is-winning-its-war-on-terror/# (accessed June 29, 2017).

8. Reuters, "Pakistani Man Arrested on U.S. Terrorism Charges," September 2, 2011, http://www.reuters.com/article/2011/09/02/us-pakistan-usa-arrest-idUSTRE7815M920110902 (accessed June 29, 2017).

9. Abha Shankar, "Trial's First Week Reinforces Pakistani Intelligence Suspicions," Investigative Project on Terrorism, *IPT News*, May 27, 2011, http://www.investigativeproject.org/2919/trial-first-week-reinforces-pakistani (accessed June 29, 2017).

10. Peter R. Lavoy, ed., *Asymmetric Warfare in South Asia: The Causes and Consequences of the Kargil Conflict* (Cambridge, UK: Cambridge University Press, 2009), p. 10.

11. Nuclear Threat Initiative, *Nuclear Security Index*, "Overview Highlights," http://www.ntiindex.org/overview-highlights/overview/ (accessed July 3, 2017).

12. "Pakistan's Future: Resilient Mess," *The Economist*, February 11, 2012, http://www.economist.com/node/21547231 (accessed June 29, 2017).

13. Stephen P. Cohen, "The Future of Pakistan," The Brookings Institution, January 2011, https://www.brookings.edu/wp-content/uploads/2016/06/01_pakistan_cohen.pdf (accessed June 29, 2017).

14. Daniel R. Coats, Director of National Intelligence, "Statement for the Record: Worldwide Threat Assessment of the US Intelligence Community," Select Committee on Intelligence, U.S. Senate, May 11, 2017, p. 24, https://www.dni.gov/files/documents/Newsroom/Testimonies/SSCI%20Unclassified%20SFR%20-%20Final.pdf (accessed July 3, 2017); James R. Clapper, Director of National Intelligence, "Statement for the Record: Worldwide Threat Assessment of the US Intelligence Community," Committee on Armed Services, U.S. Senate, February 9, 2016, pp. 26–27, https://www.armed-services.senate.gov/imo/media/doc/Clapper_02-09-16.pdf (accessed July 3, 2017). Cited hereafter as 2017 WWTA and 2016 WWTA, respectively.

15. David Wright, "North Korean ICBM Appears Able to Reach Major US Cities," Union of Concerned Scientists, July 28, 2017, http://allthingsnuclear.org/dwright/new-north-korean-icbm (accessed August 14, 2017).

16. Bruce Klingner and Sue Mi Terry, "We Participated in Talks with North Korean Representatives. This Is What We Learned," *The Washington Post*, June 22, 2017, https://www.washingtonpost.com/opinions/we-participated-in-talks-with-north-korean-representatives-this-is-what-we-learned/2017/06/22/8c838284-577b-11e7-ba90-f5875b7d1876_story.html?utm_term=.18ec48a5b73e (accessed August 14, 2017).

17. Yonhap News Agency, "N.K. Calls Itself 'Nuclear-armed State' in Revised Constitution," May 30, 2012, http://english.yonhapnews.co.kr/northkorea/2012/05/30/76/0401000000AEN20120530005200315F.HTML (accessed June 29, 2017).

18. Anna Fifield, "North Korea's Making a Lot of Threats These Days. How Worried Should We Be?" *The Washington Post*, March 11, 2016, https://www.washingtonpost.com/news/worldviews/wp/2016/03/11/north-koreas-making-a-lot-of-threats-these-days-how-worried-should-we-be/ (accessed June 29, 2017).

19. Reuters, "Head of U.S. Missile Defense Agency Says North Korea Missile Advances a 'Great Concern,'" June 7, 2017, http://www.reuters.com/article/us-usa-northkorea-missiles-idUSKBN18Y2XA (accessed July 4, 2017).

20. Dan Goure, "Why Trump Needs to Deploy Missile Defenses to Counter North Korea and Iran," *The National Interest*, February 20, 2017, http://nationalinterest.org/blog/the-buzz/why-trump-needs-deploy-missile-defenses-counter-north-korea-19510 (accessed July 4, 2017).

21. James Mattis, Secretary of Defense, "Written Statement for the Record," Committee on Armed Services, U.S. House of Representatives, June 12, 2017, http://www.politico.com/f/?id=0000015c-9f04-d070-a57d-fffe4c600001 (accessed July 3, 2017).

22. Andrew S. Erickson and Michael S. Chase, "China's SSBN Forces: Transitioning to the Next Generation," *China Brief*, Vol. 9, Issue 12 (June 12, 2009), http://www.jamestown.org/single/?no_cache=1&tx_ttnews[tt_news]=35120#.U5GOOSjb5NQ (accessed June 29, 2017).

23. For more information on China's cruise missile program, see Dennis M. Gormley, Andrew S. Erickson, and Jongdong Yuan, *A Low-Visibility Force Multiplier: Assessing China's Cruise Missile Ambitions* (Washington: National Defense University Press, 2014), http://ndupress.ndu.edu/Portals/68/Documents/Books/force-multiplier.pdf (accessed June 22, 2017).

24. 2017 WWTA, p. 6.

25. Ibid., p. 7.

26. Ibid., p. 17.

27. Ibid., p. 16.

28. North Korea Leadership Watch, "Kim Jong-un Supervises Missile Drill," March 6, 2017, http://www.nkleadershipwatch.org/2017/03/06/kim-jong-un-supervises-missile-drill/ (accessed August 14, 2017).

29. International Crisis Group, "North Korea's Nuclear and Missile Programs," *Asia Report* No. 168, June 18, 2009, https://www.crisisgroup.org/asia/north-east-asia/korean-peninsula/north-korea-s-nuclear-and-missile-programs (accessed June 29, 2017).

30. U.S. Department of Defense, Office of the Secretary of Defense, *Military and Security Developments Involving the Democratic People's Republic of Korea 2013*, Annual Report to Congress, 2014, http://www.defense.gov/Portals/1/Documents/pubs/North_Korea_Military_Power_Report_2013-2014.pdf (accessed June 29, 2017).

31. Bruce E. Bechtol, Jr., "Understanding the North Korean Military Threat to the Security of the Korean Peninsula and Northeast Asia: Declined or Evolved?" *Korea Observer*, Vol. 40, No. 1 (Spring 2009), pp. 115–154.

32. Bruce W. Bennett, "A Brief Analysis of the Republic of Korea's Defense Reform Plan," RAND Corporation *Occasional Paper* No. OP-165-OSD, December 2005, http://www.rand.org/content/dam/rand/pubs/occasional_papers/2006/RAND_OP165.pdf (accessed June 29, 2017).

33. David Albright, "North Korea's Nuclear Capabilities: A Fresh Look," Institute for Science and International Security, April 28, 2017, http://isis-online.org/isis-reports/detail/north-koreas-nuclear-capabilities-a-fresh-look (accessed June 29, 2017).

34. Joel S. Wit and Sun Young Ahn, "North Korea's Nuclear Futures: Technology and Strategy," Johns Hopkins University, Paul H. Nitze School of Advanced International Studies, U.S.–Korea Institute, North Korea's Nuclear Futures Series, February 2015, http://38north.org/wp-content/uploads/2015/02/NKNF-NK-Nuclear-Futures-Wit-0215.pdf (accessed June 29, 2017).

35. Bruce Klingner, "Allies Should Confront Imminent North Korean Nuclear Threat," Heritage Foundation *Backgrounder* No. 2913, June 3, 2014, http://www.heritage.org/asia/report/allies-should-confront-imminent-north-korean-nuclear-threat (accessed June 29, 2017).

36. Victor Morton, "North Korea Threatens Pre-emptive Nuclear Strikes Against U.S., South Korea," *The Washington Times*, March 6, 2016, http://www.washingtontimes.com/news/2016/mar/6/north-korea-threatens-nuclear-strike-against-us-so/ (accessed June 29, 2017).

37. Anthony Capaccio, "North Korean Cyber Capability Among World's Best, Brooks Says," Bloomberg, April 19, 2016, https://www.bloomberg.com/amp/news/articles/2016-04-19/north-korean-cyber-capability-among-world-s-best-brooks-says (accessed August 14, 2017).

38. 2017 WWTA, p. 7.

39. Ibid., p. 17.

40. Ibid., p. 16.

41. International Institute for Strategic Studies, *Strategic Survey 2013: The Annual Review of World Affairs* (London: Routledge, 2013), p. 32.

42. Fact Sheet, "Nuclear Weapons: Who Has What at a Glance," Arms Control Association, updated January 2017, https://www.armscontrol.org/factsheets/Nuclearweaponswhohaswhat (accessed July 3, 2017).

43. "India Condemns Pak Support to Hafiz Saeed's Rally in Lahore," *India Today*, December 14, 2014, http://indiatoday.intoday.in/story/hafiz-saeed-pakistan-lahore-rally-26-11-mumbai-attacks-jud-al-qaeda/1/405036.html (accessed June 29, 2017).

44. "Spate of Violations: DGMOs to Reduce Cross-border, LoC Tensions," *Express Tribune*, August 27, 2014, http://tribune.com.pk/story/754176/spate-of-violations-dgmos-to-reduce-cross-border-loc-tensions/ (accessed June 29, 2017).

45. International Institute for Strategic Studies, *Strategic Survey 2013*, p. 31.

46. 2016 WWTA, p. 25.

47. Major General P. J. S. Sandhu (Retd.), "Border Defence Cooperation Agreement—What Next?" United Service Institution of India, October 28, 2013, http://www.usiofindia.org/Article/?pub=Strategic%20Perspective&pubno=38&ano=2003 (accessed June 29, 2017).

48. N. C. Bipindra, "India, China Skid on Visa, Ink Border Pact," *New Indian Express*, October 24, 2013, http://newindianexpress.com/nation/India-China-skid-on-visa-ink-border-pact/2013/10/24/article1852361.ece (accessed June 29, 2017).

49. Nirupama Subramanian, "India, China Not to Use Force in Case of Face-offs," *The Hindu*, October 24, 2013, http://www.thehindu.com/todays-paper/india-china-not-to-use-force-in-case-of-faceoffs/article5266608.ece (accessed June 29, 2017).

50. James R. Clapper, Director of National Intelligence, "Statement for the Record: Worldwide Threat Assessment of the US Intelligence Community," Committee on Armed Services, U.S. Senate, February 26, 2015, p. 22, http://www.armed-services.senate.gov/imo/media/doc/Clapper_02-26-15.pdf (accessed August 5, 2016).

51. Andrew Jacobs and Jane Perlez, "U.S. Wary of Its New Neighbor in Djibouti: A Chinese Naval Base," *The New York Times*, February 25, 2017, https://www.nytimes.com/2017/02/25/world/africa/us-djibouti-chinese-naval-base.html (accessed June 29, 2017).

52. Madison Park, "Why China's New Air Zone Incensed Japan, U.S.," CNN, November 27, 2013, http://www.cnn.com/2013/11/25/world/asia/china-japan-island-explainer/ (accessed June 29, 2017).

53. Jason Le Miere, "China Claims U.S. Military Plane 'Illegally' Entered Chinese Air Defense Zone," *Newsweek*, March 24, 2017, http://www.newsweek.com/china-claims-us-military-plane-illegally-entered-chinese-air-defense-zone-573711 (accessed June 29, 2017).

54. Hans Nichols and Courtney Kube, "Two Chinese Fighter Jets Intercept U.S. Plane Over East China Sea, Officials Say," NBC News, May 18, 2017, http://www.nbcnews.com/news/us-news/two-chinese-fighter-jets-intercept-u-s-plane-officials-say-n761931 (accessed June 29, 2017).

55. Admiral Harry B. Harris Jr., U.S. Navy, Commander, U.S. Pacific Command, statement "On U.S. Pacific Command Posture" before the Committee on Armed Services, U.S. House of Representatives, April 26, 2017, p. 8, http://docs.house.gov/meetings/AS/AS00/20170426/105870/HHRG-115-AS00-Wstate-HarrisH-20170426.PDF (accessed July 3, 2017).

56. Tim Hume, "Close Call as China Scrambles Fighter Jets on Japanese Aircraft in Disputed Territory," CNN, updated May 26, 2014, http://www.cnn.com/2014/05/26/world/asia/china-japan-jets-scramble/ (accessed June 29, 2017).

57. International Institute for Strategic Studies, *The Military Balance 2014: The Annual Assessment of Global Military Capabilities and Defence Economics* (London: Routledge, 2014), p. 292.

58. U.S. Department of Defense, Office of the Secretary of Defense, *Military and Security Developments Involving the People's Republic of China 2014*, Annual Report to Congress, 2014, p. 33, http://www.defense.gov/Portals/1/Documents/pubs/2014_DoD_China_Report.pdf (accessed June 29, 2017).

59. Zachary Keck, "Putin Approves Sale of S-400 to China," *The Diplomat*, April 11, 2014, http://thediplomat.com/2014/04/putin-approves-sale-of-s-400-to-china/ (accessed June 29, 2017).

60. Xinhua, "Full Text: China's National Defense in 2010," March 31, 2011, http://www.nti.org/media/pdfs/1_1a.pdf?_=1316627912 (accessed June 29, 2017).

61. While it has long been a matter of U.S. policy that Philippine territorial claims in the South China Sea lie outside the scope of American treaty commitments, the treaty does apply in the event of an attack on Philippine "armed forces, public vessels or aircraft in the Pacific." Mutual Defense Treaty Between the United States and the Republic of the Philippines, August 30, 1951, Article V, http://avalon.law.yale.edu/20th_century/phil001.asp (accessed June 29, 2017). In any event, Article IV of the treaty obligates the U.S. in case of such an attack to "meet the common dangers in accordance with its constitutional processes." Regardless of formal treaty obligations, however, enduring U.S. interests in the region and perceptions of U.S. effectiveness and reliability as a check on growing Chinese ambitions would likely spur the U.S. to become involved.

62. 2017 WWTA, p. 16.

63. Xinhua, "China Announces Success in Technology to Refuel Satellites in Orbit," June 30, 2016, http://news.xinhuanet.com/english/2016-06/30/c_135479061.htm (accessed June 29, 2017).

64. Mei Lianju, *Space Operations Teaching Materials* (Beijing, PRC: Academy of Military Sciences Publishing House, 2013), p. 65.

65. Brian Weeden, "Through a Glass Darkly: Chinese, American, and Russian Anti-Satellite Testing in Space," *The Space Review*, March 17, 2014, http://www.thespacereview.com/article/2473/1 (accessed June 29, 2017).

66. Ian Easton, *The Great Game in Space: China's Evolving ASAT Weapons Programs and Their Implications for Future U.S. Strategy*, Project 2049 Institute, 2009, pp. 4–5.

67. Mei Lianju, *Space Operations Teaching Materials*, p. 69.

68. Peter B. de Selding, "Runaway Zombie Satellite Galaxy 15 Continues to Pose Interference Threat," Space.com, October 15, 2010, http://www.space.com/9340-runaway-zombie-satellite-galaxy-15-continues-pose-interference-threat.html (accessed June 29, 2017).

69. 2017 WWTA, pp. 8–9.

70. Stephanie Henry, "Verizon Report Describes Trends in International Data Breaches, China-Based Espionage," US–China Business Council, April 24, 2013, http://www.uschina.org/washington-update/verizon-report-describes-trends-international-data-breaches-china-based-espionage (accessed July 3, 2017); Lucian Constantin, "Verizon: One in Five Data Breaches Are the Result of Cyberespionage," *PC World*, April 23, 2013, http://www.pcworld.com/article/2036177/one-in-five-data-breaches-are-the-result-of-cyberespionage-verizon-says.html (accessed June 29, 2017).

71. Dan McWhorter, "Mandiant Exposes APT1—One of China's Cyber Espionage Units and 3,000 Indicators," Mandiant, February 18, 2013, https://www.mandiant.com/blog/mandiant-exposes-apt1-chinas-cyber-espionage-units-releases-3000-indicators/ (accessed June 29, 2017).

72. Bai Bangxi and Jiang Lijun, "Systems of Systems Conflict Is Not the Same as Systems Conflict," *National Defense Newspaper*, January 10, 2008.

73. News release, "U.S. Charges Five Chinese Military Hackers for Cyber Espionage Against U.S. Corporations and a Labor Organization for Commercial Advantage," U.S. Department of Justice, May 19, 2014, http://www.justice.gov/opa/pr/us-charges-five-chinese-military-hackers-cyber-espionage-against-us-corporations-and-labor (accessed June 29, 2017).

74. Guo Ruobing, *Theory of Military Information Security* (Beijing, PRC: National Defense University Publishing House, 2013), pp. 12–21.

75. Tan Rukan, *Building Operational Strength Course Materials* (Beijing, PRC: Academy of Military Sciences Publishing House, 2012), p. 204.

76. Nicole Perlroth and Michael Corkery, "North Korea Linked to Digital Attacks on Global Banks," *The New York Times*, May 26, 2016, http://www.nytimes.com/2016/05/27/business/dealbook/north-korea-linked-to-digital-thefts-from-global-banks.html?ref=dealbook&mtrref=news.blogs.nytimes.com&gwh=B571811569BAD1B83C5914D567DBF9E9&gwt=pay (accessed August 14, 2017).

77. Paul Mozur and Choe Sang-hun, "North Korea's Rising Ambition Seen in Bid to Breach Global Banks," *The New York Times*, March 25, 2017, https://www.nytimes.com/2017/03/25/technology/north-korea-hackers-global-banks.html (accessed August 14, 2017).

78. Jose Pagliery, "North Korea-linked Hackers Are Attacking Banks Worldwide," CNN, April 4, 2017, http://www.cnn.com/2017/04/03/world/north-korea-hackers-banks/ (accessed August 14, 2017).

79. "Cyber Attack Retaliation Against Seoul's Move to Join 'Cyber Storm,'" *The Korea Herald*, July 7, 2009, http://www.koreaherald.com/common_prog/newsprint.php?ud=20090710000075&dt=2 (accessed June 29, 2017).

80. "N.Korea Boosting Cyber Warfare Capabilities," *Chosun Ilbo*, November 5, 2013, http://english.chosun.com/site/data/html_dir/2013/11/05/2013110501790.html (accessed June 29, 2017).

81. Yoon Sangwon, "North Korea Recruits Hackers at School," Al Jazeera, June 20, 2011, http://www.aljazeera.com/indepth/features/2011/06/201162081543573839.html (accessed June 29, 2017).

82. Kelly Beaucar Vlahos, "Special Report: The Cyberwar Threat from North Korea," Fox News, February 14, 2014, http://www.foxnews.com/tech/2014/02/14/cyberwar-experts-question-north-korea-cyber-capabilities/ (accessed June 29, 2017).

83. Choi He-suk, "N.K. Third for Cyber War Capabilities," *The Korea Herald*, June 7, 2012, http://www.koreaherald.com/view.php?ud=20120607001276 (accessed June 29, 2017).

84. 2017 WWTA, p. 1.

85. 2016 WWTA, p. 3.

86. 2017 WWTA, p. 2.

87. Yuan Wenxian, *Joint Campaign Information Operations Teaching Materials* (Beijing, PRC: National Defense University Press, 2009), pp. 109–112.

88. International Institute for Strategic Studies, *The Military Balance 2014*, p. 220.

89. International Institute for Strategic Studies, *The Military Balance 2017: The Annual Assessment of Global Military Capabilities and Defence Economics* (London: Routledge, 2016), p. 320.

90. Ibid.

91. Ibid., p. 279. The Pentagon's annual report to Congress on PRC-related military and security developments contains higher estimates, including 1,200 SRBMs. See U.S. Department of Defense, Office of the Secretary of Defense, *Military and Security Developments Involving the People's Republic of China 2016*, Annual Report to Congress, 2016, p. 109, http://www.defense.gov/Portals/1/Documents/pubs/2016%20China%20Military%20Power%20Report.pdf (accessed June 29, 2017).

92. International Institute for Strategic Studies, *The Military Balance 2017*, pp. 279–284.

93. International Institute for Strategic Studies, *The Military Balance 2014*, p. 231.

94. International Institute for Strategic Studies, *The Military Balance 2017*, p. 278.

95. Ibid., p. 267.

96. Ibid., p. 303.

97. Ibid.

Conclusion: Global Threat Level

America and its interests face challenges around the world from countries and organizations that have:

- Interests that conflict with those of the U.S.;

- Sometimes hostile intentions toward the U.S.; and

- In some cases, growing military capabilities.

The government of the United States constantly faces the challenge of employing, sometimes alone but more often in concert with allies, the right mix of U.S. diplomatic, economic, public information, intelligence, and military capabilities to protect and advance U.S. interests.

In Europe, Russia remains the primary threat to American interests. The *2018 Index* again assessed the threat emanating from Russia as a behavior score of "aggressive" and a capability score of "formidable," the highest category on the scale. Moscow continues to engage in massive pro-Russia propaganda campaigns in Ukraine and other Eastern European countries and over the past year has performed a series of provocative military exercises and training missions that are viewed as warnings to neighboring countries, particularly the Baltic States. It also has increased its investment in modernizing its military and has gained significant combat experience while continuing to sabotage U.S. and Western policy in Syria.

In the Middle East, Iran remains the state actor that is most hostile to American interests. The *2018 Index* assesses Iran's behavior as "aggressive" and its capability as "gathering." In the years since publication of the *2015 Index*, Iran has methodically moved closer to becoming a nuclear power, successfully maneuvering to stabilize its program through the nuclear agreement negotiated with the U.S.; has continued to back Houthi rebels in Yemen in what some consider a proxy war between Iran and its Sunni Arab neighbors; has continued to exert influence in the region through its backing of the Assad regime and Hezbollah; and has further deepened its exploitation of instability of Iraq by providing direct support to Shia militias.

Also in the Middle East, a broad array of terrorist groups, most notably ISIS and the Iran-sponsored Hezbollah, are the most hostile of any of the global threats to America examined in the *Index*. They also are evaluated as being among the least capable. In 2017, the threat posed by ISIS decreased due to a loss of territorial control and the need to focus its efforts on defending its remaining stronghold and preserving its influence in the region.

In Asia, China moved from "aggressive" to "testing" in the scope of its provocative behavior. China continues to militarize the islands that it built on reefs in international waters and continues to claim sovereignty. It also has continued to field new equipment, most notably in naval power, perceived to be most important in its efforts to shape the Western Pacific maritime domain in line with its interests.

North Korea's level of behavior remained "aggressive" from the *2017 Index* to the *2018 Index*. Its capability level has also remained at "gathering" as Pyongyang continues to develop and refine its missile technology, especially in the area of submarine-launched ballistic missiles.

The terrorist threats emanating from the Afghanistan–Pakistan region returned to "aggressive" in the *2018 Index* after a one-year drop to "testing." However, the capability score for the region's terrorist threat dropped to "capable."

Just as there are American interests that are not covered by this *Index*, there may be additional threats to American interests that are not identified here. The *Index* focuses on the more apparent sources of risk and those in which the risk is greater.

Compiling the assessments of these threat sources, the *2018 Index* again rates the overall global threat environment as "aggressive" and "gathering" in the areas of threat actor behavior and material ability to harm U.S. security interests, respectively, leading to an aggregated threat score of "high." This score is a full category worse than the *2016 Index* assessment of "elevated," driven by increases in the capability of Russia, Iran, and China.

Behavior of Threats

	HOSTILE	AGGRESSIVE	TESTING	ASSERTIVE	BENIGN
Russia		✔			
Iran		✔			
Middle East Terrorism		✔			
Af-Pak Terrorism		✔			
China			✔		
North Korea		✔			
OVERALL		✔			

Capability of Threats

	FORMIDABLE	GATHERING	CAPABLE	ASPIRATIONAL	MARGINAL
Russia	✔				
Iran		✔			
Middle East Terrorism			✔		
Af-Pak Terrorism			✔		
China	✔				
North Korea		✔			
OVERALL		✔			

Threats to U.S. Vital Interests

	SEVERE	HIGH	ELEVATED	GUARDED	LOW
Russia		✓			
Iran		✓			
Middle East Terrorism		✓			
Af-Pak Terrorism		✓			
China		✓			
North Korea		✓			
OVERALL		✓			

Our combined score for threats to U.S. vital interests can be summarized as:

Threats to U.S. Vital Interests

SEVERE	HIGH	ELEVATED	GUARDED	LOW

U.S. Military Power

An Assessment of U.S. Military Power

America is a global power with global interests. Its military is meant first and foremost to defend America from attack. Beyond that, it is meant to protect Americans abroad, allies, and the freedom to use international sea, air, and space while retaining the ability to engage in more than one major contingency at a time. America must be able not only to defend itself and its interests, but also to deter enemies and opportunists from taking action that would challenge U.S. interests, a capability that includes preventing the destabilization of a region and guarding against threats to the peace and security of America's friends.

As noted in the three preceding editions of the *Index*, however, the U.S. does not have the right force to meet a two–major regional contingency (two-MRC) requirement and is not ready to carry out its duties effectively. Consequently, as we have seen during the past few years, the U.S. risks seeing its interests increasingly challenged and the world order it has led since World War II undone.

How to Think About Sizing Military Power

Military power begins with the people and equipment used to conduct war: the weapons, tanks, ships, airplanes, and supporting tools such as communications systems that make it possible either for one group to impose its will on another or to prevent such an outcome from happening.

However, simply counting the number of people, tanks, or combat aircraft that the U.S. possesses would be insufficient because it would lack context. For example, the U.S. Army might have 100 tanks, but to accomplish a specific military task, 1,000 or more tanks might be needed or none at all. It might be that the terrain on which a battle is fought is especially ill-suited to tanks or that the tanks one has are inferior to the enemy's. The enemy could be quite adept at using tanks, or his tank operations might be integrated into a larger employment concept that leverages the supporting fires of infantry and airpower, whereas one's own tanks are poorly maintained, the crews are ill-prepared, or one's doctrine is irrelevant.

Success in war is partly a function of matching the tools of warfare to a specific task and employing those tools effectively in the conditions of the battle. Get these wrong—tools, objective, competency, or context—and you lose.

Another key element is the military's capacity to conduct operations: how many of the right tools—people, tanks, planes, or ships—it has. One might have the right tools and know how to use them effectively but not have enough to win. Given that one cannot know with certainty beforehand just when, where, against whom, and for what reason a battle might be fought, determining how much capability is needed is an exercise of informed but not certain judgment.

Further, two different combatants can use the same set of tools in radically different ways to quite different effects. The concept of employment matters. Concepts are developed to account for numbers, capabilities, material readiness, and all sorts of other factors that enable or constrain one's actions, such as whether one fights alone or alongside allies, on familiar or strange terrain, or with a large, well-equipped force or a small, poorly equipped force.

All of these factors and a multitude of others bear upon the outcome of any military contest. Military planners attempt to account for them when devising requirements, developing training and exercise plans, formulating war plans, and providing advice to the President in his role as Commander in Chief of U.S. military forces.

Measuring hard combat power in terms of its capability, capacity, and readiness to defend U.S. vital interests is hard, especially in such a limited space as this *Index*, but it is not impossible. Regardless of the difficulty of determining the adequacy of one's military forces, the Secretary of Defense and the military services have to make decisions every year when the annual defense budget request is submitted to Congress.

The adequacy of hard power is affected most directly by the resources the nation is willing to invest. Although that investment decision is informed to a significant degree by an appreciation of threats to U.S. interests and the ability of a given defense portfolio to protect U.S. interests against such threats, it is not informed solely by such considerations; hence the importance of clarity and honesty in determining just what is needed in terms of hard power and the status of such power from year to year.

Administrations take various approaches in determining the type and amount of military power needed and, by extension, the amount of money and other resources to commit to it. After defining the national interests to be protected, the Department of Defense can use worst-case scenarios to determine the maximum challenges the U.S. military might have to overcome. Another way is to redefine what constitutes a threat. By taking a different view of whether major actors pose a meaningful threat and of the extent to which friends and allies have the ability to assist the U.S. in meeting security objectives, one can arrive at different conclusions about necessary military strength.

For example, one Administration might view China as a rising belligerent power bent on dominating the Asia–Pacific region. Another Administration might view China as an inherently peaceful rising economic power, with the expansion of its military capabilities a natural occurrence commensurate with its strengthening status. The difference between these views can have a dramatic impact on how one thinks about U.S. defense requirements. So, too, can policymakers amplify or downplay risk to justify defense budget decisions.

There also can be strongly differing views on requirements for operational capacity.

- Does the country need enough for two major combat operations (MCOs) at roughly the same time or just enough for a single major operation and some number of lesser cases?

- To what extent should "presence" tasks—the use of forces for routine engagement with partner countries or simply to be on hand in a region for crisis response—be an addition to or a subset of a military force sized to handle two major regional conflicts?

- How much value should be assigned to advanced technologies as they are incorporated into the force?

Where to Start

There are two major references that one can use to help sort through the variables and arrive at a starting point for assessing the adequacy of today's military posture: government studies and historical experience. The government occasionally conducts formal reviews that are meant to inform decisions on capabilities and capacities across the Joint Force relative to the threat environment (current and projected) and evolutions in operating conditions, the advancement of technologies, and aspects of U.S. interests that may call for one type of military response over another.

The 1993 Bottom-Up Review (BUR), conducted by then-Secretary of Defense Les Aspin, is one such frequently cited example. Secretary Aspin recognized that "the dramatic changes that [had] occurred in the world as a result of the end of the Cold War and the dissolution of the Soviet Union" had "fundamentally altered America's security needs" and were driving an imperative "to reassess all of our defense concepts, plans, and programs from the ground up."[1]

The BUR formally established the requirement that U.S. forces should be able "to achieve decisive victory in two nearly simultaneous major regional conflicts and to conduct combat operations characterized by rapid response and a high probability of success, while minimizing the risk of significant American casualties."[2] Thus was formalized the two-MRC standard.

Dr. Daniel Gouré, in his 2015 *Index* essay "Building the Right Military for a New Era: The Need for an Enduring Analytic Framework," noted that various Administrations have redefined force requirements based on their perceptions of what was necessary to protect U.S. interests.[3] In an attempt to formalize the process, and perhaps to have a mechanism by which to influence the executive branch in such matters,[4] Congress mandated that each incoming Administration must conduct a comprehensive strategic review of the global security environment, articulate a relevant strategy suited to protecting and promoting U.S. security interests, and recommend an associated military force posture.

The Quadrennial Defense Reviews (QDRs) have been conducted since 1997, accompanied in 1997, 2010, and 2014 by independent National Defense Panel (NDP) reports that have reviewed and commented on them. Both sets of documents purport to serve as key assessments, but analysts have come to minimize their value, regarding them as justifications for executive branch policy preferences (the QDR reports) or overly broad generalized commentaries (the NDP reports) that lack substantive discussion about threats to U.S. interests,

a credible strategy for dealing with them, and the actual ability of the U.S. military to meet national security requirements.

Correlation of Forces as a Factor in Force Sizing

During the Cold War, the U.S. used the Soviet threat as its primary reference in determining its hard-power needs. At that time, the correlation of forces—a comparison of one force against another to determine strengths and weaknesses—was highly symmetrical. U.S. planners compared tanks, aircraft, and ships against their direct counterparts in the opposing force. These comparative assessments drove the sizing, characteristics, and capabilities of fleets, armies, and air forces.

The evolution of guided, precision munitions and the rapid technological advancements in surveillance and targeting systems, however, have made comparing combat power more difficult. What was largely a platform v. platform model has shifted somewhat to a munitions v. target model.

The proliferation of precise weaponry increasingly means that each round, bomb, rocket, missile, and even (in some instances) individual bullet can hit its intended target, thus decreasing the number of munitions needed to prosecute an operation. It also means that the lethality of an operating environment increases significantly for the people and platforms involved. We are now at the point where one must consider how many "smart munitions" the enemy has when thinking about how many platforms and people are needed to win a combat engagement instead of focusing primarily on how many ships or airplanes the enemy can bring to bear against one's own force.[5]

In one sense, increased precision and the technological advances now being incorporated into U.S. weapons, platforms, and operating concepts make it possible to do far more with fewer assets than ever before. Platform signature reduction (stealth) makes it harder for the enemy to find and target them, while the increased precision of weapons makes it possible for fewer platforms to hit many more targets. Additionally, the ability of the U.S. Joint Force to harness computers, modern telecommunications, space-based platforms—such as for surveillance, communications, and positioning-navigation-timing (PNT) support from GPS satellites—and networked operations potentially means that smaller forces can have far greater effect in battle than at any other time in history. But these same advances also enable enemy forces, and certain military functions—such as seizing, holding, and occupying territory—may require a certain number of soldiers no matter how state-of-the-art their equipment may be.

With smaller forces, each individual element of the force represents a greater percentage of its combat power. Each casualty or equipment loss takes a larger toll on the ability of the force to sustain high-tempo, high-intensity combat operations over time, especially if the force is dispersed across a wide theater or across multiple theaters of operation.

As advanced technology has become more affordable, it has become more accessible for nearly any actor, whether state or nonstate. Consequently, it may be that the outcomes of future wars will depend to a much greater degree on the skill of the forces and their capacity to sustain operations over time than they will on some great disparity in technology. If so, readiness and capacity will take on greater importance than absolute advances in capability.

All of this illustrates the difficulties of and need for exercising judgment in assessing the adequacy of America's military power. Yet without such an assessment, all that remains are the quadrennial strategic reviews, which are subject to filtering and manipulation to suit policy interests; annual budget submissions, which typically favor desired military programs at presumed levels of affordability and are therefore necessarily budget-constrained; and leadership posture statements, which often simply align with executive branch policy priorities.

The U.S. Joint Force and the Art of War

This section of the *Index*, on military capabilities, assesses the adequacy of the United States' defense posture as it pertains to a conventional understanding of "hard power," defined as the ability of American military forces to engage and defeat an enemy's forces in battle at a scale commensurate with the vital national interests of the U.S. While some hard truths in military affairs are appropriately addressed by math and science, others are not. Speed, range, probability of detection, and radar cross-section are examples of quantifiable characteristics that can be measured. Specific future instances in which U.S. military power will be needed, the competence of the enemy, the political will to sustain operations in the face of mounting deaths and destruction, and the absolute amount of strength needed to win are matters of judgment and experience, but they nevertheless affect how large and capable a force one might need.

In conducting the assessment, we accounted for both quantitative and qualitative aspects of military forces, informed by an experience-based understanding of military operations and the expertise of external reviewers.

Military effectiveness is as much an art as it is a science. Specific military capabilities represented in weapons, platforms, and military units can be used individually to some effect. Practitioners of war, however, have learned that combining the tools of war in various ways and orchestrating their tactical employment in series or simultaneously can dramatically amplify the effectiveness of the force committed to battle.

Employment concepts are exceedingly hard to measure in any quantitative way, but their value as critical contributors in the conduct of war is undeniable. How they are utilized is very much an art-of-war matter that is learned through experience over time.

What Is Not Being Assessed

In assessing the current status of the military forces, this *Index* uses the primary references used by the military services themselves when they discuss their ability to employ hard combat power. The Army's unit of measure is the brigade combat team (BCT), while the Marine Corps structures itself by battalions. For the Navy, it is the number of ships in its combat fleet, and the most consistent reference for the Air Force is total number of aircraft, sometimes broken down into the two primary sub-types of fighters and bombers.

Obviously, this is not the totality of service capabilities, and it certainly is not everything needed for war, but these measures can be viewed as surrogate measures that subsume or represent the vast number of other things that make these "units of measure" possible and effective in battle. For example, combat forces depend on a vast logistics system that supplies everything from food and water to fuel, ammunition, and repair parts. Military operations require engineer support, and the force needs medical, dental, and administrative capabilities. The military also fields units that transport combat power and its sustainment anywhere needed around the world.

The point is that the military spear has a great deal of shaft that makes it possible for the tip to locate, close with, and destroy its target, and there is a rough proportionality between shaft and spear tip. Thus, in assessing the basic units of measure for combat power, one can get a sense of what is likely needed in the combat support, combat service support, and supporting establishment echelons. The scope of this *Index* does not extend to analysis of everything that makes hard power possible; it focuses on the status of the hard power itself.

This assessment also does not account for the Reserve and Guard components of the services; it focuses only on the Active component. Again, the element of proportion or ratio figures prominently. Each service determines the balance among its Active, Reserve, and National Guard elements (only the Army and Air Force have Guard elements; the Navy and Marine Corps do not) based on factors that include cost of the respective elements, availability for operational employment, time needed to respond to an emergent crisis, allocation of roles between the elements, and political considerations.[6] This assessment looks at the baseline requirement for a given amount of combat power that is readily available for use in a major combat operation—something that is usually associated with the Active components of each service.

The Defense Budget and Strategic Guidance

When it comes to the defense budget, how much we spend does not determine the posture or capacity of the U.S. military. As a matter of fact, simply looking at how much is allocated to defense does not tell us much about the capacity, modernity, or readiness of the forces. Proper funding is a necessary but not by itself sufficient condition for a capable, modern, and ready force. It is possible that a larger defense budget could be associated with less military capability if the money were allocated inappropriately or spent wastefully. That said, however, the budget does reflect the importance assigned to defending the nation and its interests in the prioritization of federal spending.

Absent a significant threat to the survival of the country, the U.S. government will always balance expenditures on defense with spending in all of the other areas of government activity that are deemed necessary or desirable. Some have argued that a defense budget indexed to a percent of gross domestic product (GDP) is a reasonable reference. However, a fixed percentage of GDP does not accurately reflect national security requirements *per se* any more than the size of the budget alone correlates to levels of capability. Additionally, the fact that the economy changes over time does not necessarily mean that defense spending should increase or decrease in lockstep by default.

Ideally, defense requirements are determined by identifying national interests that might need to be protected with military power; assessing the nature of threats to those interests, what would be needed to defeat those threats, and the costs associated with that capability; and then determining what the country can afford or is willing to spend. *Any difference between assessed requirements and affordable levels of spending on defense would constitute a risk to U.S. security interests.*

This *Index* enthusiastically adopts this approach: interests, threats, requirements, resulting force, and associated budget. Spending less than the amount needed to maintain a two-MRC force results in policy debates about where to accept risk: force modernization, the capacity to conduct large-scale or multiple simultaneous operations, or force readiness.

The decision to fund national defense commensurate with interests and prevailing threats is a reflection of national priorities and risk tolerance. This *Index* assesses the ability of the nation's military forces to protect vital national security interests within the world *as it is* so that the debate about the level of funding for hard power is better informed.

The fiscal year (FY) 2017 base discretionary budget for defense was $521.8 billion.[7] This represents the resources allocated to pay for the forces (manpower, equipment, training); enabling capabilities (things like transportation, satellites, defense intelligence, and research and development); and institutional support (bases and stations, facilities, recruiting, and the like). The base budget does not pay for the cost of major ongoing overseas operations, which is captured in supplemental funding known as OCO (overseas contingency operations).

In 2017, the debate about how much funding to allocate to defense was framed by the incoming Administration's campaign promise to rebuild the military. Despite repeated emphasis on the importance of investing more to fix obvious readiness, capacity, and modernization problems, the debate was determined once again by larger political dynamics that pitted those who wanted to see an overall reduction in federal spending against those who advocate higher levels of defense spending and those who want to see any increase in defense spending matched by commensurate increases in domestic spending.

The argument for significant increases in defense spending in 2017 was anchored by House Armed Services Committee Chairman Mac Thornberry (R–TX) and the Senate Armed Services Committee Chairman John McCain (R–AZ). Both released public documents early in the year that stressed the importance of rebuilding the military and set budgetary targets for the coming fiscal year that would start to do so.[8] The proposals established a spending objective of $640 billion, substantially higher than the caps imposed by the Budget Control Act (BCA) of 2011 and exceeding both the Trump Administration's recommended $603 billion[9] and The Heritage Foundation's recommended $632 billion.[10]

In testimony before the House Armed Services Committee, Secretary of Defense James Mattis and Chairman of the Joint Chiefs of Staff General Joseph Dunford emphasized the need for sustained budget growth so that U.S. forces can maintain a competitive advantage over likely adversaries. "We know now," General Dunford testified, "that continued growth in the base budget of at least 3 percent above inflation is the floor necessary to preserve just the competitive advantage we have today, and we can't assume our adversaries will remain still."[11]

President Barack Obama's 2012 defense budget, the last sent to Congress before passage of the BCA, proposed $661 billion in defense spending for FY 2018. A bipartisan consensus, as seen in the National Defense Panel report in 2014, identified the so-called Gates budget (named after then-Secretary of Defense Robert Gates) as the minimum that the United States should be spending on national defense.[12] As seen in Chart 3, despite congressional pushes toward a higher topline, both the FY 2017 enacted budget and the FY 2018 budget proposal are below this minimum.

The restrictions placed on defense spending by the BCA continue to be a major concern of the military service chiefs, who have testified consistently about the damage these restrictions are causing to readiness, modernization, and capacity for operations. The funding

CHART 3

Defense Spending Heavily Constrained by Budget Control Act

Current defense spending is far below the levels requested by former Secretary of Defense Robert Gates in 2012 and President Trump in his FY 2018 budget.

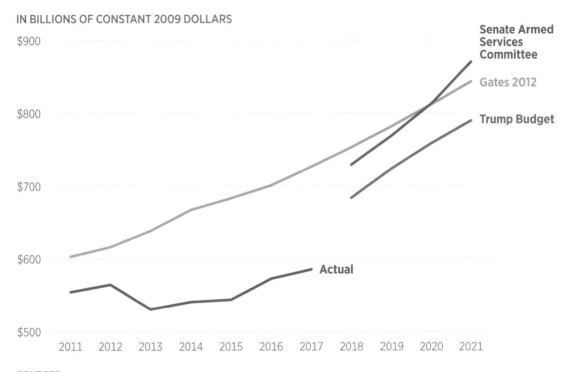

IN BILLIONS OF CONSTANT 2009 DOLLARS

SOURCES:

- Gates 2012: White House, Office of Management and Budget, *Fiscal Year 2012 Budget of the U.S. Government, Analytical Perspectives*, February 2011, https://www.gpo.gov/fdsys/search/pagedetails.action?collectionCode=BUDGET&granuleId=&packageId=BUDGET-2012-PER (accessed July 31, 2017).
- Trump Budget: White House, Office of Management and Budget, *Budget of the U.S. Government Fiscal Year 2018: A New Foundation for American Greatness*, May 2017, Table S–3, https://www.whitehouse.gov/sites/whitehouse.gov/files/omb/budget/fy2018/budget.pdf (accessed July 31, 2017).
- Senate Armed Services Committee: Sen. John McCain, "Restoring American Power: Recommendations for the FY 2018–2022 Defense Budget," January 2017, https://www.mccain.senate.gov/public/_cache/files/25bff0ec-481e-466a-843f-68ba5619e6d8/restoring-american-power-7.pdf (accessed July 31, 2017).
- Actual: U.S. Department of Defense, "Fiscal Year 2018 Budget Request," May 2017, p. 4, http://comptroller.defense.gov/Portals/45/Documents/defbudget/fy2018/fy2018_Budget_Request.pdf (accessed July 31, 2017).

heritage.org

restrictions that have caused severe degradation in military readiness over the past five years have yet to be addressed adequately by Congress. The BCA remains a major obstacle to creating predictable levels of funding for defense and will continue to harm readiness and modernization until it is repealed and sufficient funding is provided on a consistent basis for at least the next decade.

Purpose as a Driver in Force Sizing

The Joint Force is used for a wide range of purposes, only one of which is major combat operations. Fortunately, such events have been rare (but consistent), averaging roughly 15–20 years between occurrences.[13] In between (and even during) such occurrences, the military is used to support regional engagement, crisis response, strategic deterrence, and humanitarian assistance, as well as to support civil authorities and U.S. diplomacy.

The U.S. Unified Combatant Commands, or COCOMS (EUCOM, CENTCOM, PACOM, SOUTHCOM, and AFRICOM), all have annual and long-term plans through which they engage with countries in their assigned regions. These engagements range from very small unit training events with the forces of a single partner country to larger bilateral and sometimes multilateral military exercises. Such events help to establish working relationships with other countries, acquire a more detailed understanding of regional political–military dynamics and on-the-ground conditions in areas of interest, and signal U.S. security interests to friends and competitors.

To support such COCOM efforts, the services provide forces that are based permanently in respective regions or that operate in them temporarily on a rotational basis. To make these regional rotations possible, the services must maintain a base force that is sufficiently large to train, deploy, support, receive back, and make ready again a stream of units that ideally is enough to meet validated COCOM demand.

The ratio between time spent at home and time spent away on deployment for any given unit is known as OPTEMPO (operational tempo), and each service attempts to maintain a ratio that both gives units enough time to educate, train, and prepare their forces and allows the individuals in a unit to maintain some semblance of a healthy home and family life. This ensures that units are fully prepared for the next deployment cycle and that service-members do not become "burned out" or suffer adverse consequences in their personal lives because of excessive deployment time.

Experience has shown that a ratio of at least 3:1 (three periods of time at home for every period deployed) is sustainable. If a unit is to be out for six months, for example, it will be home for 18 months before deploying again. Obviously, a service needs enough people, units, ships, and planes to support such a ratio. If peacetime engagement were the primary focus for the Joint Force, the services could size their forces

to support these forward-based and forward-deployed demands.

Thus, the size of the total force must necessarily be much larger than any sampling of its use at any point in time.

In contrast, sizing a force for major combat operations is an exercise informed by history—how much force was needed in previous wars—and then shaped and refined by analysis of current threats, a range of plausible scenarios, and expectations about what the U.S. can do given training, equipment, employment concept, and other factors. The defense establishment must then balance "force sizing" between COCOM requirements for presence and engagement with the amount of military power (typically measured in terms of combat units and major combat platforms, which informs total end strength) that is thought necessary to win in likely war scenarios.

Inevitably, compromises are made that account for how much military the country is willing to buy. Generally speaking:

- The Army sizes to major warfighting requirements.

- The Marine Corps focuses on crisis response demands and the ability to contribute to one major war.

- The Air Force attempts to strike a balance that accounts for historically based demand across the spectrum because air assets are shifted fairly easily from one theater of operations to another ("easily" being a relative term when compared to the challenge of shifting large land forces), and any peacetime engagement typically requires some level of air support.

- The Navy is driven by global presence requirements. To meet COCOM requirements for a continuous fleet presence at sea, the Navy must have three to four ships in order to have one on station. A commander who wants one U.S. warship stationed off the coast of a hostile country, for example, needs the use of four ships from the fleet: one on station, one that left station and is traveling home, one that just left home and is traveling to station, and one that fills in for one of the other ships when it needs maintenance or training time.

This report focuses on the forces required to win two major wars as the baseline force-sizing metric. The military's effectiveness, both as a deterrent against opportunistic competitor states and as a valued training partner in the eyes of other countries, derives from its effectiveness (proven or presumed) in winning wars.

Our Approach

With this in mind, we assessed the state of military affairs for U.S. forces as it pertains to their ability to deliver hard power against an enemy in three areas:

- Capability,

- Capacity, and

- Readiness.

Capability. Examining the capability of a military force requires consideration of:

- The proper tools (material and conceptual) of sufficient design, performance characteristics, technological advancement, and suitability needed for the force to perform its function against an enemy force successfully.

- The sufficiency of armored vehicles, ships, airplanes, and other equipment and weapons to win against the enemy.

- The appropriate variety of options to preclude strategic vulnerabilities in the force and give flexibilities to battlefield commanders.

- The degree to which elements of the force reinforce each other in covering potential

vulnerabilities, maximizing strengths, and gaining greater effectiveness through synergies that are not possible in narrowly stovepiped, linear approaches to war.

The capability of the U.S. Joint Force was on ample display in its decisive conventional war victory over Iraq in liberating Kuwait in 1991 and later in the conventional military operation in Iraq to depose Saddam Hussein in 2003. Aspects of its capability have also been seen in numerous other operations undertaken since the end of the Cold War. While the conventional combat aspect at the "pointy end of the spear" of power projection has been more moderate in places like Yugoslavia, Somalia, Bosnia and Serbia, and Kosovo, and even against the Taliban in Afghanistan in 2001, the fact that the U.S. military was able to conduct highly complex operations thousands of miles away in austere, hostile environments and sustain those operations as long as required is testament to the ability of U.S. forces to do things that the armed forces of few if any other countries can do.

A modern-day "major combat operation"[14] along the lines of those upon which Pentagon planners base their requirements would feature a major opponent possessing modern integrated air defenses; naval power (surface and subsurface); advanced combat aircraft (to include bombers); a substantial inventory of short-range, medium-range, and long-range missiles; current-generation ground forces (tanks, armored vehicles, artillery, rockets, and anti-armor weaponry); cruise missiles; and (in some cases) nuclear weapons. Such a situation involving an actor capable of threatening vital national interests would present a challenge that is comprehensively different from the challenges that the U.S. Joint Force has faced in past decades.

In 2017, the military community continued to debate the extent to which the U.S. military is ready for major conventional warfare, given its focus on counterinsurgency, stability, and advise-and-assist operations since 2004. The Army in particular has noted the need to reengage in training and exercises that feature larger-scale combined arms maneuver operations, especially to ensure that its higher headquarters elements are up to the task. According to Acting Secretary of the Army Robert Speer and Army Chief of Staff General Mark Milley:

> In 2014, the United States Army began the transition from training for a decade-long counterinsurgency campaign to training for major combat operations. Over the next two years, the Army's challenge is to balance the requirements of remaining regionally engaged, while simultaneously preparing to meet the demands of a globally responsive contingency force.[15]

This *Index* ascertains the relevance and health of military service capabilities by looking at such factors as average age of equipment, generation of equipment relative to the current state of competitor efforts as reported by the services, and the status of replacement programs that are meant to introduce more updated systems as older equipment reaches the end of its programmed service life. While some of the information is quite quantitative, other factors could be considered judgment calls made by acknowledged experts in the relevant areas of interest or as addressed by senior service officials when providing testimony to Congress or addressing specific areas in other official statements.

It must be determined whether the services possess capabilities that are relevant to the modern combat environment.

Capacity. The U.S. military must have a sufficient quantity of the right capability or capabilities, but there is a troubling and fairly consistent trend that characterizes the path from requirement to fielded capability within U.S. military acquisition. Along the way to acquiring the capability, several linked things happen that result in far less of a presumed "critical capability" than supposedly was required.

- The manufacturing sector attempts to satisfy the requirements articulated by the military.

- "Unexpected" technological hurdles arise that take longer and much more money to solve than anyone envisioned.

- Programs are lengthened, and cost overruns are addressed (usually with more money).

- Then the realization sets in that the country either cannot afford or is unwilling to pay the cost of acquiring the total number of platforms originally advocated. The acquisition goal is adjusted downward (if not canceled), and the military finally fields fewer platforms (at a higher cost per unit) than it originally said it needed to be successful in combat.

As deliberations proceed toward a decision on whether to reduce planned procurement, they rarely focus on and quantify the increase in risk that accompanies the decrease in procurement.

Something similar happens with force structure size: the number of units and total number of personnel the services say they need to meet the objectives established by the Commander in Chief and the Secretary of Defense in their strategic guidance. The Marine Corps has stated that it needs 27 infantry battalions to fully satisfy the validated requirements of the regional Combatant Commanders, yet current funding for defense has the Corps at 24. In 2012, the Army was on a build toward 48 brigade combat teams, but funding reductions now have the number at 31—less than two-thirds the number that the Army originally thought was necessary.

Older equipment can be updated with new components to keep it relevant, and commanders can employ fewer units more expertly for longer periods of time in an operational theater to accomplish an objective. At some point, however, sheer numbers of updated, modern equipment and trained, fully manned units are going to be needed to win in battle against a credible opponent when the crisis is profound enough to threaten a vital interest.

Capacity (numbers) can be viewed in at least three ways: compared to a stated objective for each category by each service, compared to amounts required to complete various types of operations across a wide range of potential missions as measured against a potential adversary, and as measured against a set benchmark for total national capability. This *Index* employs the two-MRC metric as a benchmark.

The two-MRC benchmark for force sizing is the *minimum* standard for U.S. hard-power capacity because one will never be able to employ 100 percent of the force at the same time. Some percentage of the force will always be unavailable because of long-term maintenance overhaul (for Navy ships in particular); unit training cycles; employment in myriad engagement and small-crisis response tasks that continue even during major conflicts; and the need to keep some portion of the force uncommitted to serve as a strategic reserve.

The historical record shows that the U.S. Army commits 21 BCTs on average to a major conflict; thus, a two-MRC standard would require 42 BCTs available for actual use. But an Army built to field only 42 BCTs would also be an Army that could find itself entirely committed to war, leaving nothing back as a strategic reserve, to replace combat losses, or to handle other U.S. security interests.

Again, this *Index* assesses only the Active component of the services, though with full awareness that the Army also has Reserve and National Guard components that together account for half of the total Army. The additional capacity needed to meet these "above two-MRC requirements" could be handled by these other components or mobilized to supplement Active-component commitments. In fact, this is how the Army thinks about meeting operational demands and is at the heart of the current debate within the total Army about the roles and contributions of the various Army components. A similar situation exists with the Air Force and Marine Corps.

The balance among Active, Reserve, and Guard elements is beyond the scope of this study. Our focus here is on establishing a minimum benchmark for the capacity needed to handle a two-MRC requirement.

We conducted a review of the major defense studies (1993 BUR, QDR reports, and independent panel critiques) that are publicly available,[16] as well as modern historical instances of major wars (Korea, Vietnam, Gulf War, Operation Iraqi Freedom), to see whether there was any consistent trend in U.S. force allocation. The results of our review are presented in Table 3. To this we added 20 percent, both to account for forces and platforms that are likely to be unavailable and to provide a strategic reserve to guard against unforeseen demands. Summarizing the totals, this *Index* concluded that a Joint Force capable of dealing with two MRCs simultaneously or nearly simultaneously would consist of:

- Army: 50 BCTs.

- Navy: at least 346 ships and 624 strike aircraft.

- Air Force: 1,200 fighter/attack aircraft.

- Marine Corps: 36 battalions.

America's security interests require the services to have the capacity to handle two major regional conflicts successfully.

Readiness. The consequences of the sharp reductions in funding mandated by sequestration have caused military service officials, senior DOD officials, and even Members of Congress to warn of the dangers of recreating the "hollow force" of the 1970s when units existed on paper but were staffed at reduced levels, minimally trained, and woefully ill-equipped.[17] To avoid this, the services have traded quantity/capacity and modernization to ensure that what they do have is "ready" for employment.

As was the case in 2016, the service chiefs have stated that current and projected levels of funding continue to take a toll on the ability of units to maintain sufficient levels of readiness across the force. Some units have reduced

TABLE 3

Historical U.S. Force Allocation

Troop figures are in thousands.

	Korean War	Vietnam War	Persian Gulf War	Operation Iraqi Freedom
ARMY				
Total Troop Deployment During Engagement	206.3	219.3	267.0	99.7
Divisions*	6	7	4	1
Reserve Component Divisions Total for Strategic Documents	n/a	n/a	n/a	n/a
Total Army End Strength During Engagement, During Year of Strategy Document Active	1,313.8	1,113.3	738.0	499.0
Total Active End Strength Recommendations	n/a	n/a	n/a	n/a
NAVY				
Total Fleet During Engagement	904	770	529	297
Aircraft Carriers	6	5	6	5
Carrier Air Wings	6	5	6	5
Large Surface Combatants	37	14	30	23
Small Surface Combatants	16	47	16	9
Attack Submarines	4	0	12	12
Amphibious Vessels	34	26	21	7
Combat Logistics and Support Ships	28	29	45	42
Fighter/Attack Squadrons	21	43	22	24
MARINE CORPS				
Total Troop Deployment During Engagement	33.5	44.7	90.0	66.2
Active Divisions*	1	2	2	1
Reserve Divisions	n/a	n/a	n/a	n/a
Marine Expeditionary Force	1	1	1	2
Air Wings Active/Reserve	1	1	1	1
Total Marine Corps End Strength During Engagement by Year of Strategy Document	187.0	289.0	196.3	178.0
Total Recommended End Strength	n/a	n/a	n/a	n/a
AIR FORCE				
Bombers or Bomber Squadrons**	21	23	3	4
Fighter Squadrons	26		30	30
Active Fighter Wings	7	8	10	10
Reserve Fighter Wings				
Airlift/Tankers	239	167	388	293

* Figures for engagements are numbers deployed; figures for documents are totals.
** Figures for Air Force bombers for Korean War, Vietnam War, Persian Gulf War, and Iraq are bomber squadrons. All other figures are bombers.
*** 2014 QDR prescribed nine heavy bomber squadrons, equaling 96 aircraft.

	1993 BUR	1997 QDR	2001 QDR	2006 QDR	2010 QDR	2010 Indep. Panel	2-MRC Paper	2014 QDR	2014 NDP
ARMY									
Total Troop Deployment During Engagement	n/a	n/a	n/a	n/a	n/a	n/a	n/a	n/a	n/a
Divisions*	10	10	10	11		11	10	10	n/a
Reserve Component Divisions Total for Strategic Documents	n/a	5	8	8	18	7	8	8	n/a
Total Army End Strength During Engagement, During Year of Strategy Document Active	572.0	492.0	481.0	505.0	566.0	566.0	550.0	490.0	490.0
Total Active End Strength Recommendations	n/a	n/a	n/a	482.4	n/a	1,106.0	600.0	450.0	490.0
NAVY									
Total Fleet During Engagement	346	310	n/a	n/a	n/a	346	350	n/a	346
Aircraft Carriers	12	12	12	11	11	11	11	11	n/a
Carrier Air Wings	12	11	11	n/a	10	10	10	10	n/a
Large Surface Combatants	124	116	116	n/a	84–88	n/a	120	92	n/a
Small Surface Combatants				n/a	14–28	n/a	n/a	43	n/a
Attack Submarines	55	50	55	n/a	53–55	55	50	51	n/a
Amphibious Vessels	41	36	36	n/a	29–31	n/a	38	33	n/a
Combat Logistics and Support Ships	65	n/a	n/a	n/a	58	n/a	75	n/a	n/a
Fighter/Attack Squadrons	33	30	30	n/a	30	30	30	30	n/a
MARINE CORPS									
Total Troop Deployment During Engagement	n/a	n/a	n/a	n/a	n/a	n/a	n/a	n/a	n/a
Active Divisions*	4	3	3	n/a	3	n/a	n/a	3	n/a
Reserve Divisions	1	1	1	n/a	1	n/a	n/a	1	n/a
Marine Expeditionary Force	3	3	3	n/a	3	3	3	2	n/a
Air Wings Active/Reserve	n/a	4	4	n/a	4	n/a	n/a	4	n/a
Total Marine Corps End Strength During Engagement by Year of Strategy Document	174.0	174.0	173.0	180.0	202.0	202.0	196.0	182.0	182.0
Total Recommended End Strength	n/a	n/a	n/a	175.0	n/a	243.0	202.0	182.0	182.0
AIR FORCE									
Bombers or Bomber Squadrons**	200	187	112	n/a	96	180	200	96***	n/a
Fighter Squadrons	54	54	46	n/a	42	66	54	48	n/a
Active Fighter Wings	13	12+	15	n/a	n/a	20	20	9	n/a
Reserve Fighter Wings	7	8	12	n/a	n/a	n/a		7	n/a
Airlift/Tankers	n/a	n/a	n/a	n/a	1023	1023	1,000	954	n/a

manning. Though progress has been made in some areas due to funding provided by Congress over the past few years, the return of further cuts under the Budget Control Act of 2011 threatens to undo these gains. For example:

- General Daniel Allyn, Vice Chief of Staff of the Army, testified in February 2017 that "[t]oday, only about 1/3 of our BCTs, 1/4 of our Combat Aviation Brigades and half of our Division Headquarters are ready. Of the BCTs that are ready, only three could be called upon to fight tonight in the event of a crisis."[18]

- Secretary of the Air Force Heather A. Wilson and Air Force Chief of Staff General David L. Goldfein warned in testimony before Congress in June 2017 that "the Air Force is too small for the missions demanded of it and it is unlikely that the need for air and space power will diminish significantly in the coming decade.... We are at our lowest state of full spectrum readiness in our history."[19]

- The U.S. Navy's force reductions without a commensurate reduction in mission demand have led to a readiness crisis as well. "Maintaining the readiness of our naval forces is key to maintaining the scope and scale of operations demanded of them," Acting Secretary of the Navy Sean Stackley testified in June 2017. "We have been increasingly challenged in our ability to do so, however, by the growing imbalance between the size of the force, the operational demand placed on the force, and the funding available to operate and sustain the force."[20]

- Top Marine Corps officials acknowledged similarly continued strains, testifying in April 2017 that "today's force is capable and our forward deployed forces are ready to fight," but that "we are fiscally stretched to maintain readiness across the breadth of the force in the near term, and

to modernize for future readiness against threats we will face. The Marine Corps will require sufficient resources to remedy this situation."[21]

It is one thing to have the right capabilities to defeat the enemy in battle. It is another thing to have enough of those capabilities to sustain operations over time and many battles against an enemy, especially when attrition or dispersed operations are significant factors. But sufficient numbers of the right capabilities are rather meaningless if the force is unready to engage in the task.

Scoring. In our final assessments, we tried very hard not to convey a higher level of precision than we think is achievable using unclassified, open-source, publicly available documents; not to reach conclusions that could be viewed as based solely on assertions or opinion; and not to rely solely on data and information that can be highly quantified, since simple numbers do not tell the whole story.

We believe that the logic underlying our methodology is sound. This *Index* drew from a wealth of public testimony from senior government officials, from the work of recognized experts in the defense and national security analytic community, and from historical instances of conflict that seemed most appropriate to this project. It then considered several questions, including:

- How does one place a value on the combat effectiveness of such concepts as Air-Sea Battle, Network-centric Operations, Global Strike, Multi-Domain Battle, or Joint Operational Access?

- Is it entirely possible to assess accurately (1) how well a small number of newest-generation ships or aircraft will fare against a much larger number of currently modern counterparts when (2) U.S. forces are operating thousands of miles from home, (3) orchestrated with a particular operational concept, and (4) the enemy is leveraging a "home field advantage" that includes strategic depth and much shorter and perhaps better protected lines of communication and (5) might be pursuing much dearer national objectives than the U.S. so that the political will to conduct sustained operations in the face of mounting losses might differ dramatically?

- How does one neatly quantify the element of combat experience, the erosion of experience as combat operation events recede in time and those who participated in them leave the force, the health of a supporting workforce, the value of "presence and engagement operations," and the related force structures and deployment/employment patterns that presumably deter war or mitigate its effects if it does occur?

This *Index* focused on the primary purpose of military power—to defeat an enemy in combat—and the historical record of major U.S. engagements for evidence of what the U.S. defense establishment has thought was necessary to execute a major conventional war successfully. To this we added the two-MRC benchmark, on-the-record assessments of what the services themselves are saying about their status relative to validated requirements, and the analysis and opinions of various experts in and out of government who have covered these issues for many years.

Taking it all together, we rejected scales that would imply extraordinary precision and settled on a scale that conveys broader characterizations of status that range from very weak to very strong. Ultimately, any such assessment is a judgment call informed by quantifiable data, qualitative assessments, thoughtful deliberation, and experience. We trust that our approach makes sense, is defensible, and is repeatable.

U.S. Military Power

	VERY WEAK	WEAK	MARGINAL	STRONG	VERY STRONG
Army		✔			
Navy			✔		
Air Force			✔		
Marine Corps		✔			
Nuclear			✔		
OVERALL			✔		

Endnotes

1. Les Aspin, Secretary of Defense, *Report on the Bottom-Up Review* (Washington: U.S. Department of Defense, October 1993), p. iii, http://www.google.com/url?sa=t&rct=j&q=&esrc=s&source=web&cd=2&ved=0CCUQFjABahUKEwjj4dWf6N3HAhVEmh4KHdG1Cdg&url=http%3A%2F%2Fwww.dtic.mil%2Fcgi-bin%2FGetTRDoc%3FAD%3DADA359953&usg=AFQjCNFvzw730XRz7YRxpc5BNr5_UdfMiQ (accessed August 1, 2017).

2. Ibid., p. 8.

3. Daniel Gouré, "Building the Right Military for a New Era: The Need for an Enduring Analytic Framework," in *2015 Index of U.S. Military Strength*, ed. Dakota L. Wood (Washington: The Heritage Foundation, 2015), pp. 27–36, http://index.heritage.org/militarystrength/important-essays-analysis/building-right-military-new-era/.

4. John Y. Schrader, Leslie Lewis, and Roger Allen Brown, *Quadrennial Defense Review 2001: Lessons on Managing Change in the Department of Defense* (Santa Monica, CA: RAND Corporation, National Defense Research Institute, 2003), http://www.rand.org/content/dam/rand/pubs/documented_briefings/2005/DB379.pdf (accessed August 1, 2017).

5. The United States has not had to contend in combat with any credible air force since the Vietnam War, but U.S. Air Force planners are increasingly concerned about an enemy's ground-based, anti-air missile capability. For naval planners, ship-based, air-based, and shore-based anti-ship cruise missiles are of much greater concern than is the number of conventional surface combatants armed with large-caliber guns that an enemy navy has. Likewise, ground force planners have to consider the numbers and types of guided anti-armor weapons that an enemy possesses and whether an opposing force has guided artillery, mortar, or rocket capabilities. Guided/precision weapons are less expensive (by orders of magnitude) than the platforms they target, which means that countries can produce far more guided munitions than primary weapons platforms. Some examples: Harpoon ASCM ($2 million)/DDG-51 *Arleigh Burke*-Class destroyer ($2 billion); AT4 anti-armor weapon ($1,500)/M1A1 Abrams main battle tank ($9 million); 120mm guided mortar round ($10,000) or 155mm guided artillery round ($100,000)/M198 155mm howitzer ($500,000); S-300 anti-air missile ($1 million)/F/A-18 Hornet ($60 million) or F-35A Lightning II ($180 million).

6. One example of balancing the forces was the Army's Aviation Restructure Initiative, in which the active-duty force sought to redistribute certain rotorcraft platforms among the active-duty Army and the National Guard, a plan that the Guard has contended would reduce the capabilities it has gained during recent combat engagements, such as its pilots' proficiency in flying Apache helicopters. For more on this issue, see U.S. Government Accountability Office, *Force Structure: Army's Analyses of Aviation Alternatives*, GAO–15–430R, April 27, 2015, p. 1, http://www.gao.gov/assets/670/669857.pdf (accessed August 2, 2017).

7. U.S. Department of Defense, Office of the Under Secretary of Defense (Comptroller), *National Defense Budget Estimates for FY 2018*, June 2017, p. 1, http://comptroller.defense.gov/Portals/45/Documents/defbudget/fy2018/FY18_Green_Book.pdf (accessed July 24, 2017).

8. For the House version, see House Committee on Armed Services, *Rebuilding National Security—The Price of Freedom*, 2017, https://armedservices.house.gov/sites/republicans.armedservices.house.gov/files/wysiwyg_uploaded/HASC%20Budget%20White%20Paper.pdf (accessed August 3, 2017). For the Senate version, see U.S. Senator John McCain, *Restoring American Power: Recommendations for the FY 2018–FY 2022 Defense Budget*, 2017, https://www.mccain.senate.gov/public/_cache/files/25bff0ec-481e-466a-843f-68ba5619e6d8/restoring-american-power-7.pdf (accessed August 3, 2017).

9. U.S. Office of Management and Budget, *Budget of the U.S. Government: A New Foundation for American Greatness, Fiscal Year 2018* (Washington: U.S. Government Printing Office, 2017), p. 201, https://www.whitehouse.gov/sites/whitehouse.gov/files/omb/budget/fy2018/budget.pdf (accessed August 3, 2017).

10. Thomas Spoehr and Rachel Zissimos, "Preventing a Defense Crisis: The 2018 National Defense Authorization Act Must Begin to Restore U.S. Military Strength," Heritage Foundation *Backgrounder* No. 3205, March 29, 2017, http://www.heritage.org/defense/report/preventing-defense-crisis-the-2018-national-defense-authorization-act-must-begin.

11. Aaron Mehta, "DoD Needs 3–5 Percent Annual Growth 2023, Top Officials Say," *Defense News,* June 13, 2017, http://www.defensenews.com/pentagon/2017/06/13/dod-needs-3-5-percent-annual-growth-through-2023-top-officials-say/ (accessed July 24, 2017).

12. See, for example, *Ensuring a Strong U.S. Defense for the Future: The National Defense Panel Review of the 2014 Quadrennial Defense Review*, July 2014, p. 4, http://www.usip.org/sites/default/files/Ensuring-a-Strong-U.S.-Defense-for-the-Future-NDP-Review-of-the-QDR_0.pdf (accessed August 1, 2017).

13. Since World War II, the U.S. has fought four major wars: the Korean War (1950–1953); the Vietnam War (1965–1973); the Gulf War/Operation Desert Shield/Desert Storm (1990–1991); and the Iraq War/Operation Iraqi Freedom (2003–2011).

14. Defense references to war have varied over the past few decades from "major combat operations" (MCO) and "major theater war" (MTW) to the current "major regional contingency" (MRC). Arguably, there is a supporting rationale for such shifts as planners attempt to find the best words to describe the scope and scale of significant military efforts, but the terms are basically interchangeable.

15. The Honorable Robert M. Speer, Acting Secretary of the Army, and General Mark A. Milley, Chief of Staff, United States Army, statement "On the Posture of the United States Army" before the Committee on Armed Services, U.S. Senate, 115th Cong., 1st Sess., May 25, 2017, p. 6, https://www.armed-services.senate.gov/imo/media/doc/Speer-Milley_05-25-17.pdf (accessed August 3, 2017).

16. The Department of Defense, through the Joint Staff and Geographic Combatant Commanders, manages a relatively small set of real-world operational plans (OPLANS) focused on specific situations where the U.S. feels it is most likely to go to war. These plans are reviewed and updated regularly to account for changes in the Joint Force or with the presumed enemy. They are highly detailed and account not only for the amount of force the U.S. expects that it will need to defeat the enemy, but also for which specific units would deploy; how the force would actually flow into the theater (the sequencing of units); what ports and airfields it would use; how much ammunition, fuel, and other supplies it would need at the start; how much transportation or "lift" would be needed to get the force there (by air, sea, trucks, or rail); and the basic plan of attack. The Pentagon also routinely develops, explores, and refines various notional planning scenarios in order to better understand the implications of different sorts of contingencies, which approaches might be more effective, how much of what type of force might be needed, and the regional issue or issues for which there would have to be an accounting. These types of planning events inform service efforts to develop, equip, train, and field military forces that are up to the task of defending national security interests. All of these efforts and their products are classified national security information and therefore not available to the public.

17. For more on the potential for a hollow force, see Association of the U.S. Army, "Preventing a Hollow Force Is Army's Top Priority," May 25, 2017, https://www.ausa.org/news/preventing-hollow-force-army%E2%80%99s-top-priority (accessed July 31, 2017), and J. V. Venable, "America's Air Force Is in Bad Shape," *National Review*, June 13, 2017, http://www.nationalreview.com/article/448556/us-air-force-weakened-funding-cuts-shrinking-workforce-aging-fleet-hurt-preparedness (accessed July 31, 2017).

18. General Daniel Allyn, Vice Chief of Staff, United States Army, statement on "State of the Military" before the Committee on Armed Services, U.S. House of Representatives, 115th Cong., 1st Sess., February 7, 2017, p. 4, http://docs.house.gov/meetings/AS/AS00/20170207/105530/HHRG-115-AS00-Wstate-AllynD-20170207.pdf (accessed August 3, 2017).

19. The Honorable Heather A. Wilson, Secretary of the Air Force, and General David L. Goldfein, Chief of Staff, United States Air Force, statement on "Air Force Budget Posture" before the Committee on Armed Services, U.S. Senate, June 6, 2017, pp. 2–3, https://www.armed-services.senate.gov/imo/media/doc/Wilson-Goldfein_06-06-17.pdf (accessed August 3, 2017).

20. The Honorable Sean J. Stackley, Acting Secretary of the Navy, statement before the Committee on Armed Services, U.S. Senate, June 15, 2017, p. 5, https://www.armed-services.senate.gov/imo/media/doc/Stackley_06-15-17.pdf (accessed August 3, 2017).

21. Lieutenant General Ronald L. Bailey, Deputy Commandant for Plans, Policies, and Operations; Lieutenant General Jon M. Davis, Deputy Commandant for Aviation; and Lieutenant General Michael G. Dana, Deputy Commandant for Installations and Logistics, statement on "The Current State of the Marine Corps" before the Subcommittee on Readiness Subcommittee, Committee on Armed Services, U.S. House of Representatives, April 5, 2017, p. 4, http://docs.house.gov/meetings/AS/AS03/20170405/105768/HHRG-115-AS03-Wstate-BaileyUSMCR-20170405.pdf (accessed August 1, 2017).

U.S. Army

The U.S. Army is America's primary land warfare component. Although it addresses all types of operations across the range of ground force employment, its chief value to the nation is its ability to defeat and destroy enemy land forces in battle.

Like the other services, the U.S. Army has been required "to take risk when meeting current operational requirements while maintaining a ready force for major combat operations."[1] Fiscal challenges have strained the Army's ability to meet the national security requirements outlined in the Defense Planning Guidance as it works to balance readiness, modernization, and end strength.

Army leaders have testified that Congress "stopped the bleeding" by including additional Army end strength in the 2017 National Defense Authorization Act (NDAA) and through supplemental funding in response to a May 2017 "Request for Additional Appropriations,"[2] but significant issues of size, readiness, modernization, and operational tempo still remain unaddressed. Chief of Staff General Mark Milley has testified that the Army is too small to accomplish the missions outlined in the National Security Strategy and Defense Planning Guidance, that "modernization has been sacrificed for current operations," and that only one-third of the Army's brigade combat teams (BCTs) are at an acceptable state of readiness.[3] Acting Secretary of the Army Robert M. Speer has testified that the Army's "pace of operations is as high as it has been in the past 16 years" despite ostensible reductions in troop deployments to Iraq and Afghanistan.[4]

In fiscal year (FY) 2017, the Army's active-duty end strength was 476,000, down from a height of 566,000 in FY 2011.[5] The Obama Administration had planned to cut active Army end strength even further to as low as 450,000 by 2018.[6] Although the Bipartisan Budget Act of 2015 provided a brief period of stability for the Department of Defense (DOD), current funding levels continue to force the Army to prioritize readiness. The trade-offs in that decision were "a smaller Army, smaller investments in modernization, and deferring installation maintenance. The principal negative impacts of these trade-offs have been stress on the force, eroded competitive advantage, and deteriorating installations."[7] Army leaders have testified that if Budget Control Act–mandated budget caps return in FY 2018, the result will be a "hollow Army."[8]

Operationally, the Army has approximately 186,000 soldiers forward stationed across 140 countries.[9] This is very similar to last year's level of 190,000, reinforcing the point that the Army continues to experience a historically high level of operational tempo,[10] but does not include a probable increase of as many as 3,900 soldiers in the number of U.S. forces in Afghanistan that is reportedly near approval by the Trump Administration.[11] Of the total number of U.S. forces deployed globally, "[t]he Army currently provides 48% of planned forces committed to global operations and over 70% of forces for emerging demands from Combatant Commanders," highlighting the key role that the Army plays in the nation's defense.[12]

Capacity

The 2017 NDAA increased Army authorized end strength to 1,018,000 soldiers: 476,000 Active soldiers, 199,000 in the Army Reserve, and 343,000 in the Army National Guard, reversing years of reductions.[13] Because the outgoing Obama Administration had not requested this funding, additional funding was requested by the Trump Administration and provided in the May 2017 supplemental funding package.[14] As noted, General Milley has testified that the Army is too small for the missions it has been assigned. He believes that the Active Army should number between 540,000 and 550,000, the Army National Guard from 350,000 to 355,000, and the Army Reserve between 205,000 and 209,000.[15]

The Army normally refers to its size in terms of brigade combat teams. BCTs are the basic "building blocks" for employment of Army combat forces. They are usually employed within a larger framework of U.S. land operations but are sufficiently equipped and organized so that they can conduct independent operations as circumstances demand.[16] A BCT averages 4,500 soldiers depending on its variant: Stryker, Armored, or Infantry. A Stryker BCT is a mechanized infantry force organized around the Stryker ground combat vehicle (GCV). Armored BCTs are the Army's principal armored units and employ the Abrams main battle tank and the M2 Bradley fighting vehicle. An Infantry BCT is a highly maneuverable motorized unit. Variants of the Infantry BCT are the Airmobile BCT (optimized for helicopter assault) and the Airborne BCT (optimized for parachute forcible entry operations).

The Army also has a separate air component organized into combat aviation brigades (CABs), which can operate independently.[17] CABs are made up of Army rotorcraft, such as the AH-64 Apache, and perform various roles including attack, reconnaissance, and lift.

CABs and Stryker, Infantry, and Armored BCTs make up the Army's main combat force, but they do not make up the entirety of the Army. About 90,000 troops form the Institutional Army and provide such forms of support as preparing and training troops for deployments, carrying out key logistics tasks, and overseeing military schools and Army educational institutions. The troops constituting the Institutional Army cannot be reduced at the same ratio as BCTs or CABs, and the Army endeavors to insulate these soldiers from drawdown and restructuring proposals in order to "retain a slightly more senior force in the Active Army to allow growth if needed."[18] In addition to the Institutional Army, a great number of functional or multifunctional support brigades (amounting to approximately 13 percent of the active component force based on historical averages[19]) provide air defense, engineering, explosive ordnance disposal (EOD), chemical/biological/radiological and nuclear protection, military police, military intelligence, and medical support among other types of battlefield support for BCTs.

While end strength is a valuable metric in understanding Army capacity, the number of BCTs is a more telling measure of actual hardpower capacity. In preparation for the reduction of its end strength to 460,000, the planned level for FY 2017,[20] the Active Army underwent brigade restructuring that decreased the number of BCTs from 38 to 31. When Congress reversed that reduction in end strength and authorized an active-duty level of 476,000 for 2017, instead of "re-growing" BCTs, the Army chose primarily to "thicken" the force and is raising the manning levels within the individual BCTs and thereby increasing readiness.[21]

The 2015 NDAA established the National Commission on the Future of the Army to conduct a comprehensive study of Army structure. To meet the threat posed by a resurgent Russia and others, the commission recommended that the Army increase its numbers of Armored BCTs.[22] The FY 2018 budget will support the conversion of one Infantry BCT into an Armored BCT, marking the creation of the Army's 15th Armored BCT.[23]

In 2017, in a major initiative personally shepherded by General Milley, the Army established the first of a planned six Security Force

Assistance Brigades (SFABs). These units, composed of about 530 personnel each, are designed specifically to train, advise, and mentor other partner nation military units. The Army had been using regular BCTs for this mission, but because train and assist missions typically require senior officers and noncommissioned officers, a BCT comprised predominantly of junior soldiers is a poor fit. The Army envisions that these SFABs will be able to reduce the stress on the service.[24] It plans to activate two SFABs in 2017, but further activations are on hold until final decisions on long-term Army end strength are made.[25]

Army aviation units also have been reduced in number. In May 2015, the Army deactivated one of its 12 Combat Aviation Brigades (though retaining a headquarters element),[26] leaving only 11 CABs in the active component.[27] This left U.S. Army Europe without a forward stationed CAB, forcing the Army to rely on rotational forces from the United States.

The reductions in end strength since 2011 have had a disproportionate effect on BCTs. The Active Army has been downsized from 45 BCTs (552,100 soldiers) in FY 2013 to 31 BCTs (476,000 soldiers) in FY 2017.[28] Put another way, a 14 percent reduction in troop numbers has resulted in a 31 percent reduction in BCTs.

In addition to the increased strategic risk, the result of fewer BCTs and a reduced Army end strength, combined with an undiminished daily global demand, has been a corresponding increase in operational tempo (OPTEMPO). The Army also uses the term "dwell time" to refer to the time soldiers and units are back at their home stations between deployments. The chief personnel officer for the Army has described the current situation:

[M]any thought the dwell time had gone down because the troop levels have reduced in Afghanistan and Iraq, and that's really not the case. You know we're rotating forces right now into Korea. We're rotating forces into Kuwait. We're rotating forces into Europe along with Iraq and Afghanistan. So, the dwell time has not come down.[29]

As part of these rotations, the Army has begun to rotate Armored BCTs to Europe on a "heel-to-toe" basis, using the funding provided in the European Reassurance Initiative (ERI). The first of these rotational BCTs, the 3rd BCT of the 4th Infantry Division, arrived in January 2017 and is engaged in a series of exercises with NATO allies.[30]

To capture operational tempo, the Army uses a ratio referred to as "BOG/Dwell," which is the ratio of Boots on the Ground (BOG, or deployed) to Dwell (time back at home station). As of May 2017, Army BOG/Dwell rates were extraordinarily high.[31] For example, a 1:1 ratio for Division Headquarters means that for every year that Army division headquarters are deployed, they are at home station for a year. Primarily because of the stress on soldiers, these ratios are unsustainable.

Capability

The Army's main combat platforms are ground vehicles and rotorcraft. The upgraded M1A2 (M1A2SEP v.3) Abrams and M2/M3 Bradley vehicles are used primarily in active component Armored BCTs, while Army National Guard ABCTs still rely on variants.[32] Stryker BCTs are equipped with Stryker vehicles. In response to an Operational Needs Statement, Stryker vehicles in Europe are being fitted with a 30mm cannon to provide an improved anti-armor capability. Fielding will begin in 2018.[33] Infantry BCTs have fewer platforms and rely on lighter platforms such as trucks and High Mobility Multipurpose Wheeled Vehicles (HMMWVs) for mobility. CABs are composed of Army helicopters including AH-64 Apaches, UH-60 Black Hawks, and CH-47 Chinooks.

Overall, the Army's equipment inventory, while increasingly dated, is well maintained. Some equipment has been worn down by usage in Afghanistan and Iraq, but the Army has undertaken a "reset" initiative that is discussed below in the readiness section. Most Army vehicles are relatively "young" because of recent remanufacture programs for the Abrams and Bradley that have extended the service life of both vehicles beyond FY 2028.[34] While the current equipment is well maintained, however, "Army leadership notes for the first time since World War I, that the Army does not have a new ground combat vehicle under development and 'at current funding levels, the Bradley and Abrams will remain in the inventory for 50 to 70 more years.'"[35]

The Army has been methodically replacing the oldest variants of its rotorcraft and upgrading others that still have plenty of airframe service life. Today, the UH-60M, which is a newer version of the UH-60A, makes up approximately two-thirds of the total UH-60 inventory. Similarly, the CH-47F Chinook, a rebuilt variant of the Army's CH-47D heavy lift helicopter, is expected to extend the platform's service life at least through 2038.[36] However, at $3.1 billion, the 2018 budget request for aircraft procurement for Apache, Blackhawk, and Chinook helicopters stands at $1.3 billion less than the FY 2017 President's budget.[37] The proposed 2018 budget will further delay complete modernization of the Apache and Black Hawk fleets, respectively, from 2026 to 2028 and from 2028 to 2030.[38]

In addition to the viability of today's equipment, the military must ensure the health of future programs. Although future modernizing programs are not current hard-power capabilities that can be applied against an enemy force today, they are a significant indicator of a service's overall fitness for sustained combat operations. The service may be able to engage an enemy but be forced to do so with aging equipment and no program in place to maintain viability or endurance in sustained operations.

The U.S. military services are continually assessing how best to stay a step ahead of competitors: whether to modernize the force today with currently available technology or wait to see what investments in research and development produce years down the road. Technologies mature and proliferate, becoming more accessible to a wider array of actors over time.

The Army is currently undertaking several modernization programs to improve its ground combat vehicles and current rotorcraft fleet. However, cuts in research and development, acquisition, and procurement accounts because of budget reductions levied in previous years have significantly affected these efforts. As the Vice Chief of Staff of the Army recently testified, the modernization budget is "50 percent of what it was in 2009. In FY '17 it's $24.8 billion, it was $45.5 billion in 2009."[39] Summarizing the impact of these reductions at a November 2016 conference, Major General Eric Wesley, Commanding General, U.S. Army Maneuver Center of Excellence repeated an assessment that "of 10 major capabilities that we use for warfighting, by the year 2030, Russia will have exceeded our capacity in six, will have parity in three, and the United States will dominate in one."[40]

Army leaders have testified that they have "deferred many modernization investments which allowed our competitors to gain advantages in such areas as fires, air and missile defense, and armor."[41] As the Acting Secretary of the Army warned in June 2017, "a consequence of underfunding modernization for over a decade is *an Army potentially outgunned, outranged, and outdated* on a future battlefield with near-peer competitors."[42]

The anemic nature of the Army's modernization program is illustrated by the fact that its highest-profile joint service Major Defense Acquisition Program (MDAP) is a *truck* program, the Joint Light Tactical Vehicle (JLTV). Intended to combine the protection offered by Mine Resistant Ambush Protected Vehicles (MRAPs) with the mobility of the original unarmored HMMWV, the JLTV is a follow-on to the HMMWV (also known as the Humvee) and features design improvements that will increase its survivability against anti-armor weapons and improvised explosive devices (IEDs). The Army plans to procure 49,099 vehicles over the life of the program, replacing only a portion of the current HMMWV fleet. The program is heavily focused on vehicle survivability and is not intended as a one-for-one replacement of the HMMWV. In fact, the JLTV is intended to take on high-risk missions traditionally tasked

FIGURE 6

Army Readiness: Brigade Combat Teams

In 2012, the Army fielded 45 active component Brigade Combat Teams (BCTs). Due to budget cuts, that number has been reduced to 31.

The U.S. Army currently can field a force of **31 BCTs.**

Three BCTs can "FIGHT TONIGHT," meaning they can deploy immediately to a conflict.

10 BCTs are considered "READY," meaning they can fulfill most of their wartime missions.

The Heritage Foundation assesses the Army needs an **additional 19 BCTs**, for a total of 50, based on historical force requirements.

🏛 heritage.org

to the HMMWV, to include scouting and troop transport in adverse environments, guerrilla ambushes, and artillery bombardment.

Several issues, including changed requirements and some technical obstacles in the early development phases, delayed the JLTV program from its originally intended schedule by about one year. FY 2018 Base Procurement of $804.4 million supports 2,110 JLTVs of various configurations to fulfill the requirements of multiple mission roles and minimize ownership costs for the Army's Light Tactical Vehicle fleet.[43]

Other Army MDAPs of note in FY 2018 include the M1A2 Abrams Equipment Change Program (ECP); M2 Bradley modifications; M109A6 Paladin 155mm Howitzers (Paladin Integrated Management); and munitions including Guided Multiple Launcher Rocket System (GMLRS) and Hellfire missiles.[44]

The M1A2 is currently being enhanced with Vehicle Health Management and Power Train Improvement and Integration Optimization to upgrade the tank's reliability, durability, and fuel efficiency so that it can provide ground forces with superior battlefield firepower.[45] Similarly, the M109A6 is being outfitted with the Paladin Integrated Management (PIM) program, which consists of a new drivetrain and suspension components, to sustain the platform's utility in combat through 2050.[46]

The Armored Multi-Purpose Vehicle (AMPV), the program to replace the Army's 1960s-vintage M113 Armored Personnel Carrier, is a new start in FY 2018. The AMPV will have five mission modules: General Purpose, Medical Treatment, Medical Evacuation, Mortar Carrier, and Mission Command. FY 2018 Base Procurement dollars of $193.715 million will procure 42 AMPVs. This represents the first year of Low Rate Initial Production (LRIP). The Army acquisition objective for AMPVs is 2,897 vehicles.[47]

Significantly, the Army's rotorcraft modernization programs do not include any new platform designs. Instead, the Army is upgrading current rotorcraft to account for more advanced systems.

The Army's main modernization programs are not currently encumbered by any major problems, but there is justifiable concern about the lack of new development programs underway. In the words of an Army Deputy Chief of Staff, because of 15 years of sustained combat operations and limited resources, we have "forfeited the modernization of our weapons systems."[48]

Readiness

The combined effects of the Budget Control Act of 2011, an unrelenting global demand for forces, and reductions in end strength have caused Army readiness to decline to the point where only one-third of Army BCTs are now considered "ready" and only three are ready to "fight tonight."[49] The Chief of Staff of the Army recently testified that they "have much, much more work to do to achieve full-spectrum readiness and modernization."[50]

Congress provided much-needed relief in May 2017 by appropriating approximately $15 billion for the Pentagon in response to the Administration's request for additional appropriations, the bulk of which was targeted directly at increasing wartime readiness.[51] This, combined with the increase in Army end strength authorized in the 2017 NDAA, provided a desperately needed measure of relief. For FY 2018, training activities are relatively well resourced. When measuring training resourcing, the Army uses training miles and flying hours, which reflect the number of miles that armor formations can drive their tanks

and aviators can fly their helicopters. According to the Department of the Army's budget justification, "The FY 2018 base budget funds 1,188 Operating Tempo Full Spectrum Training Miles and 10.6 flying hours per crew, per month for an expected overall training proficiency of BCT(-)."[52] These are significantly higher than resourced levels of 839 miles and 9.5 hours in FY 2017.[53]

Nonetheless, structural readiness problems summarized by too small a force attempting to satisfy too many global presence requirements and Operations Plan (OPLAN) warfighting requirements have led to a force that is both unable to achieve all required training events and overly stressed. As a result, the Army continues to "protect current readiness at the expense of future modernization and end strength."[54] In the words of Army Vice Chief of Staff General Daniel Allyn, "fifteen years of sustained counter-insurgency operations have degraded the Army's ability to conduct operations across the spectrum of conflict and narrowed the experience base of our leaders."[55]

Recognizing the risk that degraded readiness introduces into its ability to respond to an emergent threat, the Army continues to prioritize operational readiness over other expenditures for FY 2018. A return to "full spectrum combat readiness" will require sustained investment for a number of years. As a result of years of high operational tempos and sustained budget cuts, the Army now does not expect to return to "full spectrum readiness" until "best case 2021, worst case 2023."[56]

This tiered readiness strategy means that only a limited number of BCTs are available and ready for decisive action. Accordingly, the tiered readiness model employed by the Army has resulted in approximately one-third of the 31 Active BCTs being ready for contingency operations in FY 2017 compared to a desired readiness level of two-thirds.[57]

As part of its new Sustainable Readiness Model (SRM),[58] the Army uses Combat Training Centers (CTCs) to train its forces to desired levels of proficiency. Specifically, the mission of the CTC program is to "provide realistic Joint and combined arms training" to approximate actual combat and increase "unit readiness for deployment and warfighting."[59] The Army requested financing for 19 CTC rotations in FY 2018, including four for the Army National Guard.[60] Another change in the Army's training model involves the implementation of a system of "Objective T" metrics that seeks to remove the subjectivity behind unit commander evaluations of training. Under the Objective T program, the requirements that must be met for a unit to be assessed as fully ready for combat are to be made clear and quantitative.[61]

The ongoing challenge for the Army remains a serious one: Despite increased levels of funding for training, if the size of the Army remains the same and global demand does not diminish, "at today's end-strength, the Army risks consuming readiness as fast as we build it," which means that the date by which Army leaders hope to regain full spectrum readiness will continue to be pushed back, prolonging strategic risk for the nation.[62]

Another key factor in readiness is available quantities of munitions. The Army's chief logistician warned recently about shortages of "preferred munitions—Patriot, THAAD, Hellfire and our Excalibur which are howitzer munitions," adding that "if we had to surge, if we had a contingency operation, and if there are—continue to be emerging threats which we see around the world, I am very concerned with our current stockage of munitions."[63]

Scoring the U.S. Army

Capacity Score: Weak

Historical evidence shows that, on average, the Army needs 21 brigade combat teams to fight one major regional conflict. Based on a conversion of roughly 3.5 BCTs per division, the Army deployed 21 BCTs in Korea, 25 in Vietnam, 14 in the Persian Gulf War, and around four in Operation Iraqi Freedom—an average of 16 BCTs (or 21 if the much smaller Operation Iraqi Freedom initial invasion operation is excluded). In the 2010 Quadrennial Defense Review, the Obama Administration recommended a force capable of deploying 45 active BCTs. Previous government force-sizing documents discuss Army force structure in terms of divisions; they consistently advocate for 10–11 divisions, which equates to roughly 37 active BCTs.

Considering the varying recommendations of 35–45 BCTs and the actual experience of nearly 21 BCTs deployed per major engagement, 42 BCTs would be needed to fight two MRCs.[64] Taking into account the need for a strategic reserve, the Active Army force should also include an additional 20 percent of the 42 BCTs.

- **Two-MRC Benchmark:** 50 brigade combat teams.

- **Actual 2017 Level:** 31 brigade combat teams.

The Army's current Active Component BCT capacity meets 64 percent of the two-MRC benchmark and thus is scored as "weak."

Capability Score: Marginal

The Army's aggregate capability score remains "marginal." While the Army will continue to pursue the aim of improving readiness levels in FY 2018 over the previous year, and while Congress increased end strength slightly and provided a modest amount of additional funding, the service's overall capability score remains static due to unrelenting global demands for Army forces with no additional BCTs, CABs, or Divisions to satisfy those demands. Additionally, in spite of modest progress with the JLTV and AMPV, research, development, and procurement budget levels remain well below the levels needed to begin even a minimal modernization program, thereby negatively affecting platform innovation and modernization. These subsequent reductions continue to limit the Army's development of future capabilities needed to remain dominant in any operational environment.

This aggregate score is a result of "marginal" scores for "Age of Equipment," "Size of Modernization Programs," and "Health of Modernization Programs." The Army scored "weak" for "Capability of Equipment."

Readiness Score: Weak

Just over a third of Active BCTs were ready for action according to official Army testimony by the Chief of Staff in May 2017.[65] The Army had 31 BCTs; therefore, roughly 10 of the Active Army BCTs were considered ready for combat. For that reason, this *Index* assesses Army readiness as "weak." However, it should be noted that the Vice Chief of Staff also reported in February that of the BCTs fully trained for "decisive action operations," only three were ready to "fight tonight."[66] With this in mind, *actual* readiness is therefore likely dangerously close to nearing a state of "very weak."

Overall U.S. Army Score: Weak

The Army's overall score is calculated based on an unweighted average of its capacity, capability, and readiness scores. The average score was 2.3; thus, the overall Army score is "weak." This was derived from the aggregate score for capacity ("weak"); capability ("marginal"); and readiness ("weak"). This score is the same as the score in the *2017 Index* and indicates continued concerns for the Army, particularly when it comes to capacity in light of increased demand on the service around the globe.

U.S. Military Power: Army

	VERY WEAK	WEAK	MARGINAL	STRONG	VERY STRONG
Capacity		✓			
Capability			✓		
Readiness		✓			
OVERALL		✓			

Endnotes

1. The Honorable Robert M. Speer, Acting Secretary of the Army, and General Mark A. Milley, Chief of Staff, United States Army, statement "On the Posture of the United States Army" before the Committee on Armed Services, U.S. Senate, 115th Cong., 1st Sess., May 25, 2017, p. 1, https://www.armed-services.senate.gov/imo/media/doc/Speer-Milley_05-25-17.pdf (accessed July 26, 2017).

2. Congressional Quarterly, "Senate Armed Services Committee Holds Hearing on Army Posture," CQ Congressional Transcripts, May 25, 2017, http://www.cq.com/doc/congressionaltranscripts-5110936?20 (accessed July 19, 2017).

3. Ibid.

4. Ibid.

5. Major General Thomas A. Horlander, Director, Army Budget, *Army FY 2018 Budget Overview*, May 2017, https://www.asafm.army.mil/documents/BudgetMaterial/fy2018/overview.pdf (accessed July 26, 2017).

6. Michelle Tan, "Army Lays out Plan to Cut 40,000 Soldiers," *Army Times*, July 10, 2015, http://www.armytimes.com/story/military/pentagon/2015/07/09/army-outlines-40000-cuts/29923339/ (accessed July 14, 2015).

7. Speer and Milley, statement "On the Posture of the United States Army."

8. Ibid.

9. Ibid.

10. Ibid.

11. Gregory Hellman, "White House Reported to Cap U.S. Troops in Afghanistan," *Politico*, July 7, 2017, http://www.politico.com/tipsheets/morning-defense/2017/07/07/white-house-reported-to-cap-us-troops-in-afghanistan-221216 (accessed July 18, 2017).

12. Lieutenant General Joseph Anderson, Deputy Chief of Staff, G-3/5/7, United States Army, Lieutenant General Aundre Piggee, Deputy Chief of Staff, G-4, United States Army, and Lieutenant General Gwen Bingham, Assistant Chief of Staff, Installation Management, United States Army, statement before the Subcommittee on Readiness, Committee on Armed Services, U.S. House of Representatives, 115th Cong., 1st Sess., March 8, 2017, p. 2, http://docs.house.gov/meetings/AS/AS03/20170308/105661/HHRG-115-AS03-Wstate-AndersonUSAJ-20170308.pdf (accessed July 26, 2017).

13. Lieutenant General James C. McConville, Deputy Chief of Staff, G-1, United States Army, statement "On Active Guard, Reserve and Civilian Personnel Programs" before the Subcommittee on Military Personnel, Committee on Armed Services, U.S. House of Representatives, May 17, 2017, http://docs.house.gov/meetings/AS/AS02/20170517/105910/HHRG-115-AS02-Wstate-McConvilleJ-20170517.pdf (accessed July 26, 2017).

14. Joe Gould, "US Lawmakers Reach 2017 Budget Deal Through September," *Defense News*, May 1, 2017, http://www.defensenews.com/articles/us-lawmakers-reach-2017-budget-deal (accessed July 18, 2017).

15. Congressional Quarterly, "Senate Appropriations Subcommittee on Defense Holds Hearing on the U.S. Army Fiscal 2018 Budget," CQ Congressional Transcripts, June 7, 2017, http://www.cq.com/doc/congressionaltranscripts-5117288?33#speakers (accessed July 19, 2017).

16. U.S. Department of the Army, Field Manual 3-96, *Brigade Combat Team*, October 2015, http://www.apd.army.mil/epubs/DR_pubs/DR_a/pdf/web/fm3_96.pdf (accessed July 26, 2017).

17. Ibid., p. 3-31.

18. Andrew Feickert, "Army Drawdown and Restructuring: Background and Issues for Congress," Congressional Research Service *Report for Members and Committees of Congress*, February 28, 2014, p. 18, https://www.fas.org/sgp/crs/natsec/R42493.pdf (accessed July 18, 2017).

19. The 13 percent estimate is based on a review of historical figures as referenced in U.S. Government Accountability Office, *Army Planning: Comprehensive Risk Assessment Needed for Planned Changes to the Army's Force Structure*, GAO–16–327, April 2016, p. 12, http://www.gao.gov/assets/680/676516.pdf (accessed June 21, 2016).

20. U.S. Department of Defense, Office of the Under Secretary of Defense (Comptroller), *National Defense Budget Estimates for FY 2017*, March 2016, p. 260, http://comptroller.defense.gov/Portals/45/Documents/defbudget/fy2017/FY17_Green_Book.pdf (accessed July 19, 2017).

21. Speer and Milley, statement "On the Posture of the United States Army."

22. National Commission on the Future of the Army, *Report to the President and the Congress of the United States*, January 28, 2016, p. 52, http://www.ncfa.ncr.gov/sites/default/files/NCFA_Full%20Final%20Report_0.pdf (accessed July 19, 2017).

23. U.S. Department of the Army, Assistant Secretary of the Army (Financial Management and Comptroller), *FY 2018 President's Budget Highlights*, May 2017, p. 14, https://www.asafm.army.mil/documents/BudgetMaterial/fy2018/pbhl.pdf (accessed July 26, 2017).

24. C. Todd Lopez, "Security Force Assistance Brigades to Free Brigade Combat Teams from Advise, Assist Mission," U.S. Army, May 18, 2017, https://www.army.mil/article/188004/security_force_assistance_brigades_to_free_brigade_combat_teams_from_advise_assist_mission (accessed July 19, 2017).

25. C. Todd Lopez, "End Strength Increase to Save Units, Fill Shortfalls," U.S. Army, June 15, 2017, https://www.army.mil/article/188920/end_strength_increase_to_save_units_fill_shortfalls (accessed July 18, 2017).

26. General Daniel Allyn, Vice Chief of Staff, U.S. Army, statement on "Current State of Readiness of the U.S. Forces in Review of the Defense Authorization Request for Fiscal Year 2017 and the Future Years Defense Program" before the Subcommittee on Readiness and Management Support, Committee on Armed Services, U.S. Senate, 114th Cong., 2nd Sess., March 15, 2016, p. 2, http://www.armed-services.senate.gov/imo/media/doc/Allyn_03-15-16.pdf (accessed June 26, 2016).

27. U.S. Department of the Army, *Department of Defense Fiscal Year (FY) 2018 Budget Estimates, Volume I, Operation and Maintenance, Army: Justification of Estimates*, May 2017, p. 120, https://www.asafm.army.mil/documents/BudgetMaterial/fy2018/oma-v1.pdf (accessed July 18, 2017).

28. U.S. Department of the Army, Assistant Secretary of the Army (Financial Management and Comptroller), *FY 2018 President's Budget Highlights*, p. 15.

29. Congressional Quarterly, "House Armed Services Subcommittee on Military Personnel Holds Hearing on Military Personnel Posture," May 17, 2017.

30. Jen Judson, "US Army's First Heavy Brigade Rotation in Europe Learns Newfound Agility," *Defense News*, July 13, 2017, http://www.defensenews.com/articles/armys-first-heavy-brigade-rotation-in-europe-learns-newfound-agility?utm_source=Sailthru&utm_medium=email&utm_campaign=EBB%207.14.17&utm_term=Editorial%20-%20Early%20Bird%20Brief (accessed July 18, 2017).

31. U.S. Army, "SECDEF Ordered Operational Support of Combatant Commands," July 1, 2017, p. 1, http://www.ausa-westmoreland.org/docs/ArmySupportToCombatantCommandsJul17.pdf (accessed August, 8, 2017).

32. Andrew Feickert, "The Army's M-1 Abrams, M-2/M-3 Bradley, and M-1126 Stryker: Background and Issues for Congress," Congressional Research Service *Report for Members and Committees of Congress*, April 5, 2016, p. 9, https://www.fas.org/sgp/crs/weapons/R44229.pdf (accessed July 26, 2017).

33. Matthew L. Schehl, "Army Receives First Stryker Upgraded with 30mm Cannon," *Army Times*, October 28, 2016, https://www.armytimes.com/articles/army-receives-first-stryker-upgraded-with-30mm-cannon (accessed July 18, 2017).

34. Feickert, "The Army's M-1 Abrams, M-2/M-3 Bradley, and M-1126 Stryker," p. 1.

35. David Vergun, "Four Myths About Combat Vehicles, Debunked by LTG McMaster," Army News Service, November 2, 2016, quoted in Andrew Feickert, "Selected Foreign Counterparts of U.S. Army Ground Combat Systems and Implications for Combat Operations and Modernization," Congressional Research Service *Report for Members and Committees of Congress*, January 18, 2017, p. 2, https://fas.org/sgp/crs/weapons/R44741.pdf (accessed July 26, 2017).

36. U.S. Department of Defense, Office of the Undersecretary of Defense (Comptroller)/Chief Financial Officer, *United States Department of Defense Fiscal Year 2017 Budget Request: Program Acquisition Cost by Weapon System*, February 2016, p. 1-10, http://comptroller.defense.gov/Portals/45/Documents/defbudget/fy2017/FY2017_Weapons.pdf (accessed July 19, 2017).

37. U.S. Department of the Army, *Department of Defense Fiscal Year (FY) 2018 Budget Estimates, Army: Justification Book of Aircraft Procurement, Army*, May 2017, pp. 35, 39, 59 (AH-64); 63, 72, 76 (UH-60); and 82, 85, 94 (CH-47), https://www.asafm.army.mil/documents/BudgetMaterial/fy2018/aircraft.pdf (accessed August 9, 2017).

38. U.S. Department of Defense, Office of the Under Secretary of Defense (Comptroller)/Chief Financial Officer, *United States Department of Defense Fiscal Year 2018 Budget Request: 2018 Budget Overview*, May 2017, p. 7-8, http://comptroller.defense.gov/Portals/45/Documents/defbudget/fy2018/fy2018_Budget_Request_Overview_Book.pdf (accessed July 26, 2017).

39. Congressional Quarterly, "Senate Armed Services Committee Holds Hearing on the State of the Military," CQ Congressional Transcripts, February 7, 2017, http://www.cq.com/doc/congressionaltranscripts-5036905?2&search=1T0GmDzT (accessed August 8, 2017).

40. Courtney McBride, "Wesley: Russia Offers 'Pacing Threat' for Army Modernization Efforts," *Inside Defense*, November 1, 2016, https://insidedefense.com/daily-news/wesley-russia-offers-pacing-threat-army-modernization-efforts (accessed July 18, 2017).

41. Anderson et al., statement before Subcommittee on Readiness, House Committee on Armed Services, March 8, 2017, p. 5.

42. Congressional Quarterly, "Senate Appropriations Subcommittee on Defense Holds Hearing on the U.S. Army Fiscal 2018 Budget," June 7, 2017. Emphasis added.

43. U.S. Department of Defense, Office of the Under Secretary of Defense (Comptroller)/Chief Financial Officer, *United States Department of Defense Fiscal Year 2018 Budget Request: Program Acquisition Cost by Weapon System*, May 2017, p. 3-2, http://comptroller.defense.gov/Portals/45/Documents/defbudget/fy2018/fy2018_Weapons.pdf (accessed August 9, 2017).

44. Horlander, *Army FY 2018 Budget Overview*, p. 11.

45. U.S. Department of Defense, Office of the Undersecretary of Defense (Comptroller)/Chief Financial Officer, *United States Department of Defense Fiscal Year 2017 Budget Request: Program Acquisition Cost by Weapon System*, p. 3-5.

46. Ibid., p. 3-6.

47. U.S. Department of the Army, *Department of Defense Fiscal Year (FY) 2018 Budget Estimates, Army: Justification Book of Procurement of W&TCV, Army*, May 2017, p. 10, https://www.asafm.army.mil/documents/BudgetMaterial/fy2018/wtcv.pdf (accessed July 18, 2017).

48. Congressional Quarterly, "House Armed Services Subcommittee on Readiness Holds Hearing on Current State of U.S. Army Readiness," CQ Congressional Transcripts, March 8, 2017, http://www.cq.com/doc/congressionaltranscripts-5057103?2 (accessed July 19, 2017).

49. Allyn, statement on "State of the Military," p. 4.

50. Congressional Quarterly, "Senate Armed Services Committee Holds Hearing on Army Posture," May 25, 2017.

51. Jeremy Herb, "Trump Gets a $15 Billion Defense Boost," CNN, May 1, 2017, http://www.cnn.com/2017/05/01/politics/trump-military-funding-increase/index.html (accessed July 14, 2017).

52. U.S. Department of the Army, *Department of Defense Fiscal Year (FY) 2018 Budget Estimates, Volume I, Operation and Maintenance, Army: Justification of Estimates*, p. 2.

53. U.S. Department of the Army, *Department of the Army Fiscal Year (FY) 2017 Budget Estimates, Volume 1, Operation and Maintenance, Army: Justification of Estimates*, February 2016, p. 2, https://www.asafm.army.mil/documents/BudgetMaterial/fy2017/oma-v1.pdf (accessed July 26, 2017).

54. Major General Thomas A. Horlander, Director, Army Budget, *Army FY 2017 Budget Overview*, February 2016, p. 7, http://www.defenseinnovationmarketplace.mil/resources/Army%20FY%202017%20Budget%20Overview.pdf (accessed July 26, 2017).

55. Allyn, statement on "State of the Military," p. 2.

56. Congressional Quarterly, "House Armed Services Subcommittee on Readiness Holds Hearing on Current State of U.S. Army Readiness," March 8, 2017.

57. Congressional Quarterly, "Senate Armed Services Committee Holds Hearing on Army Posture," May 25, 2017.

58. U.S. Army, Army G-3/5/7, "Army Readiness Guidance," May 19, 2016, https://www.army.mil/standto/2016-05-19 (accessed July 26, 2017).

59. U.S. Department of the Army, "Combat Training Center Program," Army Regulation 350–50, April 3, 2013, p. 1, http://www.apd.army.mil/epubs/DR_pubs/DR_a/pdf/web/r350_50.pdf (accessed August 8, 2017).

60. U.S. Department of Defense, *United States Department of Defense Fiscal Year 2018 Budget Request: Defense Budget Overview*, p. 7-6; Horlander, *Army FY 2018 Budget Overview*, p. 8.

61. Michelle Tan, "'Objective T': The Army's New Mission to Track Training," *Army Times*, October 11, 2016, https://www.armytimes.com/articles/objective-t-the-armys-new-mission-to-track-training (accessed July 18, 2017)

62. Allyn, statement on "State of the Military," p. 2.

63. Congressional Quarterly, "House Armed Services Subcommittee on Readiness Holds Hearing on Current State of U.S. Army Readiness," March 8, 2017.

64. Note that the first figures derive from an average BCT size of 4,500 and average division size of 15,000. The second set of numbers derives from the current average of around 3.5 BCTs per division and analysis of the structure of each Army division.

65. Speer and Milley, statement "On the Posture of the United States Army."

66. Allyn, statement on "State of the Military," p. 4.

U.S. Navy

In *A Design for Maintaining Maritime Superiority*, issued in January 2016, Chief of Naval Operations Admiral John M. Richardson describes the U.S. Navy's mission as follows:

> The United States Navy will be ready to conduct prompt and sustained combat incident to operations at sea. Our Navy will protect America from attack and preserve America's strategic influence in key regions of the world. U.S. naval forces and operations—from the sea floor to space, from deep water to the littorals, and in the information domain—will deter aggression and enable peaceful resolution of crises on terms acceptable to the United States and our allies and partners. If deterrence fails, the Navy will conduct decisive combat operations to defeat any enemy.[1]

The basis for understanding the key functions necessary to accomplish this mission was provided in the March 2015 update to *A Cooperative Strategy for 21st Century Seapower*.

For much of the post–Cold War period, the Navy, Marine Corps, and Coast Guard (known collectively as the sea services) have enabled the U.S. to project power across the oceans, control activities on the seas when and where needed, provide for the security of coastlines and shipping in maritime areas of interest, and thereby enhance America's deterrent capability without opposition from competitors. However, the ability of competitors to contest U.S actions has improved, forcing the sea services to revisit their assumptions about gaining access to key regions. Together, these functional areas—power projection, sea control, maritime security, deterrence, and domain access—constitute the basis for the Navy's strategy.

Achieving and sustaining the ability to excel in these functions drives Navy thinking and programmatic efforts.[2]

As the military's primary maritime arm, the U.S. Navy provides the enduring forward global presence that enables the United States to respond quickly to crises around the world. Unlike land forces (or even, to a large extent, air forces), which are tethered to a set of fixed, larger-scale support bases requiring consent from host nations, the U.S. Navy can operate freely across the globe and shift its presence wherever needed without any other nation's permission. As a result, naval forces are often the first U.S. forces to respond to a crisis and, through their routine forward deployments, continue to preserve U.S. security interests long after conflict formally ends. In addition to the ability to project combat power rapidly anywhere in the world, the Navy's peacetime forward presence supports missions that include securing sea lines of communication (SLOC) for the free flow of goods and services, assuring U.S. allies and friends, deterring adversaries, and providing a timely response to crises short of war.

A few key documents inform the Navy's day-to-day fleet requirements:

- The 2012 Defense Strategic Guidance (DSG);[3]

- The Global Force Management Allocation Plan (GFMAP);[4]

- The 2015 update to *A Cooperative Strategy for 21st Century Seapower*; and

- The *Design for Maintaining Maritime Superiority.*

The 2012 DSG issued by the Secretary of Defense describes 10 primary missions for the Navy and the other branches of the U.S. military. In addition, the U.S. Navy must meet forward presence requirements laid out in the fiscal year (FY) 2017 GFMAP, which states the force presence needed around the world as determined by the combatant commanders (CO-COMs) and the Secretary of Defense.

Capacity

The Navy measures capacity by the number of ships rather than the number of sailors, and not all ships are counted equally. The Navy focuses mainly on the size of its "battle force," which is composed of ships it considers to be directly related to its combat missions.[5]

The Navy currently sails 276 vessels as part of its battle force fleet,[6] up from 274 in 2016[7] but still well below both the Navy's fleet goal and a level sufficient to uphold a two-MRC (major regional contingency) construct. The Navy requested procurement of nine ships in FY 2018,[8] 12 ships less than the number recommended for procurement in the Secretary of the Navy's February 2017 "United States Navy Accelerated Fleet Plan"[9] and in a Congressional Budget Office (CBO) assessment of the average annual ship procurement needed to achieve a 355-ship fleet by 2037.[10] The Accelerated Fleet Plan includes one additional guided missile destroyer (DDG 51), one Expeditionary Fast Transport (EPF), and one Expeditionary Mobile Base (ESB) in FY 2018.[11] The gap between actual and desired procurement is the result of a shortfall in funding.

The largest proportional shortfall in the Navy fleet assessed in the *2018 Index* is the same as in past editions: small surface combatants (SSC).[12] This includes Littoral Combat Ships (LCS) and mine countermeasure (MCM) ships and previously included frigates. All *Oliver Hazard Perry*-class frigates were decommissioned by the end of 2015.[13] The fleet currently includes 11 MCM vessels and nine LCS vessels for a total of 20 SSC,[14] 32 below the objective requirement of 52 established by the Navy.[15]

The aircraft carrier force suffers a capacity shortfall of two hulls: 11 are currently in the fleet, and the two-MRC construct requires 13.[16] Current U.S. law requires the Navy to maintain a force of "not less than 11 operational aircraft carriers."[17] H.R. 941, introduced by Representative K. Michael Conaway (R–TX) in February 2017, would amend the National Defense Authorization Act for Fiscal Year 2016 to require that the U.S. Navy "expedite delivery of 12 aircraft carriers" and that "an aircraft carrier should be authorized every three years" to keep pace with the loss of carriers as they are retired.[18] The Congressional Research Service (CRS) has assessed that "[i]ncreasing aircraft carrier procurement from the current rate of one ship every five years to one ship every three years would achieve a 12-carrier force on a sustained basis by about 2030."[19] The Navy has said it needs to have two carriers deployed at all times while three are ready to reinforce on short notice, which is very hard to do with a fleet of only 11 carriers.

The carrier force fell to 10 from December 2012 until July 2017. During the first week of January 2017, no U.S. aircraft carriers were deployed, the first time this has occurred since World War II.[20] The USS *Gerald R. Ford* (CVN-78) was commissioned on July 22, 2017, returning the Navy's carrier force to a total of 11 ships. While the *Ford* is now part of the Fleet Battle Force, it will not be ready for routine flight operations until 2020 and will not be operationally deployed until 2022.[21]

In December 2016, the U.S. Navy released its latest study of forecasted fleet requirements. The Navy Force Structure Assessment (FSA) was developed to determine the correct balance of existing forces for "ever-evolving and increasingly complex maritime security threats."[22] The Navy concluded that a 653-ship force would be necessary to address all of the demands registered in the FY 2017 Global Force Management (GFM) system. A fleet of 459 ships, 200 fewer than the ideal fleet but thought still to be too expensive given current and projected limits on defense spending, would meet warfighting

FIGURE 7

The Case for 13 Carriers

The U.S. Navy carrier fleet is a critical element of U.S. power projection and supports a constant presence in regions of the world where permanent basing is limited. To properly handle this large mission, the Heritage Foundation recommends a fleet of 13 carriers.

3

The U.S. maintains one carrier in each of the major regions of the world.

ATLANTIC

PACIFIC

MEDITERRANEAN

+9

To be operationally realistic, and to ensure ships, aircraft, and crew are healthy and effective, three additional carriers are needed for each carrier deployed.

RETURNING FROM DEPLOYMENT

UNDERGOING MAINTENANCE

PREPARING FOR DEPLOYMENT

+1

One carrier is almost always undergoing an extensive mid-life overhaul.

🕿 heritage.org

requirements but accept risk in providing continual presence missions.[23] The Navy's final force objective of 355 ships, recommended by the FSA, was based on a minimum force structure that "complies with current defense planning guidance," "meets approved Day 0 and warfighting response timelines," and "delivers future steady state and warfighting requirements with an acceptable degree of risk."[24]

The final recommendation for a 355-ship force is an increase of 47 in the minimum number of ships from the previous requirement of 308. The most significant increases are:

- Aircraft carriers, from 11 to 12;

- Large surface combatants (guided missile destroyers (DDG) and cruisers (CG)), from 88 to 104 "to deliver increased air defense and expeditionary BMD [ballistic missile defense] capacity and provide escorts for the additional Aircraft Carrier";

- Attack submarines (SSNs), from 48 to 66 to "provide the global presence required to support national tasking and prompt warfighting response"; and

- Amphibious ships, from 34 to 38.[25]

"[O]ver the next 30 years," according to the CBO, "meeting the 355-ship objective would cost the Navy an average of about $26.6 billion (in 2017 dollars) annually for ship construction." This "is more than 60 percent above the average amount the Congress has appropriated each year for that purpose over the past 30 years and 40 percent more than the amount appropriated for 2016."[26] The Navy's SCN (Shipbuilding and Conversion, Navy) request for FY 2018 totaled approximately $19.9 billion,[27] well below the level the CBO has assessed is necessary to reach fleet goals. As noted, however, this includes funding for procurement of only nine battle force ships during this fiscal year, which will make it difficult to increase the fleet size.

The seeming anomaly of increased funding for shipbuilding without a corresponding increase in fleet force structure is due in part to the fact that a large portion of this funding is dedicated to advanced procurement of the next-generation ballistic missile submarine program (SSBN(X) *Columbia*-class) as well as such non–battle force requirements as a training ship.[28] Also, the CRS has estimated that roughly 15,000 additional sailors would be needed to man the 47 additional ships.[29] Without significant funding increases to procure more vessels across ship types each year, it appears unlikely that the Navy will reach its 355-ship goal for the foreseeable future.[30]

The Navy has not updated its 30-year shipbuilding plan to reflect the revised 355-ship force objective. By definition, the current 30-year plan is structured to achieve a fleet of 308 ships. However, with major adjustments in annual funding, reactivation of decommissioned ships, and expansion of naval shipyard workforce and facilities, a fleet of 355 ships could be achieved by 2035.[31]

Taken alone, total fleet size can be a misleading statistic; related factors must also be taken into account when considering numbers of ships. One such important factor is the number of ships that are forward deployed to meet operational demands. On average, approximately one-third of the total fleet is deployed at any given time. The type or class of ship is also important. Operational commanders must have the proper mix of capabilities deployed to enable a timely and effective response to emergent crises. Not all ships in the battle force are at sea at the same time. The majority of the fleet is based in the continental U.S. (CONUS) to undergo routine maintenance and training, as well as to limit deployment time for sailors. However, given the COCOMs' requirements for naval power presence in each of their regions, there is an impetus to have as many ships forward deployed as possible.

In November 2014, the Navy established an Optimized Fleet Response Plan (OFRP)

"to ensure continuous availability of manned, maintained, equipped, and trained Navy forces capable of surging forward on short notice while also maintaining long-term sustainability of the force."[32] The plan incorporates four phases of ship availability/maintenance as depicted in Chart 4. This results in a basic ratio of 4:1 for CONUS-based force structure required for deployed platforms. OFRP is on track to achieve the Navy's goal of "2 deployed and 3 surge ready" carrier strike groups (CSGs) just beyond 2021.[33]

As of this writing, the Navy had 104 ships deployed globally (including submarines): 38 percent of the total available fleet and an increase from the 94 ships deployed during 2016.[34] While the Navy remains committed to deploying roughly a third of its fleet at all times, capacity shortages have caused the current fleet to fall below the levels needed both for the Navy's stated presence needs and for a fleet capable of projecting power at the two-MRC level. The Navy has tried to increase forward presence by emphasizing non-rotational deployments (having a ship "home-ported" overseas or keeping it forward stationed):[35]

- **Home-ported:** The ships, crew, and their families are stationed at the port or based abroad.

- **Forward Stationed:** Only the ships will be based abroad while crews are rotated out to the ship.[36]

Both of these non-rotational deployment options require cooperation from friends and allies to permit the Navy's use of their facilities, as well as investment in additional facilities abroad. However, these options allow one ship to provide a greater level of presence than four ships based in CONUS and in rotational deployment since they offset the time needed to deploy ships to distant theaters.[37] A key example of the use of this practice is the Navy's constant home-porting of an aircraft carrier at the U.S. naval base in Yokosuka, Japan. In May 2015, the USS *George Washington* (CVN-73) departed this base to return to CONUS,

CHART 4

Navy's Optimized Fleet Response Plan

The optimized fleet response plan extends the deployment cycle for carriers and surface combatants to 36 months.

AIRCRAFT CARRIERS

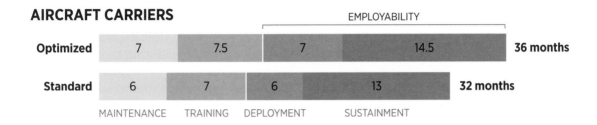

	EMPLOYABILITY	
Optimized	7 / 7.5 / 7 / 14.5	**36 months**
Standard	6 / 7 / 6 / 13	**32 months**

MAINTENANCE   TRAINING   DEPLOYMENT   SUSTAINMENT

SURFACE COMBATANTS

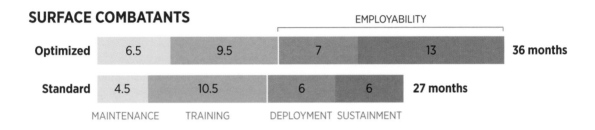

	EMPLOYABILITY	
Optimized	6.5 / 9.5 / 7 / 13	**36 months**
Standard	4.5 / 10.5 / 6 / 6	**27 months**

MAINTENANCE   TRAINING   DEPLOYMENT   SUSTAINMENT

SOURCE: U.S. Government Accountability Office, *Navy's Optimized Fleet Response Plan*, Updated Briefing for Congressional Committees, p. 12, attached to report, *Military Readiness: Progress and Challenges in Implementing the Navy's Optimized Fleet Response Plan*, GAO-16-466R, May 2, 2016, http://www.gao.gov/assets/680/676904.pdf (accessed August 16, 2017).

☎ heritage.org

---

with the USS *Ronald Reagan* sailing there to replace it.[38] The *George Washington*, stationed at Yokosuka since 2008, was withdrawn so that it could undergo its midlife refueling and complex overhaul (RCOH), the lengthy process of refueling its nuclear reactors and applying a variety of repairs and capability upgrades.

The Navy maintains that it currently will be able to meet GFMAP requirements and the 10 missions outlined in the DSG, but Admiral Richardson has indicated that the fleet will continue to be stretched to meet demand.

Capability

Scoring the U.S. Navy's overall ability to protect U.S. interests globally is not just a matter of counting the fleet. The quality of the battle force is also important in determining naval strength.

A comprehensive measure of platform capability would involve a comparison of each ship and its weapons systems relative to the military capabilities of other nations. For example, a complete measure of naval capabilities would have to assess not only how U.S. platforms would match up against an enemy's weapons, but also whether formal operational concepts would be effective in a conflict, after which the assessment would be replicated for each potential conflict. This is a necessary exercise and one in which the military currently engages, but it is beyond the scope of this *Index* because such details and analysis are routinely classified.

Capability can be usefully assessed based on the age of ships, the modernity of the platform, the payloads and weapons systems carried by ships, and the ability of planned modernization

---

programs to maintain the fleet's technological edge. The Navy has several classes of ships that are nearing the end of their lifespans, and this will precipitate a consolidation of ship classes in the battle force.

As noted, the Navy retired its entire fleet of *Oliver Hazard Perry*-class guided missile frigates in 2015. The *Perry* class is being replaced by the Littoral Combat Ship.[39] Planned capability upgrades to give the LCS fleet frigate-like capabilities include "[o]ver-the-horizon surface to surface missile and additional weapon systems and combat system upgrades" and "increased survivability...achieved by incorporating additional self-defense capabilities and increased hardening of vital systems and vital spaces."[40] However, critics of the LCS program have expressed concerns about "past cost growth, design and construction issues with the first LCSs"; "the survivability of LCSs (i.e., their ability to withstand battle damage)"; "whether LCSs are sufficiently armed and would be able to perform their stated missions effectively"; and "the development and testing of the modular mission packages for LCSs."[41]

In July 2017, the Navy released a Request for Information to the shipbuilding industry with the goal of moving forward in FY 2020 with a new ship, currently referred to as the future Guided Missile Frigate (FFG(X)).[42] The Navy stated that a reevaluation of its frigate requirements as a result of evolving threats in the global maritime environment had led to a more robust SSC with better abilities to engage in undersea and surface warfare, operate independently in contested environments, extend the fleet's network of unmanned systems, and relieve large surface combatants from routine duties during operations other than war, thus freeing them for higher-end duties. The notional FFG(X) procurement plan would purchase 20 ships over 11 years.[43]

The Administration's FY 2018 budget request includes funding for two LCSs. While the Navy has not decided on the number to be procured in FY 2019, it has stated that it will maintain the LCS industrial base until the FFG(X) contract is awarded in 2020.[44] The Navy projects that the deployable force will include 11 LCSs by the end of FY 2017 and another four, for a total of 15, by the end of FY 2018. However, this is still well below the fleet size of small surface combatants necessary to fulfill the Navy's global responsibilities (52) even when combined with the remaining mine countermeasure vessels in the fleet (11).

The Navy possesses 22 *Ticonderoga*-class cruisers.[45] To save operating expenses, it has been pursuing a plan to put half of this fleet into temporary layup status in order to extend this class's fleet service time into the 2030s—even though these ships are younger than their expected service lives (i.e., have been used less than planned). Under the FY 2015 National Defense Authorization Act:

> Congress...directed the Navy to implement the so-called "2-4-6" program for modernizing the 11 youngest Aegis cruisers. Under the 2-4-6 program, no more than two of the cruisers are to enter the modernization program each year, none of the cruisers is to remain in a reduced status for modernization for more than four years, and no more than six of the cruisers are to be in the program at any given time.[46]

In FY 2018, the Navy will continue to execute the "2-4-6" plan on seven of 11 cruisers.[47] By the end of FY 2017, the Navy will have inducted six cruisers into modernization.[48] Along with the USS *Anzio*, inducted in May 2017, the program includes *Cape St. George*, inducted in March 2017; *Cowpens* and *Gettysburg*, inducted in FY 2015; and *Chosin* and *Vicksburg*, inducted in FY 2016.[49]

In early 2016, Rear Admiral William Lescher, Deputy Assistant Secretary of the Navy for Budget, advanced an alternative to the current 2-4-6 model.[50] The alternative phased modernization plan in the FY 2017 budget request asked Congress to allow the Navy to put the remaining seven unmodernized cruisers into maintenance in FY 2017, arguing that doing so would save $3 billion in operating costs over the Future Years Defense Program. Congress had not agreed to this request as of the time this *Index* went to press.

The Navy's 12 landing ships (LSD), the *Whidbey Island*-class and *Harpers Ferry*-class amphibious vessels, will reach the end of their 40-year service lives in 2025 and are to be replaced by the next-generation LX(R) program, a ship that will be based on the *San Antonio* (LPD-17)-class amphibious ship.

Many of the other ships that the Navy sails are legacy platforms. Of the 18 classes of ships in the Navy, only seven are currently in production. For example, 66 percent of the Navy's attack submarines are *Los Angeles*-class submarines, an older platform that is being replaced with a more modern and capable *Virginia* class.[51]

The 30-year shipbuilding plan is not limited to programs of record and assumes procurement programs that have yet to materialize. Some of the Navy's ship designs in recent years, such as the *Gerald R. Ford*-class aircraft carrier, the *San Antonio*-class amphibious ship, and the Littoral Combat Ship, have proven to be substantially more expensive to build than the Navy originally estimated.[52] The first ship of any class is typically more expensive than early estimates project, which is not entirely surprising given the assumptions that must be made before actual construction begins. The Congressional Budget Office has reported that such estimates are off by 27 per cent, on average.[53] For that reason, the 30-year shipbuilding plan is often considered overly optimistic.

For example, the goal of 355 ships stated in the Navy's most recent 30-year plan includes an objective for 12 SSBN(X) *Columbia*-class submarines to replace the legacy *Ohio*-class submarine. Production of these 12 SSBN(X) submarines will require a significant portion of the SCN account if the overall budget is not increased.

The Navy's FY 2013 budget deferred the procurement of the lead boat from FY 2019 to FY 2021, with the result that "the Navy's SSBN force will drop to 11 or 10 boats for the period FY2029–FY2041."[54] This is something that the Navy will continue to have difficulty maintaining as it struggles to sustain, overhaul, modernize, and eventually retire the remainder of its legacy SSBN fleet. The *Columbia*-class ballistic missile submarine is "the Navy's top priority program"[55] and has been allocated almost $843 million in the Navy's FY 2018 request, or 4 percent of its total shipbuilding budget, for advanced procurement funding.[56]

The Navy's long-range strike capability derives from its ability to launch various missiles and combat aircraft. Of the two, naval aircraft are much more expensive and difficult to modernize as a class. Until the 1980s, the Navy operated several models of strike aircraft that included the F-14 Tomcat, A-6 Intruder, A-4 Skyhawk, and F/A-18 Hornet. The last of each of these aircraft were retired in 1997 (A-6); 2003 (A-4); and 2006 (F-14). Over the past 20 years, this variety has been winnowed to a single model: the F/A-18. The F/A-18A-D Legacy Hornet has served since 1983; it is out of production and currently flown by 13 Marine Corps squadrons, six Navy squadrons, the Naval Aviation Warfighting Development Center (NAWDC), and the Blue Angels.

The Navy is divesting itself of F/A-18 A-D variants and shifting to F/A-18 E/F Super Hornets, a newer and more capable version "that entered operational service with the U.S. Navy in 1999."[57] The F/A-18E/F Super Hornet has better range, greater weapons payload, and increased survivability over the F/A-18A-D Legacy Hornet.[58] The Navy is implementing efforts to extend the life of some of the older variants until the F-35C is fully fielded in the mid-2030s but plans to have a mix of the F-35C and F/A-18 E/F Super Hornets comprising its carrier-based strike aircraft capability.

The Navy's FY 2018 budget request includes $1.25 billion for 14 F/A-18E/F Super Hornets, and it plans to buy at least 80 more over the next five years in an attempt to mitigate shortfalls in its strike aircraft inventory.[59]

The Navy has been addressing numerous incidents, or physiological episodes (PE), of dizziness and blackouts by F/A-18 aircrews over the past five years. There were 57 such incidents in 2012 and 114 in 2016, and 52 were reported during the first half of 2017.[60] The Navy report data show that "41 percent of the total

FA-18 PEs have been attributed to breathing air delivery system (27 percent possible contamination; 11 percent aircrew oxygen system; 3 percent breathing air delivery component) and 24 percent are adjudicated to be the result of ECS component failure."[61] The report concludes that:

> To date, finding a solution to the U.S. Navy and U.S. Marine Corps' high performance jet aircraft PE challenge has proved elusive. The complexity of aircraft human–machine interfaces and the unforgiving environment in which aircrew operate will continue to generate PEs whenever systems do not operate as intended or human physiology is a factor. The number and severity of PEs can and must be dramatically reduced with a unified, systematic approach.[62]

The F-35C is the Navy's largest aviation modernization program. It is a fifth-generation fighter (all F/A-18 variants are considered fourth-generation) that will have greater stealth capabilities and state-of-the-art electronic systems, allowing it to communicate with multiple other platforms. The Navy plans to purchase 260 F-35Cs[63] (along with 67 F-35Cs for the Marine Corps[64]) to replace "a portion of the existing inventory of 546 Navy and Marine Corps F/A-18 A-D aircraft [that] will be flown through the mid-2030 timeframe."[65] The F-35C, however, will not replace all of the A-Ds.

The F-35 is supposed to be a more capable aircraft relative to the F/A-18, but at planned procurement levels of 260 aircraft, it will not be enough to make up for the Hornets that the Navy will need to replace. Transition to the F-35C is slated to begin in 2018, leading to the first operational deployment in 2021.[66]

In addition, like the other F-35 variants, the F-35C has faced development problems. The system has been grounded because of engine problems, and software development issues have threatened further delay. The aircraft also has grown more expensive through the development process. The Navy's FY 2018 budget request indicates that the service plans to buy four additional F-35Cs before the end of 2017.[67]

Readiness

Although the Navy states that it can still deploy forces in accordance with GFMAP requirements, various factors indicate a continued decline in readiness over the past year. According to Admiral William Moran, Vice Chief of Naval Operations:

> [W]hile our first team on deployment is ready, our bench—the depth of our forces at home—is thin. It has become clear to me that the Navy's overall readiness has reached its lowest level in many years.
>
> There are three main drivers of our readiness problems: 1) persistent, high operational demand for naval forces; 2) funding reductions; and 3) consistent uncertainty about when those reduced budgets will be approved.
>
> The operational demand for our Navy continues to be high, while the fleet has gotten smaller. Between 2001 and 2015, the Navy was able to keep an average of 100 ships at sea each day, despite a 14 percent decrease in the size of the battle force. The Navy is smaller today than it has been in the last 99 years. Maintaining these deployment levels as ships have been retired has taken a significant toll on our sailors and their families as well as on our equipment.
>
> The second factor degrading Navy readiness is the result of several years of constrained funding levels for our major readiness accounts, largely due to fiscal pressures imposed by the Budget Control Act of 2011. Although the Bipartisan Budget Act of 2015 provided temporary relief, in FY 2017 the Navy budget was $5 billion lower than in FY 2016. This major reduction drove very hard choices, including the difficult decision to reduce readiness accounts by over $2 billion this year.
>
> The third primary driver of reduced readiness is the inefficiency imposed by the uncertainty around when budgets will actually be approved. The inability to adjust funding levels as planned, or to commit to longer-term contracts, creates additional work and drives up costs. This results in even less capability for any given dollar we invest, and represents yet another tax on our readiness. We are paying more money and spending more time to maintain a less capable Navy.[68]

Like the other services, the Navy has had to dedicate readiness funding to the immediate needs of various engagements around the globe, which means that maintenance and training for ships and sailors that are not deployed is not prioritized. Deferral of ship and aircraft depot maintenance because of inadequate funding or because public shipyards do not have sufficient capacity has had a ripple effect on the whole fleet. When ships and aircraft are finally able to begin depot maintenance, their material condition is worse than normal due to the delay and high OPTEMPO of the past 15 years. This in turn causes maintenance to take longer than scheduled, which leads to further delays in fleet depot maintenance and increases the demands placed on ships and aircraft that are still operational. The public shipyards are undermanned for the amount of work they need to do.

Correcting this will require sufficient and stable funding both to defray the costs of ship maintenance and to expand the workforce of the public (government) shipyards. These maintenance and readiness issues also affect the Navy's capacity by significantly reducing the numbers of operational ships and aircraft available to support the combatant commanders.

The FY 2018 budget seeks to increase the public shipyard workforce by more than 1,100 workers and to provide additional funding to private yards for submarine maintenance in order to lessen the workload on government yards.[69]

A Government Accountability Office (GAO) analysis of OFRP's performance since its implementation in 2014 compared to naval readiness of the recent past yielded mixed results. The GAO found that during the period from 2011 to implementation of OFRP, the Navy's deployment and maintenance schedules were in poor condition. The three aircraft carriers that have implemented OFRP "have not completed maintenance tasks on time, a benchmark that is crucial to meeting the Navy's employability goals. Further, of the 83 cruisers and destroyers, only 15 have completed

a maintenance availability under OFRP."[70] The GAO found that these rates were better than before OFRP was implemented, but only slightly.

The Navy's aviation readiness is also suffering as a consequence of deferred maintenance, delayed modernization, and high OPTEMPO. The naval aviation community has made extreme efforts to gain every bit of readiness possible with the existing fleet, but even these efforts cannot solve the problems of too little money, too few usable assets, and too much work. As noted in Air Force testimony before the Tactical Air and Land Forces Subcommittee of the House Armed Services Committee in June 2017:

> Service life management efforts have extended the F-A-18 A-D beyond its original service life of 6,000 flight hours to 8,000 flight hours with select aircraft that may be extended up to 10,000 flight hours. Discovery of unanticipated corrosion on these legacy jets complicates depot throughput, and service life extensions for aircraft with more than 8,000 flight hours require High Flight Hour inspections, which furthers increases maintenance-man hours. These inspections assess the material condition of each aircraft and apply a unique combination of inspections and airframe modifications to maintain airworthiness certification. As of April 2017, 92 percent of the F/A-18 A-D fleet has over 6,000 flight hours and 24 percent have flown more than 8,000 flight hours; the highest flight hour airframe has attained over 9,799 hours.[71]

In short, Navy readiness levels are problematic. It is also worth noting again that the Navy's own readiness assessments are based on the ability to execute a strategy that assumes a force sizing construct that is smaller than the one prescribed by this *Index*.

Scoring the U.S. Navy
Capacity Score: Marginal

The Navy is unusual relative to the other services in that its capacity requirements must meet two separate objectives. First, during peacetime, the Navy must maintain a global forward presence. This enduring peacetime requirement to maintain a constant presence around the world is the driving force behind ship force structure requirements: enough ships to ensure that the Navy can provide the necessary global presence.

On the other hand, the Navy also must be able to fight and win wars. In this case, the expectation is to be able to fight and win two simultaneous or nearly simultaneous MRCs. When thinking about naval combat power in this way, the defining metric is not necessarily a total ship count, but rather the carrier strike groups, amphibious ships, and submarines deemed necessary to win both the naval component of a war and the larger war effort by means of strike missions inland or cutting off the enemy's maritime access to sources of supply.

An accurate assessment of Navy capacity takes into account both sets of requirements and scores to the larger requirement.

It should be noted that the scoring in this *Index* includes the Navy's fleet of ballistic missile and fast attack submarines to the extent that they contribute to the overall size of the battle fleet and with general comment on the status of their respective modernization programs. Because of their unique characteristics and the missions they perform, their detailed readiness rates and actual use in peacetime and planned use in war are classified. Nevertheless, the various references consulted are fairly consistent, both with respect to the numbers recommended for the overall fleet and with respect to the Navy's shipbuilding plan.

The role of SSBNs (fleet ballistic missile submarines) as one leg of America's nuclear triad capability is well known; perhaps less well known are the day-to-day tasks undertaken by the SSN force, whose operations, which can include collection, surveillance, and support to the special operations community, often take place apart from the operations of the surface Navy.

Two-MRC Requirement. The primary elements of naval combat power during a major regional contingency operation derive from carrier strike groups (which include squadrons of strike aircraft and support ships) and amphibious assault capacity. Since the Navy is constantly deployed around the globe during peacetime, many of its fleet requirements are beyond the scope of the two-MRC construct, but it is nevertheless important to observe the historical context of naval deployments during a major theater war.

Thirteen Deployable Carrier Strike Groups. The average number of aircraft carriers deployed in the Korean War, Vietnam War, Persian Gulf War, and Operation Iraqi Freedom was between five and six. This correlates with the figures recommended in the 1993 Bottom-Up Review (BUR) and subsequent government force-sizing documents, each of which recommended at least 11 aircraft carriers.[72] Assuming that 11 aircraft carriers are needed to engage simultaneously in two MRCs, and assuming that the Navy ideally should have a 20 percent strategic reserve in order to avoid having to commit 100 percent of its carrier groups and account for scheduled maintenance, the Navy should have 13 CSGs.

The aircraft carrier is the centerpiece of a CSG, composed of one guided missile cruiser, two guided missile destroyers, one attack submarine, and a supply ship in addition to the carrier itself.[73] Therefore, based on the requirement for 13 aircraft carriers, the following numbers of ships are necessary for 13 deployable CSGs:

- 13 aircraft carriers,

- 13 cruisers,

- 26 destroyers, and

- 13 attack submarines.

Thirteen Carrier Air Wings. Each carrier deployed for combat operations was equipped with a carrier air wing, meaning that five to six air wings were necessary for each of those four major contingencies listed. The strategic documents differ slightly in this regard because each document suggests one less carrier air wing than the number of aircraft carriers.

A carrier air wing usually includes four strike fighter squadrons.[74] Twelve aircraft typically comprise one Navy strike fighter squadron, so at least 48 strike fighter craft are required for each carrier air wing. To support 13 carrier air wings, the Navy therefore needs a minimum of 624 strike fighter aircraft.[75]

Fifty Amphibious Ships. The 1993 BUR recommended a fleet of 45 large amphibious vessels to support the operations of 2.5 Marine Expeditionary Brigades (MEBs). Since then, the Marine Corps has expressed a need to be able to perform two MEB-level operations simultaneously, which would require a fleet of 38 amphibious vessels. The 1996 and 2001 QDRs each recommended 12 "amphibious ready groups" (ARGs). One ARG typically includes one amphibious assault ship (LHA/LHD); one amphibious transport dock ship (LPD); and one dock landing ship (LSD).[76] Therefore, the 12-ARG recommendation equates to 36 amphibious vessels.

The number of amphibious vessels required in combat operations has declined since the Korean War, in which 34 amphibious vessels were used; 26 were deployed in Vietnam, 21 in the Persian Gulf War, and only seven in Operation Iraqi Freedom (which did not require as large a sea-based expeditionary force).[77] The Persian Gulf War is the most pertinent example for today because similar vessels were used, and modern requirements for an MEB most closely resemble this engagement.[78]

While the Marine Corps has consistently advocated a fleet of 38 amphibious vessels to execute its two-MEB strategy,[79] it is more prudent to field a fleet of at least 42 such vessels based on the Persian Gulf engagement. Similarly, if the USMC is to have a strategic reserve of 20 percent, the ideal number of amphibious ships would be 50.

Total Ship Requirement. The bulk of the Navy's battle force ships are not directly tied to a carrier strike group. Some surface vessels and attack submarines are deployed independently, which is often why their requirements exceed those of a CSG. The same can be said of the ballistic missile submarine (nuclear missiles) and guided missile submarine (conventional cruise missiles), which operate independently of an aircraft carrier.

This *Index* uses the benchmark set by previous government reports, especially the 1993 BUR, which was one of the most comprehensive reviews of military requirements. Similar Navy fleet size requirements have been echoed in follow-on reports.

The numerical values used in the score column refer to the five-grade scale explained earlier in this section, where 1 is "very weak" and 5 is "very strong." Taking the full Navy requirement of ships as the benchmark, the Navy's current battle forces fleet capacity of 276 ships retains a score of "marginal," as was the case in the *2017 Index*. Given the fact that the Navy has not updated its 30-year shipbuilding plan to reflect its new force structure objective, and in view of the impending need for a ballistic missile submarine replacement that could cost nearly half of the current shipbuilding budget per hull, the Navy's capacity score could fall to "weak" in the near future.

Capability Score: Weak

The overall capability score for the Navy is "weak." This was consistent across all four components of the capability score: "Age of Equipment," "Capability of Equipment," "Size of Modernization Program," and "Health of Modernization Programs." Given the number of programs, ship classes, and types of aircraft involved, the details that informed the capability assessment are more easily presented in a tabular format as shown in the Appendix.

Readiness Score: Marginal

The Navy's readiness score has returned to an assessment of "marginal," down from the *2017 Index*'s score of "strong." This assessment combines two major elements of naval readiness: the ability to consistently provide the required levels of presence around the globe and surge capacity. As elaborated below, the Navy's ability to maintain required presence in key regions is "strong," but its ability to surge to meet combat requirements ranges from "weak" to "very weak" depending on how one defines the requirement. In both cases—presence and surge—the Navy is sacrificing long-term readiness to meet current demand.

The Navy has reported that it continues to meet GFMAP goals but at the cost of future readiness. The GAO reported in May 2016 that "[t]o meet heavy operational demands over the past decade, the Navy has increased ship deployment lengths and has reduced or deferred ship maintenance"[80] The GAO further found that the Navy's efforts to provide the same amount of forward presence with an undersized fleet have "resulted in declining ship conditions across the fleet" and have "increased the amount of time that ships require to complete maintenance in the shipyards."[81] There was no compelling evidence in 2017 that this condition has improved.

Though the Navy has been able to maintain a third of its fleet globally deployed, and although the OFRP has preserved readiness for individual hulls by restricting deployment increases, demand still exceeds the supply of ready ships needed to meet requirements sustainably. Admiral Moran expressed deep concern about the ability of the Navy to meet the nation's needs in a time of conflict in this exchange with Senator Joni Ernst (R–IA):

> Senator Ernst: ...If our Navy had to answer to two or more of the so-called four-plus-one threats today, could we do that?
>
> Admiral Moran: ...[W]e are at a point right now...that our ability to surge beyond our current force that's forward is very limited, which should give you a pretty good indication that it would be challenging to meet the current guidance to defeat and deny in two conflicts.[82]

As if to sharpen Admiral Moran's concerns, the Navy experienced a number of at-sea incidents—three ship collisions and one grounding—during 2017.[83] Admiral Richardson responded by ordering a "servicewide operational pause" to review practices throughout the fleet.[84] An investigation into the latest of these incidents was underway at the time of this writing, and observers have speculated that high operational tempo and lack of funding for adequate training have contributed to poor readiness across the Navy.[85]

The Navy's readiness as it pertains to providing global presence is rated as "marginal." The level of COCOM demand for naval presence and the fleet's ability to meet that demand is similar to that of 2017 but is increasingly challenged by the range of funding problems noted in this section. The Navy maintains its ability to forward deploy a third of its fleet and has been able to stave off immediate readiness challenges through the OFRP. However, continued problems in ship maintenance and an inadequate number of hulls to relieve pressure on the maintenance cycle are jeopardizing the Navy's ability to respond effectively to COCOM requirements for sustained presence, crisis support, and surge response in the event of a major conflict.

Without increased funding for further fleet recapitalization and improvements in shipyard maintenance capacity, the readiness of the Navy's fleet will remain compromised. Admiral Moran's concerns about the Navy's ability to handle two major crises are therefore worrisome.

Overall U.S. Navy Score: Marginal

The Navy's overall score for the *2018 Index* is "marginal," the same as for the previous year. This was derived by aggregating the scores for capacity ("marginal"); capability ("weak"); and readiness ("marginal"). However, given the continued upward trends in OPTEMPO that have not been matched by similar increases in capacity or readiness funding, the Navy's overall score could degrade in the near future if the service does not recapitalize and maintain the health of its fleet more robustly than is now the case.

U.S. Military Power: Navy

	VERY WEAK	WEAK	MARGINAL	STRONG	VERY STRONG
Capacity			✔		
Capability		✔			
Readiness			✔		
OVERALL			✔		

Endnotes

1. Admiral John M. Richardson, Chief of Naval Operations, *A Design for Maintaining Maritime Superiority, Version 1.0*, January 2016, http://www.navy.mil/cno/docs/cno_stg.pdf (accessed August 16, 2017).

2. U.S. Department of the Navy, U.S. Marine Corps; U.S. Navy; and U.S. Department of Homeland Security, U.S. Coast Guard, *A Cooperative Strategy for 21st Century Seapower*, March 2015, p. 2, http://www.navy.mil/local/maritime/150227-CS21R-Final.pdf (accessed August 17, 2017).

3. U.S. Department of Defense, *Sustaining U.S. Global Leadership: Priorities for 21st Century Defense*, January 2012, http://www.defense.gov/news/Defense_Strategic_Guidance.pdf (accessed August 16, 2017).

4. The Global Force Management Allocation Plan (GFMAP) is a classified document that specifies forces to be provided by the services for use by operational commanders. It is an extension of a reference manual maintained by the Joint Staff, *Global Force Management Allocation Policies and Procedures* (CJCSM 3130.06B), which is also a classified publication. See U.S. Department of Defense, Joint Chiefs of Staff, "Adaptive Planning and Execution Overview and Policy Framework," Chairman of the Joint Chiefs of Staff Guide 3130, May 29, 2015, p. B-2, http://www.jcs.mil/Portals/36/Documents/Library/Handbooks/g3130.pdf?ver=2016-02-05-175741-677 (accessed August 22, 2017), and "Current list of CJCSG/I/M/Ns," May 4, 2017, p. 17, http://www.jcs.mil/Portals/36/Documents/Library/SupportDocs/CJCS%20Reports/CJCS%20CURRENT%20DIRECTIVES%20-%2004%20May%2017.pdf?ver=2017-05-10-100837-183 (accessed August 22, 2017).

5. U.S. Department of Defense, Department of the Navy, Office of the Secretary, "SECNAV Instruction 5030.8B: General Guidance for the Classification of Naval Vessels and Battle Force Ship Counting Procedures," March 7, 2014, pp. 1–2, http://www.nvr.navy.mil/5030.8B.pdf (accessed August 16, 2017).

6. U.S. Department of Defense, Naval Vessel Register, "Fleet Size," last updated August 14, 2017, http://www.nvr.navy.mil/NVRSHIPS/FLEETSIZE.HTML (accessed August 16, 2017).

7. "An Assessment of U.S. Military Power: U.S. Navy," in *2017 Index of U.S. Military Strength*, ed. Dakota L. Wood (Washington: The Heritage Foundation, 2016), p. 292, http://index.heritage.org/military/2017/assessments/us-military-power/u-s-navy/.

8. Allison F. Stiller, Principal Civilian Deputy Assistant Secretary of the Navy for Research, Development and Acquisition (ASN(RD&A)), Performing the Duties and Functions of ASN(RD&A); Lieutenant General Robert S. Walsh, Deputy Commandant, Combat Development and Integration, and Commanding General, Marine Corps Combat Development Command; and Vice Admiral William K. Lescher, Deputy Chief of Naval Operations for Integration of Capabilities and Resources, statement on "Department of the Navy Shipbuilding Programs" before the Subcommittee on Seapower, Committee on Armed Services, U.S. Senate, June 21, 2017, p. 3, https://www.armed-services.senate.gov/download/stiller-walsh-lescher_06-21-17 (accessed August 16, 2017).

9. U.S. Department of Defense, Secretary of the Navy, Memorandum for Secretary of Defense, "United States Navy Accelerated Fleet Plan," February 9, 2017, p. 8, https://www.blumenthal.senate.gov/imo/media/doc/U.S.%20Navy%20Accelerated%20Fleet%20Plan.pdf (accessed August 16, 2017).

10. Congressional Budget Office, "Costs of Building a 355-Ship Navy," April 2017, p. 6, https://www.cbo.gov/system/files/115th-congress-2017-2018/reports/52632-355shipnavy.pdf (accessed August 16, 2017).

11. U.S. Department of Defense, Secretary of the Navy, Memorandum for Secretary of Defense, "United States Navy Accelerated Fleet Plan," pp. 7–8.

12. "An Assessment of U.S. Military Power: U.S. Navy," *2017 Index of U.S. Military Strength*, p. 247.

13. Sam LaGrone, "Last Oliver Hazard Perry Frigate USS Simpson Leaves Service, Marked for Foreign Sale," USNI News, September 29, 2015, https://news.usni.org/2015/09/29/last-oliver-hazard-perry-frigate-uss-simpson-leaves-service-marked-for-foreign-sale (accessed August 8, 2017).

14. U.S. Department of Defense, Naval Vessel Register, "Fleet Size."

15. David B. Larter, "Frigate Competition Wide Open: Navy Specs Reveal Major Design Shift," *Defense News*, July 10, 2017, http://www.defensenews.com/breaking-news/2017/07/10/frigate-competition-wide-open-navy-specs-reveal-major-design-shift/ (accessed August 9, 2017).

16. U.S. Department of Defense, Naval Vessel Register, "Fleet Size."

17. U.S. Code, Title 10, § 5062(b), https://www.gpo.gov/fdsys/pkg/USCODE-2010-title10/pdf/USCODE-2010-title10-subtitleC-partI-chap507-sec5062.pdf (accessed August 16, 2017).

18. H.R. 941, 12 Carrier Act, 115th Cong., https://www.congress.gov/bill/115th-congress/house-bill/941/text (accessed August 17, 2017); Megan Eckstein, "House's 2018 Defense Bill Would Increase DDG, SSN Production Rates; Buy Carriers Every 3 Years," USNI News, June 20, 2017, https://news.usni.org/2017/06/20/houses-2018-defense-bill-increase-ddg-ssn-production-rates-buy-carriers-every-3-years (accessed August 10, 2017).

19. Ronald O'Rourke, "Navy Force Structure and Shipbuilding Plans: Background and Issues for Congress," Congressional Research Service *Report for Members and Committees of Congress*, June 30, 2017, p. 9, https://fas.org/sgp/crs/weapons/RL32665.pdf (accessed August 10, 2017).

20. Lucas Tomlinson, "No U.S. Aircraft Carrier at Sea Leaves Gap in Middle East," Fox News, December 30, 2016, http://www.foxnews.com/us/2016/12/30/no-us-carrier-at-sea-leaves-gap-in-middle-east.html (accessed August 10, 2017).

21. Mike Fabey, "The U.S. Navy's Most Advanced Aircraft Carrier Will Soon Face Its Greatest Challenge," *The National Interest*, June 27, 2017, http://nationalinterest.org/blog/the-buzz/the-us-navys-most-advanced-aircraft-carrier-will-soon-face-21336 (accessed August 14, 2017).

22. U.S. Department of the Navy, "Executive Summary: 2016 Navy Force Structure Assessment (FSA)," December 14, 2016, p. 1, https://news.usni.org/wp-content/uploads/2016/12/FSA_Executive-Summary.pdf (accessed August 16, 2017). Note: the full FSA was not released to the public.

23. Ibid., p. 2.

24. Ibid., pp. 2–3.

25. Ibid., pp. 3–4.

26. Congressional Budget Office, "Costs of Building a 355-Ship Navy," p. 1.

27. U.S. Department of the Navy, *Department of Defense Fiscal Year (FY) 2018 Budget Estimates, Navy, Justification Book, Volume 1 of 1: Shipbuilding and Conversion, Navy*, May 2017, p. viii, http://www.secnav.navy.mil/fmc/fmb/Documents/18pres/SCN_Book.pdf (accessed August 16, 2017).

28. See, for example, ibid., pp. xiii and 1-5 (SSBN(X)), and pp. xxxi and 241–244 (Moored Training Ship).

29. O'Rourke, "Navy Force Structure and Shipbuilding Plans," pp. 12–13; for a detailed breakout of sailors per type and number of ships, see ibid., note 26.

30. Eleven cruisers will also be placed in "Reduced Operating Status" but will be included in the ship count as they are not being retired. According to the Office of the Chief of Naval Operations, "As part of this modernization program, ships must remain in commission with a reduced crew size that matches modernization phasing and be placed in a sustainment condition where only essential maintenance, preservation, and limited hull, mechanical, and electrical (HM&E) modernization is accomplished while awaiting a depot level availability." U.S. Department of Defense, Department of the Navy, Office of the Chief of Naval Operations, OPNAV Instruction 9000.6, "Ticonderoga Class Cruiser and Dock Landing Ship Modernization Program Guidance," May 18, 2015, p. 2, ¶ 4, https://news.usni.org/2015/05/20/document-memo-on-cruiser-dock-landing-ship-modernization-programs (accessed August 16, 2017).

31. O'Rourke, "Navy Force Structure and Shipbuilding Plans," Summary, p. [1].

32. U.S. Department of Defense, Department of the Navy, Office of the Chief of Naval Operations, OPNAV Instruction 3000.15A, "Optimized Fleet Response Plan," November 10, 2014, p. 1, https://doni.documentservices.dla.mil/Directives/03000%20Naval%20Operations%20and%20Readiness/03-00%20General%20Operations%20and%20Readiness%20Support/3000.15A.pdf (accessed August 17, 2017).

33. U.S. Department of Defense, Office of the Under Secretary of Defense (Comptroller)/Chief Financial Officer, *United States Department of Defense Fiscal Year 2018 Budget Request: Defense Budget Overview*, May 2017, p. 2-5, http://comptroller.defense.gov/Portals/45/Documents/defbudget/fy2018/fy2018_Budget_Request_Overview_Book.pdf (accessed August 9, 2017).

34. U.S. Department of the Navy, "Status of the Navy," as of August 14, 2017, http://www.navy.mil/navydata/nav_legacy.asp?id=146 (accessed August 17, 2017).

35. Rotational deployments involve a ship sailing to a location for a set amount of time and returning to the United States, usually to be replaced by another ship although not always providing an overlapping or unbroken presence.

36. U.S. Department of the Navy, U.S. Marine Corps; U.S. Navy; and U.S. Department of Homeland Security, U.S. Coast Guard, *Naval Operations Concept 2010: Implementing the Maritime Strategy*, p. 26, https://www.uscg.mil/history/docs/2010NOC.pdf (accessed August 17, 2017).

37. On average, rotational deployments require four ships for one ship to be forward deployed. This is necessary because one ship is sailing out to a designated location, one is at location, one is sailing back to the CONUS, and one is in the CONUS for maintenance.

38. Sam LaGrone, "Carrier George Washington Leaves Japan for the Last Time as Forward Deployed CVN," USNI News, May 19, 2015, http://news.usni.org/2015/05/19/carrier-george-washington-leaves-japan-for-the-last-time-as-forward-deployed-cvn (accessed August 17, 2017).

39. See Ronald O'Rourke, "Navy Littoral Combat Ship/Frigate (LCS/FF) Program: Background and Issues for Congress," Congressional Research Service *Report for Members and Committees of Congress*, June 30, 2017, https://fas.org/sgp/crs/weapons/RL33741.pdf (accessed August 10, 2017).

40. Ronald O'Rourke, "Navy Littoral Combat Ship (LCS)/Frigate Program: Background and Issues for Congress," Congressional Research Service *Report for Members and Committees of Congress*, June 12, 2015, p. 15, https://news.usni.org/wp-content/uploads/2015/06/RL33741_2.pdf#viewer.action=download (accessed August 17, 2017).

41. O'Rourke, "Navy Littoral Combat Ship/Frigate (LCS/FF) Program," June 30, 2017, Summary.

42. Megan Eckstein, "Navy Slowing Frigate Procurement to Allow Careful Requirements Talks; Contract Award Set for FY2020, USNI News, May 3, 2017, https://news.usni.org/2017/05/03/navy-slowing-frigate-procurement-to-allow-careful-requirements-talks-contract-award-set-for-fy2020 (accessed August 10, 2017).

43. Program Executive Office Littoral Combat Ships, Frigate Program Office, "FFG(X) Industry Day," July 25, 2017, Slide 7, "FFG(X) Program Schedule," https://www.fbo.gov/utils/view?id=73a65bb953f970ae10c1fa82b1030493 (accessed August 17, 2017).

44. O'Rourke, "Navy Littoral Combat Ship/Frigate (LCS/FF) Program," June 30, 2017, pp. 5–6.

45. U.S. Department of the Navy, *Highlights of the Department of the Navy FY 2018 Budget*, May 2017, p. 3-3, http://www.secnav.navy.mil/fmc/fmb/Documents/18pres/Highlights_book.pdf (accessed August 17, 2017).

46. Ronald O'Rourke, "Navy Aegis Ballistic Missile Defense (BMD) Program: Background and Issues for Congress," Congressional Research Service *Report for Members and Committees of Congress*, October 25, 2016, p. 1, https://www.history.navy.mil/content/dam/nhhc/research/library/online-reading-room/technology/bmd/navyaegis_ballistic.pdf (accessed August 17, 2017).

47. Stiller, Walsh, and Lescher, statement on "Department of the Navy Shipbuilding Programs," June 21, 2017, p. 11.

48. News transcript, "Press Briefing by Rear Admiral Brian E. Luther on the President's Fiscal Year 2018 Defense Budget for the Navy," U.S. Department of Defense, May 23, 2017, https://www.defense.gov/News/Transcripts/Transcript-View/Article/1193229/press-briefing-by-rear-admiral-brian-e-luther-on-the-presidents-fiscal-year-201/ (accessed August 17, 2017)

49. U.S. Navy, "Cruisers–CG," U.S. Navy *Fact File*, last updated January 9, 2017, http://www.navy.mil/navydata/fact_display.asp?cid=4200&tid=800&ct=4 (accessed August 17, 2017).

50. Megan Eckstein, "FY 2017 Budget: Navy Wants to Modernize Last 7 Cruisers Instead of Following 2/4/6 Directive from Congress," USNI News, February 9, 2016, https://news.usni.org/2016/02/09/fy-2017-budget-navy-wants-to-modernize-last-7-cruisers-instead-of-following-246-directive-from-congress (accessed August 10, 2017).

51. This is based on a calculation of the total number of attack submarines (which includes three different classes), which was 54 as of publication, and the number of *Los Angeles*-class submarines, which was 39 as of publication.

52. Stephen J. Ilteris, "Build Strategic Fast Attack Submarines," U.S. Naval Institute *Proceedings*, Vol. 142/10/1,364 (October 2016), https://www.usni.org/magazines/proceedings/2016-10/build-strategic-fast-attack-submarines (accessed August 17, 2017).

53. Congressional Budget Office, *An Analysis of the Navy's Fiscal Year 2016 Shipbuilding Plan*, October 2015, p. 30, Figure 10, "Cost Growth in Lead Ships, 1985 to 2015," https://www.cbo.gov/sites/default/files/114th-congress-2015-2016/reports/50926-Shipbuilding.pdf (accessed August 17, 2017).

54. Ronald O'Rourke, "Navy Columbia Class (Ohio Replacement) Ballistic Missile Submarine (SSBN[X]) Program: Background and Issues for Congress," Congressional Research Service *Report for Members and Committees of Congress*, May 12, 2017, p. 6, https://www.fas.org/sgp/crs/weapons/R41129.pdf (accessed August 17, 2017).

55. Ibid., p. 1.

56. U.S. Department of the Navy, *Department of Defense Fiscal Year (FY) 2018 Budget Estimates, Navy, Justification Book, Volume 1 of 1: Shipbuilding and Conversion, Navy*, p. xvi.

57. Boeing, "F/A-18 Hornet Fighter: Historical Snapshot," http://www.boeing.com/history/products/fa-18-hornet.page (accessed August 17, 2017).

58. Vice Admiral Paul Grosklags, Representing Assistant Secretary of the Navy (Research, Development and Acquisition); Lieutenant General Jon Davis, Deputy Commandant for Aviation; and Rear Admiral Michael C. Manazir, Director Air Warfare, statement on "Department of the Navy's Aviation Programs" before the Subcommittee on Seapower, Committee on Armed Services, U.S. Senate, April 20, 2016, p. 9, http://www.armed-services.senate.gov/imo/media/doc/Grosklags-Davis-Manazir_04-20-16.pdf (accessed August 13, 2017).

59. Vice Admiral Paul Grosklags, Representing Assistant Secretary of the Navy (Research, Development and Acquisition); Lieutenant General Jon Davis, Deputy Commandant for Aviation; and Rear Admiral DeWolfe H. Miller III, Director Air Warfare, statement on "Department of the Navy's Aviation Programs" before the Subcommittee on Tactical Air and Land Forces, Committee on Armed Services, U.S. House of Representatives, June 7, 2017, p. 5, http://docs.house.gov/meetings/AS/AS25/20170607/106065/HHRG-115-AS25-Wstate-GrosklagsP-20170607.pdf (accessed August 17, 2017).

60. Zachary Cohen, "US Navy fighter pilot deaths tied to oxygen issues," CNN, June 17, 2017, http://www.cnn.com/2017/06/16/politics/us-navy-aircraft-pilot-deaths-oxygen-issues/index.html (accessed August 17, 2017).

61. U.S. Navy, *Comprehensive Review of T-45 and F/A-18 Physiological Episodes*, attached to memorandum from Commander, U.S. Pacific Fleet, to Vice Chief of Naval Operations, June 12, 2017, p. 9, https://news.usni.org/2017/06/15/document-the-navys-physiological-episodes-comprehensive-review (accessed August 17, 2017).

62. Ibid., p. iii.

63. (Author's name redacted), "F-35 Joint Strike Fighter (JSF) Program," Congressional Research Service *Report for Members and Committees of Congress*, July 18, 2016, p. 11, https://www.everycrsreport.com/files/20160718_RL30563_8bede6a87ca260a4aa655 62952c04a3ccc62fd0a.pdf (accessed August 22, 2017).

64. Grosklags, Davis, and Miller, statement on "Department of the Navy's Aviation Programs," June 7, 2017, pp. 13–14.

65. Ibid., p. 4.

66. Ibid., p. 10.

67. U.S. Department of Defense, Office of the Under Secretary of Defense (Comptroller), *Department of Defense Budget Fiscal Year 2018: Procurement Programs (P-1)*, May 2017, p. N-3C, http://comptroller.defense.gov/portals/45/documents/defbudget/FY2018/FY2018_p1.pdf (accessed August 17, 2017).

68. Admiral William F. Moran, Vice Chief of Naval Operations, statement on "State of the Military" before the Committee on Armed Services, U.S. House of Representatives, February 7, 2017, pp. 1–2, http://docs.house.gov/meetings/AS/AS00/20170207/105530/HHRG-115-AS00-Wstate-MoranW-20170207.pdf (accessed August 17, 2017).

69. U.S. Department of the Navy, *Highlights of the Department of the Navy FY 2018 Budget*, p. 3-5.

70. U.S. Government Accountability Office, *Military Readiness: Progress and Challenges in Implementing the Navy's Optimized Fleet Response Plan*, GAO-16-466R, May 2, 2016, p. 2, http://www.gao.gov/assets/680/676904.pdf (accessed August 17, 2017).

71. Grosklags, Davis, and Miller, statement on "Department of the Navy's Aviation Programs," June 7, 2017, p. 4.

72. This requirement is derived from the BUR's requirement for four–five carrier strike groups per MRC; however, this *Index* finds that this number is low by historical accounts and therefore recommends one additional carrier per MRC.

73. U.S. Navy, "The Carrier Strike Group," http://www.navy.mil/navydata/ships/carriers/powerhouse/cvbg.asp (accessed August 17, 2017).

74. U.S. Navy, "The Carrier Air Wing," http://www.navy.mil/navydata/ships/carriers/powerhouse/airwing.asp (accessed August 17, 2017).

75. The full array of aircraft actually embarked on a carrier is more than just the strike aircraft counted here and includes E-2 Hawkeye early warning, C-2 Greyhound cargo, and various helicopter aircraft, among others, that are fielded in a ratio that is roughly proportional to the number of aircraft carriers in the fleet.

76. U.S. Navy, "The Amphibious Ready Group," last updated May 26, 2009, http://www.navy.mil/navydata/nav_legacy.asp?id=148 (accessed August 17, 2017).

77. The size and capability of amphibious ships also have grown over time, with smaller amphibs like the old LST replaced by the much larger LSD and LPD classes. Consequently, fewer ships are needed to lift the same or an even larger amphibious force.

78. GlobalSecurity.org, "Marine Expeditionary Brigade (MEB)," last modified May 7, 2011, http://www.globalsecurity.org/military/agency/usmc/meb.htm (accessed August 17, 2017).

79. Congressional Budget Office, *An Analysis of the Navy's Amphibious Warfare Ships for Deploying Marines Overseas*, November 2011, p. 1, http://www.cbo.gov/sites/default/files/cbofiles/attachments/11-18-AmphibiousShips.pdf (accessed August 17, 2017).

80. U.S. Government Accountability Office, *Military Readiness: Progress and Challenges in Implementing the Navy's Optimized Fleet Response Plan*, p. 1.

81. Ibid., p. 8.

82. Stenographic transcript of *Hearing to Receive Testimony on the Current Readiness of U.S. Forces*, Subcommittee on Readiness and Management Support, Committee on Armed Services, U.S. Senate, February 8, 2017, pp. 44–45, https://www.armed-services.senate.gov/imo/media/doc/17-07_02-08-17.pdf (accessed August 16, 2017).

83. Joe Sterling, "A Spate of US Navy Warship Accidents in Asia Since January," CNN, updated August 22, 2017, http://www.cnn.com/2017/08/21/politics/navy-ships-accidents/index.html (accessed August 23, 2017)

84. Corey Dickstein, "CNO Orders Navy-wide Pause, Broad Review After 2nd Pacific Collision in 2 Months," *Stars and Stripes*, August 21, 2017, https://www.stripes.com/news/pacific/cno-orders-navy-wide-pause-broad-review-after-2nd-pacific-collision-in-2-months-1.483806#.WZxmGumQyUk (accessed August 23, 2017).

85. Jeremy Herb, "Why Are So Many Navy Ships Crashing?" CNN, updated August 22, 2017, http://www.cnn.com/2017/08/21/politics/navy-ships-crashing-readiness/index.html (accessed August 23, 2017).

U.S. Air Force

The U.S. Air Force (USAF) is the youngest of the four branches of the U.S. military, having been born out of the Army's Signal Corps to become its own service in 1947. The Air Force mission set has expanded significantly over the years. Initially, there were four major components—Strategic Air Command (SAC); Tactical Air Command (TAC); Air Defense Command (ADC); and Air Mobility Command (AMC)—that collectively reflected the "fly, fight, and win" nature of the service. Space's rise to prominence began in the early 1950s, and with it came a host of faculties that would help to expand the service's impact and mission set.

Today, the Air Force focuses on five primary missions:

- Air and space superiority;

- Intelligence, surveillance, and reconnaissance (ISR);

- Mobility and lift;

- Global strike; and

- Command and control (C2).

These missions, while all necessary, put even greater stress on the resources for which the Air Force is forced to compete in an incredibly strained fiscal environment. Using the 2012 Defense Strategic Guidance (DSG) as its framework for determining investment priorities and posture, the Air Force intentionally traded size for quality by aiming to be a "smaller, but superb, force that maintains the agility, flexibility, and readiness to engage a full range of contingencies and threats."[1]

During testimony before the Senate Armed Services Committee in June 2017, Secretary of the Air Force Heather Wilson and Air Force Chief of Staff General David Goldfein stated that "the Air Force is too small for the mission demanded of it and it is unlikely that the need for air and space power will diminish significantly in the coming decade."[2] Unfortunately, the funding available has not allowed this "too small" service to execute an acquisition program to reverse the downward spiral of aircraft availability, nor has it supported enough time in the air for pilots to sustain much more than a marginal level of readiness.

Sequestration has forced the Air Force Chief of Staff to make strategic trades in capability, capacity, and readiness to meet the current operational demands of the war on terrorism and prepare for the future. Five years of sequestration has had many detrimental effects on the ability of the service to sustain the war on terrorism, remain ready for a full-spectrum war, and modernize its aging fleet of aircraft. Presidential budgets during the sequestration years of the Obama Administration always proved aspirational, and the trades among capability, capacity, and readiness failed to keep pace with demands on the service. When funding did arrive, it was pursuant to continuing resolutions adopted well into the year of execution, making any real form of strategic planning impossible.[3]

The Trump Administration has proposed a budget for fiscal year (FY) 2018 that would begin to turn the corner in each of the three bins with a budget of $183 billion (base budget plus overseas contingency operations or OCO).[4] If executed in its current form, it would allow the Air Force to bring on an additional 4,100 active-duty personnel, fund the flying hour program (FHP) to the maximum executable level of 91 percent, and increase full-spectrum training/operational readiness accounts to $1.5 billion.[5] While this Administration appears more willing to put pressure on Congress to execute the President's budget, it is by no means certain that Congress will do so.

If the House and Senate were able to meet or exceed the funding levels in the President's budget, they would enable the Air Force to reverse several trends in capacity, capability, and readiness, all three of which are under stress.

Capacity

The trade-off in capacity has seen near-term reductions in lift, command and control, and fourth-generation fighter aircraft to ensure that the Air Force's top three modernization programs—the F-35A, Long-Range Strike Bomber (LRS-B), and KC-46A—are preserved.[6] The USAF is "the smallest and oldest it has ever been," and as the demand for air power continues to increase, capacity will continue to limit capability.[7] Unlike some of the other services, the Air Force did not expand in numbers during the post-9/11 buildup.[8] Rather, it became smaller as programmed retirement dates for older aircraft were not offset with programmed retirements. Successive delays in F-35 and KC-46 development have carried over into production, leaving both fighter and tanker fleets short of the ready numbers required to train for and execute their respective missions.

The Air Force's capacity in terms of number of aircraft has been on a constant downward slope since 1952,[9] and the number will drop again from 5,517 aircraft in 2017 to 5,416 in 2018.[10] As Air Force officials testified in 2017:

[A]dversaries are modernizing and innovating faster than we are, putting at risk America's technological advantage in air and space.... Before 1991, the Air Force bought approximately 510 aircraft per year. In the past 20 years, we have averaged only 96 per year. Today, the average age of our aircraft is over 27 years.[11]

This reduction in capacity is expected to continue because of ongoing budgetary pressure. Under spending caps mandated by the Budget Control Act of 2011 (BCA), the Air Force has shrunk from 70 combat-coded[12] active-duty fighter squadrons during Desert Storm[13] to just 55 across the whole of the active-duty, guard, and reserve force.[14] Only 32 of those are active duty.[15]

The Heritage *Index of U.S. Military Strength* assesses that a force of 1,200 fighter aircraft is required to execute a two–major regional contingency (two-MRC) strategy—a number that is also reflected in a 2011 study conducted by the Air Force.[16] More recently, the service acknowledged that it could reduce the requirement by 100 fighters by assuming more risk.[17] Of the 5,416 manned and unmanned aircraft in the USAF's inventory, 1,308 are active-duty fighters, 915 of which are combat-coded aircraft (aircraft not associated with operational testing, evaluation, or training of replacement pilots).[18] Constrained funding levels will continue to deepen the shortage of fighters and readiness levels, degrading vital air operations as well as operational testing and training expertise.

Capability

Reductions in funding brought about by the BCA and other budget constraints have forced the Air Force to prioritize future capability over capacity. This strategy centers on the idea of developing and maintaining a capable force that can win against advanced fighters and surface-to-air missile systems that are being developed by top-tier potential adversaries like China and Russia. The only way the Air Force can sustain that technological edge in the current budget environment is by reducing its fleet of aircraft that are moving toward obsolescence.

Any assessment of capability includes not only the incorporation of advanced technologies, but also the overall health of the inventory. Most aircraft have programmed life spans of

CHART 5

Lack of Procurement Has Led to Aging Aircraft Fleets

The U.S. military currently maintains several fighter aircraft fleets that were last purchased decades ago. In 1990, the average age of a fighter aircraft was 11 years. Today, it is 24 years.

NUMBER OF AIRCRAFT PROCURED ANNUALLY, BY AIR FORCE FLEET

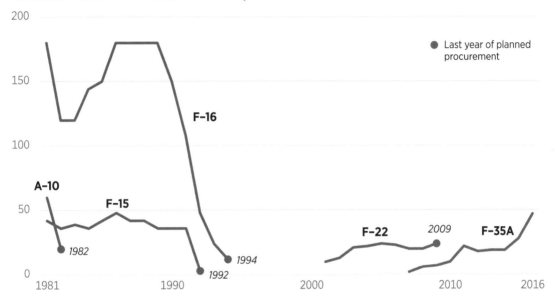

● Last year of planned procurement

F–16

A–10

F–15

1982

F–22   2009   F–35A

1994

1992

1981   1990   2000   2010   2016

SOURCES: Congressional Budget Office, "Total Quantities and Unit Procurement Cost Tables: 1974–1995," https://www.cbo.gov/sites/default/files/103rd-congress-1993-1994/reports/94doc02b.pdf (accessed June 27, 2017); U.S. Department of Defense, "Selected Acquisition Report: F–22," December 31, 2010, http://www.globalsecurity.org/military/library/budget/fy2010/sar/f-22_sar_25-dec-2010.pdf (accessed June 27, 2017); and U.S. Department of Defense, "Selected Acquisition Report: F–35 Joint Strike Fighter Aircraft (F–35)," December 2015, https://fas.org/man/eprint/F35-sar-2016.pdf (accessed June 27, 2017).

🕾 heritage.org

20 to 30 years, based on a programmed level of annual flying hours. The bending and flexing of airframes over time in the air generates predictable levels of stress and metal fatigue. The average age of Air Force aircraft is 27 years,[19] and some fleets, such as the B-52 bomber, average 55 years.[20] Although service life extension programs (SLEPs) can lengthen the useful life of airframes, their dated avionics become increasingly expensive to maintain. That added expense consumes funding and reduces the amount the services have available to invest in modernization, which is critical to ensuring future capability.

The average age of the F-15C fleet is over 33 years, leaving less than 10 percent of its useful service life remaining.[21] That same fleet comprises 57 percent of USAF air superiority platforms—a fleet reduced in size by 10 aircraft (8 percent) in 2017.[22] The fleet of F-16Cs are, on average, 26 years old,[23] and the service has used up nearly 80 percent of its expected life span. KC-135s comprise 63 percent of the Air Force's tankers and are over 55 years old on average.[24] Air Force officials have testified that "before 1991, the Air Force bought approximately 510 aircraft per year. In the past 20 years, we have averaged only 96 per year."[25]

The Air Force's ISR and lift capabilities face similar problems in specific areas that affect both capability and capacity. Of total ISR aircraft, 79 percent are now unmanned aerial vehicles (UAVs).[26] Even here, however, the numbers fell from 371 to 256[27] with the retirement of the MQ-1 Predator.[28] The RQ-4 Global Hawk is one of the more reliable of those platforms, but gross weight restrictions limit the number of sensors that it can carry, and the warfighter still needs the capability of the U-2, which is now 34 years old on average.[29] The E-8 Joint Surveillance and Target Attack Radar System (Joint-STARS) and the RC-135 Rivet Joint are critical ISR platforms, and each was built on the Boeing 707 platform, the last one of which was constructed in 1979. The reliability of the Air Force fleet is at risk because of the challenges linked to aircraft age and flight hours, and the fleet needs to be modernized.

A service's investment in modernization ensures that future capability remains healthy. Investment programs aim not only to procure enough to fill current capacity requirements, but also to advance future capabilities with advanced technology. The Air Force continued to structure its budget in FY 2017 to preserve funding for its three top acquisition priorities: the F-35A Joint Strike Fighter, the KC-46A Pegasus refueling aircraft, and the Long Range Strike-Bomber.[30]

The Air Force's number one priority continues to be the F-35A. It is the next-generation fighter scheduled to replace all legacy multirole and close air support aircraft. The rationale for a program of record of 1,763 aircraft to replace the 1,303 legacy fighters currently in the Air Force inventory has never been fully justified.[31] This has led to speculation that, at least in part, it may be an attempt to offset the Defense Department's draconian reduction of the original plan to purchase an F-22A program of record of 750 aircraft[32] to a final program of record of just 187.[33] Even so, The Heritage Foundation's analysis finds a requirement for 1,260 total F-35As.[34]

The Active Air Force currently has just 106 F-15Cs left in its fleet, and concerns about what platform will fill this role when the F-15C is retired have now manifested into a significant gap. Even with their superior technology, 159 combat-coded F-22As from the active and guard inventory would be unable to fulfill the wartime requirement for air superiority fighters for even a single major regional contingency.[35] The F-35A's multirole design favors the air-to-ground mission, but its fifth-generation faculties will allow it also to be dominant in an air-to-air role,[36] enabling it to augment the F-22A in many scenarios.[37]

Fulfilling the operational need for air superiority fighters will be further strained in the near term because the F-22 retrofit—a mix of structural alterations to 162 aircraft needed for the airframe to reach its promised service life—has been forecasted to run through 2021. As a result of the retrofit, only 62 percent (99 of 169) of the mission fleet of F-22As are currently available.[38]

As with the other Joint Strike Fighter variants, the F-35A has experienced a host of developmental problems that have caused its initial operating capability (IOC) date to be pushed from 2013 to 2016. This system of systems relies heavily on software, and the currently fielded version (3I) delivers about 90 percent of the code required to deliver full warfighting capability. The "3F" version of the fighter's software that will enable full operating capability (FOC) will be fielded by the end of the third quarter of 2017, half a year later than planned.[39] Given the age of the aircraft that the F-35A will be replacing, every slip in the Lightning II's program will necessarily affect U.S. warfighting capability. Nevertheless, experienced fighter pilots now flying the jet have a great deal of confidence in their new fighter,[40] and this program appears to be gaining traction.

A second top priority for the USAF is the KC-46A air refueling tanker aircraft. Though the KC-46 has experienced a series of delays, it reached a milestone in August 2016 that enabled low-rate initial production.[41] The Air Force awarded the contract for 19 initial aircraft in August 2016 and has programmed delivery of 70 aircraft by FY 2020.[42] It expects to have all 179 of these new tankers in service by 2028. The Pegasus "will replace less than half of the current tanker fleet and will leave the Air Force with over 200 aging KC-135s awaiting recapitalization."[43]

The third major USAF priority from an acquisition perspective is the B-21 Raider, formerly called the Long-Range Strike Bomber. The USAF awarded Northrop Grumman the B-21 contract to build the Engineering and Manufacturing Development (EMD) phase, which includes associated training and support systems and initial production lots. The program completed an Integrated Baseline Review for the overall B-21 development effort, as well as a Preliminary Design Review. The Air Force is committed to a fleet size of 100 B-21s[44] at an average cost of $564 million per plane.[45]

The B-21 is programmed to begin replacing portions of the B-52 and B-1B fleets by the mid-2020s.[46] The Air Force has 62 B-1s in the inventory, 32 of which are undergoing an Integrated Battle Station upgrade that will provide enhanced situational awareness and precision engagement capabilities, and the entire fleet is undergoing a SLEP to restore all 289 B-1 engines to their original specifications. At least some of these bombers are programmed to remain in service through 2040.[47]

The Air Force also plans to modernize the B-2's Defense Management System, Stores Management Operational Flight Program, and Common Very-Low-Frequency/Low Frequency Receiver Program to ensure that this penetrating bomber remains viable in highly contested environments. These 20 stealth bombers will be in service for the foreseeable future.

Modernization efforts are also underway for the B-52. The jet entered service in the 1960s and will remain in the inventory through 2050.

The capacity of the Air Force's bomber fleet has fallen from 290 aircraft in 1991 to 156 B-1s, B-2s, and B-52s today. The current number is insufficient to meet Defense Planning Guidance and nuclear guidance while sustaining current operational demands and maintaining training and readiness capacity.[48]

The Air Force's strategy of capability over capacity is encumbered by the requirement to sustain ongoing combat operations in Afghanistan, Iraq, and Syria. In a budget-constrained environment, the need to sustain these ongoing efforts while modernizing an outdated fleet of aircraft for operations in contested environments means that funding has to be pulled from other areas, adversely affecting readiness.

Readiness

During testimony before the Senate Armed Services Committee in June 2017, the Secretary of the Air Force and the Air Force Chief of Staff warned that the USAF is at its "lowest state of full spectrum readiness in our history,"[49] and there is an abundance of ancillary evidence to support that statement.

Full-spectrum operations include the seamless conduct of nuclear deterrence operations, continued support of counterterrorist operations, and readiness for potential conflict with a near-peer competitor. During testimony before the House Armed Services Committee in July 2016, Major General Scott West, Director of Current Operations, Deputy Chief of Staff for Operations, stated that the Air Force was "able to conduct nuclear deterrence operations and support [counterterrorist] operations," but that operating "against a near-peer competitor would require a significant amount of training" because readiness is out of balance "at a time when the Air Force is small, old, and heavily tasked."[50]

The Air Force used five areas or "levers" of readiness to inform the FY 2018 budget request:

1. Flying Hour Program (FHP), which includes funding sortie production;

2. Critical Skills Availability (pilot/maintenance specialty level training);

3. Weapons System Sustainment (aircraft availability production);

TABLE 4

Air Force: Only Four of 36 Combat-Coded Fighter Squadrons Fully Mission Capable

SORTS Score	Resource/ Training Level	Mission Capability	Active Duty Units Meeting Capability Threshold
C1	90%–100%	Can execute **all** wartime missions	4 of 36
C2	70%–89%	Can execute **most** wartime missions	Less than 18 of 36
C3	55%–69%	Can execute **portions** of wartime missions	Up to 32 of 36
C4	0%–54%	**Needs more resources** before it can execute its mission	Up to 32 of 36

SOURCE: R. Derek Trunkey, "Implications of the Department of Defense Readiness Reporting System," Congressional Budget Office *Working Paper* No. 2013-03, May 2013, http://www.cbo.gov/sites/default/files/cbofiles/attachments/44127_DefenseReadiness.pdf (accessed April 11, 2017).

☎ heritage.org

---

4. Training Resource Availability (funding for ranges, live/virtual construct); and

5. Deploy to Dwell (funding for force capacity to meet current taskings).

Flying Hour Program and Critical Skills Availability. A shortage of aircraft maintenance personnel (maintainers) has limited the ability of the Air Force to generate sorties. The Air Force was short 3,400 aircraft maintainers at the close of 2016,[51] and this shortfall has reduced flying hours to the point where fighter pilots who once averaged over 200 hours per year were fortunate to fly 120 hours in 2014.[52] In 2015, the average rose to 150 hours through combat deployments to Iraq, Afghanistan, and Syria, but the air threat there is benign, the low-threat employment is relatively undemanding, and no high-threat training is allowed. When they return home, those same pilots have to rehone their primary mission skill sets, often averaging less than one sortie a week.[53]

During his confirmation hearing for the position of Chief of Staff of the Air Force, General David Goldfein stated that his service could not surge enough combat-ready forces to execute a single MRC and still meet the remaining demand for global combat-ready forces. He went on to say that less than 50 percent of combat units are ready for "full spectrum" high-threat, high-intensity combat.[54]

In testimony before the Senate Armed Services Committee on March 29, 2017, Lieutenant General Mark Nowland, Air Force Deputy Chief of Staff for Operations, told lawmakers that only four of the Air Force's 55 total (Active, Reserve, and National Guard) fighter squadrons are at the very highest levels of readiness. Fewer than half are in the top two readiness tiers.[55]

General Nowland's reference to levels of readiness is based on the formal Department of Defense grading system for readiness, known as the Status of Resources and Training System (SORTS). SORTS assesses personnel, supply, equipment, and training levels to make a comprehensive capability assessment of fighting units. A C1 designation is the highest level and is given to units that can fully carry out their wartime mission. C2 units can carry out "most" of their wartime missions, C3 units can carry out portions of their wartime missions, and C4 units need additional resources and/or training to execute their missions successfully. Organizations with a C1 or C2 score are the only ones that are considered to be combat-ready.[56]

When General Nowland said that only four squadrons are at the highest level of readiness, he presumably meant that those squadrons are C1. Taken in conjunction with the Chief of Staff's acknowledgement that less than 50 percent are ready for full-spectrum combat, this means that as many as 17 and as few as four fighter squadrons are ready to go to war with a near-peer competitor.

The current state of Air Force fighter readiness includes many intangibles, but the things that can be measured, such as average sortie per aircraft/month and total flying time, point to a readiness level not witnessed by the Air Force since the Carter Administration.

The flight hour program is limited by combat deployments and low sortie generation rates, but the Air Force has funded it to what it assesses to be the maximum executable level of 91 percent in the FY 2018 budget request.

Weapons System Sustainment. Near-constant deployments and a shortage of maintenance personnel have severely limited aircraft availability and sortie production. While maintenance manning shortfalls are expected to begin recovering during the coming year, it will take many years to develop the experience lost over the past five years. The shortage has driven and will continue to drive aircraft utilization rates (the number of times a jet is flown each month) well below those witnessed during the hollow force of the late 1970s.

Those numbers also affect retention of fighter pilots. Lieutenant General Gina M. Grosso, Air Force Deputy Chief of Staff for Manpower, Personnel, and Services, detailed this shortfall in testimony before a subcommittee of the House Armed Services Committee on March 29, 2017:

> At the end of FY 2016 the total force including active, reserve, and guard components was short 1,555 pilots across all mission areas (608 active, 653 guard, 294 reserve). Of this amount, the total force was short 1,211 fighter pilots (873 active, 272 guard, 66 reserve). Unfortunately, our greatest concern is [that] the active fighter pilot shortage is projected [to] exceed 1,000 by the end of FY 2017.[57]

Training Resource Availability. In order to prepare for full-spectrum combat in peacetime, pilots require the opportunity to engage regularly in high-end air-to-air and surface-to-air missile platforms and simulators. The two effective methods for giving aircrew the repetitions they need to sharpen these perishable skills are through live, large-force exercises over well-equipped ranges or through a live/virtual construct.

The three exercises/ranges that have the airspace and assets required for live high-threat training are the Red and Green Flag exercises at Nellis Air Force Base, Nevada, and Elmendorf Air Force Base, Alaska. The Air Force funded 16 of these large-force exercises in 2016 and 2017 and has budgeted for the same number in FY 2018.[58]

The live/virtual construct attempts to fill the gaps between deployments to Nellis and Elmendorf through networked simulators as well as plug-and-play simulations that feed a virtual scenario and the accompanying threats into the software/cockpit displays of fighters flying "local" missions out of their home airfields. While these systems show genuine progress, the number of opportunities offered does not offset the drought in sorties, nor are they considered replacements for actual flying time by the pilots themselves.[59] The FY 2018 budget requests a total increase of $1.5 billion to further each of these efforts.[60]

Deploy to Dwell. The last of the five Air Force levers or areas of readiness is the deploy-to-dwell ratio. The projected dwell time for active-duty personnel in the President's FY 2018 budget request is 1:2 dwell or better at home for 94 percent of the deployers; 96 percent of National Guard deployers achieve a 1:5 dwell or better, and Reservists average 97 percent. On paper, these look reasonably healthy, but several facts are not immediately evident from the numbers. The major deployments do not include shorter-term dispatch to schools, exercises, and other non-elective temporary duty (TDY) assignments. For some career specialties, personnel are in such high demand that they generally do not come close to the target dwell time.

One last consideration in assessing Air Force readiness is the availability of wartime readiness materials (WRM) like munitions. Funding limitations have not allowed restocking of all WRM accounts. Munitions are being used faster than they can be replaced, and air-to-surface weapons that offer stand-off, direct attack, and penetrators are short of current inventory objectives.[61] The concurrent shortage of air-to-air weapons could lead to an increase in the time needed to gain and maintain air superiority in future environments,[62] particularly highly contested ones.

The Air Force has rapidly been depleting its wartime inventory levels of precision-guided munitions. Over 50,000 missiles and bomb-related munitions have been used since August 2014,[63] significantly drawing down stockpiles, and the rate of expenditure has only grown with time. Absent sustained and increased funding, the ongoing depletion of our munition stockpiles will continue to reduce Air Force readiness and jeopardize America's ability to meet its national security objectives.[64]

Space. Although the classified nature of deployed space assets and their capabilities makes any assessment of this mission area challenging, the constellation of ISR, navigation, and communication satellites available to the United States is arguably unrivaled by that of any other nation-state. It is an array that allows the Air Force and its sister services to find, fix, and target virtually any terrestrial or sea-based threat anywhere, anytime.

Unfortunately, the United States' historically unchecked dominance in space has also facilitated an environment of overreliance on the domain and underappreciation of the vulnerabilities of its capabilities.[65] Some space assets represent nearly single-point failures in which a loss caused by a system failure or an attack could cripple a linchpin capability. Because of U.S. dominance of space and nearly complete reliance on space-based assets for everything from targeting to weapons guidance, other state actors have every incentive to target those assets.[66]

An adversary will capture and hold the initiative by leveraging surprise and every asymmetric advantage it possesses while denying those warfighting elements to its opponents. Since Operation Desert Storm, the world, including every one of America's near-peer competitors, has watched the United States employ satellite-enabled precision targeting to profound effect on the battlefield. That ability depends almost entirely on the kinetic end of the strike system: precision-guide munitions (PGMs).[67]

China and Russia are now investing heavily in ground-based anti-satellite (ASAT) missiles,[68] orbital ASAT programs that can deliver a kinetic blow,[69] or co-orbital robotic interference to alter signals, mask denial efforts, or even pull adversary satellites out of orbit.[70] If a near-peer competitor were able to degrade regional GPS signals or blind GPS receivers, it could neutralize the PGMs the U.S. relies on to conduct virtually every aspect of its kinetic strike capability.

As General Thomas Hyten, head of Air Force Space Command, has clearly indicated, the vulnerability of the U.S. space constellation lies in its design.[71] Every satellite we currently rely on costs millions of dollars and takes years to design, build, and launch into orbit. Until the Air Force shortens that time span or diversifies its ability to find, fix, and destroy targets precisely, space will remain a dominant but incredibly vulnerable domain for the U.S. Air Force.

Scoring the U.S. Air Force

Capacity Score: Marginal

One of the key elements of combat power in the U.S. Air Force is its fleet of fighter aircraft. In responding to major combat engagements since World War II, the Air Force has deployed an average of 28 fighter squadrons, based on an average of 18 aircraft per fighter squadron. That equates to a requirement of 500 Active component fighter aircraft to execute one MRC. Based on government force-sizing documents that count fighter aircraft, squadrons, or wings, an average of 55 squadrons (990 aircraft) is required to field a two-MRC–capable force (rounded up to 1,000 fighter aircraft to simplify the numbers). This *Index* looks for 1,200 active fighter aircraft to account for the 20 percent reserve necessary when considering availability for deployment and the risk of employing 100 percent of fighters at any one time.

- **Two-MRC Level:** 1,200 fighter aircraft.

- **Actual 2017 Level:** 915 fighter aircraft.

This number is 244 fighters below the *2017 Index* number of 1,159, which was based on total active-duty fighters minus Air Education and Training Command fighter numbers.[72] Several squadrons that should not have been included in the original total within Air Combat Command have been removed from the total.[73]

Based on a pure count of combat-coded fighter/attack platforms that have achieved IOC, the USAF currently is at 76 percent of the two-MRC benchmark, and even that low number should be taken with a few caveats. The F-35 will become a highly advanced and capable multirole platform, but the 123 aircraft that have entered the USAF inventory to date[74] are only IOC and do not yet field many of the capabilities that would constitute full-spectrum readiness.

The 915 figure yields a capacity level well within the methodology's range of "marginal," but aircraft require pilots to fly them and maintainers to launch, recover, and fix them. With a fighter pilot shortage approaching 1,000 and a maintenance shortfall of over 3,000 personnel, the ability of the Air Force to meet wartime manning requirements for fighter cockpits, as well as enough maintenance personnel to repair, refuel, and rearm aircraft in line with wartime sortie requirements, continues to wane. These factors, coupled with the lack of funding for a sufficient supply of spare parts, have reduced the capacity for employment from a *2017 Index*

assessment of "strong" to a *2018 Index* assessment of "marginal." As noted above, given personnel shortfalls, the Air Force capacity score is therefore trending toward "weak."

Capability Score: Marginal

The Air Force's capability score is "marginal," a result of being scored "strong" in "Size of Modernization Program," "marginal" for "Age of Equipment" and "Health of Modernization Programs," but "weak" for "Capability of Equipment." These scores have not changed from the *2017 Index*'s assessment. However, the F-35 program has begun to show signs of strength, and the Air Force has made progress toward effective replacement of legacy aircraft.

Readiness Score: Marginal

The Air Force scores "marginal" trending downward in readiness in the *2018 Index*, the same overall grade that it received in the *2017 Index*. This assessment is based primarily on 47 fighter pilot interviews, testimony of senior leaders, and follow-on analysis of the Air Force's ability to meet full-spectrum readiness requirements in 2017.[75] The Air Force should be prepared to respond quickly to an emergent crisis and retain full readiness of its combat airpower, but it has been suffering from degraded readiness since 2003, and implementation of BCA-imposed budget cuts in FY 2013 only exacerbated the problem. Similar to the other services, the Air Force was able to make up some of its readiness shortfalls under the FY 2016 budget, but given its poor readiness assessment, much more improvement is required.

The Air Force's current deficits in both pilot and maintainer manpower are also very troubling indicators for readiness. They will strain the service in the immediate term and, if not reversed, could lead to broader readiness challenges in the future.

Overall U.S. Air Force Score: Marginal

The Air Force is scored as "marginal" overall. This is an unweighted average of its capacity score of "marginal," capability score of "marginal," and readiness score of "marginal."

While the overall score remains the same as its score in the *2017 Index*, it has trended downward, largely because of a drop in the USAF's "capacity" score for a second consecutive year. The shortage of pilots and maintainers also continues to affect the ability of the Air Force to generate the amount of combat air power that would be needed to meet wartime requirements.

U.S. Military Power: Air Force

	VERY WEAK	WEAK	MARGINAL	STRONG	VERY STRONG
Capacity			✔		
Capability			✔		
Readiness			✔		
OVERALL			✔		

Endnotes

1. The Honorable Michael B. Donley, Secretary of the Air Force, and General Mark A. Welsh III, Chief of Staff, United States Air Force, "Fiscal Year 2014 Air Force Posture Statement" before the Committee on Armed Services, U.S. House of Representatives, April 12, 2013, p. 2, http://www.dtic.mil/dtic/tr/fulltext/u2/a584783.pdf (accessed August 26, 2016).

2. The Honorable Heather A. Wilson, Secretary of the Air Force, and General David L. Goldfein, Chief of Staff, United States Air Force, statement on "Air Force Budget Posture," before the Committee on Armed Services, U.S. Senate, June 6, 2017, p. 2, https://www.armed-services.senate.gov/hearings/17-06-06-posture-of-the-department-of-the-air-force (accessed July 29, 2017); Congressional Quarterly, "Senate Armed Services Committee Holds Hearing on Posture of the Department of the Air Force," CQ Congressional Transcripts, June 6, 2017, http://www.cq.com/doc/congressionaltranscripts-5116113?3 (accessed July 25, 2017).

3. General David Goldfein, U.S. Air Force, "Rebuilding Air Force Readiness," remarks at The Heritage Foundation, Washington, D.C., April 12, 2017, http://www.heritage.org/defense/event/rebuilding-air-force-readiness.

4. U.S. Department of Defense, Secretary of the Air Force, Office of Financial Management and Budget (SAF/FMB), *United States Air Force Fiscal Year 2018 Budget Overview*, May 2017, p. 15, http://www.saffm.hq.af.mil/LinkClick.aspx?fileticket=m3vZOmfR368%3d&portalid=84 (accessed August 6, 2017).

5. U.S. Department of Defense, Office of the Under Secretary (Comptroller)/Chief Financial Officer, *United States Department of Defense Fiscal Year 2018 Budget Request: Defense Budget Overview*, May 2017, p. 2-10, http://comptroller.defense.gov/Portals/45/Documents/defbudget/fy2018/fy2018_Budget_Request_Overview_Book.pdf (accessed July 29, 2017).

6. Ibid., p. 2-9.

7. The Honorable Deborah Lee James, Secretary of the Air Force, and General Mark A. Welsh III, USAF Chief of Staff, statement on "Fiscal Year 2016 Air Force Posture" before the Subcommittee on Defense, Committee on Appropriations, U.S. Senate, February 25, 2015, pp. 9, 12, and 19, http://www.appropriations.senate.gov/imo/media/doc/hearings/FY16%20Air%20Force%20Posture%20Statement%20(Final)%20022515.pdf (accessed July 29, 2017).

8. The Honorable Deborah Lee James, Secretary of the Air Force, and General Mark A. Welsh III, Chief of Staff of the Air Force, statement on "Air Force Posture" before the Committee on Armed Services, U.S. House of Representatives, March 16, 2016, pp. 7–8, http://docs.house.gov/meetings/AS/AS00/20160316/104662/HHRG-114-AS00-Bio-JamesD-20160316.pdf (accessed July 25, 2017).

9. Technological advances in aircraft materials and structure greatly extended the service life of USAF equipment. As a result, the USAF was able to sustain its force structure while procuring fewer aircraft. See Colonel James C. Ruehrmund Jr. and Christopher J. Bowie, *Arsenal of Airpower: USAF Aircraft Inventory 1950–2009*, Mitchell Institute for Airpower Studies, November 2010, p. 8, http://higherlogicdownload.s3.amazonaws.com/AFA/6379b747-7730-4f82-9b45-a1c80d6c8fdb/UploadedImages/Mitchell%20Publications/Arsenal%20of%20Airpower.pdf (accessed July 25, 2017).

10. U.S. Department of Defense, Secretary of the Air Force, Office of Financial Management and Budget (SAF/FMB), *United States Air Force Fiscal Year 2018 Budget Overview*, p. 15.

11. Wilson and Goldfein, statement on "Air Force Budget Posture," June 6, 2017, p. 2.

12. Combat-coded aircraft and related squadrons are aircraft and units assigned a wartime mission. For the purpose of assessing capacity and readiness, this *Index* refers to combat-coded aircraft and units maintained within the Active component of the U.S. Air Force. See Report No. 112–329, *National Defense Authorization Act for Fiscal Year 2012*, Conference Report to Accompany H.R. 1540, U.S. House of Representatives, 112th Cong, 1st Sess., December 12, 2011, p. 25, https://www.gpo.gov/fdsys/pkg/CRPT-112hrpt329/pdf/CRPT-112hrpt329-pt1.pdf (accessed August 6, 2017).

13. "The Air Force in Facts and Figures," U.S. Air Force Almanac 1996, *Air Force Magazine*, Vol. 79, No. 5 (May 1996), p. 59, http://www.airforcemag.com/MagazineArchive/Magazine%20Documents/1996/May%201996/0596facts_figures.pdf (accessed August 6, 2017). The Air Force uses a variety of categorizations to describe or refer to its inventory of aircraft and units. This can make assessing Air Force capacity a challenge.

14. Wilson and Goldfein, statement on "Air Force Budget Posture," June 6, 2017, p. 2.

15. International Institute for Strategic Studies, *The Military Balance 2017: The Annual Assessment of Global Military Capabilities and Defence Economics* (London: Routledge, 2017) pp. 53–54. The 32 combat-coded fighter squadrons are the active-duty F-22A, F-15C/D, F-15E, F-16C/D, A-10C, and F-35A squadrons listed for Air Combat Command, Pacific Air Forces, and United States Air Forces Europe.

16. William A. LaPlante, Assistant Secretary of the Air Force (Acquisition); Lieutenant General James M. "Mike" Holmes, Deputy Chief of Staff (Strategic Plans and Requirements); and Lieutenant General Tod D. Wolters, Deputy Chief of Staff (Operations), statement on "Fiscal Year 2016 Air Force, Force Structure and Modernization Programs" before the Subcommittee on Airland Forces, Committee on Armed Services, U.S. Senate, March 19, 2015, p. 8, http://www.armed-services.senate.gov/imo/media/doc/LaPlante_Holmes_Wolters_03-19-15.pdf (accessed August 6, 2017).

17. Ibid.

18. The numbers for total aircraft inventory (TAI) and combat-coded aircraft for the active-duty Air Force were derived through review of U.S. Department of Defense, Secretary of the Air Force, Office of Financial Management and Budget (SAF/FMB), *United States Air Force Fiscal Year 2018 Budget Overview*, and International Institute for Strategic Studies, *The Military Balance 2017: The Annual Assessment of Global Military Capabilities and Defence Economics* (London: Routledge, 2017), pp. 53–55. Where the two publications were in conflict with respect to TAI, the SAF/FMB numbers were adopted. Neither document specifies the number of active-duty combat-coded aircraft. That number was derived by tallying the total number of fighters by type and dividing that number by the total number of active-duty squadrons flying that type of aircraft. The number and type of aircraft associated with weapons squadrons, adversary tactics, test, operational test and evaluation, and other units are not standard/determinable and could not be accessed. The associated error is minimized by totaling all like fighter aircraft (F-16, F-15C, etc.), dividing them by the total number of squadrons flying that aircraft, and spreading the error equally across all combat-coded fighter and training units. Fighters associated with non-fighter training unit (FTU) squadrons were counted as combat-coded.

19. Wilson and Goldfein, statement on "Air Force Budget Posture," June 6, 2017, p. 2.

20. "The Air Force in Facts and Figures," U.S. Air Force Almanac 2016, *Air Force Magazine*, Vol. 99, No. 5 (May 2016), p. 37, http://secure.afa.org/joinafa/AFMag0516/files/downloads/attachments/0516fullissue.pdf (accessed August 7, 2017). Age posted is "as of September 30, 2015." Ten months were added because of the delay between publication of the Air Force Almanac and this *Index*.

21. Ibid.

22. Comparison made between U.S. Department of Defense, Secretary of the Air Force, Office of Financial Management and Budget (SAF/FMB), *United States Air Force Fiscal Year 2018 Budget Overview*, p. 46, and International Institute for Strategic Studies, *The Military Balance 2017*, pp. 53–55.

23. "The Air Force in Facts and Figures," May 2016, p. 37. Age posted is "as of September, 30 2015." Ten months were added because of the delay between publication of the Air Force Almanac and this *Index*.

24. Ibid.

25. Wilson and Goldfein, statement on "Air Force Budget Posture," June 6, 2017, p. 2.

26. Comparison made between U.S. Department of Defense, Secretary of the Air Force, Office of Financial Management and Budget (SAF/FMB), *United States Air Force Fiscal Year 2018 Budget Overview*, p. 46, and International Institute for Strategic Studies, *The Military Balance 2017*, pp. 53–55.

27. U.S. Department of Defense, Secretary of the Air Force, Office of Financial Management and Budget (SAF/FMB), *United States Air Force Fiscal Year 2018 Budget Overview*, p. 46.

28. Comparison made between U.S. Department of Defense, Secretary of the Air Force, Office of Financial Management and Budget (SAF/FMB), *United States Air Force Fiscal Year 2018 Budget Overview*, p. 46, and International Institute for Strategic Studies, *The Military Balance 2017*, pp. 53–55.

29. "The Air Force in Facts and Figures," May 2016, p. 37. Age posted is "as of September 30, 2015." Twenty-two months were added because of the delay between publication of the Air Force Almanac and this *Index*.

30. Wilson and Goldfein, statement on "Air Force Budget Posture," June 6, 2017, p. 13.

31. Colonel Michael W. Pietrucha, U.S. Air Force, "The Comanche and the Albatross: About Our Neck Was Hung," *Air & Space Power Journal*, May–June 2014, pp. 133–156, http://www.dtic.mil/docs/citations/ADA602171 (accessed July 26, 2017).

32. Jeremiah Gertler, "Air Force F-22 Fighter Program," Congressional Research Service *Report for Congress*, July 11, 2013, p. 7, https://www.fas.org/sgp/crs/weapons/RL31673.pdf (accessed July 26, 2017).

33. Jeremiah Gertler, "F-35 Joint Strike Fighter (JSF) Program," Congressional Research Service *Report for Members and Committees of Congress*, April 29, 2014, p. 2, http://fas.org/sgp/crs/weapons/RL30563.pdf (accessed July 26, 2017).

34. Thomas W. Spoehr and Rachel Zissimos, eds., "Preventing a Defense Crisis: The 2018 National Defense Authorization Act *Must* Begin to Restore U.S. Military Strength," Heritage Foundation *Backgrounder* No. 3205, March 29, 2017, p. 8, http://www.heritage.org/sites/default/files/2017-03/BG3205.pdf.

35. Gertler, "Air Force F-22 Fighter Program," p. 7.

36. John Venable, "Independent Capability Assessment of the U.S Air Force Reveals Readiness Level Below Carter Administration Hollow Force," Heritage Foundation *Backgrounder* No. 3208, April 17, 2017, p. 2, http://www.heritage.org/sites/default/files/2017-04/BG3208.pdf (accessed August 8, 2017).

37. Dave Majumdar, "Can the F-35 Win a Dogfight?" War Is Boring, December 17, 2013, p. 1, https://warisboring.com/can-the-f-35-win-a-dogfight-95462ccd6745#.5pvpajaos (accessed July 26, 2017).

38.	James Drew, "F-22 Raptor Retrofit to Take Longer, but Availability Hits 63%," FlightGlobal, July 6, 2015, http://www.flightglobal.com/news/articles/f-22-raptor-retrofit-to-take-longer-and-availability-hits-414341/ (accessed August 6, 2017).

39.	Kris Osborn, "Air Force: F-35 3F Software Drop Challenges Resolved," *Defense Systems*, May 17, 2017, https://defensesystems.com/articles/2017/05/17/f35.aspx (accessed July 26, 2017); Lara Seligman, "F-35 Full Combat Capability Will Be Four Months Late," *Defense News*, March 23, 2016, http://www.defensenews.com/story/defense/air-space/2016/03/23/f-35-full-combat-capability-four-months-late/82187648/ (accessed August 6, 2017).

40.	John Venable, "Operational Assessment of the F-35A Argues for Full Program Procurement and Concurrent Development Process," Heritage Foundation *Backgrounder* No. 3140, August 4, 2016, pp. 8 and 10, http://www.heritage.org/defense/report/operational-assessment-the-f-35a-argues-full-program-procurement-and-concurrent (accessed August 7, 2017).

41.	Aaron Mehta, "KC-46 Tanker Cleared for Production," *Defense News*, August 12, 2016, http://www.defensenews.com/training-sim/2016/08/12/kc-46-tanker-cleared-for-production/ (accessed July 26, 2017).

42.	Colin Clark, "Boeing Wins $2.8B for KC-4 Tanker Low Rate Production," *Breaking Defense*, August, 18, 2016, http://breakingdefense.com/2016/08/boeing-wins-2-5b-for-kc-46-tanker-low-rate-production/ (accessed July 26, 2017); U.S. Department of Defense, Office of the Under Secretary of Defense (Comptroller)/Chief Financial Officer, *United States Department of Defense Fiscal Year 2016 Budget Request: Overview*, February 2015, p. 8-17, http://comptroller.defense.gov/Portals/45/Documents/defbudget/fy2016/FY2016_Budget_Request_Overview_Book.pdf (accessed August 6, 2017).

43..	Lieutenant General Arnold W. Bunch, Jr., Military Deputy, Office of the Assistant Secretary of the Air Force (Acquisition); Lieutenant General Jerry D. Harris, Deputy Chief of Staff (Strategic Plans and Requirements); and Major General Scott A. Vander Hamm, Assistant Deputy Chief of Staff (Operations), statement on "Air Force Bomber/Tanker/Airlift Acquisition Programs" before the Subcommittee on Seapower and Projection Forces, Committee on Armed Services, U.S. House of Representatives, May 25, 2017, p. 10, http://docs.house.gov/meetings/AS/AS28/20170525/106013/HHRG-115-AS28-Wstate-BunchA-20170525.pdf (accessed August 6, 2017).

44.	Ibid.

45.	Lieutenant General James M. "Mike" Holmes, USAF Deputy Chief of Staff (Strategic Plans and Requirements), and Lieutenant General Arnold W. Bunch, Jr., USAF, Military Deputy, Office of the Assistant Secretary of the Air Force (Acquisition), "Subject: Hearing on Air Force Bomber/Tanker/Airlift Acquisition Programs–HASC Seapower and Projection Forces," statement before the Subcommittee on Seapower and Projection Forces, Committee on Armed Services, U.S. House of Representatives, March 1, 2016, p. 4, http://docs.house.gov/meetings/AS/AS28/20160301/104353/HHRG-114-AS28-Wstate-BunchA-20160301.pdf (accessed August 26, 2016).

46.	Ibid., p. 4.

47.	Ibid., p. 5.

48.	Lieutenant General Jerry "JD" Harris, Jr., Deputy Chief of Staff (Strategic, Plans, Programs and Requirements); Lieutenant General Arnold W. Bunch, Jr., Military Deputy, Office of the Assistant Secretary of the Air Force (Acquisition); and Lieutenant General Mark C. Nowland, Deputy Chief of Staff (Operations), statement on "Air Force, Force Structure and Modernization Programs" before the Subcommittee on Airland Forces, Committee on Armed Services, U.S. Senate, March 29, 2017, https://www.armed-services.senate.gov/imo/media/doc/Harris-Bunch-Nowland_03-29-17.pdf (accessed August 6, 2017).

49.	Wilson and Goldfein, statement on "Air Force Budget Posture," June 6, 2017, p. 3.

50.	Major General Scott West, Director of Current Operations, Deputy Chief of Staff for Operations, Headquarters, U.S. Air Force, statement on "Military Aviation Readiness and Safety" before the Subcommittee on Readiness, Committee on Armed Services, U.S. House of Representatives, July 6, 2016, http://docs.house.gov/meetings/AS/AS03/20160706/105159/HHRG-114-AS03-Wstate-WestS-20160706.pdf (accessed August 6, 2017).

51.	2016 maintainer shortage statistic provided by Headquarters Air Force Deputy Chief of Staff for Logistics, Engineering, and Force Protection (HAF A4) on April 13, 2017.

52.	Julian E. Barnes, "Warning Sounded on Cuts to Pilot Training," *The Wall Street Journal*, December 19, 2013, http://www.wsj.com/articles/SB10001424052702304773104579268651994849572 (accessed July 26, 2017).

53.	Scott Maucione, "Air Force Puts a Number on Maintenance Staffing Deficit," Federal News Radio, June 16, 2016, http://federalnewsradio.com/defense/2016/06/air-force-puts-number-maintainence-staffing-deficit/ (accessed July 26, 2017).

54.	*Hearing to Consider the Nomination of General David L. Goldfein, USAF, for Reappointment to the Grade of General and to Be Chief of Staff, United States Air Force*, Committee on Armed Services, U.S. Senate, June 16, 2016, "Advance Policy Questions," pp. 7–8, http://www.armed-services.senate.gov/hearings/16-06-16-nomination_-goldfein (accessed August 30, 2016).

55. Courtney Albon, "Air Force: 1,900 Fighter Jets Is Low-end Requirement; Service Likely Needs About 2,100," Inside Defense, March 30, 2017, https://insidedefense.com/daily-news/air-force-1900-fighter-jets-low-end-requirement-service-likely-needs-about-2100 (accessed August 6, 2017).

56. R. Derek Trunkey, "Implications of the Department of Defense Readiness Reporting System," Congressional Budget Office *Working Paper* 2013-03, May 2013, pp. 5 and 11, https://www.cbo.gov/sites/default/files/113th-congress-2013-2014/workingpaper/44127_DefenseReadiness_1.pdf (accessed August 6, 2017).

57. Lieutenant General Gina M. Grosso, Deputy Chief of Staff Manpower, Personnel and Services, U.S. Air Force, statement on "Military Pilot Shortage" before the Subcommittee on Readiness, Committee on Armed Services, U.S. House of Representatives, March 29, 2017, p. 2, http://docs.house.gov/meetings/AS/AS02/20170329/105795/HHRG-115-AS02-Wstate-GrossoG-20170329.pdf, (accessed July 26, 2017).

58. U.S. Department of Defense, Office of the Under Secretary (Comptroller)/Chief Financial Officer, *United States Department of Defense Fiscal Year 2018 Budget Request: Defense Budget Overview*, p. 2-11.

59. Venable, "Independent Capability Assessment of the U.S. Air Force Reveals Readiness Level Below Carter Administration Hollow Force," p. 4.

60. U.S. Department of Defense, Office of the Under Secretary (Comptroller)/Chief Financial Officer, *United States Department of Defense Fiscal Year 2018 Budget Request: Defense Budget Overview*, p. 2-11.

61. LaPlante, Holmes, and Wolters, statement on "Fiscal Year 2016 Air Force, Force Structure and Modernization Programs," p. 16.

62. Ibid., p. 17.

63. U.S. Department of Defense, Secretary of the Air Force, Office of Financial Management and Budget (SAF/FMB), *United States Air Force Fiscal Year 2018 Budget Overview*, p. 4.

64. Bunch, Harris, and Vander Hamm, statement on "Air Force Bomber/Tanker/Airlift Acquisition Programs," p. 14.

65. U.S. Air Force Space Command, "Hyten Announces Space Enterprise Vision," April 13, 2016, http://www.af.mil/News/Article-Display/Article/719941/hyten-announces-space-enterprise-vision/ (accessed August 6, 2017).

66. Colin Clark, "Space Command Readies for War with 'Space Enterprise Vision,'" *Breaking Defense*, June 20, 2016, http://breakingdefense.com/2016/06/space-command-readies-for-war-with-space-enterprise-vision/ (accessed July 26, 2017).

67. Venable, "Independent Capability Assessment of the U.S. Air Force Reveals Readiness Level Below Carter Administration Hollow Force," p. 10.

68. Bill Gertz, "China Tests Anti-Satellite Missile," *The Washington Free Beacon*, November 9, 2015, http://freebeacon.com/national-security/china-tests-anti-satellite-missile/ (accessed July 26, 2017).

69. Weston Williams, "Russia Launches Anti-Satellite Weapon: A New Warfront in Space?" *The Christian Science Monitor*, December 22, 2016, http://www.csmonitor.com/USA/Military/2016/1222/Russia-launches-anti-satellite-weapon-A-new-warfront-in-space (accessed April 11, 2017).

70. Brid-Aine Parnell, "MYSTERY Russian Satellite: ORBITAL WEAPON? Sat GOBBLER? What?" *The Register*, November 18, 2014, http://www.theregister.co.uk/2014/11/18/russia_secret_satellite_kosmos_2499/ (accessed August 6, 2017).

71. U.S. Air Force Space Command, "Hyten Announces Space Enterprise Vision."

72. International Institute for Strategic Studies, *The Military Balance 2016: The Annual Assessment of Global Military Capabilities and Defence Economics* (London: Routledge, 2016), pp. 46–48.

73. See note 18, *supra*. This number represents total Active component, combat-coded fighters. This *Index* considers requirements such as aircraft that are needed to perform Operation Noble Eagle (ONE), an ongoing mission to defend American airspace. Details regarding ONE are limited and largely unavailable to the public. Because the exact number of Active component fighter aircraft participating in ONE is unknown, fighters that may be tasked with the ONE mission are not counted in this total.

74. U.S. Department of Defense, Secretary of the Air Force, Office of Financial Management and Budget (SAF/FMB), *United States Air Force Fiscal Year 2018 Budget Overview*, p. 46.

75. Venable, "Independent Capability Assessment of the U.S. Air Force Reveals Readiness Level Below Carter Administration Hollow Force."

U.S. Marine Corps

The U.S. Marine Corps (USMC) is the nation's expeditionary armed force, positioned and ready to respond to crises around the world. Marine units assigned aboard ships ("soldiers of the sea") or at bases abroad stand ready to project U.S. power into crisis areas. Marines also serve in a range of unique missions, from combat defense of U.S. embassies under attack abroad to operating the President's helicopter fleet.

Although Marines have a wide variety of individual assignments, the focus of every Marine is on combat: Every Marine is first a rifleman. The USMC has positioned itself for crisis response and has evolved its concepts to leverage its equipment more effectively to support operations in a heavily contested maritime environment such as the one found in the Western Pacific. Today, "there are over 34,000 Marines deployed around the globe to assure our allies and partners, to deter our adversaries, and to respond when our…citizens and interests are threatened."[1] In 2016, despite the drawdown of forces, "the Marine Corps executed over 210 operations, 20 amphibious operations, [and] 160 Theater Security Cooperation (TSC) events, and participated in 75 exercises" in addition to providing embassy security and short-term reinforcement of posts.[2]

Pursuant to the Defense Strategic Guidance (DSG), maintaining the Corps' crisis response capability is critical. Thus, given the fiscal constraints imposed, the Marines have prioritized "near-term readiness" at the expense of other areas, such as capacity, capability, modernization, home station readiness, and infrastructure.[3] This trade-off is a short-term fix to meet immediate needs: Over the longer term, the degradation of investment in equipment will lead to lowered readiness.

Capacity

The Marine Corps has continuously prioritized readiness through managed reductions in capacity, including a drawdown of forces, and delays or reductions in planned procurement. Its measures of capacity are similar to the Army's: end strength and units (battalions for the Marines and brigades for the Army). In February 2015, Marine Corps Commandant General Joseph Dunford testified that:

> Today, the Marine Corps continues to execute its end-strength reductions that began during FY12, reducing the Corps from a high of 202,000. The Marine Corps is adjusting its active duty end-strength to 182,000 Marines by 2017, emphasizing the enduring requirement to provide crisis response forces that meet today's demand. We can meet the DSG at this level, but with less than optimal time between deployments to train and allow Marines to be with their families.[4]

The Department of Defense (DOD) FY 2018 *Defense Budget Overview* reflects a slightly higher projected "Active Component End Strength" of 184,400 in 2017, a slight increase over previously projected levels due to President Trump's request for supplemental funding in FY 2017. President Trump's FY 2018 budget request would reverse planned drawdowns and support an end strength of 185,000 active personnel in FY 2018.[5]

The Marine Corps' basic combat unit is the infantry battalion. A battalion has about 900 Marines and includes three rifle companies, a weapons company, and a headquarters and service company. FY 2017 appropriations supported 24 infantry battalions,[6] an increase from 2016 levels but still down from 27 in FY 2012.[7] Although the President's FY 2018 budget request retains support for 24 battalions, under full sequestration, USMC end strength would be able to support only 21 infantry battalions,[8] which, according to General Dunford, would leave the Corps "with fewer active duty battalions and squadrons than would be required for a single major contingency."[9]

Additionally, the current population of noncommissioned officers and staff noncommissioned officers does not meet USMC force structure requirements. This will pose readiness challenges for the Corps as the shortage of "small unit leaders with the right grade, experience, technical skills and leadership qualifications" grows.[10]

In 2010, the USMC determined that its ideal force size would be 186,800 in light of the requirements of the President's National Security Strategy at that time.[11] However, given the budget pressures from the Budget Control Act (BCA) of 2011 and the newer 2012 DSG, the Corps determined that a force of "182,100 active component Marines could still be afforded with reduced modernization and infrastructure support."[12]

One impact of reduced capacity is a strain on Marines' dwell time. The stated ideal deployment-to-dwell (D2D) time ratio is 1:3 (seven months deployed for every 21 months at home), which, given current demands, can be achieved with 186,000 troops.[13] A force of 182,000, without a corresponding decrease in operational demand, would result in a lower D2D ratio of 1:2, which translates to roughly seven-month deployments separated by stretches of 14 months at home.[14]

Under current budget constraints, "Marine Corps operating forces are currently averaging less than a one-to-two deployment-to-dwell ratio."[15] A return to BCA-level budget caps in FY 2018 could reduce capacity even further, and the dwell ratio for the Marine Corps could fall to 1:1.[16] This increase in deployment frequency would exacerbate the degradation of readiness, because people and equipment would be used more frequently with less time to recover between deployments. The same problems are present across the Marine Corps' major weapons platforms, including its aviation and amphibious assets.

Marine aviation units have been particularly stressed by insufficient funding. Although operational requirements have not decreased, fewer Marine aircraft are available for tasking or training. For example, according to the Marine Corps' *2017 Marine Aviation Plan*, the USMC currently fields 19 tactical fighter squadrons,[17] compared to 20 in 2016 and around 28 during Desert Storm.[18] This change reflects the retirement of one AV-8B squadron.[19] However, this does not adequately capture the capacity challenges the Marine Corps faces, as the service has decreased the number of aircraft per squadron in order to compensate for shortages in the number of aircraft available, whether because of maintenance or procurement delays.[20] Although supplemental appropriations in 2017 provided some relief from BCA caps, the capacity challenges facing the Marine Corps will be fixed only by stable and predictable increases in the funding of both procurement and maintenance accounts.

The number of available aircraft continues to decline as procurement of the F-35B and MV-22 struggles to keep pace with the decommissioning of aging aircraft squadrons, high operational tempos, and maintenance backlogs that have limited the number of Ready Basic Aircraft (RBA) for training and operational requirements.[21] According to the *2017 Marine Aviation Plan*, the transition to the Osprey is 75 percent complete, and it is expected that the active component transition will be completed in FY 2019. However, the procurement objective could increase to 380 aircraft pending the results of an ongoing requirements-based analysis.[22]

In 2016, "shortages in aircraft availability due to increased wear on aging aircraft and modernization delays" led the Marine Corps to reduce the requirement of aircraft per squadron for the F/A-18, CH-53E, and AV-8B temporarily in order to provide additional aircraft for home station training.[23] Approximately 80 percent of Marine Corps aviation units are still experiencing shortages below the minimum number of RBA needed to account for training and wartime requirements.[24] Any reduction in Marine aviation capability has a direct effect on overall combat capability, as the Corps usually fights with its ground and aviation forces integrated as Marine Air-Ground Task Forces (MAGTFs).

Additionally, due to a chronic shortfall in the Navy's requirement for 38 amphibious ships, the USMC has relied heavily on land-based Special Purpose Marine Air-Ground Task Forces (SPMAGTFs). While SPMAGTFs have enabled the Marine Corps to meet joint force requirements, land-based locations "lack the full capability, capacity and strategic and operational agility that results when Marine Air-Ground Task Forces (MAGTFs) are embarked aboard Navy amphibious ships."[25]

The USMC continues to invest in the recapitalization of legacy platforms in order to extend platform service life and keep aircraft and amphibious vehicles in the fleet, but as these platforms age, they also become less relevant to the evolving modern operating environment. Thus, while helping to maintain capacity, programs to extend service life do not provide the capability enhancements of modernization programs and ultimately result in higher costs to maintain an older, less-capable fleet of equipment.

Capability

The nature of the Marine Corps' crisis response role requires capabilities that span all domains. The USMC ship requirement is managed by the Navy and is covered in the Navy's section of the Index. The Marine Corps is focusing on "essential modernization" and emphasizing programs that "underpin our core competencies," making the Amphibious Combat Vehicle (ACV) and the F-35 Joint Strike Fighter (JSF) programs its top two priorities.[26]

Of the Marine Corps' current fleet of vehicles, its amphibious vehicles—specifically, the Assault Amphibious Vehicle (AAV-7A1) and Light Armored Vehicle (LAV)—are the oldest, with the AAV-7A1 averaging over 40 years old and the LAV averaging 26 years old.[27] The AAV-7A1 is currently undergoing survivability upgrades, with the first round of upgrades (AAV SU) delivered to U.S. Marine Corps Base Quantico in 2016.[28] These upgrades will help to bridge the capability gap until the fielding of the ACV and keep the AAV SU in service until 2035.[29] In the meantime, the Marine Corps will "continue to spend limited fiscal resources to sustain legacy systems as a result of deferred modernization, [and] risk steadily losing our capability advantage against potential adversaries."[30] There is still no planned replacement for the LAV. Comparatively, the Corps' M1A1 Abrams inventory is 27 years old with an estimated 33-year life span,[31] while the newest HMMWV variant has already consumed half of a projected 15-year service life.[32]

All of the Corps' main combat vehicles entered service in the 1970s and 1980s, and while service life extensions, upgrades, and new generations of designs have allowed the platforms to remain in service, these vehicles are quickly becoming poorly suited to the changing threat environment. For example, with the advent of improvised explosive devices (IEDs), the flat-bottom hulls found on most legacy vehicles are ineffective compared to the more blast-resistant V-shaped hulls incorporated in modern designs.

The age profiles of the Corps' aircraft are similar to those of the Navy's. As of 2017, the USMC had 273 F/A-18 A–Ds (including one reserve squadron) and 18 EA-6Bs in its primary mission aircraft inventory,[33] and both aircraft have already surpassed their originally intended life spans. The Marine Corps began to retire its EA-6B squadrons in FY 2016 with the decommissioning of Marine Tactical Electronic Warfare Squadron 1 and has stayed on track in decommissioning one per year through FY 2019.[34] Unlike the Navy, the Corps did not acquire the newer F/A-18 E/F Super Hornets; thus, the older F/A-18 Hornets are going through a service life extension program to extend their life span to 10,000 flight hours from the original 6,000 hours.[35] This was intended to bridge the gap to when the F-35Bs and F-35Cs enter service to replace the Harriers and most of the Hornets. However, delays in the service life extension program and "increased wear on aging aircraft" have further limited availability of the F/A-18 A-D and AV-8B.[36]

The AV-8B Harrier, designed to take off from the LHA and LHD amphibious assault ships, will be retired from Marine Corps service by 2026.[37] The AV-8B received near-term capability upgrades in 2015, which continued in 2017 in order to maintain its lethality and interoperability until the F-35 transition is complete.[38] The Corps declared its first F-35B squadron operationally capable on July 31, 2015, after it passed an "Operational Readiness Inspection" test.[39] To date, three F-35B squadrons have been delivered to the Marine Corps, including two operational squadrons and one fleet replacement squadron, totaling 52 aircraft.[40]

The Marine Corps has two Major Defense Acquisition (MDAP) vehicle programs: the Joint Light Tactical Vehicle (JLTV) and Amphibious Combat Vehicle (ACV).[41] The JLTV is a joint program with the Army to acquire a more survivable light tactical vehicle to replace a percentage of the older HMMWV fleet, originally introduced in 1985. The Army retains overall responsibility for JLTV development through its Joint Program Office.[42]

Following FY 2015 plans for the JLTV, the program awarded a low-rate initial production (LRIP) contract, which includes a future option of producing JLTVs for the Marine Corps, to defense contractor Oshkosh.[43] Congressional testimony indicates that if its budget permits it to do so, the USMC may be interested in procuring a larger quantity in the long term than originally intended. Despite a delay in the program's full-rate production decision and

reduced procurement quantities in FY 2016 and FY 2017, the Corps still expects to complete its initial acquisition objective of 5,500 by FY 2023.[44] Reductions in annual procurement quantities reflect prioritization of the ACV within the USMC's ground force.[45]

The President's budget request for FY 2018 would fund the final year of low-rate initial production for the JLTV, including 527 vehicles for the Marine Corps and limited procurement quantities for the Air Force.[46] Although the Marine Corps has indicated that the JLTV will not be a one-for-one replacement of the HMMWV, there are concerns that reduced procurement will create a battlefield mobility gap for some units.[47] Program officials have reportedly discussed increasing the acquisition objective to 9,091 for the Marine Corps.[48] While this will still only partially offset the inventory of 17,000 HMMWVs,[49] the service is considering what percent of the fleet should be replaced by the JLTV and what percent of the requirement might be filled by lighter wheeled vehicles.[50]

The Corps has procured 317 JLTVs through FY 2017.[51] The lack of operational detail in the Army's Tactical Wheeled Vehicle Strategy could affect future USMC JLTV procurement and modernization plans.[52] The USMC expected the program to reach initial operational capability (IOC) in the fourth quarter of 2018, but IOC has been delayed because of Lockheed Martin's bid protest following the award of a low-rate initial production decision to Oshkosh.[53]

The Marine Corps plans to replace the AAV-7A1 with the ACV, which completed its Milestone B requirements in November 2015 and will move into low-rate initial production in FY 2018.[54] The ACV, which took the place of the Expeditionary Fighting Vehicle (EFV), "has been structured to provide a phased, incremental capability."[55] The AAV-7A1 was to be replaced by the EFV, a follow-on to the cancelled Advanced AAV, but the EFV was also cancelled in 2011 due to technical obstacles and cost overruns. Similarly, the Corps planned to replace the LAV inventory with

FIGURE 8

American Tank Loses Traction in Modernization

When it was first introduced in 1980, the M1A1 Abrams arguably became the world's most formidable battle tank. However, since then several nations have introduced new or upgraded tanks, including Russia and China.

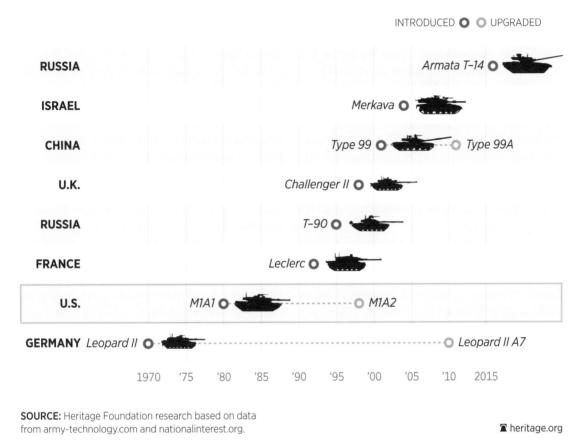

INTRODUCED ○ ○ UPGRADED

RUSSIA — Armata T-14 ○

ISRAEL — Merkava ○

CHINA — Type 99 ○ ----○ Type 99A

U.K. — Challenger II ○

RUSSIA — T-90 ○

FRANCE — Leclerc ○

U.S. — M1A1 ○ ----○ M1A2

GERMANY Leopard II ○ -------------○ Leopard II A7

1970   '75   '80   '85   '90   '95   '00   '05   '10   2015

SOURCE: Heritage Foundation research based on data from army-technology.com and nationalinterest.org.

🔔 heritage.org

---

the Marine Personnel Carrier (MPC), which would serve as a Light Armored Vehicle with modest amphibious capabilities but would be designed primarily to provide enhanced survivability and mobility once ashore.[56] However, budgetary constraints led the Corps to shelve the program, leaving open the possibility that it might be resumed in the future.

After restructuring its ground modernization portfolio, the Marine Corps determined that it would combine its efforts by upgrading 392 of its legacy AAVs and continuing development of the ACV to replace part of the existing fleet and complement the upgraded AAVs.[57] This would help the Corps to meet its

requirement of armored lift for 10 battalions of infantry.[58] As of March 2015, the USMC's acquisition objective for the ACV 1.1 was 204 vehicles for the first increment.[59] However, ACV program officials have since informed the U.S. Government Accountability Office "that only 180 AAVs would be replaced by the incoming 204 ACV 1.1s."[60] Brigadier General Joseph Shrader confirmed that this ACV 1.1 increment would not entirely replace the AAV, but rather would serve to "enhance that capability."[61]

The ACV 1.1 platform is notable in that it will be an amphibious wheeled vehicle instead of a tracked vehicle, capable of traversing open water only with the assistance of Navy shore connectors such as Landing Craft, Air Cushion Vehicles (LCAC). The ACV 1.2 platform is being planned as a fully amphibious, tracked version.[62] Development and procurement of the ACV program will be phased so that the new platforms can be fielded incrementally alongside a number of modernized AAVs.[63] Plans call for a program of record of 694 vehicles (a combination of upgraded AAVs and ACVs), with the first battalion to reach IOC in FY 2020, and for modernizing enough of the current AAV fleet to outfit six additional battalions, two in the first increment and four in the second. The AAV survivability upgrade program will modernize the remaining four battalions, allowing the Corps to meet its armored lift requirement for 10 battalions.[64] In addition, the Corps will purchase new vehicles based on the MPC concept.

The F-35B remains the Marine Corps' largest investment program in FY 2017. The Corps announced IOC of the F-35B variant in July 2015.[65] Total procurement will consist of 420 F-35s (353 F-35Bs and 67 F-35Cs). The slight change in the balance of short take-off and vertical landing vehicle and carrier variants from FY 2016 to FY 2017 reportedly reflects "evolving circumstances" and operational requirements within the service. The AV-8Bs and F/A-18A-Ds will continue to receive interoperability and lethality enhancements in order to extend their useful service lives during the transition to the F-35, and the Corps continues to seek opportunities to accelerate procurement.[66]

As the F-35 enters into service and legacy platforms reach the end of their service life, the Marine Corps expects a near-term inventory challenge due to a combination of reduced JSF procurement, increasing tactical aircraft utilization rates, and shortfalls in F/A-18A-D and AV-8B depot facility production.[67] In March 2016, Marine Corps Commandant General Robert Neller assessed that "[i]f these squadrons [in the F/A-18 community] were called on to fight today they would be forced to execute with 86 less jets than they need."[68] Like the F-35A, the F-35B and F-35C variants are subject to development delays, cost overruns, budget cuts, and production problems. The F-35B in particular was placed on probation in 2011 because of its technical challenges.[69] Probation has since been lifted, and the Corps declared IOC with its first F-35B squadron, VMFA-121, on July 31, 2015.[70]

Today, the USMC MV-22 program is operating with few problems and nearing completion of the full acquisition objective of 360 aircraft.[71] As of June 2017, the Corps had received 293 of the 360 aircraft included in the program of record.[72] Currently, there are 14 fully operational capability squadrons in the active component to meet these needs, and two additional squadrons are transitioning from the reserve component.[73] The MV-22's capabilities are in high demand from the Combatant Commanders (COCOMS), and the Corps is adding capabilities such as fuel delivery and use of precision-guided munitions to the MV-22 to enhance its value to the COCOMs. The Corps is struggling to sustain the Osprey's capability rates because of a shortfall in its "ability to train enlisted maintainers in the numbers and with the qualifications necessary to sustain the high demand signal."[74]

The USMC's heavy-lift replacement program, the CH-53K, conducted its first flight on October 27, 2015.[75] The CH-53K will replace the Corps' CH-53E, which entered service in 1980. Although "unexpected redesigns to critical components" delayed a low-rate initial production decision,[76] the program achieved Milestone C in April 2017, and the FY 2018 President's budget request authorizes $756.4 million for the production of Lot 2 aircraft, "including Advanced Procurement and initial spares."[77] The helicopter is predicted to reach IOC in 2019, almost four years later than initially anticipated.[78] This is of increasing concern as the Marine Corps maintains only 146 CH-53Es.[79] Although the Corps began a reset of the CH-53E in 2016 to bridge the procurement gap, it will not have enough helicopters to meet its heavy-lift requirement without the transition to the CH-53K.[80] The FY 2018 request would continue to fund procurement totals of 194 aircraft.[81]

Readiness

The Marine Corps' first priority is to be the crisis response force for the military, which is why investment in readiness has been prioritized over capacity and capability. However, in order to invest in readiness in a time of downward fiscal pressure, the Corps has been forced to reduce end strength and delay investment in modernization.

Even though funding for near-term readiness has been relatively protected from cuts, future readiness is threatened by underinvestment in long-term modernization and infrastructure. As General Dunford has explained, extended or long-term imbalance among the USMC "pillars" of readiness, which address both operational and foundational readiness, "will hollow the force and create unacceptable risk for our national defense."[82]

Already, modernization delays have begun to affect readiness as it becomes increasingly challenging to keep aging platforms in working order, and aircraft are retired before they can be replaced—leaving a smaller force available to meet operational requirements that in turn further increases use of the platforms that remain. According to a 2017 joint statement before the Senate Armed Services Committee, "Marine Corps operating forces are currently averaging, in the aggregate, less than 1:2 deployment-to-dwell ratio," and "[i]ndividual unit deployment tempo remains on par with the height of our commitments in Iraq and Afghanistan.[83]

The DOD has prioritized funding for deployed and next-to-deploy units. As a result, the USMC has maintained support for current operations but "may not have the required capacity—the 'ready bench'—to respond to larger crises at the readiness levels and timeliness required" or to support sustained conflict.[84]

Marine aviation in particular is experiencing significant readiness shortfalls. With a smaller force structure and fewer aircraft available for training, aviation units are having difficulty keeping up with demanding operational requirements. All of the Marine Corps' fixed-wing and tiltrotor aircraft are operating in excess of a 1:2 D2D ratio; this stress is increased by reduced procurement and workforce cuts, which contribute to readiness problems and leave fewer aircraft available for training or operations.[85] More than 92 percent of the Department of the Navy's F/A 18 A-D fleet has already surpassed the aircraft's service life expectancy of 6,000 flight hours, and "a portion of the [USMC's] existing inventory...will be flown through the mid-2030 timeframe."[86]

As of December 31, 2016, only 41 percent of the Marine Corps' fixed-wing and rotary-wing aircraft were considered flyable. Readiness rates among the Hornet fleet are even more severe, with just over a quarter of the Corps' 280 aircraft considered flyable. As a result, the Corps is 150 airplanes short of the necessary requirement to meet its flight hour goals.[87] The combination of aging aircraft and flight hour reductions can raise the risk of flight accidents attributed to both human and mechanical error. However, according to a February 2017 statement by Lieutenant General Jon Davis, Deputy Commandant for Aviation, average flight hours for the Marine Corps is "about three hours per pilot per month better than we were" in May 2015.[88]

For FY 2018, the Department of the Navy continues to prioritize immediate readiness by accepting "risk in facilities [and] weapons capacity," "delay[ing] certain modernization programs,"[89] and "protect[ing] near-term operational readiness of its deployed and next-to-deploy units" while struggling to maintain a "ready bench."[90] According to Marine Corps Assistant Commandant General John M. Paxton, "[b]y degrading the readiness of these bench forces to support those forward deployed, we are forced to accept increased risk in our ability to respond to further contingencies, our ability to assure we are the most ready when the nation is least ready."[91]

The Marines' Ground Equipment Reset Strategy has been progressing and is expected to be completed by the end of FY 2017. All of the equipment in Afghanistan was withdrawn by February 2015. As of April 2017, the Marine

Corps had reset approximately 90 percent of its ground equipment, compared to 78 percent in the prior year.[92] Reconstituting equipment and ensuring that the Corps' inventory can meet operational requirements are critical aspects of readiness.

Scoring the U.S. Marine Corps

Capacity Score: Weak

Based on the deployment of Marines across major engagements since the Korean War, the Corps requires roughly 15 battalions for one MRC.[93] This translates to a force of around 30 battalions to fight two MRCs simultaneously. The government force-sizing documents that discuss Marine Corps composition support this. Though the documents that make such a recommendations count the Marines by divisions, not battalions, they are consistent in arguing for three Active Marine Corps divisions, which in turn requires roughly 30 battalions. With a 20 percent strategic reserve, the ideal USMC capacity for a two-MRC force-sizing construct is 36 battalions.

More than 33,000 Marines were deployed in Korea, and more than 44,000 were deployed in Vietnam. In the Persian Gulf, one of the largest Marine Corps missions in U.S. history, some 90,000 Marines were deployed, and approximately 66,000 were deployed for Operation Iraqi Freedom. As the Persian Gulf War is the most pertinent example for this construct, a force of 180,000 Marines is a reasonable benchmark for a two-MRC force, not counting Marines that would be unavailable for deployment (assigned to institutional portions of the Corps) or that are deployed elsewhere. This is supported by government documents that have advocated a force as low as 174,000 (1993 Bottom-Up Review) and as high as 202,000 (2010 Quadrennial Defense Review), with an average end strength of 185,000 being recommended.

- **Two-MRC Level:** 36 battalions.

- **Actual 2017 Level:** 24 battalions.

The Corps is operating with slightly less than 67 percent of the number of battalions relative to the two-MRC benchmark. This is a slight increase in the capacity level as measured in the *2017 Index* but insufficient to justify an increase in the Corps' capacity score. Marine Corps capacity is therefore scored as "weak" again in 2018.

Capability Score: Marginal

The Corps receives scores of "weak" for "Capability of Equipment," "marginal" for "Age of Equipment" and "Health of Modernization Programs," but "strong" for "Size of Modernization Program." Therefore, the aggregate score for Marine Corps capability is "marginal." Excluded from the scoring are various ground vehicle programs that have been cancelled and are now being reprogrammed. This includes redesign of the MPC.

Readiness Score: Weak

In FY 2017, approximately half of USMC units experienced degraded readiness. As the nation's crisis response force, the Corps requires that all units, whether deployed or non-deployed, be ready. However, since most Marine Corps ground units are meeting readiness requirements only immediately before deployment and the Corps' "ready bench" would "not be as capable as necessary" if deployed on short notice, USMC readiness is only sufficient to meet ongoing commitments at reported deployment-to-dwell ratios of 1:2. This means that only a third of the force—the deployed force—could be considered fully ready. Furthermore, as of December 2016, the USMC reported more specifically that only 41 percent of its fixed-wing and rotary-wing aircraft were considered flyable. Due to the lack of a "ready bench" and a further decline in readiness levels among the USMC aircraft fleet, the *2018 Index* assesses Marine Corps readiness levels as "weak."

Overall U.S. Marine Corps Score: Weak

The Marine Corps is scored as "weak" overall in the *2018 Index*. This is a drop from "marginal" as assessed in the *2017 Index*. Absent a reduction in operational commitments and a significant increase in funding to clear backlogged maintenance and speed procurement of new platforms, the Corps will continue to struggle to improve its condition for the foreseeable future.

U.S. Military Power: Marine Corps

	VERY WEAK	WEAK	MARGINAL	STRONG	VERY STRONG
Capacity		✓			
Capability			✓		
Readiness		✓			
OVERALL		✓			

Endnotes

1. Lieutenant General Ronald L. Bailey, Deputy Commandant for Plans, Policies, and Operations; Lieutenant General Jon M. Davis, Deputy Commandant for Aviation; Lieutenant General Michael G. Dana, Deputy Commandant for Installations and Logistics, statement on "The Current State of the Marine Corps" before the Subcommittee on Readiness, Committee on Armed Services, U.S. House of Representatives, April 5, 2017, p. 5, http://docs.house.gov/meetings/AS/AS03/20170405/105768/HHRG-115-AS03-Wstate-BaileyUSMCR-20170405.pdf (accessed August 13, 2017).

2. Lieutenant General Robert S. Walsh, Deputy Commandant, Combat Development and Integration, and Commanding General, Marine Corps Combat Development Command; Brigadier General Joseph Shrader, Commander, Marine Corps Systems Command; and John Garner, Program Executive Officer, Land Systems Marine Corps, statement on "Marine Corps Ground Programs" before the Subcommittee on Seapower, Committee on Armed Services, U.S. Senate, June 6, 2017, p. 2, https://www.armed-services.senate.gov/imo/media/doc/Walsh-Shrader-Garner_06-06-17.pdf (accessed August 13, 2017).

3. General Joseph Dunford, Commandant, United States Marine Corps, statement on Marine Corps readiness before the Subcommittee on Defense, Committee on Appropriations, U.S. House of Representatives, February 26, 2015, p. 10, http://www.hqmc.marines.mil/Portals/142/Docs/CMC%20Testimony%202015/USMC%20FY16%20Written%20Posture%20Statement_FINAL.pdf (accessed August 29, 2016).

4. Ibid., p. 11.

5. U.S. Department of Defense, Office of the Under Secretary of Defense (Comptroller)/Chief Financial Officer, *United States Department of Defense Fiscal Year 2017 Budget Request: Defense Budget Overview*, May 2017, p. A-2, http://comptroller.defense.gov/Portals/45/Documents/defbudget/fy2018/fy2018_Budget_Request_Overview_Book.pdf (accessed July 13, 2017).

6. U.S. Department of Defense, Office of the Under Secretary of Defense (Comptroller)/Chief Financial Officer, *United States Department of Defense Fiscal Year 2017 Budget Request: Defense Budget Overview*, p. A-1.

7. David Alexander, "Marines to Cut Four Battalions, 12 Air Squadrons," Reuters, March 14, 2012, http://www.reuters.com/article/us-usa-defense-marines-idUSBRE82E00Y20120315 (accessed August 17, 2016).

8. U.S. Department of Defense, *Fiscal Year 2015 Budget Request: Estimated Impacts of Sequestration-Level Funding*, April 2014, p. 3-2, http://archive.defense.gov/pubs/2014_Estimated_Impacts_of_Sequestration-Level_Funding_April.pdf (accessed August 13, 2017).

9. General Joseph F. Dunford, Jr., Commandant of the Marine Corps, statement in *Hearing to Receive Testimony on the Impact of the Budget Control Act of 2011 and Sequestration on National Security*, Committee on Armed Services, U.S. Senate, January 28, 2015, p. 32, http://www.armed-services.senate.gov/imo/media/doc/15-04%20-%201-28-15.pdf (accessed August 13, 2017).

10. General John Paxton, Assistant Commandant of the Marine Corps, statement on "U.S. Marine Corps Readiness" before the Subcommittee on Readiness, Committee on Armed Services, U.S. Senate, March 15, 2016, p. 3, http://www.armed-services.senate.gov/imo/media/doc/Paxton_03-15-16.pdf (accessed August 13, 2017).

11. Dunford, testimony in *Hearing to Receive Testimony on the Impact of the Budget Control Act of 2011 and Sequestration on National Security*, p. 100.

12. General James F. Amos, Commandant of the Marine Corps, "2014 Report to Congress on the Posture of the United States Marine Corps," statement before the Committee on Armed Services, U.S. House of Representatives, March 12, 2014, p. 12, http://www.hqmc.marines.mil/portals/142/docs/FY_2015_CMC_POSTURE_STATEMENT.pdf (accessed August 29, 2016).

13. Paxton, statement on "U.S. Marine Corps Readiness," March 15, 2016, p. 8.

14. Dunford, statement on Marine Corps readiness, February 26, 2015, pp. 24–25.

15. General Robert B. Neller, Commandant, United States Marine Corps, statement on "Posture of the Department of the Navy" before the Committee on Armed Services, U.S. Senate, 115th Cong., 1st Sess., June 15, 2017, p. 9, https://www.armed-services.senate.gov/imo/media/doc/Neller_06-15-17.pdf (accessed August 13, 2017).

16. Dunford, testimony in *Hearing to Receive Testimony on the Impact of the Budget Control Act of 2011 and Sequestration on National Security*, p. 75.

17. U.S. Marine Corps, *2017 Marine Aviation Plan*, p. 54, www.aviation.marines.mil/Portals/11/2017%20MARINE%20AVIATIOIN%20PLAN.pdf (accessed August 13, 2017).

18. Congressional Quarterly, "House Armed Services Committee Holds Hearing on Aviation Readiness," CQ Congressional Transcripts, July 6, 2016, http://www.cq.com/doc/congressionaltranscripts-4922435?3&search=lXd1KGHk (accessed August 17, 2017)

19. U.S. Marine Corps, *Marine Aviation Plan 2016*, p. 39, https://www.slideshare.net/robbinlaird/usmc-aviation-plan-2016 (accessed August 18, 2017); U.S. Marine Corps, *2017 Marine Aviation Plan*, p. 54.

20. Congressional Quarterly, "House Armed Services Committee Holds Hearing on Aviation Readiness," CQ Congressional Transcripts, July 6, 2016, http://www.cq.com/doc/congressionaltranscripts-4922435?3&search=IXd1KGHk (accessed August 29, 2016).

21. International Institute for Strategic Studies, *The Military Balance 2016: The Annual Assessment of Global Military Capabilities and Defence Economics* (London: Routledge, 2016), pp. 44–45. The prior year figure was not repeated in recent testimony. Since publication of the 2016 IISS *Military Balance*, one Prowler squadron has been decommissioned, and one *Harrier* squadron has been transitioned to an F-35B squadron. Factoring in these changes, there are 60 total squadrons in the Marine Corps active component, including all fixed-wing and rotary aircraft squadrons, training and transport squadrons, and one combat search and rescue squadron (which does not include the "VIP" transport squadron). Using the same metrics, the total for 2015 based on the IISS *Military Balance* would have been 64.

22. U.S. Marine Corps, *2017 Marine Aviation Plan*, pp. 70 and 76.

23. Paxton, statement on "U.S. Marine Corps Readiness," March 15, 2016, p. 9.

24. General Glenn Walters, Assistant Commandant of the Marine Corps, statement on "Marine Corps Readiness" before the Subcommittee on Readiness, Committee on Armed Services, U.S. Senate, February 8, 2017, p. 6, https://www.armed-services.senate.gov/imo/media/doc/Walters_02-08-17.pdf (accessed August 13, 2017).

25. Ibid., p. 5.

26. General John Paxton, Assistant Commandant, United States Marine Corps, statement on Marine Corps readiness and FY 2016 budget request before the Subcommittee on Readiness and Management Support, Committee on Armed Services, U.S. Senate, March 25, 2015, pp. 10–11, http://www.armed-services.senate.gov/imo/media/doc/Paxton_03-25-15.pdf (accessed August 13, 2017).

27. General Robert B. Neller, Commandant of the Marine Corps, statement on "Navy and Marine Corps FY17 Budget Request" before the Committee on Armed Services, U.S. Senate, March 15, 2016, p. 16, http://www.armed-services.senate.gov/imo/media/doc/Neller_03-15-16.pdf (accessed August 29, 2016); Walters, statement on "Marine Corps Readiness," February 8, 2017, p. 7.

28. News release, "SAIC Delivers First AAV SU to U.S. Marine Corps Ahead of Schedule," Science Applications International Corporation, March 11, 2016, http://investors.saic.com/press-release/saic-delivers-first-aav-su-us-marine-corps-ahead-schedule (accessed June 27, 2016).

29. Walsh, Shrader, and Garner, statement on "Marine Corps Ground Programs," June 6, 2017, p. 5.

30. Walters, statement on "Marine Corps Readiness," February 8, 2017, p. 7.

31. The average age of the M1A1 was 26 in 2016. Paxton, statement on "U.S. Marine Corps Readiness," March 15, 2016, p. 15. No new M1A1 Abrams have been commissioned over the past year, so the average age is estimated as 27 in 2017.

32. U.S. Marine Corps, Concepts & Programs, "Ground Equipment Age," last revised April 3, 2014, https://marinecorpsconceptsandprograms.com/resources/ground-equipment-age (accessed August 18, 2017).

33. U.S. Marine Corps, *2017 Marine Aviation Plan*, p. 212.

34. Lieutenant Colonel Ricky B. Johnson (Ret.), "The Military Will Need the Marines' Electronic Warfare Squadrons Beyond 2019," *Marine Corps Times*, May 28, 2016, http://www.marinecorpstimes.com/story/opinion/2016/05/28/military-need-marines-electronic-warfare-squadrons-beyond-2019/84623644/ (accessed August 29, 2016); U.S. Marine Corps, *2017 Marine Aviation Plan*, p. 2.

35. U.S. Marine Corps, Concepts & Programs, "Legacy Aircraft," last revised March 3, 2015, https://marinecorpsconceptsandprograms.com/programs/aviation/legacy-aircraft (accessed July 27, 2017); Jeremiah Gertler, "Navy F/A-18E/F and EA-18G Aircraft Procurement and Strike Fighter Shortfall: Background and Issues for Congress," Congressional Research Service *Report for Congress*, December 22, 2009, p. 5, https://www.fas.org/sgp/crs/weapons/RL30624.pdf (accessed July 27, 2017).

36. Paxton, statement on "U.S. Marine Corps Readiness," March 15, 2016, p. 9.

37. U.S. Marine Corps, *2017 Marine Aviation Plan*, p. 56.

38. Vice Admiral Paul Grosklags, Representing Assistant Secretary of the Navy (Research, Development and Acquisition); Lieutenant General Jon Davis, Deputy Commandant for Aviation; and Rear Admiral Michael C. Manazir, Director Air Warfare, statement on "Department of the Navy's Aviation Programs" before the Subcommittee on Seapower, Committee on Armed Services, U.S. Senate, April 20, 2016, p. 3, http://www.armed-services.senate.gov/imo/media/doc/Grosklags-Davis-Manazir_04-20-16.pdf (accessed August 13, 2017).

39. Megan Eckstein, "Marines Declare Initial Operational Capability on F-35B Joint Strike Fighter," USNI News, July 31, 2015, https://news.usni.org/2015/07/31/marines-declare-initial-operational-capability-on-f-35b-joint-strike-fighter (accessed July 27, 2017).

40. U.S. Marine Corps, *2017 Marine Aviation Plan*, p. 232.

41. U.S. Department of Defense, Office of the Under Secretary of Defense (Comptroller)/Chief Financial Officer, *United States Department of Defense Fiscal Year 2018 Budget Request: Program Acquisition Cost by Weapon System*, May 2017, pp. 3-2 and 3-9, http://comptroller.defense.gov/Portals/45/Documents/defbudget/fy2018/fy2018_Weapons.pdf (accessed August 13, 2017).

42. Andrew Feickert, "Joint Light Tactical Vehicle (JLTV): Background and Issues for Congress," Congressional Research Service *Report for Members and Committees Congress*, May 31, 2017, pp. 1–2, https://fas.org/sgp/crs/weapons/RS22942.pdf (accessed July 27, 2017).

43. Joe Gould, "Oshkosh Awaits Protest After JLTV Win," *Defense News*, August 29, 2015, http://www.defensenews.com/story/defense/land/vehicles/2015/08/29/oshkosh-awaits-protests-jltv-win/71325838 (accessed July 27, 2017).

44. Hearing, *Marine Corps Ground Modernization*, Subcommittee on Seapower, Committee on Armed Services, U.S. Senate, 115th Cong., 1st Sess., June 6, 2017, p. 63, https://www.armed-services.senate.gov/imo/media/doc/17-56_06-06-17.pdf (accessed July 27, 2017).

45. U.S. Department of Defense, Office of the Under Secretary of Defense (Comptroller)/Chief Financial Officer, *United States Department of Defense Fiscal Year 2018 Budget Request: Program Acquisition Cost by Weapon* System, p. 3-1.

46. Ibid., p. 3-2.

47. Feickert, "Joint Light Tactical Vehicle (JLTV)," p. 1; Congressional Quarterly, "Senate Armed Services Committee Holds Hearing on the Marine Corps," CQ Congressional Transcripts, June 6, 2017, http://www.cq.com/doc/congressionaltranscripts-5117362?2 (accessed July 28, 2017).

48. Feickert, "Joint Light Tactical Vehicle (JLTV)," p. 7.

49. Hearing, *Marine Corps Ground Modernization*, p. 63.

50. Congressional Quarterly, "Senate Armed Services Committee Holds Hearing on the Marine Corps."

51. U.S. Department of the Navy, *Department of Defense Fiscal Year (FY) 2018 Budget Estimates, Navy: Justification Book, Volume 1 of 1, Procurement, Marine Corps*, May 2017, p. 271, http://www.secnav.navy.mil/fmc/fmb/Documents/18pres/PMC_Book.pdf (accessed July 28, 2017).

52. Feickert, "Joint Light Tactical Vehicle (JLTV)," p. 9,

53. Dunford, statement on Marine Corps readiness, February 26, 2015, p. 13; Feickert, "Joint Light Tactical Vehicle (JLTV)," p. 6.

54. Andrew Feickert, "Marine Corps Amphibious Combat Vehicle (ACV) and Marine Personnel Carrier (MPC): Background and Issues for Congress," Congressional Research Service *Report for Members and Committees of Congress*, June 1, 2017, p. 7, https://www.fas.org/sgp/crs/weapons/R42723.pdf (accessed August 13, 2017); U.S. Department of Defense, Office of the Under Secretary of Defense (Comptroller)/Chief Financial Officer, *United States Department of Defense Fiscal Year 2018 Budget Request: Program Acquisition Cost by Weapon System*, p. 3-9, http://comptroller.defense.gov/Portals/45/Documents/defbudget/fy2018/fy2018_Weapons.pdf (accessed July 27, 2017).

55. U.S. Department of Defense, Office of the Under Secretary of Defense (Comptroller)/Chief Financial Officer, *United States Department of Defense Fiscal Year 2018 Budget Request: Program Acquisition Cost by Weapon System*, p. 3-9.

56. Feickert, "Marine Corps Amphibious Combat Vehicle (ACV) and Marine Personnel Carrier (MPC)," pp. 1–2.

57. Lieutenant General Kenneth J. Glueck Jr., Deputy Commandant, Combat Development and Integration, and Commanding General, Marine Corps Combat Development Command, and Thomas P. Dee, Deputy Assistant Secretary of the Navy, Expeditionary Programs and Logistics Management, statement on "Marine Corps Modernization" before the Subcommittee on Seapower, Committee on Armed Services, U.S. Senate, March 11, 2015, pp. 8–9, https://www.armed-services.senate.gov/imo/media/doc/Glueck-Dee_03-11-15.pdf (accessed August 18, 2017).

58. With regard to this overall requirement—armored lift for 10 battalions of infantry—the AAV Survivability Upgrade Program would provide for four battalions, and ACV 1.1 and ACV 1.2 would account for six battalions. Ibid., pp. 7–8.

59. Lieutenant General Robert Walsh, Deputy Commandant for Combat Development and Integration; Brigadier General Joseph Shrader, Commander, Marine Corps Systems Command; and William Taylor, Program Executive Officer, Marine Corps Land Systems, statement on "Marine Corps Ground Forces Modernization, Modernization Programs," before the Subcommittee on Tactical Air and Land Forces, Committee on Armed Services, U.S. House of Representatives, March 2, 2016, p. [4], http://docs.house.gov/meetings/AS/AS25/20160302/104554/HHRG-114-AS25-Wstate-WalshR-20160302.pdf (accessed August 13, 2017).

60. U.S. Government Accountability Office, *Amphibious Combat Vehicle Acquisition: Cost Estimate Meets Best Practices, but Concurrency Between Testing and Production Increases Risk*, GAO-17-401, April 2017, p. 12, http://www.gao.gov/assets/690/684145.pdf (accessed August 13, 2017).

61. Sam LaGrone, "WEST: Marines Plan to Issue Amphibious Combat Vehicle Request for Proposal in March," USNI News, February 12, 2015, http://news.usni.org/2015/02/12/west-marines-plan-issue-amphibious-combat-vehicle-request-proposal-march (accessed August 23, 2016).

62. Feickert, "Marine Corps Amphibious Combat Vehicle (ACV) and Marine Personnel Carrier (MPC)," June 1, 2017, p. 7, https://fas.org/sgp/crs/weapons/R42723.pdf (accessed August 17, 2017).

63. Dunford, statement on Marine Corps readiness, February 26, 2015, p. 28.

64. Walsh, Shrader, and Garner, statement on "Marine Corps Ground Programs," June 6, 2017, p. 5.

65. Grosklags, Davis, and Manazir, statement on "Department of the Navy's Aviation Programs," April 20, 2016, p. 7.

66. Vice Admiral Paul Grosklags, Representing Assistant Secretary of the Navy (Research, Development and Acquisition); Lieutenant General Jon Davis, Deputy Commandant for Aviation; and Rear Admiral DeWolfe H, Miller III, Director Air Warfare, statement on "Department of the Navy's Aviation Programs" before the Subcommittee on Seapower, Committee on Armed Services, U.S. Senate, June 13, 2017, pp. 13–14, https://www.armed-services.senate.gov/imo/media/doc/Grosklags-Davis-Miller_06-13-17.pdf (accessed August 13, 2017).

67. Vice Admiral Paul Grosklags, Principal Military Deputy, Assistant Secretary of the Navy (Research, Development and Acquisition); Rear Admiral Michael C. Manazir, Director Air Warfare; and Lieutenant General Jon Davis, Deputy Commandant for Aviation, statement on "Department of the Navy's Aviation Programs" before the Subcommittee on Seapower, Committee on Armed Services, U.S. Senate, March 25, 2015, p. 10, http://www.armed-services.senate.gov/imo/media/doc/Grosklags_Manazir_Davis_03-25-15.pdf (accessed August 13, 2017).

68. Neller, statement on "Navy and Marine Corps FY17 Budget Request," March 15, 2016, p. 8.

69. Stephen Trimble, "US Military Unveils Possible F-35B Redesign in Sweeping Budget Reforms," FlightGlobal, January 6, 2011, https://www.flightglobal.com/news/articles/us-military-unveils-possible-f-35b-redesign-in-sweep-351600/ (accessed August 30, 2016).

70. Eckstein, "Marines Declare Initial Operational Capability on F-35B Joint Strike Fighter."

71. U.S. Department of Defense, *Selected Acquisition Report (SAR): V-22 Osprey Joint Services Advanced Vertical Lift Aircraft (V22) as of FY 2017 President's Budget*, RCS: DD-A&T(Q&A)823-212, March 21, 2016, p. 61, http://www.dod.mil/pubs/foi/Reading_Room/Selected_Acquisition_Reports/16-F-0402_DOC_64_V-22_DEC_2015_SAR.pdf (accessed August 30, 2016).

72. Grosklags, Davis, and Miller, statement on "Department of the Navy's Aviation Programs," June 13, 2017, p. 18.

73. U.S. Marine Corps, *2017 Marine Aviation Plan*, p. 70.

74. Grosklags, Manazir, and Davis, statement on "Department of the Navy's Aviation Programs," March 25, 2015, p. 16.

75. Grosklags, Davis, and Manazir, statement on "Department of the Navy's Aviation Programs," April 20, 2016, p. 21.

76. U.S. Government Accountability Office, *Defense Acquisitions: Assessments of Selected Weapons Programs*, GAO-16-329SP, March 2016, p. 93, http://www.gao.gov/assets/680/676281.pdf (accessed August 13, 2017).

77. Grosklags, Davis, and Miller, statement on "Department of the Navy's Aviation Programs," June 13, 2017, p. 20.

78. U.S. Government Accountability Office, *Defense Acquisitions: Assessments of Selected Weapons Programs*, p. 93.

79. U.S. Marine Corps, *2017 Marine Aviation Plan*, p. 82.

80. Lieutenant General Jon M. Davis, Deputy Commandant for Aviation, statement on "Aviation Readiness and Safety" before the Subcommittee on Readiness, Committee on Armed Services, U.S. House of Representatives, July 6, 2016, pp. [5] and [9], http://docs.house.gov/meetings/AS/AS03/20160706/105159/HHRG-114-AS03-Wstate-DavisJ-20160706.pdf (accessed August 13, 2017).

81. Another six aircraft will be procured with research and development funding, bringing the program of record to 200 aircraft. U.S. Department of Defense, Office of the Under Secretary of Defense (Comptroller)/Chief Financial Officer, *United States Department of Defense Fiscal Year 2018 Budget Request: Program Acquisition Cost by Weapon System*, p. 1-15, http://comptroller.defense.gov/Portals/45/Documents/defbudget/fy2017/FY2017_Weapons.pdf (accessed August 13, 2017).

82. Dunford, statement on Marine Corps readiness, February 26, 2015, p. 20.

83. Walsh, Shrader, and Garner, statement on "Marine Corps Ground Programs," June 6, 2017, p. 5.

84. Walters, statement on "Marine Corps Readiness," February 8, 2017, p. 9.

85. Paxton, statement on "U.S. Marine Corps Readiness," March 15, 2016, p. 9.

86. Grosklags, Davis, and Miller, statement on "Department of the Navy's Aviation Programs," June 13, 2017, p. 4.

87. Jeff Schogol, "More Than Half of All Marine Aircraft Unflyable in December," *Marine Corps Times*, February 8, 2017, https://www.marinecorpstimes.com/articles/many-marine-aircraft-grounded (accessed August 13, 2017).

88. Hope Hodge Seck, "Pilot Error Common Thread in Recent Marine Corps Crashes: General," Military.com, February 3, 2017, http://www.military.com/daily-news/2017/02/03/pilot-error-common-thread-in-recent-marine-corps-crashes-general.html (accessed August 13, 2017).

89. U.S. Department of the Navy, *Highlights of the Department of the Navy FY 2018 Budget*, May 2017, p. 1-4, http://www.secnav.navy.mil/fmc/fmb/Documents/18pres/Highlights_book.pdf (accessed August 13, 2017).

90. Neller, statement on "Posture of the Department of the Navy," June 15, 2017, p. 9.

91. Paxton, statement on "U.S. Marine Corps Readiness," March 15, 2016, p. 7.

92. Bailey, Davis, and Dana, statement on "The Current State of the Marine Corps," April 5, 2017, p. 9.

93. This count is based on an average number of 1.5 divisions deployed to major wars (see Table 3, pp. 311–312) and an average of 10–11 battalions per division.

U.S. Nuclear Weapons Capability

Assessing the state of U.S. nuclear weapons capabilities presents several challenges.

First, instead of taking advantage of technological developments to field new warheads that could be designed to be safer and more secure and could give the United States improved options for guaranteeing a credible deterrent, the U.S. has elected to maintain nuclear warheads—based on designs from the 1960s and 1970s—that were in the stockpile when the Cold War ended.

Second, the lack of detailed publicly available data about the readiness of nuclear forces, their capabilities, and weapon reliability makes analysis difficult.

Third, the U.S. nuclear enterprise has many components, some of which are also involved in supporting conventional missions. For example, dual-capable bombers do not fly airborne alert with nuclear weapons today, although they did so routinely during the 1960s (and are capable of doing so again if the decision should ever be made to resume this practice). Additionally, the national security laboratories do not focus solely on the nuclear weapons mission; they also perform a variety of functions related to nuclear nonproliferation, medical research, threat reduction, and countering nuclear terrorism, including nuclear detection. The National Command and Control System performs nuclear command and control in addition to supporting ongoing conventional operations.

Thus, assessing the extent to which any one piece of the nuclear enterprise is sufficiently funded, focused, and effective with regard to the nuclear mission is problematic.

In today's rapidly changing world, the U.S. nuclear weapons enterprise must be flexible and resilient to underpin the U.S. nuclear deterrent. If the U.S. detects a game-changing nuclear weapons development in another country, the U.S. nuclear weapons complex must be able to provide a timely response.

The U.S. maintains an inactive stockpile that includes near-term hedge warheads that can be put back into operational status within six to 24 months; extended hedge warheads are said to be ready within 24 to 60 months.[1] The U.S. preserves significant upload capability on its strategic delivery vehicles, which means that the nation can increase the number of nuclear warheads on each type of its delivery vehicles if contingencies warrant. For example, the U.S. Minuteman III intercontinental ballistic missile (ICBM) can carry up to three nuclear warheads, although it is currently deployed with only one.[2]

Presidential Decision Directive-15 (PDD-15) requires the U.S. to maintain the ability to conduct a nuclear test within 24 to 36 months of a presidential decision to do so.[3] However, successive governmental reports have noted the continued deterioration of technical and diagnostics equipment and the inability to fill technical positions supporting nuclear testing readiness.[4] A lack of congressional support for improving technical readiness further undermines efforts by the National Nuclear Security Administration (NNSA) to comply with the directive.

The weapons labs face demographic challenges of their own. Most scientists and engineers with practical nuclear weapon design and testing experience are retired. This means that for the first time since the dawn of the nuclear age, the U.S. will have to rely on the scientific judgment of people who were not directly involved in nuclear tests of weapons that they designed, developed, and are certifying.

Not all of the existing inactive stockpile will go through the life-extension program. Hence, our ability to respond to contingencies by uploading weapons kept in an inactive status could decline with the passage of time.

The shift of focus away from the nuclear mission after the end of the Cold War caused the NNSA laboratories to lose their sense of purpose and to feel compelled to reorient and broaden their mission focus. According to a number of studies, their relationship with the government also evolved in ways that reduce output and increase costs. The NNSA was supposed to address these problems but has largely failed in this task, partly because "the relationship with the NNSA and the National security labs appears to be broken."[5]

In 1999, the Commission on Maintaining U.S. Nuclear Weapons Expertise concluded that 34 percent of the employees supplying critical skills to the weapons program were more than 50 years old. The number increased to 40 percent in 2009.[6] On average, the U.S. high-technology industry has a more balanced employee age distribution.[7]

Both the lack of resources and the lack of sound, consistent policy guidance have undermined workforce morale. The Congressional Advisory Panel on the Governance of the Nuclear Security Enterprise recommended fundamental changes in the nuclear weapons enterprise's culture, business practices, project management, and organization. Others proposed moving the NNSA to the Department of Defense.[8]

Another important indication of the health of the overall force is the readiness of forces that operate U.S. nuclear systems. In 2006, the Air Force mistakenly shipped non-nuclear warhead components to Taiwan.[9] A year later, it transported nuclear-armed cruise missiles across the U.S. without authorization (or apparently even awareness that it was doing so,

mistaking them for conventional cruise missiles).[10] These serious incidents led to the establishment of a Task Force on DoD Nuclear Weapons Management, which found that "there has been an unambiguous, dramatic, and unacceptable decline in the Air Force's commitment to perform the nuclear mission and, until very recently, little has been done to reverse it" and that "the readiness of forces assigned the nuclear mission has seriously eroded."[11]

Following these incidents, the Air Force instituted broad changes to improve oversight and management of the nuclear mission and the inventory of nuclear weapons, including creating the Air Force Global Strike Command to organize, train, and equip intercontinental-range ballistic missile and nuclear-capable bomber crews as well as other personnel to fulfill a nuclear mission and implement a stringent inspection regime.

The success of these changes has been limited. In January 2014, the Air Force discovered widespread cheating on nuclear proficiency exams and charged over 100 officers with misconduct. The Navy had a similar problem, albeit on a smaller scale.[12] The Department of Defense conducted two nuclear enterprise reviews, one internal and one external. Both reviews identified a lack of leadership attention, a lack of resources to modernize the atrophied infrastructure, and unduly burdensome implementation of the personnel reliability program as some of the core challenges preventing a sole focus on accomplishing the nuclear mission.[13]

The ICBM Force Improvement Program was initiated and mostly implemented throughout 2014 and into 2015, and the Air Force shifted over $160 million to address problems, modernize certain facilities, and generally improve morale. The Air Force has also seen an increase in badly needed manpower—but not nearly enough to alleviate manpower concerns. If changes in the nuclear enterprise are to be effective, leaders across the executive and legislative branches will have to continue to provide sufficient resources to mitigate readiness and morale issues within the force.

Fiscal uncertainty and a steady decline in resources for the nuclear weapons enterprise (trends that have begun to reverse in recent years) have negatively affected the nuclear deterrence mission. General John E. Hyten, Commander, U.S. Strategic Command (STRATCOM), testified in April 2017 that:

> For decades now, we have held a military advantage over our adversaries, both from a nuclear and conventional standpoint. That is starting to change. As our nation rightly focuses on combating violent extremist organizations and the states that support them, other adversaries have taken the opportunity to develop advanced nuclear and conventional weaponry that rival many of our systems.[14]

The Trump Administration has inherited a comprehensive modernization program for nuclear forces—warheads, delivery systems, and command and control. The Obama Administration included this program in its budget requests, and Congress to a significant extent has funded it. Because such modernization activities require long-term funding commitments, it is important that this commitment continue. At the same time, the Trump Administration has an opportunity to reassess the U.S. nuclear force posture, including some of its more misguided elements like discounting Russia's aggressive policies toward the United States and U.S. allies in Europe.

Implications for U.S. National Security

U.S. nuclear forces are not designed to shield the nation from all types of attacks from all adversaries. They are designed to deter large-scale conventional and nuclear attacks that threaten America's sovereignty, forward-deployed troops, and allies.

U.S. nuclear forces play an important role in the global nonproliferation regime by providing U.S. assurances to NATO, Japan, and South Korea that lead these allies either to keep the number of their nuclear weapons lower than otherwise would be the case (France and the United Kingdom) or to forgo their development and deployment altogether. North Korea has proven that a country with very limited intellectual and financial resources can develop a nuclear weapon if it decides to do so. Iran continues on the path to obtaining a nuclear weapon, and the Joint Comprehensive Plan of Action might make reaching this goal easier by providing Iran with money and access to advanced technologies.

This makes U.S. nuclear assurances to allies and partners ever more important. Should the credibility of American nuclear forces continue to degrade, countries like South Korea could pursue an independent nuclear option, which would raise several thorny issues including possible additional instability across the region.

Certain negative trends could undermine U.S. nuclear deterrence if problems are not addressed. There is no shortage of challenges on the horizon, from an aging nuclear weapons infrastructure and workforce to the need to recapitalize all three legs (land, air, and sea) of the nuclear triad, and from the need to conduct life-extension programs while maintaining a self-imposed nuclear weapons test moratorium to limiting the spread of nuclear know-how and the means to deliver nuclear weapons. Additionally, the United States must take account of adversaries that are modernizing their nuclear forces, particularly Russia and China.

Since 2010, when the most recent Nuclear Posture Review (NPR) was concluded, the global strategic security environment has become increasingly dangerous. Russia is now engaged in an aggressive nuclear buildup, having added new modern nuclear systems to its arsenal since 2010. Concurrently, Russia is using its capabilities to threaten the sovereignty of U.S. allies in Eastern Europe and the Baltics. China is engaging in a similar nuclear buildup as it projects power into the South China Sea. North Korea and Iran have taken an aggressive posture toward the West as they attempt to shift from nuclear proliferators to nuclear-armed states.

Deterrence is an intricate interaction between U.S. conventional and nuclear forces and the psychology of both allies and adversaries that the U.S. would use these forces to defend the interests of the U.S. and its allies. Nuclear deterrence must reflect the mindset of the adversary the U.S. seeks to deter. If an adversary believes that he can fight and win a limited nuclear war, the task for U.S. leaders is to convince that adversary otherwise even if U.S. leaders think it is not possible to control escalation. The U.S. nuclear portfolio must be structured in terms of capacity, capability, variety, flexibility, and readiness to achieve this objective. In addition, military requirements and specifications for nuclear weapons will be different depending on who is being deterred, what he values, and what the U.S. seeks to deter him from doing.

Due to the complex interplay among strategy, policy, actions that states take in international relations, and other actors' perceptions of the world around them, one might never know precisely if and when a nuclear or conventional deterrent provided by U.S. forces loses credibility. Nuclear weapons capabilities take years or decades to develop, as does the infrastructure supporting them—an infrastructure that the U.S. has neglected for decades. We can be reasonably certain that a robust, well-resourced, focused, and reliable nuclear enterprise is more likely to sustain its deterrent value than is an outdated and questionable one.

The U.S. is capable of incredible mobilization when danger materializes. The nuclear threat environment is dynamic and proliferating, with old and new actors developing advanced capabilities while the U.S. enterprise is relatively static, potentially leaving the United States at a technological disadvantage. This is worrisome because of its implications both for the security of the United States and for the security of its allies and the free world.

Scoring U.S. Nuclear Weapons Capabilities

The U.S. nuclear weapons enterprise is composed of several key elements that include warheads; delivery systems; nuclear command and control; intelligence, surveillance, and reconnaissance; aerial refueling; and the physical infrastructure that designs, manufactures, and maintains U.S. nuclear weapons. The complex also includes the talent of people from physicists to engineers, maintainers, and operators, without which the continuous maintenance of the nuclear infrastructure would not be possible.

The factors selected below are the most important elements of the nuclear weapons complex. They are judged on a five-grade scale, where "very strong" means that a sustainable, viable, and funded plan is in place and "very weak" means that the U.S. is not meeting its security requirements and has no program in place to redress the shortfall, which has the potential to damage vital national interests if the situation is not corrected.

Current U.S. Nuclear Stockpile
Score: Strong

U.S. warheads must be safe, secure, effective, and reliable. The Department of Energy (DOE) defines reliability as "the ability of the weapon to perform its intended function at the intended time under environments considered to be normal" and as "the probability of achieving the specified yield, at the target, across the Stockpile-to-Target Sequence of environments, throughout the weapon's lifetime, assuming proper inputs."[15] Since 1993, reliability has been determined through an intensive warhead surveillance program; non-nuclear experiments (that is, without the use of experiments producing nuclear yield); sophisticated calculations using high-performance computing; and related evaluations.

The reliability of nuclear warheads and delivery systems becomes more important as the number and diversity of nuclear weapons in the stockpile decrease, because fewer types of nuclear weapons mean a smaller margin of

U.S. Military Power: Five-Grade Scale

VERY WEAK	WEAK	MARGINAL	STRONG	VERY STRONG

error should one type be affected by a technical problem that requires the repair or decommissioning of a weapon type or its delivery system. Americans and allies must be confident that U.S. nuclear warheads will perform as expected.[16]

As warheads age, they become less able to perform their mission as expected, and this can complicate military planning significantly. Despite creating impressive amounts of knowledge about nuclear weapons physics and materials chemistry, the U.S. may not be completely certain about the long-term effects of aging components that comprise a nuclear weapon. According to former NNSA spokesman Bryan Wilkes, for example, "We know that plutonium pits have a limited lifetime."[17] A plutonium pit is a crucial component of a nuclear weapon,[18] and with life-extension programs introducing new components to warheads whose radiological effects are not fully known, the level of uncertainty has increased.

The United States has the world's safest and most secure stockpile, but security of long-term storage sites (including overseas sites), potential problems introduced by improper handling, or unanticipated effects stemming from long-term handling could compromise the integrity of U.S. warheads. The nuclear warheads themselves contain security measures that are designed to make it difficult, if not impossible, to detonate a weapon absent a proper authorization.

Grade: The Department of Energy and Department of Defense are required to assess the reliability of the nuclear stockpile annually. This assessment does not include delivery systems, although the U.S. Strategic Command does assess overall weapons system reliability, which includes both the warhead and delivery platforms.

Absent nuclear weapons testing, the assessment of weapons reliability becomes more subjective, albeit based on experience and non-nuclear tests. While certainly an educated opinion, it is not a substitute for the type of objective data obtained through nuclear testing. Testing was used to diagnose potential problems and to certify the effectiveness of fixes to those problems. Given that modern simulation is based on nuclear tests that were conducted primarily in the 1950s and 1960s, using testing equipment of that era, there is a great deal that modern testing equipment and computer capability could teach us about nuclear physics.

"[I]n the past," according to the late Major General Robert Smolen, some of the nuclear weapon problems that the U.S. now faces "would have [been] resolved with nuclear tests."[19] By 2005, a consensus emerged in the NNSA, informed by the nuclear weapons labs, that it would "be increasingly difficult and risky to attempt to replicate exactly existing warheads without nuclear testing and that creating a reliable replacement warhead should be explored."[20] When the U.S. did conduct nuclear tests, it frequently found that small changes in a weapon's tested configuration had a dramatic impact on weapons performance. In fact, the 1958–1961 testing moratorium resulted in weapons with serious problems being introduced into the U.S. stockpile.[21]

In fiscal year (FY) 2017, the NNSA assessed that the stockpile is safe, secure, reliable, and effective.[22]

The lack of nuclear weapons testing creates some uncertainty concerning the adequacy of fixes to the stockpile when problems are found. This includes updates made in order to correct problems that were found in the weapons or changes in the weapons resulting from life-extension programs. It is simply impossible to duplicate exactly weapons that were designed and built many decades ago. According to former Defense Threat Reduction Agency Director Dr. Stephen Younger, we have had to fix "a number of problems that were never anticipated" by using "similar but not quite identical parts."[23] The high costs of having to certify weapons without nuclear testing are resulting in fewer types of weapons and, consequently, a greater impact across the inventory if there is an error in the certification process.

"To be blunt," warned Secretary of Defense Robert Gates in October 2008, "there is absolutely no way we can maintain a credible deterrent and reduce the number of weapons in our stockpile without either resorting to testing our stockpile or pursuing a modernization program."[24] The U.S. is pursuing warhead life-extension programs that replace aging components before they can cause reliability problems. However, the national commitment to this modernization program, including the necessary long-term funding, continues to be uncertain.

In light of our overall assessment, we grade the U.S. stockpile as "strong."

Reliability of U.S. Delivery Platforms Score: Strong

Reliability encompasses not only the warhead, but strategic delivery vehicles as well. In addition to a successful missile launch, this includes the separation of missile boost stages, performance of the missile guidance system, separation of the multiple re-entry vehicle warheads from the missile post-boost vehicle, and accuracy of the final re-entry vehicle in reaching its target.[25]

The U.S. conducts flight tests of ICBMs and submarine-launched ballistic missiles (SLBMs) every year to ensure the reliability of its systems. Anything from electrical wiring to faulty booster separations could degrade the efficiency and safety of the U.S. strategic deterrent if it were to malfunction. U.S. strategic, long-range bombers regularly conduct intercontinental training and receive upgrades in order to sustain a high level of combat readiness, but potential challenges are on the horizon.

Grade: U.S. ICBMs and SLBMs are flight tested annually, and these tests were successful

in 2016. To the extent that data from these tests are publicly available, they provide objective evidence of the delivery systems' reliability and send a message to U.S. adversaries that the system works. The aged systems, however, occasionally have reliability problems.[26] Overall, this factor earns a grade of "strong."

Nuclear Warhead Modernization Score: Weak

During the Cold War, the United States maintained a strong focus on designing and developing new nuclear warhead designs in order to counter Soviet advances and modernization efforts and to leverage advances in understanding the physics, chemistry, and design of nuclear weapons. Today, the United States is focused on sustaining the existing stockpile, not on developing new warheads, even though all of its nuclear-armed adversaries are developing new nuclear warheads and capabilities and accruing new knowledge in which the U.S. used to lead. Since the collapse of the Soviet Union, nuclear weapons and delivery vehicles have not been replaced despite being well beyond their designed service lives. This could increase the risk of failure due to aging components and signal to adversaries that the United States is less committed to nuclear deterrence.

New weapon designs could allow American engineers and scientists to improve previous designs and devise more effective means to address existing military requirements (for example, the need to destroy deeply buried and hardened targets) that have emerged in recent years. New warheads could also enhance the safety and security of American weapons.

An ability to work on new weapon designs would also help American experts to remain engaged and knowledgeable, would help to attract the best talent to the nuclear enterprise, and could help the nation to gain additional insights into foreign nations' nuclear weapon programs. As the Panel to Assess the Reliability, Safety, and Security of the United States Nuclear Stockpile noted, "Only through work on advanced designs will it be possible to train the next generation of weapon designers and producers. Such efforts are also needed to exercise the DoD/NNSA weapon development interface."[27] Other nations maintain their levels of proficiency by having their scientists work on new nuclear warheads and possibly by conducting very low-yield nuclear weapons tests.

Grade: The lack of plans to modernize nuclear weapons—life-extension programs are not modernization—and restrictions on thinking about new designs that might accomplish the deterrence mission in the 21st century more effectively earn nuclear warhead modernization a grade of "weak."

Nuclear Delivery Systems
Modernization Score: Strong

Today, the United States fields a triad of nuclear forces with delivery systems that are safe and reliable, but as these systems age, there is increased risk of significantly negative impact on operational capabilities. The older weapons are, the more at risk they are that faulty components, malfunctioning equipment, or technological developments will limit their reliability in the operating environment. Age can degrade reliability by increasing the potential for systems to break down or fail to respond correctly. Corrupted systems, defective electronics, or performance degradation due to long-term storage defects (including for nuclear warheads) can have serious implications for American deterrence and assurance. If it cannot be assumed that a strategic delivery vehicle will operate reliably at all times, that vehicle's deterrence and assurance value is significantly reduced.

The U.S. Air Force and Navy plan to modernize or replace each leg of the nuclear triad in the next several decades, but fiscal constraints are likely to make such efforts difficult. The Navy is fully funding its programs to replace the *Ohio*-class submarine with the *Columbia*-class submarine and to extend the life of and eventually replace the Trident SLBM, but existing ICBMs and SLBMs are expected to remain in service until 2032 and

2042, respectively, and new bombers are not planned to enter into service until 2023 at the earliest. Budgetary shortfalls are leading to uncertainty as to whether the nation will be able to modernize all three legs of the nuclear triad, but the U.S. Strategic Command says that a triad is a "requirement."[28] This requirement, validated by all U.S. NPRs since the end of the Cold War, gives U.S. leadership credibility and flexibility, attributes that are necessary for any future deterrence scenarios.

Maintenance issues caused by the aging of American SSBNs and long-range bombers could make it difficult to deploy units overseas for long periods or remain stealthy in enemy hot spots. At present, the United States can send only a limited number of bombers on missions at any one time. As Bradley Thayer and Thomas Skypek have noted, "Using 2009 as a baseline, the ages of the current systems of the nuclear triad are 39 years for the *Minuteman III*, 19 years for the *Trident II* D-5 SLBM, 48 years for the B-52H, 12 years for the B-2, and 28 years for the *Ohio* Class SSBNs."[29] Remanufacturing some weapon parts is difficult and expensive either because some of the manufacturers are no longer in business or because the materials that constituted the original weapons are no longer available (for example, due to environmental restrictions). The ability of the U.S. to produce solid-fuel rocket engines and possible U.S. dependence on Russia as a source of such engines are other long-range concerns.[30]

Grade: U.S. nuclear platforms are in dire need of recapitalization. The U.S. has plans for nuclear triad modernization in place, and funding for these programs has been sustained by Congress and by the services, notwithstanding difficulties caused by sequestration. This demonstration of commitment to nuclear weapons modernization earns this indicator a grade of "strong."

Nuclear Weapons Complex Score: Weak

Maintaining a reliable and effective nuclear stockpile depends in large part on the facilities where U.S. devices and components are developed, tested, and produced. These facilities constitute the foundation of our strategic arsenal and include the:

- Los Alamos National Laboratories,

- Lawrence Livermore National Laboratories,

- Sandia National Laboratory,

- Nevada National Security Site,

- Pantex Plant,

- Kansas City Plant,

- Savannah River Site, and

- Y-12 National Security Complex.

In addition to these government sites, the defense industrial base supports the development and maintenance of American delivery platforms.

These complexes design, develop, test, and produce the weapons in the U.S. nuclear arsenal, and their maintenance is of critical importance. As the 2010 NPR stated:

In order to remain safe, secure, and effective, the U.S. nuclear stockpile must be supported by a modern physical infrastructure—comprised of the national security laboratories and a complex of supporting facilities—and a highly capable workforce with the specialized skills needed to sustain the nuclear deterrent.[31]

A flexible and resilient infrastructure is an essential hedge in the event that components fail or the U.S. is surprised by the nuclear weapon capabilities of potential adversaries.[32] U.S. research and development efforts and the industrial base that supports modernization of delivery systems are important parts of this indicator.

Maintaining a safe, secure, effective, and reliable nuclear stockpile requires modern facilities, technical expertise, and tools both to repair any malfunctions quickly, safely, and securely and to produce new nuclear weapons if required. The existing nuclear weapons complex, however, is not fully functional. The U.S. cannot produce more than a few new warheads per year, there are limits on the ability to conduct life-extension programs, and Dr. John Foster has reported that the U.S. no longer can "serially produce many crucial components of our nuclear weapons."[33]

If the facilities are not properly funded, the U.S. will gradually lose the ability to conduct high-quality experiments. In addition to demoralizing the workforce and hampering further recruitment, obsolete facilities and poor working environments make maintaining a safe, secure, reliable, and militarily effective nuclear stockpile exceedingly difficult. The NNSA's facilities are old: Upwards of 50 percent are more than 40 years old, nearly 30 percent date to the Manhattan Project of the 1940s, and 12 percent are considered excess or no longer needed.[34] As a consequence, the NNSA had about $3.7 billion in deferred maintenance at the end of FY 2015.

Since 1993, the DOE has not had a facility dedicated to production of plutonium pits, one of the main components of America's nuclear warheads. The U.S. currently keeps about 5,000 plutonium pits in strategic reserve. There are significant disagreements as to the effect of aging on pits and whether the U.S. will be able to maintain them indefinitely without nuclear weapons testing. Currently, the U.S. can produce no more than about 10 plutonium pits a year at the Los Alamos PF-4 facility. Infrastructure modernization plans for PF-4, if funded, will boost that number to about 20 by the middle of the next decade and to between 50 and 80 by the end of the following decade. Russia can produce around 2,000 pits a year.[35]

Manufacturing non-nuclear components can be extremely challenging either because some materials may no longer exist or because manufacturing processes have been forgotten and must be retrieved. There is a certain element of art to building a nuclear weapon, and such a skill can be acquired and maintained only through hands-on experience.

Grade: On one hand, the U.S. maintains some of the world's most advanced nuclear facilities. On the other, some parts of the complex—most importantly, parts of the plutonium and highly enriched uranium component manufacturing infrastructure—have not been modernized since the 1950s, and plans for long-term infrastructure recapitalization remain uncertain. The infrastructure therefore receives a grade of "weak."

Quality of People Working in the National Nuclear Laboratories Score: Marginal

Combined with nuclear facilities, U.S. nuclear weapons scientists and engineers are critical to the health of the complex and the stockpile. The 2010 NPR emphasizes that:

> [A] highly skilled workforce [is] needed to ensure the long-term safety, security, and effectiveness of our nuclear arsenal and to support the full range of nuclear security work to include non-proliferation, nuclear forensics, nuclear, counter-terrorism, emergency management, intelligence analysis and treaty verification.[36]

The ability to maintain and attract a high-quality workforce is critical to assuring the future of the American nuclear deterrent. Today's weapons designers and engineers are first-rate, but they also are aging and retiring, and their knowledge must be passed on to the next generation that will take on this mission. This means that young designers need challenging warhead design and development programs to hone their skills, but no such challenging programs are in place today. The NNSA and its weapons labs understand this problem and, with the support of Congress and despite significant challenges, are taking steps to mentor the next generation.

The U.S. currently relies on non-yield-producing laboratory experiments, flight tests, and the judgment of experienced nuclear scientists and engineers to ensure continued confidence in the safety, security, effectiveness, and reliability of its nuclear deterrent. Without their experience, the nuclear weapons complex could not function. A basic problem is that few scientists or engineers at the NNSA weapons labs have had the experience of taking a warhead from initial concept to a "clean sheet" design, engineering development, and production. The complex must attract and retain the best and brightest. The average age of the NNSA's workforce remained 48.1 years as of April 2017.[37]

Grade: In addition to employing world-class experts, the NNSA labs have had recent success in attracting and retaining talent. However, because many scientists and engineers with practical nuclear weapon design and testing experience are retired, nuclear warhead certifications will rely largely on the judgments of people who have never tested or designed a nuclear weapon. Management challenges and a lack of focus on the nuclear weapon mission contribute to the lowering of morale in the NNSA complex. In light of these issues, which have to do more with policy than with the quality of people, the complex earns a score of "marginal."

Readiness of Forces Score: Marginal

The readiness of forces is a vital component of America's strategic forces. The military personnel operating the three legs of the nuclear triad must be properly trained and equipped. It is also essential that these systems are maintained in a high state of readiness.

During FY 2017, the services have continued to align resources in order to preserve strategic capabilities in the short term, but long-term impacts remain uncertain. Continued decline in U.S. general-purpose forces eventually could affect nuclear forces, especially the bomber leg of the nuclear triad. Changes prompted by the 2014 Navy and Air Force cheating scandals have begun to address some of the morale issues. A sustained attention to the situation in the nuclear enterprise is critical.

Grade: Uncertainty regarding the further potential impacts of budgetary shortfalls, as part of the overall assessment, earns this indicator a grade of "marginal."

CHART 6

Putting the U.S. Nuclear Arsenal in Context

The U.S. has 1,797 nuclear warheads deployed. Combining those with arsenals from NATO allies France and the U.K. totals 2,207 warheads—1,375 warheads below Russia's estimated total. Additionally, NATO's combined arsenal protects 1.09 billion people in 30 countries, while Russia's arsenal protects only its population of 124.9 million.

RUSSIA ARSENAL: 3,587+ WARHEADS

NATO ARSENAL: 2,207 WARHEADS

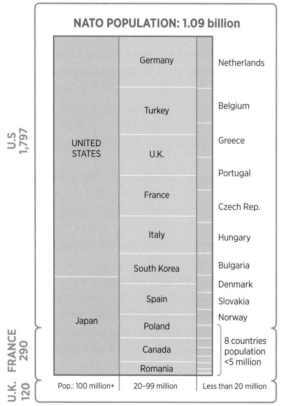

NATO POPULATION: 1.09 billion

U.S 1,797

FRANCE 290

U.K. 120

UNITED STATES	Germany	Netherlands
	Turkey	Belgium
	U.K.	Greece
	France	Portugal
	Italy	Czech Rep.
	South Korea	Hungary
	Spain	Bulgaria
		Denmark
Japan	Poland	Slovakia
	Canada	Norway
	Romania	
Pop.: 100 million+	20–99 million	Less than 20 million

8 countries population <5 million

RUSSIA POPULATION: 124.9 million

NOTES: Figures are from 2015. Warhead totals are estimates.
SOURCES: U.S. Department of State, "New START Treaty Aggregate Numbers of Strategic Offensive Arms," July 1, 2015, http://www.state.gov/t/avc/rls/240062.htm (accessed September 3, 2015); Amy F. Woolf, "Nonstrategic Nuclear Weapons," Congressional Research Service *Report for Members and Committees of Congress*, February 23, 2015, https://www.fas.org/sgp/crs/nuke/RL32572.pdf (accessed September 3, 2015); and Terry Miller and Anthony B. Kim, *2017 Index of Economic Freedom* (Washington: The Heritage Foundation, 2017), http://www.heritage.org/index.

heritage.org

Allied Assurance Score: Marginal

The number of weapons held by U.S. allies is an important element when speaking about the credibility of America's extended deterrence. Allies that already have nuclear weapons can coordinate action with other powers or act independently. During the Cold War, the U.S. and the U.K. cooperated to the point where joint targeting was included.[38] France maintains its own independent nuclear arsenal, partly as a hedge against the uncertainty of American credibility. The U.S. also deploys nuclear gravity bombs in Europe as a visible manifestation of its commitment to its NATO allies.

The U.S., however, must also concern itself with its Asian allies. The United States provides nuclear assurances to Japan and South Korea, both of which are technologically advanced industrial economies facing nuclear-armed adversaries and potential adversaries. If they do not perceive U.S. assurances as credible, they have the capability and know-how to build their own nuclear weapons and to do so quickly. That would be a major setback for U.S. nonproliferation policies.

Grade: At this time, most U.S. allies are not seriously considering developing their own nuclear weapons. European members of NATO continue to express their commitment to and appreciation for NATO as a nuclear alliance. Doubts about the modernization of dual-capable aircraft and even about the weapons themselves, as well as NATO's lack of attention to the nuclear mission and its intellectual underpinning, preclude assigning a score of "very strong." Additionally, the perception among some that America has accepted Iran's nuclear program may encourage other countries in the Middle East region to seek similar capabilities. Thus, allied assurance remains "marginal."

Nuclear Test Readiness Score: Weak

Testing is one of the key elements of a safe, secure, effective, and reliable nuclear deterrent. While the U.S. is currently under a self-imposed nuclear testing moratorium, it maintains a low level of nuclear test readiness at the Nevada National Security Site (formerly Nevada Test Site). This approach is questionable with regard to its efficacy in assuring that the U.S. has the timely ability to conduct yield-producing experiments should it discover a flaw in one or more types of its nuclear weapons that requires experimentation to correct. The U.S. might need to test to develop a weapon with new characteristics that can be validated only by testing and to verify render-safe procedures. Yield-producing experiments can also play an important role if the U.S. needs to react strongly to other nations' nuclear weapons tests and communicate its resolve or to understand other countries' new nuclear weapons.

Current law requires that the U.S. be prepared to conduct a nuclear weapons test within a maximum of 36 months after a presidential decision to do so. The current state of test readiness is between 24 and 36 months, although both the NNSA and Congress required the NNSA to be ready within 18 months in the past.[39] The U.S. could meet the 18-month requirement only if certain domestic regulations, agreements, and laws were waived.[40] Because the United States is rapidly losing its remaining practical nuclear testing experience, including instrumentation of very sensitive equipment, the process would likely have to be reinvented from scratch.[41]

"Test readiness" refers to a single test or a very short series of tests, not a sustained nuclear testing program. Because of a shortage of resources, the NNSA has been unable to achieve this goal. The test readiness program is supported by experimental programs at the Nevada National Security Site, nuclear laboratory experiments, and advanced diagnostics development.[42]

Grade: As noted, the U.S. can meet the readiness requirement mandated by the law only if certain domestic regulations, agreements, and laws are waived. In addition, the U.S. is not prepared to sustain testing activities beyond a few limited experiments, which certain scenarios might require. Thus, testing readiness earns a grade of "weak."

Overall U.S. Nuclear Weapons Capability Score: Marginal

Though modernization programs for warheads and delivery systems are uncertain, the infrastructure that supports nuclear programs is aged, and nuclear test readiness has revealed troubling problems within the forces, those weak spots are offset by strong delivery platform reliability and allies who remain confident in the U.S. nuclear umbrella. The commitment to warhead life-extension programs and modernization of nuclear delivery platforms is a positive trend that should be maintained. Averaging the subscores across the nuclear enterprise therefore results in an overall score of "marginal."

U.S. Military Power: Nuclear

	VERY WEAK	WEAK	MARGINAL	STRONG	VERY STRONG
Warhead Surety				✔	
Delivery Platform Reliability				✔	
Warhead Modernization		✔			
Delivery Systems Modernization				✔	
Nuclear Weapons Complex		✔			
National Labs Talent			✔		
Force Readiness			✔		
Allied Assurance			✔		
Nuclear Test Readiness		✔			
OVERALL			✔		

Endnotes

1. "U.S. Nuclear Forces," Chapter 3 in U.S. Department of Defense, Office of the Secretary of Defense, Office of the Assistant Secretary of Defense for Nuclear, Chemical, and Biological Programs, *The Nuclear Matters Handbook, Expanded Edition*, 2011, http://www.acq.osd.mil/ncbdp/nm/nm_book_5_11/chapter_3.htm (accessed September 17, 2014).

2. George C. Marshall Institute, "LGM-30G Minuteman III," Missile Threat website, https://missilethreat.csis.org/missile/minuteman-iii/ (accessed June 13, 2017).

3. "Test Readiness," in Chapter 1, "Safety, Security, and Reliability of the U.S. Nuclear Weapons Stockpile," in National Research Council, Committee on Reviewing and Updating Technical Issues Related to the Comprehensive Nuclear Test Ban Treaty, *The Comprehensive Nuclear Test Ban Treaty: Technical Issues for the United States* (Washington: National Academies Press, 2012), http://www.nap.edu/openbook.php?record_id=12849&page=30 (accessed June 13, 2017).

4. Memorandum, "Report on the 'Follow-up Audit of the Test Readiness at the Nevada Test Site,'" U.S. Department of Energy, Office of Inspector General, Audit Report No. OAS-L-10-02, October 21, 2009, http://energy.gov/sites/prod/files/igprod/documents/OAS-L-10-02.pdf (accessed June 13, 2017).

5. Statement of Dr. Charles V. Shank, Senior Fellow, Howard Hughes Medical Institute, and Co-chair, National Research Council Committee on Review of the Quality of the Management and of the Science and Engineering Research at the DOE's National Security Laboratories–Phase 1, in *Hearing to Receive Testimony on National Nuclear Security Administration Management of Its National Security Laboratories*, Subcommittee on Strategic Forces, Committee on Armed Services, U.S. Senate, April 18, 2012, p, 5, http://www.armed-services.senate.gov/imo/media/doc/12-28%20-%204-18-12.pdf (accessed June 13, 2017).

6. Task Force on Leveraging the Scientific and Technological Capabilities of the NNSA National Laboratories for 21st Century National Security, *Leveraging Science for Security: A Strategy for the Nuclear Weapons Laboratories in the 21st Century*, Henry L. Stimson Center *Report* No. 71, March 2009, p. 11, http://www.stimson.org/images/uploads/research-pdfs/Leveraging_Science_for_Security_FINAL.pdf (accessed June 13, 2017).

7. Ibid.

8. The report also recommends that the Department of Energy be renamed the "Department of Energy and Nuclear Security" to "highlight the prominence and importance of the Department's nuclear security mission." Congressional Advisory Panel on the Governance of the Nuclear Security Enterprise, *A New Foundation for the Nuclear Enterprise: Report of the Congressional Advisory Panel on the Governance of the Nuclear Security Enterprise*, November 2014, p. xii, http://cdn.knoxblogs.com/atomiccity/wp-content/uploads/sites/11/2014/12/Governance.pdf?_ga=1.83182294.1320535883.1415285934 (accessed June 13, 2017).

9. Associated Press, "US Mistakenly Ships ICBM Parts to Taiwan," March 25, 2008, http::/www.military.com/NewsContent/0,13319,164694,00.html (accessed June 13, 2017).

10. Associated Press, "Air Force Official Fired After 6 Nukes Fly Over US," updated September 5, 2007, http://www.nbcnews.com/id/20427730/ns/us_news-military/t/air-force-official-fired-after-nukes-fly-over%20us/#.WT (accessed June 13, 2017).

11. U.S. Department of Defense, Secretary of Defense Task Force on DoD Nuclear Weapons Management, *Report of the Secretary of Defense Task Force on DoD Nuclear Weapons Management, Phase I: The Air Force's Nuclear Mission*, September 2008, http://www.defense.gov/Portals/1/Documents/pubs/Phase_I_Report_Sept_10.pdf (accessed June 13, 2017).

12. Kevin Liptak, "U.S. Navy Discloses Nuclear Exam Cheating," CNN, February 4, 2014, http://www.cnn.com/2014/02/04/us/navy-cheating-investigation/index.html (accessed September 11, 2017).

13. U.S. Department of Defense, *Independent Review of the Department of Defense Nuclear Enterprise*, June 2, 2014, http://www.defense.gov/pubs/Independent-Nuclear-Enterprise-Review-Report-30-June-2014.pdf (accessed June 13, 2017).

14. General John E. Hyten, Commander, United States Strategic Command, statement before the Committee on Armed Services, U.S. Senate, 4 April 4, 2017, p. 4, https://www.armed-services.senate.gov/imo/media/doc/Hyten_04-04-17.pdf (accessed June 12, 2017).

15. R. L. Bierbaum, J. J. Cashen, T. J. Kerschen, J. M. Sjulin, and D. L. Wright, "DOE Nuclear Weapon Reliability Definition: History, Description, and Implementation," Sandia National Laboratories, *Sandia Report* No. SAND99-8240, April 1999, http://www.wslfweb.org/docs/usg/reli99.pdf (accessed June 13, 2017).

16. U.S. Department of Defense, *Nuclear Posture Review Report*, April 2010, https://www.defense.gov/Portals/1/features/defenseReviews/NPR/2010_Nuclear_Posture_Review_Report.pdf (accessed June 13, 2017).

17. "Test Site Is Finalist for Nuke Bomb Plant," *Las Vegas Sun*, September 27, 2002, http://lasvegassun.com/news/2002/sep/27/test-site-is-finalist-for-nuke-bomb-plant/ (June 13, 2017).

18. Jonathan E. Medalia, "U.S. Nuclear Weapon 'Pit' Production Options for Congress," Congressional Research Service *Report for Members and Committees of Congress*, February 21, 2014, http://fas.org/sgp/crs/nuke/R43406.pdf (accessed June 13, 2017).

19. Major General Robert Smolen, USAF (Ret.), Deputy Administrator for Defense Programs, U.S. Department of Energy, National Nuclear Security Administration, remarks at AIAA Strategic and Tactical Missile Systems Conference, January 23, 2008, https://www.aiaa.org/uploadedFiles/About-AIAA/Press_Room/Key_Speeches-Reports-and-Presentations/Smolen.pdf (accessed June 13, 2017).

20. Thomas Scheber, *Reliable Replacement Warheads: Perspectives and Issues*, United States Nuclear Strategy Forum Publication No. 0005 (Fairfax, VA: National Institute Press, 2007), p. 2, http://www.nipp.org/National%20Institute%20Press/Current%20Publications/PDF/RRW%20final%20with%20foreword%207.30.07.pdf (accessed September 17, 2014); Thomas D'Agostino, "Presented at the Woodrow Wilson International Center for Scholars—The Reliable Replacement Warhead Program," June 15, 2007,
http://nnsa.energy.gov/mediaroom/speeches/06.15.2007 (accessed September 17, 2014).

21. National Institute for Public Policy, *The Comprehensive Test Ban Treaty: An Assessment of the Benefits, Costs, and Risks* (Fairfax, VA: National Institute Press, 2011), pp. 24–25, http://www.nipp.org/wp-content/uploads/2014/12/CTBT-3.11.11-electronic-version.pdf (accessed June 13, 2017).

22. U.S. Department of Energy, National Nuclear Security Administration, *Fiscal Year 2017 Stockpile Stewardship and Management Plan—Biennial Plan Summary*, March 2016,
https://nnsa.energy.gov/sites/default/files/nnsa/inlinefiles/FY17SSMP%20Final_033116.pdf (accessed June 12, 2017).

23. Stephen M. Younger, *The Bomb: A New History* (New York: HarperCollins, 2009), p. 192.

24. Robert M. Gates, speech delivered at Carnegie Endowment for International Peace, Washington, DC, October 28, 2008, http://archive.defense.gov/Speeches/Speech.aspx?SpeechID=1305 (accessed June 13, 2017).

25. Robert W. Nelson, "What Does Reliability Mean?" in "If It Ain't Broke: The Already Reliable U.S. Nuclear Arsenal," Arms Control Association, April 1, 2006, http://www.armscontrol.org/print/2026 (accessed June 13, 2017).

26. For example, the U.S. lost contact with 50 intercontinental-range ballistic missiles in October 2010. For more information, see NTI Global Security Newswire, "Air Force Loses Contact with 50 ICBMs at Wyoming Base," October 27, 2010, http://www.nti.org/gsn/article/air-force-loses-contact-with-50-icbms-at-wyoming-base/ (accessed June 13, 2017).

27. Panel to Assess the Reliability, Safety, and Security of the United States Nuclear Stockpile, *Expectations for the U.S. Nuclear Stockpile Program: FY 2001 Report of the Panel to Assess the Reliability, Safety, and Security of the United States Nuclear Stockpile*, 2002, http://fas.org/programs/ssp/nukes/testing/fosterpnlrpt01.pdf (accessed June 13, 2017).

28. Admiral C. D. Haney, Commander, United States Strategic Command, statement before the Committee on Armed Services, U.S. Senate, March 10, 2016, p. 3, http://www.armed-services.senate.gov/imo/media/doc/Haney_03-10-16.pdf (accessed June 13, 2017).

29. Bradley A. Thayer and Thomas M. Skypek, "The Perilous Future of U.S. Strategic Forces," Petroleumworld`s Opinion Forum, May 2008, http://www.petroleumworld.com/sunopf09050301.htm (accessed June 13, 2017).

30. Sydney J. Freedberg Jr., "Fading Solid Fuel Engine Biz Threatens Navy's Trident Missile," *Breaking Defense*, June 16, 2014, http://breakingdefense.com/2014/06/fading-solid-fuel-engine-biz-threatens-navys-trident-missile/ (accessed June 13, 2017).

31. U.S. Department of Defense, *Nuclear Posture Review Report*, April 2010, pp. xiv–xv.

32. Andrew C. Weber, Assistant Secretary of Defense for Nuclear, Chemical, and Biological Defense Programs, testimony in *Hearing to Receive Testimony on Nuclear Forces and Policies in Review of the Defense Authorization Request for Fiscal Year 2014 and the Future Years Defense Program*, Subcommittee on Strategic Forces, Committee on Armed Services, U.S. Senate, April 17, 2013, http://www.armed-services.senate.gov/imo/media/doc/13-22%20-%204-17-13.pdf (accessed June 13, 2017).

33. John S. Foster, Jr., "Nuclear Weapons and the New Triad," in conference proceedings, *Implementing the New Triad: Nuclear Security in Twenty-First Century Deterrence, Final Report*, Institute for Foreign Policy Analysis and International Security Studies Program of the Fletcher School, Tufts University, December 14–15, 2005, p. 69.

34. U.S. Department of Energy, National Nuclear Security Administration, *Prevent, Counter, and Respond—A Strategic Plan to Reduce Global Nuclear Threats, FY 2017–FY 2021*, March 2016,
https://nnsa.energy.gov/sites/default/files/nnsa/inlinefiles/NPCR%20FINAL%203-31-16%20(with%20signatures).pdf (accessed June 13, 2017).

35. Robert G. Joseph, "Second to One," *National Review*, October 17, 2011,
http://www.nationalreview.com/article/304310/second-one-robert-g-joseph (accessed May 22, 2015); Oleg Bukharin, "A Breakdown of Breakout: U.S. and Russian Warhead Production Capabilities," Arms Control Association, October 1, 2002, http://www.armscontrol.org/act/2002_10/bukharinoct02 (accessed June 13, 2017).

36. U.S. Department of Defense, *Nuclear Posture Review Report*, April 2010, p. 41.

37. U.S. Department of Energy, National Nuclear Security Administration, workforce data as of April 1, 2017, https://nnsa.energy.gov/sites/default/files/nnsa/multiplefiles/nnsa_fy17_0.pdf (accessed June 12, 2017).

38. U.K. House of Commons, Foreign Affairs Committee, *Global Security: UK–US Relations, Sixth Report of Session 2009–10* (London: The Stationery Office Limited, March 28, 2010), http://www.publications.parliament.uk/pa/cm200910/cmselect/cmfaff/114/114.pdf (accessed June 13, 2017).

39. Mary Beth D. Nikitin, "Comprehensive Nuclear-Test-Ban Treaty: Background and Current Developments," Congressional Research Service *Report for Members and Committees of Congress*, September 1, 2016, http://fas.org/sgp/crs/nuke/RL33548.pdf (accessed June 15, 2017).

40. National Research Council, *The Comprehensive Nuclear Test Ban Treaty: Technical Issues for the United States*, p. 30.

41. John C. Hopkins, "Nuclear Test Readiness. What Is Needed? Why?" *National Security Science*, December 2016, http://www.lanl.gov/discover/publications/national-security-science/2016-december/_assets/docs/NSS-dec2016_nuclear-test-readiness.pdf (accessed June 12, 2017).

42. U.S. Department of Energy, National Nuclear Security Administration, Nevada Field Office, "Stockpile Stewardship Program," August 2013, http://www.nv.doe.gov/library/factsheets/DOENV_1017.pdf (accessed September 17, 2014).

Glossary of Abbreviations

A

A2/AD	anti-access/area-denial
AAMDS	Aegis Ashore Missile Defense System
AAV	Amphibious Assault Vehicle
ABM	Ansar Bayt al-Maqdis
ACF	Army contingency force
ACV	Amphibious Combat Vehicle
ADIZ	Air Defense Identification Zone
AEHF	Advanced Extremely High Frequency (satellite system)
AEW	airborne early warning
AFAFRICA	U.S. Air Forces Africa
AFP	Armed Forces of the Philippines
AFRICOM	U.S. Africa Command
AFSOC	U.S. Air Force Special Operations Command
AIP	Air Independent Propulsion
AIT	American Institute in Taiwan
AMDR	Air and Missile Defense Radar
AMPV	Armored Multipurpose Vehicle
ANSF	Afghan National Security Forces
AN/TPY-2	Army Navy/Transportable Radar Surveillance
ANZUS	Australia–New Zealand–U.S. Security Treaty
AUSMIN	Australia–United States Ministerial
AOR	area of responsibility
APC	armored personnel carrier
APS	Army Prepositioned Stocks
AQAP	Al-Qaeda in the Arabian Peninsula
AQI	Al-Qaeda in Iraq
AQIM	Al-Qaeda in the Islamic Maghreb
ARG	amphibious ready group
ASBM	Anti-ship ballistic missile
ASEAN	Association of Southeast Asian Nations
ASW	anti-submarine warfare
ASUW	anti-surface warfare
AW	air warfare

B

BBA	Bipartisan Budget Act of 2015
BCA	Budget Control Act of 2011
BCT	brigade combat team
BDCA	border defense cooperation agreement
BJP	Bharatiya Janata Party
BMD	ballistic missile defense
BUR	Bottom-Up Review
BVR	beyond visual recognition

C

C2	command and control
C4ISR	command, control, communications, computers, intelligence, surveillance, and reconnaissance
CA	civil affairs
CAB	combat aviation brigade
CBO	Congressional Budget Office
CCT	Combat Controller
CELAC	Community of Latin American and Caribbean States
CENTCOM	U.S. Central Command
CFC	Combined Forces Command (South Korea–U.S.)
CIA	Central Intelligence Agency
CJTF-HOA	Combined Joint Task Force–Horn of Africa
CLF	Combat Logistics Force
CMRR	Chemistry and Metallurgy Research Replacement
CMT	combat mission team
COCOM	Combatant Command
CONUS	continental United States
CPMIEC	China Precision Machinery Import–Export Corporation
CPT	Cyber Protection Team
CSF	coalition support funds
CSG	carrier strike group
CSO	Critical Skills Operator
CT	counterterrorism
CTC	Combat Training Centers
CTF	Combined Task Force
CTIC	Counter Terrorism Information Center
CVN	Aircraft Carriers

CVW	carrier air wing
CW	chemical warfare
CYBERCOM	U.S. Cyber Command

D

D2D	deployment-to-dwell
DA-KKV	direct-ascent kinetic-kill vehicle
DDPR	Deterrence and Defense Posture Review
DIME	diplomatic, informational, military, and economic
DMZ	demilitarized zone
DNI	Director of National Intelligence
DOD	U.S. Department of Defense
DOE	U.S. Department of Energy
DOS	denial of service
DDOS	distributed denial of service
DPRK	Democratic People's Republic of Korea (North Korea)
DTTI	Defense Trade and Technology Initiative
DSG	Defense Strategic Guidance
DSR	Defense Strategic Review

E

EAS	European Activity Set
EBO	effects-based operations
ECP	engineering change proposal
EDCA	Enhanced Defense Cooperation Agreement
EEZ	exclusive economic zone
EFV	Expeditionary Fighting Vehicle
EOD	explosive ordinance disposal
EMD	engineering and manufacturing development
EMP	electromagnetic pulse
ERI	European Reassurance Initiative
ESG	Expeditionary Strike Group
EUCOM	U.S. European Command
EW	electronic warfare

F

FATA	Federally Administered Tribal Areas
FCS	Future Combat Systems
FOC	full operational capability
FONOPS	freedom of navigation exercises
FTA	free trade agreement

G

GAO	Government Accountability Office (formerly General Accounting Office)
GATOR	Ground/Air Task Oriented Radar
GCC	geographic combatant commander
GCC	Gulf Cooperation Council
GCV	Ground Combat Vehicle
GDP	Gross Domestic Product
GFMAP	Global Force Management Allocation Plan
GEO	geosynchronous orbit
GPF	general purpose forces
GPS	Global Positioning System

H

HA/DR	humanitarian assistance/disaster relief
HEO	highly elliptical orbit
HMMWV	High Mobility Multipurpose Wheeled Vehicle ("HUMVEE")
HVE	homegrown violent extremist

I

ICBM	intercontinental ballistic missile
ICS	industrial control systems
IDF	Israel Defense Forces
IED	Improvised Explosive Device
IFV	infantry fighting vehicle
IMF	International Monetary Fund
INEW	Integrated Network Electronic Warfare
INF	Intermediate-Range Nuclear Forces (treaty)
IOC	initial operating capability

IRGC	Islamic Revolutionary Guard Corps
ISAF	International Security Assistance Force
ISIL	Islamic State of Iraq and the Levant
ISIS	Islamic State of Iraq and Syria
ISR	intelligence, surveillance, and reconnaissance

J

JOAC	Joint Operational Access Concept
JeM	Jaish-e-Mohammed
JP	joint publication
JSF	Joint Strike Fighter (F-35 Lightning II)
JSOC	Joint Special Operations Command
JSTAR	Joint Surveillance and Target Attack Radar System
JLTV	Joint Light Tactical Vehicle
JTF North	Joint Task Force North
JuD	Jamaat-ud-Dawa

K

KATUSA	Korean Augmentees to the United States Army

L

LAC	Line of Actual Control
LAF	Lebanese Armed Forces
LAV	Light Armored Vehicle
LCAC	Landing Craft Air Cushion Vehicle
LCS	Littoral Combat Ship
LeT	Lashkar-e-Taiba
LHA	landing helicopter assault (amphibious ship)
LHD	landing helicopter dock (amphibious ship)
LNG	liquefied natural gas
LoC	Line of Control
LPD	landing platform/dock or amphibious transport dock (amphibious ship)
LRA	Lord's Resistance Army
LRS-B	Long-Range Strike Bomber
LRIP	Low-Rate Initial Production
LSD	landing ship, dock (amphibious ship)

M

MAGTF	Marine Air-Ground Task Force
MANPADS	man-portable air-defense systems
MARCENT	U.S. Marine Corps Forces Central Command
MARFORAF	U.S. Marine Corps Forces Africa
MARFOREUR	U.S. Marine Corps Forces Europe and Africa
MARFORPAC	U.S. Marine Corps Forces, Pacific
MARSOC	U.S. Marine Corps Special Operations Command
MCM	mine countermeasure (ship)
MCO	major combat operation (see MRC, MTW)
MCMV	mine countermeasure vessel (ship)
MDAP	Major Defense Acquisition Program
MEB	Marine Expeditionary Brigade
MEF	Marine Expeditionary Force
MISO	Military Information Special Operations
MNLA	National Movement for the Liberation of Azawad
MNLF	Moro National Liberation Front
MNNA	major non-NATO ally
MOJWA	Movement for Oneness and Jihad in West Africa
MPC	Marine Personnel Carrier
MPS	Maritime Prepositioning Ships
MRC	major regional conflict (see MTW, MCO)
MRAP	Mine-Resistant Ambush-Protected (vehicle)
MRBM	medium-range ballistic missile
MRF	Marine Rotational Force
MTW	major theater war (see MCO, MRC)

N

NAP	National Action Plan
NATO	North Atlantic Treaty Organization
NAVAF	U.S. Naval Forces Africa
NAVEUR	U.S. Naval Forces Europe
NDN	Northern Distribution Network
NDAA	National Defense Authorization Act
NDP	National Defense Panel
New START	New Strategic Arms Reduction Treaty
NNSA	National Nuclear Security Administration

NPR	Nuclear Posture Review
NPRIS	Nuclear Posture Review Implementation Study
NSC	National Security Council
NSR	Northern Sea Route
NSWC	Naval Special Warfare Command

O

OAS	Organization of American States
OCO	overseas contingency operations
OEF	Operation Enduring Freedom
OIF	Operation Iraqi Freedom
O-FRP	Optimized Fleet Response Plan
ONA	Office of Net Assessment
ONE	Operation Noble Eagle
OPCON	operational control
OPLAN	operational plan
OPTEMPO	operational tempo
OSCE	Organization for Security and Co-operation In Europe

P

PACAF	U.S. Pacific Air Forces
PACFLT	U.S. Pacific Fleet
PACOM	U.S. Pacific Command
PAF	Philippine Air Force
PDD-15	Presidential Decision Directive-15
PIM	Paladin Integrated Management
PLFP	Popular Front for the Liberation of Palestine
PLFP-GC	Popular Front for the Liberation of Palestine–General Command
PKO	peacekeeping operation
PLA	People's Liberation Army
PLAAF	People's Liberation Army Air Force
PLAN	People's Liberation Army Navy
PLO	Palestine Liberation Organization
PNI	Presidential Nuclear Initiative
PNT	positioning, navigation, and timing
PRC	People's Republic of China

PRT	Provisional Reconstruction Team
PSA	Port of Singapore Authority
PSF	Peninsula Shield Force

Q

QDR	Quadrennial Defense Review
QNSTR	Quadrennial National Security Threats and Trends

R

RAF	Royal Air Force
RBA	Ready Basic Aircraft
RCOH	refueling and complex overhaul (nuclear-powered ship)
RDJTF	Rapid Deployment Joint Task Force
RFP	Request for Proposals
RMA	revolution In military affairs
ROK	Republic of Korea (South Korea)
RP	Republic of the Philippines

S

SAARC	South Asia Association of Regional Cooperation
SAM	surface-to-air missile
SAR	search and rescue
SBIRS	Space-Based Infrared System (satellite system)
SCN	Shipbuilding and Conversion, Navy (budget category)
SEAL	Sea Air Land operator (Navy)
SEATO	Southeast Asia Treaty Organization
SFA	Strategic Framework Agreement
SIGINT	signals intelligence
SLBM	submarine-launched ballistic missile
SMU	special mission unit
SOCAFRICA	U.S. Special Operations Command Africa
SOCCENT	U.S. Special Operations Command Central
SOCEUR	U.S. Special Operations Command Europe
SOCPAC	U.S. Special Operations Command Pacific
SOF	U.S. Special Operations Forces
SOP	Standard Operating Procedure

SORT	Strategic Offensive Reductions Treaty
SOTFE	Support Operations Task Force Europe
SPE	Sony Pictures Entertainment
SPMAGTF	Special-Purpose Marine Air–Ground Task Force–Crisis Response–Africa
SRBM	short-range ballistic missile
SSBN	ballistic missile submarine, nuclear-powered
SSGN	guided missile submarine, nuclear-powered
SSN	attack submarine, nuclear-powered
SSP	Stockpile Stewardship Program
STRATCOM	U.S. Strategic Command
SUW	surface warfare

T

TACAIR	tactical air
TAI	total active inventory
TANAP	Trans-Anatolian Natural Gas Pipeline
TAP	Trans-Adriatic Pipeline
TCO	transnational criminal organization
TPP	Trans-Pacific Partnership
TTP	Tehrik-e-Taliban Pakistan
TLAM/N	Tomahawk Land Attack Missile/Nuclear
TMP	technical modernization program
TNW	tactical nuclear weapon
TRA	Taiwan Relations Act
TRANSCOM	U.S. Transportation Command
TSOC	Theater Special Operations Command

U

UAV	unmanned aerial vehicle
UAE	United Arab Emirates
UCLASS	Unmanned Carrier-Launched Airborne Surveillance and Strike
UNASUR	Unión de Naciones Suramericanas (Union of South American Nations)
UNC	United Nations Council
USAF	U.S. Air Force
USAFCENT	U.S. Air Forces Central
USAFE	U.S. Air Forces Europe
USARAF	U.S. Army Africa

USARCENT	U.S. Army Central
USARPAC	U.S. Army Pacific
USAREUR	U.S. Army Europe
USASOC	U.S. Army Special Operations Command
USFJ	U.S. Forces Japan
USFK	U.S. Forces Korea
USNAVCENT	U.S. Naval Forces Central
USNORTHCOM	U.S. Northern Command
USSOCOM	U.S. Special Operations Command
USSOUTHCOM	U.S. Southern Command
USW	undersea warfare

V

VEO	violent extremist organizations
VLS	vertical launching system

W

WGS	Wideband Global SATCOM (satellite system)
WMD	weapons of mass destruction
WRM	wartime readiness materials
WWTA	Worldwide Threat Assessment

Appendix:
Military Capabilities and Corresponding Modernization Programs

As mentioned in the Methodology, this *Index* measures the capability of the U.S. military based on the current state of its combat equipment. Four factors are key to this assessment: the age of key platforms relative to their expected life span, whether the required capability is being met by legacy or modern equipment, the scope of replacement programs relative to the operational requirement, and the overall health and stability of modernization programs. This appendix presents each of the services' principal combat platforms and corresponding modernization programs, scoring them in each of the four factors.

ARMY SCORES

Main Battle Tank

PLATFORM	Age Score	Capability Score	MODERNIZATION PROGRAM	Size Score	Health Score
M1A1/2 Abrams Inventory: **775/1,609** Fleet age: **27/6.5** Date: **1980** The Abrams is the main battle tank used by the Army in its armored brigade combat teams (BCTs). The Abrams went through a remanufacture program to extend its life to 2045.	④	④	None		

Infantry Fighting Vehicle

PLATFORM	Age Score	Capability Score	MODERNIZATION PROGRAM	Size Score	Health Score
M2 Bradley Inventory: **6,547** Fleet age: **12** Date: **1981** The Bradley is a tracked infantry fighting vehicle (IFV) meant to transport infantry and provide covering fire. The Bradley complements the Abrams tank in armored BCTs. Originally intended to be replaced by the Ground Combat Vehicle (now canceled), the Bradley underwent a remanufacture program to extend the life of the platform. The Army plans to keep the Bradley in service until 2045.	④	❶	Ground Combat Vehicle (GCV) was canceled. Concept design contracts were awarded in May 2015 for a Future Fighting Vehicle.		

Armored Fighting Vehicle

PLATFORM	Age Score	Capability Score	MODERNIZATION PROGRAM	Size Score	Health Score
Stryker Inventory: **3,892** Fleet age: **11** Date: **2002** The Stryker is a wheeled armored fighting vehicle that makes up the Stryker BCTs. The program was considered an interim vehicle to serve until the arrival of the Future Combat System (FCS), but that program was cancelled due to technology and cost hurdles. The Stryker is undergoing modifications to receive a double-v hull (DVH) to increase survivability. The Stryker is expected to remain in service for 30 years.	④	③	None		

See Methodology for descriptions of scores.   Fleet age—Average age of fleet   Date—Year fleet first entered service

Armored Personnel Carrier

PLATFORM	Age Score	Capability Score	MODERNIZATION PROGRAM	Size Score	Health Score
M113 Armored Personnel Carrier Inventory: **3,000** Fleet age: **18** Date: **1960** The M113 is a tracked APC that plays a supporting role for armored BCTs and infantry BCTs. The APC was also to be replaced by the GCV. Plans are to use the platforms to 2045.	④	①	**Armored Multi-Purpose Vehicle (AMPV)** Timeline: **2018–2035** The AMPV will be adapted from an existing vehicle design which allowed the program to bypass the technology development phase. The FY 2018 President's budget requests funding for the initial procurement of 107 vehicles. IOC is not expected until 2022.	②	⑤

PROCUREMENT

2,897

SPENDING ($ millions)

$552 $13,375

Light Wheeled Vehicle

PLATFORM	Age Score	Capability Score	MODERNIZATION PROGRAM	Size Score	Health Score
HMMWV Inventory: **150,000** Fleet age: **9.5** Date: **1985** The HMMWV is a light wheeled vehicle used to transport troops under some level of protection. The expected life span of the HMMWV is 15 years. Some HMMWVs will be replaced by the Joint Light Tactical Vehicle (JLTV).	②	①	**Joint Light Tactical Vehicle (JLTV)** Timeline: **2015–2035** Currently in development, the JLTV is a vehicle program meant to replace some of the HMMWVs and improve reliability and survivability of vehicles. So far the program has experienced a one-year delay due to changes in vehicle requirements. This is a joint program with USMC. Low rate initial production was awarded to a single contractor in August 2015.	①	④

PROCUREMENT

2,690   46,409

SPENDING ($ millions)

$1,965 $23,311

See Methodology for descriptions of scores.   Fleet age—Average age of fleet   Date—Year fleet first entered service

ARMY SCORES

Attack Helicopter

PLATFORM	Age Score	Capability Score	MODERNIZATION PROGRAM	Size Score	Health Score
AH-64 A-D Apache Inventory: **450** Fleet age: **16** Date: **1984** The Apache is an attack helicopter that makes up the Army Combat Aviation Brigades. There are currently two variants, the AH-64A and AH-64D. The AH-64A is being retired. AH-64D makes up the 82 percent of the inventory and entered service in 1998. The expected life cycle is about 20 years.	①		**AH-64E Reman** Timeline: **2010–2024** The AH-64E Reman is a program to remanufacture old Apache helicopters into the more advanced AH-64E version. The AH-64E will have more modern and interoperable systems and be able to carry modern munitions. The overwhelming majority of AH-64Es will be from remanufacture.	②	④

PROCUREMENT
287   347

SPENDING *($ millions)*
$6,580 $8,017

PLATFORM	Age Score	Capability Score	MODERNIZATION PROGRAM	Size Score	Health Score
AH-64E Inventory: **146** Fleet age: **3** Date: **2013** The AH-64E variant of the Apache is a remanufactured version with substantial upgrades in powerplant, avionics, communications, and weapons capabilities. The expected life cycle is about 20 years.	⑤		**AH-64E New Build** Timeline: **2013–2028** The AH-64E New Build pays for the production of new Apaches. The program is meant to modernize and sustain the current Apache inventory. The AH-64E will have more modern and interoperable systems and be able to carry modern munitions. Very few AH-64Es are being built compared with the remanufactured variant.	②	④

(Capability Score for Attack Helicopter: ②)

PROCUREMENT
37   26

SPENDING *($ millions)*
$539 $1,984

Medium Lift

PLATFORM	Age Score	Capability Score	MODERNIZATION PROGRAM	Size Score	Health Score
UH-60A Black Hawk Inventory: **802** Fleet age: **24** Date: **1979** The Black Hawk UH-60A is a medium-lift utility helicopter. The expected life span is about 25 years. This variant of the Black Hawk is now being replaced by the newer UH-60M variant.	①		**UH-60M Black Hawk** Timeline: **2005–2030** Currently in production, the purchases of the UH-60Ms are intended to modernize and replace current Black Hawk inventories. The newer M variant will improve the Black Hawk's range and lift by upgrading the rotor blades, engine, and computers.	⑤	④

PROCUREMENT
873   494

SPENDING *($ millions)*
$15,844 $10,817

PLATFORM	Age Score	Capability Score
UH/HH-60M Black Hawk Inventory: **700** Fleet age: **9** Date: **2006** The Black Hawk UH-60M is a medium-lift utility helicopter that is a follow-on to the UH-60A. As the UH-60A is retired, the M variant will be the main medium-lift rotorcraft used by the Army. Expected to remain in service until 2030.	④	

(Capability Score for Medium Lift: ③)

See Methodology for descriptions of scores.   Fleet age—Average age of fleet   Date—Year fleet first entered service

①②③④⑤
Weakest ⟵⟶ Strongest

Procurement ■ Through FY 2017
and Spending □ Pending

Heavy Lift

PLATFORM	Age Score	Capability Score	MODERNIZATION PROGRAM	Size Score	Health Score
CH-47D Chinook Inventory: **75** Fleet age: **27** Date: **1962** The Chinook is a heavy-lift helicopter. It has an expected life cycle of 20 years. The CH-47Ds were originally upgraded from earlier variants of the CH-47s.	**1**		**CH-47F** Timeline: **2003–2018** Currently in production, CH-47F program is intended to keep the fleet of heavy-lift rotorcraft healthy as older variants of the CH-47 are retired. The program includes both remanufactured and new builds of CH-47s. The F variant has engine and airframe upgrades to lower the maintenance requirements. Total procurement numbers include the MH-47G configuration for U.S. Special Operations Command (67 total).	**5**	**4**
CH-47F Chinook Inventory: **360** Fleet age: **4.4** Date: **2001** CH-47F is "a remanufactured version of the CH-47D with a new digital cockpit and modified airframe to reduce vibrations." It also includes a common aviation architecture cockpit and advanced cargo-handling capabilities. The expected life span is 35 years.	**5**	**5**			

PROCUREMENT

534 9

SPENDING ($ millions)

$14,528 $132

Intelligence, Surveillance, and Reconnaissance (ISR)

PLATFORM	Age Score	Capability Score	MODERNIZATION PROGRAM	Size Score	Health Score
MQ-1C Gray Eagle Inventory: **105** Fleet age: **3** Date: **2009** The Gray Eagle is a medium-altitude long-endurance (MALE) UAV used to conduct ISR missions. The use of MALE UAVs is a new capability for the Army. The Gray Eagle is currently in production.	**5**	**5**	**MQ-1C Gray Eagle** Timeline: **2010–2016** The MQ-1C UAV provides Army reconnaissance, surveillance, and target acquisition capabilities. The army increased its acquistion objective of the MQ-1C from 167 to 204 in 2017.	**5**	**4**

PROCUREMENT

193 11

SPENDING ($ millions)

$5,506 $207

SOURCE: Heritage Foundation research using data from government documents and websites. See also Dakota L. Wood, ed., *2017 Index of U.S. Military Strength* (Washington, DC: The Heritage Foundation, 2017), http://index.heritage.org/militarystrength/..

See Methodology for descriptions of scores.   Fleet age—Average age of fleet   Date—Year fleet first entered service

NAVY SCORES

Procurement ■ Through FY 2017
and Spending ■ Pending

Aircraft Carrier

PLATFORM	Age Score	Capability Score	MODERNIZATION PROGRAM	Size Score	Health Score
Nimitz-Class Aircraft Carrier (CVN-68) Inventory: **10** Fleet age: **26.5** Date: **1975** The expected life of the *Nimitz*-class nuclear aircraft carrier is 50 years. The class will start retiring in the mid-2020s and will be replaced by the *Ford*-class carriers.	③		**Ford-Class Aircraft Carrier (CVN-78)** Timeline: **2008–2018** Currently in production, the *Ford*-class will replace the current *Nimitz*-class aircraft carriers. After a year-long delay, the first ship of its class was commissioned on July 22, 2017. The *Ford*-class will increase aircraft sorties by 25 percent, require a crew of several hundred fewer sailors, and be able to handle more advanced weapon systems.	①	②
		①			
Ford-Class Aircraft Carrier (CVN-21) Inventory: **1** Fleet age: **0.2** Date: **2017** The expected life of the *Ford*-class nuclear aircraft carrier is 50 years.	⑤				

PROCUREMENT   2   1

SPENDING ($ millions) $28,516 $17,219

Large Surface Combatant

PLATFORM	Age Score	Capability Score	MODERNIZATION PROGRAM	Size Score	Health Score
Ticonderoga-Class Cruiser (CG-47) Inventory: **22** Fleet age: **27.1** Date: **1983** The *Ticonderoga*-class guided missile cruiser has a life expectancy of 35 years. There are plans to lay up half of the cruiser fleet to modernize it and extend its life into the 2030s. Two cruisers began modernization in FY 2015. There are no replacements currently planned.	②		**Zumwalt-Class Destroyer (DDG-1000)** Timeline: **2007–2009** The DDG-1000 was designed to be a new-generation destroyer capable of handling more advanced weapon systems with modern gun systems and a hull design aimed to reduce radar detectability. The DDG-1000 program was intended to produce a total of 32 ships, but this number has been reduced to 3, essentially ending the acquisition program. The first DDG-1000 was commissioned in October 2016.	①	①
Zumwalt-Class Destroyer Inventory: **1** Fleet age: **1** Date: **2016**	⑤				
		④			

PROCUREMENT   3

SPENDING ($ millions) $21,859 $955

PLATFORM	Age Score	Capability Score	MODERNIZATION PROGRAM	Size Score	Health Score
Arleigh Burke-Class Destroyer (DDG-51) Inventory: **64** Fleet age: **15.6** Date: **1991** The *Arleigh Burke*-class guided missile destroyer is the only operating class of large surface combatant currently in production. The DDG-51 has a 35-year life expectancy.	③		**Arleigh Burke-Class Destroyer (DDG-51)** Timeline: **1985–2022** The DDG-51 has been procured since 1985, but was restarted in FY 2013 to make up for the reduction in DDG-1000 acquisitions. Future DDG-51s will be upgraded to a Flight III design, which will include the Advanced Missile Defense Radar (AMDR), a more capable missile defense radar. The DDG-51 will make up the bulk of the Navy's large surface combatant requirement of 88.	④	④

PROCUREMENT   77   9

SPENDING ($ millions) $87,180 $23,951

See Methodology for descriptions of scores.   Fleet age—Average age of fleet   Date—Year fleet first entered service

Small Surface Combatant

PLATFORM	Age Score	Capability Score	MODERNIZATION PROGRAM	Size Score	Health Score
Littoral Combat Ship (LCS) Inventory: **9** Fleet age: **3.5** Date: **2008** The Littoral Combat Ship includes two classes: the *Independence*-class and the *Freedom*-class, both of which are in the early phases of production. The ship is expected to have a service life of 25 years. The LCS is designed to meet multiple missions and make up the entirety of the small surface combatant requirement. LCS 7 was commissioned in October 2016.	⑤	②	**Littoral Combat Ship (LCS)** Timeline: **2009–2025** The LCS program is in the early stages of production. The LCS is intended to fulfill the mine countermeasure, antisubmarine warfare, and surface warfare roles for the Navy. It will be the only small surface combatant in the fleet once the Navy's frigates and MCM ships retire in the coming years. The program is facing controversy due to cost growth, development issues, and requirements issues for survivability and strike. A modified LCS classified as a frigate was announced to fill out the remaining 20-ship small surface combatant requirement in late 2014.	②	❶
Avenger-Class Mine Counter Measure (MCM-1) Inventory: **11** Fleet age: **25.2** Date: **1987** Designed for mine sweeping and hunting/killing, 11 of the 14 *Avenger*-class ships built are still active. The class has a 30-year life span. The remaining MCMs are expected to be decommissioned throughout the 2020s. There is no replacement in production for this class of ship, but the Navy plans to fill its mine countermeasure role with the LCS.	❶				

PROCUREMENT	SPENDING *($ millions)*
28 12	$20,319 $8,665

SSGN Cruise Missile Submarine

PLATFORM	Age Score	Capability Score	MODERNIZATION PROGRAM	Size Score	Health Score
Ohio-Class (SSGN-726) Inventory: **4** Fleet age: **32.2** Date: **1981** Rather than retiring the four oldest *Ohio*-class ballistic missile submarines early, the Navy converted them to SSGN-726 guided missile submarines, equipping them with conventional Tomahawk cruise missiles rather than Trident ballistic missiles tipped with nuclear warheads. The SSGNs provide the Navy with a large stealthy strike capability. The conversion began in 2002 and was completed in 2007. Since the conversion, they are expected to be retired in the late 2020s. The Navy has no planned replacement for the SSGNs once they retire.	②	❶	None		

See Methodology for descriptions of scores.   Fleet age—Average age of fleet   Date—Year fleet first entered service

NAVY SCORES

Attack Submarines

PLATFORM	Age Score	Capability Score	MODERNIZATION PROGRAM	Size Score	Health Score
Seawolf-Class (SSN-21) Inventory: **3** Fleet age: **17.2** Date: **1997**			**Virginia-Class (SSN–774)** Timeline: **1998–TBD**	⑤	④

Seawolf-Class (SSN-21)

Inventory: **3**
Fleet age: **17.2**   Date: **1997**

Larger and equipped with more torpedo tubes than the U.S. Navy's other current nuclear-powered attack submarines, the class was canceled after three submarines were purchased due to budget constraints in the 1990s. The *Seawolf*-class submarines are expected to be retired in 14 years. Meant to replace the *Los Angeles*-class, the *Seawolf* has been replaced by the *Virginia*-class attack submarine.

Age Score: ③

Los Angeles-Class (SSN-688)

Inventory: **35**
Fleet age: **27.5**   Date: **1976**

The *Los Angeles*-class comprises the largest portion of the Navy's attack submarine fleet. The class has a 30 year service life. Of the 62 built, 25 have been decommissioned and one was converted into a moored training ship. The last *Los Angeles*-class submarine is expected to retire in the late 2020s. The *Virginia*-class is replacing this submarine class.

Age Score: ①   *Capability Score:* ②

Virginia-Class (SSN-774)

Inventory: **13**
Fleet age: **6.8**   Date: **2004**

The *Virginia*-class is the U.S. Navy's next-generation attack submarine. The life expectancy of the *Virginia*-class is 33 years. The *Virginia*-class is in production and will replace the *Los Angeles*-class and *Seawolf*-class attack submarines as they are decommissioned.

Age Score: ④

Virginia-Class (SSN–774)

Timeline: **1998–TBD**

Size Score: ⑤ Health Score: ④

The *Virginia*-class is on a production schedule of two per year. The program has been mostly successful. However, the current program of record purchases 33 total submarines, which is not enough to replace the decommissioning *Los Angeles*-class submarines and will create a shortfall in attack submarines. There are reportedly plans to restructure the program to increase the number of submarines in the SSN-774 class to 48.

PROCUREMENT

26   22

SPENDING (*$ millions*)

$78,687 $85,636

See Methodology for descriptions of scores.   Fleet age—Average age of fleet   Date—Year fleet first entered service

NAVY SCORES

SSBN Ballistic Missile Submarine

PLATFORM	Age Score	Capability Score	MODERNIZATION PROGRAM	Size Score	Health Score
Ohio-Class (SSBN) Inventory: **14** Fleet age: **26.7** Date: **1984** The SSBN Ohio-class is one of the three legs of the U.S. military's nuclear triad. The Ohio-class's expected service life is 42 years. The Ohio-class fleet will begin retiring in 2027 at an estimated rate of one submarine per year until 2039. The Navy plans to replace the Ohio-class with the SSBN(X) or next-generation "Ohio replacement program."	②	①	**Columbia-Class (SSBN-X)** Inventory: **14** Fleet age: **26.7** Date: **1984** In January 2017, the SSBN Columbia-class was designated a major defense acquisition program. This also marks the entry of the program into the engineering and manufacturing development phase. The ships will begin construction in FY 2021. **PROCUREMENT** 12		

Amphibious Warfare Ship

PLATFORM	Age Score	Capability Score	MODERNIZATION PROGRAM	Size Score	Health Score
Wasp-Class Amphibious Assault Ship (LHD-1) Inventory: **8** Fleet age: **20.4** Date: **1989** The Wasp-class is the Navy's current amphibious landing helicopter deck, meant to replace the Tarawa-class LHA. This ship has a 35-year life span. This class is no longer in production and will be replaced by the new America-class.	③		**America-class (LHA-6)** Timeline: **2007–2017** The America-class is in production with two LHA-6s already procured. There has been significant cost growth in this program resulting in a Nunn–McCurdy cost breach. The program is also experiencing a 19-month delay because of design problems. One problem was caused by the level of heat from the F-35B STOVL's exhaust. The LHA-7 will follow designs from the LHA-6; FY 2017 funded the procurement of the third and final America-Class LHA.	①	①
America-Class Amphibious Assault Ship (LHA-6) Inventory: **1** Fleet age: **2.9** Date: **2014** The America-class, the Navy's new class of large-deck amphibious assault ships, is meant to replace the retiring Wasp-class LHDs. The lead ship was delivered in April 2014. The America-class is designed to accommodate the Marine Corps' F-35Bs.	⑤	①	**PROCUREMENT** **SPENDING** (*$ millions*) 3 $9,037 $2,014		

See Methodology for descriptions of scores.   Fleet age—Average age of fleet   Date—Year fleet first entered service

(1) (2) (3) (4) (5)

Weakest ⟵⟶ Strongest

Amphibious Warfare Ship

PLATFORM	Age Score	Capability Score	MODERNIZATION PROGRAM	Size Score	Health Score
San Antonio-Class Amphibious Transport Dock (LPD-17) Inventory: **10** Fleet age: **6.6** Date: **2006** The San Antonio-class is the replacement for the Austin-class LPD and makes up most of the LPD inventory. The LPDs have well decks that allow the USMC to transfer the vehicles and supplies carried by the ship to the shore via landing craft. The LPD can also carry 4 CH-46s or 2 MV-22s. The class has a 40-year life expectancy.	(5)		**San Antonio-Class Amphibious Transport Dock (LPD-17)** Timeline: **1996–2016** The LPD-17s are replacements for the San Antonio-class LPDs. All 13 LPD-17s have been procured. **PROCUREMENT** ▬▬▬ 13 **SPENDING** ($ millions) ▬▬▬ $22,451 $103	(5)	(4)
Whidbey Island-Class Dock Landing Ship (LSD-41) Inventory: **8** Fleet age: **28.6** Date: **1985** The Whidbey Island-class is a dock landing ship, which transports Marine Corps units, equipment, and supplies for amphibious operations through use of its large stowage and well decks. The Whidbey Island-class and Harpers Ferry-class ships are to be replaced by the LX(R) program, which is in early developmental stages.	(3)	(3)			
Harpers Ferry-Class Dock Landing Ships (LSD-49) Inventory: **4** Fleet age: **21.3** Date: **1995** A follow-on to the Whidbey Island-class, the Harpers Ferry-class LSDs have a larger well deck with more space for vehicle stowage and landing craft. Like the Whidbey Island-class, these ships should remain in service until 2038. The Whidbey Island-class and Harpers Ferry-class ships are planned to be replaced by the LX(R) program, which is in early developmental stages.	(3)		N/A—LX(R) not yet a Major Defense Acquisition Program (MDAP)		

See Methodology for descriptions of scores.   Fleet age—Average age of fleet   Date—Year fleet first entered service

Airborne Early Warning

PLATFORM	Age Score	Capability Score	MODERNIZATION PROGRAM	Size Score	Health Score
E-2C Hawkeye Inventory: **51** Fleet age: **31** Date: **1964** The E-2C Hawkeye is a battle management and airborne early warning aircraft. While still operational, the E-2C is nearing the end of its service life and is being replaced by the E-2D Advanced Hawkeye. The E-2C fleet received a series of upgrades to mechanical and computer systems around the year 2000.	①	②	**E-2D Advanced Hawkeye** Timeline: **2009–2024** Meant to replace the E-2C, the E-2D Hawkeye is in production. The original plan was to purchase five per year until 2023. DOD plans to make up for the cut in FY 2017 by purchasing six units.	⑤	④
E-2D Advanced Hawkeye Inventory: **25** Fleet age: **3.5** Date: **2013** A more advanced version of the E-2C, the E-2D provides improved battle management capabilities. The program recently started production.	⑤				

PROCUREMENT 46 | 29
SPENDING (*$ millions*) $13,926 | $8,081

Electronic Attack Aircraft

PLATFORM	Age Score	Capability Score	MODERNIZATION PROGRAM	Size Score	Health Score
EA-18G Growler Inventory: **117** Fleet age: **4** Date: **2010** The EA-18G electronic warfare aircraft replaced the legacy EA-6B Prowlers. The platform is still in production and is relatively new.	⑤	⑤	**EA-18G Growler** Timeline: **2006–2016** The EA-18G Growler has been in production for several years, with few current acquisition problems. The program total of 160 is an increase from previous years, which estimated the Navy would purchase 88. All 160 have been procured.	⑤	④

PROCUREMENT 160
SPENDING (*$ millions*) $14,861 | $517

See Methodology for descriptions of scores.   Fleet age—Average age of fleet   Date—Year fleet first entered service

①②③④⑤
Weakest ←——→ Strongest

Procurement ■ Through FY 2017
and Spending ▨ Pending

Fighter/Attack Aircraft

PLATFORM	Age Score	Capability Score	MODERNIZATION PROGRAM	Size Score	Health Score

F/A-18 A-D Hornet

Inventory: **230**
Fleet age: **25.5**   Date: **1983**

The F/A-18 is the Navy's older carrier-based fighter and strike attack aircraft. The Navy has been trying to extend the life of the later variants (C-D) from 6,000 flight hours to potentially 10,000. However, some are being retired and eventually will be replaced by the F/A-18 E/F Super Hornet and F-35C variant.

① (Age Score)

③ (Capability Score)

F/A-18 E/F Super Hornet

Inventory: **561**
Fleet age: **14**   Date: **2001**

The F/A-18 E/F Super Hornet is a newer, more capable version of the Hornet. The Navy is aiming to have a combination of Super Hornets and F-35Cs make up their carrier-based strike capability. The F/A-18 E-F has an expected service life of 20 years.

② (Age Score)

F-35C Joint Strike Fighter

① (Size Score)   ① (Health Score)

Timeline: **2009–2033**

The F-35C is the Navy's variant of the Joint Strike Fighter. The Joint Strike Fighter faced many issues during its developmental stages, including engine problems, software development delays, cost overruns incurring a Nunn–McCurdy breach, and structural problems. The F-35C variant was always scheduled to be the last one to reach initial operational capability (IOC). Like the other variants, the IOC date was pushed back three years from March 2015 to late 2018.

PROCUREMENT

65   195

SPENDING (*$ millions*)

$122,580 $283,901

NOTES: The total program dollar value reflects the full F–35 joint program, including engine procurement. The Navy is also procuring 67 F-35Cs for the Marine Corps. Age of fleet is calculated from date of commissioning to January 2016.
SOURCE: Heritage Foundation research using data from government documents and websites. See also Dakota L. Wood, ed., *2017 Index of U.S. Military Strength* (Washington, DC: The Heritage Foundation, 2017), http://index.heritage.org/militarystrength/.

See Methodology for descriptions of scores.   Fleet age—Average age of fleet   Date—Year fleet first entered service

AIR FORCE SCORES

Strategic Bomber

PLATFORM	Age Score	Capability Score	MODERNIZATION PROGRAM	Size Score	Health Score
B–52 Inventory: **58** Fleet age: **53.7** Date: **1955** The B-52, the oldest of the bombers, can provide global strike capabilities with conventional or nuclear payloads, although it largely has made up the core of the strategic bomber force. The aircraft entered service in 1955 and was in production until 1962.	①		The B-21 is intended to replace the Air Force bomber fleet. The program is not yet a major defense acquisition program.		
B–1 Inventory: **61** Fleet age: **29** Date: **1986** The B-1, originally designed to carry nuclear weapons, was reconfigured for conventional weapons in the early 1990s. The program entered service in 1986 and completed production in 1988. The B-1B will remain in service until 2040.	③	①			
B–2 Inventory: **20** Fleet age: **22.1** Date: **1997** The B-2 bomber provides the USAF with global strike capabilities. It can carry both nuclear and conventional payloads. Initially deployed in 1997, the aircraft communication modules are being upgraded. It is expected to remain in service until 2058.	④				

See Methodology for descriptions of scores.   Fleet age—Average age of fleet   Date—Year fleet first entered service

AIR FORCE SCORES

① ② ③ ④ ⑤
Weakest ⟵⟶ Strongest

Procurement ■ Through FY 2017
and Spending ▢ Pending

Ground Attack Aircraft

PLATFORM	Age Score	Capability Score	MODERNIZATION PROGRAM	Size Score	Health Score
A-10 Thunderbolt II Inventory: **143** Fleet age: **34** Date: **1977** The A-10 is the only USAF platform designed primarily for close air support and does so with a variety of conventional munitions. The USAF has proposed retiring the aircraft earlier than the planned 2028 date for budget reasons.	②	①	**F-35A** Timeline: **2007–2038** ⑤ ① The F-35A is the Air Force variant of the Joint Strike Fighter program, a multirole fixed-wing aircraft. It is currently in early stages of production. The program has faced many issues including a Nunn–McCurdy cost breach during development, grounding due to engine problems, and software development problems. The F-35A achieved IOC on August 2, 2016.	⑤	①
F-16 Inventory: **570** Fleet age: **26** Date: **1978** The F-16 is a multirole aircraft that was built between 1976 and 1999. It has received various upgrade blocks over that time. The aircraft was expected to last about 30 years.	①	①	**PROCUREMENT** 178 1,585 **SPENDING** (*$ millions*) $122,580 $283,901		
F-35A Inventory: **123** Fleet age: **2** Date: **2016** See Ground Attack Modernization Program entry. The USAF has received a small portion of a projected 1,763 total aircraft for the program.	⑤				

Fighter Aircraft

PLATFORM	Age Score	Capability Score	MODERNIZATION PROGRAM	Size Score	Health Score
F-15 Inventory: **313** Fleet age: **28.7** Date: **1979** The F-15 is a legacy fighter that performs air superiority missions. It is no longer in production. The newer F-15E Strike Eagle variant is to operate until 2025 to supplement the F-22.	①	②	None		
F-22 Inventory: **166** Fleet age: **8.9** Date: **2005** The F-22 is the preeminent air superiority fighter aircraft. The stealth aircraft completed production in 2009 after a dramatic cut of its overall order from 750 to 187. It is currently being modified.	⑤				

See Methodology for descriptions of scores.   Fleet age—Average age of fleet   Date—Year fleet first entered service

AIR FORCE SCORES

Tanker

PLATFORM	Age Score	Capability Score	MODERNIZATION PROGRAM	Size Score	Health Score
KC-10 Inventory: **59** Fleet age: **31.6** Date: **1981** An aerial refueling tanker supporting the USAF's Mobility and Lift mission, the KC-10 was deployed in 1981. The aircraft was purchased to increase the number of tankers available, which the Air Force posited did not meet current requirements. The aircraft is no longer in production, but is planned to remain in inventory until 2040.	③		**KC-46** Timeline: **2015–2027** The KC-46 is meant to replace the KC-135. The program entered low rate initial production in August 2016 after having been delayed by a year due to "design changes and late parts." This is a top program for the Air Force and has an aggressive development and test schedule that may be problematic.	①	③
KC-135 Inventory: **155** Fleet age: **55** Date: **1956** The KC-135 supports the mobility and lift mission by providing the joint force aerial refueling capability. The KC-135 makes up the bulk of the aerial refueling capability. The aircraft was initially deployed in 1956, completing production in 1965. The aircraft has undergone several modifications, mainly engine upgrades to improve reliability. It is expected to be in service until 2040, but excessive usage has created many reliability issues due to problems from wear and tear, such as corrosion and fuel bladder leaks.	②	① (between rows)			

PROCUREMENT

38   141

SPENDING ($ millions)

$12,970 $31,505

Heavy Lift

PLATFORM	Age Score	Capability Score	MODERNIZATION PROGRAM	Size Score	Health Score
C-5 Inventory: **36** Fleet age: **36.5** Date: **1970** The C-5 is the USAF's largest mobility and lift aircraft, enabling it to transport a greater amount of cargo (270,000 pounds) compared with other transport aircraft. Originally deployed in 1970, the aircraft has undergone three modification cycles. The latest started in 2009 to upgrade the platform to a C-5M. The modification program is currently ongoing. The aircraft will remain in service until the 2030s.	②	②	**C-5 RERP** Timeline: **2008–2014** This program is modernizing the C-5 to improve "reliability, maintainability, and availability." The C-5 is having its engine replaced with the new F138. The new engine experienced several issues that are in the process of being mitigated.	③	④

PROCUREMENT

52

SPENDING ($ millions)

$6,936 $6.8

See Methodology for descriptions of scores.   Fleet age—Average age of fleet   Date—Year fleet first entered service

AIR FORCE SCORES

Heavy Lift

PLATFORM	Age Score	Capability Score	MODERNIZATION PROGRAM	Size Score	Health Score
C–17 Inventory: **162** Fleet age: **13** Date: **1993** The C-17 is a large fixed-wing transport aircraft in support of USAF's mobility and lift mission. The aircraft can lift 170,900 pounds and land on short runways. The aircraft entered service in 1995. The program was expanded from 120 aircraft to 223 aircraft. The procurement program for the C-17 was recently completed. The aircraft was originally planned to last 30 years, but more frequent usage may shorten that life span.	③	⑤	None		

Medium Lift

PLATFORM	Age Score	Capability Score	MODERNIZATION PROGRAM	Size Score	Health Score
C–130 H/J Inventory: **13/85** Fleet age: **23.9** Date: **1956** The family of C-130 aircraft supports the USAF's tactical mobility and lift capability. Unlike the other transport aircraft, the C-130s can land on rough dirt strips. It can carry about 42,000 pounds and is expected to last 25 years.	①	⑤	**C–130J** Timeline: **1994–2023** The program provides the Air Force with an upgraded medium-lift capability. The C-130J can lift over 40,000 pounds of cargo. The frame supports various other types of aircraft, such as the USMC tanker KC-130J. There are few issues with the current acquisition of C-130Js.	④	③

PROCUREMENT

154   15

SPENDING (*$ millions*)

$12,620 $3,184

See Methodology for descriptions of scores.   Fleet age—Average age of fleet   Date—Year fleet first entered service

Intelligence, Surveillance, and Reconnaissance (ISR)

PLATFORM	Age Score	Capability Score	MODERNIZATION PROGRAM	Size Score	Health Score
RQ-4 Global Hawk Inventory: **36** Fleet age: **6** Date: **2011** The RQ-4 is a unmanned aerial vehicle (UAV) that supports the USAF's ISR mission. Unlike the MQ-1 or MQ-9, the RQ-4 is a high-altitude, long-endurance (HALE) UAV, which in addition to higher altitude has a longer range than medium-altitude, long-endurance (MALE) UAVs. Originally deployed in 2011, the new Block 40 version is being procured. The life expectancy of the Global Hawk is 20 years.	④		**RQ-4** ④ ① Timeline: **2002–2012** This program consists of Block 20, 30, and 40 RQ-4 UAVs. This program had a Nunn–McCurdy breach in 2010. The DOD proposed ending investment in the RQ-4 Block 30, but was rejected by Congress. The program procured 45 platforms, a reduction from 63. **PROCUREMENT** ▬▬▬▬ 45 **SPENDING** *($ millions)* ▬▬▬▬ $9,129	④	①
MQ-1 Predator Inventory: **110** Fleet age: **9.4** Date: **2005** The MQ-1 Predator is a MALE UAV that supports the USAF's ISR mission. The MQ-1 is being replaced by the newer MQ-9. The expected life span of the MQ-1 is 20 years.	③	③	**MQ-9** ⑤ ③ Timeline: **2002–2017** The MQ-9 is in production. It has experienced delays due to manufacturing and testing problems. The Air Force completed acquisition of 347 aircraft with procurement of 24 aircraft in FY 2017. **PROCUREMENT** ▬▬▬▬ 347 **SPENDING** *($ millions)* ▬▬▬▬ $8,661 $4,262	⑤	③
MQ-9 A/B Inventory: **225** Fleet age: **6** Date: **2007** The MQ-9 Reaper is the replacement for the MQ-1 Predator to fulfill the USAF's ISR mission. The UAV is in production.	④				
RC-135 Rivet Joint Inventory: **22** Fleet age: **53** Date: **1964** The RC-135 is a manned ISR aircraft. It was originally fielded in 1964. The Air Force plans to keep the system in service until 2018.	①		None		
U–2 Inventory: **27** Fleet age: **33.6** Date: **1956** Initially deployed in 1956, this manned ISR aircraft can operate at high altitudes and long ranges. The U-2 has undergone a series of modification programs since 1967 to extend the life of the aircraft.	②				

See Methodology for descriptions of scores.   Fleet age—Average age of fleet   Date—Year fleet first entered service

AIR FORCE SCORES

Procurement ■ Through FY 2017
and Spending ▪ Pending

Command and Control

PLATFORM	Age Score	Capability Score	MODERNIZATION PROGRAM	Size Score	Health Score
E-3 AWACS Inventory: **31** Fleet age: **38**　Date: **1978** The E-3 is an airborne warning and control system (AWACS) that provides USAF with command and control and battle management capabilities. The aircraft entered service in 1978. No longer in production, the current inventory is undergoing modifications to upgrade computing systems. The fleet is currently intended to remain in service until 2025.	①	②	None		
E-8 JSTARS Inventory: **16** Fleet age: **15.7**　Date: **1997** The E-8 is a newer command and control aircraft that provides battle management and C4ISR capabilities, mainly by providing ground surveillance to various air and ground commanders in theater. The aircraft first entered service in 1997 and is not currently in production. The Air Force plans to retire the JSTARs in the early 2030s.	③				

See Methodology for descriptions of scores.　　Fleet age—Average age of fleet　　Date—Year fleet first entered service

AIR FORCE SCORES

Space Superiority

PLATFORM	Age Score	Capability Score	MODERNIZATION PROGRAM	Size Score	Health Score
Global Positioning System (GPS) Inventory: **32** Fleet age: **22** Date: **1990** GPS satellites are part of USAF's air and space superiority mission and provide the joint force with navigation data. The GPS constellation was completed in 1995. It is currently being updated by the follow-on GPS III. These satellites have an average lifespan of 7.5 years, although the newest Block IIF has a 12–year life span.	①	③	**GPS III** Timeline: **2012–2014** GPS III is a more advanced GPS satellite to replace the legacy systems. It was expected to start launches in 2016. However, as a result of technical issues during development, the first launch is now expected to take place no earlier than 2018.. **PROCUREMENT** **SPENDING** (*$ millions*) ████████████ ████████████▒ 8 $4,789 $650	⑤	③
Spaced-Based Infrared System (SBIRS) Inventory: **2** Fleet age: **n/a** Date: **2010** The SBIRS satellite system, part of air and space superiority mission, provides early missile warning for missile defense and battlespace awareness purposes.	⑤	③	**SBIRS High** Timeline: **2009–2013** The SBIRS High constellation is a multipurpose program that will fulfill the requirements not only of ballistic missile defense, but also of other general defense needs, such as space surveillance and battlefield awareness. The program is in production and struggling with recurring cost overruns. The program should be completed by 2019. **PROCUREMENT** **SPENDING** (*$ millions*) ████████████ ███████████▒▒ 4 $2,153 $1,305	⑤	②

NOTE: The total program dollar value reflects the full F–35 joint program, including engine procurement.
SOURCE: Heritage Foundation research using data from government documents and websites. See also Dakota L. Wood, ed., *2017 Index of U.S. Military Strength* (Washington, DC: The Heritage Foundation, 2017), http://index.heritage.org/militarystrength/.

See Methodology for descriptions of scores.   Fleet age—Average age of fleet   Date—Year fleet first entered service

MARINE CORPS SCORES

Main Battle Tank

PLATFORM	Age Score	Capability Score	MODERNIZATION PROGRAM	Size Score	Health Score
M1A1 Abrams Inventory: **447** Fleet age: **27** Date: **1989** The M1A1 Abrams Main Battle Tank provides the Marine Corps with heavy-armor direct fire capabilities. It is expected to remain in service beyond 2028.	**2**	**1**	None		

Light Wheeled Vehicle

PLATFORM	Age Score	Capability Score	MODERNIZATION PROGRAM	Size Score	Health Score
HMMWV Inventory: **17,000** Fleet age: **9.5** Date: **1985** The HMMWV is a light wheeled vehicle used to transport troops with some measure of protection against light arms, blast, and fragmentation. The expected life span of the HMMWV is 15 years. Some HMMWVs will be replaced by the Joint Light Tactical Vehicle (JLTV).	**2**	**1**	**Joint Light Tactical Vehicle (JLTV)** Timeline: **2015–2022** Currently in development, the JLTV is a vehicle program meant to replace some of the HMMWVs and improve reliability, survivability, and strategic and operational transportability. So far the program has experienced a one-year delay due to changes in vehicle requirements. This is a joint program with Army. The Marine Corps has indicated that it will likely increase its total acquisition objective in the future.	**1**	**4**

PROCUREMENT
■▢
323   5,177

SPENDING ($ millions)
■▢
$1,965 $23,311

NOTE: JLTV spending figures reflect the full joint program spending.

See Methodology for descriptions of scores.   Fleet age—Average age of fleet   Date—Year fleet first entered service

MARINE CORPS SCORES

Procurement and Spending ■ Through FY 2017 □ Pending

Amphibious Assault Vehicle

PLATFORM	Age Score	Capability Score	MODERNIZATION PROGRAM	Size Score	Health Score
AAV-7A1 Inventory: **1,311** Fleet age: **40** Date: **1972** The Amphibious Assault Vehicle transports troops and cargo from ship to shore. The AAV-7 has been through a service life extension to extend the expected life to 42 years.	①	①	**Amphibious Combat Vehicle (ACV)** Timeline: **n/a** The Amphibious Combat Vehicle is now a major defense acquisition program. The ACV is intended to replace the aging AAV. The program is expected to reach Milestone C in 2018. The president's FY 2018 budget request supports initial procurement of 26 vehicles.	②	n/a
LAV-25 Inventory: **252** Fleet age: **26** Date: **1983** The LAV is a wheeled light armor vehicle with modest amphibious capability used for armored reconnaissance and highly mobile fire support. It has undergone several service life extensions to expand its life span to 42 years and will be in service until 2035.	②	①			

PROCUREMENT   694

SPENDING (*$ millions*) $465 $1,452

Attack Helicopters

PLATFORM	Age Score	Capability Score	MODERNIZATION PROGRAM	Size Score	Health Score
AH-1W Cobra Inventory: **109** Fleet age: **25.3** Date: **1986** The Super Cobra is an attack helicopter that provides the Marines with close air support and armed reconnaissance. The Super Cobra will remain in service until 2021, when it will be replaced with the AH-1Z.	①		**AH-1Z** Timeline: **2004–2020** The new AH-1Z Viper program is part of a larger modification program to the H-1 platform. The new H-1 rotorcraft will have upgraded avionics, rotor blades, transmissions, landing gear, and structural modifications to enhance speed, maneuverability, and payload. The AH-1Z started out as a remanufacture program, but that was later changed to a New Build program because of concerns over existing airframes. While costs have increased, the program has not met the APB breach threshold.	⑤	③
		②			
AH-1Z Viper Inventory: **52** Fleet age: **3.9** Date: **2010** The AH-1Z Viper is the follow on to the AH-1W Cobra attack helicopter. The Viper will have greater speed, payload, and range, as well as a more advanced cockpit. It is expected that the AH-1Z will fully replace the AH-1W Cobra in 2021. The expected operational life span of the Viper is 30 years.	⑤				

PROCUREMENT   119   70

SPENDING (*$ millions*) $10,655 $1,417

See Methodology for descriptions of scores.   Fleet age—Average age of fleet   Date—Year fleet first entered service

Airborne Electronic Attack Aircraft/ Ground Attack Aircraft

PLATFORM	Age Score	Capability Score	MODERNIZATION PROGRAM	Size Score	Health Score
EA-6B Inventory: **18** Fleet age: **29** Date: **1971** The Prowler provides the USMC with an electronic warfare capability. It will be retired in 2019 and will be replaced by the F-35B.	①		**F-35B/C** Timeline: **2008–2033** ③ ① The Corps is purchasing 353 F-35Bs and 67 F-35Cs. The F-35B is the USMC version of the Joint Strike Fighter program. It is meant to replace the AV-8B Harrier, completing transition by 2030. The Joint Strike Fighter has had many development issues, including a Nunn–McCurdy cost breach and major development issues. The F-35B in particular has had software development problems and engine problems that led to grounding. The Marine Corps announced IOC of its second F-35B squadron in June 2016. The F-35C will not reach IOC until 2018.		
AV-8B Inventory: **131** Fleet age: **20.2** Date: **1985** The Harrier is a vertical/short takeoff and landing aircraft designed to fly from LHA/LHDs. It provides strike and reconnaissance capabilities. The aircraft will be retired around 2024.	②	①			
F-35B Inventory: **43** Fleet age: **2.6** Date: **2015** The F-35B is the Marine Corps' short takeoff and vertical landing variant meant to replace the AV-8B Harrier. Despite some development problems, the F-35B achieved IOC in July 2015.	⑤				
F/A-18 A-D Inventory: **251** Fleet age: **25** Date: **1978** Many aircraft in the F/A-18 fleet have logged about 8,000 hours compared with the originally intended 6,000. The fleet life has been extended until 2030. This is necessary to bridge the gap to when the F-35Bs and F-35Cs are available.	②				

PROCUREMENT

107   313

SPENDING ($ millions)

$122,580 $283,901

See Methodology for descriptions of scores.   Fleet age—Average age of fleet   Date—Year fleet first entered service

MARINE CORPS SCORES

Medium Lift

PLATFORM	Age Score	Capability Score	MODERNIZATION PROGRAM	Size Score	Health Score
MV-22 Inventory: **250** Fleet age: **5.2** Date: **2007** The Osprey is a vertical takeoff and landing tiltrotor platform designed to support expeditionary assault, cargo lift, and raid operations. The program is still in production. The program life expectancy of the MV-22 is 23 years.	④	⑤	**MV-22B** Timeline: **1997–2031** The Osprey is in production, and the platform is meeting performance requirements. The modernization program is not facing any serious issues. Procurement figures include 48 Navy MV-22s and 50 of the carrier variant CV-22s.	④	③

PROCUREMENT   391   67

SPENDING *($ millions)* $46,694 $9,456

Heavy Lift

PLATFORM	Age Score	Capability Score	MODERNIZATION PROGRAM	Size Score	Health Score
CH-53E Super Stallion Inventory: **146** Fleet age: **27.9** Date: **1981** The CH-53E is a heavy-lift rotorcraft. The aircraft will be replaced by the CH-53K, which will have a greater lift capacity. The program life of the CH-53E is 41 years.	②	❶	**CH-53K** Timeline: **2017–2028** The program is in development. It is meant to replace the CH-53E and provide increased range, survivability, and payload. The program still has not fully developed the critical technology necessary. The program experienced delays and cost growth.	⑤	③

PROCUREMENT   2   192

SPENDING *($ millions)* $6,288 $24,872

Tanker

PLATFORM	Age Score	Capability Score	MODERNIZATION PROGRAM	Size Score	Health Score
KC-130J Inventory: **48** Fleet age: **9.2** Date: **2004** The KC-130J is both a tanker and transport aircraft. It can transport troops, provide imagery reconnaissance, and perform tactical aerial refueling. This platform is currently in production. The airframe is expected to last 38 years.	④	⑤	**KC-130J** Timeline: **1997–2028** The KC-130J is both a tanker and transport aircraft. The procurement program for the KC-130J is not facing acquisition problems, but experienced decreased procurement quantities in FY 2014 and FY 2015.	④	③

PROCUREMENT   57   47

SPENDING *($ millions)* $4,479 $5,300.7

NOTES: The total program dollar value reflects the full F–35 joint program, including engine procurement. As part of the F–35 program, the Navy is purchasing 67 F-35Cs for the U.S. Marine Corps, which are included here. The MV-22B program also includes some costs from the U.S. Air Force procurement. The AH-1Z costs include costs of UH-1 procurement.
SOURCE: Heritage Foundation research using data from government documents and websites. See also Dakota L. Wood, ed., *2017 Index of U.S. Military Strength* (Washington, DC: The Heritage Foundation, 2017), http://index.heritage.org/militarystrength/.

See Methodology for descriptions of scores.   Fleet age—Average age of fleet   Date—Year fleet first entered service

About the Honorable J. William Middendorf II

J. William Middendorf II was prepared for tough decisions and leadership early in his career. He was a naval officer in World War II and by the age of 40 had founded a company with a seat on the New York Stock Exchange.

He could have settled for business success, but he decided instead to pursue a career in public service. This led him into a series of high-level Administration positions where he helped to shape America's national security during the most consequential moments of the Cold War.

At a time when the Soviet navy was threatening to overtake the naval power of the United States, Middendorf worked to maintain America's competitive edge. As Secretary of the Navy under Presidents Richard Nixon and Gerald Ford, he supported the development of vital programs, most notably the Trident missile for Ohio-class submarines, the Aegis missile defense system, and the F/A-18 combat jet.

Middendorf continued to advance national security as Ambassador to the Organization of American States, where he resisted the expansion of Soviet and Cuban influence in Latin America. He was also a tireless advocate for economic freedom in Latin America and later travelled with a Heritage delegation to urge post-Communist leaders in the former Soviet Union to adopt free-market economics.

His decision-making, relationship-building, and statesmanship on the international stage have enhanced America's security and stability during a volatile period in our history. Throughout his brilliant career, he has been devoted to his family and has pursued lifelong interests in art and music. He also has been a proud member of The Heritage Foundation Board of Trustees since 1989.